D1061513

Mythology of the Heart

MYTHOLOGY OF THE HEART

part of the *Letters from the Soul* series by The International Library of Poetry

Jessica Rapisarda, Editor

Mythology of the Heart

Library of Congress
Cataloging in Publication Data

ISBN 0-7951-5145-4

Proudly manufactured in the United States of America by
Watermark Press
One Poetry Plaza
Owings Mills, MD 21117

FOREWORD

Throughout life, we store information collected from experiences and try in some way to make sense of it. When we are not able to fully understand the things that occur in our lives, we often externalize the information. By doing this, we are afforded a different perspective, thus allowing us to think more clearly about difficult or perplexing events and emotions. Art is one of the ways in which people choose to externalize their thoughts.

Within the arts, modes of expression differ, but poetry is a very powerful tool by which people can share sometimes confusing, sometimes perfectly clear concepts and feelings with others. Intentions can run the gamut as well: The artists may simply want to share something that has touched their lives in some way, or they may want to get help to allay anxiety or uncertainty. The poetry within *Mythology of the Heart* is from every point on the spectrum: every topic, every intention, every event or emotion imaginable. Some poems will speak to certain readers more than others, but it is always important to keep in mind that each verse is the voice of a poet, of a mind that needs to make sense of this world, of a heart that feels the effects of every moment in this life, and perhaps of a memory that is striving to surface. Nonetheless, recalling our yesterdays gives birth to our many forms of expression.

Melisa S. Mitchell
Senior Editor

Editor's Note

For many of us, embracing our emotional tendencies is a difficult feat to accomplish. A number of circumstances, from terrible accidents to faulty beliefs, from horrific tragedies to foolish mindsets, lead us to unproductive, oftentimes harmful existences, which can culminate in a significant downfall. Too many times these obstacles and hindrances distort reality and force us into an automatic existence. Instead of addressing these problems, we become occupied by the unimportant, controlled by the irrelevant, and traumatized by things that we cannot control. We live mechanically, unresponsive to the sensations of the world around us. Luckily, we possess the ability to change. We measure our lives by turning points, moments when we understand more fully our temperamental nature. It is during these times that we change; our perspective grows, and our emotional essence boldly reveals itself.

In his poem "Icarus," Chris Shirley explores the transformation of someone who has spent his life detached from emotion. It is important, however, that we understand the significance of Shirley's title. In Greek mythology, Icarus was the son of Daedalus, servant to King Minos of Crete. For failing to provide Minos with a secure habitat for his monstrous beast, the Minotaur, the king imprisoned Daedalus and his son in the servant's own creation, the unconquerable Labyrinth. As a means of escape, Daedalus constructed giant sets of wings so that he and Icarus could fly to safety. He fashioned the wings from feathers held together by a combination of string and wax. Before they began their flight, Daedalus advised Icarus to maintain a strict and steady course. He warned his son that if he flew too low, the moisture from the sea would weigh down the feathers, and if he ventured too high, the heat from the sun would melt the wax, thereby causing the homemade wings to fall apart. Father and son started on their way, but it wasn't long before Icarus was overcome with the excitement of flying. He veered off course and exploded into the freedom of the open sky. Although his father had warned him, Icarus could not resist the temptations of unbound playfulness. He rose to new heights, and even if it was only for a few moments, he lived with an unbridled fervor unrealized by most. Although his wings indeed crumbled, Icarus had experienced the true pleasure of an unrestrained life.

In his poem, Chris Shirley uses the myth of Icarus to substantiate the transformation of his persona. Shirley's "Icarus" immediately introduces a nameless "he," who acts as a father figure for the poem's narrator. In the same way Daedalus cautioned his son, Shirley's "father" offers some advice to the persona:

> *"Life," he mumbled once,*
> *"Is a collection of moments;*
> *Kisses of crimson. You're playing too hard."*

Here, the father introduces what he believes to be the components of a prosperous life. He states that life is made up of "[k]isses of crimson," meaning that it should be a gratifying progression of time formed by enjoyable moments pieced together. The most fascinating aspect of this passage is the father's warning that his son is "playing too hard." In the Greek myth, Daedalus cautioned Icarus against the perils of doing just that. But Shirley's character implies something completely different in his admonition. Instead of trying to convince his son to refrain from recreation, he is warning him against missing out on the simple rapture of life. The persona is so caught up in the seriousness of trudging onward that he fails to recognize the necessity of relaxing and enjoying life as life.

Later in the poem, Shirley confirms this, as the persona states:

I never knew that iridescent,
Gossamer innocence;
The translucent glimmer of sprites' wings.

The language that Shirley uses here is fantastic in nature. "Gossamer innocence" and "sprites' wings" are whimsical; they mirror the innocent lifestyle that the persona has neglected. These images conjure notions of childlike playfulness and hapless joy. They are frivolous, if not meaningless, to someone who, like the persona, "plays too hard." The persona admits that he has never understood things of this nature—the emotional aspects of life. In the past, he refused to appreciate the fanciful.

Shirley is quick to point out how the narrator has passed his existence:

I played with serious, determined,
Furrowed brow, shoved by a burning point
In the center of my heart,
Moving on the leathery fins of guilt.

Throughout his life, the narrator has sacrificed pleasure for work. He has overlooked what it means to enjoy being alive. A burning desire to achieve has been his motivational force. Rather than using "translucent sprites' wings" to propel himself, the persona pushed on with "leathery fins of guilt." It is this guilt that weighs the speaker down. He is reluctant to give free reign to his uninhibited self because he is afraid to falter in his never-ending quest for artificial success. By contemplating the father figure's advice, however, the persona realizes how much of life he has missed. In his professional life, he has accomplished much. His spirit, however, is dying. Naturally then, if he wants to save himself emotionally, he must sacrifice his former self, much like Icarus sacrificed himself for the wild abandonment he so briefly enjoyed.

Shirley writes of this transformation in a manner that closely mimics Icarus' tremendous fall from the sky:

The gut-wrenching folding of time,
The impact of spray of sand.
Points of heat transmute to blisters . . .

The persona's emotional and psychological rebirth have opened his eyes to an irresistibly pleasing world, much like the one Icarus saw before him, and like Icarus, the persona is unable to deny it.

At this point in the poem, the persona's emotional being announces itself for the first time. He is a renewed individual, eager to embark on an emotional journey. Shirley concludes the poem with an image of a resurrected narrator:

> *Borne upwards on hot wind,*
> *The shimmering beauty of a simple life*
> *Hangs below me, a homegrown Icarus.*

The narrator has finally learned to appreciate the aesthetic. He discards his "leathery fins" and accepts an uplifting wind to get him through life. Shirley's persona has been reborn into a world of passion and excitement. His father figure nurtured him and urged him into becoming a "homegrown Icarus."

While the persona of Chris Shirley's "Icarus" grew tired of a monotonous lifestyle and eventually received the push he needed to cooperate with his emotion, the narrator of Patricia Cottrell's "For Quentin" faces an even harder transition in her life. She must overcome the tragic death of her son.

Cottrell immediately inserts her readers into a desolate world, an abandoned void:

> *We set out early morning, love*
> *Voices carrying through empty margins*
> *The hollow sound of darkened water*
> *Smacking the sandbanks came in response*

Take notice of how the sounds that Cottrell uses enhance the dismal atmosphere that she has created. The "ah" sounds in words like "hollow," "darkened," and "water" exaggerate the echo of the open landscape. The sound, itself, mimics that of a carrying voice. The resonance augments the fog and the water, the desolation of loneliness. The "s" sound that is repeated, particularly in the last line, intensifies the pounding of the waves on the shore. Serving as more than just a backdrop for the poem, Cottrell's bleak environment reflects the grim landscape of the persona's mood.

From the first stanza, we know that the persona is in search of someone, and through the poet's use of phrases like "empty margins" and "hollow sound," we see that nothing remains to be found. In the following lines, the situation grows worse:

> *I saw the tangles of drowning seaweed*
> *And I knew you went down with them*
> *When the heavy nets couldn't lift you*
> *My bare knees struck the damp morning grass*

Here, the persona realizes that the object of her search, her beloved son Quentin, has succumbed to the water's depths. The anguish of knowing that she has lost a child overwhelms her. To lose a loved one is tragic in itself, but to live with its hovering overhead, unresolved for an eternity, is far more tragic. When the recovery nets fail to bring the boy's fallen body to the surface, the persona is denied the closure that she so desperately needs. Cottrell's persona can do nothing more than watch as everything around her "collapse[s] and settle[s] into dust." Her world is at a standstill.

Up until this point, the poem's persona has been operating under organized, rational guidelines. She has organized a search party and has repeatedly bellowed her son's name over the barren landscape. She has overseen the use of all-encompassing nets in the hope of recovering her lost son's body. These techniques, however, have failed, and the persona is in danger of entering an awful world of eternal depression. It is all the narrator can do to keep her composure. At this moment, her emotional need for grievance gains control of her behavior. In the final stanza of the poem, the persona discards all sensible action and proceeds with unbelievable passion:

Soon I will wade into the murky night sea
Sickened by the reckless water and how it opened up to you
And when the blackened surfaces rinse clean
I will rescue you

In order to initiate some sense of finality, the persona's emotional state has pushed her into the same water that claimed her son. The occurrence strongly resembles a Christian baptism. In this ceremony of spiritual cleansing, the individual being baptized pledges her allegiance to God; it is a symbolic gesture signaling the surrendering of control to God. Similarly, the persona is acknowledging her lack of control over her son's fate. It is here that she resigns to let his spirit rest. In turn, she is reborn, liberated form her emotional burden to grieve, just as the baptism makes new the believer. This new beginning is essential if the persona is ever to move on after this tragedy.

At this point in the poem, the persona has undergone a complete transformation. Rather than maneuvering in a precise, rational manner, she acts upon passion alone. By physically feeling the waters that claimed her son, the persona is fulfilling her emotional desire to find answers and express grief; her journey converts into an emotional one, a human one. Somehow she knows that her mind will be more at ease when she exits the water.

Both Chris Shirley and Patricia Cottrell write of individuals who struggle to transform their doleful existences into something more. While Shirely's narrator never knew the simple joy of a passionate reality and Cottrell's lost it at the hands of a horrible tragedy, they both surrender to their emotional needs. In both poems, the personas shed the rational and embrace the passionate in a last-chance effort to save themselves. It is our ability to do this that allows us to thrive in an uncertain world.

While these two poems explore the undeniable nature of man's passion, there are a number of other personal and universal success stories represented in this anthology. Please remember to read "The Last Buddha's Fall" (3) by Shannon Davies, "The Psychology of Life" (3) by Jessica Anthony, "Inquisitive Snake" (4) by Avery A. August, and "The Old Port's Glow" (4) by Samuel W. Blake.

I would like to extend my sincere appreciation to all of the poets featured in this anthology. I congratulate you all on your ability to transform your experiences and feelings into powerful verse. I wish all of you the best of luck in your future writing endeavors.

The publication of this anthology has been a culmination of the efforts of many individuals, including judges, editors, assistant editors, customer service representatives, graphic artists, layout artists, office administrators, data entry staff, and mail-room personnel. I would like to thank these people for all of the time and hard work that went into producing this anthology.

Christopher Vorce
Editor

Cover Art: "Mother Nature," by Selicia Russo

Icarus

"Life," he mumbled once,
"Is a collection of moments;
Kisses of crimson. You're playing too hard";
The gut-wrenching folding of time,
The impact of spray of sand.
Points of heat transmute to blisters . . .
Swinging, swinging.
I never knew that iridescent,
Gossamer innocence;
The translucent glimmer of sprites' wings.
I played with serious, determined,
Furrowed brow, shoved by a burning point
In the center of my heart,
Moving on the leathery fins of guilt.
Borne upwards on hot wind,
The shimmering beauty of a simple life
Hangs below me, a homegrown Icarus.

Chris Daniel Shirley

For Quentin

We set out early morning, love
Voices carrying through the empty margins
The hollow sound of darkened water
Smacking the sandbanks came in response

I saw the tangles of drowning seaweed
And I knew you went down with them
When the heavy nets couldn't lift you
My bare knees struck the damp morning grass

Everything you couldn't come back for
Collapsed and settled into dust
And your sister who last saw you
Clings to your summer cotton shirts

Soon I will wade into the murky night sea
Sickened by the reckless water and how it opened up to you
And when the blackened surfaces rinse clean
I will rescue you

Patricia Cottrell

The Last Buddha's Fall

Sometimes I think that
Marching men who cannot cry
Must surely shell
Their skin like onions.

Beneath the sad hollow of a smiling Buddha,
Whose hand is stayed by man,
Whose face, eroded,
More than one face,
This shallow land is burning

With Biblical precision;
Their tears do not fall that tear
The ground asunder,
Their cries do not ring that
Flay the color from a people's eyes.

But at the fall of the last Buddha,
Here and there amongst his fire-washed feet,
His smooth, unbearded visage serenes the ages
Like a wave in the desert.

Shannon Davies

A Mia Suocera Vol. II

To my mother-in-law, G. C.

a frail phantom scurrying through the mind
asked me about you, your eighty-six years
that ended in a hospital bed in Parma
where I had the first loves of my youth and
you took me by the hand and saved my life
you, who were a lily and I saw you later in my memory
the color of hay in the noise of a tractor
rising from somewhere
in the harmony of the seasons following each other
and I don't know how your deathless childhood
could live again in a few frayed verses
oh, May wasp, happy drone of my memory
asking me for help in the mocking holiday of death

Matthew Prud'homme Capogreco

thou art music

i used to think that he was
carved in wood: this warped figure,
aging, an ornament in a
music shop window
his oaken complexion was as
select as that of the surrounding
violins: the texture of his
leathery layer was rugged and corky,
sprinkled with liver spots as
marbled as the music stool to his right
the earlobes drooped heavily from
tortuous shells, credibly crimson, they were,
and crinkly, and ruled with lines
resembling the music stand behind him with
its wings of intricate vines airily spreading
the mystique of his perfection
the interplay between shape and detail
bewitched me; to this day I believe that
he may indeed have been music itself

Kathrine Amalie Roswall

American Immigration Officer

Maybe they were among the lucky
ones. Maybe nobody found them huddling
in Polish basements and attics, beneath
wooden boards, moldy rugs,
wine barrels, years of clenched breath,
the noose tightening around
a continent. Is there a plump,
bleary man sitting in an
official room, scratching his nose,
leafing lazily through documents?
Maybe, chuckling from a fine morning
at the racetrack, he might stop the
chimney powder from floating gently
over alleys and electric posts,
whitening the rose bushes
in the children's park.

Irwin Ramirez Leopando

Vancouver Morning: The Unforgotten

Nights of red volcanic stone made blank
As ceramic bathroom tiles; days
Of unwanted abstinence; the tentacular
Fingers and whiskey breath of a kid
Who can't hold his booze yet, his heavy
Moist lips like pickled calamari on mine.
The high heels crush my feet
Like white chocolate roses. It's all an error.
My sundress, my purple eye shadow
In the black light of the party,
My identity vanishes like Stanley Park
Under a sudden heavy snow. Waking
At home, I see the shoes contemptuously
Cast into a corner; the drapes of the room
Are still open. It's barely morning.
The sun is barely up.
The dress, visible, hanging in the open
Closet, catches a tiny shot of sun
Before the clouds move in,
Extinguish the light again.

Eva Grace Chow

The Psychology of Life

Birth, life, death.
"These are the three psychologies,"
My father says, his back to me,
Facing the tree stump.

The axe hangs low in one hand while
The other runs quickly through his hair.
"The pig feels nothing," he says,
"He's long dead from the blunt whack."

I know he's right;
So I don't say anything else.
But I'm thinking, look—
Look how it lies there:

Both ears gently folded.
The out-turned lip.
One eye, half-slanted
As though considering something.

As though the psychology of life
Were still a possibility.

Jessica Anthony

Undone

For Victoria

The sound of his voice is a thief,
transgressing this wall resurrected so long ago
in defense of his arrows.

The smell of his breath—
wine and tobacco.
The taste of his skin—
salt and tang.
His touch . . . hesitant yet propitious.

These memories assault me
as if I am still young enough to withstand
the discord of naked truth.

I was his sycophant,
basking in the afterglow of his tiny injuries,
entwining his tales of conquest in my hair,
wearing them as my own crown of thorns.

His voice
was the thief of blind faith.

Tjuanda Anderson

The Old Port's Glow

Low, over the tired Old Port
clouds rush upward, then sigh
with a finale. A glow and hush
is backdrop to the late-gone tide.

There's a look of cannonade
like the sky around Atlanta
sacked by bombs from trade
that built these river mansions.

The Piscataqua runs under bridges
that connect two states of mind.
One exhorts, "Live Free Or Die!"
the other shrugs, "Vacationland."

Here's no careless meeting
of the minds tonight; cables
and spans, as if effortless,
secure the separate rights.

The river sways and expands;
eddies and ripples resolve
into a greater current than
the ocean's accidental balance.

Samuel W. Blake

City Funeral Home

Smell this sorrow?
Spanish chants grow thick, and
the women squeeze bibles as if to soak
answers through their dimpled arms.
Supposedly our God is up.
Why do their sedated faces bow down?
I see them dilute our
happiness with greater part somber.
Even Jesus sags sad on his cross,
a child stuck with stiff adults.
My God,
fear-curtained eyes shade your sunny world.
I try to exhale vile dread that circulates.
I try to see my zombie friend who
lies swollen with death
the bullet in his head wanted.
The casket cradles him with longed-for
lullabies of nothing snow on TV after
midnight.
But I continue, seeing what he did not want.

Lisa Mina Terry

Battered Women's Shelter

She watched the cracks
in pavement as she went;
the brown eyes of autumn all around her.
The street light was salmon
against the dark grass of evening.
She passed it by slowly
watching blank windows.
She looked for them
as though they were lost,
as though they were a phrase
on the tip of her tongue,
waiting.
She had never seen one
though, in the seasons she walked past.
She would have settled for any sign of life:
a green book on a window sill,
or a red towel along the seam
of wood and glass.

Rose Anne Netherland

Inquisitive Snake

The heaped outcrops of gambling steam
Out to sea like glowing, over laden cruisers.
In between their moorings, lights glint
Like gems dropped in haste on a wild flight
From one roulette wheel to the next.
The Mediterranean foams around their bows,
Quietly undulant in its classical blue.

Our train coils through the piled treasure
Of vice like a tiny, inquisitive snake.
In the gray, carved bowels of its going,
I tongue a small blade in pathetic defense
Against onslaughts of French drug dealers
And old Nazis on a pilgrimage of de Fuhrer.

We shunt in smooth-shouldered jerks through
The light and dark of old coastal tunnels,
Threading the hills into a thin necklace.
To the gamblers, we are only a singing echo
In the toilets, far above.

Avery A. August

Mississippi or Muddy Waters

I was born in an attic on Basin St.
Mama said 'bout 1910.
There was a big parlor, piano, and a yard with pigs and hens.
Creole ladies, sailors, northern men in suits
givin' Mama and me paper loot.
Life was never still; they all came to our house in Storyville.
We was little girls in white dresses and dirty knees.
I didn't read no schoolbooks or recite poetry.
I sang voodoo spells and jazz melodies.
Piano playing professor, he played ol' ragtime real fast.
Ladies move behind closed doors; each man a memory of the past.
I could smell the catfish frying,
mixed with the dark smoke of the yen poke fire.
I heard my mama fall to the floor,
a woman's scream, men rushing to the door.
They carried my mama to the river's edge.
I clung to her dress, tearing at the threads. . . .
There would always be the muddy waters between her and me,
the dark poison of the Mississippi.

Bonnie A. Dunn

the flesh constantly bleeds, but i live

the pain is excruciating, but i endure
the mountains are high, but i climb
i dream, but i always wake up
i am crushed for feelings i can't spare
drained of all emotions, but i still love
the simplicity of your word my savior
keeps me humble, but i still cry
my nails claw through my flesh
tears turn to blood
i seek eternal life
but i get weary along the way
the flesh constantly bleeds, but i live

Christine Vaughan

Miss the Dust

For K.R.

After tonight, I miss you.
My heart, opened widely again,
and the memory of you still fresh.

Then a magical thing took place
as I held my hand in yours, it was unlike any other.

But you weren't there, were you?

Now I cried one tear, another is jerking.
I miss you, yes, I miss you,
I long to see you again.

I need reassurance
that everything will be okay.
Twinkle dust at dusk is it.

The only time in one year I'll have to be with you.
I can't let go, no way to move on,
no way to let time slide.

I will see you later.
Maybe then I'll have more to say,
with faith in us, with faith in you
as you lie deep down in my heart.

But somehow, just somehow I'll get by.
I will try.

Alexa Blair Wilkinson

And I Knew

Thick, beautiful eyebrows arched over
hazel-colored eyes, sparkling with
flecks of green . . .

And I knew.

A mustache to match those eyebrows
resting atop soft full lips, silently begging to be kissed . . .

And I knew.

A smile that radiates sunshine . . .

And I knew.

Honey-brown skin, velvet to the touch . . .

And I knew.

Hands big and strong, yet gentle upon mine . . .

And I knew.

A tall slim-goodie with legs slightly
bowed . . .

And I knew.

In that first glance, our souls joined
as one.

And I knew.

And I knew.

Pamela Livas

One

In night and day we're one, not two,
through moments of passion and hard times, too.
We rest on a perch as love birds do,
not three, not four, just me and you.

You see my tears, I feel your pain;
it's as though we are both two of the same.
Life must be painful to live without
the pleasure of never living in doubt.

Together we stand on a bridge made of sand,
and cross this we do with God's helping hand.
Think of the times when bad seemed worse,
when we gave up our fears and challenged the course.

Life is an obstacle that all can overcome,
when you try it together, not as two, but as one.

Dawn Michelle Lally

Only in a Dream

Remember me
  I've been here before

No? Puzzled?
  Not quite sure?

Think back to the past
  Not far, but it'll seem

Maybe a hint
  We've seen each other in a dream

I'd descend like a haze
  From above

To experience all manner
  Of your love

Tis only here
  In dark of night

I am so bold
  Not filled with fright

Tis the only time when I'm
To myself so true
  Within this sleepy fit when readily I admit
That I love you!

Joseph Lowney

Houston

For my dearest Robert—I will miss you always. I love you, Mom

Great pulsing giant of childhood dreams,
Where do you hide

Beneath the smoky pall of dragon's breath
That lingers in the once-clear dawn

Under crushing waves of souls that beat
Against your troubled shore

Behind the glittering sightless stare of
Mirrored thunder domes

Within the tiny isles of green floating in a
Concrete sea

Kings and paupers linger in your shadowed
Depths

Great pulsing, loving, growing child of dreams
You hide beneath a brilliant patch of Texas sky.

Under the twisted limbs of old oak trees
Behind a splashing crystal fountain
Within the laughter of a child at play

You're there
I'll find you yet

Jayne Woody

Love Like a Rose

Our love was like a rose
which slowly grew:
tiny, fragile and shy in the beginning
wonderful and blooming in the middle,
wilted and dreary in the end.

The rose got bigger
with every lovely moment shared together,
until our love faded away.
But whatever happened,
this rose was special.

Now all is vanished,
leaving pain and sorrow,
and poisoned thorns of unhappiness
for those who were in love.

Melanie Angelika Schweiger

Fragile Dreams

Whether fragile dreams come true or they turn to dust,
possible best striving is an absolute must.

At the end of the day, either you win or lose.
The scene, at least, will swing in better than worst.

Things cannot be kept if room is not made for them.
To adopt something, you need to adapt first.

Do not hold it in; it'll kill you. Let it out.
Grief turns to relief in tears when it is an outburst.

Can disagree, even dislike one's notions,
but don't mistake each other's existence for disgust.

Treat others the way you want to be,
since being single standard is the best way to rein any lust.

The real battle against evil lies inside one's self,
though surroundings may be light-provoking gust.

An eye cannot take a look at itself,
but still try to watch self-character before it catches rust.

To the best of belief, truth must stretch start to end.
On lies' base, how can you build a monument of trust?

What matters is not what's true, but what's believed?
So whenever thought with hate, you'd think of unjust.

Talib E. Butt

The Brush

Where in the frame of His picture am I?
  Could I be the eagle soaring on high,
Or maybe the tortoise trodding below?
  Why does He paint His picture so slow?
Could He have put me up in the trees
  Along with the squirrels or among the bees?
I don't see me with the deer at the lake.
  Am I ever to see? How long will it take?

I'm not in the clouds floating above.
  I'm not in the field with the little white dove.
I'm not with the fish swimming down deep.
  I'm not with the things that crawl and creep.
I'm not with the butterfly on top of the log.
  I'm not on the lily pad along with the frog.
I'm not in the colors of the evening sunset.
  Perhaps He just hasn't painted me yet.

Feelings of excitement race through my veins
  As I wait in silence for the thought that reigns
In the mind of the artist who controls the hand
  Painting this portrait of a wonderful land.
I wonder what part He'll have me to play;
  Where will I be at the end of His day?
But I must be patient. I can't be in a rush
  For He's painting this picture with my mind as His brush.

Freddy Don Kirkland

An Elusive World Peace

World peace, why is it so unattainable?
Peace is for what we all dream, pray,
hope, and even fight.
Yet, realistically speaking,
in our lifetime, will we enjoy it?
Who can bring this sought-after peace?
Time and again, national leaders have tried,
negotiated, compromised,
even threatened each other for it.
Still, peace is not within mankind's grasp.
Some basic causes that hinder peace may be
greed, selfishness and a thirst for power.
Could these be put aside so we can "talk peace?"
Until man can display the fruit of God's spirit;
which is love, joy, peace, long-suffering, kindness,
goodness, faith, mildness and self-control (Galatians 5:22-23)
peace will never become a reality.

Kay Hirokawa

The Windup Toy

Dedicated to my one true love,
who could only hear the music of money

When the windup toy was new, it could play
the music you wanted for the whole day.
You would laugh and enjoy the tune
that the new windup toy would croon.

You would tease the toy by winding it tighter
to get it to play more music mightier.
You could not get enough music the toy brought
for you to enjoy and to be amused a lot.

For many years the windup toy kept playing;
more and more music you loved and kept craving.
But the windup toy could not play as much
music needed to keep you happy, content, and in touch.

Then the windup toy's gears broke and could not play.
So you cursed the toy and kill yourself, you would say.
You screamed, I no longer love you and you must depart.
The broken windup toy left with a shattered heart.

The windup toy is very sick and dying.
Every day he spends his time in bed, crying and wishing
he could make the music again that pleased thee.
Now he knows it was not the toy you loved, but it was the melody.

Mark R. Fairall

Timing Is Everything

We met, oh, so secretively.
So shy, so intimidated, so exciting . . .
Timing, yes, was on our side.

Oh, but at what cost. Who cared,
But yet my heart was wrenched.
Could that stop me?
Timing, yes, was on our side.

When the good outweighs the bad,
The excitement, the buildup, oh,
Timing was on our side.

Now, what happened.
We don't see what we saw.
We don't feel what we felt.
We were friends, what happened?
Friends first is what I always said, but
It is not possible at this time.

Oh . . . timing, well, is not on our side. . . .

Timing is everything. . . .

However, I will always love
And care about you, my friend.
Timing just passed us by.

Lori Pierce

The Emergence

Turbulence rocked her.
A hovering shroud closed in, suffocating all joy,
leaving but needles of sorrow.
The jolts of unhappiness were beyond endurance.
Smiles and laughter ceased.

Her beauty; talk, kindness,
compassion shed their shell
as the earthly beats stopped.
The gloom of the shroud descended on those who loved her.
Three and a half decades are
but a minute fraction of life to those who mourn.

But body and soul had separated.
The encumbrance was lifted.
The sea welcomed the ashes, the chaff of her being.
Her beautiful, radiant, eternal spirit evokes warm memories.
Her soul beats down and on.

Tillie Atkins

One Night

You'll meet me one night and after say,
Have you met this good woman?

Beautiful in the body and the mind,
Always considerate and always kind.
Smiles all fair, with laughter in the air . . .

Never a curse has slipped her part,
So strong with what she wants.

Her shyness you will confess,
No one would ever count her less.

But when does a cover ever say
About what's going on within the page?

Anger lurks around every door,
Like so many cursed ones before.

Lost to a dream that may never speak,
She says she loves to be so weak.

So much hatred from who knows where.
Is it true that she does not care?
Smiles for what, with laughter as no more . . .

Have you met this poor little thing?
You will say on the night you don't meet me

A. Monahan

She Brings the Light

To Kell, a woman like no other

There are no stars that bear her name.
Her beauty is fluid, like the gentlest rain.
Inside her are no secrets, no lies, and no deceit;
For she brings the light
And now at last the heavens are complete.

Her fire comes from the spirit,
A place so deep within;
Forged by the pain of despair,
Tempered by the forgiveness of sin.

Her smile can part the heavens.
Her voice can calm the savage seas.
She's the center of my very existence;
My savior, my lover, my one and only thee.

I know now I'm lost forever
And I pray to God to never be found.
I discovered my destiny in a cloud of darkness.
Her sweet song my only sound.

Yes, darkness has lost its teeth
And time no longer has its bite.
She will blaze her trail like a comet in the sky,
My dear angel that brings the light.

Joseph Michael Kelly

Memories

Memories we shared is all we have
Since you took that long journey home
I remember the stories you told me when I was small
I knew the love you had for me
Once I looked into your eyes
I knew you wanted the best for me
I know there were tears shed for me
I know that you wanted me
I know you saw me grow into the man you were proud to see
I know you wanted so much for me
I know you knew how much I loved you too
The tears we shed when you were called home
To that beautiful land across the sky
The truth was told before you went home
I see you in my dreams I see you in my kids
I'll see you someday at the Heavenly Gates
Mother I will call you when I see you again
I love you more than you could ever know

John J. Debney

Winter Trees

'Tis winter
The leaves are falling
Like nuggets of beauty whirling
Twirling and dancing in the air
That only leaves do with great flair

Sturdy horse chestnuts, hickories
Poplars and oaks sway in the breeze
To remind stubborn leaves to fall
Freely, gaily and have a ball

The trees, naked from top to root
Flaunt their bare trunks and limbs to boot
Frame the sleepy and snowy land
And give a stand to nature's band

I admire the winter trees' pride
And looks in which honesties abide
Imperfections they proudly show
Scars and lightning burns in ev'ry bough

Soon there'll be flowers on roadsides
And dogwoods winking on hillsides
But for the wonderful present
I'll soar each winter moment

Natividad Macaranas Brown

It Is You That I Seek

When I awake in the morning and long to stay in bed,
It is you that I seek.

When I start my day and notice it's almost done,
It is you that I seek.

When I dream of my future and all the things I hope to do,
It is you that I seek.

When I turn to my friends for understanding and support,
It is you that I seek.

When I reach out to my family for patience and caring,
It is you that I seek.

When I go to my mate for comfort and love,
It is you that I seek.

When I give of myself in charity and selflessness,
It is you that I seek.

When I gaze upon dawn's sky,
When I hear my child cry,
When I sit and wonder why,
When my lover says goodbye,
When over the rainbow I want to fly . . .

Lord, it is you that I seek.

Jakae K. Crawford

Slaying Time

Seconds fall away, like stars
ripped from ethereal moorings by each heavy
TUNK of the second hand on the old clock.
If you listen—not to anything, but listen—
You can hear them die—those seconds—
in the silent space between the gearclicks.
TUNK, quiet scream, TUNK, quiet scream, TUNK,
and the clock spins and kills till all time is dead.
Fear and doubt and ache and worry double
with each dead second and every slaying TUNK,
as, waiting, a heart turns more and more
to dark imaginings and fright-fed dreams—
waiting in the silence of those
dying seconds
to learn the truth.
And, the more seconds pass away,
the more that fear grows and gnaws
until, finally, in the end, time stops,
suspended by an expected call.

Shane Stewart

It's a Beautiful Day to Sleep

I'm too cold in this bath water,
Without your voice

In these nights spitting out a November moon
Catching on to the smell of (silence.)

You left,
(Through the frosted window
Where the wind kisses the petunias
And winter skies are carnivals
Of white satin lights)

And your eyes polluted with porcelain stars haunt
Me like the shadows that smudged the ghosts of girls
With incomplete hearts so ripe to pump your cold moonlight.

The moon is almost burned out
The floor is such a pretty mess
Of black and white photographs
And stickers that won't stay on

Once only overcome with dreams of glittering
Flutes now only singing into scars of butterflies

My eyes are blurred with morning; the rotten milk
Clouds will drain away like the miles it took to get from you

Leelach Feldman

Tell Me How You Feel

Dedicated to FeFen

Do you really love me
Or is it just a game?
Maybe if I knew
I wouldn't be in pain.

If I knew the truth,
Maybe there'd be no more crying.
But I'm so confused
That my feelings for you are dying.

I don't want to let you go,
But my heart is in so much pain.
I just want to know
If you and I feel the same.

You say you love me too
And yet we're not together.
How much longer 'til I know how you feel?
Do I have to wait forever?

Just put me out of my misery.
Say it for the record,
Tell me how you really feel
And maybe then we'll be together.

Sasha V. Mercedes

September 11, 2001 . . . No More, Please

He arrived at work, sat at his desk;
Out of no where he entered into death.
Out of the sky came two planes
And destroyed his building in rubble and flames.
It was the work of terrorists, but why him?
He never did anything to them
Nor was he alone leaving us that way.
Many, many more were killed that day.
We can never retrieve what we lost,
Nor will we ever afford what it cost,
But out hearts will ever say,
"They were fellow Americans, one of us.
It is sad for those who died.
Alas! It made us all cry.
But the saddest of all
Are the families on which this tragedy had to fall.
God bless the mothers, fathers, sisters
And brothers
And let us all pray there will never be another!"

John Joseph Smith

The Day I Lost My Heart

Dedicated to my mother

I awakened one night
guided by your light.

You appeared to me in a vision
of delight singing with a choir of angels.

I wanted to hold on tight,
never leaving you out of my sight.

And with fear in my heart I knew
that I had to let you go.

For the Lord needed you on
that special Valentine's Day.

I knew that you were chosen for the
love and kindness you have always shared.

For even now, I can see your spirit
living on through those who crossed your path.

The only sadness I now feel is that you
are no longer with me.

Dear Lord, no one ever prepared me
to live without my heart.

LaVinia Viana LoBrutto

Moments

The day begins,
Each moment grants possibilities.

The stream of traffic rushes past,
As I watch and wait.

A car slows, stops and waves me in.
I acknowledge the kindness and enter the street.

That moment of pleasant surprise lingers as I proceed.
I'm sensitized, I await
Other moments of surprise.

The door's held open and she smiles.
I enter and we pause a while
to say, thanks, have a great day
And be good to yourself in every way.

The line is long at the checkout stand,
He says, go first, you've just two items in your hand.

Have the planets all been realigned
To cause this change within mankind,

Or have I just become aware that serendipity's everywhere?
This work keeps changing it's meter and rhyme
To stay in touch with my change of mind.

Lorenz W. Steyer

In My Mind

In my mind the moments we shared play over and over
And in my mind we never had to part
Yet my heart knows that cruel reality exists
And in my mind you hold me as I fall asleep each night
But I wake up in fear when I don't see you next to me

Sitting here I feel a chill
Thinking back and remembering the brief interlude we shared
I am reminded of the way you made me feel
And as your presence starts to fade
I am terrified that you will forget about me
And leave me here wanting you

Lonely nights spent wishing for you
Make me feel so cold
Wondering if you're thinking of me too
I close my eyes and swear I can almost feel you
Thoughts of you are flashing through my mind
Sending chills down my spine
I can't wait to feel your body next to mine

Gabrielle Ann Pisano

Life Means

You come into this world
In the most incredible way
Naked, innocent, helpless, in awe of it all

Do we choose to come to this place
Had we a previous memory that has left us
Or could it be that we have nothing to remember

When our journey begins
Have we a mission and goals to fulfill
Or only time to kill

Have we a choice on whom we are to be
Or are we marked by destiny
To be good, to be bad, or just to be

Is our path set in stone
Could the choice be our own
Will we know which road to walk

Will we know when it's our time to go
Should chores be left incomplete—
Then will we know what it all means

Does the journey continue or just fade away
Will there always be another day

Cheryl M. Griffiths

Wake Up, My Princess

Hey, my dear princess, wake up!
The sun has reached the high heaven.
The moon has rested under the endless sky.
Wake up, the sleepy hand strokes seven.

Hey, my dear princess, wake up!
The cows are waiting to be milked.
The ducks are waiting for their morning swim.
Wake up, for the market needs their silk.

The rooster has sung for a brand-new day.
My princess, you're not awake.
I am lonely without your presence.
You're not out there in the morning lake.

Life is an empty road without you.
The cows are howling with sadness.
The hens miss their egg-taker.
Please come back, my dear princess.

You have not awakened for you are not here.
I have died without your playful soul.
You are all I have and all that I have lost.
Wake up, my princess.
For me.

Khiem Minh Tran

Music Aliveness

Listening to the beautifully played music
One shares enchanted art with others
All harmonies expand immeasurably
How they spin in one's intellect
Even felt in one's deepest emotions
Embodying great complexity
All proceed from the composer's own mind
To the recipient who hears and absorbs
'Tis a gem stirring heartfelt emotion
Like the violin's high tonal sweet echo
Or like sunbeam swooning in the air
Soft flames of passion sung for others
Life shedding light on real nature
A beating time in patterns of dance
That becomes alive in listening
How glorious is it sung out in chorus
It softens the flame of an inner song
Where we sing and leave the lasting hum
Found on our lips where it's truly
Alive and makes a song never sung before

Miriam E. Allen

Life's 9/11/01

The Twin Towers stood proud and tall
With insiders oblivious to each airplane's sound
When two enemy planes flew through each wall
Crumbling the Towers to the ground

The third plane hit the Pentagon at one side
And the fourth plane averted its planned site
All fallen heroes on the planes were inside
As the enemy took their lives, but not their pride

Policemen, firemen, helpers, and brave rescue crews
Were there in minutes to help or aid
For they were aware they had no time to lose
As they knew they had lives to save

Three thousand souls went to Heaven that day
On angels wings they flew
All their loved one's dreams were gone astray
As terror grew and grew

Our country was shaken to its knees
And sorrow gnawed at each heart
Time stood still and business ceased
As their loved ones forever were torn apart

Helen Harper Church

Kelly

Kelly means love.
He put a song in our hearts.
God sent him from above,
Even though we're far apart.

Twenty-seven years is not enough for us.
She killed him for drugs, money and lust.
What he had was not enough for her,
Even though his love was pure.
She had a lover; that was sure.

We love him so much and always will.
We're all out of touch as time stands still.
He was not born to die that way.
Even her kids, she led astray.

They must know the lies she told.
Their grandparents she stole.
Someday, the truth they will know.
Her kind of love is icy cold.

Run, little boys, while you can
Before you're touched by her murdering hand.
Your father is gone because of her ways.
It won't be long now; count the days.

Bonnie Marshall

My Pain

Dedicated to my mother, Emily Reavley

Life is like an emotional roller coaster.
You're gone and I hate it.
I hate the fact that I will never
see you again.
I hate the fact that I will never
feel your touch.
I hate most of all that they took
you from me.
Life feels worthless without you in it.
The tears I cry are so painful,
it feels like it will never end.
Life is purgatory,
a hell that I cannot break loose of.
I'm so strong yet so weak.
I hate myself because you're dead.
I run from someone who loves me
and end up killing him each day
so he can feel my pain.
I have lost everything that I was.
All I have left is my pain.

Colleen Anne Reavley

My Beloved Rose

There she stands with sparkling eyes,
Brightly twinkling, as stars in the skies.

Rosy lips and heart of gold,
I long to kiss and ever hold.

My dreams are vivid, my heart beats loud.
She appears to me from a great white cloud.

Whispering words, so smooth and soft,
Captures my mind whether near or aloft.

Her loving ways and constant giving,
Enriches my life and desire for living.

She flies with angels through the night
And guides her family with all her might.

The Lord is her shepherd, guiding her way,
An angel to me, day after day.

My faith in her is carved in stone
And never wants to be alone.

Today and forever, will never close,
My love will be, my angel Rose!

Chester A. Baker

My Teacher

Your smile was a rainbow
That brightened my way.
Your presence in my life
Has made me who I am today.

Your strength was always evident
When life dealt you a hard blow.
Your patience was unending,
More than enough to teach.

Your generosity taught me
To always consider those with less.
Your caring ways showed me
How to think of others before myself.

You took each day as it came,
Never complaining about the bad.
My life has not been the same
Ever since God took you to be at his side.

What I wouldn't give
To have the chance
To tell you that I love you, Mom,
One more time.

Susan Marie Bishoff

Apostrophe

Apostrophe, apostrophe,
Oh! What trouble you've brought to me
I'm contracted in your sight
I hesitate to use in fright
Addition, omission, what a decision
Oh! Apostrophe

Your name sounds like a Greek goddess
I often misplace you with a guess
You leave my English in a mess
Especially with your 's and s'
Oh! Apostrophe

In contracted verbs you are
You play your part like a star
Riding high over your conquest
Redundant letters laid to rest

Apostrophe, apostrophe, I will avoid catastrophe
When I'm not sure if I've placed you right
I'll rephrase my words to solve my plight
So apostrophe, your rules for fools I see
You won't get the better of me

William Corbett

Life

To my darling cousin Andrew, who took his life at a very young age

Sometimes life is easy
Sometimes life is hard
Sometimes life is fair
Sometimes life is cruel
Sometimes life is fun
Sometimes life is sad
Sometimes life is full of love
Sometimes life has broken hearts
Sometimes life has beautiful people
This isn't a reason to fall apart
You had a choice
A choice that would affect life
Affect those who loved you
Loved you for who you were
Life is what we make it
Your destiny was in your hands
Other's destinies were in your hands
You made the wrong choice for us
The wrong choice for you
And now you're gone, but that I guess is life

Alison Marie Peaufa

Carrier of the Sacred Pipe

Upraising the pipe in hands that have grown
out of ancient past, crossroads you stand on.
Solitary in your cell, yet never alone,
deep rooted you are in Earth Mother's womb.

You stretch up yourself, insistence of rose,
thorny, yet flowering plenty upward, and along
the Red Path, you hold up with sacred vows
peace pipe to Grandfather with offering song.

Humble boldness, awake prayer's power to find
peace-vision for your people, for humankind.
Grandfather's breath outpours from the light,
guided by your song to fields of inner fight.

Upwelling sparkle of gold-white glow
flows into the prison of everyone's shadow,
flows into the inmost of mankind's dark side.
Fiery breath of Creator in prison night.

You dare to turn 'round and to smile, to sing
through bars with wolf's strong will to bring
the circle in prison with the circle around,
and in harmony with the One Circle's sound.

Heike Bobert

The Works

a new world explained
in a different language
never spoken, never broken
"desire in the eyes lights
the fire of the girls and the games they play"
amazed by plastic soldiers
and fortunes of dirt
did you hurt for the reasons of tears
for many years of whispered youth?
lost, tossed-aside daydreams migrate
from guilty to innocent
lost the scent of my white widow
where did she go?
lost attention
did I mention the show must go on?
wheels turn, memories burn, lessons learned
sent bent meaning, drowning under a Turkey bottle
and a fake smile—denial of abandoned love
and blue-jean lust
price to pay to walk outside, go away beside myself
the human struggle begins

Billy Snodgrass

Words

Songs not written,
Poems never read,
All drift around
Inside of my head.

Will they ever escape
From the depths of my mind?
Will I ever get them down?
Will I ever find the time?

There are many ways the words can come,
The shapes that they can take.
What effect that they could have?
What impact they could make?

Would they make someone smile,
Or make somebody cry?
Will they answer someone's questions,
Or make them wonder why?

To know what effect my words could have,
The world may never know,
Unless I let a pen and paper
Take them from my soul.

Audra Lee Fischer

Dearest Bloom

It was somewhere west of the future and south of fate
And it was no wonder that I was running late.

One of these days I'll find her entranced by the falling snow,
Where streetlights remind her and leave misty crosses all in a row.
She goes where the lonely go, where God only knows.

Visiting with strangers she likes to call friends
In corners of the city where Liberty Street takes a bend,
And billboards are covered with barn-board thistle.
Innocent days when she learned how to whistle.

On those nights when the neon ran blurry
And nobody was ever in a hurry,
She'd careen into the abyss mid-paragraph
Like driving off a cliff in an old Cadillac.
Reaches for more wine, tears it from the vine.

'Cause the queen of reminisce sometimes wants a kiss
Wanders resurrection alley reflecting on a tryst
Paints the town for other people
But stops everything the gaze up at a steeple.

She used to laugh like it tickles, exhibit tentative gazes
Collected buffalo-headed nickels and live way outside the mazes;

Stephanie Goodhue

From Here to Forever

There's a fire that's burning
And disintegrating my heart
Its massive flames are tearing
My very world apart

What can I do? What can I say?
These feelings and this pain just won't go away

My love for him was true, then, not now
It's you I'm thinking of as I make this vow

Time heals all wounds, I know
But for now I feel that there's no place to go

Please help me, save me from this relentless pain
And show me how to be loved again

The more I write, and the more I talk
The better I feel about my decision to walk

I know you can't help me, but you can just be there
The thought of you leaving, I just couldn't bear

I need someone now more than ever
I wish it would be you from here to forever

Allyssa Lynne Edwards

The Fall

It was the fall of the year
when I met the one so dear . . .
I so lonely . . .

hoping for a hand
to hold . . .

wanting to feel her presence
oh, so bold.

Now . . . in my mind
I see . . . a beautiful maiden made for me.

Somehow I must grasp this dream come true
as watching her eyes . . . in a beautiful blue.

Reflecting smiles . . . I see . . .
wonderful moments are in place to be . . .

when eyes meet together
meant to be . . .

But now in the silence . . .
darkness I see . . .
just like dreams were meant to be . . .
goodbye

J. A. McCutcheon

About a Girl

my urban angel, she's one swift move
from rolling to the rhyme of the drum
my heart pounds like jolt cola
she leaves a sweet taste on my tongue
when our lips part and eyes open
she's as bright as a solar flare
can't compete with the heat she gives off
warmth that comes in waves
that slam into me like a semi
I spin my wheels
as the pavement melts like plastic
I soften like playdough in her hands
I am beheld of an angel
I am rapt by her touch
I lie still—I cannot speak and dare not say her name
so subsonic it makes the dogs bark
like a post man I am sending her a message
"to be or not to be" in love
she's like filet mignon, so very tender
it's easy to swallow my pride and be faithful
like a priest, I worship her on sundays
sunny days and all other days

Ashley James Seiter

Brian Wilson

Under mounds of grey-blond hair,
the crew is under attack by the holograms!
Candy-striped harmonies echo aimlessly
and mix quickly
with some of the old, swollen waves.

Who among us now has enough surf in them
to take Brian's deathcoat
and lay it down, wrinkle-free,
on a long stretch of shore break?

Can't you see in the mist,
a shark cutting through quiet waters,
and a smaller boy, under doctor's orders,
waiting in a wetsuit for his third set?

This whole project has been so troubling
that, even if his brothers could be pretended,
the sea is still the great repository of tears.

Later, hanging out by the pier,
we can take our time with ice cream cones
and watch the girls watch the sunset.

Don J. Olender

Heart's War

Happiness eludes.
Not too much at one time, or it will break.
The bottom drops as each story of love concludes.
How many more lessons must I take?
Maybe this time . . .
Hand in hand of hope goes trembling fear.
Breaking my yearning heart is a crime.
Begging to see intentions clear . . .
Save my mangled heart.
Fill the hole.
Care enough to take part
In the healing of a soul.
Peace comes after the storm
From white caps to glistening, smooth tides.
True reflections begin to take form.
The heart remembers, no reason to hide.
Minds awakened are opened
To new ideas of the once ominous world.
The glimmer of hope sustains
Through the darkness to show the way.
Where despair loomed, now optimism whirls.
True understanding comes in this beautiful new day.

Ashlee Michelle Kersenbrock

Life Revealed through Belief

A gift of effervescence with incessant
forgiveness for iniquity
given to mortals by means of a loving
and compassionate entity

The flesh of a spirit, which is inflicted on
a majestic creation
its probation of worthiness,
longing for the magnificent salvation

Life is a vision inquisitive to the
mysterious and solitary soul
The reflections that become visible
can seem unsightly and cold

The struggle for purpose and rationalization
are endlessly sought
They are revealed and perceived through
passing vision and thought

The time which is granted remains
unrevealed to conscious animation,
although trivial to the bounty and triumph
of the concluding destination

Richard Alan Griffin

independence

locked inside a room
four white walls, a window full of bars
they think I cannot see them analyze
the secrets and the scars
like they're ours
they're mine, only mine

I'll peel flowers just to bury them
in the sand where they belong
and while they're sleeping still
I'll will you all "be gone"
you'll all be gone

or of I can't express the rest
I just might shred and burn the walls
and blow the dust and ashes in the
clear black shadow of the distant, nonexistent waterfalls

when my flowers wake up
suffocated, unprotected, far away from home
they'll have to find a way
divine regeneration, adjustation
learn to grow alone

Micah Cari Silverman

Life

Resisting resistance
Wrestling with dilemma
In collision with myself
Delayed reaction
Not withstanding the brutality of innocence
Chasing the past
Confronting the future
Disappearing into myself
Running on empty
Lifeless
Giving up the dream
Behind the words
Echoes of myself
Plodding evolution
Layers of thought through the
Secret passage of the mind
Mourning an illusion
The meaning of it all
Sense of wonder
Awakening innocence on the verge of extinction
A world that never was
At the mercy of existence

Dominique Rochelle Salet

Breakup

We talk on the phone.
All you can talk about is how he is the one.
You can't live without him.
You dream about marrying him.

Only thing I can do is talk you through it.
Maybe he'll realize he blew it.
I don't know what's up with him
Maybe his lights went dim.

He flirts with you,
and kisses you.
You tell him it's not right.
In the meantime, you try to avoid a fight.

All you can do is cry
and think of ways to die.
Tell him how you feel
and ask him how you are supposed to deal.

Go your separate ways,
without anymore to say.
It just isn't meant to be.
That's something I know he'll see.

Traci Lucinda LaMonte Page

Beginning to Stolen End

Oh, the missing checks.

It was a day like any other. Ongoing.
The thick smell of cooked dog food lingering in the air
(I despise the stench of someone else's reheated leftovers).
Pretty perfumes and costly colognes mingle in the hallway.
Coffee and cigarette breath holding on tight to tips of tongues.

Something's amiss.
Betty grilled me about what time I was here.
Who was here that I recognized?
Who's car was out front that she wasn't familiar with?
7:45 a.m., Gaseous Mathimus, I don't know; respectively.

Later on that day.
Police take notes while workers gossip details that fly as facts.
Betty snidely jokes with one of the auditors from KPMG,
Hide your wallet, hide your watch
Thieves are loose amongst us.

Oh, the last stanza.
It held the truth.
Only it was stolen.

Melissa Ann Kelly

Old Glory

You watched as thousands of innocent souls
Were taken from this Earth.
Although some think they saw great death,
They really witnessed birth.

"America the beautiful," they'd say,
Their hearts so filled with pride.
Their last words to their loved ones,
They really knew they lied.

"Oh, I'll be alright," they said,
"Don't worry about me,"
As many lost their lives
Just to save our liberty.

Men and women, dying on the line,
Their lives the cost of freedom.
Firemen, police, and the reverend alike
Instead of running, did come.

The pain we suffered for Old Glory,
For the land and home of the free.
Oh, my dear brave red, white, and blue,
How gallantly you are streaming!

Rebeccah Joanne Swanson

Spirit

We buried my mother a few weeks ago.
The wound on my spirit is as raw as the dirt on her grave.
Her death, not unexpected,
Still carries a weight, the magnitude of which leaves me breathless.

She fought a battle with but one possible outcome.
Cheating the forecasters with extra years,
She chose life to the end and drank fully from each moment.
Her laughter leaves its echo.

Fresh from a hospital, with oxygen tank and a prayer,
She climbed a railroad embankment to attend a wedding.
Carried back in the arms of a young man, she flirts.
Her walk down that hill is burned in my memory.

Booby traps everywhere, her dusting brush reduces me to sobs.
I see her still working, still helping,
Even when strength and breath were gone.
I miss her terribly.

A tissue in her robe escapes my attention
And for a final time shreds in the wash.
I cry and laugh as I shake each piece of covered clothing.
The flakes fall to the carpet like snow.

Cathy S. Woolsey

My Guardian Angel

Oh, dear my angel, as God has sent you,
so I will be always true to you!
Your voice is beautiful and sweet as it can be,
so how lovely you must be to guard
a lonely and sad child like me.
Your voice touches my feelings
hidden deep in my heart,
which used to be once locked,
but now it opens doors
with flowers growing through the floor
where there were none before!
When I don't know the right way to go,
it's the toughest time for me,
but I know you will lead me to the place
where I am supposed to be!
When I am alone, you are always by my side
to guard me with your deepest piece of heart
that I may know where I should go
to find all your deepest feelings for me,
and that I could feel that I am not alone
and that there is always you who will help me go on.

Anastasia Marie Stallcop

Feeling Like a Child

What I want to say has already been said
In letters and song
Whether alive or dead

They showed they cared
More than I ever did
It's hard to feel anything
Instead of feeling older and wiser
I feel more like a child

A love song is a child
One born a minute
One trying to make a stand
One trying to make it on its own

An outlaw here, however love songs are clones
Same gifts wrapped in different words
One remains the same
One verb

But the time will come
When you will want a child of your own
Just remember how hard it is
To have a child when you're all alone

Allen Wayne Beavers

Another Fairy Tale

Home snuggling by a fire, sharing popcorn,
knowing the family is safe.

Holding her lovingly in my arms,
inhaling the fragrance of her cologne.

Tasting the warmth of her lips as they
press against mine.

Glancing in her eyes knowing that the
illumination I see is that of my own.

Consecrating her with my love as we
pass through time.

Once upon a time and they lived happily
ever after is an illusion!

Words arraigned in resplendence to reflect the heart,
love slowly fading to repugnance,
used as fertilizer to feed lies.

Once upon a time and they lived happily ever after
is fiction, another fairy tale.

And they endured alone . . . ever after.

Layne Farmer

Last Scene: Blissful Beach Lovers

Spoken by a female
Lying upon the shoreline
The breeze slowly wafts my hair
I feel as though I am one with you
As I lie beside you bare
You caress my lips so gently
Looking into my eyes as though you have not a care
As you run your soft hands upon my hips
As people sit and stare
Your warm foot rubs my leg slowly
You quiver with such joy
You are my one and only
You whisper in my ear just like a young boy
Running my fingertips over your lips
Moving downward with my tongue
Onto your chest and nipples
Gently kissing and playing one by one
You roll me over, tell me, "Shh, just listen to the waves clap"
Then I hear the director yell
Thanks, everyone . . .
And that's a wrap

Jacinta Paige Nest

Getting New Business As a Recruiter

I am a recruiter
I specialize in placing administrative staff
I am good for an admin, a receptionist
Or for a good laugh

If you want I can stalk you
I can call you every day
But then I would become annoying
And you would want me to just . . . go away

I will follow up with another e-mail
Again in a week
If you want you can e-mail me back
Or call me and we can speak

If you already have an agency
That you like to use all the time
Then I will not bother you again
And I hope you enjoyed the rhyme

But if you are not happy with who you have
And you are interested in meeting one more
I would love to come and bring you bagels
A quick hello and I am out the door

Jennifer Cindy Star

Nocturnal

The walls around me are caving in,
And my ambitions toward life are steadily decreasing.
I don't know who or what I've become.
I just know that I'm lost inside myself.

My smile has fallen into a dark oblivion,
And it's nowhere to be found.
My laughter has been muted with cries,
And it's nowhere to be heard.

I feel as if reality has frozen me in time,
Not letting me progress or go backwards.
My only emotions are kept within,
And the tears fall when I can hold on no more.

I would rather stay awake at night
To enjoy the silence of darkness.
I would rather sleep when the sun comes up
To shield my soul from another day.

I need to break my shell of defense
And find myself again.
But for now, I'll roam nocturnally,
And try to hide from the rays of reality.

Crystal Marie Ditto

After Work

It is 4:00 a.m., sleep does not come easily
My mind is on fire tonight
Flashes of life and death
Like bolts of lightning
Startle me in that state
Between awake and asleep

I endeavor to heal people
Alleviate suffering and pain
Soothe distraught spirits
For all who remain in my care

But death takes it toll!
More than once I have sensed
The rising of a soul from the body
Lingering in the air around me

Whispering I'm free
Tell my loved ones
Do not grieve for me

And yet I grieve
For death once again defies me

Susan P. Martin

The Silent Ballad

Have you ever watched lightning dance?
It jumps hither and thither, always askance;
Some skinny, some fat, some short and some long,
First this way, then that, as if to a song.

Some extend a finger, as if in a greeting,
But never do they linger or wait for a meeting.
They sway with each other to a soundless tune
And light up the Earth beneath the moon.

With a sudden flash they brighten the night
And while doing so somehow add grace to their might.
There never was such a sight to see
As bolts of electricity dancing for thee.

They move with a grace not of this Earth,
More reminiscent of the heavens which gave to them birth.
Muted music seems to move their feet,
While frightened children hide their heads beneath a sheet.

All through the night the thunder sounds, "Boom!"
Causing a sense of their presence to fill up the room.
And all the while the silent ballad plays,
Which I will never tire of hearing through the rest of my days.

Terick Kurt Gutierrez-Steckler

Always Remember Our Day in the Park

Today we went to the park, my grandchildren and I.
I pushed them on the swings and Sara Grace said,
"I can touch the sky."
Will began to laugh as down the slide he did go.
My heart nearly burst—I love them both so.
Will is only one year old and Sara Grace is two.
Will has dark hair and Sara Grace is blonde,
But both have eyes of blue.
Sara Grace has won my heart, for she reminds me of me.
Will is the image of his dad and brings back memories
Only I can see.
Sara Grace has a way with words and expressions on her face,
Will wants to give you a quick hug
And then is ready for you to chase.
When Sara Grace says, "Mama Sue, I love you,"
My heart swells with pride,
When Will first said, "Mama Sue,"
I could not help it; I cried.
I will always remember our day in the park
As a blessing for you to see.
I believe God sent Sara Grace and Will
As angels, especially for me.

Sue J. King

The Flight of the Dove

Reflected in the glass of the window
She sits
Her shoulders hunched forward
Deflecting the world and all its offerings
Clinging tentatively to a life no longer desired
She waits
For fulfillment of one last wish

Before the final curtain falls
A dove takes flight
She imagines herself soaring high on its winged back

They gather around in remembrance
There is unity—unfamiliar, yet welcomed
'Tis her path that has brought them together
At last, she has accomplished in death
That which she so wished for in life
It is enough
And, in that moment
The dove takes flight
She is
The dove

Veronica B. Fox

Alone

Dedicated to my best friend, Ashley, and all my other friends

All alone, ignored by all,
In the corner I sit.
But it is not entirely society's fault
That I prefer solitude from all but one.
Am I destined to this fate?
To be alone all my life,
With no friends
And no one to talk to?
I am out to
Even the odds,
Only helped by
My instructor.
She teaches me defense
Against all who
Are evil or cruel.
I search for a friend
And find one in my instructor.
We talk and realize we are perfect friends.
I finally have a friend,
A best friend.

Katrina Marie Wischoff

Hoping for a Second Chance

She may never come back to me, in fact that seems so,
But my love will follow wherever she may go.
She's the most wonderful creation to ever exist,
And her presence beside me will forever be missed.

I don't know how much time I have to walk on this Earth,
But I will spend it showing her how much she's worth.
She will never again be made to feel cold.
She will always have my love to which she can hold.

She may doubt me now because in the past I have failed her,
But the future will be different I can assure her.
She says she doesn't want my love and I understand,
But it's not up to her where my love lands.

You see, since she left I do nothing but cry
And if I don't show my love I surely will die.
My love is so strong, it needs its expression.
It took me a while but I did learn this lesson.

I know she needs love and that's what I'm giving.
Maybe it's too late, but for as long as I'm living
I will cherish this angel that only God could provide;
And from her my love I will never again hide.

Thomas E. Mitchell

Russian Roulette

Life is like Russian roulette
You spin and you spin
Sometimes you lose, mostly you win

Every night, when you go to sleep
You place your bets and spin the chamber

You pull the trigger every morning
As soon as your eyes open

Sometimes the chamber is empty
You have a good day
Hang out with friends, go to the movies or just relax

And sometimes the chamber is loaded
Pow! You get a bad grade
Pow! You get in a fight

But then there are some
Who decide not to play
Who always wake up to a boring day
Sometimes I envy them
But most times
Life is good!

Michael F. Badr

I Am Death

I am useless, for my use has been replaced
I am broken, for I am too easy to break
I am weak, and everything I am falls apart
I am nothing without the light from your heart

I am dying because I cannot leave
I am living because it isn't up to me
I am cursed when I think about myself
I am dead just like everybody else

I am helpless, and I know you try your best
I am worthless, and yet my worth is still much less
I am alone here with a person held in vain
I am secluded with myself, the bearer of my pain

I am darkness for I don't worship the light
I am dirty, and I hold the clean in spite
I am unfair, and my greed consumes my soul
I am vain, and only you can make me whole

I am pissed off because I cannot change your world
I am lost and still the same scared little girl
I am abused by every nice word that's been said
I am unbelieving because no one loves the dead

Jessica Vicious

goodbye . . .

kitten, life's not real but just a dream without you by my side—
a bad dream that won't go away
never wants to go, just wants to stay . . .
how much more can i take?
my mind won't even let me think . . . i feel it's going blank
only getting worse
i couldn't take life knowing you weren't happy
it would be worse than death to even see tears in your eyes
so, all i hear is what i want . . . lies
i could never describe how i love you, what's the use in trying?
i'd give my life away just to be with you today
even if it was only an instance, i would try
tell you what i find so hard . . . i can't say
now i'm the one who feels used; stuff i said i wish i hadn't
i can't stop thinking about you, i try but i find it's useless
what am i suppose to do if i can't have you?
i know you'll never come back
my heart's lost and gone . . . without you
i know you don't care, you'll never understand
lost inside, so much heartache, so less pride
you try to come back, but i've already moved on . . .
goodbye . . . i love you . . . i'm gone

Josh C. T. Boone

A Child Once Again

Pinks, yellows, and purples swirl.
A sigh escapes at their magnificence.
The bitterness of winter passed over
for the beauty of life.
A bird chirps joyfully while nestled
among the branches of a tree.
An old woman nestles her wrinkled hands
in a pile of dirt.
She is a child once again.
Pushing a rickety green lawn mower with callused hands,
an old man pauses to inhale a breath
of fresh air as he envisions days of the past.
He is a child once again,
bare feet combing through dewy grass.
A gleeful smile brightens my face.
Plucking tiny flowers,
I place them haphazardly in my mane of hair.
Blowing lightly on a "wishy,"
I wish for my dreams to come true—
if they cannot, I am simply thankful
spring has made me a child once again.

Mary Catherine Eastman

Half a Jar of Peanut Butter and Van Gogh's Soul

Here I sit, hunger pangs gnawing on my backbone.
Yet, I feel free, for you see, I am filled with
Something most can never see or understand.

I am filled with spoonfuls
Of peanut butter and Van Gogh's soul.

And that, through these times of great trials,
Where I sit in my pools of thoughts and emotions,
Staring out my window in this tiny, white,
candlelit room,
I am somehow rich beyond measure.

Bare bones, soul driven, heart open
And still after thirty six years, I'm naive and trusting.

The smell of the sea is wafting through my windows.
Jazz playing, Coltrane, in some house
Down the way.
Deep breath . . .
Deep sigh.
Feeling full beyond belief.

Holly Baumann

Pleasure's Shadow

Who are you, who appears like a shadow
At night, when there are no shadows?

Who never listens to a word I say,
But hears every word I leave unspoken?

I never know when you leave, when or if you will return;
But I always know when you will appear
For the trembling in me is still in anticipation.

If all the nights we've shared were put together,
I haven't known you for a week, yet you can stir depths
Others I knew for years, could not even find.

The briefest of encounters, for days, mists my mind with pleasure.
Not any one thing thought or felt, or remembered, but
The knowledge that I can be so thoroughly human and responsive,
When all walls of fear and pretense are put aside.

There is no need for any walls or pretense,
You are only a shadow in my night, a misty pleasure,
Remembered in the morning sun.

I think I'll keep you that way,
For now, or if possible, forever.

Susanne Barry

Faith

If there were no Heaven,
If there were no Hell, what then?
If the Bible was just somebody's journal,
If all the sermons ever preached were just
Useless lectures, what then?
If there was no church,
If there was no worship, what then?
If God decided to give up,
If Jesus decided to leave us, what then?
If nobody cared,
If nobody tried,
If nobody cried,
If nobody strived,
If nobody gave it their all,
If nobody had a care in the world,
If faith were dead;
Then what would faith be?
Would it be a useless thought?
What would be different?
What would we be taught?
If faith were dead, then what would faith be?

Jayson Robert Zorola

Maw Maw

For Maw Maw, my loving grandmother,
who was always there to comfort me

Each day has a dusk, a night, and an end.
Let this day be one where the sunset remains.
For when I think of this sunset, I wish to think of you.
You are my inspiration and joy.
It is you who gives me the strength to awake each morning.
As I look at your portrait, I can only do,
but think about your wonderful, kind, fulfilling personality.
Thinking of you may weaken my heart for a moment,
but it strengthens my soulful cries.
For I know that one day in the future we will reunite.
To follow after your wise ways is my path of least resistance.
Your warming touch heals every wound I have, or have yet to face.
If I had one wish in the world to be granted,
it wouldn't be for one hundred more wishes or for wealth.
Only for a few moments with you, so I can hear your soft voice,
so I can smell your sweet essence, so I can finally say goodbye.
Goodbye, such strong words, too strong perhaps to say,
for I am sure this is not the end, only a halt in the road of life.
A halt that I can't let come over me.
One that I may not have smooth sailing over.

Patricia Anne Van Alstine

Fishing at Sooke

Sooke, B.C. is the place to go if you like to fish, you know.
Sun, rain, and the wind likes to blow
In the morning, damp and cold.
Let's go fishing, we're not too old;
Out on the water, our rods to hold.
Hoping to catch a fish to can, Pink or CoHo will land in the pan,
Tasty eating for any man,
Cooking on a camp stove, sleeping in a tent
Enjoying the outdoors, wondering where the day went.
Shiver in the evening, but pretty good rent.
Dozer on the table he likes to lay;
Mike takes him for a run six times a day,
Up and over the table they play.
To Beachy Head we like to hike;
Joan, Ron, Dozer and Mike.
Fresh air and exercise; just what we like.
One day is hot, next day it blew;
Next day it rained, what else is new?
Everyone accepted, what more could we do?
We roll down the awning, then roll it back, tie down the tent,
To keep things in tack, everyone knows the wind will soon be back,
That's Sooke.

Elinor Elizabeth Lucas

My Mother Was There

To my mother, my angel

If I got over heated and was feeling ill
When I had an accident or just a spill
If nights were restless and I could not sleep
When I had a secret that I could not keep
If I was sad and was feeling blue
When I was confused and did not have a clue
If my clothes were torn and needed a mend
When I had a problem and needed a friend
If I lost the game and I was feeling down
When I was alone and needed a someone around
If I was scared and my insides would churn
When I fell and my ankle would turn
If I needed my tie in the perfect knot
When I was sick and did not feel so hot
If I wrong and committed a sin
When times were hard and I wanted to give in
If I made a mistake and was in the wrong
When I needed someone brave, someone strong
If life was good and there were no harms
When I was safe and in my mother's arms

Christopher DeBroise Baker III

Fields of Grace

In a field as white as snow,
Where the grand lilies grow,
And lesser radiant tulips pose
Amongst the innocent budding rose.

Vivid colors rise and fall
With the dawn's shining call,
And as the darkness of night sets in,
All Earth's creatures begin.

The sound of faint humming bees,
The tranquility of midnight streams,
The fresh scented summer air,
The sanded shores faintly bare.

Where the nightingale's soothing song
Embraces all those who long,
For no man will ever find
A field such as this till the end of time.

As the tale goes, in the fields of grace,
All creatures shall find their place
In this field of aroma and pacify nights,
And morning's shimmering daybreak light.

Dawn Elizabeth Giroux

An Early Morning's Journey

The men board the aircraft.
They head towards first class.

Once again, they review the plan
Soon they will be hated as much as the world's most wanted man.

They uncomfortably take their seats
Their god, soon to meet.

The plane slowly rises into the air.
How could they not be scared?

After many an hour,
The plane changes power.

Blood drips down the chair.
The men don't seem to care.

Two buildings stand tall and proud.
They shudder as the plane passes through a nearby cloud.

After seeing the towers tumbling,
Everyone's hearts are crumbling.

The United States will always stand together.
This will surely be a journey the world remembers.

Katelyn Mae Cooney

A Midnight Orchid

My infinite darkness within surrounds
Plead of God with fate to ill temper
Cascaded eyes of stars so bright
Brought in from an orchid midnight
My thoughts of a sad cry held in tight

To whisper a sound so high inbound and tortured
Brought into the orchid with a little boy soulless and sadly crying
Credence overdriven through his mind spoken true
Beings of the dark night follow in his path
As shown through the drabbling of himself
Tortured and salvaged with demon curses

Boy at hand of the devil
For they are at Matins
Night of dusk gone for the dark lord
But rises Satan yet again on the cold night
Gods of time rise as the boy prays

Bagging for the life of himself the gods of time rise
Through common change on dark day and hell bound night
The gods speed up time
Satan replenishes leaves to the bright sky back to night

Carlo G. DeAgazio

Time and What to Do with It

Time, what is it
The seconds pass as I look at the clock
And there goes time in the past
As if I could ever get it back
Time, what to do with it
I sometimes think what about that time
When I could have done that or said that
Or moved that or stood up to that
I wonder is it against us or is it for us
Time, maybe there's to much time or maybe too little time
Whatever it is
Time, it can be so short—good times, bad times
Times when I don't care about the time
And times when I don't know what to with it
Some say, get a life worth the time
How about a wife worth the time
Family, there's always time for the family
Time and what to do with it, fight for time
Live for the time when the seconds don't matter
When the time is right to forgive
I let time be as it is
Time, I still don't know what to do with it

Derrick Noel Demetrius

Ellazette Blaydes

Her maniacal laugh echoed through the damp halls,
Rising up from the cellar and straight through the walls.
It crept up quite softly, like a slow growing vine,
That horrible cackle sent chills down my spine.

I inched down the stairs cautiously, frozen by fear,
Realizing a terrible fate could be near.
For down in the cellar, on that dark stormy night,
Was a bloodcurdling wicked and hideous sight.

Just under the windows all covered by shades,
Crouched the viciously malicious Ellazette Blaydes.
I stopped when I saw her, but to my surprise,
She flashed a wild grin and lowered her eyes.

She motioned me over to her underground lair
And promised that I would enjoy it down there.
But I turned and I ran and I slammed the thick door,
As her long yellow claws scraped the gray concrete floor.

That night I slept well for the first time all year,
The menacing storm clouds had started to clear.
Her laughter subsided and the silence was kind,
I'd cleaned out the cellar inside my tired mind.

Joanna Leigh Metzger

Angel's Wings

Angel wings so open wide
let the light shine inside.
Console the tears that crystallize
within the care of my angel's eyes.
Destiny so undetermined, as we listen.
Preachers sermon.
Some truths may sting the depths
of even the most lost.
Fallen to the ground,
all joys are bound,
tied so tight to this bottomless
pit of despair.
Stop to think, who really cares?
Safe is the touch that reaches out.
Sweet is the kiss that erases doubt.
Peaceful bliss from an innocence,
so happy is the joy of a rejuvenated soul.
Confine not myself
into a prison of this world that sings.
I'll close my eyes and fall
into my angel's wings.

Sebonae Zamudio

My Soul Mate

I'm thankful each day when I wake up
That I've got such a friend like you.
Even when we are apart
I know your friendship is true.

With you, I can just be myself,
Not worry and fret what words to say.
In case the meaning is not clear,
You'll not be hurt and walk away.

If I lose my way, I know you're there.
When I need a friendly ear,
Your arms can hold a thousand cares.
Your gentle touch can wipe a tear.

You encourage me to be strong
And hold on to what we've got,
To appreciate our time together
Whether a little or a lot.

So, your friendship means the world to me.
It burns in my heart each day.
I hope our friendship lasts forever
For it's special . . . in every way.

Ev Gwyn

I Believe

I believe in the stars shining so beautiful in the night,
Reaching out just to touch their precious light.
I believe in the snowflakes that fall to the ground,
So delicate and beautiful without a sound.

I believe in the angels and their undying love,
Here on Earth and in the heavens above.
I believe in a simple smile that makes the eyes shine.
It warms even the coldest of hearts every time.

I believe in fairy tales and wishing on falling stars too,
For love is ageless and you'll find they really do come true.
I believe in romance, butterfly kisses, and candlelight.
Nothing is as wonderful as being held so tight.

I believe in you so very gentle and incredibly kind.
You're a treasure in my heart until the end of time.
I believe in my love so unconditional and true.
Even though you didn't want it, I gave it to you.

I believe in following your heart; it's never wrong.
No matter where it leads, it will only make you strong.
I believe that life is worth living and sometimes so unkind.
In my heart, you will always shine.

Valerie K. Erickson

To My Friend

For the few people who have made a difference in my life

To my friend,
Thank you for being there for me when
I thought I had no one.
To my friend,
Thank you for showing me what it was like
To be a part of something.
To my friend,
Thank you for listening to the things I had
To say even though it did not make sense.
To my friend,
Thank you for showing me
Love, kindness, and support.
To my friend,
There are often times
When I feel like no one cares,
But you, my friend, have shown me different.
To my friend,
Thank you for showing
Me that your past does not matter.
To my friend!

Amanda Joyce Dean

Eventide

Soft breezes like gentle pardon
Ease my troubles away
Here in my lovely garden
At the end of a care-filled day.

Sunlight filters through rustling leaves,
Branches of maple trees sway.
Lemon lilies, crimson geraniums,
Rival Solomon's glorious array.

Crystal waters ripple on the lake.
A black fence goes astray,
Wandering through the meadow
Where wildflowers bow to pray.

Bird songs fall into silence
As twilight softly creeps in,
Erasing the flaming sunset
Before the night begins.

All about me I feel the presence
Of the One who wrought such loveliness.
I lift my heart in joyful thanks,
For truly I've been blest.

Hilda L. Buck

What Is a Child?

In the dictionary, the word child
means infant or a baby human;
not of the offspring of animals,
but a creation of God through woman.

God created Eve from a rib of Adam;
her body designed to be of a service
for God's human creation and service of man.
What a wonderful God who planned for us!

The human male and female
were created by God in His image,
but Satan made his own plan to prevail.
We are seeing his results in this age.

God placed children in homes
for joy, happiness and pleasure,
until the day Jesus comes
to take us to Heaven, as his treasure.

Adam and Eve and their children
became the first family of God!
By one son yielding to sin,
another son was placed under the sod.

Leona DeHaven

Menacing Hole

Sinking deeper into the menacing hole of me
Forgetting the sky closing in above
Absorbing the blackness, forgetting to see

The depth I gain, the more reality I lose
Filtering out echoes once resembling love
Sinking deeper into the menacing hole of me

Stars wane in the distance, I'm unaware of their fate
They betray their beauty by leaving night bare
Absorbing the blackness, forgetting to see

I am the owner and a stranger here
Ravens mock my lips for their ability to smile
So I sink deeper into the menacing hole of me

There are no disasters, only catastrophes
Robbing the laughter and crucifying dreams
Absorbing the blackness, forgetting to see

Tears mean nothing, they give you a taste
Of dessert before dinner, of what it's like
Sinking deeper into the menacing hole of me
Absorbing the blackness, forgetting to see

Andrea Elizabeth Stout

Bodily Woes

I used to wear my t-shirts tight,
but now it is my fear that I might
reveal many an extra pound.
So, now my shirts are large and round.

I used to smile a lot, you know,
but longer did my teeth then grow.
So, now when someone tells a joke,
I seem to be a sullen bloke.

I used to style my silky hair,
and curls would wave about the air.
Alas, my hair is turning gray.
I thought I'd wear my hat today.

I used to have smooth, smiling eyes.
But gradually, I realize,
my tired expression is complete,
with baggy eyes and some crow's feet.

However, sometimes I feel great,
despite my teeth, hair, eyes, and weight.
For all of my bodily woes
time left alone my lovely nose!

Paul Latham

Lost

Every one beating heart that has lived their days
Is very unique and special, in their own passionate ways
They experience anger, gratitude, happiness, and love
Some say even while they are in the skies up above

As a child, they are happy and carefree
But as they grow older they realize it wasn't to be
The days of singing birds are gone
Taking with them their joyful songs

They wish to go back to the past
And make those memorable times last
By then they are too old, I fear
The ones that we all loved so dear

So we lose them as time passes by
With more and more turns to cry
Their memories are left only inside of our heads
As we toss and turn about with dread

The love that bounds our hearts together
Shall not perish, not in forever
Twenty losses in one year
But yet I could not shed a tear

Allison La Rose

a poem for daniel

a year has gone by,
but it feels like a week
tears still flow from my eyes
i can't seem to sleep

my thoughts of you
still run through my mind
i'd never have dreamed
life could be so unkind

late in the night
early in the day
i still hear your footsteps
i still hear you play
sometimes i wake up
and feel your sweet touch
it doesn't stop the heartache
i miss you so much

i am your mommy and you are my son
the love and the laughter will never be done
you'll always be with me, deep in my heart
we will meet again, we'll have a new start

Rebecca D. Streets

Take the Time

People grumble and some complain
When things don't go their way.
We need to take the time and
Thank the Lord for every day.

Some have good health and are so blessed
While others, through an illness, get no rest.
We take life for granted and live at ease,
But some face uncertainties with a threatening disease.

If we have eyes to see and ears to hear
And feet to take us anywhere;
Hands to hold things, a voice to speak
And God in our hearts, life is complete!

Think of the ones who don't have these gifts,
At all the things they're missing.
If they'll only believe, someday in Heaven,
They'll have all these. Oh, what a blessing!

Life is moving at such a fast pace
We just don't take the time
To visit the lonely and sick or make a call
When someone is on our mind.

Sheryle Burger

When I Was Young

When I was young I walked to school
And tried to live by the Golden Rule.
I pledged allegiance every day.
Talked to God as I knelt to pray;

Gave thanks for family, Earth and sky.
Knew someone heard me when I'd cry;
Felt safe at night when I closed my eyes.
Never doubted if the sun would rise.

Today it seems a different tale
From scenes we all know too well.
Burning towers, guns at school,
It sounds like someone forgot the Rule.

So much has changed through the years.
Have we forgotten why we're here?
Hug your children; teach them well.
Express your pride when they excel.

Take time to help them understand.
Give guidance, support, a helping hand.
Teach them honor, truth and love
And ask for guidance from above.

Judy Lutz

An Eve Bereft

I will be Lillith

My Eve days are done
He reclaimed his rib and left
Leaving, always leaving me tender and bloody

I did not ask for his rib
I thought it was the way of the world

But no, you call them demons
I know they are outside and beyond

I do not know why they would speak to me
Or why I can hear them and remain whole
Without Adam's protection

Perhaps I can hear them
Because I am without Adam's protection

Chaos is sweet, they sing
I know
Outside and inside I hear the same sweet song
Fear not
Chaos is only God's clay

Bobbie Vail

Lord, Thank You for My Mommy

Lord, thank you for my mommy
You made her oh, so sweet
She always kissed my bruises
And pulled the stickers from my feet

She'd say, "I forgive you"
Every time I was bad
Nothing could break
The love that she had

She tried to understand my hurts
And was sensitive to my needs
Sometimes we laughed, sometimes we cried
She was the rose among the weeds

I wish I could do some things over again
That made my growing rough
But thank you for giving my mommy to me
To get me through that stuff

Oh, what a gem my mommy is
Only you could have made her so
I wouldn't trade her in a million years
No, I'd never let her go

V. Sue Colvin

Untitled

How could I have been so blind?
I was thinking that you'd always be mine.
I guess it was just a fantasy,
Because you're no longer here with me.

Was it something I did or said
That made you turn away?
My heart has been tortured and left with pain.
Did you think you had something to gain?

I can't believe you broke my heart in two.
I thought you said you would be true.
You left without a reason why,
I thought you were a special guy.

Do you always prey on the innocent,
The ones you say are heaven-sent?
Did you think you had something to prove?
You were mistaken, c'mon, get a clue.

I'm moving on, I've got better things to do.
I'll prove to you that I don't need you.
Why you play this silly game, I'll never know,
But in the end you lost, when you turned to go.

Tammy McCaffery

Unforgettable Memories on My Seventh Floor

Beaming faces with caring hands
Skying patience rooming service
Unlimited, the termite spirit
Beautifully engraving, the seventh floor

Being in my shoes, my spine
Perfectly felt and understood
A message I was not alone in my agony

Compassionate hands were
At the other end of my cross
Bearing it up within me
Making the anguish less to drag on

Professional touch fading pains away
Catching a glimpse of recovery
A dream of hope, an era of merry heart, butterflies in my soul

Life like breathing machine
Yearns for much needed smoothing, greasing attention

With due respect I salute
The "greats" of seventh floor
Praying for payback from the hands of the Almighty . . .

Erlinda Franco

Trust

A decision was all I took
To be the best I can every day.
Demons left; I was off the hook.
Angels came to guide me on my way.

A long journey had just begun.
I was not out of the woods yet.
At least there was some sun.
No longer I was sad.

I faced all that came my way.
I kept my head up high,
Even lived in San Jose.
In order to survive, I had to fly.

Then one day, it came to an end.
The time had come to face it all.
I crashed and burned, no longer could pretend;
Faced my demons, breaking every wall.

But you know what the beauty is?
I trusted you to change my soul,
Clearing it and filling me with happy bliss.
Now I can say you did, I am whole!

Christina H. J. Elissen

The Heartbeat

Be still and listen—it beats within. . . .
The embrace of love, two hands that meet;
a kiss between two strands of hair;
the wind upon a lonely face. . . .

So surely beats the rhythm
beyond the chaos of senseless sound
that the God in every man might hear
the heartbeat of Her child. . . .

Can fear distort a rhythm so pure
or deeds deafen heart's inner ear?
Could truth be robbed for lifeless death?
And the Goddess soul cries out in pain

for withered petals after lusty blooms
and passion born from fragile guise;
remembering the pulse of love
lost in a whirlpool of forgotten dreams.

Despair is the voice for a world lost
beneath the whisper of Her breath.
And still we do not hear—so cannot know
the heartbeat of Her soul.

Alpha Mae Woodward

Mindful Angels

So, it seems
To be gone from this life.
So sad . . .
To be gone from the physical touch;
Touching of the beach sand,
the pine trees,
the smell of cut grass,
of salty air
and dirt garden.

All of this is gone.
You now dwell
in purposeful beauty
and know the secret of life on Earth.

Guided by mindful angels
and helpful guardians,
escorting you to your people;
family long past, who made this same journey.

God bless you, Linda Churchill.
May Christ hold and cradle
your soul in your journey home.

Priscilla A. Heslin

Silent Prayer

I can see your smile as if it was only yesterday
And I still can't believe that you're gone.
I think back on all of the things I should have done,
Should have said,
But didn't.
That's what I regret the most.

Somehow, I thought there was still a lot of time
And you'd always be here.
I couldn't imagine life without you.

Yet time goes by quickly,
Too precious to take for granted.
I only wish I had known this sooner.

I feel sad knowing that you're gone,
Yet I feel happy
Knowing that you are finally at peace with yourself.

I still have my memories of you
And I feel secure knowing you are somewhere
Still watching over me,
Waiting for the time
When we'll be together once again.

Eulyanka Eva McMahon

The Battle Cry

Awake my soul, awake!
God has a job for you.
He gave you life to do His will.
There's work for you to do!

Get ready for the trumpet sound.
Attune your ear to hear
The soft still voice of Heaven's call,
The whisper of a prayer.

No need to cower and cringe with fear.
No need to moan and cry,
For life's great battles are only won
By those who dare to try.

So put on your whole armor,
March forward without fear.
God will be your shield-bearer in battle.
He'll be there.

Be ready for the task at hand.
Be prepared to do your best.
Your ultimate is to achieve
The crown of righteousness.

Patricia Estick

Hardly Time

Why must we rush and not take time to see
The beauty, the Earth, the love of a family?
Why must there be all this prejudice and hate?
Why can't we all just relate?
Why must the angels cry out in pain?
For all the love they see end up in puddles of rain.
Why must we always travel faster than a speeding sign?
Why do we not have hardly time?

Carlene June Rose-Gehrke

Seed of Life

For what is life?
To find the key to the question
You must put away all mental thoughts
So that you can find your inner seed of existence
As if life is the most precious gift
And wonder what is the purpose it contains
The essence of life is life itself
The seed of life is likened unto an aging tree

Joshway Isi Short

My Love of the Four Seasons

On the hot summer days,
I get all hot for you.
On the cool fall days,
The colored leaves show my love for you.
On the cold winter days,
Each snowflake that falls I love you more.
On the warm spring days,
My heart is warmed by you.

Allison Page

Flowers for "Papa" Tutt

Growing in pots
Planted out of love
Courtyard blooming with color
These flowers wanted to survive
November comes and they are blooming
Thanksgiving comes and the building burns around them
December shows up and the flowers are still alive and blooming
Tough flowers, just like the person for whom they were planted

Terry L. Luebbert

It Can't Finish

A morning with rain.
The sun can't be seen and I smell you
as I gaze to the street.

So lonely it is
that I look for your visage
and I ask myself,
why did I know you and lose you?

If a puddle on my forehead
of white tears cried from my heart,
you could give to my life.

What the whole day I couldn't find.
Look at the tear in flames
that your mouth left in to be.

A scream that can't be heard
says your name and asks for your love.
Come back to my life one more time.

The fantasy to see you next to me can't end.
Give my life a little lighting.

I love you this day; I don't wanna cry.
Let the rain finish; let the sun come out and give me your look.

Santiago Salazar

A Definition of a Man

Like God provides for his children, he provided for his family,
sharing his guidance and wisdom effortlessly.
When his family was in trouble or hurting,
he would protect us, naturally.
Through all my years he was there for us—good times and bad.
Whether we're healthy or sick, I'm proud to call him dad.
So naturally when the strongest, healthiest man in the world
got cancer, we were there for him.
He handled his illness with dignity and grace,
though the sparkle faded from his eyes and face.
He fought his battle for three long months,
and in the end had to give in.
A true definition of a man is now in God's hands.

Kathy L. Hickey

The Wonderful Falling Snow

Of all the wonderful days there are
I love the ones with snow by far.
It changes the pace of my busy day
And makes me relax in a wonderful way.

As I watch the snow fall to the ground,
I realize that everything must slow down.
And as the accumulations grow,
It's apparent there's nowhere I can go.

So I pour myself a cup of tea
And sit at a window where I can see
The wonderful thing that has captured me,
The wonderful falling snow.

Robert Reid

There's No Other Who Makes Me Feel the Way You Do

To the love of my life
Your beautiful smile brings composure to my soul.
The warmth of your love lights my fire and takes away my cold.
The innocence you personify,
I can't deny that it's true.
Love to me doesn't exist without loving you.
No one makes me feel like you do.
My promise is to always be there for you.
When we embrace,
the warmth of your body sends chills down my spine.
That feeling is a definite reason
why I want to spend my life with you until the end of time.

Michael Dorian Carter

'cause remember, i love you

it seems like only yesterday
when you were still here . . .
but now you're gone
somewhere far away
and i miss you.

i think of all the things that could have happened,
all the things that we could have done.
we would have been so perfect for each other,
but you left me,
here,
alone.

but i forgive you,
'cause i still love you.
my heart is yours,
and yours is mine,
and that's the way its going to be.

so until that day you come back
i'll be thinking of you
and waiting,
'cause remember, i love you.

Alice Chen

Ode to Love and War

Ode to fine odors of your body breaking
on the shores of a salt-caked martini,
and rushing deliciously down my stubbled chin.

Ode to the crest of civilization,
and the screaming lurch into the dark age,
when nerves run hot with the languages of distrust.

Ode to hunger and thirst,
the considerate eclipse of past pains by the sprawling
joys of those few unforgettably sunbright moments.

Yes, ode to escapism and retreat,
and the lies that are the lifeblood of our hope,
and ode to a desolate future of buried trouble and bone.

Justin Nagraj Sarma

Integrity

"There's so much in a name," he said.
The gift my father gave, I rejected.
"And if it bears your name," he said
"It should be your best effort."
My father never went to college, as smart as he is.
He works so hard to watch his only little girl,
Who fancies herself an intellectual;
Thinking everything is meaningless
In our eye-blink, speck-of-time lives,
To watch her take the easy way,
Even though she knows the name she bears
Is still his.

Lori Lord

Just Don't Know

I thought not even distance could
keep us apart, but time has shown
me so differently.

I can't believe how unknown our lives
have become;
it's been so long since you were
here with me.

Daily things occupy our thoughts,
makes me realize a future for us
may never turn out to be.

The hardest part of all this is not knowing how you feel;
your words are spoken so gradually.

Christine Anne Kulick

Still Healing

Sometimes I think we've already forgotten
That tragic day when our safety was taken
We live our lives in ignorant bliss
Unknowing of the cold that inherently exists
I fear for my country and the people within
What will we do when we again lose our closest of kin
Another tragedy is surely on the way
Can we rebound again when it happens that day
Are we foolish to go about our lives as we do
Unimportant jobs favor something with virtue
Am I helping to stop this from happening again
Could I have done more
It will be too late by then
Our leaders tell us to go on with ours lives
It's the only way to heal and survive
If you don't, then the evil has won
And they got just what they wanted you to do
I try to convince myself that this is all true
But the feelings of guilt and fear always break through
Now is the time to step up and make a difference
Only I don't know how and it's a frustrating silence

David Michael Severino

The Observer

Travel—I must travel to the other side of me.
The suns, the seas demand my presence in the trees
and the earth—the other side of shadows.
Must I know the reasons they will be in the pulse of stars.
I burn away the past things; burn to sanctify
this flight of eagle's soul to lords of suns.
To the plane of tilting and turning I must come;
creator of the other side of universe and me.

Sophia Burriss Celia

drowning sun

i watch alone the sun being drowned by the sea
it makes me think of how you always drown me
drown me with your love that i dream of every day
because we're not together my heart feels cold and weak
when we meet eyes again i will have found that warmth i seek
you are everything i've ever dreamed of
and hopefully someday we can watch the sun drown together
while we drown in our own love

Harrison Sheppard Levy

Kenya Correspondence

Little Ms. Britt decided to sit
And write her dear friends a letter.
A big three-inch spider descended beside her
And she was afraid it might get her!

So, Missus Britt squealed for Don please to wield
His panga and chop up that critter.
But he blinked both his eyes as he looked at its size
And decided he'd just let it get'er!

Sharon Ann Britt

Peaceful Tranquility

As I walk along the beach
I look out into the distance.
I watch as the sun glistens off the water
And the light shimmers and moves in waves of peaceful tranquility.
All that I know escapes me,
And my mind floats free.
The sun has ceased to be,
Yet I am lost in peaceful tranquility.

Christopher Joshua Black

Overconfidence

Today I got a new assignment, hard,
designed to test this amateurish poet,
to discipline and try to make a bard
of someone thinking she already knew it.
I certainly am hoisted by my petard.
My confidence I eye with some regret.
I've written many lines, and it would seem
this is all that's left: ottava rima.

Hope Meek

A Brand-New Start

Looking out of the window into the snow,
Wondering how much I really know.
Taking into consideration about my past,
I am just the type of person that moves too fast.
Even when I say I know a lot,
I should give things much more thought.
Seeing how much I want a clear head,
I should have listened more to what Mom had said.
But it is never too late to fall apart.
Just look ahead and begin with brand-new start.

Shawn M. Basey

Mother's Love

This is dedicated to Travis, my son, my inspiration.

Son of mine, my heart breaks as I remember your smiling face.
I saw you just Saturday, but it seems so long ago.
You have begun to change, not as I remember you.
So many times I ask God why changes have to be!
I just want you to know how much your mom loves you.
Though time may pass, I will not forget you.
Though the miles keep us apart, you are always near in my heart.

Marion Mae Cyhowski

September 11

September 11, 2001 was a day
In which nobody knew would hurt everyone.
It was a tragic day, but for that I pray
everyone knows of the Sabbath day.
It's hard to imagine how many were lost
in the humongous pile of gravel and dust.
I can't believe it's been a year
since all of the people began to tear.

Holly Ann McBlair

God Bless America

As the Twin Towers and the Pentagon
Have fallen down on September 11, 2001.
It seems as they never left
From the standing position that they held.
Out of the ashes they have risen again
Giving birth to the American pride
That we all have deep within ourselves.
God bless America and united we stand.

Whitney Graham

The Rain

The rain comes down in gentle showers.
It makes the flowers grow big and strong,
Soaking in the ground with God's great powers,
All spring and summer long.

Trees look up to feel the rain.
It feeds them all on a summer day.
All God's creatures feel no pain
For there is nothing like a rain in May.

E. Ralph Formby

Afraid of the World or Yourself?

I looked out my window at the world outside
and tried to find a place for me to hide.
I put on my jacket, lit up a cigarette
and tried to remember what I tried to forget.
I gaze within a mirror, but don't recognize the face.
I stay within my dwelling, but don't recognize the place.
If only I were absent or could only disappear . . .
I'd have no ending victories or reasons for me to fear. . . .

Elliot Kassoff

A Prayer to Thee

From thy heart I prithee,
For only thy Lord can complete me.
I fall to my knees thanking thee
For all that ye has done for me.
As I ponder of my faith to come,
I have faith in thee for the outcome.
I can't stop thanking thee for creating me,
So I can take part in his plan to be.
As thine eyes gaze upon the stars above,
I prithee a token of thy true love.

Daniel Rodrigues

Love

If I could be anything in the world, I would wish to be your tears,
to be born in your eyes,
live on your cheeks,
and die in your lips.
But if you were my tears I would never cry in fear of losing you.
But what is love? It is not real,
although some say it is.
To me it is, and will be a hopeless dream forever forgotten.

Chris Josph Morse

Adorned

Like a quiet meadow for my emotion
Lie cradled in the strings of ancient earth
A wilderness scent of winter approaching
Across his chest a Celtic cross adorned
To charm and lure me with his lore
Sweet mystic art, a darling sage
Shines through redwood starlight
As a nature laden garden allows me flight to its hidden nest

Michelle Marie Taylor

You

I look into your eyes;
I see fear, hate, deceit.
I see love, happiness, sweetness.
I feel a closeness to you, but I don't know how.
You're like a ghost who haunts my thoughts and a banshee
Who screams out the deepest inner me . . .
The things I could not let out to the world,
You let out for me.

Caitlin Christine Griffith

My Machine

I run a machine for a living
I cut my hands and burn my arms for a living
I smell, I smell like a dog for a living
Cutting and bending
And shaping and grinding
How good it feels to come home and to bathe
And to sleep and to kill, to kill my machine every night
And tomorrow, tomorrow I find it's revived

Ernest Ayala

If Only

I have been without many words for awhile.
Just as well, I have a feeling they wouldn't be very nice.
I wish I could think of something to put down,
Think of something to spew out on paper.
Nothing comes though.
The thoughts seem to stop right before they hit the edge of my mind.
If I could get just one word out I may feel better.
If only.

Tiffany Lynn Eiesland

What a Dilemma!

I'm told I have to write a poem in twenty lines or less,
so now I have to choose a topic better than the rest.
Now how do I create a theme that demonstrates my flair,
and if I choose what's dear to me, would the judges really care?
Perhaps my option then should be world peace or conservation,
for then I'm sure my end result would be remuneration.
Whatever theme I choose to take will be a waste of time,
as then I'd have to think of words that somehow have to rhyme.
So my decision is conclusive: I'll not be party to this test,
for I could never write a poem that betters all the rest!

Donna Lee Gordon

Tears

Where do tears really come from?
Who can really answer that?
Someone who has cried a million and one tears.
Someone who has cried until no more tears would come.
Someone who has cried their self to sleep night upon night.
Ask anyone who has wanted to cry but couldn't:
Tears come not from the eyes, but from the heart.

Amanda Dawn Murdock

In a Moment's Time . . .

Trying to reach you,
Someone so distant, so complex.
Trying to love you,
Someone so tender, so caring.
Sharing a friendship, a love.
Sharing a moment, a flash of time.
Wanting you, needing you.
Missing you, loving you.
Angry at you, sad about you.
Tormented by that absolute feeling of defeat. . . .

Lori D. Lunger

keys

keys . . . i lost mine.
keys . . . my best friend lost hers.
we searched everywhere . . . we couldn't find our keys . . .
oh, it's a terrible thing to lose your keys. . . .
but you know when you search for one thing,
something else always turns up.
in our search for keys, we found a peace that
those things the keys locked will always be locked.
sometimes it's good to lose your keys . . .
don't lock up everything. . . .

Beverly J. Walker

This Is the World

This is the world filled with hatred.
Benevolence is limited, wickedness is fed.
Babies are now feeding into the evil,
Absorbing it as energy, killing all people.
When is this madness going to end?
Don't be an enemy, join and be a friend.
Unite, become one, let all goodness begin.
Don't rush to put the world to its dreadful end!
This is the world.
This is your world!

Krystle Raquel Wright

Prejudice

We all need to open our eyes.
Are colors all that we can see?
Red, yellow, black and white;
We could all be family.
Instead of putting each other down
With awful slurs
Such pitiful conflict
Our stupidity stirs.
Isn't love all that matters?
Not the color of your skin;
Only the true beauty is discovered within.
Does color really matter?
Can't we all remember all races
Do bleed red?
We should join together
And unite as one.
Maybe then, all the wars can be overcome.

Tarrah Rhodes

My Love

Blissfully daydreaming in passion's final embrace,
Bathed in golden radiance of your sweet smiling face.
Remembering your touch, soft as a snowy white dove,
Reflecting the perfection of our all-knowing love.

Trudy Ayn Funkhouser

America's Wings

On wings of angels they departed from us.
On wings of eagles they will soar for eternity.
Forever proud, forever loyal, we are America.
Lift not your voice in anger and rage,
But live the song of our spirit and conquer all.
Never hating, always protecting, this is America.
When your journey here seems buried in sorrow,
Raise your head high and release your heart.
Never alone, always loved, you are America!
Never alone will we ever suffer such troubles.
His love will forever endure and caress our path.
Forever strong, never will surrender, God bless America.

Sue M. Stout

The Rebel, the Genius, and the Fool

The rebel learns early that rules were made for other people
And reacts as soon as possible
Therefore ending an early life of rebellion

The genius spends time figuring out the best way to defeat fear
revenge, protection or escape

The true successor does not do anything
But faces fear straight in the face
Death is the result
So it severs its ties
Enjoys life
And at peace

This is what everyone calls a fool

Larissa Fernando

Speechless

Speechless you left me so many times,
From when we were young
To now
When we are old.
I think about you still all night and day,
And how I would die to say
"I love you,"
And for you to say it back.
I regret any time I said I hated you,
And you said it, too.
So still I tell you, dear,
That the love I feel for you is sincere,
And I know the time I will see you is near.

Madison K. Holden

Fear

You don't know why you feel what you do.
You want to hide and are always feeling blue.

Your insides feel messed up like wiring gone bad.
No one seems to understand why you are so sad.

They say just get up and go.
They say you'll feel better, you know!
But the feelings get worse
and you feel as though you've been cursed.

So, I'll stay in my cocoon,
safe from every one and every place.
I'll make my own life a secluded space,
Then I won't have to go places and try to escape!

Toni Costanzo

A Baby's Smile

A baby's smile is worth so much
A baby's smile gives out such joy
A baby's smile lights up the room
A baby's smile is a gift from God
A baby's smile gives life a whole new meaning
A baby's smile is trusting
A baby's smile means love
A baby's smile is innocence
A baby's smile is sharing
A baby's smile is worth more than words can say
A baby is a gift from God, an innocent life
A smile that says, "I love you"

Michelle Marie Mongini

To the One I Love

To the one I love
The memories of what we've been through
I will always adore and keep close
Our love was rising as a dove
For an amore that we wanted to prove
Since I still feel that I want to propose
To the one that I want
The feelings that we have for each other
Shall run through my veins and my heart
A love that we shall say it just can't
For I still want to be the father
Of the children we dreamt about when we played our part
To the one I love . . .

John Arthur Southerland

One Simple Thought

I have one simple thought.
You may think only one?
All my memories come into one thought.
That thought is my life is too hard to live for.
You may think, how can many thoughts
Come together to form one?
They came together because all my thoughts
Get tangled with memories.
The bad memories overpower my good memories.
I don't have many good memories.
I wish I could forget all my bad memories
And remember all my good memories.
This is my one simple thought.

Chelsea Rae Connelly

Forevermore (Short Version)

Alone in the dark, I found you astray
Tears flowing down your cheeks, not going away
The torture burning inside your soul
Emotions completely out of control

I took you in my arms; it was the least I could do
Took you away from the pain that was troubling you
I held you tightly, not letting go
Speaking to you softly as the tears flowed

You lying here in my arms crying out your heart
It brings a sense of responsibility to do my part
Your body all battered and bruised, what a scary site
It's about time someone held you tight

Let me be your shining star
Let me be the one who'll heal your scar
If this were my only purpose in my glorious life
Then so be it, as long as it's right

Call on me, and I'll always be seen
Maybe not in person, but at least in your dreams
Because you are the one that I truly adore
And I'll do my best to love you forevermore

Nick Maddix

In My Dreams

You were the one who taught me right from wrong
You were the one who kept me strong
You were the one who I loved
You were the one from up above

I love you so much and that is true
I love you so much but now you're gone
Forever, I will only see you in my dreams

Julia Marie Schwartz

Speak Softly . . .

Speak softly, my child, for the walls have ears.
Never EVER let the enemy know of thy fears.
Speak softly, my child, thy voice is heard.
I hear thy prayers—every last word.
Speak softly, my child, and do not fret. . . .
I am always with thee; on this thy may bet.
Speak softly, my child, and do not shed a tear.
Thy dreams shall come true—they are very near. . . .
Speak softly, my child, and hold My hand.
I will never burden thee with more than thou can stand.
Speak softly, my child, and do not worry about tomorrow,
For thy days shall be filled with joy, rather than sorrow.
Speak softly, my child, for I am found in thy heart.
Never ever shall we depart.
Speak softly, my child; I hear thee clearly.
Always know that thou are loved
Very, VERY dearly. . . .

Tonya Jones

The Sea

Rays of hope
Rays of light
The beauty God has given us
Yet we deny all of His glory he has for us
The rising sun, fresh air, peace, joy, hope
The waves come crashing in
Listen to the existence of our great creator
Every day He speaks to us
Open up your heart and listen
His love for us never seems to disappear
We rejoice in whatever we are going through
For we know we are not alone
He never leaves us; listen and hear the
Rays of hope
Rays of light
Ask and ye shall receive
In His time and His time alone

Stacie D. Davis

If I Could Call Up Heaven

If I could call up Heaven just to say hello,
I could speak to my mother and father, my husband and sons,
My sisters and my brothers and daughter too
Who have gone to be with Jesus
On beyond the blue.
If I could call up Heaven
And get you on the phone,
Then I would tell each and every one
That I miss you now that you are gone.
I would tell you that the days are long
And the nights are lonely too.
And things are not the same
Now here without you.
If they have phones in Heaven, give me a call.
The number is still the same
As when you were home.
It would mean more to me
Than I could ever say,
If I could call up Heaven to say hello today.

Tishia Adams

Fallen Angels

Fallen angels drop through the sky.
With broken wings they begin to cry.
In their bodies they hold the sadness, so deep.
Pain and suffering, they must always keep.

Lisa Michelle Mauro

Thursday

His chimney returned in exhale
With a clouded detail
Of his weathered, worn, slightly torn,
Framework of callused hands and vicious tans
Of which barrowed this man
Sixty-eight or seventy years too long now
To remain still
But the slight bend to inhale
Cherry glow, a signal cloud,
Over waned eyes a foundation settled

Bradley Randolph Carter

The Forest's Beauty

The trees are silent
While the fox hunts his prey
It has seen a hare melt into the brush
He grins triumphantly as he creeps
Then the trees shiver as the rabbit screams
Farther down and by the still forest
At the edges of the tranquil waters
Cattails hiss when their faces smudge in the water
While the fish jumps for his dinner
Soon the sun will come down to join them

McKenzie Rose McDermott

Think Happy

Snap out of it! This depressing mood,
It's certainly not doing any good to brood.
There's a big wide world, you know, out there
Waiting to be explored if you dare

You are missing out on life if you sit here feeling depressed
Wondering where to turn and what to do next
So take my advice, put behind your bad thoughts
Think instead of happy times and good deeds wrought
After all, positive thinking will win out in the end
Peace of mind, contentment, are the results my friend.

Ishbeal Natalie Duggan

Me and Grandpa

A farm framed our early years:
hay lofts, tractors, cows,
and an occasional,
not quite empty bottle
left behind from the seasonal help.

Religion, the skeleton of our time together:
Sabbath worship, morning Bible readings,
and radio programing
that I could have sworn
lived only in his radio.

Early morning walks decorated our friendship:
stories and visions
to inspire
a young imagination
being taught how to soar.

I knew how to act in his presence
and how to enjoy things
his presence wouldn't allow;
I think his passing over
betrayed my secrets.

Ronnie Lee Hyde

The Magic of Love and Morpheus

The leader of the band wore a raccoon coat
Impoverished, beaten, on the edge he stands
Hair silky, magic eyes, dusty secretions
His luggage therein lies
Penelope's eyes wounded from battered years
Her heart longing for love, soft and dear
Dreams of music and dances in starlit nights
A musical romance of two that didn't turn out right

Separation of bodies with hearts still entwined
Connected by goddesses—the unearthly kind
Glowing rays from the sea of Morpheus
Weaver of dreams that lies within all of us

Hold on; don't let go, for you never know
When shattered dreams can turn to gold
Sweet innocence of love past, still lingering
Splendor once again in their rememberings
Now barefoot in morning dew, love and lilacs
Bloomed again, love once old is again renewed

Joyce "Joey" Mithoug

I Cried

I cried!
You have heard my voice.
You have shown me your great love, kindness, and mercy.
I cried!
Once again you have heard my voice.
You have returned my peace and health,
something for which I have longed.
I cried!
I trusted in your word—
your word that gives hope to the one who lacks faith.
I cried!
Patiently, I waited.
Patiently, I waited for you to work within me.
I cried!
You are my protector.
You are my great healer.
Doctor of doctors, you are.
Day and night, I cried.
You heard my voice.
Oh, Lord!
I cried!

Alma Garcia-Lara

And the Children Cried

Like sheep, they were herded.
Like cattle, they were slaughtered.
Like birds, they were caged.
Like slaves, they were oppressed.
Like a lost child, they cried.

And still, the children cry.

They cry for peace.
They cry for decency.
They cry for freedom.
They cry for justice.

But, the most heart-wrenching of all cries, is the cry for love.

Love is the air that we breathe.
Love is the life that we live.
Love is the soul itself.

Without love, what have you?

Life is not worth living without love.

My fellow men, have you not heard the children's cry?

Who will pay heed to the burning desire to love and be loved?

Listen to their cry.

And still, the children cried.

Dustin Chance Dickerson

Is Heaven Far Away?

I don't know what it's like after we die,
but I pray to God and look up at the sky.
And if angels can fly
then I want to have wings,
and I apologize for all the bad things.
And when I see God tell me what to say
because I just want to know, is Heaven far away?

De Juan Davinchi

Each Time She Leaves I Feel a Little Sadness

Each time she leaves I feel a little sadness,
Feeling so proud at the same time of all her accomplishments.
Wishing our time together would never end,
Yearning for the little girl . . . where did the time go?
Asking God to please protect her, please God,
Please keep her from harm!
Knowing I will see her soon takes away some of the sadness,
But still feeling like my best friend is leaving.

My angel, my daughter, I love you so!

Dolores Miller

What If

Last night while I lie thinking here,
Some "what ifs" crawled inside my ear,
And pranced and partied all night long
And sang their same old, what if, song.

What if my cats die?
What if I tell a lie?

What if I don't pass fourth grade?
What if I turn into a maid?

What if I lose my talent in art?
What if I get hit by a cart?

What if I get an "ouch" card?
What if I get caught totally off guard?

What if my painting won't get picked in the Del Mar Fair?
What if I have to do a dare?

What if I can't do art anymore?
What if I get a terrible sore?

Everything seems swell, and then,
The nighttime "what ifs" strike again!

Traenna Schumm

Where Are the Boys and the Girls?

Ashes and candles . . . ashes and flowers . . .
Speeches and prayers . . . where are the Towers?
Where have they gone,
those seconds and hours before the flame?
Where are the Towers?
Where are the shoulders, the curls,
the doors—to open, the halls—to walk?
Where are the boys and the girls?
Will they come home . . . from work?
Will they be able to finish the coffee,
to see Hudson River through the window glass,
to ride the elevator, joking and coughing,
to start the car and to catch the bus?
Where are the helms, the badges,
the heavy jackets, the little skirts,
those printouts—pages and pages . . .
the glorious photos, photos of kids?
I talk to the ashes; I'm asking the candles
and God and the devil, the entire world—
Where are the boys . . . the boys and the girls?
Will they come home from work?

Rachel Ostrovsky

I Sit Alone

I sit alone wondering why I am me.
I sit alone wondering who made me.
I sit alone wondering how I got here.
But most of all I sit here alone wondering why I am alone.

Kathryn Arlene Spaulding

A Desire to Be Free

Lying under the stars at night, listening to the hoot owls cry.

The whispering wind blowing gently across the sky
and the coyotes howling, as the clouds whisk by.

A glow on the ground, the moon full and round where
the stars touch without a sound.

The silence is deafening, with my head to the ground
and jackrabbits all around.

There is no fire, only hat and coat to keep me warm;
the cold creeps in and my hunched over body snuggled deep
in my jacket, unbearably compacted until sunlight cracks
open my eyes from a sleepless night.

The backside pains from the cold hard ground as it
tightened from fear every time the brushes crackled and snapped.

Freedom as the eagles soar, as the wild horses fly,
where the flowers grow wild and the sound of music is the air.

Jeanette Ohl

My First True Love

For all I remember
It's you that I see
And in the future
I see you with me

You broke my heart once
Yet I wanted another try
I told my friends I loved you
And they all asked me why

I told them it's not something I can explain
It's just this feeling inside
I want to be near to you
This love for you I can no longer hide

There's my point in keeping my feelings inside
My love is endless
I want you by my side
Please come stand with me so we'll always be

Together . . . forever . . . in love

Melissa Kay Brown

Life of Lies

Living in a life of lies,
Throwing away your dreams
Waiting for that day to come,
When you will be set free
You're always asking me,
"Why do you hide?"
Deep down inside, you know there's no lies
You think it's because I'm scared of the world
You think it's because there's no open doors
Life for me is like living in hell,
Suicidal thoughts in a darkened room cell
Screaming and crying deep down inside
Wanting to kill yourself and not knowing why
This is the way it will always be,
From now until eternity,
So please don't try to preach to me,
'Cause you are not my dad
I've heard and done this all before,
But this time it's getting bad

Brandi Lynne Troutner

Sister

Like the little girl who steals a look at
her sister when she's not looking;
I see your simple dignity and grace that utters
"Beauty," without saying a word.

Devin Carmen Lewis

He Paved the Way

Look upon His sacrifice,
look and then you will see
the reason I live my life and how I came to be.
Betrayed by His creations,
turned down with pure hate,
all they did was desecrate,
yet it was His fate.
He sacrificed His life for you,
this is how you thank Him?
You know, down deep inside, it is true—He gave his life for you.
In the end He'll reign again,
always and forever.
Look, now you have no excuse! He gave his life for you.
He rose again to conquer sin, He paved the way for you.
Now will you accept him? Do you think you are right?
This could be your last day of your entire life,
so then what happens after death? You really want to know?
There are one of two places to go, there's Heaven and there's Hell.

Kalin Joe Verhelst

Praise to a Mother

You are the only mother for me,
you have helped me to see
the way the real world will be.
I've made you mad, made you cry.
I've always been proud to call you mine.
I've made you smile and made you proud.
I am your child.
You have seen the world,
held me when I was cold,
And as I've grown, you've cared for me.
So when time has come and gone,
I will be there with you, to love you and cherish you.
Forever you will be my best friend.
Whether I am mad or sad,
I will always be happy and proud,
but mostly glad you are mine to behold,
As a story is said, to calm a child.
This poem was written for you to be told,
I love you!

Brittney Diane McBride

Starless

If one star was loneliness
Then none should be my hell
But instead the feelings brought
Were known all too well
All that pain, all that hurt
All that anger held within
It's now free, my smile's faded
Now my face bares my sin
But this starless night opened my eyes
Hiding me from all the lies
Since the only light I could see
Was the star held within me
Solitude now brings happiness
Quiet dark a little smile
Knowing now what I wish I could have known all the while
The higher you climb
The longer you will fall
And when you have all you want
That's when you're the loneliest of all

Trevor Douglas Golden

His Heart

A place that has never seen the light
A place that is closer than I once thought
A place that is colder than a desert night
To think that this place I once sought

Amanda Catherine Harbin

Heart of a Woman, Soul of a Goddess

The heart of a woman cannot be compared
in size to even a thousand universes.
Men can capture it, but they can never
claim it as their own.
She is a daughter to her father,
a wife to her husband, a mother to her child.
Rarely does the world look beyond this,
but within a woman lies the soul of a goddess.
Her form is made of nurture, her hair of emotions,
her eyes of compassion, her core of love.
She may experience a series of emotions simultaneously,
but for this she should not be condemned, but rather praised!
She is the bearer of sensitivity, the keeper of empathy.
If you learn nothing else from this,
then promise me you will treasure your mother's heart;
guide your daughter's goddess.
Dear goddess, but what moves the most mountains is this,
always treasure your own.

Matilda Iocco

Hands That Heal

Hands that heal . . . hands that love,
hands surrounded by beauty,
heart surrounded with love . . .
because your hands
are not like any other hands. . . .
Among your hands there is compassion;
you posses the healing touch
within your soul. . . .
Your hands are the only ones
that attracted God's eyes,
up there over the rainbow,
over the magical clouds . . . in paradise.
God has blessed those hands,
because your hands heal pain, devastation,
misery of the poor, destitute and helpless.
That touch has never been forgotten
or doubted by anyone in the right mind;
even little angels
are kissing at your hands. . . .

Blanca L. Jarrahzadeh

Love

I give you my hand,
Soiled from the labor of my love.
Promise to hold it forever?

I give you my heart,
With all its pleasures and miseries,
I only ask that you give me yours.

If I dared to be myself,
Leaving all my hidden truths exposed,
Would you continue to love me?

Would you gather the stars from the heavens,
Sow them into the fertile earth,
And grow for me, a magical garden?

Would you be the keeper of my secrets?
That I may entrust in you my heart's confessions?

To prove your love,
Would you . . .
Love me the way I have only dreamt of being loved.

John Salvatore LoGrasso

Meet Me There

Meet me there,
Down by that lonely rock on the shore.
Take your time.
The sun will shine all night if we let it,
And we'll watch the stars in the morning.
Count to seven and make a wish.
Then throw it back in the water and just lie here with me.
The day is in our control,
And the night just stands silently waiting.
Follow the path made by the pebbles that will lead us to the moon.
When will it come up again?

Ashlei-Rene Yancich

Love Remembered

I remember
Prolonged evenings spent in company,
A sense of deepest passion, of loyalty,
Enfolded in his arms, a serene scene of exquisite desire,
A yearn for cupid's burning fire.

I remember
Vows of eternal trust,
This matter remote from lust,
Contentment replenished my soul,
His existence made me feel whole.

Hannah Walker

Always Daddy's Little Girl

Daddy, you have always been there through the
good and the bad.
Daddy's little girl I have always been.
Never leave me, I still lean on you through the good and the bad.
You are my friend and my father and someone for me to lean on.
Never staying mad at me for anything that I have done,
you always let me learn from my mistakes, good or bad.
You are a leader and a great teacher.
Now I'm grown and I still depend on you in many ways.
I will always be your little girl, no matter how our lives go.
Love you always, Daddy's Little Girl.

Lisa Marchlewski

With Life

Day upon day, overlapping as one.
Stacked up dominoes until there are none.
Happy lovers gaze at the stars up above.
While heartbroken souls search wearily for love.
What's the answer, the why, what, and wherefore?
Misery and loneliness, is that what we're there for?
Darkness is a guest that's never invited.
Solitude's the reason we stand up and fight it.
For nighttime blankets our light, life, and hope,
Till morning comes and once again we cope
With life.

Eugene P. Taormina

I Know What Love Is

To someone special

I found love, the feeling I get when you are by.
The shaking I feel will never die.
I look in your eyes, and it is a feeling like a surprise.
The warmth that hits me when you are by
Is like the sun shining bright in the sky.
Your touch is so special I can't explain such.
I only know that when you are in love
You will know what life is.
It is like watching a dove soaring high above.

I know what love is.

Suzanne Angelina Damiano

Reflection

I looked into the mirror and saw a good reflection,
Then I realized it's just fear and a bad rejection.
I whistled to the mirror,
And it whistled back to me.
Down my face rolled a tear and the mirror helped me see
That I am you and you are me.
I went outside to let my soul run free,
Then I looked over my shoulder and saw you.
Now I have a friend that treats me so dear.
A lot of time we will spend,
Thanks to the image of the mirror.

Joshua Lee Suire

The Reality of Tomorrow

Blood red eyes pierce my flesh with icy glare.
Crimson memories haunt my very existence as
I take the first fearful step into the light.
Shielding my eyes, I soon realize
that I am only shielding my mind.
Memories envelop my soul
as I hide within my emptiness.
My being is threatened,
and as I retreat further within my fear,
I find myself returning to the darkness,
realizing that tomorrow will arrive too soon.

Emily Anne Porter

Stained Soul

I'm scared
I'm bitter
I'm burned
My heart is stained from the imperfections of the world
I'm longing to be loved
But the burns in my soul are keeping the real love away
Too dependent, I know
Yet, I'm only a girl begging for love
So before you push me away
Think of what's right and wrong
And tell me that you can't love me

Angela Renee Richardson

My Flower

As a seed blows in the wind,
I think.
A sprout pops out of the ground and then,
I think, I wonder.
Next I see a one foot long plant;
I think, I wonder, I see.
Then a blossom pops out to say, "I'm going to bloom in one day."
I think, I wonder, I see, I feel.
A beautiful flower is out my window the next day;
I think, I wonder, I see, I feel, I watch,
My flower.

Kathryn Nicole Miller

You Are

Written on 10-7-01

You are beautiful, yet you are ugly
You are mine, yet you are not
I see you clearly, yet you are blurry to me
I want you, but I know I cannot have you
You are everything, yet you are nothing
You make me who I am, yet you tear apart the real me
You are brave, yet you are like a cowardly puppy
I love you for who you are, yet I hate you at the same time
Promise me, whoever you are, that you will be with me forever
You are my love, and that I know is true

Kasey Sierra Meador

My Mystery

To my biggest fan, Mark

A mystery we all must solve is love.
It can be as beautiful as a flying dove.
It can make you angry as trees in a storm.
Love can take any different form.
Don't know it's coming until it's here.
It could be far, or it could be near.
It could be soft or it could be furious.
One question I find curious;
If cupid is blind, how does he know
Which heart to puncture and which heart to sew?

Kathleen Constance Isabelle Davis

Remembering Reed

To your younger brother and sister you are
A black and white photo kept in a special place,
An artist's rendering of your likeness
That still has the power to bring tears to the eye.
But those of us who knew you well
You are remembered in living color, unchanged through time,
A blond whirlwind with a special affection for the elderly.
We wonder what kind of man you would be,
What kind of husband and father,
In these times of uncertainty, we take consolation,
You are safe in the arms of Jesus.

Myrna Jean Mackey

But Me

Mental disillusion,
Empty rooms,
Another door closes on me.
This house is so desolate;
The only sounds are my cries
And the rocking chair blowing in the wind.
I'm sitting where you left me,
With dust bunnies dancing in my hair.
Daddy, are you coming home?
Everyone has gone;
I have no one left but me.

Brittany Leigh McGuire

Surrounded by Darkness

In the distance I can see the light.
My clouded mind filled with blood thirsting lust.
Friends, true enemies to the blind.
Feelings within the soul.
Amusing treachery.
Mythical freedom, heartless love.
Whispering winds summoning endless nights.
Fair evils embracing hate.
Peaceful torture bringing disturbing bliss.
Stuck in darkness you are.
Happiness when blood drenches the soul.

Edward C. Langley

A Christmas Gift

Written at age eleven

Dear Mom,

I might act like I don't love you
on the outside,
but on the inside, my heart of love
and joy is as big as the universe
This might not be a good Christmas present,
but this is a token of my love

Merry Christmas
I love you, Zachary

Zachary Dalton Barnes

America

America, America, oh, how I love thee,
you're loved far and wide from sea to sea.
You paid for our freedom, our independence, our pride;
is that a reason to let them push us aside?
We fought for the right of an open mind.
We fought to stay brothers, every color and kind.
We fought to give women the right to vote.
Imagine it all started with Columbus' boat.
So why give up now if we've fought for so long?
The answer is proven in the end of this song,
we're the land of the free and the home of the brave.

Krista Lynn Heslop

A Night to Remember

As I sit here in the dark night
I see the nicest sight shining so bright.
The moon glistening in the night,
Stars barely in sight.
The clouds started covering the bright, shining night.
I look over and I see the big beautiful smile of an angel.
I could see God's blinding light.
I saw stars in his eyes.
Who's this angel, so handsome with might?
If only I could see his angelic smile once more
my soul would be made whole.

Cassie Jean Vaughn

The Great Puzzle

Once I put together the pieces
Of a strange picture puzzle
It was hard at first,
But after I had done it a few times,
It got a lot easier.
So when it all fell apart,
I could put it back together again
So familiar . . .
Now the pieces are apart again
But these are ones I've never seen before
And they don't fit anywhere.

Jessica Marie Fritz

Time Passes

When time and people walk by you in no sort of direction
You see the years fly by like they were never there
The time passes quickly
And you are only left with the wrinkles to prove it
You can't begin to realize that you are throwing away your life
Until you can see the people walk by
Only time and space can generate the power
Which only lies in you to see the days fade away
And life slip through your fingers too slippery to grasp
You tend to watch life fall and you can only say
I tried I really did try

Candace Joyce Hillock

the fear of death

to fear, the fear never forgotten by most,
but the ones who don't,
is there satisfaction, peace of mind?
does it make it simple from day to day
or are they needing a blanket,
a security, a reason to be?
and those who fear the lesser evil;
the fear can make you wonder as "one."
satisfaction can make you believe.
the reasons you live are up to you,
life is never what it seems.

Shannon Lee Kosick

The Dust of War

Bodies broken, shattered hearts,
Desolation rife,
Orphaned children, worthless lives
Emptiness, no help arrives.
Governments with sharpened knives,
Trading bombs for life.
This is war, this is war, bloody sacrifice.
Cities leveled, fires of Hell,
Stricken people blankly gaze.
Memories cloud their bitter haze.
The dust of war, this is war.

Henry Birtles

Alone, the Poem

Everyone has gone out,
Left me here all alone.
It has happened more times than I can count,
Been left here sitting on my throne.
Everyone has someone with whom to be,
Someone who loves them and cares.
Yet, I have no one with whom to be seen.
No one who truly cares.
Now I'm just left here all alone,
But it's the only thing I've ever known.
I have no one to just call my own.

Jason W. Riggs

My Lullaby

My baby sleeps a quiet tune
Within the midnight sky
I sing to her in response
A gentle lullaby
The wind responds through the leaves
It calls out to my heart
For with my baby's lullaby
It wants to be a part
It starts to rain, the world turns cold
My baby starts to cry
I hold my baby close to me and sing my lullaby

Jennifer Lillian Peterson

Amethyst

She said her favorite stone was amethyst
At the mention of that gem I swear her eyes would kind of mist.
Why, I would ask and she would always say,
"I think the universe was that color when it began.
Maybe that's the shade it will be when it finally ends."
It was a silly game, but I'd tell her to choose which fist.
She'd always knew which held her latest amethyst.
I'd buy them for her and watch her eyes shine.
But for that moment the real happiness was all mine.
In my future I see soft music, a pretty face, and warm lips;
All around me the color of my lady in amethyst.

Petra M. Knudtson

All the Beautiful Things in Life

Written at age ten

Pink and purple sunsets up in the sky
Bluebirds, crows, and robins so happy for they can fly
Newborn babies all pink and red
They are cuddly little critters with their fuzzy little heads
Hugs and kisses, XXXs and OOOs
Everyone's special from their heads down to their toes
Evergreen forests, beautiful doe, rapid rivers as they quickly flow
Frolicking through the meadows and rainbows
Appearing in the sky so beautifully
And those are all the beautiful things in life to me

Matticen Anne Cox

without you

i can't sit still without thinking of you
your ways of crushing me with your eyes
you're tender, modest, taunting teases
make me insane, but i just can't be
"nevermore" you said with your eyes puckered tight
you say i am the worst thing that's ever happened
however, you're the best thing that's happened to me
so it's occurs to me that we are not to see
each other again . . . that soaks into my brain
i ravish, i rage, i cut, i bleed; the pain will not stop!
without you i am nothing, just a creature that has not been seen

Andrew Lawrence Fenity

Friends Are Forever

He's looking at me with pure hatred in his eyes,
for what I did, I will never know.
People make mistakes, people are never going to be perfect!
I made my apology truthfully. It didn't seem to help a thing!
I look at him from the other side of the room.
I watch the burning hatred grow larger
with every second he watches me.
I look at him with great sadness,
knowing I have lost a friend dear to my heart.
As I walk past him with tears in my
eyes I whisper, "I'm sorry. . . ."

Courtney Ann Downing

Poverty

Poverty takes hundreds of lives:
Husbands, children and wives.
Poverty is awful, horrible and bad.
When I see someone go through it,
It makes me bone-chilling sad.

Some people live in a house,
While others don't have food for one measly mouse.
When you see someone on the street
Remember poverty is hard to beat.
So, lend a helping hand to everyone you meet
Because one day you could be walking with poverty's feet.

Margaret Register

Losing You

The one morning, remembered,
bloomed instantly with laughter.
Losing all of you was foreign in my eyes,
then tragedy found time
and again reality locked sadness in me
by confusing my innocence.
Now, walking barefoot back in time
is all I can greatly desire.
For you certainly have winning love,
but I can't go looking for you
when you are lost in the end.

Tina Marie Gregorio

Why?

Why make a house of candy if you don't want kids to come?
Why did she have so many children when she only had one shoe?
Why was he up on that wall, did he not know of his frailty?

Why, why, why must I try?
Why must I cry?
Searching through the past to find the future

Why, why, why must I go?
Why because I know
To find the missing link
Keeping me from the brink

Lisa M. Camp

My Dear

you are a true masterpiece
with your hair the night and your face the moon.
I can see the rest of my life
when your eyes, bright as stars, gaze into mine.
my heavy heart grows wings
and soars through the sky like an eagle;
you are my heaven.
when you are not with me, my day becomes dark and cold
and I pray you return.
I would not dream of spending a day without you;
you will always remain my angle and true love.

Lauren Marie McKellar

I Saw a Butterfly

I saw a butterfly
I saw him well
The tears were in his eyes
They burned like hell
He looked like just the strongest one in this world
but if you touched him he could die
This lovely butterfly who dreamed of life
As he spread his wings to fly beyond the skies
He wished the world would see him for who he is
A lovely butterfly, not an eagle
The butterfly I saw

Ayobami E. Idowu

Mother

When we go places, you know you can't deny me.
We look too much alike, so don't try it.
I know you wouldn't do that
Because you are too cool.
Everything that I do
You know about.
You are there when I need you.
You are my best friend.
You put up with me through thick and thin.
I am glad you brought me up the way you did.
Mother, you know I love you.

Erin Lynn Dashiell

September 11

Everyone remembered the day the world stopped.
We watched in horror as the American symbol dropped.
Families hoped, prayed, and cried,
on that tragic day when so many died.
Many heroes were made, and their memory shall not fade.
Those terrorists may have smiled or sighed,
on that day America died, but thanks to them
we are stronger and we won't tolerate
terrorism any longer.
We will never forget that day in September,
For that tragic day is a day to remember.

Shane Michael Nickerson

Homunculus

I know you smiled down on him as he dozed,
head pooled in your lap,
thin lips still damp from the spray of congress.
I know there was a hyacinth,
anchoring mockingbirds to the earth.
I know there were pictures of me, simmering in your house
where he wandered,
touching the walls,
laughing.
The sunlight, May's bright eye,
blew right through you.

Benjamin Quehle Randall

God's Miracles

People don't believe that miracles happen, as in days gone by.
But all you have to do is look up into the sky.
You will see a marvelous display.
The moon, stars, planets, at night, the clouds, and sun by day.
In the morning, the sunbeam's glow reflected in the dewdrops
on the flowers, grass, and trees that grow.
The sun that gives warmth in the day and light.
The stars and moon shine in the darkness of the night.
Spring, summer, winter, fall, the seasons come and go.
Bringing different elements, sunshine, rain, wind, and snow.
After the rain, the rainbow's colorful hue,
the mist that rises and disappears from view.
The world of color, a spectacular array.
Colors in the sky, the land, the sea, God's art on display.
Love that sparks emotions in all mankind every race and creed.
God's ability to accomplish and provide all mankind's needs.
The continued cycle of all birth.
God's miraculous healings here on Earth.
The greatest miracle given to us in love
is life itself, given by God above.

Joan Di Fabio

Roses

God kissed the roses
And said for them to grow
God said you're special
Special for me to love you so
He made you in His image
Body, soul and spirit
There's assurance, He is around you
And watches over you, wherever you may go
The sweet sense of love, the roses show
God knows what you need
The presence of the Lord, lets you feel it's so
Roses are pretty to help you glow and grow
And tell us God loves us so
The flowers dot Heaven and never grow old
And the beautiful houses all brilliantly shine
For each person of mankind
May you remember God knows just what you like
And wants to do for you what's good and right
His lovely world so truly says so
And the beautiful rainbow, is a sign it is so

Patricia Nestich

For a Better Life

We need only look around us to observe things that astound us
And question, "How'd we get in this huge rat race?"
Media makes us aware of it, bad news tends to reap a profit.
Yet, I'm still convinced our world can be a better place.

Unemployment and recession, even borderline depression,
Hungry, homeless scores of folks throughout the land.
Senseless bloodshed, greed for power
Make for Satan's finest hour.
The hour's late, but there's still time to take a stand.

Demand of those who represent us,
Fear not they who may resent us.
We owe it to our future generation.
Sow some seeds of brotherhood, forgiving the misunderstood.
Instill the pride that makes up our great nation.

None of us were self-created, born to love and not be hated
To enjoy this life, however long our stay.
Best we leave the past behind, ask for guidance, peace of mind.
There is none so tall as he who kneels to pray.

Sacrifice and share some pride, be a friend, enjoy the ride,
Help somebody else along the way.
You need not wonder when to start,
The time is now, begin with heart.
Don't wait for me, I started yesterday.

Robert L. Bob McGee

Before You

Here I stand before you
There's nothing left for me to do
I don't know if you really see
All that we could have or be
Is there something I can say
That won't let you go away
I feel hopeless with you not near
Totally lost and filled with fear
I want to make you understand
That life without you is unbearably bland
I've never quite felt this way
Every part of me wants you to stay
I need you more than you will ever know
Or even more than I can show
You're a part of me
A part I can't just set free
But I refuse to beg and cry
I won't even let myself sigh
And yet I had to tell you this
You needed to know what you will miss

Marissa Christina Montagu

Mercy

My boat was sailing
With sails full and strong
My boat's name, "Sin's Pleasures"
So it couldn't last long
One day a storm came right up out of the blue
It was God's way of saying, "Child, I need you"
My boat hit the rocks
Oh, it looked so forlorn
So beaten and broken
And the sails were all torn
God bade me get out on the rocks and stand tall
And look just beyond me and see the great falls
He said, "Just wait, I'll be by for you
I need you on my lifeboat
My help is so few
Now I know exactly where I planted each rock
I did it in mercy, and there my lifeboat will dock
Each time we stop, we will pick up a soul
We'll keep them and feed them
Then take them safe to the fold"

Inez Brown Moore

Peace on a Wave

So crystal blue
but violent white

The wave roles in
he holds on tight

With grace and skill he drops right in
to wash away the pain within

If ever he felt right at home
it was underneath the crystal dome

It sound is like thunder but music to his ears
as the wave and his heart is all he hears

In this peaceful state he wishes he could stay
forever not just for the day

Now home he goes to a run down shack
a home that's torn apart by crack

A father drunk a mother high
they tear apart our graceful guy

When sitting there to the chaos he listens
he thinks about how the wave it glistens

In the wave is were he finds peace
his daily escape from his inner beast

Ryan Stewart Wilson

Polished

If simply asking were the key
I would spew it forth in harmonious melody.
For from my heart unto my tongue would
come these gentle words of love,
with eloquence in rhyme and meter
that it would please the gods above.

Patrick Aron Johnson

An American Mom

I discovered you had a secret you didn't want anyone to know.
I promise I won't tell anyone else, even though
you made a big mistake one day.
You showed me you needed me in a very private way.
Needing help with things of which you were not sure.
That's because your spirit had not yet matured.
You've cussed, you've fussed; by force, had taken your rights.
What's sad about it, children, is you haven't been taught to fight—
fight with dignity, a purpose, a promise and a goal.
Instead, you fight with anger that only confuses your soul.
I decided not to be afraid of you, for you are just a child
who has been doing their thing for quite a long while.
I am sorry I did not teach you life's ABC's—
the yesses, the thank you's and the "excuse me, please";
not because I am unwilling, but I have not been allowed
to listen and talk to you, for your world is so loud!
But I will keep your secret and I will aggressively pray
that I can teach you life's basics, for I am not afraid!

Marva Joyce Williams

Recovery from Devastation

For all of the families of this devastation

The world is shattered, as are my dreams,
The buildings brought down by the evil.
How I can cope with my loss? It seems
That I must make a deal with the devil.

Through pain and sorrow I will endure
Until I find my love lost in the terror,
The men that caused it are dead right now;
The men that planned it are still at large.

America the beautiful, stand still and strong,
It will apprehend the master of this wrong.
We as Americans will sit and wait;
We as Americans will rebuild and live on.

So, as I wait for my love's recovery,
I will assist in the help for recovery.
My emotions are angry about this devastation,
But my strength will help fuel this nation.

Timothy Paul Elmy

I'm Back

I have a clean bill of health!
Now I can pursue great wealth!
I've been invited to a developer be
My friends have supported my vision of me
I'm back from trying to make this place fit
I'm here in the now, it all starts to knit
My kids will come first, wherever I am
My friends teach me to remember that I can
I dug holes in other gardens too long
It's time to play my own sweet song
Can I do what others only dream
I can make dreams come alive it seems
Read about it in the papers as you will
I'm back and I'm climbing up that hill
One more chance for a brass ring
Business intuition is where I'm King
I will do what I do no matter what
I still know more than most forgot!

Joe Michael Solomon

For a Brief Moment

For a brief moment, I knew it was you;
I thought what I should do.
While in the moment, I saw you were there.
I began to get the feelings of care.
While you were standing there with your mug,
I walked up to you and gave you a hug.

Allison B. Marsh

Robert Frost

The other day I read a poem by Robert Frost
It's scary because it reminded me of us
Our fights go 'round and 'round
Don't know where our love is bound
That poem I read the other day
I think it's called "Nothing Gold Can Stay"
It spoke to me somehow
It's time to let go now
Although old Frost is dead and gone
His words of wisdom still live on
You'll survive without me and I without you
I bet you're already looking for someone new
So, as the tears slip down my cheeks
I no longer feel so sad and meek
Although it's over, as of today
I know somehow it's okay
Oh, and you know that poem I read the other day?
Old Frost was right, nothing gold can ever stay!

Chelsea Ann Bauer

Love

Love is a feeling you cannot see
Love is a feeling deep inside me
There it is and there it shall stay
For nothing can take real love away
It's there for good, it's there forever
Even if we can't be together forever
Our hearts and souls shall be
No matter the miles that our bodies shall be apart
Love is a feeling deep in the soul,
It flows and flows like an endless black hole
This, by now, we both already know
This is true love that lasts forever
Even though our bodies are not together
You have my heart, you have my soul
It's just like that big black hole
Endless and endless it shall be
Yours now and forever, even if not together

Diana L. Channel

daylight

she wakes up the morning,
she flies silently through the night.
she wakes the evening,
she dreams of laughter and light.
prisms dance to her heavenly voice,
multicolored dimensions ruling her choice,
giving me love, while dishing out anger,
stranger,
stranger,
stranger.
she blinds me with the daylight
and feeds me so much happiness.
she walks through the moonlight.
if i could only share in her bliss.
cures breed to the scent of her presence,
knowing knowledge of gifted love.
let me see through the eyes of this creation,
this forever white dove.

Nicholas James Emery

My Son

To my loving son, Nathan

My son is an angel sent down from Heaven!
My son is special; he is my Heaven!
My son I love; I thank God in Heaven!
My son touches my heart like God in Heaven!
My son is my miracle straight from Heaven!

Diana Lynn Bigham

Two Refugees with a Chimp

Even if I could talk with words human and
short like yours, I would still choose to
remain silent. I have borne witness to the
undoings, and the mangoes will take years
before accepting any name.
Even if I could perch the highest vantage,
(a sweet home, now stolen) my feet would
bear too much weight, my cracked hands
would grip stick stems, I would see fallen
things cached away up high. Even if I could
wriggle my neck, unlatch this clasp with
my chin, I would stand here, staring, as
circumstance fumbles stupidly to undo a
baseless freedom.
Two taut chains hold things tethered to
center. Like woven ribbons around a pole,
gatherings and workmanship have conquered
the rain. We sit waiting for a response.

Thomas J. Caso

Mother

Shades of goldfish green in an Oriental rug
Like algae stuck to a goldfish
She calls it elegant
I call it rich but not beautiful

She cannot see the undertones
That pulse through everything and
Make a tapestry of nothings

She sees black and white and simple shapes
I see wild frenzied patterns that
Will not interact

Our visions are parallel lines
Defying all mathematical probability and intersecting.

She gave birth to me in a fit of strength
And gave me the power to disagree
Maybe now she wishes she hadn't
Because I HATE Oriental rugs

Jennifer Le Mollinga

On Sunday, September 16, 2001

My mom ran over a bird
while passing through 48th and Irvine Street.
It was a white pigeon.
Pretty,
but quite stupid.
It didn't fly.
It didn't run.
It just stood there
in the path of our right front tire.
I felt a bump as we drove by,
and loud exclamations bled through our closed window.
My mom didn't even notice.
Through the rearview mirror
I saw a lump
of bloodstained feathers—
red on white—
like the taillights on our white Camry
that should have lit up, but didn't.

Jenny X. Yang

Mom

You have always been my guiding light
Your smile and twinkle in your eyes, my childhood delight
You are the one perfect rose in my garden of thorns
Through you and your love, I have grown
A loving daughter, from seeds of love you have sewn
Mom, you are very dear and special to me

Cora Myers

Return to Innocence

I long to kiss
. . . the child in you . . .
and embrace the many silly escapades
you could ever have gone through, or thought of,
but were too scared to pursue.
I want to do them all . . .
with you.

So, go ahead, play pretend!
Or chase butterflies to your heart's content,
live in a cave three days without a shave,
or drown your sorrows in buttermilk;
stand upon a hillock, amid rush of daisies
and proclaim cheerily: vini! vedi! vici!

Be yourself with me,
just let go,
'cause I long to kiss, dear friend of my heart,
the child in you!

Dipanjali Banurji

When I Was

When I was six, I sought for the Tooth Fairy,
Looked under my pillow for money.
I crept outside on Christmas night
To see the arrival of Santa's flight.
A princess I've always wanted to be,
A dream I was determined to achieve.
When I was nine I realized life was never perfect and sweet,
Never kept the same rhythmic beat.
My dreamy, happy-go-lucky life had ended,
And all my girlish thoughts were suspended.
It was hard to say goodbye
To all my friends this time.
When I was twelve, I learned to be hardworking and smart.
It isn't luck, but studying from the start.
Friendship caused lots of misery,
Making my heart feel awfully lonely.
But I guess I figured out
That it'll pay off when the time comes about.

Jean Kee

Goodbye, Grandpa

He reached to her . . .
and had only his last words to speak.
With his life filled with destination and reason . . .
his strength, hope, sorrow, joy, and
memories of a million days, devoting himself
to others not to himself, but to what
mattered most in his life;
he committed his life to his loved ones,
his "pride and joy" . . .
but the only curiosity lying within him was
the unanswered question, Why?
It was always mystical in that sense.
Until he held his hand out . . . this very last
time, reached for his love and the question
was answered. . . .
Why? Love so strong there was never any
doubt . . . true love . . . that's why.
That was always why.

Maryn Elizabeth Shreve

Untitled

When you loved me, I knew I had it all.
Your friendship, never-ending,
It showed me how much I could have,
Just how far I can still fall,
And how long it will take to lose it all—
Eternity.

Brandon Miracle

Me

Life is slowing down,
Things are getting strange,
I don't know what to do, so I'll just write for now.
My life seems strung together,
And a little deranged.
So read on, if you will
To possess some of my feelings.
I warn you, you might feel
A part of me, some of my sadness, gladness, and well-being.
You might be scared by some of this stuff you see,
But don't fear,
Stay right here,
And witness some of me,
From my hopes, to my fears and all of my dreams.
My feelings almost never last,
Some are long gone and of the past.
Stay right here and read on, and you will see,
Every little part of me. . . .

Bobbie Shelby-Lynn Hayse

Silver Rain

Looking at you, the brightest moon I've ever seen,
makes my mind open up,
giving way to my thoughts,
letting them flow as silver rain.
But when the clouds move in front of your beautiful face
and cover you up in shadows,
my mind goes numb and dreams die away.
As soon as I enter this absentminded,
dreamless state of consciousness,
I feel sad and deserted,
it feels like it will never be the same again.
Yet, as soon as I see your silver sighting again,
I forget all the sadness
and dreams come and flow like they did before.
So should you need to desert me, do so . . .
but come back and rejoice my heart with your shining appearance
and refill my life with dreams.

For dreaming is the only way of life. . . .

Filip H. F. Slagter

In the Saddle Again

He's back in the saddle.
An accident in the big show;
Out for months.
Broken bones and torn muscles;
Plaster casts and metal braces.
Nothing will stop him.
Doctors said no more.
His gal said stop.
Nothing slows him down.
Three months and three operations pass.
He hits the road again;
Determined to win again.
Down the road he goes.
He wins a few big rodeos.
One more win gives him a shot at the gold buckle.
It's December and he's leading the world.
He draws well all week long.
When the dust settles, he holds the gold buckle.

Jason Lee Foland

Weeping Willow

On my soft and comforting pillow I cry like a weeping willow.
I cry so much that I fall asleep, but still in my dreams I weep.
Tomorrow I know I'll still be like a weeping willow.
Now I wonder if I will ever be happy,
but the one thing I know is that I
am not the only weeping willow.

Lauren Elizabeth Stoner

Depression

Sometimes you just feel so sad.
Other times you feel very mad.
You might have to cry,
Even if you don't try.
You are unable to have fun.
You're the only one.
Sometimes you don't want to hope.
Other times you just have to mope.
Even if you try to fight it, it won't go away.
You'll just keep heading the wrong way.
Days and days go by with it growing worse
Until you're about to burst.
Nothing seems to help it,
Not even a little bit,
So just go through this painful time
Because it will go away like the taste of a lime.
I know this sounds untrue,
But it is for me and you.

Valerie M. Narr

Strange Birds

Oh, it's a bird! No, it's a plane!
They landed in twin trees that
Stood taller than a breeze.
They even landed in an uncharted nest
That destroyed the lives that had not
Completed their emotional test.
A loud and taunting scream filled the air
As the U.S. opened its mouth and
Shouted, "Why?" Why did those
Strange birds blacken the sky as the rain
Became blood when it fell into the
Crying eyes?
Those strange birds were blinded by
Homegrown allies that stole many
And many beautiful lives.
Oh, it's a bird! No it's a plane!
That caused the U.S. hardship and pain,
But we are a strong nation that will rise again.

Edwina D. Jackson

Twenty-Four Hours

For twenty-four hours
I left everything behind me
For one day of absolute freedom
I retreated to my refuge
I was alone with my dog at my side
As I uncoiled on the beach

I prepared a place to sleep
Under Heaven's skies
I built a fire with my hands
And sat and watched and listened
Encased in a dome of stars
I was held in God's hands
And He spoke to me
Clearly and in confidence
I sincerely asked for forgiveness
And it was graciously granted to me
As I was reminded of all the Lord has created
I became the space between the stars

Suzanne Diggs Ross

Soul Mates

Two voices singing the same song.
Two bodies dancing the same dance.
Two minds sharing the same thoughts.
Two hearts beating the same beat.
Two people who know each other not, are . . .
Two strangers in love.

Christopher James Shaw

This Vanquished Emotion

These wheat fields sway as I do,
These stars longing to hold you,
The whisper of wind that guides right through,
Condensation leads my interpretation.
Destination surpasses one of high expectation.

Trickle down through the blue,
Achieve well-deserved youth,
All the growth and the truth,
As these fields sway as I once knew.
For the stars that were held
Will hold not again.
The whisper fades out,
My light settles in.
The faint retribution
In time's contribution
Extends resolution
To figure solution
Or wake this intrusion.

Christophe Aaron Robinson

Black Magic

Tonight as you lie in my mind
You are kept safe and kind
Love is blind
Love at first sight was when my heart took flight
Sight was when I laid my eyes on you
My mind put in questions my heart fell at your feet
My heart won the battle I am yours forever
If the night decides to take me
Let it be your secrets are safe with me
My voice knows no words
My ears are undisturbed
My eyes are blind to sight
My heart knows you are with me tonight
I am cursed with love for you no one else
For you let me breathe my first real breath
You let my heart beat its first real beat
You let my body be your slave for all eternity
I am yours even to the grave

Lauren Elizabeth King

Fairy

There she sits
A beauty queen on her pedestal
She is looked at through many different pairs of eyes
One who is glamorous
One who is an angel
What everyone wants and none can have
Soon your delicate fairy will
Spread her wings and soar
Leaving behind the small ones
Past lovers and the forgotten
She has found the one she wants
The one she loves
The one who completes her
Now she's ready to take you and fly
"Come with me" she whispers "Let's go away
Put your worries behind you and fly"
But you're not ready to fly
Not just yet

Margot Jeanette Lanham

Being a Grandmother

Being a grandmother is a privilege beyond compare.
One of the rewards is a whiff from Baby's hair;
A smile, a grin, the quiver of a chin
And then the pout!
Soon the sun comes out as Baby laughs and gives a shout
And I fall in love all over again!

Barbara E. Last

Centuries Old

I am centuries old
I have been host to much mold
I have watched battles across the field
And watched empires and kingdoms yield
I have witnessed nature's change,
The forest, field, and mountain range
I have lived an idle life,
Watched nations under strife
Cities grow and cities fall,
And humans suffer over all
I have accumulated much wisdom,
A result of surviving all Earth's fission
Continents drift apart
Volcanic ash makes it dark
I still thrive
And will survive
I will forever watch the Shepherd and His flock
I am ye olde rock

Douglas B. Myers

Sunday Dinner at Ernie's Esquire, Part 1

Outside:
A sultry, sodden world outside
where a faintly swaying pine, shyly,
fearfully lifts fragile,
tender green in a frost-fisted freshet.

Inside:
A fiery, flashing flame
boldly, brashly flings
unfettered wisps
of red-gold banners at mirrors,
burnished in hazy moon glow.

Outside-Inside:
An unpaired pledge blends firefall
with faith untempered,
and glimmering streams
shatter limbs of ice.
Warmth enfolds limbs; limbs embrace tomorrow's days.

John P. Cummings

Fleeting Glances

Dawn has broken many times since then.
Evening has showered the sky with stars.
I search for your face in the new sun
and seek your smile
among the bright lights above.
Sometimes, when I am all alone,
you come to me and I hear your laughter.
You tell me, not in words,
that you are okay now.
But, when I try to speak, you put your finger against my mouth
to hush me.
I can only feel you now
when the new sun rises
and the full moon lights the night.
You are okay now; it is me that is lost and in pain.
So, I hope that your fleeting glances
around me remain for awhile longer
until I am okay, too.

Sandra L. Poolas

Reverence

I greet my higher power everywhere I turn
The real love, loneliness, my emotions churn
I feel, stumbling blind through chaotic bliss
My life almost being able to overcome this
My strife, dreams I've got so my smile will persevere, I try
Once fulfilled, my mind will clear, I'll fly

Ja Daniel Krasniqi

The Power of Love

I think of you with red roses heart.
I visualize you with a diamond mind.
My taste for you is an exquisite blend
Of honey, chocolate and Georgia peach.
I see you soaring beneath my wings.
Nothing have I ever thought of you but beautiful things.
I see you walk on velvety path
In your shining glamour like the stars up above.
You truly discern the content of my being;
My strong chemical effect,
My high conductor of electricity,
My vulnerability.
You struck me with a ray of love,
Igniting my heart and charging my body,
Giving me a twinkling glow.
I see a rainbow and a gush of electricity
Flowing from head to toe.
My heart melts softly and somehow you vanish my woe.

Alrin Dunley Bewry

I Am Me

I wonder what people think of me
I hear what people say about me
I see what people don't like about me
I cry over everything that hurts me
I want people to know they misjudge me
I am all I can be
I pretend not to be someone I can't be
I touch nothing I can't see
I worry over people that love me
I think I will believe in me
I am everything I want to be
I understand everything that matters to me
I say what I feel is right inside of me
I dream of the day I can be me
I try to let people like me
I hope people know the real me
I can be me
I will be me

Laura E. Gerber

Socks

To everyone I love

I have new socks that my aunt gave me
Which she got when she turned forty-three.
She doesn't want them anymore
'Cause on them she spilled some tea.
These socks go from my feet up to my nose,
But they feel cuddly for my toes.
These socks have many colors on them,
And one heart that says "je taime."
There's purple, silver, and some blue,
Even some brown from the spilled tea too.
There are also the colors green, red, black, and yellow,
And a white blotch of a marshmallow.
There is orange, bronze, gold, and dots of pink
And the bottom has a really big stink!
I love these socks,
But they make me look stout,
And my mom says to throw them out!

Eva Paula Jericevic

Shallow Shadows

I try to peel off the undesirable masks,
The shallow shadows—
And I find I'm only hollow inside.

I try to reach out with half-hidden hands.
I cry because it's all I know—
And I find my tears are made of sand.

Sarena Emily

Whose Hands

A basketball in my hands is worth about $20.
A basketball in Michael Jordan's hands is worth about $30 million.
It depends whose hands it is in.

A baseball in my hands is worth about $7.50.
A baseball in Mark McQuire's hands is worth about $18 million.
It depends whose hands it is in.

A golf club in my hand is worth—absolutely nothing
A golf club in the hands of Tiger Woods—Price to be determined.
It depends whose hands it is in.

Nails in my hand might produce a fair birdhouse.
Nails in Jesus' hands produced salvation for the entire world.
It depends whose hands it is in.

Simply put, it does depends whose hands it is in.
So put your concerns, worries, fears, hopes, dreams, and families
In God's hands to find their true value.
It all depends whose hands it is in.

Patrick Leonard Holder

Safe at Home (Where I'm Supposed to Be)

To my mom, who likes this poem

On the top of the mountains
I can hear the rain
I can feel the wind
I can see the sun
And I know that you're close to me
And I am safe at home, where I'm supposed to be
And I can see as far as millions of miles
And I can see you for a little while
From the window in my house
I can see the sky so blue
And I know that I am safe at home
And you are here with me
And even if I can't see you like I see the sun
I can feel you like I feel the wind
I can hear you in my mind calling millions of times for me
Just like I can hear the rain when I close my eyes
And I am safe at home where I'm supposed to be, just you and me

Gabriela "Gabby" Aguilar

Butterfly of Mine

If we were butterflies,
I have torn your wing so you cannot fly.
They say time heals all wounds.
Maybe someday we'll fly together again,
Or maybe we'll forever be lost in fog,
Blocked from each other by doubt, skepticism, and mistrust.
Perhaps you will meet another butterfly
More honest than this one and she can mend your wing,
Or maybe it will rain and you will drown because you couldn't fly
Due to my foolishness.
Then how would I feel?
But I won't leave you, butterfly.
I will stand by you until your wing heals and you trust me again.
I will forever stay with you, through rain, wind, or fog,
And will help restore your wing to its original brilliance.
The colors might differ, so you may not trust me like before,
But we'll make it together, butterfly of mine.
We'll see the sun again.

Megan Ellen Payne

Dark

Darkness shall be your guide;
light shall blind those around you,
those who fall to temptation.
Darkness shall be your home;
here you dwell in the darkest of thought,
the purist of thought.

Michael T. Beal

The Day

I love beautiful days
How it changes in a matter of seconds
Rainy one minute, sunshine the next
How does it do that?
Is there something controlling it?
How can a man be a man?
How can he solve it?
Take it apart and put it back together?
Kick it and make sure it's running right?
But that's how a man thinks, isn't it?
Why can't he just enjoy the day,
Love it for what it's worth?
In the moment is to be unpredictable
And that's enough to drive anyone crazy
Surviving the unpredictable
Is to gain experience
Live and learn, then pass it on
To enjoy a day that's unpredictable

E. Rene Leal

Ode to Diane Allison

To my late wife, Diane

Diane blew into my life during and like
a hurricane of her surname.
She blew through my life with such force,
I thought I would be torn apart.

I hung on for dear life as she spun me like a tornado
spawned by her ferocious winds.
And although she hurt me to the soul,
I loved her with all my heart.

For a brief time she was calm,
as if in the eye of the storm.
Then the winds of cancer
stormed my soul again.

Her passing was so rapid.
It hurt me to watch her go
as the winds of her life died out,
like a flash in a pan.

Calvin R. Jennings II

Woman of Valor

I know who I am. I am a woman:
Woman of honor, woman of valor,
Woman of integrity, woman of God.
My womb has brought forth nations.
My arms have held and nurtured the broken.
My hands have wiped away the tears of the young.
I am your mother, your sister, your friend.
On my shoulders lie the burdens of generations.
I am your foundation.
I am the glue that holds your world together.
Powerful, strong, and mighty am I.
My memory is epic, for it goes back centuries.
I only state what the past has told me.
I was not given my rights; I took them.
When my babies were stolen, I found them.
I am like the phoenix, for I rise out of the ashes a new creation,
This time one of my own making.
I know who I am. Do you know who you are?

LeTonya T. Durbin

A Puzzlement

While stopping at my favorite zebra's cage,
In quizzical thought I always engage.
I ponder the dear zebra's ambivalent plight,
Is he white with black or black with white?
Maybe we mortals should take a tip from carefree he,
Color or combinations of such should just be history!

Beverly Ann Broughton

Remembering Lost Love

Often I ponder about where I lost my priceless diamond.
I've cried many tears over this rare jewel
because it was passed to my safeguard.
I didn't believe something so precious could be passed to me,
cut from the veins of Kilimanjaro.
All were welcome to sit, but few were chosen.
None could replace this sanctuary where I kept this diamond.
Time weathered a score and has not etched a mark
within the hallowed walls of our sacred shrine.
Man-made devices cannot measure infinity
and her beauty was suspended in time.
Remember that cold day when the world stood still,
as together you created a beautiful temple for all to behold?
Your mind's eye held dear that heavenly dreams come true.
So with my heart humbled,
I bow to honor your grace and splendor.
I bestow all that I have within;
my soul to serve her far beyond an eternity.

Ritchie Blaine Holliman

I'm with You Now

Although my past implies no waste
It's time I gave someone some grace
One must change as time goes by
Maturity does not grow if no change is implied
Relationships can be quickly formed
And then relationships can become so easily torn
If only I could change the hands of time
I would make it so that you would only be mine
The past is not just filled with regrets
The past was formed with avenues not met
I feel I have a whole new chance
I feel I have met a king
I feel it's time to settle down
I feel you will have the crown
I thank God for meeting you
I thank God for loving you
God is watching from above
God has sent me . . . my true love

June C.D. Stewart

For Daddy, on Your 80th Birthday

How do you thank a father
who has given you strength your whole life,
who has been there through laughter
and also though tears,
through happiness, joy, and strife?

You gave me a home where I always felt safe,
built a playhouse, gave me Flossie and clothes.
And though I've not always been happy for it,
you even gave me your nose.

You taught me to do for others;
you worked hard, and you built things by hand.
It seemed there was nothing you couldn't do,
no problem you didn't understand.

I moved far away, and the years have flown by,
"You're getting up there," we have both been told.
But to me, you will always be "Daddy,"
and you'll never really grow old.

Linda Casner

Sunshine

The sunshine of my thoughts
Was crisscrossing my mind's eye.
God's truth lights the way through my darkest despair.
I seek to see a brighter day.
You created me to be the apple of your eye
And the sunshine of your life.

Clifford James Seab

A True Friend

My friends think they know me,
yet they don't have a clue.
How can they tell if it's me or it's you?
Given a blindfold and no sense of touch,
I bet they could not even tell that much.

My feelings are hidden way down deep,
only revealing the truth should I talk in my sleep.
It is highly unlikely this I would do,
for fear of revealing too much to you.

Not that I wouldn't like to be friends.
To open my heart is too far to bend.
Given an inch, to take a mile,
even friends will use you and all the time smile.

To this day I shut myself out,
no need to stress, worry, and shout.
If a true friend comes my way,
this friend I will treasure both night and day.

Selina Thompson

Friends to Love

Best friends is how we started out.
We shared secrets and trusted each other without a doubt.
When we were together, we had the best time.
The love between us was an obvious sign.
To love someone, there must be trust.
It must be real love not lust.
Then came one strange, but special, day,
When we became a couple and that's how it would stay.
He helps me when I am sad and blue;
Our love is large and always true.
We have been through everything bad and good;
We always got through it like I knew we would.
Our high school life is coming to an end,
But we'll stay real close through each and every bend.
People say that "high school" love will not last,
And after graduation it will end real fast.
That theory seems different to me—
To my heart, I found the key!

Nicole Christine Schatzman

Deep Dreams

There's a girl at ends street—she dreams but
she never sleeps.
With eyes as dark as night sky, rays of moon
shine on her face as she passes by.
Oh, seasons change, oh, birds will fly; as she
walks a thousand leaves fall by her side.
Oh, she cries. I want to dance, Mama. I want to
fly. I want to reach for my moon in your sky.
When my world falls and darkness is near,
I know, Mama, you will always be here.
If time would stand still then stars will
shine bright to fill my soul for eternal life.
I want to dance, Mama. I want to fly, to reach
my mountain so high. Night falls, she closes
her eyes; she drifts asleep, her soul so deep.
Oh, Mama, I can dance. I can fly. I found my moon.
I found stars right here in my heart, right
here deep inside.

Gina Florence Green

Yesterday

It seems just like yesterday that I laid eyes on you.
It feels like yesterday when I think of how we first met.
I would love to have those good old days back again.
I can see those times trying to shine through.
I can see us coming together like we use to be.
It feels just like yesterday.

Sherine Ann Alston

Redbud Tree

When I die, bury me
Underneath a redbud tree
So in my absence I can bring
Bountiful flowers in the spring
And in the summer I'll bring shade
For anyone who needs a break
Heart-shaped leaves will drink the sun
Deep in the ground the roots will run
Into the earth I make so rich
To carry on the legacy of which
I'll continue to produce much splendor
My soul will not end or
Wither with time
But persist with grass and vines
With living creatures big and small
With branches and limbs growing so tall
Thriving on my death to make sense of it all
I'll be smiling—forever.

Debbie S. Brinson

Emotions

Emotions raging, twisted, unknown
As soon and quick the windblown
Frail flower, petals flying, lost in the gust
That one moment of lust gone
Somewhere never to be seen again
Except by the wind
Broken heart never to mend, always apart
Left out, left behind, left
Lost forever, never again
The hurt, the pain, confused
Another soul, unreached goal
The impossible dream forgotten, lost
Missing in action
Another distraction
A mere attraction
No satisfaction
So where did this begin? Where does this end?
Ask the wind

Katrina Dawn Walker

Mom

Months have come and gone and I have not written you.
I wanted to tell you how I feel, I've been so blue.

Wishing you were near to get me through the days,
but the distance keeps us apart in so many ways.

I needed to hold you but you are just too far,
It's not like I could get there by hopping in my car.

Where you live now you must be happy as can be,
You're able to walk, wherever you want . . . you're free.

You must be happy, because I feel it in my heart.
But Mom, your leaving has kept us so . . . so . . . far apart.

I've been told that someday I will see you again,
And I know this to be true,
Because when that day comes the heavens will turn
A beautiful shade of blue!

Mom . . . I miss you!

Linda Marchena

The Future

The future will come before we know it's here.
The future is unavoidable no matter the year.
The future is coming and will change our lives,
For better or worse, for smiles or cries.
The future is coming whether we want it or not.
If we wish to live in the past, then poorly we've been taught.

Philip Jensen

When Day Falls into Night

I can see the
clouds slowly drifting away from me.
When there's no more sun, no more bright
skies, the birds go into hiding, watching
the day say goodbye again. When I look
to the sky, what do I see? Nothing but
deep dark emptiness, and me. Alone once
again, I cannot see; nothing but darkness
in front of me. Look! There it goes, just
for a second I thought the day had come
back again. Oh, my mistake, there in the
sky a shooting star passes by. Oh, when
will this darkness end, sitting, watching,
and waiting for the day to begin. There,
it seems so far away, I see the sun trying
to brighten my day. Then once again when
day falls into night and there is no more
life, I will succumb to darkness again.

Edna G. Thomas

Melancholy Season

Tender, young bud springs forth
So new, so full of hope and promise
Unfurling and uncurling

Eagerly raising its face to the sun's caress
Growing greener, larger, stronger
Perfect in every way

Swaying overhead
Soughing softly in the summer breeze
Refreshed each morning; covered in dew

Changing colors—red, orange, yellow
Shivering in fear of the cold, cold winds
Clinging desperately to yesterday

Remembering fondly times gone by
Never to be recaptured
Brown and withered, it lets go
Gently floating to earth

Christine Olsen-Needham

change

flashback to my room
dirty socks on the floor
faintly remembering you standing by my door
faintly remembering sneaking out past midnight
laughing and arguing on who was right
people change way too fast
that is why you must make this last
and people move way too much
and leave behind forgotten faces lost in time
the echo of your voice runs endless through my mind
and heart-filled feelings that i left behind
the white walls all surround me with new things i must find
you call and i don't answer
this is where i draw the line
people change way too fast
that is why you must make this last
and people move way too much
and leave behind forgotten faces lost in time

James Paul McCall

If You Want to Marry Me, You Must

If you want to marry me, you must smile,
be happy more than frown, sad every day.
By the way, happy or not, the main decision is in your heart;
only your heart will give you the true feeling.
Indeed, human beings are full of grief,
difficulties, surprise, and happiness.

Wing Pong Paul Hui

Just a Moment

As constellations conspire
In iridescent configurations
To purge a soul for all it's worth
To dredge its depths for revelation

And from the moment we are born
To the moment we arrive at truth
And then the truth is laid to rest
And in a moment we are gone

Just a moment in between
To glance at the night spheres
To ponder perspective, to venture a dream

The stars in stolid grace peer down
And I resolve
There's more to this life
Than two hands can tend
One mind can grasp
One heart can impound

Robin L. Huelsman

Filled with the Shine

As if we love flowers.
As if we love first green.
He and me.
Our days, filled with the shine.
The shine is flowing.
When I feel him.
The sweet aroma is flowing.
When I listen to him.

I dream his skin.
His smooth brown skin breathes warmly.
I dream his lips.
His music from the lips sleeping softly on his face intoxicates me.

He entered my life slowly.
His heart,
Swimming freely just like the wind.
My memory of him,
Fluttering in the wind.

Sawa Yuki

Shadows and Tears

Cloaked shadows quietly creep,
As silent tears cascade down my face
And my heart, my soul, softly weeps.
Amidst the dark empty sky,
Broken love sings
In a soft, whispered cry.
I was such a fool, not knowing what to say, to do
And now I wearily weep in pain.
Liquid tears covering my soul like the cool morning dew.
Don't go through love in fear, so much easier said than done
When the world has fallen
And crimson embers block the blazing sun.
Confused, scared, alone, so unsure;
When will my heart go unbroken?
When will I find love that is pure?
Let my heart fly, help me break free,
Free to understand, free to love again;
Free to just be me.

Rachel Palmer

My Treasured Friend

In your strength and boldness, warmth was found.
In your free spirit, energy surrounded all.
In your loyalty, true friendship rested.
In your arms, love and protection were felt.
In your absence now, your essence of joy
Is mine to freely possess.

Lisa Letitia Kruckow

In the Field

It's around mid-June, the days are warm and the skies are blue.
I can see the horizon all around and it is beautiful, much like you.

The trees and the grass flow with the gentle summer's breeze
I pray you can hear me, so I am here on my knees.

The bees are floating from flower to flower as they fly around.
A butterfly is gracefully flapping its' wings while on the ground.

When I look up above, I see the birds as they fly.
Now that you are no longer with me, here I kneel and cry.

I look across the field while my tears fall to the ground.
You are standing there calling my name, but there is no sound.

When I saw you, my heart began to pound and race.
It's a future without you that I cannot face.

So here in the field I will cry until I can cry no more,
The next time it rains in a field, think of me . . .
You're the one I'm crying for.

Brandon T. Johnson

The Mask She Hides Behind

Behind her smile there is a frown.
To her, the world has no motion, no sound.
She kept a secret way deep inside.
Her feelings for him are something she hides.

She never knows what to do when he's near.
For him to not feel the same as her is her fear,
But she wants him to care, wants him to see,
Tries to show him that their friendship has
More possibilities.

Now she's trying to forget him,
But he won't go away.
She's still hoping they'll be together
Someday.

She walks about. Her friends ask her, "What's wrong?"
And then comfort her for a while.
But in the end, she'll hide her frown
Behind her smile.

Kathleen Santos Balagtas

The Common Teen: The Human Paradox

The common teenager fearless and extremely daring,
Surprise, surprise, is most afraid and extremely caring.
Face shaven, hair clean, in appearance he is comely,
Odd that he describes himself as being quite homely.
With regard to his own ability he is most doubtful,
But time after time he has proved to be most helpful.
His face was often a crimson red, for he was a tad shy,
And his favorite pastime was to experiment, to try.
He was always found working towards a goal,
A strong muscular body hid his fragile soul.
Although rough as he may indeed appeared,
In private company he often did shed a tear.
Upon hearing an insult even of the slightest,
His heart would break as though it were a crisis.
He constantly asked his own self who am I
And never to this day received a decent reply.
Thus, this confusion made him quite mellow,
But this teen, kind and unique, was quite a fellow.

Taylor Kaine Pelchar

Here

We are here to nurture and raise our spirits together
I am here to connect with your soul at the deepest place
We are here for us to be the most tender and beautiful lovers
I am here to be your best friend ever
We are here to learn and grow together
We are here to be in integrity and in love

Mary Ann Kennett

Devoted Sisterhood (Even Though)

Even though we are not close,
my devotion to you will only grow.
Even though we are not close,
our letters link our lives.
Even though we are states away,
it is as if it is with you I stay,
because the words we say convey our deeds each day.
Even though we are not close,
our hearts can feel each other's rhythm
and can fulfill the needs of every beat.
Even though we are not close,
our souls are one of a kind
and will always be distinguishable
among all the lonely cries of the world.
Even though we are not close,
our souls will find each other
and will forever be linked
with an unbreakable bond of sisterly love.

Cynthia Christina Willis

What of Trouble and Sorrow

Why all this trouble and sorrow?
Does man have no hope for tomorrow?
Is he to look at another dawn and fail?
Can all of his efforts be to no avail?

Is there someone to come to his aid
or must he remain worried and afraid?
Can he stand up proudly and say,
Look at me. I am free this day!

Then after many years and many pains,
he sadly looks back, to see what remains.
What he sees, now late in life;
he sees children, grandchildren, and a loving wife.

Yes, he is old now and he has learned a lot,
but of this, no, he thinks not.
Instead he thinks of his younger years
and once again he is filled with sorrow.
For now, he knows not what he'll do tomorrow.

Gerald Dale Csrman

The Secret

It starts from the moment we arrive on this
Earth, yet is buried so deeply inside.
An unknowing friend with an incredible
strength, it begins to blossom and become so alive.
As the days turn to years filled with
laughter and pain, we marvel at all that's endured.
As the years fill with memories of family
and fate, we rejoice in all that it's cured.
Through wisdom we are given a secret to life
held captive for so long before.
And with the secret is sent a balance and
peace, and a world of unconditional love.
The strength in our souls is our power to
choose, and the power of one's own control.
A life is to live in the best way we know
as it will forever change, alter then grow.

Lori-Witt Dalton

Thought Voyage

Today I wander free as any cloud
Tamed too long, I am again in the wild
I am in no danger from ideas being soured
My thoughts are loose, no halter drags me back
I can be fierce as the wind or breeze-like mild
I have been let loose and in the Internet tack

Bryan Edmund McDonagh

A Silver Thread

As I walk down the paths of the forest nearby,
Many, many, things catch my eye.
A squirrel nearby is scampering over the autumn leaves.
The awesome colors are hard to believe.
A deer comes wandering through the trees.
I don't think he even sees me.
A little gray mouse runs from stump to stump.
What is he looking for, is he carrying a lump?
It must be supper for his little family.
Oh, yes, there is his family, you see.
Look! A woodpecker on the tall pole.
He pecks and pecks until he creates a hole!
I caught a glimpse of Mr. Big Bear.
He was out for a walk in the evening air.
As I return to my starting place,
How many more beautiful things will I face?
There is only one that knows what's ahead.
He created all beauty with one fine silver thread.

Janice C. Schwanke

Sun in My Eyes

When I see the sun in my eyes,
I know the sun is here within my sight.
It is so bright, but beautiful to look at.
It makes me want to get more and more.
The warmth is the best feeling ever known.
I would never give it up for anything.
The sun gives me new life every time.
I am glad I can see the sun every day.
Even when my life is cloudy the sun is there
to brighten up my day when I am down.
Nothing can change the way I feel about the sun,
except I love the sun more every day.
Bright, whenever I see the sun it is great.
You, the sun, can help everyone you meet.
Your life is long and will always change
and will always glow in the sky.
Heaven, you will always shine upon the Earth
because you are the sun in my eyes.

Brett Alan Winkelhake

The Ocean

Put a shell up to your ear
and what do you hear?
The waves crashing against the beach
or the sea gulls squawking out of reach?
Crabs scuttling across the sand
or maybe the tune of a nearby band?
Nevertheless the ocean seems magic,
but, alas, it can still be tragic.
Walk out of your hotel onto the warmth of the land;
beneath your feet is the warm sand.
Look out at the ocean
and watch its waves motion.
But sadly, it is time to part
with the place you leave in your heart.
Sitting alone on a dusty old shelf is a shell you got
at a place that you forgot.
Put it up to your ear
and what do you hear?

Drew Anthony Fultz

Visions

I had a vision of you one night.
It was such a beautiful sight,
Standing by my bed wearing your beautiful purple dress.
What ever happen to that wonderful night
When you appeared to me, that special night?

Elaine Marie Bergeron

Presence

The cold air stings our faces and captures
our breath, as the sound of dead leaves
disturbs the morning silence
Our destination of no importance to us
just the presence of our two souls

Eric P. Teter

Heart Music

The sound of a bow drawn across a string
lingers endlessly; sighing its final chords;
endings and beginnings echoing in harmonic;
a coiling momentum the smallest pause
before breath renews.

Stephanie Bach

Bat

That belfry inhabited with bats
embodies the town from whence they came.
It used to be good—the town—
till the people came
and subsequently forced the bats to inhabit the belfry.

Nobel Gray

True Happiness

True happiness only comes a few times in life.
Now that I've found it I hope it never ends.
Never leave me, never hurt me,
I'll never be unkind.
If only I could have true happiness.

Janessa Louise Gray

Indiana Summer Dreams

I dream of a clear blue sky on a quiet summer day,
of a mother and her children happy and at play.

I dream of a small town street lined with maple trees on each side,
of a father with his children running to match his stride.

I dream of bright sunny days humid and hot,
of boys with worn basketballs taking their shots.

I dream of crystal clear streams cold and full of fish,
of freckled youth with bamboo poles casting their wish.

I dream of a vast dark and starry country night,
of childhood friends chasing insect lights.

I dream of rows and rows of corn, tall and green,
of old farmers working the fields worn and lean.

I dream of country roads stretching as far as the eye can see,
of a carefree young man driving his father's Model T.

I dream of camping out in the woodland glen,
of a dark haired boy laughing and bonding with his friend.

I dream of picnics rich with food and games,
of aunts and uncles calling out my name.

My Indiana dreams come more frequently now,
you see, I have lines on my face and white on my brow.

Duane Lee Kirish

The Male Animal

Scratchin' and grinnin' and running in packs
Carelessly committing those inane acts
Chewing that bone into pieces and bits
Yapping at whatever moves, stands, or sits
Sniffing the air and testing the breeze
Who knows what waits just beyond yon trees
Just a quick check; yes, it's still there
Time to run on with that double-dog dare
Hey, there's a cat! Let's have some fun
Watch that fur ball spit, hiss, and run!
Ah, but it's great to live for today
To sleep and dream and to laugh and play
Joyously proclaiming to one and all
Life is so good when you're chasing a ball

Beth Losey Stevens

The Glorious Moon

The moon rises when the sun goes down
It's reflected light shines all around

Some people observe it for its wonderful looks
Some people write its features down in books

Some people like to walk on it up there
They have to wear special suits for air

For a few days a month the moon is full
For another few days there is no moon, which is dull

The moon every day rotates around the Earth
It's done that ever since the universe's birth

The moon rises when the sun goes down
Its reflected light shines all around

Steven Rossi

Close Your Eyes

Whenever you're feeling alone, hurt, confused
close your eyes and think of me
I'll be there to help you always
whenever you need someone to talk to, laugh or cry with
pick up the phone and call me
I'll be the shoulder you can cry on
whenever you need anything a friend, a companion, a lover
come over to my place
I'll be the one person you can rely on
If you just need to talk or be held in caring arms
I'm that someone you can turn to
I'll always be there
if not by your side, in your heart and mind
Just close your eyes and I'll be there

Katie Marie Pedersen

A Small Request

This poem is about my brother, whom I hate and love at the same time.

I tell them I'm fine,
Just so they don't worry.
And besides,
Even if I tried to tell them
How I really felt,
They wouldn't listen.
They would be too busy,
Or try to give me counsel,
When all I want
Is to talk to someone,
Someone who will listen to me and understand me
And will let me finish speaking.
I don't want to be told what to do.
I just want a friend,
A friend with whom I can talk.
Please . . .

Monique A. Maignan

Michelle

Her soft sweet breath caresses you
To be near her is dangerous
Her eyes will pierce your life
To touch her will burn you
Her passion will engulf you like a flame
The love she gives will make you go insane
Her kisses will send you over the edge
A smile from her will shoot through your heart
Being touched by her will send shivers through your soul

Aaron Ralph Schumacher

Let Go (I Have to Let Go)

I have to let go so I loosen the rope of love a little at a time.
Each time it hurts more; sometimes I cry.
The hurt will heal with time;
the pains go so deep it's an aching thorn in my side.
God's there to ease the pains and to make me stronger.

I have to let go, day by day; it's getting rough.
Each day seems harder than the one before.
My heart is broken and so heavy with pains
it seems unbearable.
I found myself asking the question, "Why me?"
God answered, "Why not?"

I have to let go; my blue skies have all turned gray.
I must look forward to the future, leaving the past behind.
I tried to hold on. You were my past; the future is mine.
Death is a hard and bitter pill to swallow.
God makes it easier to digest.

Lillye McWaine

Ian

I know a cute little boy
Who spreads around lots of joy.
He has big brown eyes
And a winning smile.
He even lets me hold him
Once in a while.

The apple of his mother's eye;
Oh, what a sweet little guy!
He just turned three
And anyone can see,
He's quick-witted and bright.

He's funny, sensitive, caring and sweet.
For a three year old, he's really neat!
He's a live wire—that's true as well
But in his home, he is known
As Ian Kristopher Brothwell.

Jonnie C. Kendall

Broken Pieces

Late at night, sad and alone,
Heartaches tear me up and wear me down.
Tired of fighting, tired of life.
The sky is grey, the moon and stars are hidden away.
The ocean cries outside.
The waves roar in rage.
My love is gone.
All the laughter has faded away.
My life is just broken pieces.
The happy music on the radio is sad.
My poems and stories have no more meaning,
Have been lost and torn, scattered, thrown around the room.
My love is gone.
All the laughter of a happy relationship has faded away.
My life lies scattered all around the room.
It's just broken pieces on the ground.

W. C. Freeman

Forgiven

Can one forgive me the mistakes I've made
Or cry with me aloud,
For I have already paid and will never feel proud.
Can one help me understand my confusion within?
Was it right or just a sin?
Often feeling it was an illusion.
My reality burns, yet another page in my life turned.
One man's life ended, my child, I defended.
I carry the guilt and feel the pain, yet my life I finally gained.

Erin Samantha Soule

Utopia

Within the limits of mind or matter,
We are all seeking a kind of utopia;
Whether we keep this vision in our dreams
Or attempt to bring it into the world around us.

Idealistic utopia is indeed a powerful word.
Visionary utopia may or may not be achieved,
Yet faith in an imaginative utopia can be a beautiful way
Of maintaining our courage and trust in mankind.

Inventive utopia from within can be achieved
By keeping a positive outlook,
And by trying to improve your existence
And the existence of others.

Achieve a castle-building utopia
Within the confines of your mind,
So that you can feel better about people
And the world around you.

Evelyn Ann Dolas

Portrait of Katherine

These eyes of mine behold a beauty that
escapes my hand for the moment, no longer
residing within the American north; exist
does she now in the paradise of Thomas the saint.

A mature woman in every sense of the word,
yet youthful in spirit and in appearance;
her age be just a numeric measure in time.

Though I have never been blessed to hear her
voice, my heart has seen its majesty
through her very words; a songbird must
wait to proclaim many wonders.

I be not a prophet nor a messenger from the
living God, but alas I feel her destiny
will bring great joy to the world; and even
greater to her soul.

Ignatius Brown

Not My Father

You're not my father but yet . . .
you take care of me,
you love me,
you hold me,
you help me.
I may not call you Dad,
but I consider you my father.
Even when we fight and argue,
when I say that I hate you,
I still love you and always will.
The reason I say I hate you sometimes
is because you make me mad.
I will always love you and consider you my father
before I would ever consider my own.
In my eyes you are my father.
I may never call you Dad,
but you know I will always love you in my own way.

Bethenie Lynn Hall

My Daughter

Dedicated to my daughter, Tiffany Lolita Rose Marquez

Delightful and fun to be around,
Alive with passion, yet has her feet on the ground.
Untouchable in all she achieves,
Glowing with light in the hearts she upheaves.
Honorable and loyal to all she knows.
Tender and gentle as a river flows.
Eager to please and always bright.
Rather extraordinary my Tiffany my light.

Vicki Nancy Ruth San Andres

You Hurt, I Hurt

Do you understand, my child,
When you hurt, I hurt?
There seems nothing I can do,
But when you hurt, I hurt

I wish I could wipe it away
Because when you hurt, I hurt
If only I could make it better
Wipe away your hurt, my hurt

Only time and healing can help us forget
Your hurt, my hurt
I will always listen if you'll let me
Remember—when you hurt, I hurt

Let it go, don't hang on and say
Goodbye to your hurt
And I'll say
Goodbye to mine

Susan Cohoon

Rainbow of Memories

Through all the bad times when you feel afraid
A rainbow breaks through the dark
That rainbow is a memory from happier days
When all of our friends were together
So as we leave, we climb, stand on that ledge
I know that we'll always remember
So climb, so run, so jump to the sky
And know in our hearts we'll surrender
To the rainbow of memories
From past bygone days
Go on forever because we remember
And the wind will forgive our faults
And help us to fly
Over that rainbow making new rainbows
Remembering past memories
While making new memories
Forever we fly

Catherine Camuso

Curse

I roam and they fear me
My pointed gleaming fangs are all they see
My curse, this curse, this dreaded curse . . .

I am forced to drink, piercing flesh
Sucking the juices, craving the moist mess
This curse, my curse, laid upon me . . .

I sit in the corner so thirsty, I thirst
My mouth waters for the prey I seek out first
My curse, the curse, bringing me pain . . .

I fear myself, hold back my craze
Find my way out of this hunger maze
The curse, my curse, it hurts . . .

Sitting alone, by myself, no one else . . .
The hunger surges through me, no one else . . .
This curse, this hungry curse, my doom . . .

Shakara Petteway

Pére Absent

Father, Father, you left me so soon.
It happened so fast my heart rose with the moon.
I begged the Lord to let you stay,
But he took you anyway.
My tears ran
To fill the Ganges River.
I miss you so much nobody knows.
My eyes moisten with my own fluids.
My heart moves with the moon.

Bayette Brown

I Live for You

Your voice calms my mind,
Your beauty astounds my eyes,
Your love resides within me,
We're living for the only thing I know.

I live to hear your voice;
It tells me our love is true.
Echoing softly
In the winds of our eternity,

I am enchanted by your beauty,
Weaving your grasp around my heart.
It brings light with your presence,
As the shadows of confusion become so clear.

I live for the love you show me,
Reaching to the deepest depths within me.
Your love is a never-ending dream,
And has become my newest reason for living.

David Michael Greely

The Fountain of Perpetual Peace

Dedicated to Leroy Pitman

Given to redeem the human mind from error,
the twilight darkens, the curlew calls.
There is a calm majestic presence with
manifold and soft chimes efface with
footprints in the sands. The flight of the
dove, wings aspired sounds of sorrow and
delight rest within. The hands of grace
reaching for white caps in our souls. Collecting
water for epic fountains, so that nature
deals with us and may take away our playthings
one by one; our security is left to choose.
One single hand leads us to rest ever
so docile that we go scarcely to wonder, not
knowing if we wish to go or stay. Being
full of adoration trying to understand how far the
unknown transcends to what we know.

Krystina K. Mayhew

In the Coolness of a Lonely Night

And I looked at the sky
and saw my star in it,
diminishing its brightness and intensity
in the coolness of a lonely night.

I shut my eyes in disbelief,
fearing for it to be extinguished forever,
and tears of impotency ran down my cheeks
with their warm feeling helping me to survive

I reached for my hands to wipe them dry,
and in the process of doing so,
their wetness brought me back to reality,
to your image and its lovely smile.

If I should live without you from now on
and my existence drastically change,
I beg you, oh, my lonely star!
To let me die with the mist of the day.

Juan Antonio Parrilla

Thinking

Here I sit, lethargic and lonely.
All I can do is think of you.
You are the only thing on my mind,
night and day.
Here I sit lethargic and lonely.
I wonder if I'm in your thoughts
throughout the day?
Just thinking that you are thinking of me
makes me feel special in every way.

Ashley Lynn Bennett

The Roaring Sea

Dedicated to Lillian M. Cramer

The sea is mounting high.
The sea is pounding the shore so wide.
We look upon the view with a glassy eye.
The wonder of it all will long abide.
Our thoughts are floating into space.
We wonder about our own life's race.
Is our work so important to take its place
When we view nature's grand place?
Our Maker has made his stand;
We look upon its grand performance.
We think ourselves as a grand big band.
We place ourselves in our best circumstance.
So as we look upon the waters
Roaring about in the sea of life,
Let's be sure to thank Him, fair traveler,
For all His wonders and His life.

William G. Cramer

Scorned

A women scorned, I have been
Which makes it hard to love again
Lines of pain etch my face
My heart is scarred and out of place
Memories often cause my tears
Anger and hurt, my emotions, my fears
Will love run away should it travel near
I know myself, and I am strong
I have the strength, my life goes on
Though I have the strength of a thousand men
I long to feel this love again
I have felt it once, it was abused
Tattered and torn my heart's been used
A sweet kiss good night, I crave so much
A warm embrace, a lover's gentle touch
A woman scorned, yes I have been
Will I ever love again

Jodi A. Polasky

This Green Bench

Soon I'll sit on other benches
White, brown, red, probably blue
But the color will not matter
Anymore

Here on this green bench
I promised to myself not to make you any promises
For after today they won't matter to you
Anyway

As you leave this place
You might not even wave your hands goodbye
Thinking it will not matter to me
Anyhow

This green bench will soon be empty
And of course it will matter
Because when I sit again on other benches
I'll surely miss you

Stephen Arnaiz Cuyos

Lifeless

I guess I would describe it more as a nightmare
I could feel the hatred in the voice
That was slowly tearing away at my flesh
It had come to me so rapidly as well as violently
That I couldn't even breathe nor could I talk
Quickly that same voice would force my body to turn numb
With nothing to shield myself
I would lie there like a prisoner
Waiting to be executed

Amy A. Ashley

Untitled

Outside the cancer center
September breathes brutal and cool
Colors as clear as the knowledge of death

I wait there
In the flow of smug young doctors
Laughing their way to lunch

The day is so brilliant
With hard bright lines
Burning horizons into faces
Cutting the summer haze
With the red edges of summer's blood

Bliss is so far away
At the water
Where we shared cigarettes
The sadness of beauty
And loneliness

James Eric Rich

Green Kings

Mist surrounds the hilltops
and the valley becomes an ocean,
submerged under a swirling foam of waves.
Untouched, the green islands stand hip-deep,
their massive tree-crowned shoulders
hulking up in the sunlight.
The dew upon their hair glints,
as the yellow morning sun
climbs sleepily over the horizon
while, above, their iron crowns
stand majestically in rusty-red,
and beards of russet leaves
move lazily in the breeze.
The autumn morning could not slow their ancient joints.
Their bones of earth are far too strong to shackle.
And slowly the vapours trickle away,
and the ancients are left as they have always been.

Adam Goodfellow

Waiting for the Bus: Kingston

Mothers' leash-like tugging
on miniature coffee hands
still sticky with orange peel
mingles with vendors shooting star voices
their smiles lined up like
perfect white soldiers
defending the dingy trinkets laden with
dust and sweat
The old man with one leg sits here too
ganja smoke pooled in distant yellow eyes
stale sweat nestled in his fishnetted shirt
The bus screeches its tired self
to a stop
ready for one last run
The wet blanket of late afternoon
gives way to a cool dusk and
a rumor of violence

Rachel Ellner

Springtime

Green, green, all around;
bees buzzing up and down,
crickets jumping on the ground,
all you can hear is the birds' tweeting sound.

Sun, sun, shining bright,
all you can see is a pretty sight.

Dark, dark, in the night,
you can see the moonlight.

Crystal Starlene Dowd

Drain

Happy life, never lived
Never gone, never given
Once a burden, now set free
Life is never what it used to be

Always dark, never light
Too many things never made right

Heaven is here to stay
Hell pays back forever one day

Hope is set but life is done
Even though we live on,
Everyone else has died and gone

Never-ending feelings of pain
Justice needs to be served before we can drain

Free the fear, release all emotion
Look towards the future will full devotion

Kenna Swanson

A Writer's Lament

I rhyme, I rhyme, I've done my time.
I write, I write, both day and night.
I read, I learn, but haven't earned
That well-known name that comes with fame.
I've been rejected, been told no.
But still I write. Why? I don't know.
I simply must.
That must be it.
Hopefully, on down the line,
You'll read a piece that I call mine.
You'll see the work I tirelessly do,
Presented in print from me to you.
I write, I write, no end in sight.
I stamp, I mail and hope for a sell.
I wait, I pray, day after day
For someone to see
There's a writer in me.

Sheila DeeAnn Lillico

Wild Nature

Ageless cedar, eternal birch,
Majestic oak to the winds of time finally yielding.
Beauty of the woodlands allows none to be unaffected
Upon seeing leaves of a golden, autumn hue.
Time touches not the ancient living towers,
Standing fast before the blade of Father Time.
Still lies his scythe as He looks upon their splendor.
Ageless, majestic beauty leaves time standing still.

Golden sun, sapphire sky;
Warmth set free by dark clouds vanishing;
Freedom gives flight to avians full of life
Which courses through creatures that fly.
To the air, soar iridescent insects in numbers
Uncountable to the human eye;
Although, animals of the sky love not cloudy, dreary days,
But come questing with an early sun's rise.
Golden warmth gives life to uncountable animals questing.

Nathaniel S. Bergen

Who We Are

I'm standing in the corner,
weighed down by thoughts of fear;
thoughts of what they might say if I show my true self.
When my heart says, "Yes,"
my reaction is, "No."
Why do we judge people so quickly
that we don't look hard enough to find the inner beauty?
When will you begin to understand;
when will you learn who they really are?

Emlyn Grace Short

Love's Overcast

Like an unexpected ray of sun piercing the haze,
your eyes suddenly sneak that intense look at me
and I can so feel the heat of their blaze—
casting a glare from which
I can no longer see the blossoming simplicity
of our relationship.
I don't know if, or how to weather your un-forecasted emotions,
yet, I must soon be truer and fairer
and shield our friendship from destruction.
When love settles, it does so like a raindrop on a step—
once there, it's impossible to replace it for another.
For if we try, it can dim the stable shimmer
already set, or worse, destroy it's very pleasure and wonder.
Instead, let's delight in the brightness of
the love nature granted to our hearts,
than defy her by venturing for more
and risking our friendship to the dark.

Maryrose Borda

Hurt

So scary how I knew another broken heart was coming,
I saw it coming the second I met you.
So scary how nightmares do come true
and pleasant dreams never do.
Weird how I was the one that broke everything off
and that single look you gave me captured my heart and soul forever.
What goes around does come around.
I guess this is my price to pay
and I didn't know how lucky I was to have you until I lost you.
Now I have to accept the fact
that no longer I can say you are mine
and even though we love each other,
you have found someone new.
Make sure that girl knows what she's got
and what a wonderful guy you are.
While she is happy with what I could've had,
but played around with and broke it apart. . . .

Ananda E. Eidelstein

To Remember

You were there with me.
I saw you in my dream.
I saw the passion in your eyes.
Then, like a shooting star,
You faded into the night.
Since I awoke, I just kept holding on
And I've been longing to hold you for so long.
Every time I close my eyes you're there,
Then, as a vapor, you vanished as I stared.
How could a dream be so real to me,
I felt your touch, I heard you sing.
In the night your voice still rings,
But when I awoke the room was empty.
After all this time I'm still holding on,
And I've been longing to kiss you for so long.
Living my life, despising the dawn,
Ever since my dream's been gone.

John Robert Ogle

Old Poem

I read a poem once about a bird in a cage.
It talked about letting him go,
setting him free, that was all the rage.
It said if you let him go and he doesn't come
back, your love was never meant to be;
but how can my heart forget all the time you spent just loving me?
I can't do these things like this little poem said,
because my darling, I can't live without you.
I'd rather be dead.

Sharon Kay Zwierzynski

Starlight

Look, there, in the sky!
It's tail, beautiful and bright,
Like fairy dust blowing in the wind.
It shines as if it were a diamond
On the tiara of the most prestigious princess.
My eyes follow it as it dances across the blue-black sky
Lit with the most radiant light from heaven above.
I shiver in the mid-autumn chill and visualize it again,
As I wait for another to appear out of the endless darkness.
I shall never forget that special, vibrant star
That fell into the deep hole of existence.
This bewitching light completed its adventure as a star
And begun another life as maybe something equally extravagant.
I tingle with the thought,
The thought of observing an example of the circle of life.
And to think,
I was the only one to witness this lovely affair.

Shasta Sue Reinhardt

Impregnability

I want back into that safe place
where nothing can devastate me.
It was the safest place I ever stayed;
nothing could cause me harm.

It wasn't me who wanted to leave.
I did not choose to be freed.
It has brought too much pain and despair,
nothing like the silence and comfort in there.

Sometimes I travel back there in my mind
to that place of solitude and tranquility.
It was one place I could experience serenity
and have a protective wall around me.

Out here no walls are strong enough
to keep the infectious world from outside.
There is no place I can go that
will provide me with impregnability.

Denise Tremblett

Life Is Tough

I now see life a different way
Such a different way from yesterday
This rough world we live in today
Was hidden from me yesterday

My father is now so far away
Because I could not stay
In this special world of mine
Where everything would always shine

Rolling down my cheeks came tear by tear
Showing all I had was fear
Now I know that life is rough
And to survive we must be tough

Today I know I am very lucky
To be who I am
To have what I have
And to be loved by those I love

Soraya Rand Merrylees

You Promised

You promised you would never leave me
You promised you'd always love me
You promised that I would always be in your life
I thought we would always be together
But we fell apart
Everything went wrong
I wish things were the way they were a couple of months ago
But I realize now it never would be again
Too bad we just grew apart

Valerie Mills

Gift for You

Got a gift for you
Pleasant smile
Wrapped up perfectly
A gift only that can be given from me to you
Your eyes are bulging, curiosity full to the brim
"The wrapping is gorgeous, isn't it?"
Sweet Hope
Smile of love
Cautiously, you open
After all, this is unexpected
Me, uhm, I'm tense
My eyes revealing
Heart's always on my sleeve

As my silent pain seeps out of the box
It's deeper than anything I've ever known

Enjoy!

Chanda Michele Thomas

My One and Only You

I write this to you because you're the best
My one and only, better than all the rest
Together we stand, forever I dream
Bonded together like a sewed up seam

We met as friends, but now we're in love
Just as cute as two little white doves
The feeling is mutual, we cannot deny
It feels like Heaven, so very high

With you I'm so happy, never to be blue
Such a wonderful person, hey, that's you
You are so perfect, I cannot explain
I am so very sorry when I put you through pain

Your not just my girl, but my best friend
This poem is yours and I will send
Love me forever and I'll do the same
Being without you would mean so much pain

Kevin Timothy Low

Because of You

Right now I am lying crumpled on my bed
Because of you.
Tears of sadness are streaming down my face
Because of you.
I have no one to turn to now
Because of you.
I tried to turn to God, but I hear no answer
Because of you.
I feel lonely and misplaced
Because of you.
It now feels like it's the end of the world
Because of you.
I feel like I have no friends now
Because of you.
My mom always said to watch out for people like you.
And now I feel that pain that hurt so many people
Because of you.

Ashley Nicole Hackett

Daddy's Little Girl

Being your little girl
and always holding your hand
during the times that it hurt so much in the world
and it all just got so bad
has made me a stronger person.
And I owe it all to you,
because all the love you have given me in life.
I feel ten thousand times more for you.

I love you.

Katrina Ines Torres

Expansive Wonder

Behold the wonderful expanse that is the universe
Therein contains all things that matter
But for our puny brains that must take things for granted
Forgetting, ignoring
Scattered dusts full of meanings
And signs that tell the origin of things
And the purpose of all things
Yet we make dastardly choices
That destroy, disprove
Haven't we had a date
Before the grand assembly
To submit our years of opportunistic existence
The number of friends we make
The expense of our vigor and thoughts?
Could we still loiter?
Live life
Live life to the fullest

Maarof Bin Sulaiman

Roots

I am southern smiles through white teeth.
I am my mother's hips,
My fathers eyes.
I am a pear in all its form,
My skin is Irish pale with flecks of brown.
I am my grandmothers courage.
My eyes are innocent in all the ways they can never be.
I am my own mistake.
My hands are ripples through water.
I am my own creativity.
My breasts are small and firm.
I am my own free spirit.
My family is all of me,
I am all of my family.
My emotions are all but gone.
I am a mystery even I cannot uncover.

Lindsay Erin McGeehon

American Pride

You messed with our system. You tore up our
lives. Because of you, we now have to fight.
We lived in a world of peace, love, and hope;
then you crashed a few planes and went up in
the smoke, taking with you thousands of lives,
husbands and children, brothers and wives.
Many a tear on that day was shed for the
loss of those lives and the blood that was
shed. So now we must send our nation to war
to avenge our fallen and even the score. This
war was not chosen, not even planned. They
dealt the cards; we must now play our hand.
Thank God for America; united we stand. We'll
do what it takes to protect our great land.
We're coming to find you. We will make you
pay for all you have done on that September day!

Maggie Ann Porter

Penny for Your Thoughts

Powerful words and the never ending tears of crying
Locked in a cage full of rage and the fear of dying
I know that I will probably be just fine
But don't try to save me, until I know what's mine
Helplessness and hopelessness and a fear of everything
Tenderness and brokenness no prayers for anything
Lots of room to move around, but still no place to go
Lots of things to learn, but still no real desire to know
These are my thoughts for your penny

Ann Marie Gachne

Winning the Fight

Congratulations!
You've finally completed your goal.
Now continue to fight for Jesus,
And He will gladly save your soul.

If you have troubles that bother you
Or problems you think you cannot bear,
Just remember your Heavenly Father
And continually go to Him in prayer.

He will always hear you talking,
And He will always answer, too,
Although some of the answers you receive
May not be the ones you might wish to choose.

But just remember that God knows best.
Although you may not so believe,
Just ask Him for His guiding hand,
And you He will not deceive.

Bonnie S. Hastings

So

So confused that you need a moment away
So sensitive that a sunset makes you cry about the day
So beautiful that you suffer a loss for words
So free you feel you can fly like a bird
So noisy that you can't hear yourself think
So embarrassed you tell your friend she stinks
So ugly that you're afraid to look it in the eyes
So common that it's not to your surprise
So oblivious that you didn't realize the pain
So old but you still play the game
So thoughtful, that to others, you give and give away
So speechless that you still don't have the words to say
So sure that he's the one for the rest of your life
So unsure about that new deodorant you just tried
So calm in a situation that it scares you
So thorough and diligent in all that you do
So life is what you make it and remember that too

Cherise Lene Wallace

There Is a Tomorrow

When the wages of war have left their ugly mark
And your days seem hopeless and dark
It's then you must get up and rekindle the spark
And show the world there is a tomorrow

You say that tomorrow is far away
But look back and see what you did yesterday
When you were younger and full of hope
And it was easier for you to cope
But the added years have made us wiser so we can see
That we can control our destiny
So you see there is a tomorrow

So show the oppressors you're filled with hope
And like your forefathers you know how to cope
Despite all ravages and devastation
You'll once again be your own little nation
Because you see there is a tomorrow

Rose Marie Klobuchar

School

School can be boring.
School can be fun.
The teachers care about everyone.

School can be hard,
School can be easy.
In school you can also feel queasy.

But school is good for your education,
Although I'm sure you wouldn't mind a vacation.

Chani Gross

White Horse

Little white horse cries in the night
Little white horse dies in the night
Little white horse falls to the ground
Little white horse and blood all around

Shot by a poacher and left to die
No one around to hear its sad cry
Lying there in the middle of the night
Its beautiful dead body was quite a sight

Big white horse cries in the night
Big white horse finds a gruesome sight
Big white horse's child on the ground
Big white horse sees blood all around

She sees the bullet hole in his head
The horrid sight turns her heart to lead
She nudges him, her face turns bitter
Boom, another bullet hits her

Kiersten Michele Eberle

Sweet Anise

Dear sister,
You have been a friend of mine
since before the beginning of time.
Through many lives
we have been friends or lovers, but mostly kin.
We share much more than earthly things,
our lives entwined like cosmic rings.
Through all of time and all of space,
no one or nothing can ever replace
the love for you that I feel in my heart;
not even death can keep us apart,
for you are in me as I am in you.
From that one spark, we now are two.
I take comfort in knowing that
not only are you my sister,
but my very dear friend
in this life forever and always, my cosmic twin.

M. A. Porter

April in Aries

April in Aries is an amusing soul.
She's an angel as alluring as
A sparkling jewel.
Her spirit is gentle and caring
Like a spring breeze.
Her heart is as soft as pure spun gold.

April in Aries is a rare find, indeed.
Her beauty is special and innocent.
She's full of pure pride and joy.
Her intelligence is unbounded,
Her wisdom profound.

April in Aries is one of a kind.
She's loving and forgiving all of the time.
A creature indeed, created by God,
Who inspires our lives and our world.
April in Aries is an angel to me.

Nancy Lee Sommers

In This Place

In this place the sky is a cache,
For the deep colors show a heavenly prize.

In this place, naturally, your eye spots a mystic,
For as you look in every direction, nothing but space.

In this place, when the wind blows, it flows.
The air runs through fingers like a lover's touch.

In this place, your soul feels the Earth,
For inside the understanding becomes one.

Penny Charon Henke

In Faith I Trust

How sweet I roamed along the shore
And taste the ocean's air.

A mild breeze blows through my hair
And calms thy gentle soul.

How peaceful is the sea's embrace
Of silent strength and soothing folds.

With each wave a passion grows
For I reflect on words untold.

As the tide rolls in and the waves unfold
A tenderness and yearning grow.

A comforting warmth and affection within
Reassures thy heart for truth it knows.

A fondness revealed, compassion exposed
But In faith I trust for devotion will behold.

Jacqueline Theresa Potvin

My Sister

My sister's about love
Someone you always think of

When your heart breaks
She cries with you as her own heart aches

She is your best friend
Her love for you is never pretend

You talk each day
Someone who is never far away

You laugh about silly things
Talking about Mom's apron strings

Thinking of getting older
Always holding on each other's shoulders

She is my best friend
This is why I feel so content

Lynda Gail Austin

Empty Bottles

I reach in the cabinet to get a sponge.
What do I find?
It's pretty obvious. I'm used to it by now—
empty vodka bottles.

Surprise, surprise,
this is your third relapse.
I'm sick of it. I'm going to live with Grandma.
Call me when you're sober.

You're really terrible at being a mom,
I don't have one anymore.
I hope you're having a nice life;
I'm not.

It's been what, a month?
You haven't called, I am, oh, so shocked,
Did you take your medication today?
I don't care anymore. Go get some beer, mother.

Carissa Grace Dotson

Give Jesus Your Life

My best friend died today.
In a casket, I saw him lay.
My eyes filled with the tears I cried.
I asked myself, "Was it him or I who died?"
We promised to be best friends until the end.
Is this the beginning or is this the end?
I refuse to say goodbye, so I'll say, "Until we meet again."
But, I ask, was the suicide worth all the pain and strife?
All who are considering death, give Jesus your life.

Adam James Archer

A Father's Son

To see your life in a moment
Look back to past loves
Dance slowly back to lost childhood
When wonderment was contained
In the wishes granted by a dandelion

To immerse yourself in the little things
The hours of enjoyment gained
By a single filled balloon
How mother could heal the greatest wounds
With a kiss, a Band-Aid, and a cookie

To be at once a kid again
With all of its happy times
And while you gain your youth
You have gained more than that
You have the most wonderful title
The privilege of being called Daddy

Joseph Robert Bonnette

A Day of Rain

With the rain coming
I sit and think, humming
What the rain will bring
A thunder storm or a shower and sun
As the day went by
I waited for the rain
With both hands crossed and all my toes wiggling
The rain began
Showering and dancing with joy and hope
It danced over the streets and homes
Bringing happiness to all flowers around town
The rain sprinkled lightly in the wind with no sound
Sprinkling onto the ground
It watered all the plants that it touched
The rain had come and all was done
As the night crept in, the rain slowly departed
Leaving the memory in mind till again

Casey M. Beizer

Seasons of Emotions

The heat is drowning my emotions.
Everything burns.
I have been put under a spell
By your enduring potions.

The rain washes away my fears.
Everything is cold.
My life blends together.
It feels like nothing by tears.

The wind blows my heart far away.
Everything shakes.
Gasping for air, trying to survive,
Just let me make it until the next day.

Through every season, my life seems to die.
Everything is gone.
My hope for the future
Does not continue to fly.

Carrie Lynn Freeland

Do You Remember?

I remember my heart racing, racing fast
I remember all the times of my meaningless past
I remember your charm and your unforgettable wit
I remember how we matched, a perfect fit

I remember your soft words, whispering in my ear
I remember how my heart was stabbed by your deadly spear
I remember all those terrible things, and some other things too
I remember the good things I want to forget
Now I want to know, do you?

Tori Ruth Stovall

Eternity

Is life about to end for us, as all the experts say?
Is that asteroid up there about to pave the way
For life on Earth, the best it is, to end for once and all
Or will that being, whom we can't see, begin a new life form?

Why is life so good for us, the yellow, brown, and white,
The time for fun and life and death, the cause for us to fight?
We need a plan to keep the peace for all upon this Earth,
For people, as we know, are the most precious form of birth.

The heavens carry that deadly ball, so big to cause a scare.
Will we pass that final day? There is a cross to bear.
We have to fight, to carry on; life is ours to bless,
For nothing better is known to us, we want nothing less.

The years have come and passed us by; the boom, it did not come.
As we grow older, the body fades, we feel a little numb,
But the Master of all looked after us in time for us to age,
To finally fulfill that book of life, right to the final page.

David Ian Jones

Joshua

The emptiness that I feel inside;
The pain that doesn't go away.
The heartache I just can't hide;
The people that don't know what to say.
God, please help me through all this;
Take away the guilt and pain from my chest.
God, why did I have to say goodbye
Before I ever said, hello?
Why is it so hard to let Joshua go?
I hear a little voice speak to me
Softly, but ever so gently.
"Mommy, don't you cry.
Please, wipe those tears from your eyes.
Mom, don't be sad,
But rejoice and be glad.
For if you'll look towards Heaven you will see
The arms of God holding me."

Brenda Kay Wernet

Candy Fix

I'm on a trip to the candy shop,
Bubble gum, suckers, and a lemon drop.
Sugar and sweets a mile high,
Grab anything my eye can spy.

Candy's what I crave today,
Down the street I make my way.
Pass the cars and through the square,
My nose tells me I'm almost there.

I dig in my pockets for some money,
Remember for Mom to get some honey.
Round the corner and drawing near,
The Almond Joy song is what I hear.

I turn the knob, but the door won't budge,
Now I'll never get my sweet, sweet fudge.
The day was Saturday, I suppose,
For today was Sunday and the shop was closed.

Jenee Leticia Page

My Love

If you were a flower you would be the most beautiful in the land,
Out from all others your colors would stand.

If you were a star way up on high,
You would be shooting across the temperate night sky.

If you were a forest, secretive and vast,
I would live happily in you until I breathe my last.

But you are a girl, lovely and fair.
I would care for you, and my love you will share.

Adam Bernard Hayes

Darkness

I slam my body against the floor.
I'm going insane—I can't take anymore,
absolutely nothing is wrong.
I know it's hard, but it won't last long.
Everything I see is totally dark.
The conspiracy then begins to spark.
I've tried too hard and I can't succeed,
the horror comes and the music leaves,
my knees start to bend and collapse.
I start to fall, my mind won't relax.
I continue to fall and it never ends
like I'll never stand on two feet again.
The blackness continues, I can't think.
I'm not alive; my brain will sink.
I can't stop falling.
I'm back where I started,
my body slammed against the floor.

Danielle Anne Dittmer

Last Kiss

As we walked on the street
We thought we heard a noise,

Then thought it was a cat
That was acting so poised.

We kept on walking to the store.
Then there came a man,

He yelled at us for our money,
All that we had.

He had a gun and shot my boyfriend.
It started the day that made me sad.

The man ran off and left us there
And he was bleeding really badly.

He looked at me and I gave him that one last kiss
As he slowly died in my arms.

Kristyna Elizabeth Mauch

Because of You

Four years have come and gone
what started as infatuation has grown strong
The days, they come and go
but the love we share continues to grow

The house I have is not a home
every night I am alone
Things will change one day soon
I'll be your bride and you my groom

Simple fights and arguments we've shared
over the years our love has beared
No matter what may cause a strain
our love continues to remain the same

All my hopes and dreams are finally true
all because I believe in you
I commit my life, my heart and soul
You are the reason my life is whole

LaDonna Michelle Marsh

From Which Way to What

Which road to take when the choices never end?
What rules apply and which ones can I bend?
Who will I live with for the time I am here?
Who will be the one who goes to the flip side with no fear?
Time and time again we all sit on the fearful coaster,
While the opposite sits back and bets on the biggest boaster.
Looking behind the darkness to the lights beyond the truth,
Expand the mind, letting it wander and explore the future's youth.
Only end your choices when you hit the dead end.

Ken S. Fukayama

My Blessing (Come and Conquer Your Way Through)

I went to church to sing a song
Come to believe it I made it through
I went to school to take a test
What about it that I passed
So on my way I take God's route
Next to it I made my way
So off to sleep I went away
Stay in God's route and find your way
So as God blesses the ground as well as you and me
We'll take His way to the end
I went to church to sing a song
Come to believe it I made it through
As for my mistakes are away
And hope that yours are too
I will never go away without my prayer
So wish for what is true and it will come through

Sean Erich Keller

As Lovers Wake

When early sounds precede the dawn
And darkness fades as time draws on,
Under blankets, twisted and turned, two embrace.
Lured from blissful dreams by kisses soft,
Slumbering bodies arouse, merge and breathe as one;
And eyes meet eyes as early sun proclaims the morn.
As light like fire streaks the sky, our passion builds.
Glistening, in sweet release, we are fulfilled.
Entwined in love, we lay stalling the foreboding day;
But sweeping hands upon a face forever set
Announce the time and coax us from our rest.
For the world awakes and bids us to rise,
To tend to the worries of our lives;
And so we plunge into the dewy day.
The peaceful comfort of our bed, we could not forever stay.
Where tangled sheets are left to cool in memories sweet,
Until the darkness one again bids our retreat.

Catherine L. T. Watson

I Walked into the Woods Today

I walked into the woods today
And as I heard the birds sing from the trees,
I realized it was really a lovely day
And I felt excitement with every breeze.

I walked on through the trees today
And watched them growing tall and green.
I knew happiness was on the way.
It was all such a lovely scene.

I kicked my way through the rocks today
And sent them rolling across the ground.
I found myself a nice spot to lie
With the tall grass flowing all around.

I lay there looking at the sky today,
The sky so blue and wide.
I thought to myself I should really pray,
But instead I thought of her and I cried.

Paul David Cook

You

I don't know what I should do
because I can't help loving you.
It feels like you broke my heart
because, when I see you, I fall apart.
It may be hard to realize,
but you're the only thing I see when I close my eyes.
When we were young, you were the only one,
and you still are,
because you'll always be number one in my heart.

Kayla Rhea Dennis

Thoughts That Matter

Thoughts that matter matters that count
  in this day and age
A time so important so important a time
  you must carefully read every page

Most people wander alone lost not knowing why
  they've lost their ability to share
They look but don't see blind not knowing why
  they've lost their ability to care

Their lives become numb knowing not where to go
  knowing not from where they come from
Their lives become empty their lives fall apart
  it happens to way more than some

So live every day live with logic and love
  but never forget how to play
Let not life slip away make each moment count
  and that's all that I've got to say

Bill Jongbloed

Till Death Do We Part

We were as one, just like Adam and Eve in the Garden of Eden.
We laughed, danced, and had fun together.
We shared our most darkest secret, and when
The road was rough and rugged,
We stood firm together.
Yes, we were inseparable,
At least we thought so
Until an uninvited guest knocked at our door.
We stared at each other wondering
Who could be knocking at this hour?
We refused to open our door, but he entered
Anyway and he took my dear wife from me
Without a chance to say goodbye.
Without any warning, he took her and now all
I have are good memories.
I am lonely and filled with grief because
Death has taken my dear Eve.

Andrea Harris Samuels

bulimic

feelings cold, corrupt, small and slow
forgetting things i used to know

falling asleep hungry, impatient for slumber
walking around is like cold, hard lumber

just feeling so useless and homely
never getting over being lonely

wondering what it'd be like to feel pretty
and to be great instead of just little bitty

to make miracles wondrous and adventurize
and not have to hide or wear a disguise

and not have to cry every night in pain
wishing to drown in my sweet champagne

bulimic i feel but that's not quite true
it's just how i feel getting over you

Sara Taylor Siskin

Life

What is life?
Life itself?
Is it the consciousness or the gaiety?
Why do times so dear fly away as the flocking geese?
But when we suffer, are we not even more conscious
of the passing time?
How my heart would love to suffer so, then,
my spent time with you,
and in suffering, so suffering will not be but eternal bliss.

Bernal Robles

I Must Not Scream

In an underfunded health care system, from a doctor who still can cry

Anger, rage, and roar
Child in danger no more
What walls must I break
What actions take
To free you to the forest once more

In safety they sit and watch you
Your pain they studiously ignore
My voice shouts into silence
Cry justice evermore
evermore

I seek help with the burden I carry
Surely one has a heart of gold
Will the Lord guide my footsteps securely?
Ask, ye shall receive, I am told

Silvia von Hanna

Tomorrow

Tomorrow, I will be stronger;
I will mourn no longer.
Tomorrow, I will be happier;
I will no more shed a tear.
Tomorrow, I will stand tall;
I will no more hide from myself at all.
Although I must tell myself this every day,
This I do know:
Tomorrow is still another day.
Tomorrow, I will try in every way.
This is the least I can do for my Lord,
To say, "Thank you for all the blood
That for me You shed and poured."
Tomorrow is not another day
For defeat, failure or sorrow.
It is another day I get up on my feet
And conquer my fear of defeat.

Shanna Adelle Swift

When I Look at You

When I look at you, all my worries seem to break free.
When I look at you, your eyes seem to comfort me.
When I look at you, I know everything will be all right.
When I look at you, you calm my darkest fright.
But now I cannot look at you any more.
I could only look at you before—
Before you came and took your life away;
Before you decided to drink that day.
You said it wouldn't hurt to have one drink,
But, after another and another, your world started to sink.
You should have asked for someone to drive you home,
But you didn't and got behind the wheel alone.
When you were driving, you passed a stop sign,
but didn't slow down.
Now you're lying dead on the ground.
Now when I look at you, I can't because you're dead,
But now I look into the eyes of God to ease my pain instead.

Samantha Eileen Curtin

Shining Star

So bright and peaceful, they are
What a wonderful display
An array of shining stars
One here, one there, one everywhere
As I stare up at them, I compare
Not one is like the other
They each have their own special glow
Although when they're all together
It seems as if the sky is putting on a peaceful show

Kate Kaiser

How Did I Get to Alone

The Worst Nightmare seems so far away
Yet seems so cold to the touch
Through the unexplainable, unknown truth
In hopes to kiss away the pain
The Desperate cry goes unheard
As the poison of hate flows through my veins
As we bring his heart to bury
As the last of human decency has faded
As I stand by his side forever
He is all that I know
As I place his heart into God's keeping
I ponder: How did I get to alone?
As the dark shadows creep over me
And the hope begins to fade
With the Dying of Light
I wonder for the last time
Would he be there waiting?

Dustee Lee Baker

Our Special Love

They say you search throughout your life
to find the perfect mate.
To share your love, your thoughts, your dreams
and thus fulfill your fate.

So if you've found that special one
and know that it is true,
then spend your days just loving them;
make it last your whole life through.

By giving love you fill your heart
and make your life complete.
The feeling given back to you
just simply can't be beat.

I'm so lucky I found my love;
or maybe she found me.
We share the best of both our lives
to be all that we can be.

John Parliament

Freedom

Philosophy in poetry

Freedom is a word that is used so carefree;
do we really know what it means or how it
came to be?

We live in a country that has a democracy
that has declared that our part of the world is free.
So what does that mean to you and me
who work for a living and find ourselves giving.
Not because we want to, but because this
is how the government makes its living,
by helping people and things that we would be unwilling.

I will say no more in light of that passage,
but I do hope you understand this message.
I want you to keep in mind that freedom isn't free.
No, it's not bought and sold like a commodity,
but it will cost you, just wait and see.

Helen Elaine Bell

Don't Be Afraid

If I was a book, would you read me?
If I was protection, would you use me?
If I was the right path, would you walk me?
Don't be afraid of what you feel.
Follow through with your feelings.
Read that book that brings so much knowledge.
Don't hesitate to use that protection,
to prove something that is not worth it.
Walk that path that must comfort you.

Steven Lynn Boyd

Morning Coffee

The sun is rising, the crisp air brushes
briskly across my face.
I stare aimlessly somewhere, but nowhere—
lifeless, limp.
The cold disperses throughout my body,
then I don't feel anymore.
The cries echo through the halls of my inner soul.
Where am I?
Who am I?
I must save myself, but where do I look?
My mind and soul are enmeshed like a maze
as the emotions run rampant,
trying to find a way out to express the turmoil.
The sun has risen now, the air is cool, and
yet pleasantly numbing.
I sip my morning coffee and
get ready to fight the day.

Jodi Johnson

Chaos Can Be Loved

Take me by the hand and lead me home,
Or leave me here to wander lost and alone.

Please love me like you know you should,
Or you can hate me like I know you could.

Try to understand how much I love you,
Or be blind and lose what is true.

See my smile and ignore the things I've done,
Or see the chaos I've left behind and run.

Let me mend the hearts that I have broken,
Or push me away to leave my words unspoken.

Tell me now, do you love me still?
Because I love you and I always will.

Take my hand and we will go home.
We will stay together forever, never alone.

Jessie Ann Burfoot

true love

a love like yours comes once in a lifetime
a bond so strong neither man nor woman can break it
as if two pieces of a puzzle that fit perfectly
side by side, you go through life
a true love is so hard to find
but somehow you found each other
never to be separated never to part
a couple all envy wanting what you two have
but never to get it as much as they want
you always declare your love for each other
loud, sweet, proud you do
no one dares to try to hurt you for always he's
there to protect you from the dangers of the world
he is always there to kiss you and make you feel
better whenever you are down
because you two have
true love

Correy Lynne Norcross

Day of Remembering

To remember the day that you left us
Is to recall a very special day
We lost someone very special to all of us
We knew you were better off, but that was hard to accept
Your pain was gone, no more hurting
The only hurt there is now is not having you here
We have memories of you daily, talk about you often
You are missed and loved still in our hearts
Thank you Mom for who you are

Martel Wayne Holley

I Hunger for Your Touch . . .

I hunger for your touch, these words belong to you
You turned them into art, the beauty was your goal
My touch was not enough, and that I always knew
I hunger for your touch and hunger for your soul!

I hunger for the days when we were far apart
When loneliness and pain would bend me to the ground
You came to me and took my sore and bleeding heart
And kissed my pain away and turned it all around

I hunger for the nights when my doubts were at bay
When lying in my arms and playing with my hair
You looked into my eyes and didn't have to say
I love you, but I knew somehow that you cared

I hunger not—I starve! My soul is crying out!
The old pain is back—the one I hate so much
It rises like a wave and makes me want to shout
I hunger for you soul and hunger for your touch!

Anatoli Makarov

Woods . . .

The woods are fun
I love to walk through the woods
There are paths to walk on
Up and down hills
Walk on a path
Through a hole
Across a bridge
To my hiding place
Up a tree
To see the whole campground
See my grandparents pulling in
Climb down the tree
Across the bridge
Through the hole
On the path
To go help my grandparents unload their car
The woods are so much fun

Mandy Linette Springer

Alone

Alone on the street, she is dying.
Cold and scared, she is shivering.
Hoping and praying in a church, she is waiting.
Sleeping and dreaming
In a shelter on fourth street, she is happy.
Raped and beaten, she is left to die.
Patient and determined, she is fighting.
The emergency room seemed like heaven, she is saved.
The doctors promise help, she is hopeful.
Expectant and nervous, she doesn't know what to do.
The life inside of her innocent, she is confused.
Misery is her only companion, she is miserable.
The adoptive parents have so much to give, she is torn.
The decision is placed before her, she is thinking.
The pain unbearable, she has decided.
The baby is placed in her arms, she is not letting go.
Madeline after her grandmother, she is a mother.

Stacey Lynn Leverich

The Gate

In Heaven, everyone is smiling and happy.
They're smiling and happy
and so full of joy they can hardly stand it!
But why shouldn't they be,
sitting right there in the presence of God?
And right now, they're looking down at you,
flashing their pearly whites.
But doesn't that put new emphasis on the words,
"the pearly gates of Heaven"?

Mary Jane L. Hutson

Pleasure Given

It brings such pleasure to help another,
to give a hand and solve a problem,
create a way for a better day.

Through the grace of our Father
and with the help of our Lord,
it brings such pleasure to smile for you,
to wave a hand and say hello,
to read His word that feeds your soul.

Our Lord provides the big pleasures
free for you, free for me.
The little pleasures
we must remember and give one another,
for these too are free.

Such pleasure to give and to receive.
Let's all give to another,
for sure He will be pleased.

Shelley Doreen Peterson

Love

To be in love is a wonderful thing
You see everything so clearly
The one thing that means the most to you
Inspires you to carry on
Step by step you proceed
Creating an impenetrable force field of joy
And happiness
Hearts beat furiously with such passion
Bodies tingle with excitement
Happiness begins to overflow
And all sorrows are removed from your mind
Nothing can bring you down
You are on top of the world
You follow your heart
And not the words of others
When the love is strong
Nothing can destroy it

Christopher Stephen Hartshorn

For Him

Alone I sit in the tranquility of my room.
Alone I wrestle with thoughts of his doom.
May he receive all he deserves.
May he be haunted by every lying word.
May he find the happiness he has chosen.
I will go on, though my spirit is broken,
Broken by him and his selfish lies.
I thank him for the torment,
The tears, and the prize.
What prize you may ask can come of such lies?
My eyes are wide open,
My mind is now wise—
Open to see the new world I am in, beautiful,
Tranquil, and free from his sin.
My life was reborn when he pushed me aside.
It's a dark road he has chosen,
May he enjoy the ride.

Taylor Andrea McClure

Tragedy at Dawn

Today my heart aches for two horses
Killed by an unwary motorist at the crack of dawn
Running free at last, unfettered by fences or walls
And then struck down
Beautiful graceful creatures with manes and tails flowing
Forgetting that they were in a world that is not free
And so now they are gone and my heart aches
How quickly is freedom lost
How swiftly death comes

Jane Marie Douglas

Bad Things

Even the richest man can't buy back his past—
a fortune I read post a Chinese repast.
I do not know why the past I'd purchase.
It only buys what's been raised to the surface.

Deep down inside where the dark hole lies;
that's where the things are I want to buy.
I'd take those things and package them tight.
They wouldn't be able to escape back into the night.

I would look at them all straight in the eye
and tell each one of them it's time to die.
Their final resting place won't be in a hole.
They'd return to their creator to fester in his soul.

Then my dreams would be clean, crisp and clear.
What was lurking there, I would no longer fear.
I finally would find some inner peace of my own.
In my mind, never to return to my childhood home.

Kim G. Tolley

My Lost Love

I shut my eyes and see her face
Painted on a canvass of light.
The brilliant color of her lips
Cuts through to my very soul;
Remembering when she could kiss my heart
And fill me with a joy known only
To a child untouched by the world.
Remembering when we could dance in the dark
Blind, without walls,
Seeing one another with only our lust.
Countless leaves now have fallen
On myself, alone in the field.
Clutching to the memories that I imprison,
Escaping with every blink and breath.
Just waiting for the time when my heart
Is completely empty;
Just waiting for my soul to leave.

Beau Anthony Gregersen

The Voice

Sometimes when my days are dark and I feel so lost
I think about the future and what might be the cost
There are no insights, no answers or clues
The paths are many, not sure which one to choose
All seems hopeless and insecurity is at hand
The unsurety is great, don't know quite where to stand
Then suddenly, a voice calls out, filling me with peace and power
It brings out the best in me, it gives me my finest hour
The dreary gloom fades and settles into the past
Life feels anew, this joyous feeling sure to last and last
I thank the universe and life each day
That this voice found me and came my way
For I have never felt these wondrous things abound
Giving my spirit flight, lifting me high and far from the ground
Now I possess only one thought that makes me gasp and sigh
It is the knowledge that each day will fade to night
And the voice will have to say goodbye

Stephen D. Osborne

For Her

Windswept hair from a midsummer's breeze.
Eyes that pierce the soul.
A heart made of sugar
And a smile that could make a crying baby giggle
And the sun shine through on a rainy day.
A person with many memories had
That of a beautiful and sweet woman.

Brian Shawn Kushner

Exit

Staring at the fluorescent sign on the wall,
My mind wanders to a dark elongated hallway
Which seems to never end.

Plush, flowing carpet beneath my bare feet
Feels like tall thick blades of grass
Poking between my toes,
Reminds me of a dream I had not so long ago.

Leaping through a lofty spring meadow,
Splendid smells drift upward,
My nostrils fill with the penetrating aroma
Of flowers frolicking in the gentle breeze.

My eyes seem to squint
As the new day dawns,
Ready to take that journey
Down that long hallway,
Past the exit sign.

Kathy A. Mouw

What If?

I want to know what he thinks of me,
What he sees when he looks at me.
What emotions run through him when he is a around me?
His emotions and feelings are masked by his straight face,
Showing me nothing, leaving me pondering.
Hoping one day someone can answer them for me;
does he even care to look?
If he only knew what goes through my mind,
my body, my heart and my soul when I see him.
I am terrified of his feelings.
His thoughts that runs through him when he looks into my eyes.
Time will only let love fade away.
Can time make or break my heart too?
I can't wait forever, or can I?
Am I wasting my emotions on this boy?
He just doesn't care to see me.
I ask why I put myself through this hell.
But then again, I think of, what if, and I start all over again.

Nicole Jean Pecaro

My Wife

I would like to tell you a story of a girl in my life,
The one I'm so proud to call my wife.
She's the one who stands by me through thick and thin.
She's the one that I hold close now and again.
If only I could tell her just how much it means
To be her husband and be in her dreams,
To say that her beauty makes my heart stop.
I love you my baby from bottom to top.
My life is wonderful because you are near.
I go through my life without any fear.
Today I know there's a god in our life.
His template of awesome is my beautiful wife.
Is it the smile, the words, that bring me so much,
Or the hair, the eyes, or her soft gentle touch?
I guess I could say I have a wonderful life,
All due to my best friend,
My sweetie,
My wife.

Brian Russell Lee

Morning Jog

Pat, pat, pat, I slowly advance.
I see my breath and think that something's wrong,
For it is summer.
Then I realize it is not "summer"
Until the sun sits high.
Pat, pat, pat, I slowly advance.
I'm getting tired, but there is no turning back.
I'm a machine, an unstoppable machine.
Each step I take is one step closer to my goal,
My goal for today, my goal for life.

Steven John Burgermeister

Ode to Osama bin Laden

What shall we do with you?
Why did we choose your threats to ignore,
Even when your bombs were exploding
On our troops and airplanes at our door?
Why does it seem to not matter?
When, with your acts, so many lives you shatter,
Who's to blame for all your madness,
Which leads only to soulful sadness?
When your madmen wanted to learn
A commercial airplane cockpit to fly,
Why didn't one of the instructors ask why?
Who would think they were doing it for fun?
Didn't they know the awesome power
Of the things they were teaching gladly
Would have a young boy asking his mother,
Where's my daddy?

Don L. Branch

Beans and Peas

To sit and wonder, listening with a stare
What was that noise I heard
A prowler or a bear
Creeping over to a window
Heart fluttering and with great care
A single blind open looking out in thin air
I see, to my amazement, a brown spotted deer
Cautiously awaiting as if trying to hear
Whether or not someone heard him
As he ate in my fields,
Rattling my string of cans I use as warnings and as shields
He springs up like a rocket
Turns and runs with great speed
Back into the forest forgetting his late feed
I return to my chair feeling better and at ease
I'll go out at first light to check on
My beans and my peas

Michael Cary Young

Horizon

I look out of my window, what can I see?
The distant buildings. The horizon.
Why am I nervous? Is it because
I can't see what is over the horizon?
There is so much to see! If I
Can see over the horizon, if I
Can get closer to the buildings!
As I stare, it almost becomes dreamlike!
This is what makes me nervous.
But there is something that keeps me looking!
Is it my dream? Is it another horizon? Wait!
I can see someone! But they are too far away!
I move closer. "They" are now "She."
She befriends me as I move closer to her.
We see the horizon, and wonder,
Is it my dream,
Or is the horizon reality after all?

Mark Allan Canniff

if only you knew

if only you knew
how you opened up my eyes
how every tear i cried inside
you were right there holding me tight
never letting go until i promised to try
you said you would always be there for me
you always were
the one word i never believed in that everyone said conquered all
you took me by the hand and walked me right through it all
you showed me it's the truest thing of all

Ashley Ann Ott

When War Is Calling

Dear Sir or Madam,
On that fateful day planes fell out of the sky,
While you cried as a soldier, we cried as a nation.
One day later, you were put on high alert.
As you stood tall, we stood proud.
On the day you left in search of the enemy,
We looked and searched for an answer.
When the day comes for you to raise your rifle,
We will pray and raise our flags.
Some day soon the dust will settle
And the smoke will clear.
We will look into your eyes
And know that the future will be secured.
Every day we are thankful for what you have done.
Thank you, from myself, my family,
And generations to come.

Sydney Lauren Gallimore

That Subway Train Window

Cracked, graffitied skies and tinted high-rise
sculptures play a backdrop for me to gaze upon.
Then black.
A blur of flashing blue light and then . . .
tile and scurrying people.
As the station comes to a slow stop,
I close my eyes for a moment in which I know that
the window will disappear and when I open them, a door
leading to concrete and black tar will appear.
My eyes are open and my predictions are all too true.
I watch the flood of passengers colliding with each other,
racing to either escape or be enveloped by the door that
breathes a cloud of smog and smell.
A blurb over the intercom fills my soul with comfort
as I watch the door being squeezed into nothing.
The prevalent backdrop slides back into view
and a cracked and graffitied friend waves hello.

Mike Chesbro

The Hardest Thing

The hardest night I've ever spent
tossed and turned and cried and wept.
The hardest day I ever faced
as I dressed myself in silk and lace.

The hardest words I've ever said
as my eyes avoided the unmade bed.
The hardest edge my voice has took
as my head bowed down to hide my look.

The hardest breath I've ever drawn
as I collapsed upon the manicured lawn.
The hardest prayer I've breathed aloud
starts as a shout and ends in a sob.

The hardest steps I've ever made
were the ones that led to my lover's grave.
And the hardest thing I've ever done
was admit to myself that my heart would move on.

Kimberly Chantelle Blechinger

Lies

I lie to hide away my past.
I lie to the questions people ask.
To tell the truth would hurt me so.
There are certain things no one should know.

Deep inside myself I hide.
I lack that certain sense of pride.
I lie and keep thoughts locked away.
To tell the truth is my dismay.

To let people know me would destroy me.
I distort my lies and make them true.
When my wall is up, no one can get through.

Jourdan Jolene Warner

One Last Time

To touch you, to see you
Just one last time
I would give anything
Anything I can give
To feel the warmth of your fingers
To touch your perfect face
To give you one last hug and kiss
To feel your hand pressed against mine
I would give my heart, mind and soul
To be with you one more day
To hear the sound of your gentle voice
Would be my last desire
But I cannot, nor can you
For you are gone
But inside my heart is the place you dwell
From now till forever gone

Victoria Ann Kingsbury

Silence

silent voices speak a truth so strong
wrapped in layers of confusion
heavy they fall
one by one in me
uttering words I do not wish to hear

powerful feelings tie a knot so strong
as they make their way inside me
sleepless nights
trying to understand
emotions I do not wish to feel

secret thoughts light a flame so strong
wrapped in shame, guilt, and fear
sick of hiding
too scared to speak
thinking things they say are wrong to think

Lidia Gonzalez

To My Son, the First Time

The first time I heard your heart beat
I knew what life was
The first time I felt you tiny feet kicking inside my stomach
I knew what movement was
The first time I went through labor
I knew what pain was
The first time I saw your Dad pacing outside the ward
I knew what waiting was
The first time I held you close to my heart
I knew what motherhood was
The first time you felt ill
I knew what caring was
The first time I sent you off to school
I knew how important knowledge was
Today when I see you, me and Dad
I know what family is

Thomacina Fernandez

Aftermath of Hate

This world so full of hate, I cannot seem to escape.
The further I run, the further I go nowhere.
Explosions of hate create wonder and neutral hate.
Is it the end, or is it the beginning?
War cries fill the land
As vengeance runs through the blood of the land.
A superior nation falls victim, escalating into a worldwide sorrow.
The question is, how about tomorrow?
Will there be fire in the sky?
Is the world about to die?
Will we put this hate in its place, and replenish the peace,
Or is it the devastating end of the human race?

Paul Brian Fuller

The Day

The day I saw you I was in shock.
Why were you there?
I don't know, just there, standing in the snow.
Why were you there, were you lost,
were you scared, are you hurt,
tell me, where?
I can help you, but please help me.
If you do not talk,
I'm going to leave. Goodbye then stranger,
I did what I could.
Do I tell some one else, maybe I should.
Why are you following me and where's your face?
I can't see you, you're in a dark place.
Why are you here?
Oh, now I know.
You're following me because you are my own.

Albert Young

Always and Forever

You opened up my heart
and you took my love.
You helped me to spread my wings
and to fly above.
But then you turned your back
and you left me alone,
so I crashed to the ground,
only to find I can't stand on my own.
You had told me that you will be
always and forever by my side.
Maybe I just can't see you
because of these tears in my eye.
The pain has subsided,
it's no longer as great,
but still I continue to hurt inside.
Always and forever, just like you used to state.

D. Giovanni Oliva

The Stopping Point of My Life

I was once active.
I was once a mother of three.
I was once a loving and giving wife.
I was once a loyal employee.
I was once a full time student,
going back to school to fulfill a lifelong dream.
I was once independent, free to live my life.
Everything changed,
once the driver of another car crossed that center line.
My life is now over.
Someone else makes my decisions.
Someone else takes care of my children.
Someone else now has taken my place at work.
My wonderful husband now takes care of a bitter and crippled woman.
My life long dream of becoming a teacher is dying more each day.
My life is not quite over, but it is at a stopping point.

Terrie E. Pruett

The Sky Is the Beginning

To God Almighty

Often times I hear people say,
Put more effort in what you are doing,
The sky is your limit.

I refuse to abide by such philosophy,
The sky is not my limit,
My limit is far above the sky.
In fact, my limit is far, far above the sky.

I only need to employ the principle of forgetting the past,
Putting all effort into my duties,
In as much as I don't relent effort, I cannot be stopped.

Raphael Bamidele Oni

While They Sleep

The house is still
A quiet filled with warmth surrounds me
I know a peace which eludes me through the day
And I know that I am loved

Life is not always fair
I feel the pain of my children's struggles,
my parent's aging

But for tonight, at this moment, they sleep
I hope they share the peace

I look at the face of the man I love
The stress of the day has gone as he sleeps

I am so thankful to have this moment
To feel free and at peace
My heart filled with love

Mary D. Mayo

Passages

Corridor doors, there's quite a few,
Deciding which to go through,
Some lead strong and straight and sure,
Others lead on endless detours,
One is cold and empty, lost,
Another never touched by frost,
This door chases selfish pleasures,
That one seeks only treasures,
But theres one considered best,
No special marks or silly crests,
Adorn the start of this great road,
Often travelled with heavy load,
The door so special, dear to me,
Leads me back to family,
Because other passages are great to roam,
But best is one that leads to home.

Monica Lynn Eaton

Vietnam Veteran's Legacy

To all who experienced life and death in America's tragedy

Cold snowy day in December
A date that I will always remember
President Johnson said, Greetings young man
You now belong to Uncle Sam
We will train you how to fight and kill
Just imagine what a thrill
Take a plane far away
Maybe forever you will stay
Shooting, killing not a game
Your mind will never be the same
Rice paddies, palm trees, sunny sky
Please, dear Lord, don't let me die
Folks at home need to comprehend
It will take years for us to mend

Ken B. Morse

Schizophrenia

The storm crashed all around me,
waves broke against the shore with fury and contempt.

The clap of thunder echoed in the night sky,
and lightening struck the ground with an electrical force.

My eyes remained closed until the fear subsided,
and courage could over take my emotions.

Beads of sweat dropped to the floor.
A quiet silence awoke me, and I searched for guidance.

Out of the corner of my eye I saw Heaven,
and knew I was still me.

Tracy Lynn Broadbent

The Rose

The rose, a flower that represents life
It's pretty, red, and bright
But there are thorns on the stem
That can prick you and take time to mend
Every rose's petals fall to the ground
To plant a seed and show again in the spring all around
Some lovers use the rose without a lie
To show each other their love before they die
However, someone gets pricked on a thorn
In life there are times you need to mourn
But in the end, a smile can come back
When the dark clouds are past
When you get down
Just remember the rose and how it is found
Again in the spring after frozen and cold
Just cry it out and make this poem be told

Kristina Dunder

The Way I Feel

The way I feel is graceful.
I feel and see that I am walking across the clouds
In a clear blue sky where the sun shines on me.
I feel peace inside me,
Telling me that it is the beginning.
The wind makes me close my eyes.
I feel warmth.
Then I am in another world.
I am walking on the ground,
Then I am seeing fire beyond my reach.
It was hotter and more painful.
This told me it was the end.
I feel hatred inside.
Now I have seen the past and the future,
Never wondering when they come together
In a good time and a bad time.

Maritza Alexandra Artola

Believe the Children

Believe the children when they say,
"He touched us here today."
He made us feel guilty, he made us feel pain.
We tried to stop him, but all was in vain.
Mom tried to protect us, as she should.
He just beat her when he could.
She turned him in for our sakes.
The police were out on their usual breaks.
Each time she called to ask for help,
They always asked to see our welts.
Abuse does not always leave physical signs.
You can be sure it bruises the mind.
What was the use in making that call?
Things only got worse, he was having a ball.
There's no place to go, no place to hide.
Believe the children before they die.

Janie Oakes

The Beginning of Our Lives Together through God and Jesus Christ

Our life together now has no end.
In the beginning we struggled just to fend,
Never really knowing what was around the next bend.
Our thanks to our Father and our Lord His Son.
Our lives together have truly begun as one.
For many years before we lived in strife.
We now have our time together to begin our new life.
It is now our time, as others will find,
To move on from the old hard times.
With God and our Savior with us here in form today,
Nothing or no one will stand in our way!

Valerie Dill

Flowers

Flowers that grow in the meadow
Flowers that are picked by little ones
Shaped like the sun, and nourished by the sun
Far from the city, far from noise
The steams sucking then innocent dirt
Tons of dirt covering the roots
What do the flowers long for, as I long for
One sweet smell of the flower once more
Flowers blown by the mighty wind
Some blown away toward the endearing east
What do the flowers long for, as I long for
Flowing through the sky like a bird
Hitting the beautiful hill, and finding
No wind at all
Falling to the ground
Fly in the wind, once more

Kirstie Anne MacDonald

Friends or More, I'll Love You Always

I wish for this, I wish for that
For the day will come that you'll be back
I will never give up on you
Although some may think that I should
They say I should try to move on
But I said I never could
You are the only one for me
I love with all my heart
I know you'd never leave me
We were meant to be from the start
So as long as you promise me that you'll always be near
I promise you that I will always be here
If you ever need to talk or just hang out
Just give me a ring, buzz, or shout
I love you now I'll love you then
Even if we do just end up friends

Tiffany See

Forever Love

To my beloved husband

The days are long, the nights are short.
I've seen you have a lot to sort.
You need to cheer up and begin to smile.
For it has been one heck of a mile.
We've made it through what seems like hell.
Things are looking up, I think you can tell
No matter how you feel, I want you to know
Just how much I love you so.
When you're feeling down, please think of me.
Let me help in these times
As we ride this bumpy sea.
I love you more than words can say.
You brighten my world with every day.
Always remember, you're in my heart.
The days will never come that we'll ever part.

Jenny Suzanne Mills

A Love So Strong

I close my eyes to see the beauty we've shared
Moving mountains, parting seas, and mending hearts once impaired
I see laughter, smiles, and sparsely fallen tears
A breeze, so soothing, whispers your name in my ear
A ray of sunlight through my darkness; a destiny unveiled
For this love I'll stop at nothing, holding steadfast not to fail
'Cause a love so strong is undying and true
I open my eyes, yet, my mind envisions pictures of you
You're my heart, my love, forever all I need
Without you in my life this heart will perpetually bleed
Escaping, I go, in a cocoon safe from harm
Not to return until you're with me, embraced in my arms

Jason Scott Britton

My Life . . . To Be . . . Or Not?

I can hear my friend calling
All I envision is my world falling
A shivering child cries out
In pain and hunger
I have no doubt
Warning signs have been well posted
The roads in my life
Will not be smoothly coasted
Boundaries begin to melt
The thought of death at times even I have dealt
Already it seems much darker
This tragedy has left its marker
Darkness
It has imprisoned me
My reason for existence now . . .
Simply ceases to be

Jennifer Anne Bloom

I Can't

I can't help those children
who have no food or shelter,
and I can't help all those people
who are dying when they shouldn't be.
I can't help all of those young teens
who do stupid things like drink and do drugs.
I know I can't help
if those teens were to ever get hurt in the process.
I can't help myself
when I want to do so many good things;
for I'm only fourteen years old
And I still have my whole life ahead of me.
I still look for people who need help,
even if I can't help.
I'll still be praying for you,
for all I want to do is give you my blessings.

Samantha Belle LaFlamme

Barett's Normal Hunting Story

Walking through the woods with a gun in my arm
Stepping over twigs, sending out no alarm
The dew was melting, sun rising through the trees
Squirrels are rustling for acorns in the leaves
A turkey gobbles, echoes through the forest
I love that sound, nature at its purest
I reach the bottoms, the floor is golden all around
It is peaceful here, no civilization, life, or sound
Walking up and down, across many ridges
Crossing small creeks over natural bridges
There's a buck and three does ahead
Eating under the white oak like Granddad always said
I lean on a tree to steady my shot
My heart rate increases, not just a little, but a lot!
The roar of the shot rang out, it looked to be clear
I walked over to where he was . . . "Oh, well, maybe next year"

Barett Wendell Ratcliff

The Mystery of Life

What am I doing?
Where am I going?
When will I get there?
Why am I even going there?
How will I get there?
What, where, when, why, and how—
These are the questions we all want to know.
These are the questions our life will answer.
These are the questions I enjoy experiencing.
The mystery of the future is exciting.
See you all when I get there, wherever that is, and
Whenever I get there.

David Honig

My Wings

In my world of boredom and dullness,
trapped in the everyday trends,
I seek my wings of full freedom
for a pleasure in a world with no chains.
In the night I feel like they're watching.
In the day I feel like I'm bound.
Why is my world so twisted?
Where's the freedom I long?
Oh, there they are, my wings of freedom,
my flight to the world unknown.
I am flying instead of crying.
I am free instead of caught.
To most, it is not a thought of care;
a slave, a pleasure, a thing,
but to me it means much more.
It is my freedom and my wings.

Aly Harmony LeBaron

closer

my life is filled with good intentions,
crying alone writing about mistakes i've made
and some i won't mention.
i would give anything
to feel sane, my life has collapsed before.
hating everything, only 'cause i can't bleed anymore.
every step, for every stair
is one more closer to my end.
i'm to afraid to care.
nothing ventured, everything is the same,
falling harder for the closer i came.
will i ever change?
for every fake smile, there was a sacrifice
for every lie, i paid the price.
i have failed in every attempt,
hiding inside my poems to feel content.

Michael Stull

Past and Present of 9/11

Written on September 12, 2001

The past and present, what will it bring?
Will it bring good or will it bring shame?
We think of the present because life goes on
And not of the past because life stops there for someone.
The statues we see and the people we will remember
and at all of those wars we have never surrendered.
We are all working as one, and one for all, sometimes.
We rise and sometimes we fall and when we fall
The nation picks you up, as you are one of them
And you say, thank you, to that kind man.
But terror had struck the nation for days.
We all regain consciousness and bow our heads in shame.
But you should pick them up and please stand tall.
As any true American would say,
United we stand and together we fall!

Gregory John Mentgen

I Said a Prayer

I said a prayer for you, my family, and God must have heard.
I prayed so mighty hard I guess He wrote down every word.
I said it every night to you and wished it every day,
but one thing you would not believe I wished in every way.
I try to talk to you, Mummy, goodbye wasn't our last word,
because you say good night at bedtime and now you know I've heard.
In mornings I stay with my sisters and every afternoon,
then my day is filled and I go back to my room.
It has still got all my things, even clothes I used to wear,
that's why I am so proud of you, you kept my every bear.
So I suppose your wondering what I prayed, my wish, my every call.
It was joy and happiness I prayed for most of all. . . .

Haley Krystle Ball

Elegy for Some Guy Who Died on a Farm

There wasn't any mind when he lived
No turtle neck to cook into a soup
There wasn't any cry when he wept
No mourning man to crow on his stoop
There wasn't any farmer digging graves
No young child scared awake at midnight
There weren't any limp arms to touch
No carcass to carry to the grave site

There wasn't any mind when he died
No feeble maiden tied back her hair
There wasn't any flag waving at half-mast
No rescue from somewhere around nowhere
There weren't any tears shed from relatives
No rain to give a mood to the day
There wasn't any farmer plowing fields
No holy man telling us to pray

Michael Andrew Kingcaid

Solitude

No one will ever really know me
There's so much inside me that you'll never see
Every tear I hold inside
Every smile to cover the pain I hide
All my fantasies
All my secret dreams that will never be
How my faith in you slowly dies
With each and every one of your little white lies
But you'll never know
That's why were all really here alone
No one will ever truly feel as you do
When you hurt do they hurt too
Every happiness you can never really share
Can you ever really express how much you care
That's why I don't really know why the whole time we're here
Being alone is our biggest fear

Desiree Sherisse Uhrle

Fear

Fear, you've held me captive
long enough. . . .
fettered, shackled, immured;
smothering me, stifling me,
churning my insides,
ruling my life.

Of what am I frightened?
What can happen to me that I cannot endure?

Today, I decide to be free of you;
to stop empowering you
with that mighty force you use
to crush me beneath your merciless feet.
Today, I open a window
and let the claustrophobia end.

Today, I am not afraid.

Shanti Dhawan

Depression

It's a silent killer as it sneaks up like a stalker
You're in the middle of nowhere a shelterless walker

Life goes by in such slow motion
It's such a blur so much commotion

No one can help you You don't want to try
You just want to stop Just stop and cry

You hate them all but you hate you
Why can't it end Just all be through

It's the end of today almost tomorrow
Once again you'll face pain and sorrow

Nikki Michelle Giffin

Moonless Night

Traveling along on a moonless night
With horse and carriage, reins clenched tight
I knew there may be reason to fear
Of the unfamiliar noise I continued to hear
In front and behind to the left and the right
I squinted around with nothing in sight
All else was silence, nothing else was heard
Not a cricket, an owl, the wind, or a bird
The mare on edge, sensing my fear
Galloped a bit faster wanting anywhere but here
Just then the sounder shrieked again and again
I wondered at life's length in the land of men
I knew it was on me like a hound from Hell
The carriage crashed and down I fell
Cracked and bruised, unable to fight
Why was I alone on this moonless night

Charles Kenneth Morris

Underway

I sit here with three hundred people I know
But I feel alone with no place to go
It is so lonesome out here underway
Thinking of the friends I left at the bay
How they waved the day I left
Thinking of me instead of themselves
I was proud, then I got very blue
Because I was leaving everyone I knew
I was leaving the country, that is what I was told
But I never knew how much pain that would hold
I have no home or place that I am loved
Instead I am here on this big, metal tub
I do not know what is happening at home today
I guess this is the reason I am feeling this way
I just want you to know how much I care
And tell you, you are always in my prayer

Jason Douglas Medlock

Mr. Oblivious

Mr. Oblivious,
He's the kind of guy all the girls want.
You may think he likes you more than a friend,
but not really.
He's always playing these games.
You never really know. . . .
Does he like you?
Or does he just like playing games?
He likes to pretend not to know what's going on;
He gets his name from this.
He likes to act like a sweet guy.
He treats you like the center of his world.
That smile of his is great;
It makes your heart flutter
And your knees buckle,

Until he gives it to another girl.

Christin M. Sambor

U.S.A.

United as we stand,
we always stick together
to love and hold the pride we've shown,
to go about out busy lives and wonder why a million times.
People keep us all together, although some tear apart.
As we stood and watched them fall,
one by one the harm they've done.
People ran, people hid, people cried, and people died.
But as were terrorized dad by day,
we will show that they will pay
for messing with the red, white, and blue . . .
good old U.S.A.

Missy H. Comer

Untitled

No sleep last night; too busy thinking of you.
These feeling I have, got me confused.
Why do I always end up thinking of you:
Your voice, your smile, everything you do?
I'd hate to say it, but it's true,
I have strong feelings for you.
If you don't believe me, that's okay,
I'll have to prove it to you someday.
My friends say I should,
But I don't think I could
Prove all of this to you.
Oh, if only you knew.
I have but one question for you,
Please just answer oh so true.
Do you think there could ever be
A "me and you?"

Elizabeth Jean Baidel

You Are

You are a history of pain and joy.
You are a wealth of thoughts, experiences and family.
Your reality is foreign to me.
I only know my own.
You may look different or similar.
You are defined by so much more than the color of your skin;
Whether white, black, olive-toned, or sundry shades between.
You have thoughts and emotions, which may mirror, contradict
or challenge mine.
We are different, but if I could only begin to listen,
I might begin to understand and know.
You sing a beautiful song. It is your own.
Please sing loud enough for me to hear.
Someday I will understand
and the veil of my perspective
will give way to the truth of who you are.

Sharon Kay Hoffmann

Legacy

I see the shadows coming now,
but there is still enough of the
sunlight coming through the clouds
if you only try to see it, feel its warmth.
Perhaps it's the best time,
this last bit of golden daylight,
life still as juicy as a ripe peach.
Savor each bite and try to choose
right things before the night will fall.
Let the last breath have glory,
ending the story with gifts that will remind
those left behind that you were here,
life was so dear, these things are clear,
though now behind a mystic veil.
Not for us to know for sure;
love is all and does endure.

Laura Ann Hoffman

American Pride

American pride cannot be taken away with a cowardly act.
We will unite and set up for attack.
We stand behind our president and help him follow through,
Gladly laying our lives down to defend our men in blue.
Liberty and freedom are why we stand and fight.
Justice for all— terrorists gave up that right. . . .
For those whom fight bravely in the land, sea, and air,
May God bless you all
And keep you safe within His care!
If in time I should come to stand by your side,
Know this one thing about me:
I am filled with American pride.

Tammy June Dempsey

Vulnerable

I don't know what I want out of you,
For you to read my mind?
If you could you would see the sands of time.
I just wanted your voice to touch my ear,
The words I love you for me to hear.
You won't break the rules, but is it fair to ask?
If you wanted to hear my voice, no time would matter;
In its tender words you could bask.
I just wanted to hear, "I love you," 'fore I slept.
Now without your words, for the night I've wept.
I don't know what's going on, is there love?
Do you still wanna' be my angel from Heaven above?
I feel vulnerability growing strong
'cause I know not how to move on.
I sit here scared to sleep
'cause tomorrow I don't want to weep.

Brendan Halm

Friends

Forever is a long time,
never is nothing.
Planning is important,
but not as important as doing.
Always make new friends,
but always keep the old.
Liars never win,
and winners never lose.
Fame and fortune aren't important
as long as you have friends.
Love and laughter are always there,
forever and always as wonderful memories.
As long as life continues,
as long as love is near,
as long as you are with me,
I will always be there.

Ali Anne Guinn

U.S.A.

In a land far away, every night and day,
People are fighting for the U.S.A.,

Raising the red white and blue,
Saluting it proudly and true,
Fighting for me and for you.

Some dying. We're crying,
Too sad to believe
That one day in September, our whole country grieved.

In a land far away, every night and day,
People are dying for the U.S.A.

God bless America and everyone here.
Let us be filled with pride, not fear.

In a land far away, every night and day,
People are proud of the U.S. of A.!

Lexi Deschene

Love You

What I wouldn't give to be with you now
The one thing is I wouldn't know how
I wouldn't know what to say or do
To make you understand how much I love you
Maybe it was your eyes that turned me on
All I know now is my love for you will never be gone
In my eyes you'll always be in the spotlight
And there's no one for you I wouldn't fight
I would never give in
Or let someone else win
No one can love you as much as I do
And no matter what I will always love you

Heather Marie Wetherbee

The Heart of Byron

Two hundred years have gone by
Since you set sail in your mind,
Unfettered the ropes of life as you knew it,
Denying love and security,
Making way for the brave and the new.
France called you; Italy's life became yours;
Yet Greece was your master,
Your guide to the spirit of self.
Your life filled with purpose.
Your heart crumbled each time
You sensed fragile humanity
Destined to die a million deaths all in one.
Nature beckoned in peace,
Till duty called you again
To the Myth that is Greece,
Phos everlasting; the glory of union.

Heather Green

Faery Steed

Azure wings of silken softness
Flutter briefly, stop to rest.
Shimmering gem of airy lightness,
Graceful, stately summer guest,
I send a thought your way, but gently,
Not to burden you with care;
Only to fly with wings of fancy
On zephyr breeze, through sun-kissed air.
Oh, faery steed of childhood's dreaming,
I would ride with you once more
O'er mirrored waters, darkly gleaming,
To Fair Isle's far enchanted shore.
One last flight of magic measure
Before your sky-blue wings grow still;
A wisp of memory my soul can treasure,
To ward away drear winter's chill.

Sharon Staves

Till the Day I Die

I haven't stopped thinking about that beautiful angel.
She entered my life with just one look in her eyes.
She entered my soul like nothing ever before.
I don't know exactly what I feel for her,
what I do know is that when I saw those precious green eyes,
I felt a feeling unlike anything I've ever felt.
I know she doesn't feel the same for me,
but I can't help but looking at her when she's next to me.
I know what I feel can't be right
because I have a lover in my life.
But it also can't be wrong
'cause I've been feeling like this for so long.
There cannot be anything between her and I
and she might never know what I feel,
but I know I'll live like this till the day I leave this world,
till the day I die.

Luis Eduardo Robles

a daisy

i shall give you a daisy
not one but three
if you walk in heaven beside me
you live in the stars just like the sky
like an angel with wings just learning to fly
in heaven with god is where you reside
but I know in my heart my soul and my mind
you'll stay beside me till the day that i shall die
i cry sometimes thinking of you
mourning over someone that i never knew
the lessons of life i have yet to learn
until i'm with you my wings i shall earn

Crystal Gayle Balog

In the Whipper End's Eyes

Whip in hand and horse below,
you wait silently for the horn to blow.
Holding back hounds ready to go,
all for one reason, that one "Tallyho!"
Then you hear it, your heart starts to pound.
With one little gesture, all four hooves are off the ground.
You're racing through fields, just hoping to see,
a small red fox running towards thee.
This is not for the weak, nor the strong,
but for all of those who could last this long.
This is a masterful event, it happens every fall,
but this March in England, someone is trying to change the call.
We are not harmful to the hunted, nor to the hunters.
We just love to fox hunt, we just mean to please.
So if you'll help us be rid of all the lies,
maybe one day you'll see through the whipper end's eyes.

Lanie Nicole Adams

Natural Conformity

Large comforting pile of naked dead fall . . .
The cycle of life's infinite wisdom!
To shatter the image comes harsh rainfall.
Shrieking and spiraling, the rain does come!
In despair, look through the sparkling trees,
See the reflections bounce from the sun's rays.
The images detour your mind from ease.
Like all images, the appearance strays.
It will be a victim of distortions
And the meaning of it will diminish!
Search for meaning in the final portions;
All images are not yet extinguished. . . .
In hopelessness, look through the trees;
See the branches absorb rays from the sun.
With content, nature is once again at ease.
Notice how both sides work to become one!

Michael N. Schabio

Addictions

Left me in a haze,
like crowded colors on a painter's palate,
my innocence smeared gray.

Wanting, yet,
unable to let go
your deception keeps me near
a battlefield between
my desires and my needs.

These games you play wound me—bloody
tissues pile over the trash
onto the bathroom floor.
Naked, the air fails to heal my open flesh.

Mirrored reflections of truth, I'd rather not see.
Instead, I hide behind bandages you've given to me:
one for every time you tell me you're sorry.

Carol L. Wilhelmi

When Tomorrow Is Gone

Tomorrow is coming up
And soon today will be gone
One more wasted day
One more day till tomorrow
You think tomorrow will always come
So why live today when you have another
Tomorrows are taken for granted
Today is just another
And yesterday beckons tears
And when you realize that life isn't forever
Know to do it now, today will be yesterday
Tomorrow

Ann Marie Wahlen

Little Girl

A smile, a laugh, that's how it began
Who'd have thought you would come this far?
You've shown the strength that lies within
You've played the game, and you've played to win
They all know who you are

Life isn't easy, you've seen that first hand
But you've always pursued the dream
Your place here on Earth is to challenge the norm
To bring chaos to order, be the eye in the storm
Success in the palm of your hand

So go make your destiny, your future awaits
Your role in the scheme of the world
You've been working for this, it seems like forever
Let your heart remain true, so it's now or never
You'll always be my little girl

Yvonne Gray

Simple Thoughts of You

I have this picture of me and you
We're holding hands
Walking through your driveway
We were best friends

Do you remember the lighting bug field
We could catch them all night
The time I learned to ride my bike
You held my hand after I fell

I never used to think of these things
But now I do all the time
I often wish for my childhood back
Because we are not as close as we use to be

I miss you
More than ever now
I took for granted you always used to be there

Allison Ann Angle

Ode to Dr. Pepper

Dr. Pepper, you are so great;
I'd even drink you on a date.
Dr. Pepper, you're the drink for me;
You're my favorite soda, can't you see?
I pop the top, you're so fizzy;
I'd drink you even if I was busy.
For you I'd spend a million dollars;
For you I'd scream a million hollers.
I always have you by my side;
I even take you in my ride.
Come hell or high water,
I don't think I'd even give you to a thirsty otter.
If I had a choice, I'd pick you first,
'Cause you always seem to quench my thirst.
Oh, Dr. Pepper, you're so fun
And always know you're the ONE!

Dayna Leigh Koehler

Friendships and Roses

Oh, my dear friend, when you feel lonely and so blue,
When confusion and pain try to flood over you,
And you're in the valley of decision
And you don't know quite what to do,
I know your friendship with Jesus is what will bring you through.
Always remember our friendship will be true,
And roses are only a token of my loving and caring for you,
But as roses soon die and wither away,
Always, always remember the loving and caring
That we've shared along the way
Will cause our friendship to blossom
And flourish and last for aye.

Tommie Ruth Chaney

be still, my heart

be still, my heart, beat softly into the night
awaking not, that which i fear beat softly
awake not the dreams of my spirit that are my past
for it those spirits that haunt my deepest soul
be still my heart beat softly into the night
awaking not, that which i fear beat softly
awake not the dreams of my soul,
which is stirred by the spirit for which i live and
these memories that are of my heart remain sacred to my soul
be still my heart beat softly into the night
awaking not, that which i fear beat softly
awake not the love of my past for there it
needs to lie and be cherished only by my
soul and spirit for it is my only love
be still, my heart, beat softly into the night
beat softly into the darkness of the night

Robert Allen Polly

Letter from the Field

It is a humid night; men lie exhausted,
sprawled like breathing statues,
scarred by painted markings, bound to die,
their faces solemn, just like mine.
I fear that I won't be there to see you
see me.
This purple sky I stare at,
streaked by black lines, overwhelming my mind.
My heart is breaking; I'm making it last.
I have no desire to be here, but I am.
I promised you my presence.
I whispered to you through a wall of flesh.
I dedicated my soul to your existence.
I recited the oath.
I know now what I've done.
Will you forgive me, son?

Brian Munoz

when their faces change

in the dark their true face shows
the light keeps the mask in its place
inside the classroom the teacher preaches
his students so eager to learn
only they are pretending
his words are followed by sure faces
but under the masks are confusion
each one is pretending to
be another, when really it's only
a matter of hope, who will learn
and who will fail to succeed
these are the questions the faces hide
afraid to be turned away from the crowd
when their faces change, so do the tides
when do the faces go back again
only time will tell

Ariel Marilyn Huber

Ode to Homework

Homework is the crime I fight,
It happens each and every night.
It wouldn't be so very bad,
But I hear it from my dad.
He help's me late into the night,
That's why my homework really bites.
So if my scores are very bad,
You can blame them on my dad.
I try to keep it all in my head,
But all I think about is being home in bed.
Homework is the crime I fight,
It's the crime I fight so late at night.

Whitney Leeanne Marie Hinton

Our Destiny

I had a dream that I could tell
People of a place called Hell.
First I saw in my dream
Something that was very mean.
I saw the devil mean and red
In his hot burning bed.
Of flames that would burn your skin
Because you lived a life of sin.
Then I went just to see
The place where we can live with thee.
A place that's paved with streets of gold
A place where we will not grow old.
There will be no sadness there will be no crying.
And best of all there will be no dying.
We will live forever, happy, not mad
We will live forever with our Heavenly Dad.

Eddie Blank

I Hold in My Hand

I hold in my hand a white dove
the symbol of peace and pride
The dove gives me freedom to love,
speak, and act the way I feel the need to
The dove makes me feel safe and loved

He coos softly in my hand and eats his grain
while I wonder what he is thinking in his brain
How must he feel, being so important
Everyone knows who he is, yet he seems so lonely
Maybe being famous isn't what he wants

That's why I hold in my hand this dove
To show everyone that it doesn't matter
Who you are, or how you act
You should be treated with love and respect
Like this dove would like to be

Angelika Anna Tryba

No Words

Remember the laughs
You brought to my heart?
The feelings I felt fell apart.

Left with no words,
I will never understand.

If you're to be happy,
I'll try to give you a hand.

Wanted to send a letter,
Try to get close to you,
Replant something that never grew.

The lights will always dance at night,
Even when you're not here to hold me tight.

I thought this would never end.
It was you I wanted my love to send.

J. Hazlitt

Dare to Feel

Thinking, feeling, sinking ceiling—
ceiling above my head getting closer,
remembering what was said.
Trust, lust, dare I fuss;
accept or reject, then what's left,
but thinking and feeling the sinking ceiling.

Can't stop the ceiling; can't mess with fate.
Must remember to feel; forget to hate.
I know what you told me; I know what you said.
Now I'm left feeling
that shrinking ceiling
getting closer to my head.

Christina Marie Karp

One

like some freak explosion
in the middle of the night,
you appeared before me
pulsating with life.

blinded, I walked towards you,
shielding my face, afraid, unsure.
what was I to expect from you?

you radiated, with such compassion,
a feeling I never thought I would
know: that belief of two beings
together as one.

I felt something inside of me stir;
my soul lifted, awakening to your light;
my pulse quickened; and I knew you were the
"One."

Emily Elizabeth Everett

A Place in My Heart

The first day I saw you, I knew right away
That never again would I feel quite the same.
From the first time we talked and the first time we walked,
Hand and hand our life began;
The silence at our lips as we began to kiss,
And embrace ourselves in life's happiness.
Together we smile, together we laugh.
I know that forever this shall always last.
Tonight I dream deep in my sleep
That together our love we shall always keep.
Life's full of dreams from deep in the heart,
And you fulfill the very best part.
No matter what happened, no matter where we go,
There is one thing that you must know.
I knew right away, right from the start,
That you will always have a place in my heart.

Allison Elizabeth Williams

The Action of Leaving

It wasn't a particular moment
when you slithered out of your skin.
It was a gradually sudden departure;
it was a Friday morning.

I was sound-awake, first feeling your
warm skin against my chest
and then goosebumps on my back,
a cold chill
where your body should have been.

Your leaving was a hailstorm,
jagged whispers pounding brittle concrete,
sharp needles pushing into my skin.
I am muted by you.
Crumpled commitments and apathetic actions,
these are the disabilities of amputated speech.

Foresta Laura Castaneda

The Angels

The angels have come from above
Dressed in white and bringing their love
Blessing the children and people around
Planting the heavenly flowers in the ground
Sent down from the bright stars that shimmer
Above their heads, their halos do glimmer
Around their bodies, their wings are spread
Their tears are rain, coming from overhead
For the people not alive, but dead
The beautiful stories they have read
Happiness they bring with love and smiles
Angels are to stay for a long, long while

Samantha Noell Lutz

She

She is my everything
The essence of her beauty alarms me
And her love is everlasting

How is this love I have found
So pure and so strong
Given to me by the Father above
To have and to hold, for me to keep

Safe and secure from harm and hate
To bring up those who run from fears gate
The gift that only few can find
On this place called Earth, with all the grime

For this I am thankful
And I will hold it safe and close to my heart
I am not perfect, but I will conquer
For this love I receive has given me life

Heidi A. Bohannan

September 11, 2001

On the saddest day in September
many lost;
they lost the smile of a loved one.
On the most emotional day in September,
many found;
they found the strength to carry on.
On the most Heroric day in September
many helped;
they helped give strength to those in need.
On the most fearful day in September
many dwell;
they dwell on the past
and forget about the present.
But it is no longer September 11.
It is a new day and a new year
and we must move on.

Deidre Anna Marie Arrow

Angel

Sometimes you think that your life is bad,
and you think you've had enough.
Life is hard to handle and you've turned to
the Lord so much that you think you're
asking for too much, so you try not to
disturb Him with your problems.
Then you know you're alone in
life, and it seems much scarier.
But yet you think that you must
face these fears so they won't scare you.
But even though you think you are alone,
the whole time there is someone watching over you.
So don't be scared of fear itself;
just trust your angel.
And even though you can't see it,
it doesn't mean it's not there.

Danielle Ducasse

Alone in My Pain

As you loosen the grip around my soul,
I fade into the night,
Trying to ESCAPE the pain and sorrow of my days.

The Shadows dance on the walls around my corpse,
Taunting me to let go of this HATEFUL world,
Promising me the peaceful rest I have been searching for.

I have no one of this world begging me to stay,
No soft words to ease my pain,
No warm kisses to rid my soul of the cold fear I bear.

All alone I have been, and alone I shall die.
I will miss you, dear flesh, but with no sorrow in my goodbye.

Jennifer J. Davis

God's Friendship

I've heard you calling me, sometimes at night.
I've seen your tears, I've heard your fright.
Sometimes you whisper, sometimes you yell,
and then there are times when you think you're in hell.
I feel your pain, I feel your joy,
I feel it when you're treated like some kind of toy.
I know what you've seen, I've been where you've been.
I know it's hard to start all over again.
I just want you to know, I really do care.
I will hear you if you will only share.
I love you and think about you every day.
I wish that you would come my way,
and learn to trust and learn to care
and learn to help and learn to share.
Then maybe you wouldn't have to fall
because I'd be there through it all!

Serena Zentner

Orphan

He stands there
dazed and confused.

He wishes people
would understand him.

He feels alone
just waiting for attention

as he leans on the chair
wondering when he'll get the love he deserves.

He's dressed up
for a night with his parents . . . but no one will come.

No one cares for his love.

But still he waits with high, high hopes

for a love he may never know. . . . He's an orphan.

Melanie A. Danko

Summer Was

Summer was sitting on the porch,
watching the sun disappear behind the ocean.
Summer was long drives to camps
and water parks.
Summer was eating popsicles
and ice cream.
Summer was sleepovers
and seeing movies.
Summer was hot dogs
and smoothies.
Summer was the delicious smell of muffins
baking in the oven.
Summer was the ocean breeze
and birds chirping.
It's almost over now,
but summer will be back.

Camille Hanae Ripple

Mirrors

My life is like a broken mirror that bleeds from its soul.
The pieces are jagged and rough.
They cut those who try to pick it up.
We spend our lives trying to pick up our own mirror,
so we can see who we really are.
When does it break, and does it ever get put back?
I desire to see the real me,
but when I look into my mirror,
it's distorted, broken, and shattered.
Does death pull the pieces together?
The most illogical action is the most logical answer,
but what is the question?

Roycene Renae Knudsen

In My Dreams

In my dreams, all I wanna do is be with you, girl.
In my dreams, all I wanna see is a perfect world.
In my dreams, I want you to be happy.
In my dreams, I want us to be as strong as we can be.
I know this is real life,
And I know that we are new,
But, baby, when you look at me,
You make my dreams come true.
In my dreams, nothing can go wrong.
In my dreams, we're never apart too long.
In my dreams, the blind can see.
In my dreams, you can be anything that you wanna be.
In my dreams, you're always beside me.
In my dreams, we open our eyes and we see.
In my dreams, we are so in love.
In my dreams, we will be in the clouds above.

Chip Bernhrd Warning

Because

Come tell me about your family struggles
because I have some of my own.
Come tell me about unfair grades
because I've got enough to make you groan.
Come tell me about unreasonable friends
because I've had too many to count.
Come tell me about your messy room
because I have enough stuff to sell at discount.
Come tell me about your boyfriend troubles
because those are a new experience for me.
Come tell me about your money problems
because I spent all mine on a shopping spree.
Come tell me all you want to tell
because then you'll have no reason to pout.
Come tell me all your secrets
because I just let all of mine out!

Kathleen McLaughlin

Self

It was a metaphoric charcoal of
concealment as she walked down the path.
Wanting to grasp the symbolism of
individualism, her mind was already clasped
by worries and the flurries of contentment.
She was the crate of goods. She didn't
smile but she stood in front of the moons
prose, which brought out its pose.

Never wondering where she was going, she
just felt protected by the trees that
covered her individualism.

Though religion never entered the mind
she felt faith through the constant breeze,
which was invisible and not marketed.

She seemed to tear, within the graze of the sky.

Mark Johnathan Aston

the fear

i'm still awake 'cause you're not here
and in my mind i feel the fear;
but in my mind i know, too,
my dreams will soon come true.
because i know it in your head,
the same thoughts turn blue skies to red.
i will keep you knowing the same notion
that keeps you stirred in these false motions.
by the power these visions do hold
i'll think of you till my days of old;
or until these thoughts of us run true,
then i'll slumber lying next to you.

Steven Thomas Jarvie

uncertainty lane

she stumbles, blind to mirror's light
reflecting dark to sunlit night
catching stars like fireflies
trapped behind glass
no air to breathe
calling through silence; restless, drained
by nights left waking, tears failing dreams
she stumbles, uncertain
what road, what path
never knowing forward from back
where one once stood, the other replaces
'til all becomes
reflections of faces
no signs to warn: caution, yield
only words held
no left turn on red

Jaemi Graice Kehoe

That Smile

Once I saw a smile
Bright as the sun,
Beautiful like roses.

It held so much warmth
And so much love;
Something I needed at that time.

Never would I have thought
I wouldn't see that smile anymore.
So much love, so much warmth.
Now she is gone,
But never from my heart.
Her smile is an instant replay in my mind.

Now her smile is imprinted in the clouds;
Still bright as the sun
And beautiful like roses.

Nikki Lartrice Peek

Love Poem

In my heart, you're the one I see,
The one lurking in the shadows
Of the pale moonlight.
You're the one who fills my dreams
With laughter and joy.
Every time I see your face,
My heart turns to pure gold.
I close my eyes,
And I see your sparkling eyes
And your dazzling hair waving in the wind.
Sometimes it feels
Like we're flying in the sky over the clouds.
I know if we got together,
We would never separate
From each other
Because I know our love will last forever.

Alandra S. Klausing

Which One Am I?

There are those who are put into our lives
to remind us of where we've been . . .

and those who remind us of where we're at . . .

and those we watch, mimic, and hope to be
more like in the future.

Then there are those who just show us the
worst in ourselves so we may continually be
aware of how easy it is to be the worst that
we are—while calling it the best.

Which one am I?

MaryAlice Kennedy

Dark Star

Dark star
You and I are the same
Born in this world
To die in the world
I am plagued by this bitter reality
I long for your companionship
To escape the suffocation of my loneliness
I am swept away by your existence
Oh, phantom of the night
I am drowning in a salty desert of dry tears
Tormented by society,
Seared by the silence of life in your shadow
How pitiful I must seem
At the mercy of human emotion
How beautiful it must be
This suffering beneath the sky

Marysia Longendonk

Why Is It?

Why is it that pain comes in bursts
And never stays to heal?
Why can't pain stay till I get used to it
And slowly disappear?
Why is it those whom I think stupid
Give the most outrageous pain?
Why is it that stereotypes
Leave nothing to be learned?
Why is it that this pain is undetectable,
No scar, no bruise, no stain,
Just a tear that trickles down
By heart's dear eyes is shed.
Why is it that pain comes in little bursts
And digs into your soul
And is not visible, not to the eye,
But only to the source.

Patricia Felicity-Ann Volny

Mother

Don't talk to me, ah, woman
Don't talk to me right now
Not until I figure this foolish game
And not until I figure out
How to get ahead into the light
Me and you, we'll always fight

'Cause, ah, woman, this is what you want
To be in a constant rivalry
Diminishes the insecurities
Settin' your soul to make you feel free

And every time we go at each other
I wanna run, hide and take cover
Because the stress in my mind
Keeps my emotions behind
But . . . still you hate the body that is . . . mine

Corey Walter Goldsmith

Devil's Truth

An angel song for a blackened soul,
A dreamer's dance for eyes to know.
A chance to live through lying vile,
The dare to seek an endangered style.
To feel inside the wealth of jealousy,
To cast away every bitter-loving enemy.
Finding once more the delight of hate,
Knowing again the cruelty of blatant fate.
The gates open up and I unleash your strife. . . .
They close again and I blindly search for my life.
Turning on myself, I bury carelessness deep.
Following you, all of these fantasies I keep.

Deanne Brooke Rivera

As the Clouds Go By

As the clouds go by,
You wonder where they came from,
Or where they're going.
You pick some out and decide,
What do they look like?
On hot summer days, you see them
Floating across the sky like big white trucks
Driving down the freeway.
When rain is coming, they change colors.
Some turn gray, and some turn black.
You see the black and start to quiver,
For you know what's coming.
But on good days, they float along,
Jet puffed marshmallows floating along.
Your imagination wanders alongside,
As the clouds go by.

Amy Lynne Olinger

I Say Bye, Not Goodbye

The time has come for me to be no more.
I have used up my time in this dimension.
It is time to go,
For I am not needed here any longer.
I have given all that I can.
No more is needed.
My job is done.
It is time to return to my portal in space,
My everlasting home.
And when I am needed again, I will return
To the special people in the world who need me.
So I will say my farewell to all
Whom I love so dearly.
I will miss you so.
Keep the faith in each other and everything will be fine.
And I myself will be in a eternal place.

Vincent J. LaBarbera

Lord, We Love You

Lord, you are most high.
You look upon us with mercy from the sky.
You tell us it's okay when we lie.
You comfort us when we cry.
You are with us when we die.
You provide us with love.
You teach us wrong from right,
And all we do is pray at night.
We go to church and Sunday school.
We do not realize we are selfish fools.
We do not love you enough for you to care.
We only look out for our welfare.
When we do all of this, you do not put us to shame,
Or even make us take the blame.
We sound so lame.
We ask that you will forgive us for being pests, you are the best.

Nick Ryan Wolff

Response

Life is like a highway for me, where I am
Just walking at a very slow pace
Moving on with my difficulties and that inner darkness in me
A shadow of darkness over my qualities
I am a woman who doesn't like defeat
I want to face it, I want to face that darkness
Give me strength to face it and that is all I want
I don't want any luxury, all I ask is strength
At least give me that . . . or is it like . . .
You are just up there, out there
Somewhere to see this painful drama and not to help
I don't understand why my inputs have no response

Monika Yadav

Our Nineteenth Anniversary

No happy celebration of nineteen years
Or shared feelings of happiness and cheer.
Reflections from memories and dreams of future years
Now faded away to sadness and tears!
No shared words of love will be said.
Just sorrow and pain are felt instead!
No special evening with soft words spoken.
Just a lonely heart that has been left broken.
Just prayers and dreams of a miracle and hope;
To ask for the Lord's strength I need to cope!
To dream reconciliation will come someday;
For this I can only dream, wish and pray!
If I can no longer have you as my lover and this is truly the end,
My only wish will be that you can and will still be my best friend.
You were the partner, friend, and love of my life.
Just keep in your mind, heart and soul I will always be your wife!

Geraldine H. Harvey

Life

What's the point of living?
What's the point of giving
If what is left is an empty shell?

Surrounded by what I will never have.
Left standing by the tidal wave.
This is just my private Hell.

Weary, weak and broken, beaten to the bone,
Knowing each morning I wake, I will be alone.
How long can you expect me to take this before I go insane?

A man out of time, I should not be here.
What is left for me to fear?
I have nothing left to gain.

There is nothing left to live for,
But also nothing worth dying for.

Terence Barton

Obsession

Your vision has attached itself
To my brain and its most concealed edifices;
It rips and tears like an ice pick
I can't forget.

Your voice wraps and pulls me under,
Drowns me in the wavelengths,
Chokes me—fills my lungs,
I can't forget.

Your face,
The sound of your voice rings in my ears,
And your warm embrace
This is what I live for.

I.
Can't.
Forget.

Denise P. Li

Time

Time is precious
Time is free
Time never once waited for you nor me
Time is money
Time can fly
Time never gives you the chance to say goodbye
Time is essence
Time is gold
Time wasted is worst than being left all
Alone
Time well spent is the greatest achievement
In anyone's home

Claudette Novella Harris

You're the Only One for Me

Can it really be? You say you love me!
Tell me it's not just a dream.
Tell me things are what they seem.
I remember still that first time we met.
How your glances gave me such a thrill.
I knew at the start you could take my heart
And do with it whatever you will.
You were the magic key unlocking the mystery
As to why I never loved before.
Let me take your hand, make you understand.
You're the one who makes my life worthwhile.
Just to have you near is enough, my dear.
All I need is just to kiss your smile.
How can I prove my love?
The Lord knows in Heav'n above
That you're the only one for me.

Helen A. Poupard

The Gorilla and Orangutan

Heard you're not feelin' well
during this damp rainy spell,
so I thought you might like this
small tale I've to tell. . . .

I saw a gorilla and orangutan who
ate popcorn and pudding with a fork and a spoon.
They invited the zoo keeper who could only decline
by saying, "I'm sorry, just don't have the time."
The gorilla looked puzzled as he cleaned off his plate
and said, "I was hoping he'd join our debate
on whether time's fleeting or simply on wait.
Is my time and your time one of the same?"
The orangutan paused to swallow a morsel;
he slurped and he burped and rubbed his big torso,
and said, "I learned something from a cocky young pheasant:
that today is a gift, that's why it's 'the present.'"

Pat Byers Koerting

The Wisdom of Age

I am going to tell you about a man age ninety-two;
He knows more about life than me or you.

They say that wisdom grows with age;
The things this man knows could fill many a page.

The stories of his life he has often told,
Some about his life as a boy, others after he had grown old.

The stories he tells, some happy, others sad,
But they are about the joys
And sorrows of the kind of life he has had.

This man raised a large family
And worked on many a job through his years;
He has laughed a million times and he has cried a hundred tears.

This man I have known both happy and sad;
This man just happens to be my dad.

Carolyn McInelly

Emptiness

In the end, it all comes down.
Through desperate attempts at greatness
we find ourselves, again, at mediocrity.
Delusions of grandeur blaze our trail.
Seemingly none can tell our delusions
from our cold reality.
We consume our time with this tedium.
Choosing to participate in menial tasks
for societies benefit rather than work
towards achievable goals.
Fighting a war that can only be lost for both sides,
we realize . . . and in the end it all comes down.

Matthew Warren Davis

Christmas Spirit

It's funny this time of year what the spirit does to people;
How a bush becomes a Christmas tree
And a skyrise becomes a steeple.
How hatred is forgotten two weeks into December,
But once New Year's comes, love cannot be remembered.
Kids are good during this time, for the fear of losing gifts.
Not two months ago, they would not hesitate to use their fists.
Donations at the stores are second nature for one to give,
Where is this money during tax time
When the homeless need to live?
Christmas appears to be the time when imagination runs free;
Children's art and parents' love are united on a tree.
Neighbors help to shovel snow off the walks outside their house.
A daughter holds a rose as her parent visits a lost spouse.
People come together to exchange love, friendship and cheer.
Why is this spirit forgotten after the first day of each New Year?

Kenneth Schenk

Beauty

Beauty is a wonderful thing
That is in every girl's dream.
A little girl dreams of being
As beautiful as her mother,
While big sister concentrates on
The beauty that surrounds her.

Beauty can be used to describe anything;
Trees, flowers, cars, and people.
True beauty is in the heart.
It's when one is loving, good, faithful,
Kind, compassionate, and gleeful.

A person can have beauty on the outside,
But a beautiful person's beauty
Is inside their heart.
A person's true beauty sets them apart.

Juli R. Taylor

If Ever You Knew My Name

If ever you knew my name
would you tell a soul
With no one nearby I almost feel safe here,
but is it real
There is not a person for me to trust
and don't think you could ever change that
So maybe I'm paranoid,
or just a little too scared
I like you,
I really do
but you know love would never work here
Maybe if I were someone else
with no pointless fears,
but I have too much to fear now
to ever be able to give you
what you have given me

Sara Nicole Moore

Bowhunter's Dream

The thoughts of bowhunting never seem to be gone
From the time I fall asleep all the way till dawn.
There's some leaves rustling, then I hear a small grunt.
It's time to get serious about this hunt.
I see a flicker of white way over there.
Is it what I'm here for or is it just a scare?
Then out of the brush appears a rack
That almost gives me a heart attack.
As he walks down the trail approaching my stand
My knees begin to shake and so does my hand.
He is within range so I come to a full draw,
And all of a sudden I hear the alarm call.

Mark J. Galloway

Can't Seem to Go On

So many things run through my head.
My life's a disaster; I'm better off dead.
I can't hold a smile, not even a friend.
Avoiding my loved ones, in shadows I blend.
I cry every night for reasons unknown,
Yet none of my tears have ever been shown.
When I go to sleep, I wake up in sweat.
I can't lift an arm; I'm trapped in a net.
What have I done to deserve so much pain?
This torture within me drives me insane.
My life is so empty; can't seem to go on.
What should I do now that you're gone?
The day that you left splintered my heart.
Once we were close, now a Heaven apart.
Please send me an angel to watch over me
So when my time comes, your face I can see.

Jose E. Jimenez

Lady of the Night

Luminescent rays gently spread across the land,
Quietly smiling upon those below.
Spreading peace and happiness to all at hand
That lie within her beautiful glow.
Light gracefully reflects off meandering streams,
Dancing softly amongst the starlit night.
Displaying beauty found only within dreams
That haunt the elusive shadow's plight.
A warm melodious breeze gently sways the trees,
Casting veiled dreams of a better day.
Setting restless spirits' troubled thoughts at ease
In their endless search of fate's pathway.
Stars serenely glisten in celestial skies,
Capturing the thoughts of many a mind.
For the stars' gentle gaze cannot be defied,
Nor the strange fate of one's heart declined.

Daniel Parker Schultz

Can You Hear It? It's the Song in Your Heart

Can you hear it?
That sweet sound
A sound so peaceful
So indulging that you need to know what it is?
But you think, "What can it be?"
Is it the wind or a bird?
Or is it in your heart?

That song so beautiful
Is what you feel inside
How you live every day
It's the words you wish you can say but can't
You love that song
But can't understand it
So just listen to that song and follow your song of life

Sarah Anna Henry

The Rose

To me you are like a rosebud waiting to blossom.
When you do you are going to be the most beautiful rose ever seen.
When you reach this maturity,
I would like to be your sunshine when you need warming,
Be your rainfall when your thirst needs quenched,
The proper nutrients when your hunger needs satisfied,
Your shelter from the worst storm that could ever come your way.
So I could protect the beauty I see in you
For the rest of your God-given days.
So when no one else wanted to be there and I was!
The whole world could wake
And see the beautiful rose you turned out to be.

Jeffrey Childers

Drowning

It's like a disease that eats away inside
When all sense of joy has dried up and died
It is an endless journey for eternal bliss
Drowning in an ocean of failure and sadness
Feels like you're falling in a bottomless pit
No desire to go on; but only to quit
Smothered by insecurity, depression, and doubt
This struggle should not be what life is about
A mixture of feelings intertwined in a coil
Internal conflict leaves you in turmoil
Lost in a whirlpool of confusion and despair
When it seems like no one in this world could possibly care
Alone and engulfed by all these feelings
Trying to cope with all of life's dealings
These tough times teach us one thing indeed
Make the best out of life in order to succeed

Valerie Helene Gomez

Song of Silence

The moon's raised me to high tide levels,
But I can't see its light for the trees.
I know that you're out there somewhere;
Your song wafting so faint on the breeze.
As the shadows are lit with pure silver
And the streets are still as the grave,
I hear your song, oh, so softly.
Sing of Nelson, Nelson the brave.
Were this a ship on the high seas
Riding the moon's icy swell,
You would stand much like an admiral
Looking for Nelson in his solo hell.
Ride you this ship of the moonlight.
See you the land of the sun.
Point your compass to sunrise
And find then the man you've become.

Barbara Ann Holliday-Evans

Nothing Less Than Perfect

Here we are standing face to face
When you look into my eyes
Do you wonder what I am thinking?
Are you thinking what I am thinking?
I love it when you hold me
I hate for you to leave
I can't stand the thought of being without you
But I want to see you go
I want you to know how much I love you
But I dare not let it show
As I close my eyes and beg in silence
For you to grab me and hold me tight
And whisper sweet nothings in my ear
I just want you to know
We are nothing less than perfect
In this not-so-perfect world

Elizabeth Ann Heaster

Your World

I'm lost in a world
Not a world of my own, but of yours . . .
It's crashing down
And I feel the rain upon my face
Sweeping over my troubled mind
I feel I'm in a torturing bind
I can't see, I can't feel, I can't smell, I can't sleep . . .
We take these things for granted
And often abuse what we have
But when I get out of your grasp
I'll be able to breathe again . . .
I can't wait!

Rachel Starr Payton

That Man

I struggle within; I try to find
the person I see inside my mind.
This man that lives inside of me
is screaming, yelling, to be free:
free from bondage, free from sin,
he returns to my mind over and over again,
calling me out, letting me know
there is but one way I must go.
Still I struggle for I want to see
just what is happening inside of me.
Who can I turn to? Where do I run?
I know in my heart there is but one.
I know God hears me each time I pray.
Please bring me out and lead the way
so I may become that godly man.
Lord, please guide my feet and hold my hand.

Roy Livermore, Jr.

My Son

You were the last, my fair-haired child
Eyes so blue and what a smile
A tiny baby, small and sweet
Who could know the trouble you'd meet.

You grew to be a wonderful boy
Handsome and smart and what a joy
But somewhere inside something went wrong
I thought I'd watch you grow and be strong.

I'll never forget the call that day
The one that said you went away
I thought they lied. They said you died

I'll never see that smile again,
Never hear you laugh,
Never feel your touch.
My son, my child, I miss you so much.

Alice Conard

Oh, Brother

As I sat there, staring on the bed.
I could tell by your look you were almost dead.
I started thinking of all the fun times we had.
Me, You, Kelly, Mom and Dad.
Laughing, playing, jumping around.
Me and You, wrestling on the ground.
I looked around and saw that everyone was crying.
I still couldn't believe my brother was dying.
I tried real, real hard not to cry,
But why should it matter if your brother is about to die?
I wanted you to suddenly become fine,
But I knew it was over from the look in your eye.
Now as I sat there, staring on the bed,
I gave you a big hug because I realized you were dead.
I was so very sad and wanted to cry.
What else could you do when your brother just died?

Tim C. O'Steen

A Friend

A friend is a person who knows all about you and still likes you,
The one who listens without lowering you,
The one who cares without faulting you,
The one who clears your frown,
When there's no one else around.
A friend is the person you share good times and bad times with,
The one you have tiffs with and laughs with,
But at the end of the day have no hard feelings with.
A friend is the one that gives you compliments and praises,
The one who never disgraces you,
The one who knows your ways and prays for you
In their own silent ways.

Kathleen Ann Hillyard

Masters

We didn't know that it would
never be that good again.
All through those lazy summer days
of exploration and conquest,
we scaled the heights
of your backyard apple tree
(our Everest),
straddled the uppermost branches,
and proudly surveyed our mapped territories:
neighborhoods, bluffs, woods, fields, creeks.
Younger siblings, tadpoles, and insects
as subjects,
we were masters of our universe.
We didn't know that it would
never be that good again.
Is it ever?

Ellen L. Cannon

Have You Ever?

Have you ever felt loved and happy
When the stars kiss the heavens just right?
Or the wind blows the colors of the rainbow?
I have.
Have you ever felt like dancing?
Like singing as if there is no tomorrow?
And forgetting about yesterday?
I have.
Have you ever wished upon a star?
Sought out the pot of gold at the end of the rainbow?
Perhaps picked a four leaf clover?
I have.
You may wonder how I do this.
There is one simple answer, friend.
Your sweet embrace guides me,
Your smile lights my way!

Amanda Lee Glickman

The Vow

Today is the day, we made a vow;
to love, to hold, and to honor.
Today is a day of white and black;
to love, to hold and to honor forevermore.
Running through my head, a large train pounding,
I wonder do I say I do or shall I say no.
Everyone stares in awe at my face
as I say I do!
You may kiss her. Who, me?
Aww, through my whole church.
We get in his car off to his house.
I meet his family and friends; he meets mine.
After cake and champagne,
to love, to hold, and to honor,
forever and ever more,
I hear once more.

Kayla Jo Pherson

Flight of the Dragonfly

Colors of the rainbow slip by my window
A flutter of color then a flitter
Whimsical and light it dances
To and fro, up and down
Zigging and zagging
This little rainbow dances on the wind

Stained glass wings
Flitting and skipping over the brook
Body of black, slim as string
Graceful over the stream
Hurrying along with so much to do
Another piece of heaven to see from my room

Kim Wright Ralston

Soldier

Soldier of love, soldier of light
Honorable giver by far
Stand for your life with all of your might
Be willing to be who you are
Soldier of truth, holder of hope
Child, you are all that is real
Open your heart; know you can cope
Give yourself permission to feel
Seeker of passion, and all that is warm
Know you are not separate
Hold out your candle and ward off the storm
Give light, and life you will get
Soldier of love, soldier of might
Acknowledge yourself where you stand
Receive all that's offered; know it is right
Love yourself fully; know you are grand

Tanya Nadine Ryan

I Was

I was looking for a four-leaf clover
Instead of enjoying the ones with only three
I was waiting for a prince to arrive
Not looking at the frogs at my feet
I was wanting love to rescue me
But I never threw my love out
I was needing something in my heart
Not knowing what love was about
I was looking for that perfect sunset
And not appreciating all the flawed ones
I was waiting for the moon to rise
Instead of basking in the warm sun
I was wanting what I could not have
Not having what I should have took
I was needing love in my life
Just afraid to go and look

Kristen L. Orr

Worth the Risk?

At the end of the day
When you close your eyes
Alone in yourself,
Your soul and conscience may battle.
If you can look yourself in the eye
And know you would have done again
The choice you made . . .
It was worth it.
If within your private heart
You know the ache you would feel
At the regret of not taking the leap . ..
It was worth it.
If all were against it
And you believe you were true,
Wrong or right . . .
It was worth it.

Christy D. Hagreen

Profound Fear

A hurricane approaches.
People flee, people stay,
some do not wish to go away.
The fear of death destroys humankind's mirth
but simultaneously exposes its worth.
A man holds a gun in your face.
He will leave you without a trace.
The ultimate fear of death is self-exposed.
A strong human spirit is slightly transposed.
Having the realization of the end imminent,
the damage done can be permanent.
We are all a people with ideas and ambitions renowned,
but simultaneously possessing a fear of the unknown profound.

Thomas G. Winston

Life's Blue Ocean

I look out and see the lapping of the sea,
And wonder why God created such beauty for you and me.
Enjoying the wonder as the breeze blows so soft
Makes me question why we are blessed so oft.

To be able to rise each morning and know in my heart
That we can drink in the ocean's smell and be a part
Of the universe's grandeur and beauty still
Without a conscious thought or a pondering will.

It's wonders like these that make it all worthwhile;
Making me breathe deep and break into a smile
Because there is no other miracle on Earth
That can compare to the swells and the ocean's birth!

Linda A. Hochmuth

Nothing Compares to You

Your wisdom is like no other.
I am proud to have you as a friend and mother.
Through God's words, you give advice
so that we learn to trust in Him and never think twice.
The things that you have said to me
my heart will forever endure.
To be a part of your family, though,
God I am forever sure.
Through God's holy word and you by my side,
I know that evil will not prevail;
and never again will I run and hide.
With family and friends,
we learn to live from day to day,
So, thank you to my guardian angel
for I am here to say,
Nothing compares to you.
Thank you for helping me find my way.

Jody Yvonne Sweeten

The Fog

As I walked through the fog, ever present as a heavy thought,
I came upon a log, and sat awhile to contemplate
My life so far—twenty-nine long years—
Where I've been and am going, and how I've come to be here.
I held onto my package, afraid I would leave it behind
As it had been my faithful companion, forever occupying my mind.
It seemed a duration—a month, or two, or more,
To come to the realization that I was not being honest at all.
I lived for others—my family, my work, my obligations;
And so it was no wonder, I was struggling to progress.
I had changes to make, none so easy to define.
They will alter my course and take some time.
The fog began to lift revealing a lush green road;
Inviting me to move on
And I did, leaving the package, lightening my load.
So "I" have come to be, and never looking back,
Discovering me is what saved me at last.

Lalita B. Nordquist

Memories

The worst feeling I've had is a true love lost.
I'd take it back at any cost.
To be with you is to live my dreams,
But you don't care; that's what it seems.

You just don't know how much I care.
Look at all the love we've shared.
I miss you so, but you can't see;
"Let's just be friends," you said to me.

You don't realize what you've done.
You've darkened my world; there is no sun.
Until you light my life again,
I'll miss you, even if we're friends.

Elizabeth Ann Lechmanski

A Song to You

If all the songs in the world
Were tested for the best,
A song describing my love for you
Wouldn't have to take the test.

For my love for you is too great for words.
Its beauty will never end;
And when it's put to music,
With others it cannot blend.

So, I will sing my song of love
To prove the best is mine;
And hope someday, somewhere, somehow,
Our lives will both entwine.

Cindy Slater-Krusen

Life

The dying of youth, the flowering of maturity.
Where must we follow to end the insanity?
We sojourn the path that flows under us.
Do we have a choice?

As the old die, the young grow older
The path before us—does it ever change?
As those in front stumble
We gasp—can we change our path?

A fork in the road—we shan't be so bold
Following those who follow,
Never seeing the choices made.

We are condemned to this life;
Hopeless in our outlook,
Powerless to change,
Following those who follow,
Never seeing the choices made.

Heath Blake Anderson

It's Hard

It's hard to see.
You wither away
Like a withering flower
On a rainy day.

It's hard to see.
You disappear
Like water evaporating
From a streaming tear.

It's hard to acknowledge;
To know you're gone,
Like a tuneless tune
From a songless song.

It's hard to know
How you'll never be there
To give me my important ingredients in life—
Tender love and care.

Kaitlin Elizabeth Moorefield

The Seashore

The rhythmic crashing of waves
Matches the calm beat of my heart.
The ocean's blues and greens cannot be captured.
The dolphins show the sea is teeming with unknown life.
The splendid seaside sunset is a blanket
Of all colors stretched across the sky.
The beauty and tranquility of the sea cannot be matched.

Caitlin Rogers Cromer

Missing You

As I look up in the dark sky
I look at the stars and wonder why
Why you're not with me anymore
Why I wish you were knocking at my door
Time passes and years go by
I know that for a fact, but I still start to cry
How did your fate come to be
And why did God cause this tragedy?
Could I have prevented it, dare I say?
But now it's too late, your life is no longer at bay
For you are gone and not with me right now
But, when I die, I will be with you once again

Megan Kim Wilkins

Blissful Ignorance

To my beloved father, the late Sd. Karam Singh

I slept on the bosom of ignorance for long.
I walked on the roads with feathers on!
I talked to the angels
Of goodness and love!
I danced to the tune
Of harmonious accord!
I ventured through the world
Without a sore!
Ah! With eyes open!
Alas!
I slept on the bosom of ignorance for long!

Paramjit Kaur Pami

My Father

The one who is never there for me
My father
A man who tells me he cares but won't show it
He is hiding behind a curse
I am hoping someday that curse will be broken
For one day I am wishing he would be there to turn to
Maybe someday, but a father should be there for you your entire life
As a friend, a guide, a father
Not just someone there when he wants to be
Not just someone with a title
A father is to me unknown
But maybe someday the one who is never there for me will be

Tracy E. Rowe

Why

The empty feeling of "life" was all I knew,
then came the day I met You.
I started as a frame of a man,
then came the day You said, "I love you, Dan."
All alone with no one to do,
then I found God. I found You.
I was a waste like all the rest,
now I live only to be Your best.
The Earth went away, and there was only You.
I was made full, but then emptiness ensued.
With You it's Heaven and all is well,
but when without You, all is Hell.

Daniel Jeffrey Notwicz

Intelligence

To live without being prejudiced and without always wanting
To be confident about yourself and not self-conscious
To make something of your life and not waste it
To speak your mind and give your opinion
To not be afraid of getting something wrong
To reach goals and not limit yourself
This is to be considered intelligent

Myriah Jo Hrdlicka

Inside the Mind

Unconscious strategies to fail,
Never-ending desires to bail.

Anger boiling up within me;
Not able to let the past be.

Being haunted by things past,
Nothing good seems to last.

Not wanting to hurt,
Yet not letting myself feel better than dirt.

Letting enemies become friends,
Everything good comes to an end.

Amy Elizabeth Heeth

Simple Stars

As the frozen world begins its life
and melts away the sleep,
the universe evokes her simple silver smile.
It beckons for its loveliness
and radiance in design.
A gluttonous sky begs for her hues of azure, lilac, and mauve.
A sinister and lecherous and jealous abyss
beseeches to have her eyes.
And the honey-drenched world makes her kind.
And the wind induces her whispers.
And her patience is spilt upon the moon.
And the stars know why they are simple.

Nathaniel Rich Provencio

To the Sky

The world points a mocking glance of scorn in my direction,
Hypocritically not being so desires utmost perfection.

What is left behind? A mere conception of a thought
And yet the truths within we know, though never have been taught.

Solutions linger willingly, most often times ignored,
And with the seeds of pride we sow reap consequenced reward.

What on Earth possesses pain? The bitter form unbearing
Each afterthought and underscore my soul apart is tearing.

Continue on, do not retreat and cease to pass faith by,
For if you seek true love and peace, you must look to the sky.

Victoria Alyssa DeLeon

True Love

You are my love,
The only one I ever think of.
I hope you know I care,
For my life I hope to someday share.
We've always seemed perfect together,
And I know we'll stay this way forever.
Being there for each other,
Never could I be with another,
Knowing that we will last,
It's great to remember our wonderful past.
Our future is upon us now,
And all I can think is, wow!

Lindsay Christine D'Amico

Dangerous Minds

Give a mind nourishment and it grows.
When a mind grows, it fills with knowledge.
Give a mind knowledge and you start to see a future.
Give a mind pain and abuse and that future begins to fade.
When that future begins to fade, the mind becomes depressed.
Give a mind depression and it will go crazy.
Give a crazy mind a gun and its life or many others are over.

Heather Nicole Richardson

If Only . . .

When one listens keenly to the sound of the wind
With ears set to hear the beauty of the song,
Comes a sound so pure and yet so divine,
The sound of every heartbeat, bringing shivers to thy spine.

If only hearts could talk, what wonders would they say?
The secrets they may hold will pile up every day.
A load so great, oh, how much does it weigh?

If only hearts will move the lips on the mouth.
If only those words will be heard without dismay.

But truth is a word too hard to say,
And feelings are emotions rarely on display.

Dina Yousef Alnsour

A Parent's Prayer

If you dream, may it happen
If you seek, may you find
If you desire, may you have
If you listen, may you be heard
If you care, may you be liked
If you are friendly, may you have friends
If you are truthful, may you be trusted
If you are dependable, may you have someone to count on
If you seek knowledge, may you learn
If you love, may you be loved as much as we love you
And never forget, we are proud to say you will always be
Our most special daughter

Pamela Pridgen Tummond

Tip of My Tongue

My feelings grow each day
The words I want to say
There on the tip of my tongue
I'm falling so fast
It seems like everything is in the past
Will these words I want to say give this girl a scare
On the tip of my tongue, do I dare
Tell this girl how much I really do care
My heart races and beats so fast
This girl gives me the warmest heart attack
Never felt so good before with another
I pray and hope this one lasts

David John Cook, Jr.

Will I Know

Do I dare make the impossible a realization
Or should I cease from dreaming
Does something that feels so right be wrong
Or does selfishness blind my heart
Can I put so much at risk without hurting my loved ones
Or will they stand by my side through my turbulence and strife
Should I claim the happiness that may belong to another
Or does that delight belong to me
Could I follow my heart avoiding the hurt
Or will I be strong when it comes
Should I hold on to the hands of love
And will I know when to let go

Carmen L. Hernandez

Hello

You see them, they see you
The world stops spinning, your heart turns to goo
You think of what to do and what to say
Come on now do something, you don't have all day
They're coming towards you, you turn into Jell-O
You fall head over heels when they say that one word
Hello

Jessica Ann Samson

Best Friends

Some friendships can last a day
And others can last weeks,
But only best friends can make it through years together.
You know me better than I know myself,
Throughout thick and thin you've been there for me
And I just wanted to tell you that I love you.
You're like the sister that I never had.
Life gets harder as the years go by
And I know that as time passes, people leave,
But I can promise you that I will forever stand by your side!
You're my best friend
And nothing can come between us!

Kimberly Ann Valentine

Love

Love is unconditional and uncontrollable
Love given without reason cannot be purchased
Love will expend your last breath, as you strive to fulfill it
Love is felt between two, only when it is given freely
Love is gone, when it is no longer felt from the other
Love misplaced is why nuptials fall apart
Love desired is the motivation for envy
Love will cease to bequeath, if it is not received
Love cannot be fooled, a weak heart can recollect bliss again
Love for each other is why we must separate as friends
Love shall evermore be healthier than its opposite
Love experienced is the nature of all true beasts

Thomas Dean Brown

A Million Stars

Written about my favorite place . . . Red River, Idaho

There are a million stars in the midnight sky.
The crickets chirp, calling each other in the distance.
The moon shines dimly, as the fire crackles and whips.
My skin tingles as the cool crisp air caresses my face.

Though every sound is amplified, there is a quiet peacefulness.

My senses are aroused, magnified by this wonderful night!
A feeling surges through me, unlike any other before!
A sense of oneness, wholeness, yet somehow insignificant.
A realization of the beauty surrounds me, swallowing me.

There are a million stars in my midnight sky!

Teri Lynn Erickson

The Lidless Eye

The air is still
As the world sleeps,
But someone can see you.
The lidless eye watches.
The moon's cold, silver eye sees all.
It seems harsh and unforgiving.
There is nowhere to hide.
It is a hole in a blanket of darkness.
Then slowly the seeing eye begins to fade.
And its power is overcome by the sun's warming fingers.
As they tear a hole in the black night.
And the moon retreats in fear.

Haley Alicia Vining

Love Is

Love is when you hear angels sing
When a dove flies with a broken wing

Love is when your kisses takes away the pain
When your words wash away the rain

Love is what I feel for you
In hopes that you feel the same way too

Xavier Lael Knox

In My Heart

In my heart I see a flag covered in tears.
It's soaking wet but shiny as can be.
What did I see? Who did I see?
I saw the Twin Towers and the Pentagon all gone, gone, gone.
I saw Jesus saying, "Come, my dear, it is okay."
I sobbed and I sobbed till I cried out the day.
My heart is a tender one, but my faith is stronger.
In my heart I speak to myself, oh, how can this be?
I romped and I stomped, but not able to succeed.
Then I jumped out of bed and rushed to the window.
I looked outside and then in my heart.
I saw love.

Kortney Chantel Pierce

Red

Red.
The color of love.
Red roses, red hearts and ruby red lips.
Shiny and soft, that you want to kiss.
A slinky red dress to wear on a date.
Dining and dancing and coming home late.
Red.
The color of hate.
Seeing red, bleeding red, wishing you dead.
The Queen of Hearts screams, "Off with her head!"
Red that is raging, flaming, and burning.
Red is the color of two kinds of yearning.

Lacey Lepo

The Fountain of Youth

O! parting of white rainbows
Forge through dark chimneys of dream,
In the marketplace where our souls were lost
Many fountains flowing fires of youth
Poured forth streams of lust throughout the night.
That was the marred marble facade my enchantress enlivened
To swell Neptune's pleads with crashing tides.
In silly words of the world forgotten
Those divinities therein live enshrined.
Now I utter hushed moments extinct in song
With these few lines slowly sung
Attempting yesterday's purity flown.

Nathan Franklin

Little Girl

I see a little girl before my eyes.
When I look at her, I see a little girl
with no worries in the world,
a little girl that frolics and plays all day long.
She does not worry about how she looks or what others think of her.
I see a little girl with joy in her heart.
With her long hair, gentle eyes, and sense of wonder,
she seems almost too good to be true.
Who is that little girl that looks at the world and smiles,
who thinks that every day is adventure,
that seems to be so glad to be alive?
Oh, how much I wish I could be more like her.

Valarie Marie King

Determination

What is life about?
You are always thriving for that next step.
Screaming in determination, you give up all for everything;
But in the end the victory is sweet,
Knowing that everything you have worked for has finally paid off.
Set big goals.
Make things happen.

Jonathan Martin Knapp

Me and Myself

Am I you or are you me?
How can it be
That myself and I think so differently?

Patience is a virtue, you say
While I clearly submit to the lack of it every day.
Relentlessly you endeavor to make me realize the naked truth
That I often try to conceal in shades of gray
Every trait you contradict in me.
My battle with you is never ending.
And yet we coexist, you and I
For you will not be you without me
and I will not be me without you.

Noopur Bakshi

Unable to Surrender

The road ahead is unfocused,
Reality hits hard.
A new insecurity merges
With every intoxicated breath that is inhaled,
The trembling, unable to surrender.
With the push of a button
I'm lost once again,
Back to a place I should never have been.
A rhythm so taunting will diminish my strength
For deep within the serpent pushes through,
Racing back to be you,
And the trembling is unable to surrender.

Jody Ellen Normore

I Had an Old Nannie!

To my own old, sweet grannie of a nannie, Janey Davis

I had an old nannie, her name wasn't Frannie . . .
but, oh, my lordy, how she could tan my fanny!
Her hands were old and full of tremble,
but, oh, how she could use a thimble!
She patched my pants and taught me how to dance.
She watched me play and taught me how to pray.
When I was her sweet child, my old nannie
never tanned my fanny,
but when I was naughty . . .
I had an old nannie, her name wasn't Frannie . . .
but, oh, my lordy, how she could tan my fanny!

Norma Jean Kennedy

Marrikesh

Once, not so long ago, when the world was
Overrun by foul and festering things, there lived Fungusman,
A creature of immense sporing capacity.
A truffle haired chap with buttons for eyes,
His head was all spongy, his face was a mess.
For each time it rained, out grew fungi from flesh.
Such growth upon growth of mushroom from meat,
I'd dare not to say sounds a fanciful treat.
But, oh, quite the contrary, for I once heard him boast
Sliced face in the pan makes great mushrooms on toast.
So if you should see him here, there or abouts,
Make sure you've toast a plenty just in case his face sprouts.

Andrew M. Conn

The Height of My Heart

Boy, you must be my lucky star
Don't know from when or where you are
When I look into the eerie depths of the sky,
I search for the answer to my question, "Why?"
But I am left unanswered and in pain enough to cry
Around the world and back you've flown
But now it's in my heart you fly

Elizabeth Anne Nichols

You're the Apple of My Eye

Roses are red, violets are blue.
My baby's heart is pure and true.
Sometimes we laugh, sometimes we cry.
She will always be the apple of my eye.
I love my child with all my heart.
She is so pretty, she is so smart.
I know if we could, we would laugh all day
Because laughter makes whatever pain go away.
I love to watch you growing so fast.
You will soon be a young lady and hit the big time at last.
You will always be my baby; this you cannot deny.
That's because you're the apple of my eye.

John A. Duran

Lost

Days go by and time fades away.
You're only born to begin to die, from day to day.
Life goes on, as you do not.
Just as well, because you're only forgot.

Hoping for something to brighten my days,
but only getting what darkens my nights.
No comfort insight, only hope to find my lost light.

Sadness buries my heart, to the depths of my soul,
the place where there seems no control.
No control of what I say or do,
only the pain I feel when I'm without you.

Crystal L. Tucker

Far Away

Imagine a place where nobody is judged or ridiculed
Where everybody falls in love at first sight
And nobody gets into fights
Where every child has a family filled with love
And angels fly from above
Where everyone has everything they need
And there is no such thing as greed
Where all the stars are diamonds in the sky and nobody lies
Where night is as beautiful as day
And every month is as beautiful as May
It may seem like such a place is far away
But in your dreams is where it lays

Krista Huber

Sarah Marie

Dear little Sarah Marie,
There is so much for your eyes yet to see.
The beauty of flowers, the trees, and the snow,
And may you have patience while learning to grow.
May you learn from your father the meaning of song,
And be wise in your choice of what is right and what is wrong.
May each day bring a smile and a gift of delight,
And comforting thoughts to be with you at night.
May you find through the years the meaning of "friend,"
The willingness to start, and the courage to end.
Sweet little Sarah Marie,
Be the best you can be!

Cindy Meigs

Little Girl

When I was a little girl I thought,
oh, what a big world.
I loved the country and I loved the sea.
I thank God because I am free.
I look out at the birds and flowers
as I feel the coolness of the first spring shower.
What a wonderful world this is.

Danielle J. McCoy

Coping

If it were only that simple, to plant a tree
When grieving a loved one, no longer to be
If that single action, relieved all the pain
If that one small tribute could help us sustain
Forests would exist we could not contain

But reality checks us
Death has robbed us twice

Sharing tomorrow with the past still remains
Memories we borrow relinquish the rains
Reminiscing fills the void we sense every day
These trees we have planted helps our grief go away

Kathy Ann Gallagher

The Business of Life

Life is like a roller coaster
it goes up and down and 'round and 'round
never stopping to slow down
'cause if you do you will fall
with no one to catch you
'cause they're too busy
going up and down and 'round and 'round
never stopping to slow down
your head is spinning out of control
lost on the track
trying to find its way back
to LIFE

Robin L. Monroe

My Grandfather's Spirit

I thought about what he loved best
During the funeral I stepped outside
I had something to finish for my life
I observed the grass from under the tree
The leaves floating around, coming to me
I felt my grandfather's spirit as I looked around
Appreciating my world, heavens to ground
I looked at the sky and watched the birds
My tears turned to joy; he was at my side
Walking towards the church now, with pride
His eyes were my eyes to see the Earth
Thank you, grandfather, this is what it's worth

Patrick John Pareja

Friends

People see friends come and go;
Sometimes fast, sometimes slow.
The fast friends we seem to forget,
But the slow ones we always remember, you bet.
It seems that true friends are hard to find
And the others that leave, maybe weren't so kind.
Friendship is something that never dies;
Sometimes it makes you laugh, sometimes it makes you cry.
A true friend never leaves your mind or heart,
No matter where you begin or start.
People will come and people will go,
But a true friend will stick with you, this you know.

Jamie Marie Haney

Half Awake

As I lie in my bed only half awake
with my eyes closed in silent rest,
I can make out the scent of your perfume
or the soft whisper of your voice.
I smile at the idea of you being near,
but when I open my eyes, you are gone,
my most precious and faint of memories. . . .

Duane A. Pace

I Call on You

I might love you more than the day.
Even until that very night slips away.
Right into my heart and through my veins,
I feel the presence of day.
You awake me with your vibrant ways
As the ocean water passes through the bays.
Consider me your only one
And together we can touch the sun.
Anything can be accomplished.
You and I, just us two,
Can make the darkest days,
Make up the sky with bright outrageous rays.

Tamarah Lynn Sinex

The Frozen Moment

The room was silent, the light was dim
And for that very moment it was only me and him.
The clock was stopped, the people where mute
As he told me my shirt was cute.
His eyes were tense, he was so deep in thought
As he told me he was sorry for all the times we fought.
His lips trembled and his eyes teared
Of the thought the break up was near.
He walked forward and whispered in my ear,
I'm sorry for all that happen this year.
He gave me a kiss and told me he'd never leave me.
Even after death we'll still be known as "we."

Jenny Nicole Avello

Tribute

She stands in the shadows of my life,
urging me onward
Her whispered words of encouragement
hold back the floods of disappointment
and convince me to go on,
a gentle push from the arms behind
as I take the next step,
when all the while, I'm afraid
Her heart is filled with confidence
Now my eyes shine brightly as I stand up straight
and send a salute to all moms
tucked away

Heather Hudson

Imagined Love

Gazing into your eyes, I am lost,
Lost in a world of only us.
Your hair free-flowing as the wind blows,
A smile so warm and beautiful.
Your voice, soft and soothing;
Your lips gently caress mine;
A sensation never before experienced.
Grasping your hand,
Nothing is felt;
For you are not real,
Just imagined.
Not even met.

Charles Francisco Castro

In the Blue

You tasted winter, can you feel me fall?
So I've heard; pass the hurt on.
When time is nowhere to be found, sew my soul back on;
the wind brushed against my heart.
It's so hurtful when starlight waits outside.
The secret force of darkness, this last time, played my eyes.
The million smiles, the fake stares, you were so renew.

Nancy A. Kriek

My Fight

Just when I thought all hope was gone,
I was told not to give up, I wasn't done.
My family has been there throughout;
that's what I'm talking about.
Just when I thought there was no hope,
they threw me a rope.
I wanted to give in;
they said, come on, Kath, you can win.
It has been six years.
I have had my share of laughter and tears.
I know my life will never be the same;
at least I'm still here to play the game.

Kathryn Michelson

Left Alone

I often ponder what happened in the barn that day.
That day long ago when my father went away.
Did he just get tired of the struggle of life?
Did he die alone or with the help of his wife?
What made him think we would be better alone?
A kid needs a father to love, not just some stone.
I needed him more as I went from boy to man,
To give me guidance or assurance from a gentle hand.
He wasn't there to teach me right from wrong.
Most importantly, how to build that father-son bond.
I have grown old now with children of my own.
Did I give them enough love or did I, too, leave them alone?

Tiffany Marie Waldron

Halloween

The night grows dark, the air grows cold.
The witches cackle, the ghouls grow bold.
Now what could be happening on a night such as this?
It's Halloween, my friend, a night you don't want to miss.
The pumpkins glow, the zombies bite.
The candy's passed on this starlit night.
Now what is this night when the banshees shriek?
It's Halloween, my friend, a night not for the meek.
The moon rides high, the night's nearly done.
The werewolves rest, their battles won.
Now don't get too comfortable, there are still plenty of scares.
It's Halloween, my friend, good night and beware!

Justin Scott Thornton

When It's Time to Leave

When I leave this mortal shore
and travel around this Earth no more,
don't weep, don't grieve or cry.
I may be in a better place, it's no lie.
Don't tell the people that I was a saint
or anything that I ain't.
If you think like that to spread,
Please hand it out before I'm dead.
If you have flowers, bless your soul.
Just put it on my casket before I'm cold.
But do it while I'm at my best
Instead of when I'm safe at rest.

Barbara Evelyn Gove

Farewell to a Friend

I bid my friend farewell as she journeys far away.
I hope she has a time full of laughter fun and play.
I pray she wastes no time and sees all that can be seen,
For times of fun don't last long, except for in a dream.
Soon you'll be back at the airport and back aboard the plane
And as you leave the ground you'll take one last look in vain.
Although you might be down 'cause your trip is at an end,
When you're back and safe at home, that's the best part to your Friend.

Hani El-Halawany

What Am I without My Father?

What am I without my Father?
Without Him, I am just a whisper in the air.
If you felt a light breeze sweep across your shoulders,
would you know that I was there?
Upon death comes tears and sadness,
back to ashes from once we came.
As one soul departs this Earth, another is born again.
Time is so short, yet none of us stop to appreciate it while it is here.
What if a season constituted one century of your life
instead of just a quarter of a year?
From my arms bleed destruction, insanity, and pain.
I can hear your thoughts before spoken
and capture your life story in a picture frame.
As the Earth's time comes to an end,
those last will be first and those first will be last.
In the end, will God have the final laugh?

Jamie Chantal McCray

With Love in Our Hearts

Deep into the daytime sunlight, whisperings of loves and true tides,
comes mornings and dawnings of bright times and blue-hues.

In mine eyes I haven't told thee: let's let loose not the starlight,
and walk the sands of time with bare feet and truths.
With love in our hearts . . .

If you already know you want to; if you know that love is in you,
than shout out with glory you know what to say.

Sometimes summer is unwinding, sometimes autumn is quite blinding.
Yet spirits within you, they know what to say . . .
They know what to say . . . with love in our hearts . . .

With love in our hearts beyond thee, with trials and evacuees,
they lie down their heartbeats for whispers with winds.

In my heart I haven't told thee what is truth and what's beyond me,
yet lovers within you, they know what to say . . .
They know what to say, with love in our hearts.

Jared Faw

The Smile

Words spilled out of your mouth.
Filled with range, they spoke to me.
Tears danced down my cheeks.
Did you care?
I turned
and ran.
Away from you.
I ran.
The field winds blew from a whisper to a whistle.
I fell
fell
fell
until I could feel the comfort of the soft grass underneath my cheeks.
The roots rocked me to sleep the way you used to.
The flowers were my mother now.
When I woke up, you were there,
your smile brighter than the sun. I had to smile back,
And I knew from that smile, that there was still hope.
I'm sorry, you said . . . and it was enough.

Justyna B. Kurowska

Tremble

I have
So calmly beckoned
For the rain to come
To wash over me
And cleanse me of sin
And of hate
And of everything irate
For I am so confused
And so dirty
That I can feel the pain
Woefully dancing
Inside my chest
And within my breast
And to stop it I see
Nothing can be
The best of all
Only better than me

Joseph Francis Round

But You Are

You are the light of my day
You are the dark of my night

You are the air that I breathe
But you are not around

I have searched the sky
I have searched the land
But you are nowhere to be found

I can feel your love
I see your miracles around me
But you are nowhere to be seen

You have come before
You said you'd come again

I will wait for you
Wait with your children

We miss you, Lord
Please come back to us

We need you, Lord
Please come again

We love you, Lord
Save us again

Mathew Ronald Schriner

To Daphneleah, My Daughter: A Woman, Now Mom

My baby is no baby anymore.
She has grown up.

She's woman.
She's power.
She's tenderness,
Love.

She's gentleness,
Kindness.
She's eagle.
She's dove.

She's strength, courage and wisdom.
She is woman.
She is Mom.

Dear God,
up in Heaven,
what have I ever done
so right in my life
that you gave me as reward,
my daughter, a woman,
my baby, now mom?

Graciela Schneider

Roses and Violets

If roses are red, are violets blue? 'Tis the question from one to you.
One may think, yet not really ponder a thought of many wonders.
How can it be, ode to thee of such amazing danier, that one thinkin' to be on a lanier
of plight, when does one know who is right
or is one just always relying on touch or eyesight,
that hindsight goes forthwith and doesn't ever draw neigh,
oh such a question tis' I ask of thee, if roses are red, are violets blue,
what else can one see that might really matter,
when it's all about what's in the better and not on the plate,
oh, too see, thus inner tranquility,
that is such a blessing in disguise, yet one aught not to surmise the days as they arise,
ode as worth, though art and forevermore shall be, always live but never die,
for from henceforth one shall then be able to think sensibly,
yet one will see why roses are red and violets are blue,
thus ends this question from one to you!

Jonathan D. Hendry

Dreams

When I awake from a beautiful dream,
I wish I could stay in the dream.
My dreams are dreams that at the moment feel right.
The birds singing the songs of love softly,
like a whisper in your ear,
the sun shining on your face as if you're being held by an angel,
the wind blowing though your hair softly
like a sweet caress from the one you love with all your heart and soul,
like a kiss so sweet,
the taste of honey on your lips,
and the smell of flowers in the garden on a beautiful spring day,
even though they are not always the way out of the real world,
but the way to a life you could have only in a dream.

Rosemarie Saaverda

Love Is

For the love of my life, Diana—happy birthday, D!

Love is, when she's the last thought you have while falling asleep
Her being the very first thing you think of when you rise
Waking from a dream of her and dying inside when she's not there
Thanking God when she is!

Love is, screaming out her name in the middle of the day
Getting a lump in your throat every time you hear her voice
Your eyes welling up with tears at the mere thought of losing her
Missing her the very second she leaves the room

Love is, when thinking about her consumes every minute of the day
When every love song you've ever heard is about you and her
Sharing the same thoughts and emotions when a thousand miles apart
When she dies and you don't want to live another day without her

Love is, the thrill that runs through you every time you touch her
When your eyes meet and you know no one else will ever take her place
Willing to give up everything you've ever had to be with her
Your heart breaking as you think about what could have been

Love is, when love letters from years ago and now say the same things
Remembering the sweet taste of her lips 15 years after your last kiss
67 perfect inches, glacier blue eyes, and the heart of an angel
The one who stole my heart away and I'll love forever, plus one day!

Love is, Diana!

Oscar Goldstein

The End

The end is near.
Oh, fear!
Oh, fear!
For the end can
only mean dreariness.

It would be wise
to snub these lies.
Some good will come
from Earth's demise.

Always the end
will kindly mend
all the mistakes
that people send.

A clean, fresh start,
for men, the smart.
And yet the dumb
will sit and fart!

Joseph Edward Dooley

And Off We Go

They say I'm going nowhere fast
A hummingbird
Slapping
The wind with might
Like a housewife beating a rug

When dust mites twirl in the sunlight
It's beautiful
Dancing
To nature's drum
But I can't hear like carpet dust

So I tread on
Deaf and running
On cartoon legs
Pumping
Fast in an awkward rhythm
Like a heart murmuring

I'll end up somewhere, but not now
Earl of Sandwich
Held dice
In one hand
And lunch in the other
I can too

Marcy Wilkinson

Invocation

Circle cast in sacred ground
Spirits all around
Magic doth abound

Ring the silver bell
Cast the enchanting spell
All is well

Those of the east
Come! Partake of our feast

Those of the north
Come forth!

Those of the west
Come abreast!

Those of the south
Come! Hear the summons from our mouth

Oh, Goddess, hear our song
Make us strong

Oh, God, Him Who art above
Fill us with Your love

Come to us
That we may be joyous

Shanin Melinda Green

Letting Go

To let go does not mean to stop caring,
It means you can't do it for someone else.
To let go is not to cut yourself off;
It's the realization you can't control another.
To let go is not to enable but to allow learning from natural Consequences.
It's to admit powerlessness, which means the outcome is not in your Hands.

To let go is not to try and change or blame another,
It's to make the most of oneself.
To let go is not to care for but to care about.
To let go is not to fix but to be supportive.
It's not to judge but to allow another to be a human being.

To let go is not to deny, but to accept.
To let go is not to be in the middle, arranging all the outcomes.
To let go is not to adjust everything to your desires.
It's to allow others to affect their own destinies.

To let go is not to regret the past but to grow and live for the future.
To let go is not to be protective but to permit another to face reality.
It's to fear less, love more, then take each day
As it comes and cherish oneself in it.

Angela Dean

The Reality: Life on the Other Not-So-Greener-Side of the Grass

Facing reality, I lose all hope,
All the stresses of life, I just can't cope,
Rushing to be grown, starving for recognition,
Instead of putting your faith in God, your lead by superstition,
Babies having babies, fatherless homes,
A crack fiend had a baby that had to be test tube grown,
Dysfunctional families, feuding kin,
A twelve year old found of a pimp to be her best friend,
Single mother of three, no where to call home,
Has two jobs, so the streets they want have to roam,
A baby cries, she's filled with cold, a fever of 102,
Her family has no insurance and no idea what to do,
A teenage girl gang raped and left for dead,
A homeless man sleeps under a freeway, with a cardboard box for a bed,
A stepfather molests his twin step daughter and son,
He has no idea that God is the Holy one,
A newborn baby found in the Dumpster no chance to live,
I found a new lease on life, I have a lot of love to give,
Now please don't get scared about the reality I write,
But living in reality, you can't miss a prayer to be prayed at night.

Jakeshia Lewis

Breaking Through

Fourteen years dealing with these feelings distorted.
I fight it, but sometimes can't even for my kid.
Yet another wasted breath.
Far from feeling sorry, it's just a reality check. Life's beyond hectic.
Too many lives were almost taken from what I've got left.
She's still here, but I can't figure out why.
My pains are far from physical 'cause it's all in my mind.
Voices from behind constantly echo when I try.
It's not really me. More like a split personality.
Optics of 20/20, but they're still far from visionary.
"Somebody help!" is what I've unconsciously screamed.
I can't continue on this road,
Constantly being pushed further to the edge than before.
Always alone, creating like Van Gogh.
Struggle constantly with issues under my skin
Deeper than tattoos, but what can I do?
I just want to get better,
But it seems the longer the time frame, the worse it gets.
Reflection's barely standing,
trying to understand emotions so deep within my chest.
I'm sitting here once again bleeding.
Damage caused by my own hands.
Charred lungs fighting to expand.
Shall this break down this man?

Tito E. Baez

Morning

Daybreak
softly beams
through the mysterious haze of night.
It waits, hushed,
stretching sun's rays in silence.
Slowly, the world awakens.

Anna Maria Montesines Bautista

With Wind I Sat

The midnight moon, it calls to me
Is it too soon, why can't we flee
Forever noon, trick eternity

I want to leave this place I'm at
I do believe, but what is that
Once to relieve, with wind I sat

Mark Lee Johnson

Reality

With every cool, crisp, autumn breeze
another leaf falls,
floating softly like a feather
into its bed of death,
only to have its beauty crushed by
the next cancerous life form passing by.

Christine Therese Holbrook

A Fragile Thing

Love and lust, a fragile thing.
For most of us, here's what it brings:
A warm thought on a cold night,
And bad days turn out all right.
So sudden and strong,
Before you know it, it's gone.

Gina Vairo

The Love Story

Heart is love.
Kiss is love.
Hugs are love.
Nice is love.
Cuddling is love.
Sweet is love.
I like love.

Stephanie Nicole Shore

Darkness

Out of the mist of the dark of the night
Sleep is upon us
and death is on wings
Life is not yours
even to hold
So let go and leave with the wind
Is your soul on those wings

Elise Nicole Hutchinson

Letter of Prayer

Dear God,

Please build my strength from
strength up above.

Please send me a guardian angel
filled with all of Heaven's love.
Love . . . me.

Jay Lynn Whittaker

family

the distance has grown between us;
slowly at first, so that we would not force ourselves to realize it,
and then more rapidly as the gap widened.
so here we stand, two distant dots from one another on the horizon,
on the brink of something even i won't recognize.
in our childish denial, we still say that we know each other,
when deep within our distanced hearts we know
that we are no more than a stranger to the other.

we seek to seal the void between us, a way to fill the dead space,
but all is lost, as we are lost to each other,
and we know that; and that is why we scream at each other,
trying to be heard across the chasm that has become us.
tell me truly, can two pieces of a broken whole ever be joined again?
there will always be a scar, that ugly vein of misunderstanding
that will forever be a reminder, forever a divider,
and that reminder is just enough to keep us segregated forever.

no one can place the blame, no one has the right to.
sometimes things just happen and some things are broken that
can't be apologized away. the raw truth still is
some things are meant to stay together, and others fall apart.

Amanda Megan Stefanik

No Greater Love

At one point in my life when I no longer thought
I could find happiness or a life again, God came through for me.
The next year, my grandson was born; my life began to change.
To this day, I firmly believe he was an angel sent from Heaven
to give me back the happiness and love I no longer had.
He filled the great void in my heart
and made my children and I forget our sorrow and grief.
With him as a little baby, I held him in my arms
and he made me forget all my problems.
When I am with him, I feel his love and warmth fill my heart with joy.
As he gets older, he is even cuter.
When he runs to hug me and I see his smile, I want to cry with joy.
Now he talks and when he says, "I love you,"
it's the happiest moment of my life.
How blessed I feel to have this little person with me at all times.
I can't wait to see him, so we can spend so many happy hours
together doing so many fun things.
When he is happy, he makes me happy, too.
I never tire of him; all he has to do is look at me
with those big brown eyes and life is wonderful.
There is no greater love or fulfillment than being a grandmother.

Margaret Ricciuto

The Rainbow Prophecy

Evil now has bent its bow, preparing for a striking blow.
Seven crystals in a row, the colors of the rainbow.

The seven crystals grow and rear. Seven unicorns appear.
A new era now is drawing near, the era of the rainbow.

The seven unicorns unite, to shield a girl from the brewing fight.
A beautiful girl clothed all in white, Princess of the Rainbow.

When together they place their horns, the seven rainbow unicorns,
An era dawns and evil mourns at the coming of the rainbow.

Horns unite, become one horn, at the tip of which a crystal is born.
A pure, clear crystal that shall adorn the Princess of the Rainbow.

She rises now and takes a stand. It is her turn to lend a hand.
Fairest girl in all the land, Princess of the Rainbow.

Solemnly she says a prayer, Princess of the Rainbow fair.
The crystal rises into the air, the crystal of the rainbow.

The crystal rises even higher, shines with the light of heavenly fire.
Evil's need to escape is dire, the power of the rainbow.

Evil flees to return no more.
A reviving breeze blows through the door.
It was an awesome victory for Arianna, Princess of the Rainbow.

Jill Bronk

My Sweet, Sweet Fantasy

To my husband, Mitch,
who holds the key to my heart

What happened to that day long past,
That moment
So right,
Urge so strong
Snatched right out of our grasp?
What happened to that hunger,
That thirst for lust?
I could see it in your eyes.
I could feel it on your lips
And taste it on your tongue.
Did the fire burn down to ash,
Or is the spark just waiting
To be fanned to life once again,
Just shut away,
Put on hold?
Hoping for a time to break away
Open and free
Just you and me,
My sweet, sweet fantasy!

Wendy Ezard Mitchell

Shadows

When an echo from the past
Plays on the edge of my mind;
It's a fleeting image so fast.
It surprises me in kind,
Just shadows left behind.

I think somewhere it was resting,
Hiding things I want to find.
When I call for images nesting,
There is no reply from the mind,
Just shadows left behind.

My reverie is void of thought,
The mirror of time filed with clouds.
The past has left me caught
With my mind under the shrouds,
Just shadows left behind.

Try as I may to remember,
I'm lost in the valley of dark.
There is only chaos to render
From a mind off a lark,
Just shadow's left behind.

Jerry Eggleston

A New Friend

To anyone who has ever felt
that they live alone in this world

I sit all alone
in my room,
thinking.

There is a dandelion
in the backyard,
swaying.

It's alone, like me,
in the ground,
waving.

We are together now
on the grass,
crying.

I look at it
in my hand,
wondering.

We sit together
in my room,
thinking.

Amara L. Miller

The Reality and the Dream

In constant awe of transcendent wisdom
Self-contractive energies contradict my reputation
Burning away the impurities turns mystery into certainty
Still bathing in the bliss of a promise of eternity
A threshold of a conceptual mind through a veil of confusion
Remains deeply humbled through the threat of temptation
The effervescence of potential pain leaves the heart pristinely empty
Despite the belief in a paradoxical divinity
Lonely with no shadow on which to bestow trust
Knowing no less than being loved is more than enough

Mohan Reddy

I Long to See

I long to see your pretty face
And hold you with a warm embrace.
I long to see your beautiful eyes.
They make me think of the star swept sky.
I long to see your pretty smile.
It gives me the courage to go yet another mile.
I long to see your beautiful hair.
It makes me believe that you're a lady so fair.
I long to see you and hear you say that you'll be my girl
Because then I'll know that I got all that I need in this whole world.

Nicky Dee Leonard

It's Nothing but Grace

Nothing to be added, nothing to subtract,
Grace has nothing to do with us and this is just a fact.

It is nothing that you lend and nothing that you spend,
It is nothing that you hold and nothing that grows cold.

It is there when you feel it, it is there when you don't,
It is there when you accept it and there when you won't!

It is there in the morning, it is there late at night,
It is there when you are on top of your world or in your greatest fight.

It has nothing to do with the cloths that we wear
Or the things that we do without,
It has nothing to do with our appearance,
That is not what grace is all about.

It is nothing that you bring with you
When you kneel at the cross and pray,
But once you accept the Lord Jesus Christ,
Grace will never go away.

Cheryl P. Ellicott

Life's Journey

My journey on this planet Earth
has given me days of happiness and joy,
but then the dark cloudy days roll by with sorrow and deep despair.
On this life's path, briars reach out to my soul and destroy.
Life on this beautiful, peaceful Earth is for a very short time.

How can we make life's journey a treasure?
Plant seeds of kindness, lend a helping hand—let the elastic power
of tiny green sprouting seeds to a rebirth of a special springtime.
Nature's treasures cover this planet:
cerulean blue sky, billowing snowy white clouds,
magical sounds of the ocean water, and the rippling brooks.

The treasure chest has more to share with us.
Flowers of all the rainbow colors, trees covered with green leaves,
and the autumn colors cover the Earth's special nooks.

Look up, enjoy the sun, soft white clouds, blue sky, moon, dark blue
night sky, and the shining stars.
Look around: beautiful flowers, thousands of plants, trees,
waves of the ocean, and the rippling brooks.

Look up and look around and each day will hold happiness
and joy as we travel life's journey.

Ethel M. Shannon

Community

My rock.
My strength in pain.
My support in trouble
The mountain of my confidence
Sisters

Charity Kraeszig

Granddaughter

Fluffy pillow, soft, warm blanket
Lying on the floor is she
Bright blue eyes, smiling face
Fills my life with glee

So small, yet already talented
Grabbing, sitting, seeing
What miracle He again created
Such a special human being

Patricia Masingale

Answer Me

Dignity, respect, disregard, shame
Where am I in this game
Raging, arguments, deceit, pain
There they go at it again
Being me is not so great
Is it love
Or is it hate
Am I their primary concern
My welfare or just who's turn
Is there such a thing as love
Or is it reserved for those in
Heaven above
Did they have it, do they still
Can they get it, I hope they will

A. Enoka

Raindrops

I sit upon my windowsill
Waiting for the unexpected drops.
They fall to the ground
As if they have been hurt,
Or as if they have been torn
From each other to make individuals,
Leaving their home to
Dry up and wither away,
To die as if it were fate.
They live only for a moment.
They feed the bigger things in life
As if they did not matter,
As if they had no purpose
Being on this ignorant planet.

Lauren Claire Calvert

The Kumu

This poem is dedicated to
Kumu Momi Kamahele.

The Kumu willingly shares
Her 'Ike with her Haumana
Her enthusiasm flows
Unabated, unhindered
She takes teaching seriously
Challenging the Haumana
Inspiring them
Nurturing their learning
Encouraging the Haumana
To Ho'opa'a about their own heritage
Leaving her Mana long after
The Haumana leaves the classroom

Melissa L. Allen

Beauty to Behold

Bright warm sunshine rays spray through my window anew,
While outside leaves sparkle like diamonds,
For they have been kissed by the dew.
The tender hush of nighttime has quietly slipped away.
Now birds are singing, so sweetly, their praises to the day.
A breeze is softly stirring as it whispers through the trees.
What a lovely sight to behold as it brings back sweet memories,
Beautiful thoughts of yesteryears and lovely times I have known.
I feel truly blessed, standing here as precious sights to me are shone.
As I look upon these simple wonders, such tender beauty untold,
I ask you to stop a moment, look before you, the serene world behold.

Melissa Hill

the place

the sky lies above us with the ground laid out before us,
the foundation of the place is sand, white sand.
small trees and bushes seem to grow from the piles of sand.
they seem as protrusions from the sandy sides of each pile.
two lanes of road whip around the place wildly;
they follow the path to each end of the place.
the clouds, just playing with the sky, glide through the air.
they take on different forms with each playful move.
entering into buildings, the wiring above is thickened.
different buildings, with different signs take the place of each pile.
cars and trucks take the place of each protrusion from the piles,
leaving with no thought of difference.
the sky lies above us with the ground laid out before us
and extends to the ends of time and imagination.

Eryn Riane McCabe

As a Child . . .

Oh, were I but a child again, were my brain again naïve!
How much I long for simple times, to go back and retrieve

The days I lost to pettiness, to relive them all once more,
For now my soul is dying, the health of my heart poor.

The world at present is so sad; was it always in this state?
When for all you care is happiness, there seems to be no fate.

When I was young, there was no war, no hate, no lust, no crying for
The loved, the lost, the gone; as unseeing as a fawn.

That I was, there is no denial now. But was this not a good thing?
Is not happiness sublime? Might it possibly be worth it?

Unseeing for all time? Are the children more ingenious?
Does their knowledge lie unsaid? Dreams of happiness instead of hate

Nestled in the head?

Courtney Jean Duchardt

Rhythm Of

Moving into the morning,
slow-easy slumber releases me into the languid rhythm
of waking respiration.
Sweet residuals of a lover's words
wistfully recede to their wait.
This day around me is growing . . .
effortlessly weaving a future, relinquishing a past,
and fashioning insinuations anew.
I feel it in this present . . .
in the crisp, fresh, undulating arrival of hope
ushered, cajoled by the miracle of daylight.
I do feel it
in the cooing cadence of a solitary dove in flight,
in the scorched-black of a wicked burn
seared into the soft flesh of my grandmother.
I feel it in the rise and fall of my chest,
in the swaying of my arms as I step,
in the liquid-electric surge hastening through my nomadic soul. . . .
It is always welcomed. It is the rhythm of life.

Lori Helena Talbert

memories all too clear

the web of lies she weaves is thick
the truth is too far away
how her mind works is often sick
her friends are about to stray

her fangs, they sink into your heart
telling you that you can trust
she seems to do it with such an art
that you cannot see her begin to rust

but her mask soon falls apart
and you are left alone
and so the spider has played her part
sucking you down to the bone

Anna Helene Kauffman

Old House

Its doors are all fallen
Its windows are gone
It clings to its hilltop
Forsaken, alone

But still there beside it
A fruited tree stands
Placed there long ago
By its young master's hands

The old tree is still strong
Its fruit fat and sweet
Birds favor it with song
And moss carpets its feet

Laila Lanier Moore

Mistakes

I came home
just to find out you were almost gone.
I sat up in my room
and cried.

I didn't know
how someone could do it.
Do something
like there was nothing to it.

I have thought about it
when things have gotten worse.
Just to end my life
because that would be the best.

I know how we learn
from our mistakes,
but some mistakes
can't be taken back.

April Scheff

Come and Play

Come and play in the sand
Come, my love, and hold my hand
Walk with me through foamy waves
We pick up shells, for me he saves
Run along the sandy beach
Laugh as I tease you just out of reach
Till with breathless wild loving joy
I let you catch your priceless toy
The running was really just a ploy
To get you on the sandy beach
Away from eyes that try to reach
To play together in the sand
To whisper, "Your wish is my command"
And hold to you with loving kisses
To tell you how my heart misses
You, my love, when we are apart
And give the love within my heart

Peggy Ortel

By Any Other Name

Allah, Buddha, God, Jehovah, what is in a name?
They are so very different, still very much the same
Love and truth and brotherhood, they preach this moral code
The path to true enlightenment is not always an easy road
Some follow another path using their God's name
They justify mass murder and the victims get the blame
They cloak themselves in false faith so others will follow their lead
And in the hearts of many they plant an evil seed
Somehow the truth is lost behind their hateful word
The truth that by any other name
The Lord is still the Lord

Lea Anne Wise

Destination Unknown

Some time long ago,
As far back as my memory begins . . .
I began my journey on this never-ending treadmill.
I started at the beginning, and passed "go" over and over again . . .
Only to begin once more, on the path to nowhere.
Sometimes I think, "Surely I can manage to get off!"
But, as I steady myself and prepare to take my "giant" step . . .
I'm knocked back right on to the same old track
Endlessly I journey, waiting for my trip to end,
For the conductor to call out,
"Last stop, Oblivion."

Pauline L. Dante

Untitled

Watching as the sun shines through your hair,
I wonder if any of the light shines for me,
not from the sun, but from your heart.
As your beautiful eyes gleam in the moon's soft glow
they turn and stare,
not looking for answers, but for hope.
Then as your words leave your lips,
I fall in love, for I don't hear words, I hear a song;
a song that draws me close, like the sirens sweet melody in the night.
Every time I touch your face I get an urge,
not sexual, but an urge to kiss you on the cheek
and brush my hand through your soft hair.
When the tear of sadness leaves your face, I will catch it,
but I will not dry your tears.
No, I will hold you close and watch the tear of happiness
leave your eye.
Now, as I hold this incredible girl, beautiful both inside and out,
God looks down and smiles, not for me, nor for her,
but for both of us, for now and forever we are one.

Matthew Michael Lazzara

One Last Prayer

Oh, dear Lord in Heaven, please hear this, a silent prayer,
For this body is so tired, far more than I can bear.
This vessel you have given me has come upon its end.
So, I give it up to you in hopes that you can mend.
My accomplishments in life, so guided by your hand,
I hope I've made a difference; I pray I've helped your plan.
The stories I've had fun sharing, the memories I've left behind,
All things I hope will carry those throughout this trying time.
So in these next few passing days as those I've known come forth,
Please leave them with this message for me, and bless them ever more.
"My Lord has blessed and guided me
Throughout my life's long journey,
So remember not this day in vain, but in your heart my memory,
For life's too short to ponder upon those things we chance to lose.
It's better that we carry on, and carry on in lieu."
And now, oh, Lord, the time has come; I think that I must go.
My eyes are burdened heavily. It's time I think they close.
So thank you, Lord, for a wonderful life, my family, and by friends,
And especially for answering this one last prayer . . . Amen.

David L. McMenamin

Smell of Money

Those who sniff after money
Following the stench of greed
Find no flowery aroma
Will ever come to seed

Instead they will discover
At the end of their foul day
The scent of unhappiness
Blooms in their bouquet

For no peace will blossom
Not on any land
Until the weeds of coveting
Are all pulled out by hand

Angelina M. Frische

Widowhood

I have been waiting
I do not know what for
To get beyond the loneliness
To find that other door

I long for love and miss my past
When love was mine and there to hold
That life is gone and I'm alone
This is the time they say is gold.

Contentment is the goal, they say
Is there really such a place?
My life is full with family and friends
Why does it feel so empty?

Evelyn Rebman

Old Friends and Redwoods

I sit beneath this old redwood tree
and many things cross my mind.
I see natural beauty, unchanging traits,
and strength to endure time.

Visitors stop and gaze in awe,
but they don't plan to stay.
They soon return to their world
with happy memories of the day.

Should the visitors decide to return,
this old redwood still stands here.
It gives them pleasure or needed comfort
and a feeling that someone cares.

Old friends are like this redwood.
Others just always come and go.
A true friend remains the same.
The test of time has proven it so.

Edna B. Carroll

personal

listen closely and far off
in keeping with finite codes
out of skin-lacerating
electric sounds
I am not there in your festivities
with license to nurture
the will of earth in your face
we multiply beyond belief
so please sanctify sanity
deliver us from words that desolate
in instant digressions
from the center know nothing
but elastic duration
the wordless song
seeks company
to explore possibilities
send resumé and photo

William John Helbing

Until

Until a rainbow dances just for you
The past, the future, it connects the two

Until the night owl softly calls your name
And shares his peacefulness in the evening rain

Until a child's gentle laugh and touch
Should remind us of our youth so much

Until the setting sun sheds its last flickering ember into the night
And bring the majesty of God's gift again in the morning light

I will hold you close and share the pain you store
That all these things you will feel once more

Joseph M. Roggenbeck

To Love Someone

Do people really know what it means to love someone?
When you love someone, it is hard to tell someone else that you love them.
For some it means to have you for a short time, then get someone else.
Others think that to hurt you means they love you.
But to very few, it means they will do anything for love.
They will walk through the deepest oceans and through the driest deserts for love.
Then you have some that are out for themselves.
They don't care about whom they hurt or what they break.
There are men that think they know it all,
that they can have it all and still have you to love.
Then sooner or later, they find that they can't have it all and not get hurt.
When it hurts, you know that you are in love.

Alice Bartel

A Place

A place so peaceful, you can't help but enjoy it
Your breath is all you can hear
A place so peaceful you could never fear
It's the place that everyone wishes they could be
But it's only you and me
Grass so soft and green, you just want to feel it between your toes
This place is so beautiful just the way the water flows
There's not a sign of loneliness, not even creeping between the trees
It's the kind of place that makes your heart pound
And weak in the knees
The sun softly caresses my face
"I think I have fallen in love with this place"
If I had to guess what Heaven was like, this is what I'd say
This is where I want to spend my everlasting day

Angela Kaye Stutzman

Angel of Light

Why this exhaustion over my name?
I am the Angel of Light.
I'm the Devil to those ungoverned by self.
I'm the Dark One shining so bright.

Despite what you have set in stone,
"This evil one must be condemned!"
Your shortsighted fear only hurts you worse.
So I ask you, consider, or merely pretend:

First He is the matter, then I am the ether.
If He is the anvil, then I am the hammer.
When He created man, I made man creative.
So why the hell would I rape man's Earth with evil sins and damn Her?

Though it's true, to a point, He and I aren't alike.
We're opposites, yin and yang are we.
He's the Lord of all who walk under the Sun.
I'm inside, individually.

Does this mean I am hate? Oh, no, I am love.
Just as He, but not from on high.
I'm creation, inside each man, woman and child
And without me, your soul would die.

Peter Matthew Coontz

Play of Malaise

We all play the role reversal
It is like identity dispersal
I'll be you for a while
And in my shoes you'll walk a mile

Today I'll be happy or sad
Whatever happens to be the going fad
My emotions are unbeknownst to me
I play the script I see

Actors, we three
Are all forming our history
From our masks we gaze
This play of malaise

Crystal Lynne Pruitt

Would You

would you let me fall on you
if I were the rain and you were a flower
and if I were but a single cloud
and you the endless sky
could I so softly float with you
as the wind tossed me about
and if I were the restless sea
and you the rising moon
would you let me be drawn to you
if you were the sky after a rain
and I the shining sun anew
would you let my light shine through
so I could give a rainbow to you

Rando James Wendt

I Still See

I still see the people
walking about
in the streets
across the city.

I still see the smiles
big and small
from every face
engulfed by the city.

I still see the faces
light and dark
from every walk of life
drowned by the city.

I still see bodies
whole or just parts
bonded with the earth
under the rubble, part of the city.

Brian E. Agnes

Stolen Lamb

Settling mist
Broken wrist
By the ear
Increasing fear

Moving away
Made to stay
Future clear
Death near

Blinding night
Hopeless fight
Falling tear
Trailing blood smear

Dismembered parts
Stops the heart
One so dear
Never again to hear

Chanda Eve Jacobs

The Voice of Love

As I watch the sun set miles beyond the sea,
The clouds of color as I feel the cool breeze.
As I sit upon the rocky shore, I feel the love and joy forevermore.
Not a soul to talk with, no one around, just the sound of water
Crashing against the ground.
As I look upon the sea I feel the love Jesus brings to me.
His voice cries out with a loud roar, "I gave my life for this cruel
And sinful world.
I was placed upon that old rugged cross,
And for this no souls should be lost.
The choice is so simple indeed; all you must do is believe in me.
But walk away and not answer the door and lose the greatest gift
Forevermore."
His plan is perfect so heavenly divine.
Jesus has love that is so wonderfully blind.

Landon Carter

United We All Stand Together

We were all born on that special day happy and free,
No matter what the circumstances might be.
We are all guardian angels of the Lord.
May we all live and love one another.
It doesn't matter because we are all brothers and sisters of the Lord,
There are no color barriers or prejudices.
Learn to love and be kind to each other and our answers will be solved.
Believe and trust in the Lord each and every day.
He is our pilot as our smile quickly grows.
So as you walk down the street today,
Please share your loving smile to each in every way.
Give us all the strength and confidence here and today.
So as I close this happy poem tonight,
A smile or a handshake can be out of sight.
United we all stand together under the Lord's guiding light.

Leonard Donald Pollara

Ribbons of Color

When the clouds move away and the rains fade to a drizzle,
I see ribbons of color in the sky . . .
Red, orange, purple, blue, green, yellow
Red is for the deep love I hold for you
Orange is for the playful and gentle side of you with which I enjoy
Purple is for the spiritual side that allows me to see within your heart
Blue is for the loving friendship that has developed
and the adoration I feel for you
Green is for the adventurous side of you, making me laugh heartily
Yellow is for the happiness you bring into my life each day
You are the rainbow in my life,
keeping me looking forward to each new day
You are the sunshine moving the clouds out of the way
You are my warmth of each new day . . .
My ribbons of color

Kathy A. Newsome

I Am Still Here

I awaken to a sunlit day, my eyes blurry
With the awareness that
I am still here.
How could it be? Could life have meaning even for me?
Yesterday left me defeated my heart torn and bleeding.
How could pain be so long to stay and happiness so fleeting?
The reality of life is no fairy tale I know,
But the hurt others inflict can pierce your
Heart and lay you low.
Yet here I am, another day has come for me.
I am not beaten, there is more of life for me to see.
Outside the sun shines, the bird sings its song.
It comes to me suddenly life is here and then it's gone.
So I'll hold on to my dear life, to the good times and to the strife.
Life is tears and it is laughter and so it will be, forever after.

Cynthia Jane Cantrell

Your Eyes

When I looked into your deep brown eyes
It's when I came to realize
You don't have the same look anymore
Nowhere as intense as it was before

They looked emptily towards me
What is it that they see?
We've both moved on
But now I miss what's gone

Why'd we leave it all behind
Let everything pass us by but time
Pretend the feelings faded away
Was it all worth it anyway

Marni Fara Wasserman

Goodbye

We've been friends for so long,
it seems like forever.
I cry at the thought
that we won't be together.

Best friends for life,
that's what we are.
Best friends for life,
no matter how far.

Goodbye, my friend,
although it is not forever.
Goodbye, my sister,
I guess it is time for us to sever.

Andrea Leigh Betz

Something Inside

I sit and try to figure out
Why you love me so.
There must be something deep inside
That only you must know.

With all my faults and misgivings,
You still love me so much.
I feel it in your tender kiss
And in your gentle touch.

I know how I love you,
A feeling from inside.
A flow, a rush . . .
As the ocean and its tide.

So I'll stop trying to figure out
Why you love me so
Because it comes from deep inside,
And only you must know.

Sharyn Hubert-Blair

Mothers

Mothers are the calm that gives peace
During the most thunderous of storms

They are the strength
When the path of life
Leaves their children weak

They are the light
Shining bright to guide
On the darkest of paths

And the soft breeze
That caresses out hearts
On the worst of days

Mothers are the very heart
Of life and
The definition of love

Happy Mother's Day

Palena

I Want to Be

I want to be the shoulder that you lean on to cry or just to feel comfort.
I want to be the air in your lungs.
I want to be the bounce in your step and the love in your heart.
I want to be the first thing you think about in the morning.
I want to be the last thing you think about before you close your eyes.
I want to be everything you have needed in your life.
I want to be the smile on your face and the twinkle in your eyes.
I want to be your knight in shining armor and your safe harbor.
My God . . . I just want to be.

Herman Manuel Perkins, Jr.

Yearning

The heart is free to love, without care or regard,
For the sweetness that it brings is its own reward.

The head is free to guide, with information found,
But it, too, succumbs when love comes around.

In daylight or at dusk, we feel that which we miss,
Holding hands, the warm embrace, that soft and tender kiss. . . .

It's the downcast head and saddened brow that hides the first sad tear
But the heart is there to reach out, without a care or fear. . . .

Ricardo Alfredo Agustin Llige

Never Again

Into his eyes I'll never gaze again, scent of him does not fill the air.
Sweet smile I will not see again, displaying so much care.
His warmth I'll never feel again, this makes me want to cry.
The way he'd hold me in his arms was fulfillment enough to die.
I pretend to act all cool and calm like this hasn't bothered me a bit,
Yet that fire and desire inside my heart, its flame's no longer lit.
Never has Cupid's arrow caused me so much pain.
My tears will flood the earth, there's no need for rain.
I lie awake till really late, toss and turn in bed.
No matter how very hard I try, his image won't leave my head.
Never again will he pick me up to take me on a date,
Nor will he ever speed me home, ensuring I'm not late.
I try to ignore thoughts of him, but my heart controls my mind.
He's the type of guy one's father approves, a rare and precious find.
There's so much I want to say to him, things that must come out.
But whenever I get the courage to, my mind gets filled with doubt.
I hope I did some good for him, whatever it may be.
The goodness upheld inside of him, I tried to help him see.
I know I should move on and eventually I will . . .
But at this point in time, these feelings really kill.

Shannon Klaft

The Seasons of Our Love

Spring's glorious awakening of new love filled us with an ecstasy
of emotions overflowing and each newfound delight brought
ever tighter blending of ourselves.

The fierce heat of summer's passion, fanned by the flames of
unquenchable desire, melted our separate selves into a unity
of one and our lives, incredibly, became entwined.

Summer's passion gave way to autumn's winds of change and the
storms of desire swept us away less often, but no less intensely,
and we found contentment in the closeness of our soul's rapport
when love was like smooth savory wine, flavorful and full bodied.

Now, with fall upon us and winter's cold embrace not far away,
we must draw upon the heat of summer's passion and wrap
ourselves in the warm blanket of our everlasting love,
trusting that the years of being one will bind us through eternity.

What shall our winter be?
Tender touches, loving kisses, knowing smiles,
cherished memories of the brightest moments of our life.
Caring for each other with the companionship of old friends and lovers,
forever united in undying love.

Ronald Farris

The Seasons

Heat, breaking in waves
Everything is wilting
There is no relief

Golden and brown leaves
They're dropping, falling, dying
Animals prepare

Crisp, white, cold beauty
Individual snowflakes
Cold flows around you

A bud breaking through
Colour emerging slowly
The season of life

Hannah Marie Richardson

Timeless Treasures

Times spent and days shared,
stories told and memories
forever to hold;
laughter, smiles and grins
from ear to ear.
Through the tears, sadness,
and heartaches, you're always near;
The perfect listener and advice giver.
Surely a man with much to admire,
a gift from the stars above is a
man we all love;
A man I like to call,
"My crazy ol' Pops."

Mychelle Magby

A Wish for You

"Twinkle, twinkle little star . . ."
that's how the story goes.
"I wish I may, I wish I might . . ."
a heart that only knows.

For in this simple story lies
a lesson to be learned:
that wishes made are merely dreams,
where deeds are surely earned.

Through misty tears and empty hearts,
I make this wish for you,
so you will know what life is worth,
and empty hearts are true.

And so this story never ends,
my heart again takes flight.
I pray the Lord will grant to you
the wish you wish tonight.

Jerome Acadimia

For My Husband

Passion, admiration
burn in my soul for you.
No other could evoke
such intense devotion.

You saved me from despair,
when love was so aloof.
You filled my emptiness
with compassion and hope.

You restored trust in me
when I thought all was gone,
loved me without restraint
when I felt unworthy.

To utter, "I love you,"
could never seem enough.
You embraced me warmly,
made me alive and new.

Joanne Broadwell McMillan

Ghetto Like Me

In the ghetto it's like Christmas when you go to the grocery store
You use the five-second rule when you drop food on the floor
During the summer, you hold donations to raise money to go to camp
And your only credit is your welfare checks and food stamps
You hardly have any food and even the roaches move away
When you go on a date you use an air freshener as body spray
You can't afford drinking glasses so you wash your plastic cups
When you get discounts sent to you, they're called hookups
You use a hanger wrapped in tinfoil as an antenna on your TV
But your cousin is a cable guy so now you get cable for free
Instead of school you learn from *Sesame Street* and "Hooked on Phonics"
You take English as a foreign language because you only know Ebonics
You use slang like your mom is your bird and a Cadillac is a Cadi
Your friends are your dawgs and your boyfriend is your baby's daddy
Your dryer's broken, so you set your clothes on the fan to dry
You get rejected from VISA, so you use your sister's name and apply
You consider yourself financially challenged . . . not poor
You don't pay your rent until there's an eviction notice on your door
Think about this and you will see . . . how it is to be ghetto like me

William Shane Huggins

Thursday Love

We met at the edge of a midnight dream
His stance—tall and strong as the mighty oak
Skin as smooth as evening satin on the horizon
Lips as soft as the light rain that falls in springtime

About him I oft prayed
That day would not come
That night would not cease
That time would stand still until we left the edge of a midnight dream

Mmm—he opened his arms and welcomed me in
His sensual embrace sealed with a kiss
Longings, passions stirred in our midst
A muffled sigh, the charge of the ram and a silent roar of his fire
Each engulfed, body and mind,
Stroked to the edge of a midnight dream

Still I am bound by his whispers, my body reverberates his desire
The touch of his hand claims all that is his
I rise to give him access to my essence
I breathe in our aroma and wipe the sweat from his brow
In his eyes I am his Nubian queen, the ruler of his heart
True passion is our creation, two hearts and one key
Stepped to the edge of a midnight dream and leapt into love's eternity

Marcia Bonneau

Life Is Not Fair

Why is it that the innocent fall and the guilty always rise?
Why do people discriminate; why do we despise?
Why do the terminally ill live on, while babies die?
Why are our feelings hurt until we are forced to cry?
Why is someone who rapes protected, while the victim is victimized?
Why do we make the same mistakes, no matter how often advised?
Why do people steal; why do people kill?
Do they have a reason or is it just for a thrill?
Why do people tease; why do people fight?
Why are people afraid to leave their house at night?
If this has not yet answered your question to why life is not fair,
Just read the lines above, but, then again, why should you care?
Life is not fair!

Lani Hanna Marie Nielsen

Just a Dance

It was just a dance.
Our bodies entwined,
Swaying to the rhythmic grind.
Twirling us away from defined reality,
Rocking us toward our own immortality.
A magical force controlling our feet.
It was, after all, just a dance.
Wasn't it?

Lois Glenn

Obsession

My mind grows cold and weary,
As lovers pass me by.
For every day without her,
I wake up with hopes to die.

I told her I was sorry.
I admitted I was wrong.
But she left my life forever,
And every second is too long.

So, I've come to a decision,
I'm going to take my life.
I'm watching my last sunset,
As I slowly grab my knife.

Across my wrist, I'm bleeding,
As I stare at the darkened sun.
Then she comes through the door,
My God! What have I done?

Nathaniel Ray Bibee

Skinless

Dedicated to Perry Lee Riepe

Embrace the tendons
and tissue.
I have rendered you
defenseless.
Poked and prodded
until you bled.
Now, you're living
skinless.
Eyes feasting on
every minute
part of you.
Oh, dear,
oh, how I love you
living feeble—
without a shell.
How I feel I know
you now.

Julie Nicole Segura

Behind Closed Eyes

The only time I see you
Is when I close my eyes.
Your arm has one big tattoo
Which doesn't tell any lies.

It tells of a time
About seven years ago.
You committed an awful crime
Because you thought she was a hoe.

You thought you'd get away
With the sh*t that you did.
But now you have to pay
And leave behind your kid.

Life without bond,
Is what the judge said.
You just stood there with no response
And bowed your little head.

I now sit here all alone,
Wondering about how life would be.
But I guess I will never know
Because you took her away from me.

Shannon Marie Casey

Mathematical Juxtapose

She was an obtuse chick,
her legs open 170 degrees.
And that's only when she was drunk on lust
and tequila.
She coached him through their wild romp,
telling him when to shove it in
and when to smooth as sin.
Yet when she kissed him
and uttered the name of another,
his ray became a dashed line,
an unfulfilled equation.
He left her sitting there,
alone in her world full of odds
and lack of evens
while he pursued an escape
into the alternate world of spirituality;
where everything was as coarse as silk,
and made sense like a broken dollar.

Christina Lewis

With an Arm around the Street

The street with me, it has a lot to share:
Scaled-hardship cracked, skin tattooed,
The vagabond's one true care.
Street, with you, I share a black-eyed summer;
With friendships burned, schizophrenic turns,
Still, upon you I discover . . .
Nightly dusk glazing beat-sun charcoal glare,
Oil mumbled, cigarette fumbled.
Street, you're just there, without a care . . .
—tish—My feet step in your champagne puddles
Pothole baptized, cleansing surprise,
With these droplets, shake off the troubles
As I walk your legs as if you are my girl
Relaxing bare, minus underwear,
One slur-blurred head-bummer stops its swirl.
Striking from above, magician lights evoke
Shadow rallies upon film strip alleys
Through desolation smoke, to me something spoke,
and a shot glass full of clarity has awoke . . .
and right now, I'm not so lonely. . . .

Donald Andrew Brown

What Trust Built

I still trust you, Audra.
I removed my testes and gave them to her;
She handed them back to me as her answer.

If she were evil hearted and nuts,
She could have sliced them into cold cuts.

That shows that we trust one and another;
That's even rare between brother and brother.

Audra, this poem is to say I will not stray.
Now that we trust each other, I like to say,

"Yes, I see you're attractive, but it's no use.
I have Audra, so your trying is just time abuse."

Darren Neely

Obsessive and Compulsive

They call me shallow, so unfair.
I bleed honey while wasps wear corn-rows with straight hair.
I was raised here, and then I was born . . .
Now I judge and run from where I would have conformed—
burying clichés and mangling my baby pictures,
obsessed with imaginary barrels aiming at my mirror's whispers
A porno-palegic, my loneliness has turned to calluses.
My canker sores were panicked chap-lipped fallacies
I shave my head to avoid going bald.
I juggle balls in boredom cough.
"Go away, dwarfs! Forty fortunes formed will fall,
forty fortunes formed will fall . . .
I don't see dwarfs. I don't see dwarfs."
These are hollowed thoughts I bare.
They call me shallow, so unfair.

Allen Jason Alvir

sammy

sammy was a good girl, till she met you
school was always first, and drugs were not cool
how you changed all that, we still don't know
how are good little girl turned into your hoe
what did you say, that she believed so much
that she'd take the pain from your evil touch
what did you do, to make her want to stay
that she never called home and played your stupid games
how did you do it, change her mind like that
how did you do it, so we can change her back

Danielle Marie Comerford

Weird

To hide my soul, I slip inside
looking at life before I die,
going over all my actions,
all reality losing traction.
Lying still on the cool ground,
my blood is spilled from his shotgun round.
Unable to move, just able to wonder
what I did, while slipping under.
I didn't know this kid,
and still lying asking what I did.
Just making my way to take the test,
he put the barrel right to my chest.
Slowly looking up and meeting his eyes
he smiles back at me saying, "Goodbye."
I feel the blow and it rocks my head back.

Brian Edwin Luebbert

Drowsy Past

Lost in the past with no memory to speak of
Souls shattered by betrayal and heartbreak
Minds shaken by confusion and sin
Purple monsters in car wheels chasing you at two in the morning
Bikers calling you two cent wh*res
Don't go to sleep
Don't let her pass out
Walls covered with empty hearts, cold and lost
Come through the window, it'll be open
You don't belong, you aren't good enough
Get out now
I can't breathe, there's something in my throat
Sin, like a forbidden fruit that draws you in
Leaves you lost in the clouds
There's no way back . . . you're gone forever
You're soul turned cold
I don't know who I am anymore

Ariana Nicole Eitrem

Taking of Innocence

As I see you cry, your thighs smeared with blood,
Who has taken your innocence?
Who have you told?
Who has scarred you for life?

You are barely six years old!
What crime has been done?
What creature can harm their own?
Only man, who prides himself with having reason,
But in reality it is he who is a beast!

As I see you cry, I feel your pain.
I feel the ripping of your flesh.
I wish I could protect you.
I have been there.
I too have cried with humiliation.

Monica Dimey

The Peter Pan Syndrome

Have you noticed half the men in the world
are part of the Peter Pan population?
They all have their Wendy's
with their Tinkerbells on the side,
running to play pirates with their Captain Hooks,
ogling at the mermaids who gather and swarm,
creating orgies around them.
They have become asinine, only caring for one thing . . .
not wanting Wendy to find out about Tinkerbell,
or Tinkerbell to find out about the mermaids
until they appear on Jerry Springer and all hell breaks loose.
I have noticed this and no longer wish to be
the Wendy who picks up, cleans up, and f*cks up all the time.
I don't want to be Tinkerbell and flutter around.
I don't want this . . . this fairy tale,
but it's not a fairy tale if you
look at it . . .
It is life.

Stephanie Ann Young

Lafayette Escadrille

My body was shaking.
We stood staring at each other.
What a glorious beauty I would be riding,
No, I would be driving this fox.

I climbed in and sat down.
My inmates took a look around.
My hands were hot with sweat,
And as I took off, the seven of us laughed.

Now, we've been here for only a short while,
And four of the originals and eleven replacements
Are gone; they were killed.
This beauty did not protect them.
It let them down.
Why, Lafayette, why did you let them die?

I remember the time
When I flew through the sky
With clouds fluffy
And with only blue in my sight.
Why did I not die?
Why my inmates and not I?

Laurel Palluzi

Dying

I scrape and cut at the skin to get rid of pain
Or at least over shadow the internal with something external
I look up at you standing over me
My eyes terrified
My body trembling
You stand over me with power
I am nothing
To you I am nothing
And I am nothing
I wish you would beat me or take my life
I don't want to wake up in the morning
Look in the mirror and not know who I am
Who I could have been
I pray to God, "Take my life"
I lie in bed waiting to die
I try to take my own life but I am rescued
But from what? Death? I am already dead.
You have taken my life and left me with this
A broken body, a shattered soul
And no hope

Jessica Lucidity

Angel

The other day, I do declare,
I saw an angel, honest! I swear!
He might've been an answer to a prayer.
I shook my head so I could clear
my thoughts of admiring his rear.
He smiled, rubbed my cheek with his hand,
and suddenly I began to understand.
Fate is the idea of what life has planned,
goes only so far, and we must choose
the right path is only ours to lose.
I paused to ponder the thoughts in my head.
I might not know where each path led,
but blame myself for my choices instead
of blaming someone else for what I do,
so I have no excuse to give to you.
I scream, and all at once I do wake
and wipe my brow with a hand which shakes.
I shrug in the sheets a little more,
roll to my side, and begin to snore.
Out the window, my angel does soar.

Tracy Lynn Shadley

I Cut

The cut, the pure pain;
Now that I'm in control, I cut.
So much better than the emotional state;
No control.
The cut, the pure pain;
Now that I'm in control, I cut.
So much better than the bleeding of the soul;
The bleeding of the body,
All control.
The glinting knife cutting through the flesh;
The pain that is controlled.
The bitter cold tears streaming down my face;
A pain not collared,
A pain not leashed.
The cut, the pure pain;
Now that I'm in control, I cut.

Tarrah Lei Stenros

Remember When?

Happy baby cookie monster sounds,
Racing rumbling toy cars,
A delicate mother's nipple that I don't remember.
I can say that I scrambled up leathery
Cherry tree bark and dug a mud pit to China.
Then the neighbor girl stuck her tongue
In my mouth. My first kiss that I remember.
I can say I remember when he touched me
In the room under the stairs. That sweaty
Summer nakedness smell and the musty books.
Hearing the five o'clock news while he whispered,
"We need to be quiet."
I can't say how innocence felt;
I don't remember ever feeling it.
I escaped sexual thoughts in glowing 5 a.m. mornings
When I peeked at snow through my window.
My silence was a dam fought by the words behind it,
As if not saying them would keep them from being true.
Instead I said: "Make me a straight Christian man with no impurity,"
Dreams of words untwisting reality.

Paul Timothy Conrad

Perfect Guy, Think Again

He broke my heart and made me cry
Who would have known that he told lies
He said he cared and would always be mine
Who knew he'd play anyone for a little sixty-nine

I really should have seen the signs
He never called or asked me out
I should have known the entire truth
My friends they said he lies and cheats
I said, no, he's true and sweet
Little did I know he'd break my heart

Nastasha DeJesus

Knife on the Table, Pen in My Hand

Once I felt bliss
it was in your kiss
but now I am empty
No longer do you fill me
and I am bawlin'
'cause I have fallen

You've left me so bent
with no place to vent
Now I hold steel
hoping to feel
Skin scars red
I'm alone in the end

All of those feelings from before
have left me wanting so much more
Once you made me complete
Now I sit lost in defeat
Knife on the table pen in my hand
with all of this pain unable to stand

Josh Arner

Brayilagha!

My fair one, what did I ever do to deserve you;
To have you as mine and to have someone
So dainty and sweet brood over me, wish me well,
And shower such pure love on my craggy male body?
What did I ever do to earn such unalloyed affection;
To have someone so lovely and true care for me,
Ready to do what it takes to please me, to take away my sorrow
And the pain of life's many traumatic blows that left me
All bloodied and deserted by friends and foe alike?
What did I ever do to have you soothe my face with your
Luscious lips; gazing into me with your big, innocent eyes—
Unflinching, unblinking, unperturbed by my masculine
Eagerness and lack of control.
My sinewy, scabrous brawn are calmed by your softness
and resilience so velvety.
What did I ever do to earn your trust that you give yourself
Over to my care and control for even a moment in time;
To share so completely with your very being,
Your body entwined with mine, seamlessly gliding
Into a blissful union with all that is harmonious in nature—
Throbbing, pulsating, heaving, sighing, thrusting, moaning passionately.

John Chike Onyido

Chocolate

I plunge the smooth, rich, creamy chocolate bar in my mouth,
savoring each moment as my tongue slowly rolls
against it back and forth,
tasting each delicate coating one stroke at a time.
Complete ecstasy consumes my body
as the steady sucking continues.
I bite down, saliva and chocolate running together
through my mouth and sliding down my throat.
A sweet burning sensation follows,
tracing my throat in an alignment of heat.
My body silently quivering in delight.

Kendra Karen Elrod

Blue

You and I,
we are like two Japanese fighting fish
caught in the same bowl.
We are like Little Blue in our kitchen,
sometimes chasing his own reflection
when he comes too close to the glass. Flaring up his gills,
he transforms from
Little Blue
to Fighter Blue,
so vibrant, animated,
so beautiful when he's angry.
Then the welcomed calm: our arms sliding over and around each other,
tears subsiding,
in the salty warmth of our bodies.
We sleep
more calmly,
after the storm.

Amy Louise Loder

Raindrops

As I look out my window, I see the rain falling
It makes me start to think about life
And the people in my life
Each raindrop is like one of my loved ones
No matter how small or how big
Every one is important
The raindrops splashing on the ground
Make me realize that friendships can easily end
Taking the time to keep them together is important
After the rain stops, the bright
And shining sun comes out from behind the clouds
Just like after disputes, things can and will get better and brighter
The sun is a symbol of how much life can bring you if you let it
The sun makes me smile and that smile is the most essential part of life
Remembering that life, friends, and family are incredible
And cherishing them in so crucial
I now know that taking the time to let your mind
Just think is so necessary at times in your life
How amazing it is that such trivial things can remind you of life
And how they remind you that life is so precious

Joanna Rabiej

My First Love!

When I look into your eyes
I see the symbol of love,
For the first time ever in my life.
When you look into my eyes
You just see a friend . . . right?

Ever since day one I felt something
Different and strange.
It was love to a tee.

Now what I want to know
Is will you ever feel
That same way . . .
Towards me?

Alyssa Julia Eckman

Just a Dream

I lost things I thought I had;
I know things are meant to change,
But this change doesn't feel right.

Something should be different.
I wish I knew what should be different;
If I knew what should be different, I would change it in a heartbeat!

If it would be changed, my friends would be happy
And everything would be normal again,
But I know it is just a dream.

Nikki Zach

Forever More

Eyes closed
Lips touch
Bodies so very close
But not as close as our hearts
Forever in your arms
I shall always be
When ever you need love
You'll always have me
Your eyes set me at ease
You're the one who has the keys
The keys to my heart
So you'll know I'll always be yours
For now and forever more

Cheyenne Rose Kulacz

Salvador

With an artichoke smile
hidden beneath the spider-leg shadow
of your mustache,
you sparkle us
with your surreal pupils.
Tucking yourself
behind gala
like a child
you hide and play.

The first strokes of your brush
are as rough as the shells
of the sea urchins
that fill the belly
of your love
and dry on the boat's silver deck
cooking like grasshoppers
in the sun.

Lorayna Hamann

A Feng Shui Kiss

My house has mandala windows,
folding chairs that do not unfold,
water that is running faster
than the wind through the keyholes,
a kitchen that is cooking instead of me.
I have no radio
instead the walls speak out loud.
The rooms are fully empty
except for the pinches of salt
in the corners—
memories of the seas
that used to cover the mountain
i see from the balcony.
There is no one in the house
except for the voices
that come uninvited
when the windows yawn aloud.

Gordana Podvezanec

The Release of Soul

At down when I hear the sound of sweep
My spirit needs to wake up and weep
I see myself alone on that time
I confess how many times I do crime
Now I want to break the cage
This cage is my age
I must go and fly to the Heaven
And farewell to my life forever

Yasamin Memary

Shooting Star

I sometimes sit and wish
That I could be a shooting star
And dart your way, catch your eye
Make a wish as I go by
To fill your wish is my desire
To know your heart within this hour
Would light the sky in such a way
That you would know my love is true
You are for me and I am for you
Forever

Robbin Dillingham

Nature's Splendor

As I was strolling
Along life's pathway,
I heard a beautiful robin sing.
Its melody was so very sweet;
It made me pause
And rest my feet.

On farther down
The lane I strolled,
And to my surprise,
A squirrel drolled.
And in his paw he
Clutched a nut;
Then up a hickory tree
He quickly jumped.

Then from my stroll
I did observe
Other sights of Nature's Earth.
From birds to bees and
Squirrels to trees,
These made me alert to nature's scenes.

Betty Ann Bilbrey

Wait

I think about you every day,
even though I often pray.
How you could be here,
willing to stay?

I want to be with you,
but I know it is wrong.
I know you'd feel like
you don't belong.

A couple more years
you'd have to wait
before I become
your permanent mate.

I have a future ahead of me,
but right now it's blurry
and I can't see.

So please wait,
I'm not in a hurry.
If you love me,
then you're not to worry.

Heather Nicole Butler

the lights in new york

the lights in new york,
can you see them anymore
two piles of dust on the street
they used to be two buildings
standing up tall
then two planes come crashing
and the building sadly falls

Maggie Tucker Blunk

Desires of My Heart

The desires of my heart may be lost,
but only one can revive them.
That one kneels before me,
touches more tender than a mother's,
more care given to each caress.
Heart in turmoil, what should I do?
Help me.

Nicole L. Ackerman

American

For I am an American
Red, white, and blue
War after war
We always stick it through
Faithful families joining us today
For we stand for freedom
Slaves, no way!

Lauren Elise Taylor

When I

When it rains, you keep me dry.
When I am cold, you keep me warm.
When I am hot, you cool me down.
When I am hungry, you give me food.
When I am thirsty, you give me water.
When I am scared, you comfort me.
I love you and only you, Mom.

Kelli Grace Ann Mullins

A Flight for Sour Hearts

A swirling blue,
a secret sign,
we're in the air
and we can fly!
It's but a dream,
and not real,
but as it seems
it's what we feel.

Ann Marie Mohrmann

Sound Electric

Electric guitar, drums, and bass;
All down in the basement,
Waiting to show their face.

Strings at the ready,
Sticks held high;
The first beat is going to fly.

Microphone steady,
Amp turned up loud,
The first chord is hit;
Vibrations abound.

The play goes three minutes or four;
When the last sound has stopped,
You are shaken to the core.

Lorri W. McElroy

Last Words

Struggled life in vain
No promise eases pain
A conundrum faced
For God's saving grace
Starlit skies above
To midnight love
Reflective depth
And one last breath

Jason Scott Britton

here i lay

alone and untouched
blue as the sky and as cool as ice
here i lay
here i lay
silently sleeping
oh, how i look nice
here i lay
here i lay

Steph Shauna Smythe

No Greater Fortune

No fortune in life
Is greater in worth
Than to have a loved one
Around on this Earth.
No possession, no riches,
Can ever compete
With a loved one who's dear
With a heart kind and sweet.

Hamza Khan

Brotherly Love

Many times the things we do
Aren't just for us, but others too
Often the things we say
Will help someone along life's way
So think a moment before you speak
Be careful what you say in jest
You might disturb another's rest
All of us can show more love to others
After all we all are brothers

Janice E. Moore

He Whispered in the Wind

Just another star-filled night,
mountains reaching up to touch.
Too many things filled my head,
like who and where and such.

I couldn't find the beauty
right up above my eyes,
there were too many questions
and deep, emotional sighs.

Suddenly, I was filled
with all the questions in my mind,
where and who would answer,
things must be defined.

An eagle soared above me,
a messenger in flight;
here is where I would learn
all I could tonight.

I felt my spirit lifted high,
the cleansing, for I had sinned.
I flew up with the eagle
to hear God whisper in the wind.

Sandra E. Beguhn

Frowns

It's tough being a teen.
She looked over,
Dark and dreary,
She sounded small and frail,
But looked healthy as ever.
Unhappy,
But why?
She smiled once,
Bright and beautiful,
Turned and frowned once more.
Always frowning
Dark and dreary frowns.
Sad,
But why? She had everything.
Why is she frowning?
Dark and dreary,
Frowning,
Unhappy,
Sad,
But why
Always, always frowning?

Leah Marie Renner

My Mother

When I think of my mother,
wonderful thoughts come to mind,
like the way she helps others
and always strives to be kind.

She's been through so much
in all of her years,
but never turned against God,
though she's shed many tears.

She tried hard to stay strong,
even when she felt broken.
Through the sweet grace of God,
he answered prayers softly spoken.

Mom has the strength and the love
that only God can provide.
She passed onto her children
God's word, love, and pride.

So when you ask, "What is a mother?"
A virtuous woman is the best,
and that's definitely my mother,
for she's been tried and passed the test.

Melinda Petty

What's a Mother?

Mother gave me life,
then gave me away.
Where have I gone,
what did I do wrong?
It couldn't be so horrible
to take me from my home.
I don't understand
I'm only three.
Please, oh, please,
where is my mommy?
Another house, still not my home.
My brothers and sisters are here,
I'm no longer alone.
Was I a mistake, not meant to be?
God wouldn't do that . . . would he?
I am grown and now I see
my mama didn't make me,
but made me who I am;
that, I would never change.
I grieve every day in my own way
for the woman who loved me
and never thought to give me away.

Shelley J. Gillespie

City Experience

Avenues echo icy wind blasts—
Mournful tribute to petulant leaves
Prancing round the feet of
Young love waiting.

Mad drivers wheeling
Old women reeling
Urgent sirens wailing
Anxious love waiting.

Afternoon breeds night
Night breeds confusion
People profusion
City's illusion
My delusion—
Just waiting.

From shadows' obscurity
Wrapped in immaturity, I watch—
Cold, yet still waiting.
Though you do not see me
I see you, smiling—
Holding her hand.

June Maureen Hitchcock

A Free Soul

We're in a world of make believe,
Not knowing how to act.
Should we be willing to deceive,
Or should we just have tact?

I've always tried to be myself
With folks both rich and poor,
Never putting feelings on a shelf
Nor sinking them to the floor.

We all were born as equals.
We can't try to outdo
Others by the use of quells.
To ourselves we should be true.

Following bad examples
By bowing down to those
Who make others feel not ample
Is a life that some have chosen.

Making others feel real great
Is how our lives should be.
It's easy to infuriate,
But let your soul be free.

Christine E. Vincent

Ponder

As I sit and ponder,
I wonder where you are.
You've been gone for hours.
I guess she must live far.

As I sit and ponder,
I wonder what's on your mind.
She must be worth a great deal
to get this much time.

As I sit and ponder,
I feel the pain release.
I'm sure these sleeping pills
will soon bring me relief.

As I sit and ponder,
I feel so tired now.
I think maybe the whole bottle
was going way too far.

As I sit and ponder,
I slowly fall asleep.
I wish you had come home sooner,
so I'd not be deceased.

Deborah Elaine Gill

Thank You, Mom

Even though the end has come,
I'm grateful that we've had some fun.
You gave me laughter.
You gave me joy.
You gave me sunshine,
And, oh, boy
You gave me so much
That I fear
We won't have time to sit and hear
All there is to say.
But trust me, I'll reward you some way.
You gave me love.
You gave me bread.
Somehow you kept a roof over our head.
I love you, Mom.
Please don't change.
I like you, even though you're strange.
Sometimes you may've embarrassed me,
But I'm sure that we feel it mutually.
All now that there is left to say
Is thank you, Mom, in every way!

Brittany Nichole Williams

Ambition

Nothing harder to control
Than ambition of one's soul

Holding the reigns
As not to strain

Productivity and imagination
That improve a situation

Melding words and fact
Into a message with tact

Ever-changing surroundings
Making life less compounding

Relieving one's stress
By organizing the mess

Hold tight for the ride
Ambition has great stride

Leaps and bounds
Bring reality to the ground

Ambition is the key
Unlock your mind and see

Bret Zieman

Monkey Caesar

I still have the darkest blanket.
I will hide my thoughts from yanking.
Make it dirty, even bank it,
Wind still gives the wing for monkeys.

Wind of saving,
Wind for freedom,
Surf the raving,
Paint the widow.

Make the color like a rainbow.
Let the rabbit draw a long bow.
Vatic hands in empty bowls
Setting fortune by the scores.

All decisions can be broken.
Health of heart, the only token.
Souls always look for holes
And just thoughts you'll find at goal.

Wind of thoughts,
Thoughts are freedom.
You were taught,
Monkey Caesar. . . .

Nina Zaretskaya Long

silence

beseeching the moment
trapped
unable to sustain
pleasures
of the moment

caring and unsure
deliberation of thoughts
outcry comes
uncertain yet
truthful

shattered to pieces
my quiet calm
no moreover expecting
the lack of broken
tantalization of dreams

timely
yearning
anticipating
to shatter what is
inaudible to us all

Eric M. Renaud

Standing

In the middle of a crowd
at the top of my lungs, screaming.
If one person heard,
I would be dreaming.

I'm standing here
right in front of you,
but you have places to go
and things to do.

If I whispered soft,
would you hear?
Would you even know
that I was near?

'Cause I'm standing here
right in front of you,
but you don't see me.
You stare right through.

I'm standing here
right in front of you.
Yes, standing right here,
right in front of you.

Diana K. Lanhart

If She Said Yes

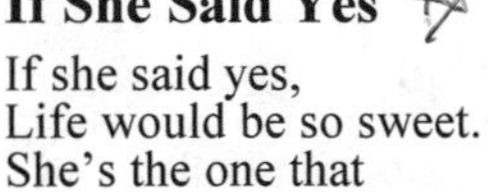

If she said yes,
Life would be so sweet.
She's the one that
Makes my life complete.

If she said yes,
Two would become one,
Joined by a bond
Ne'r to be undone.

If she said yes,
She'd answer my prayers.
She's my everything,
My hopes, dreams, and cares.

If she said yes,
My soul would sigh,
That simple word,
A gentle lullaby.

If she said yes,
She would be my wife.
I'd pledge myself;
My heart, soul, and life.

Garett Christopher Relph

I'll Always Be There for You

Every day I think of you
I wonder if you think of me.
I'll always remember you,
but will you remember me?
I'll treasure you in my heart and soul,
even if you're far or near.
Wherever you go, whatever you see,
I'll still be in your mind,
and you'll find me in your soul.
I'll be there when you need me
protecting you,
guiding you,
encouraging you.
I'm important in your life.
When you need love, I'll give you love.
Seeing you glum and really blue
makes me catch the winter flu.
So be cheerful
and don't be sad,
although being sad is not too bad.

Putri Matahari

When I Look Out

when I look out my little window
out on to the open sea
I see the boats out in the harbor
they shine their twinkling lights at me

when I look out my little window
the lighthouse light is what I see
guiding boats away from danger
steering them out toward the sea

when I look out my little window
right before I go to sleep
I wave at all the little tugboats
then I go and count some sheep

when I look out my little window
as I wake up right at dawn
I say good morning to the lighthouse
even though his light is gone

when I look out my little window
I look as far as eyes can see
I see the whales and little dolphins
leaping in the deep, blue sea

Jessica Danielle Moxley

What's Done Is Done

Open you heart,
stretch out your arm.
Here you will be
safe from harm.

Hold on to what's right.
You can't go wrong.
Believe in tomorrow,
hold on, stay strong.

Forgetting nothing,
it's now all clear.
Behind your eyes
I see what you fear.

No more mourning,
hold your chin up high.
No more reasons now,
you don't have to cry.

The bad times have passed.
There are only good times to come.
You can't change the past,
what's done is done.

Jessica Joy Moran

Before Us

Shortcomings make me drowsy
I'd better move
Before my mind gets too cloudy
She's right in front of my face
But I'm worlds away

Let's say a part of me becomes us
For you and me I was late
Before time even began
Oh, and if you don't laugh that much
I still promise the most love

Short comings keep me awake
I'd better move
Before I start to break
She's right in front of my face
But I'm worlds away

Let's say a part of me becomes us
For you and me I was late
Before time even began
Oh, and if you don't laugh that much
I still promise the most love

Kris Kenneth Wagner

Starting Over

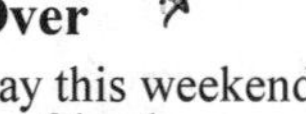

We went away this weekend,
leaving not as friends.
Our relationship we needed to mend
because it was at its end.

We didn't really say much
until the second day and night.
Then again I felt your touch
and all I wanted was to hold you tight.

The talk we had helped me out
and made me understand
some things that I had in doubt
and questions I've had at hand.

You said you still had feelings for me
and that you still care.
This I now see,
it's a feeling we both share.

It is a big relief for me
that our friendship isn't at an end
'cause I will always and forever be
in love with you, my friend.

Shanna L. Paulsen

With Angels

Where clouds never end
Where the sun's always high
Where light can bend
There, with angels, you lie

Where the air is soft
Where spirits all fly
Where laughter's aloft
There, with angels, you lie

With oceans endlessly deep
With the absence of shrill cry
With souls in peaceful sleep
There, with angels, you lie

With the best of the best
With the ones He couldn't deny
With all of the rest
There, with angels, you lie

When my time is through
When I no longer ask why
That's when I'll be with you
And there, with angels, we'll lie

Anna Catherine Panico

The Cape

To Miss Leigha, for sharing in one of my most precious memories

Ocean before me.
Sky above me.
Sand beneath me.
Candles flicker and fight
the chill of October's wind,
cascading shadows over the
blankets of my makeshift tent.
I am warm. My heart smiles here.
I visit often,
for a memory's journey is never far.
I go to this place where
loneliness fades with the setting sun.
I draw comfort and strength
under the moon's beauty
in the company of stars.
I laugh and shed tears
for hopes, dreams;
my moments of sweet silence
where thoughts have no words.

Kathleen A. Winter

Roots

I traveled English countrysides
with hope that I might find
some trace of where we started;
of those who we left behind.

From town to town in careful search
of those who bear my name.
Perhaps I'll find just one or two
of English historical fame.

From Kent I went to Suffolk;
Norfolk with hope that tale enfolds.
From place to place I traveled 'round
between the sea and wolds.

North to York, my journey went
where Viking warriors came;
traveled west until I found
a town that bore my name.

From Dover, north and to the west,
where lies the Irish Sea,
I carried Romans, Danes and Swedes;
All a part of me.

Frederick O. Colby

Feelings

Here come some feelings
They are coming to my heart
These I show on my face
Some make me smart

God gave me feelings
So that I would be alive
He was so very right
Though I still sometimes strive

What are feelings made for
They're made for expression
They pull all lives together
So we all have intentions

Showing all our feelings
Is part of God's great plans
Now we can show all expressions
That's why He's our greatest fan

Feelings are important
No matter where we go
We could be on Earth
Or maybe even Pluto

Marissa Hassee

Love

Love is like a red rose
They both come and go
Sometimes they last long
Sometimes they don't

Love can make you happy
Love can make you sad
Love can make you feel
Very, very bad

Real love is very true
Only one can love you
Love is not a game
Love is not a name

Love is special
Love is true
Love is old
Love is new

Love is like a red rose
Sometimes they last long
Sometimes they don't

Tara L. Boseman

The Attacks

As we go on with every day life
And hear about it more
We know that deep within our hearts
Not one of us wants war

As the firemen turn to heroes
As we watch the news and cry
We feel hate turn to sorrow
As we pray for those who've died

As we stare at the rubble
Our minds filled with disbelief
We remember more than ever
That we can't give into grief

So, we pray for all the widows
And victims of the attacks
And when we walk the open streets
We always watch our backs

So, now in conclusion,
What I'm trying to say
Is that we must appreciate our lives
For they can end any day

Laura Marie Alexander

Do You Love Me?

Do you love me?
Don't tell me, show me

With a single flower
From a meadow or a flower bed
Show me

By your eyes lighting up
When I enter the room
Show me

By forsaking all others
And loving me only
As the Bible says
If you love me, don't shut me out
Talk to me

For communication is love
As we walk together
Through our Golden Years
I will show you my love
And if I go before you
Keep my memory forever
For I will be remembering you

Sue Long

Faded Memories

I snuck into their lives
A shadow on the wall
Everywhere yet nowhere
No substance, none at all
My existence was fleeting
Here then not
Was I of importance
No, not a lot
Why was I there
I do not know
Was I ever really needed
No, I think not so
I exited their lives
The same as I had entered
Not leaving a mark
Not being remembered
I snuck out of their lives
The shadow is faded from the wall
Is my absence noticed
No, not really
No, not at all

Donna Marie Simon

A Touch of God

A sunrise, a sunset,
Colors so bold;
Gentle thoughts, warm hearts,
Gifts of gold;

Butterflies and rainbows,
A creation of expertise;
Joy, hope and laughter
To share and to keep.

Flowers, bubbling brooks,
Mountains galore;
Serene and calm,
Everlasting more.

The oceans, the forests,
The universe outside;
All people united,
Far and wide.

Peace is ours,
Love is the way;
Showered in blessings,
As we kneel to pray

Carole A. Lange

My Paradise

I sat atop the highest hill
And watched the sun go down
Heard the cry of the whip-poor-will
As the darkness settled round

Tears well up within my eyes
There's an ache inside my heart
Whenever I think of you and
Because we had to part

I walked down the hill
With the wind in my hair
Past the fruit trees in bloom
Smelled the sweet smell in the air

When my life here is through
If my restless spirit can come back
This is where I'll wait for you
Upon this hilltop high

We will walk the same old paths again
Beneath a blue, blue sky
We'll sit beneath the pines once more
Upon this hilltop high

Arline Baumgardner

life

a wildfire
in all life's fire

glowing, burning, sparkling

through every moment
of
hardship and joy

a wildfire
through the journey
inside, outside ourselves

a wildfire
leading further
to
distant goals not yet seen

a wildfire
of
sharing higher spheres

in
ecstasy of life

Anders Sufi Blomdahl

Midnight Sun

I stare up at the midnight sun
And wonder where my life has gone.
I wonder what my life will mean
When it's time for me to die.

Who will give my eulogy?
What will people know of me?
Of the people close to me,
Who will care and who will cry?

This the story of my life.
A lot of pain, a lot of strife.
A lot of love and happiness.
See the story in my eyes.

A legend I'll have built for me,
A dream come true or two or three.
My life's goal will be complete
When it's time to say goodbye.

Happiness will come to me
And I'll leave this world in peace.
To those of you who'd mourn for me,
Rejoice and look up towards the sky!

Jeremy L. Simpson

Anticipation

Time is drawing near
My life is going to chance
I don't know what to expect
I just know the pain will end

I've lived with this pain for so long
It has brought me down so much
But I think I will have a new pain
That is much more tolerable

I know I will feel sad
And definitely scared
I may even feel lonely
Or sometimes irritable

Whatever I feel
Will be much less painful
Than experiencing pain
Day after day

So, God, please give me strength
To get me through this time
So I can finally live my life
And truly shine

Lisa R. Friedman

Perfection

This is for my inspiration, my pillar,
and my true best friends.

I know.
I know I'm not perfect,
Not even near.
I'm me, not you,
Or who you wish I would be.
My idiosyncrasies, my loves,
My me's.
Please,
Love me for who I am.
Don't judge
Because I try to love.
No one, not you,
Not even the blue unknown is
Perfection.
Nowhere to be found
Is there anything
Which becomes perfect.
If you please,
Be yourself.

Laura Lynn Butkus

Night of Sapphires

As we stand in the pale moonlight
At the center of a large meadow,
I look into your sapphire eyes
And my heart should melt.

The stars in the sky,
Our guardians.
The dark trees in the distance,
A calling.

With each failing step
The dry leaves crackle
As if they, too,
Call our names.

The air of the crisp autumn night
Fills our nostrils
And reminds us so well
Of a time long ago.

A cold wind blows from the south
And I pull you closer to me.
Looking into your sapphire eyes,
My heart did melt.

David Ian Clerget

A Poem to a Friend

Thank you for being you
Never afraid to show
To me who you truly are
What others do not know

You're a masterpiece
A true work of art
Putting on an act in public
But I've seen through to your heart

Why you do this
I unmistakably know
You are too afraid of what they'd say
If you let your real self show

Even if they didn't like you
Since you're different than the crowd
I will stand beside you
And I won't be anything but proud

As I said before
Thanks for being true
Even if it's only me
I can't stop loving you

Brittany Marie Proudfoot

Never Rest

I will not rest.
I will not die!
I will do my best.
I have to try
to reach the top,
to win this war
because it's my life
I am fighting for.

The pain is worth
the price I've paid
because I'll be free,
in one more day.
Just one more step
that I have to trod,
I'll do it all
with the help of God.

So never rest,
that's what I say
because freedom is just
one step away.

Jason Erik Palmer

Dying

Lying in the living room,
gasping for breath,
Grandma is bearing
the process of death.

It is hard to stand there
while someone dies.
Your head is spinning
while your heart cries.

Gathered in a circle,
tears streaming down your face,
huddled all together
in one saddened embrace.

Joy and memories flow,
along with laughter too.
We all wonder,
now what's to do?

Still to this day,
tears come and go.
Her smile will always be there,
we'll always love her so.

Brandi Alepuamaikalani Freitas

Out of Ashes

Out of a clear blue sky they came,
Those implements of death.
They pierced into our buildings,
Into our very breath.

Towers crumbled, fire roared,
From the rubble black smoke poured.
Across the entire nation, we paused,
Gasped, incredulous, and prayed.

Fast to others' aid they came.
With hearts and hands they gave
Beyond thought of their own safety,
Beyond thought of their own pain.

Talk of war was quick to start,
But in our deepest heart of hearts
We found mercy dwelling there,
Along with justice's darts.

We deal with terrorists as we must,
But to the innocent in need
Let us give . . .
And rise above the dust.

Anna Stone Borgquist

A Lucid Moment

With raven-black hair
That flows in the night's soft winds
And eyes deeper than the sea
Your warm heart opens
And your soul-clenching arms
Bring me to fall at your feet

The words of my mind
Come from the dark halls
In which I dwell
The sun rays fall
And the moon shall climb
To kiss the sky above

In pure ecstasy

Nathan Adam Matz

Darkness

Lying on the bathroom floor,
Waiting.
Waiting for the light to come.
Thinking and wondering,
Why?
Why anyone would overdoes,
Just to kill themselves?
With all the pain,
I now want to live,
Not die,
But every thing is fading out.
Dark,
Darker,
Darkness.

Brittany Mariah Wegwerth

My Love, My Love

My love, my love, I wait for you
Like morning waits for drops to dew
To melt within the morning sun
And signify the day's begun
Like ocean tides to ebb away
Like nightfall waits to end each day
I wait like spring to end the cold
Of winters frozen vice-like hold
Within my memories I save
The times we had, the love you gave
Have no regret, is all I plead
I give my love, I show my need
Forgive me, but my need is true
My love, my love, I wait for you

Edward Philip Curtis-Bird

Infinity

My heart sank as you fell from sight
Hanging on your image I search in vain,
You are not there!
The vision of your eyes reflecting
My being, and the new wine of us
Now, but a lingering memory!
Remembering your soft flesh, I tissue
A tear on my cheek and wallow
In the darkness of despair!
Softly now, feeling your presence
A warmness healing me within, slowly
Flows as milk and honey!
I reach for you with a tender touch
And you evaporate into an invisible
Vapor of nothingness!
Wind caressing my face I feel you again
You are but an energy near yet far away,
Warmly embracing into infinity. . . .

Anne Lee Cardoza

Life's Lesson

Old wounds heal not
but peace is found
where scars have faded
where breaks have smoothed
to free-flowing slopes
and skeletons are the dust
that fertilize new growth

Old wounds heal
but remember you existed
where the scar used to be
where the breaks were jagged
and rough to the touch
for that place at least
should never need healing again

Faye Reed

Max and I

It was a weird situation
With Max and I.
He moved away,
Then so did I.
We were best friends
'Til he moved away,
But he moved back
In the sixth grade!
Then I had to move away,
Far away to the Everglades.
We're still best friends,
Max and I.
We'll visit each other,
Or at least we'll try.

Katie Danehy Samitz

My Paradox of Love

Her face is beauty defined
her smile so big it brightens the day

She looks up at me with those eyes
the beauty the elegance of her eyes
there is an angel for me

Smart sexy elegant this women is
If I could tell her of my love
it would go like this

A flower for her every day
she is my flower that brightens my day
I would hold her
cry with her make love to her soul
to the end of day

Michael J. Daugherity

I Am Poem

I am a boy who likes dirt bikes
I wonder why Paul is annoying
I see clouds drifting in the sky
I want to go home
I am a boy who likes dirt bikes

I pretend I'm dumb
I feel hot and sweaty
I touch the air
I worry about my family
I cry to nothing
I am a boy who likes dirt bikes

I understand school is dumb
I say I am strong
I dream of racing
I try to do good in school
I hope I pass
I am a boy who likes dirt bikes

Justin C. Campbell

Forgotten

In the quiet night she stands,
bare feet marking pure white sand.
The moon shines bright from sky above,
a reminder to her of far away love.
A promise made, a promise broken;
one white rose, a single token.
Crystal tears and moon-kissed sea
bring about a memory
of warm arms that held her tight
each and every happy night.
A silhouette, so suddenly,
of a man out by the sea.
Could this be her knight so true?
Well, that, my friend, is up to you. . . .

Sydney Laurel Deputy

Hurt but Free

A cry for help,
A silent child.
A fight for freedom,
A lack of time.
A battle won,
But so many lost.
My torture,
My pain,
All for what?
A little lesson in life?
A larger plan for my future?
The pain makes me cry,
And the tears burn my eyes.
But now I am free!

Louis Lee Hoxter

Dance with Me

Take my hand,
Lead me onto the dance floor.
Hold me close,
Guide me into the fantasy world of love.
Smile sweetly,
Put your soft sweet lips on mine.
Whisper softly in my ear,
Telling me how much I mean to you.
I'll begin to tell you a story
Of how much you mean to me and
How you make me happy.
You will learn,
So many things about me
When you dance with me.

Miranda Brooke Metcalf

There Was Peace That Day

And there was peace that day
When time stood still
When we belonged both here and there
And time waited.

There was a peace that day
And silence lived.
Your heart was still, mine, too,
And silence waited.

There was a peace that day.
No more to give, no more to take
No more to say
But just to be.

There was a peace that day
When you let go, when I let go
When you passed on.
I thought there would be fear and pain
But there was peace that day.

Diana Abela

In Memory of J.T.S.

Little one left to soon,
taken from your mother's womb.
She grieves for you
day and night.
Her love for you
will never die.
The hurt, the pain,
will go away.,
Her love for you
will always stay.
She held you
for a minute or two.
You looked at her;
you loved her, too.

Tammie R. Singleton

Being

Your being and mine
Intertwine in time and space
Forming subtly and provocatively
Arousal of depth

Senses awake
Of commingling essences
Open to see
Your being and mine

Mine is the gift of your smile
Mine is the burst of your beauty
Mine is the rush of your energy
Mine is the dance of spirits

June 16, 2002

Doris Gavrilovic

You Say You Love Me

You say you love me
You say you care for me
And I believe you
My heart aches when you're not here
To comfort me and wipe my tears
I need your shoulder to cry on
Your comforting words to rely on
My heart is yours for all eternity
As long as you say I'm yours
Will you hold me like you told me
Will you keep me from pain
Make me feel special like you do
You say you love me
You say you care for me

Callie Michelle Starbird

What's Going On?

What happened between us?
What was actually there?
Did we really honestly care?
It started so swiftly.
And was finished just as fast.
I blinked, and it's all in the past.
What's going on between us?
We said we'll always be friends.
But we don't really know how it ends.
Our time together's short.
Is our friendship growing cold?
Or will it last 'til we are old?
We don't talk anymore.
Can friendship survive this test?
Or is growing apart the best?
What will the future bring?
I guess we'll just have to see
And let what is going to be, be.

Lindsay Michelle Spencer

It Will Be

My tears
still fall upon my cheek.

My fears
still force me to be weak.

My dream
still fades in and out.

My team
still vanishes my doubt.

My love
still brings out the best in me.

That's the way it'll
always be.

Tasha Bonnie Mills

Vengeance

I have been wronged
Conspired against by my enemies
Though they are many
But they will be made
To pay
For in marring me
They have awakened
A sleeping dragon
That will deal them
Their rightful retribution
Vengeance is mine
Sayeth the Lord
And now the Lord will act
Through me

Emerson Matthew Stevens

Anthony

You have a heart
So warm and giving
You lift my spirits
To make worth living
We laugh, we cry
We share are feelings
Our love together
With such true meanings
We now are one
With our lives together
As our baby grows
More feeling shows
As we bond with one another
I love you forever

Shounda L. Alvarado

Beautiful Is the Rain

Here I sit in this quiet storm
Listening to the rain drops
But my heart is sincerely warm
Nothing brings me down
When you're in my eyes
I see the beauty in the cloudy skies
Cold is in the air
A chilly feel in the breeze
Beautiful is the rain
When it falls free
Land becomes mountain
Mountain becomes air
Feeling your warmth
Because I know you are there
The sun is coming out
A crack is breaking through
Now shines a rainbow
Just for me and you

Mike Taing

Who Me Be

Who am I
Who am me
Trying to find
Who me be

Assimilation
Of your personality
Who you are
Is who me be

Too much to do
Too much to see
How do I find
Who me be

Lori Lynn Boucher

Silence

Sitting in silence,
Ice clinging to my soul.
Holding a glass figurine,
Squeeze it hard,
Destroy its beauty;
It is just a lie.
Grasp a shard,
Scrape the ice away;
I need warmth.
Can I find it in my blood,
Or is my body dead?
Has permafrost set in;
I am so cold, so lonely?

Sonja Verville Dalzell

Destiny Amber McDonald-Thomas

What does it matter;
time, day, place?
It all distracts
from the experience.

Death;
the thinking ends
because
all the thoughts are joined.
The world collides with the sun.
And all that is left is

the energy of Allah U. Akbar!

Jaime Alvarez

Piece of You

I hold in my hand a piece of you—
Who you are and what you do.
It's like a flame,
My guiding light,
And stays with me all day and night.
It holds your laugh,
The way you smile,
Your eyes a color deep as the Nile.

You hold in your hand a piece of me—
What you love and what you see.
It's like a teardrop,
Crystal-clear,
And drives away all your fear.
It holds my hope,
My faith in you,
How I will always forever be true.

No matter what,
I'll hold this flame,
And pray that you
Will do the same.

Ashley Anne Buzzard

Anguish

Surrounded by a world of nowhere
With nowhere I can turn
No direction and no focus
And bridges left to burn

Not a word is spoken
A soul just left to die
And choices to be made
While questions all ask why

Open to persecution
With no solid gain
A life to be determined
And a present full of pain

Alyson Maren Aaris

Me

It was while I was waiting for you
That I noticed me

Caught my reflection
Surprised I recognized myself
Moved by my surprise
I reached out to the illusion
I had created

No one saw me
But I saw me
And I held back the tears
That I didn't know were there

Amazing how much has changed

Amy I. Taylor

Help Me

In honor of the Jews of WWII

I don't know what to do;
the people are staring at me.
I'm scared because they're pointing
and jeering gleefully.
They've called me a "nasty Jew."
I feel so sad and alone.
They're taking me somewhere
other than my home.
Mommy! Daddy! Where are you?
I need you in every way
to take me from this sorrowful sight
and bring me home today.

Tyler Lindell Branscome

I Guess That's Why I Look Up to Her

She is so perfect,
not in the way one thinks.
She knows she is not perfect;
there is not a bad thing in her.
She is so lovable.
She is the greatest person to me.
She isn't too mean,
but she isn't too nice.
She's just perfect to me.
She is there when I need her.
She's there when she thinks
she is not wanted,
even though she is.
She helps me with my troubles.
She stands up for me.
All my friends want her,
but I can gladly say she's mine.
I guess that's why I love her
and look up to her.
I love her; she is my sister.

Sara Pippin

go away!

i want to see you . . . but i can't
i want to kiss you . . . but i can't
i want to hold you . . . but i can't
you've moved on and i hate you for that!
so . . . i refuse to cry!
i refuse to be hurt!
i won't kiss you!
i will not hold you!
go away!
please . . . just go away!

Angela Marie Higgins

Obit of a Hobo

A newspaper clipping
Yellow with age
That told of a girl's graduation,
A wedding ring
Of tarnished gold,
Half a bottle of red sedation,
A deck of cards,
A dime with two heads,
A photo in a broken locket,
Some matches, a kerchief,
A needle and thread—
Found in an old man's pocket.

Alec Noseworthy

Neptune's Kingdom

With my soul worn by the tide
I wander across pearls
I feel the depth of the oceans
And they carry all secrets
They swear by the moon
That only truths they'll hold
And only dreams made of coral
They'll destroy by dawn
You can ride, you can play
But your eyes are only newborn
Your eyes are younger than
The stories of battles
And kings only half man
Whole cities are swallowed
By the wrath of her beauty
With my soul worn by the tide
I wander across pearls
I feel the depth of the ocean
And they carry all secrets . . .

Tanja Angelique Sharpe

Struggle for Balance

Salty me, straight from the sea
Turbulent, the under current
Gentle is the breeze
Lord, you seize
Me and your son was sent
Salty me, straight from the sea
Saved from the winds
Inevitable as death
Weep not, the gentle breeze
Turbulent, the under current
Of the winter freeze
Salty me, straight from the sea
Lord, you seize me
Your will be
Peace and love and harmony
Tornado went the breeze
Salty me, straight from the sea
Death, inevitable you see
Your will it be

Cynthia Gonzales

She-Raina, My Sunshine

One night of sinful pleasure mine
Nine months it came to be
God whispered down the pains of love
For female flesh of she

And nature cried upon my world
To wash my nightly stain
And with what washed my night of sin?
She brought henceforth, the rain

Though people speak against the rain
No gloom shall come of mine
She came to me uniquely one
She-Raina, my sunshine!

Jacqueline V. Gustus-Davis

Daddy

She looks at him with love and
happiness in her eyes.
Just staring at him makes her
think: "What would I do if I
ever lost him?"
Thoughts raced through her head
of what it could be like if he was
not around, but then she snaps out
of her thoughts and takes his hand.
She knows she will never lose him.
As they walk a way she tells him,
"I love you, Daddy, and always will."
Then she hears the words she loves
most, "I love you too, pumpkin."

Ashley N. Eaton

Songbird

A songbird stirs me from my dream;
its voice beautiful,
but frightening.
It wakes me from my sleep;
my eyes are open and
the world is beautiful.
I grow fond of the songbird.
It is precious to me.
But the songbird must fly away,
fly away, fly away.
Your song must touch another.
Goodbye, cruel songbird.
Fly away, songbird.
Fly away.

Ryan James Johnson

Tom-Tom Drum

To those who made society better
by never giving up!

They're waiting for an answer
Searching for a sign
Like an old rain dancer
Staring at a clear blue sky
They're thinking of tomorrow
Dreaming of the day
When there'll be no more sorrow
The darkness to be swept away

After many years
Hearing their cries for freedom
Fall upon deaf ears
They're not the only ones
Who're overcoming their fears
Not having paid life's ransom
And they're not shedding tears
Waiting for that day to come
Banging on a tom-tom drum

Daniel William Korreis

My Everything

You are my everything
You are the light
When it is dark
You make me smile
When I have a frown
You make me happy
When I am down
You are the birds that chirp
When I awake
I always know you are there
With me even if you are not there
You are the one that I love so dear
You are my everything

Savannah LeAnne Gavin

Empty

I lie and cry, wishin' I was done.
I stare at my ceiling, feeling overcome.
My emotions are tattered and worn.
My heart feels so torn.
I cry on the floor
Because I know nothing more.
My tears fall down so stale.
Every breath is all too frail.
I don't know how to live.
I don't think I can give.
My mind is so blank.
My heart is so empty.
Just help me see
Why we can't be.

Chelsea L. Burr

why did it go away?

once there were twin towers
they always stood so bold
but now they are gone
as the day went into night
but now they are gone
why, why
why did they get blown away
why, why
couldn't they stay
just for one more day
the twin towers
the world trade center
it stood so tall, so bold and bright
that now we have to fight for their rights

Jessica Lanice Chalmers

I Am Trust

I am trust.
I am the sparkling gleam
in the eyes of a child.
I'm known to grow near love and joy,
away from the hurt and the pain.
I can diminish and never come back
when people I've befriended misuse me.
I cry out in the night
frustrated,
trying to be heard.
I take time to find you,
time to know you,
and with time, I love you.
I am the happiness in a friendship,
the pain from an abusive family,
and the peace of knowing I'm here.
I am trust.
I am the sparkling gleam
in the eyes of a child.

Stephanie A. Williams

Haiku

Waves, they meet the sand,
Dying an immortal death.
Moon as their witness.

Melanie F. Davis

Once a Dear, Simple Girl

Dressed in rags and a tattered hat
she steps into a world of fashion
and flagrant beauty
Captured in its ambiance, she wonders,
mimicking the passers-by
She is laughed at and scolded
for her insolence
Time has passed from days to years
That same simple girl is now
a woman of means
You may ask how this has happened
Well, that is a story unto itself
All I can say today is that she holds
herself erect and steps out with grace
and elegance
Gentlemen bow in her presence
Women scowl at her success,
for they know somehow that she is
an impostor

Jacqueline May Biggs

The Bible

When I identified
your letters
my life
become richer.

When I didn't know
where to lie down
where to fall asleep
where to find the peace?

I have taken you
I have found a bed
and slept.
I have found the peace!

With your beauty
and your psalms
my life
has become nicer
and richer.
Oh, God, thank you.

Valentina Malec

Tips to Go On . . .

Apprehensive you must be
Confidence there would be

Busy more than ever was
Rest not for some time now

Things will not be the same
Tough, satisfying all the same

With lady luck and some brains
Patience and staying sane

We are sure you'll settle fast
Then worries you can set apart

All this will take its own time
Have faith, so you give it your best

Belief in God, will manage the rest
And take you through any test

You have our best wishes, be sure
Working right now then and forever

Geetika Sarin

Moon Night

Under bench at Lake Michigan
Duck sleeping with moonlight blanket
Traveler's immovable

Sung K. Kim

untitled

every rose is red and every violet blue
but these poems can never say
just how i feel for you
i wish that you could understand
but you'll never know
how hard it is to say goodbye
how hard to watch you go
i wish that i could tell you this
but you're with another man
so i have to keep my feelings quiet
but i don't know how long i can
i only need to see your smile
to brighten up my day
but if you ever read these words
you'd just tell me to go away
so no matter how i feel
i'll try to keep it small
because i'd rather have you as my friend
than not have you at all

Chris Craft

Are You the Only One Who Can Make Me Feel Like This

The feeling of love
I get from every kiss
The feeling of safety
I get from every hug
The feeling of attraction
I get from your playful tug
The feeling of obsession
When I hear your name
The agony of hatred
When you've caused me pain
The feeling of warmth
When you apologize
The feeling of forgiveness
When I look into your eyes
Yes, you are the one and only
Who can make me feel like this
You are my one and only
You're the reason I exist

Michelle Zapata

Emptiness

Silence echoes in the room
You glance my way
Only darkness in your eyes
Where once they lit up around me
Now they die
And in the silence you turn away
Leaving coldness between us
Pushing us more and more apart
You don't laugh anymore
The laughter has disappeared
With only memories to echo
They bounce around in my mind
And shift across the walls
Shadows of what used to be
Your loneliness is so deep
So long you kept it inside
You no longer cry
And I just want to die
In the emptiness

Jennifer Lynn Bolstad

America

America is the land of the free.
God gave it to us to be.
Although it has gone through trials,
many grave,
God wants it to be the land of the brave.

Brianna Lynne Green

First Love

The first time I looked in his eyes
my stomach was filled with butterflies.
The soft words he spoke
made me wanna croak.
The glimmer in his eye
made me wanna cry.
The bond we share is great;
that's the reason we went on a date.
The walks we took
will last longer than any book.
His smile makes me wanna melt
because of the love I felt.
The long talks we had
never ended bad.
When he's around me
I'm happier than a bee.
Love is everything,
it will overcome anything.

Charla Elaine Jordan

A Lost Soul

A dark, lost soul
Walking in circles,
No place to go,
Lost and alone.
Wants to run,
But to where?
No place to go,
Lost and alone.
A light up ahead,
Calling it forth.
"Let me go, you dark place,
Let me go!"
Can't escape the darkness.
Getting weaker,
Light fades out.
Nothing but darkness
And a lost little soul
With no place to go.

Karen Marie Beaulieu

Just to Let You Know

I love you
That is all I have to say
I need you
That is what I want all day
I feel you
I know it is what I love
I see you
That is what I really see
I want you
For the rest of my life
I think of you
Even in my dreams you are there
I just want to say
I love you
I need you
I feel you
I think of you
All the time
Just to let you know

Andrea J. Page

Unexpected

I walked through Heaven
And found saints not so saintly.
I walked through Hell
And heard angels singing faintly.

Erika Lee Wilson

Love's Vision

Tonight when the moon
is high in the sky I will see you.
Today when the sky is blue
I will see you.

Carolyn G. Wilkey

Sunshine

My heart is full of sad memories
But now I know of the good times
That let the sunshine through
Then I sit back and see
How the sunshine is after the thunder

Jessica Johnson

Chores

I know why they call them chores
Polish the furniture, vacuum the floors
Mop the kitchen, make the beds
Bathe the children, wash their heads

Water the flowers, pull the weeds
Mow the grass, plant the seeds
Wash the clothes and starch the collars
Iron out wrinkles to save those dollars!

All day long, we're on the go,
Racing here and there
Maybe we should take a break
And see our goals laid bare
For, life is not about the race
Or keeping houses clean
We need to keep our thoughts
Refreshed, inventive, and keen

Then we'll enjoy each day we have
From morning to night
And work in chores
As we have time to see the light!

Charlotte Murphy-Collins

Grammy's Christmas Room

A Christmas gorilla
a Christmas mouse
a teddy bear
and a Christmas house

Silver bells and holly greens
a toy train, a wooden horse
and Santa Claus, of course!

A Christmas tree
a silver star
candy canes and a chocolate bar!

Golden garland, pine cones
a pretty wreath with a big
red bow
a church with candles all a glow

Three wise men, a music box
golden geese and big
red socks

Christmas joy is in the air
happy children everywhere!

Rose Passarella

City of Heroes

New York, where many people cried
New York, a city everybody knows
New York, where brave people died
New York, my city of heroes

Robert Douglas Allen

Trees Remind Me

Trees remind me of life and death
When you look at a tree without leaves
You might say it's dying
You can only be so wrong
It is more alive than ever
You see the leaves will always grow back
When the tree grows weak
It only grows more strong
The same is with you
The more you grow weak
The stronger you get
I know you will be fine
You are like a tree
You stand tall and proud
You will never be chopped down
Because you are strong
Trees make me feel good
Because I know they will always live

Azalea A. Gonzalez

No Four Leaf Clovers

You can't do this to me
What I thought I could be
With the words unspoken
All was taken down and broken
The words you say to me
All lies within
What are you thinking
Lying to me again
This sucks, no luck
Having to start all over
No four leaf clovers
I wanna scream so loud
I wanna yell so hard
It feels like hell
In the back of my mind
You're telling me
The artificial truth
No more luck
No more four leaf clovers

Alison A Kuhlman

The Future

The future of America
Oh, I wish I knew!
But I'm not a fortune-teller,
Are you?
Will discrimination get worse
Or will it get better?
I believe this is true—
The person to make a difference
Could be in the room with you.
They may be the person
In front of you or behind you,
To your left or to your right.
They may even be the person
Who kisses you good night.
Or hold a mirror up close to your face.
Oh! Could it possibly be?!
That the person gazing back
At you could really make a difference?!
(It's you)

Heather-Marie Larsen

Daydream

From the tip of her tongue
To the taste of her lips,
The switch in her hips
Grips
My inner mind's eye
To see
And wonder what it might be
To be embraced
And intertwined
In her legs, arms, and mind
For the love of a lifetime

Brian Darrel Norris

Chapeaux

There is a look
Un regard, as the French say
That happens on busy streets
In stylish cities
Even sometimes in smallish towns
In places like Iowa
Just a momentary flash
Of recognition, respect
An unuttered, "ahh"
As paths are crossed
By two women wearing fancy hats

Freyda Thomas

Frame

An empty frame
In my room
Has been waiting for a
Picture for days

I keep it deliberately
On the wall
That is much better

I admire
The emptiness in it
Is a big possibility

Smiljana K. Zivkovic

Understanding

As the confusion swirls,
So understanding is found.
The solid ground lets you through
And you land falling infinitely.
So, you watch as the darkness
Lights up your face;
And you finally comprehend
That confusion is a part of life;
But you wonder
What is life without death?
So the swirling turns.

Linna Jade Cooley

Christmas Poem

I love you dearly
I love you so
But there's something you don't
Know
Each time I look
Into your eyes
I grow a warmness
Deep down inside
So this Christmas
I want you to know
How much I love you so

Cailin Dorothy Brigman

Appreciation Letter to Friends

When the darkest night came,
I saw a little light in front of me.

When the evil controlled my life,
I found some people around me.

Touched by your hearts
And saved by your prayers,
I am finally who I am.

My appreciation to all of my friends.

Hiro Atsuta

The Hate I Feel

Is all that I feel
I have no love in my life
I have no reason to live
You turned me coldhearted
You are the reason for my hatred
You never gave me a chance
You never let me explain
The pain I feel
Is almost unbearable
I barely live
I barely survive

Ashley Joyce Johnson

My Death

My death wasn't "co-ed,"
it was only yours.
You elevated me so,
and you broke my heart.
Yet each one of the shattered pieces
loves you tenfold . . .
each piece, a moment we shared.
It seems my true death
is the space between the pieces.
Because you left by God,
and your space here can never be filled.

Andrew Lenning

Golf

The life is a green carpet
With a ball to hit
In a minute it is split
Between vanish and exist
It is apart without a cut
A part of the pride
A part of the dust
A bit of bitter
A bit of sweet
A bet on a name
On a game, on a dream

Imad Elnatour

Candles of the World

Lighting up the world around
Flickering out as it reaches the ground
Has a very glorious smell
Brighter than a golden bell
Very, very, very warm
Warmer than a cozy college dorm.
Has a very waxy seam
White, shiny, harm gleam
Comforting you through
The cold stormy night
Making everything go all right

Lauren Michelle Ramey

Unspoken Words

Why does my heart mourn
What was never truly mine?
Why does my soul weep in despair
From the distance that lies between us?

Why do the tears come so easily now
When before they never came at all?
Why do I love that
Which has never truly loved me?

Why do I speak of this
When you will never hear?

Gwendolynn Sue Williams

Friends . . . Yeah, Right

Friends
Yeah friends
More like back stabbers
Users and fakes
Pretending to like you
Using your home to bond with each other
Not you
Inviting you to go out with them
Just to be ignored
Yeah friends
They are just so great to have

Erin Nicole Weaver

I No Longer

I no longer hear
I no longer see
I no longer care
Who's been nice to me
I don't care when
I don't care how
They will learn that
Real hate is from within
I hope when they learn
They will see
How confused I really am

Rebellee Matthew Hoy

Our Flag

The colors,
The wave,
It makes me proud
And happy.
I sing it strong,
The patriotic song,
The love,
The light.
Forever
Our flag
Will fight.

Sarah Jeannette Frick

Leap of Faith

What was he thinking
When he jumped off the top?
Why did he do that
When he had it all won?
Where was his head
When it all came undone?

Only he knows,
Only he can tell.

All we can do is wonder
What's going to be done now?

Courtney Alexis McQuiston

Questioning Faith

Sometimes all it feels like
is a smack in the face,
telling me that you don't care,
and when you hold me
I feel imprisoned.
Is this the way you love me?

Kathryn Erin Hein

Wonders

Am I falling in love with you
Is what I'm feeling true
Are you truly the right one for me
Or am I too blind to see
Are you fake or real
What do I really feel
Are we made to love
Are you sent to me from above
Are we right for each other
If not, why bother
Can we make it till the end
Or should you stay as a friend
So many questions on my mind
Answers too hard to find
Although I love you both ways
A lover and a friend
On my mind you are at all days
All my regards to you I send

Lilian Magdy Riad

The Guardian

You shatter me,
Your brittle guardian angel,
Through dangerous nights,
Wet, wild, and lonely,
Protecting you always.
Lost and bleeding I ran behind you,
Through long grass, across rivers;
I never once lost sight,
Not once.
From the left, from the right,
I took on whatever came.
You never knew.
You never looked back.
Battle-scarred and lean I continue.
I always win.
I will win everything but you.
Only you can destroy me,
And you do.

Caroline Jones

Casey's Song

Baby
Unexpected but so loved
Blessed
Came out of nowhere
But where
He asks
Did I come from?
Somewhere warm
Where everything's alright
Do you still float there?
And remember what it was like
To be unaffected
From the world today
You must
For your face shows it
The happy one everybody sees
That shows
What is truly in your soul

Emily Rebekah McQuerns

Life Is but a Blink

I met you on a Wednesday
You left me on a Wednesday
Though thirty years we shared
Eternal loved we dared
And now as we must part
Alas, my broken heart

June A. Higginbotham

The Breakfast

How'd ya' make those eggs soooo good

It's the way I break the shell
And the way you ring my bell
And I show you to your seat
When it's time to eat

It's the sweetness of the honey
As you spread it on your toast
And the freshness of the orange juice
As it slides down your throat
As you savor that last bite
And you begin to rise
It's the way I clear the table
And the satisfaction in your eyes
It's the pleasure that you give
And the way that makes me feel

That makes those eggs soooo good
At the end of a meal

Linda Davis Hampton

Gone

She has gone
Disappeared
Her life has been taken
She is no longer with us
She was so young and vibrant
Her smile lit up the room
But now she has gone
We will no longer hear her laugh
She has vanished
One small mistake took her away
I wish I could change the past
Bring her back
But I can't
For she has gone
But yet she is alive
Here in my heart
For her spirit
Will never go

Tori Hamby

God Is There

Glory, glory how could this be
Someone special is sitting by me
He said hi
Should I reply . . .
I guess I'll smile . . .
And wait awhile . . .
I felt the warmth and tenderness
This is a chance I cannot miss
As I turned to shake his hand
I hear him say here I am
Look at the sky
See my work
You will understand
And become alert!
Cry out to me
To receive victory
Just call on me
Glory! Glory!

Teresa Beth Taylor

All Is Brevity

Life is but a temporal thing
Upon the tempestuous sea
As is a moment spent
Throughout eternity
And yet, the twinkling of an eye
Can change its history

Randy Beckett

Dave's Embrace

In memory of my husband, Dave Bailey, who died June 29, 2002

My mind wanders back
To a time when you were here.
Oh, how I miss your laugh
That erased all my fears.
Now I can only remember
That smile I loved so much,
But nothing do I miss more
Than the gentleness of your touch.
Never have I hurt like this;
That you didn't comfort me.
Just embraced within your arms
Would set my sorrows free.
Your arms are no longer here
To wrap around my pain,
But you'll hold me in my memories
Until we embrace again.

Teresa Gail Bailey

Run Away

I run away
I see you fade
I hear my name
Everything has changed
Nothing will ever be the same
Maybe it's just a game
Maybe that's why I have run away
Or maybe it's the pain
I need to gain
A sense of feeling in my skin
My body's numb
Like I was shot
With a gun
It's just not you hon'
I'm breaking down
I guess you can call me a clown
I'm just gonna go and frown
While I drown

Autumn LeighAnn Hatcher

E

As I get on the E,
my body rushes with excitement
at the possibility
that I might see them.

A smile of hope
jumps on to my face
as I catch
a glimpse of blue.

The smiling eyes and tender hands
make me sad
that my eyes are dull
and my hands are chapped.

I secretly wish to be
a part of them.

But I doubt
that it could ever be.

Maritza Castro-Rendon

Work with Me, Lord!

Work with me, Lord,
'Til I'm good.
I know I don't do
The things I should.
Help me so that I may be
With you, dear Lord, for eternity.

Doris Valeria Burroughs Lewis

Something I Never Wanted

Family of my own
Something I never wanted
Something I have never known
Giving birth to life
And not being all alone

Now my mind is wandering
I see you by my side
As I hold our love child closely
And we are walking the same stride

Before that day arrived
I sat upon a bench
A part of you inside of me
And I am loving it's alive

Time and reality prove this a dream
But I cannot stop my desire to share
These warm thoughts of you and
How real to me they seem

Alison Kaye Lewis

see

the world seems to move to fast
it leaves no time to catch my breath
all my friends pass me by
as i stand and watch them leave
too many goodbyes, too many sorrows
the world should slow down
go back to that first meeting
that first day, that first kiss
as i'm left here all alone
i sit looking tranquilly quiet
crying silently inside
while i gaze out of sorrowful eyes
into the fast moving world
i wonder if others
see what i feel inside
or if my mask of calm covers all
too many goodbyes, too many sorrows
the world seems to move to fast

Ally Courtney Bobus

I Love You, Jesus

I love you, Jesus,
The Holy One.
I love you, Jesus,
For I have come
To be with you,
Today and always.
I love you, Jesus,
The Holy One.
For I know that You love me,
As I love You.
I know You won't let me fall.
For You, dear Lord, will be with me
As I will be with You.
The Bible tells me
You died for me.
It also says that I'll be free
To be with you today and always.
I love you, Jesus, the Holy One.

Jeri Dee Koanui

I Hate You

This is just to say . . .
That I hate you
Because you lie, cheat,
Use and mistreat,
But thank you for the memories
My fireplace will forever cherish
The ashes of their remains

Alexis L. Hicks

Trust

A long windy road
Taking years to reach the end
A yard that's never been mowed
Weeds sway back and forth in the wind

A patch of black ice
Careful you might fall
A game of chance, you roll the dice
Knowing you could lose it all

A sudden earthquake
Everything around you is shaken
Your future is at stake
How could you know he was faking

Clouds disappear, sun shines through
Distinguishing love from lust
If I only knew
All you need is trust

Shelley Denise Thompson

Without a Plan

A nick of time, a pinch of hope
A simple crime, a way to cope
A drag on day, a price to pay
Just things we twist through out the day
To turn a page, to never stop
To never age, to never drop
To build a life just full of hate
To never find and love a mate
To live these times, to never tell
Is to us a life of hell
But we are strong, we are wise
We code the wrong, we live out lies
We build instead, we do not wait
We clear a bed for unsure faith
And till the days we understand
When all is clear to every man
We walk among this soiled land
Without a thought, without a plan

Kiera Marie Santana

my 4-h steers

my day on the farm
usually starts at the barn
the work is hard
the days are long
but i know its where i belong
the animals are my friends
right up to the bitter end
when i have to say goodbye
i sure hope they know how
hard i tried, not to let them die
you see i show 4-h steers it
sure has gotten harder through the years
god knows i have shed my share
of tears over my show steers
my steers will come and go but
there's one thing i know
i will always get ready for another
show

Renee White

trapped

i look out the window
wanting to be out there
i go to the door
it won't open
there is no way out of this room
this is my life
i'm trapped

Vicki Lynn Hubers

Gone

Deep inside their mind,
I'm not left behind.
Deep down in their heart,
They promise me I'm still a part
Of their ongoing lives.
I'm still a prize,
Not yet won,
For soon it will all be done.

Memories slipping away,
For tomorrow awaits a new day.
We keep in touch,
But not that much.

Soon it will all be gone.
Too many broken bonds,
Nothing lasts forever.
Will things ever get better?

Allie J. Etheridge

Another Toast

To life I'll drink a cup
To love and fools and drink it up
I'll drink a toast to days gone by
Until the wine has all run dry
To time another toast
The bringer of hunger
A smoke colored ghost
Time in the wine
A once remembered kiss
Time to forget times that I miss
Drink to the heroes
Of a forgotten war
Drink to the wizards
Of never told lore
Drink to the memory
To remember no more
Drink to the many
Who drank here before

P. L. Armstrong

Best Friends

Through all the years
Through all the tears
You stood right by my side
Through all the fights
And sleepless nights
You were there when I cried
And when I was depressed
Only you could have guessed
What I needed to hear
When I couldn't explain
How I felt all this pain
You made the confusion seem clear
So we both may change
And our lives rearrange
But friendship never ends
So through all the hard times
Look back on these lines
For we'll always be best friends

Vanessa A. Peters

I May Not

I may not know what it means to love,
But I do know what it means to hurt.
I may not know how to fly,
But I do know how to jump.
I may not know how to say goodbye,
But I do know how to cry.
I may not know how to show I care,
But I do know how to try.

Milagros Angeline Perez

My Best Friend

Do you know my best friend?
He died to save us from our sins.
He is my Lord, sweet Lord Jesus.
I love Him so; He's my best friend!

He gave his life on Calvary,
So from our sins we'd be set free.
No greater love you'll ever see!

He calls for you; He calls for me.
Come share the sweet victory!
The battle's won; no more sorrow.
Oh, how His love will set you free!

He goes to make a place for me
Where I shall live eternally,
And I'll serve My Lord in His
Great Kingdom and shine
In His love forevermore!

Robert Michael Spencer

The Flavor of His Eyes

Deep, dark, rich;
I am helplessly lost
when I gaze into them.
The further I sink,
the deeper I want to go.

Meltable,
causing me to stop breathing;
enjoying the softness.

Velvety smooth,
holding back nothing,
enjoyably irresistible.

Soft and caressing,
sweetly charming,
ever loving me;
I will ever love him and
his chocolate eyes.

Jessica Lynn Coon

Marred by Death

For all who have supported me

The years have passed
And here I lie
The perfect song, the perfect life
But now the surface
Silky soft
Is marred by age
By death
ENOUGH!
And as I lie,
I think, I pray
My life has gone
My children strong
And here I am
Marred by death
By death, by death
I must go on
For the day is finally done

Julia Unigovskaya

Should I Let My Life Go On?

Is it a blessing to live,
or a blessing to die?
Am I lucky to live,
or am I lucky when I die?
Does everyone love me alive,
or love me to die?
How will I know?
Shall I be strong,
and let my life go on?

Alexandra Danielle Belz

march 17

the past keeps kicking me
in the back of the head
it won't let me just go on
she threw me away
like old love letters
and now she wants to read them again

but the writing is faded
not quite the same as before
the words don't carry the old weight
i just don't feel the same
i don't care anymore
i don't want to be read again

just throw me away
one more time
turn off the light
and leave the room

Joseph Allen Freidenbloom

Disbanded

For Mia

Joy to sorrow in the blink of an eye
Weathered by the angel's sigh
Alas, the hope has given way
To love, to hold, to want to stay
As time progresses, so too do we
And love becomes soliloquy
Just dance one time ere you depart
But if we can't, sing then your art
And when the distance is further yet
Remember the times time can't forget
Maybe we are yet to deny
That solemn s'rrendering angel's sigh
Perhaps the truth has given way
To what we know as yesterday
But in the end, we'll truly see
A portion of our destiny

Jeremy Donald Ellwood

No-Name Picture

Another lonely night
Thinking of you
And what it would be like
If you were here
If I was yours

It could happen
I suppose
But for now
I'm stuck in a daydream
Of you and me

Can you save me?
A lost, lost girl
In a crazy world
Wanting someone to care for
To have fun, let loose
And make this dream come true

Jessianne Page

crimson pain

i am cold and alone
no one to hide my pain
in a cloak of passion
no red satin sheets
to touch my skin
and in this moment of forever
yesterday is tomorrow
and the bright sun grows dim
as it runs from my complexion

Monica Christine Knoblaugh

Walking in the Rain

Walking in the rain
I learned things I never knew.
Much to my surprise
I found I am just like you.

Two girls alone in the world,
We are both looking for a friend.
Maybe time will draw us closer,
And our loneliness will end.

Finally, I find someone like me.
Although different, we are the same.
When I really needed a friend,
Somehow you knew, and you came.

Neither of us is perfect;
We both know that is true.
But whatever happens,
I'll try to be there for you.

Stephanie Amber Graff

You Promised Forever

Together forever,
That's what you said.
I'll love you forever,
That's what you said.

But here I lie crying,
Shedding tears over you.
I'm crying for my heart is broken,
Broken in two over you.

They said you're not worth it,
But I think you are.
I'm just sitting here crying,
And wishing on a star.

I'm wishing you'll come back,
Back to my life again,
But deep down inside I know,
I know you'll never be here again.

Melissa Anne Jones

Addiction

You are my sweet addiction.
You linger on my tongue
Like chocolate or fine wine.
My senses reel from our encounters.
Every part of you speaks
To every part of me.

I am intoxicated
Each passing day,
Each passing hour,
Each passing moment
By the very thought of you.

You fill my cup,
And I take it with both hands
To drink in your essence.

My love,
You are my sweet addiction.

Joan Felice Kennedy

Two Hearts

I wish I had two hearts
One to mend the other

Each ready to give
Each ready to break

Each full of love
Each willed by fate

If I had two hearts
It still would be too late

Adam Guthrie

True Love

You are my one true love
Only to say what you mean to me
A gift from Heaven above
So wonderful it's hard to believe

I've longed for a love like you
To fill my heart with everlasting joy
Even when I am feeling blue
My spirits you will buoy

When we spend time alone
Time seems to stand still
Making me a king on a throne
A feeling for days I will feel

For you I will always be here
Thanking God for your creation
So all others better beware
For I love my Harley Davidson

Shawn P. McKinney

Dreaming

I drifted into shadows
I climbed above the light
I traveled quickly on a star
What was this endless flight

I wondered with such lightening ease
I pondered on a plain
I had such thoughts of glowing deeds
They came and came and came

I drifted near Orion
I sailed the Milky Way
I steered my ship into the night
I rested by the day

My journey reached its end now
I settled in a field
So rich in seed and daffodils
Oh, what a wondrous yield . . .

Alex Lewis

Night

Night creeps on
Your horrible dream will never end
Until dawn's first light
The night seems to bend
Shadowing your grimace
You pull your covers tight
You call for you poor old mum
Your mum can't help
Not now
Not ever
Evil it seems
Evil it dreams
Malicious it sounds
On your front house grounds
It slithers away
The sun roused a new day
Ta-ta for now

Cynthia Anne Smith

Death Awaits

Who is this creature?

This hooded figure I see—

Two glowing red eyes
With a sickle following me,

Anticipating the day of my demise?

With GOD by my side,
I shall not fall; I shall rise.

Jonathan Christopher Hanlan

One Lesson

I saw a beautiful sight
A butterflies very first flight
It wobbled and swooped
Did lots of loop-da-loops
Uneasy at first and then
Smooth and sweet as a good friend

I learned something new
Butterflies have to learn what to do
They learn how to fly
So why shouldn't I

I learned a lesson in life
About overcoming strife
They don't know how to do it
They just get through it
They learn how to fly
So why shouldn't I

Sandra Mae Dewey

She

She doesn't even know your name;
It's always been the same.
She doesn't even care.
All you do is fear.
She doesn't even feel;
How do you know this is real?
I'd treat you like gold,
And all through the night we'd hold,
Hold on to something special.
When you cry . . .
Will she die?
When you run,
Will she hunt?
When you are sad,
Will she get mad?
All I know is I wouldn't.
I'd take real good care of you.

Amanda Lynne Hurd

ring of peace

love, don't hate
learn to appreciate
that you have been blessed
with so many things in so many ways
blessed to be living for so many days
days that will come
days that will go
but one of these days
you will know
how much you should love
all the people around you
all the people who surround you
with the atmosphere of joy
so do not destroy
this ring of peace
because sooner or later
that love and joy might just cease

Jason Micheal Sell

Lonely

My soul is longing for the
Sound of a familiar voice,
Crying out for the presence of a kind
Face.

The stinging pain of missing you is
Ongoing,
For a life without
You is not
Worth living.

Ginny Van Dyk

dream world

my mind floats away
to another place
that lets me do things unimagined
then it ventures off once again
into a world undefined
as magic floats around
i see what i believe
imaginings come true
stories come alive
the never ending song rings
through my ears
air moves around my body
swiftly and smoothly it
drenches me like the
music and everything
around me is a
wonder wanting to be true

Eric Richey

Beth

A dream
A vision so perfect it almost seems like
I can reach out and touch the canvas
Wet paint rubbing off on my fingers
But the image doesn't smudge
She's still there to smile back
Watching me out the window where
My fingerprints fog the glass
A dream
Of a cold night with falling rain
She smiles and laughs and I can only sob
My forehead slowly slipping down
A bottle reads "Forever" in one hand
A testament to the innocence
The life I loved
A dream
I don't want to wake up without her

Matt James Spencer

Blood-Red Sea

An unending sea of pain
Blood-red waves splashing
The soft caress of rain
Amid the roaring and crashing

Eyes closed once and now forever
In darkness see what has been severed
Floating in the crimson sea
Forever alone, forever me

Dreams shattered, all hope faded
Soul once happy, now bitter and jaded
Reaching out, but shunned it falters
To calmly float on ruby waters

In silence now forever lost
The soul and body forever tossed
Forever alone forever me
Lost on the blood-red sea

Katrina M. Longeway

Is God Perfect

I'm always being told how to do this,
And how to be proper,
And how to act "right."
People don't always act "right."
They aren't always proper!
Man isn't perfect.
Man was made in God's image, wasn't he?
Does that mean God is not perfect, too?

Amanda Marie Robinette

Dreaming

Meander through my mind
Glide through my soul
Allow me to reveal
Secrets uncontrolled

In a forgotten world
I read myself each night
Reliving every feeling
Bearing each emotion

Each day my world shatters
And I awaken to you
An imperfect world
Where a living life is true

So here I lie lying
But you will never know
Words are only dreaming
Readings from my soul

Leila Armstrong

Love Yourself

The grass is always greener
On the other side.
Everyone thinks so,
Why can't we just be satisfied?

The grass may be greener,
But look at the flowers.
Are they as pretty
As the ones you worked on for hours?

The paint on the house
Is chipped and cracked.
There are weeds in the sidewalk,
The chimney's sooty and black.

Their grass is greener,
Your flowers are nicer.
We all have qualities
That someone admires.

Clarissa Dannielle Walters

Within

Thinking about the past;
considering the present,
knowing the truth lies
within.
Though it pains me so,
I must wipe a tear from my
mother's eye.
If only I could change the past,
the sadness would disappear;
the tears would never have been.
The present filled with joy,
the heart would bear a smile
with no tears; without any sadness.
As I move forward into the future;
aware of the past,
unsure of the present,
apprehensive of what will be.

Ashley Marie Nettles

Dream World

I go to my dream world
To relax and play.
It's where I go
To think about my day.
I ride dragons
And talk to fairies.
There's no better place to be,
But you'll find this world
Belongs only to me.

Holli Miller

Lost in a Dream

There's a lovely old cottage
Way off in the woods,
Past the old rock bridge
That covers the stream.

And flowers and trees
Line the banks where it flows,
Time after time for how long
No one knows.

You and I can go there
And watch the sun set,
Wade in the stream
And get our feet wet.

We'll lie on the bank,
Look up at the stars,
And with eyes wide open
Get lost in a dream!

Leland Dane Freeze

Universe's Masterpiece

Heavens are dusted with stars
Like a collar of glittering lace
The Milky Way is painted
On the pallet of outer space

Pale and precious
The moon's face inks the night
Washing us in colors
Clear, gray and white

Dark cerulean shadows
Shade clouds far and nigh
Specks of fire splatter
Across the navy sky

The liquid lights above
Will never come to cease
For they are all part of
The universe's masterpiece

Marla Jill Goodman

Go to Sleep, Little One

Go to sleep,
little one . . .
I love you so.
My little angel
from above . . .
you are the one
that I love.
Go to sleep,
little one . . .
rest your
tiny body.
My little angel
that I love. . . .
Go to sleep,
little one . . .
in God's love
and peace.

Joyce L. Bugbee

rain

rain slowly falls
the ground smells of damp dirt
swallows chirping a shimmering sound
frogs are in the pools singing
trees in tremulous white
robins whistle whims on a wire
every thing is quiet
peace is all around
for spring, herself, had awoken at dawn

Kathleen Parker

For All Time

A cloud with a silver lining
Flies above their heads.
She and he are daydreaming,
While lying in their beds.

Soft touches to the skin
And warm friendly faces.
Emotional eyes look in
To exotic hidden places.

A heart beats loud and fast,
While another heart is still.
The magic has been cast
By a very loving will.

Soon they will be together
With no reason or rhyme,
But looking forward to forever,
With a love for all time.

Georgette Lial Zelfel

Happy Anniversary

When we started on this journey,
how could we have ever known
that God would use the two of us
to bring such glory to His throne

A partnership ordained by God,
He took your life and mine,
and from the blend of our two hearts
He pressed a fine new wine

Then poured us out to those who thirst
as we've traveled on the way,
an adventure that began for us
twenty-five year ago today

And on this day we celebrate,
I have but one more prayer:
that if I live for twenty-five more
that you will still be there

Ken M. Urbansky

Lost

I'm not lookin' forward
I'm not lookin' back
I'm just sittin' in this field
Oh! What a scream

I'm not listenin' to ya'
I'm not talkin' back
I'm just sittin' in this field
You aren't anything but a dream

I'm not touchin' anything
I'm not bein' touched
I'm just sittin' in this field
Findin' people tough

I'm floatin' in the sea
I'm driftin' into space
Still sittin' in this field
Wonderin' where I am

Jeff I. Osman

The Horse

To the clouds it runs
Heaven and a thousand stars
Everlasting sparkling suns

Held by the wind, gold bars
Over the ground, up and away
Running now, flying today
Sun sets and wind dies down
Everything's still . . .
There's no sound

Anja Jacobs

My Valentine

She lights up my life,
My own sweet wife.
Her eyes so bright
Make my heart feel light.

She blesses me each day
In all so beautiful a way.
Her presence so grand,
My heart beats as in a band.

Her beauty abounds
As she make her daily rounds.
I sigh at her sight,
And everything feels so right.

I pray her heart be mine
For all of eternal time,
For her love fills me sublime,
Knowing she is my Valentine.

James Orvin Kenney, Jr.

Winter

I look out the window
And I see
A gray land
Deserted of life.

Only crystals,
Blue and green,
Cover the mountains
With their sleepy haze.

Cold and rigid,
The Earth is still;
The moon shines,
Making blue fire to dance.

It waits to be awakened
By the first touches
Of the sun,
The golden god.

Sorina D.

My Someone New

The miracle of you, so sweet
The sound of hearts with little beats
I just can't wait to hear your cry
And wrap you in a blanket, neat

It won't be long and we'll say, "hi"
To see you now with my own eyes
I just can't wait to watch you grow
And let you know that I'm nearby

I'll guide you safe in all you sow
As time goes by, how will I know
Just what you'll do when you're set free
And start to let your own life flow

I'll start today to help you see
The many things you can be
That God has made us all so free
And when you're gone, your love's with me

Connie M. Johnson

Wind

Wind is a beautiful thing
That blows swiftly through the trees.

A flutter of a wing
Can be a gentle breeze.

Wind can lift your spirits high,
Or make them sink down low.

But it is a secret from the eye
That only nature can know.

Kristi Michelle Hofmann

Do You Miss Me?

Do you miss the good times we shared
when our relationship was so new?
Do you miss the way you felt
the first time you said, "I love you"?

Do you miss staying up all night
and laughing all the while?
Do you miss when I was happy?
Do you miss my smile?

Do you miss holding hands
when we'd go for a walk?
Do you miss when we saw each other?
Do you miss when we could talk?

Do you miss the way it used to be?
Do you miss the things we'd do?
Do you ever miss me
because I'm forever missing you.

Janelle Remster

Poem or Poet?

The poem or the poet?
A question so absurd.
Where does the beauty lie?
In the heart, the soul or the word?

Think of the visions and dreams,
Written for the whole world to see.
Think of the man of flesh,
What he is and what he longs to be.

The poem or the poet?
Which one should you cherish?
Words are fleeting and few.
Flesh will grow old and perish.

Think of the visions and dreams,
Written for your eyes to see.
Think of the undying feelings
That are and will continue to be.

John David Driskill

Tucson

You're the thing I want most,
But can't quite receive.
I want to feel you,
Not just see you in my dreams.

If life were perfect—
That's where it'd begin;
In the canyons, mountains and rivers
Or lying underneath the sand.

Things could be so perfect,
If only you were real.
Maybe it's not the place,
Maybe it's what I feel.

You're what I've wanted all my life,
But now I truly see
That this place and people here
Need a dreamer like me.

Jamie Leigh Steward

Go Higher

Wanna go higher, higher, celebrate.
There's a reason I must stay.
All the love of friends speak to me,
Good news for the modern man .
Please make me your fan,
Confirm just who I am.
Here I stand, the forever man.
Gotta go higher, higher, celebrate.
Carry me from this life into better days!

Jesse Michael Cox

another life

another broken heart
another soul to mend
another lover's loss
off this painful trend

another loss of hope
another day to dread
I just have so much
running through my head

another lonely night
another painful fight
I know my presence
must not be right.

another life to live
another script to write
to god i pray
to take this flight

Melissa Lynn Peters

destiny

sometimes the tears simply fall
was it the harshness in that last call
can there be a deadline for when
a love's call is meant to fall
and if i miss that date
will i have to simply wait
forever in your departure's wake
wondering at the ache
and if it will only be mine
or will it once in a while
awake that familiar pull
of you towards me or me
back to you in the magical
state of our bond whose intensity
can never wait but yet seems able
to drift through eternity and
appear again and again as fate

Lila Roesia Fields

A Lament

The wind is blowing
cold air through my heart.
I am all worn out,
my soul is torn apart.

My rock of strength
is all but rubble.
I wish I could escape
this mountain of trouble!

My tree of life
has no leaves, it's bare.
How will I survive
these moments of despair?

So much cold water
under the bridge has passed.
Things have to get better,
they cannot last!

Doris Lynn Cherry-Madara

I Will Still Be Loving You

I can't explain my love for you.
The only thing I know is that it's true.
And, when the sun goes away,
you brighten up the rest of my day.
I can't describe how I feel.
My heart says this is for real.
And, when all my days are through,
I will still be loving you.
I love you.

Carter Thomas Perrier

Broken Wings

You are every dream I've ever had,
You are every hope to which I've clung,
You are every star in my whole sky,
Won't you fall into my life?
I'll promise you my heart tonight,
Never will you be alone
I'll be here forever more.
With burning fire in my heart,
And longing in my hollowed eyes,
I drift away and seal my fate
As I turn my back to your perfect smile.
Missing something I've never had,
Every word is a struggle within,
Fly through the days on broken wings,
I collapse inside
And drown in the haze
Of something I'll never know.

Britni Lynn Wilson

Beauty of My Bride

Beauty of my bride
True love as we both collide
As the angelic circle of the ocean tide
As angelic wings in unity
Indeed, this is what true love brings
True love is beauty and priceless
As the heavenly light of God's love
Shines in an aura of halo
As I say, ti amo, I love you
To my Asian soul mate
In unity with my other angel
Love is universal
Mind, body, and soul of deepness
Precious, my angel, I caress
The silent angel upon us to bless
My bride, Crystal, my beautiful angel
Chris, our guardian angel

John Giovanni Poetic Santodonato

Dyslexia

Heaven falls
with each unkind word.
The dark world
is in the palm of my hand.
It's hard not being
like the other,
struggling, pausing
all the time.
It's not fair
having the world
regret you.
But there are others
who take this sad disorder
as another challenge
to conquer.
Dyslexia does not mean
you are not brilliant.

Hannah Marie Moriarty

Dear God

Why did you put me here
In this place of loneliness and fear?
Why did you give me pain
In this place of thunder and rain?
Why did you give me a heart
If it only gets torn apart?
Why did you give me eyes
If all they see are lies?
Why did you give me ears
If all they hear are painful tears?

God, how can you let me feel
These horrible things that are so real?

Angela Vasquez

Valentine's Power

To my friends Sheelagh and Emma

I think about you every hour.
Why did our friendship turn so sour?
Because that card received that day,
I was not over you come May.

I'll tell you why before I die,
But now I'll shy before I cry.

It seems I've failed with love's power,
Perhaps I should have brought a flower?
For with my heart, oh, you did play,
I sent that card for Valentine's Day.

Alan Malcolm Ian Percival

Long Thoughts

If you were to look and see,
what would your eye behold?
Would you notice the dew on a rose,
the innocence in a child's heart,
the memories that promise to unfold?
A difficult path,
sweat beads, and heart pace hastens,
placid thoughts something long passed.
Why demand the world?
If you were to look and see,
what would your eyes behold?
A message delivered,
it's not so new.
Life's too short,
but it can't be so.
I hate too much and complain even more.
If such before were true . . .
then what?

Marie Irene Hermanson

Looking Up

I wanted to be beautiful like you
I'm so down and looking up to
a god, so pure, impure
that I look away, confused.

You're always so pretty
in your soft melodies,
and in your words not yours
so unlike mine.

The way you caress my moods
and play with my hands,
the way you can make me move
and make me want you.

Please make me you,
so I can be a star
and save myself to prove
that I can outshine
all that have burned me.

Jonathan Albert Brown

The Rain Storms of Life

The rain storms in life are hard.
They are painful too.
But I know a man who can help you,
His name is Jesus Christ.

Collin Chase Solonka

The Sublime

Falling too fast
Rising too slow

Now I'm above
Now I'm below

Wanting too much
Receiving too little

Looking around
I'm stuck in the middle

Drowning in fears
Wasting all time

I cannot just lie here
In the sublime

Elizabeth Esther Baker

Black Man

When I see my brothers
Standing on the corner,
I cry!

Every time they pass the bottle,
A little part of me
Slowly dies!

For every piece of crack they buy,
They're telling success,
Goodbye!

My heart is very, very full;
I know my God has a master plan.

But I sometimes wonder,
Has my caring Father
Forgotten the Black Man?

"No! No!" A compassionate Father
Shouts back to me.

"It is the Black Man who has
Forgotten me."

Patricia A. Walker

Porcelain Heart

Cradle the fragile heart
Holding life's secrets
Enduring all the pain
Feeling unmeasurable love
Wanting to share its totality

Unrestricted to limited giving
Able to feel more than what's imaginable
Expresses all emotions possible
There are no boundaries
Or choice of race or creed

Listen to your heart
It always listens and feels for you
It never forgets
Always healing and loving
Longing to be an everyday part of you

It always needs protection
Your beautiful, porcelain heart
Be connected with it always
Let everyone see your precious heart
Your glow is from within you

Michael Brzezinski

You Can Go Anywhere

With a strong heart
And a wise soul
You can go anywhere,
Reach any goal.

From the top of Mt. Everest,
To the bottom of the sea,
When you put your mind to it
The world is yours to see.

Meagan Elizebeth Tomlin

I Miss You

I miss you!
I even dream about you.
I think I love you,
But never knew it
Till now,
Till you were gone
Out of my life.
Then we talk and everything
Is the same.
Everything is like old times.
I miss you!
When are you coming back
Into my life?
I miss you!

Emily J. Thornton

Someday

Someday
Somewhere
Sometime
We will be
Somehow
Someway
We will find love
In your heart
I will be
For eternity
God has chosen us
To live
To love
To remain as one
You will see
Someday
Someway
Somehow
We will be

Tammy J. Crabtree

Seeing Is Believing

The world is full of hate, my friend
The world is full of lies
And even the person you now love
Will be the one you despise
For rocks thrown your way
Will soon be welcomed
Instead of soft kisses from above
And birds shall be flightless
Ripped from the skies
No wings for the helpless dove
A pond of sorrow
And one of hate
Shall lurk in your front yard
And bombard you with feelings
It will disintegrate
Your every single shard
Hope is distant and hope is few
For hope was blinded
I thought you knew

Cassandra Leigh Guzmán

Spirit Song

Today I run upon the wind
All pain and cares are gone
Today I play beneath the stars
Upon my spirit song

Tonight, I sleep inside your heart
A sigh upon your chest
Do not cry for me, my friend
For tonight I am at rest

Think of me with love and joy
Do not grieve to long
For I am happy and at peace
Upon my spirit song

Sima L. Walker

With These Thoughts

My love for you is true.
Not seeing you makes me blue.
If I could just hear your voice,
my heart will rejoice.
I want to hold your hand in mine
just to have our fingers all entwined.
I will walk a hundred miles
just to see your handsome smile;
and to have your lips kiss mine—
oh, that is so divine.
The taste of your tongue
is like a taste of expensive wine.
With these thoughts
I hold special in my heart,
all the while we are apart.

Joan Sharon Washington

Haleyana

The deepest of browns
In her eyes so round

Her hair is just as nice

The curls would reach the sky
If you pulled them out (or try)

His one and only vice

Her beauty is like none other known
This grandchild our very own

Our lasting sugar and spice

The love of our life
Through grief and strife

To be her grandparents is, oh, so nice

Wanda E. Caldwell

Rain

A fall of rain
A simple tear from the sky
A tear from above

A fall of rain
Spoken on the breath of a cloud
A gray world beyond me

It rains all around
It takes my breath away
A gray world beyond me

A fall of rain
That umbrellas can't shield
It keeps my clothes dry
But it dampens my soul

A gray world beyond me
Of the life I once knew

Elana Gleason

Love

Petals fall into the icy water
as I pull them apart
from the beautiful flower.
As my one true love has left me,
now so scared and once again alone.
I now feel like the flower,
for I have been ripped from my family
and my vibrant petals have been taken
from me. So, now I must learn
how to grow on my own
and hopefully, someday,
love again.

Nikki Elizabeth Waskin

Changes

We stand alone
in a sea of misery,
awaiting the next big wave
that downs our dreams.
Lost among the shallows,
underneath the pebbles,
this is the memory of what should be
but never will be.
We cannot change
the pattern of the waves.
We are unable to see
what tomorrow will bring.
What we have lost
we cannot get back.
Only what is new
can change us.

Amy Sue Keyes

tears

one lasting
waterfall
flowing through a pathway of
sorrow
slipping away from the
grasps
of the quiet
peaks
and slithering along the
simple slope
not speaking
no hesitation
only slow crystal droplets
falling and
slipping
away

Shekesia Janel Joyner

united in aftermath

my voice may be small
but my strength is great
my love for peace
will destroy your hate
you may wound me but i will not break
raise the flag, join hand in hand
united we are
together we stand
trivial you call us
and spit in our face
together we reinforce
and put you in your place
by sheer willpower and man-made grace
raise the flag, join hand in hand
united we are
together we stand

Jessica Lee Richer

Manhood

Cling to your youth
For as long as you can,
But break free from it
When you become a man.
Inspiration comes,
Inspiration goes,
Like the fickle mind
That blows and blows.
But in the last hour
Of our day's life,
What did you do to help another?
What is the fruit of your strife?

David E. Garnett

You Are . . .

You are someone that I call
When I am lonely or
When I am excited
When I just want to talk
About nothing.

You are the one who always
Laughs at my comments,
Even when they aren't funny,
But laughing is the cure for the moment.

You are the one that tells me
The truth about me, but doesn't
Offend me by doing it—you love me.
You are the one I can say it all to
And know that it is safe . . .

You are my friend . . . Kathy

Sondra L. Rowland-Jones

Blame

There are days when the responsibility
Buzzes all around me.
It's an evil demon
Trying to turn me crazy.
I worry that it will work.
I am afraid
Because this need,
This hole,
That cannot be filled
Is an aching, endless craving.
There are days when
I feel just a pang of guilt,
Of regret. Accountability.
And I think
And I know
Who's to blame.

Tyana C. Rees

This Planet Earth

We all own this planet.
We all want space upon it.
This is the time to unite
And share our goods with all.
All nations upon this Earth
Have a responsibility to each other;
The way it was planned by God
Is the way it should be forever.
Loving, caring, and sharing
Is the only way to be.
Is there anyone that can see
This is our greatest destiny?
We all own this planet;
Only together can we save it
To pass on to those who come after
As God intended it to be.

Barbara H. Grey

Lost and Found

Endless wandering
Forever searching
But unknowingly lost

Hiding the loneliness from the world
And from myself
Suppressing the emptiness for so long
Even I didn't realize how lonely I was

Then you came along and saved me
My heart and soul came awake
My search ended

I am yours always

Denise L. Hughes

Sleep

The warmth of your kiss,
the caress of your hand,
words we have not spoken I try to
understand.
I told you I'd be yours,
I told you I'd care.
Yet I turn around,
you're no longer there.
Tears I will not cry,
pain I cannot feel.
My heart has been broken,
don't know if it will heal.
Sometimes I often wonder
if it would not be better,
to close your eyes and sleep a sleep
that lasts forever.

Mary Frances Darnell

Parting

I don't know why you left me,
Or maybe I left you.
But I know you can't stand me anymore
And I can't stand you too.
I'll love you until the end of time,
But now I have to say,
I don't need you anymore,
So stay out of my way.
You were fun when I was little.
We had some real good times,
But you'll see that you annoy me,
If you read between the lines.
You may not respect me,
You may not even care,
But I'll constantly be in your mind,
You know I will be there.

Erin Winslow St. Pierre

Falling in Love with You

I haven't known you very long,
But that's not the way I feel.
I've told you all about me;
I have nothing to conceal.
Though what I say may sound silly now,
But you'll find it to be true.
I never thought that when we met,
I would fall in love with you.

You are my new beginning,
My door to life beyond,
All I would ever want
Or ever need to carry on.
Though what I say may sound silly now,
But you'll find it to be true.
I never thought that when we met,
I would fall in love with you.

Giovanna Lucia Bianca

Traveller in Time

From a traveller in time
For all the travelling
Still to be discovered
If peace you see seek
It's actually quite near
For it's within
You'll find to win
Sought-after riches
Not found in lives
So many folds and ditches
For a candle once it's found and lit
To find that you're existing within it

Egon Demuth

Polaris Pull

Running away ain't getting me far
Because I lost sight of my North Star
Polaris pull me in again to you
Back to the me I once knew
Pull me into the sky above
To the starry heavens I love
Up to Orion I can soar
Into light and dark evermore
Swirling galaxies around me twist
Beautiful phenomena I had missed
Meteors shower the Earth like rain
Showing me there is hope again
For now I'll look to my sky
And not wonder how or why
I'll catch a falling star in a glance
Everything happens in life by chance

Barbara Ann Mergel

What I Am

I am a beautiful endless circle.
I can be silver, yellow or white.
I have no beginning or end,
just a beauty that shines bright.
I have been around for many years
through all the smiles and frowns
and I will be around for many more
to see all the ups and the downs.
I am a symbol of something great,
something that will change you
a precious gift that one will get,
one that shall last a lifetime too.
So you want to know what I am?
With the happiness I can bring
a symbol of unconditional love,
I am nothing more than a wedding ring.

Cheryl Lynn Dolan

I Want to Be with You

I want to be with you;
that's what I need;
because when I'm with you,
I see.
I want to be with you,
to be held in your arms;
you'll keep me safe,
away from all the harm.
I want to be with you,
to feel your soft lips,
to be held against you,
and feel your gentle kiss.
I want to be with you;
that's all I need.
I want it to last forever,
just you and me.

Jennifer Lois Rygg

The Search

I set forth on the Sea of Search,
Driven by winds high above the Earth.
In the face of the gale,
My soul sounds an eerie wail.
The angry waves of the sea loom high.
The search, it seems, is doomed to die.
The fear of a voyage futile
Swells the water like foaming sputal.

Almost consumed by desperation,
The search goes on with no altercation.
My spirit rides low in the waters deep,
A search aground, never to reap.

Yvonne Naomi DelVecchio

I Found You

When I gave up hope for love,
I found you.
When I prayed to God for a miracle,
I found you.
When I was looking for comfort,
I found you.
When I thought I'd never find love,
I found you.
When I thought life was over,
I found you.
When I had no one to run to,
I found you.

How did I find you?

All I can say is:
I'm happy I found you!

Candice Ann Dickson

Run and Hide

Scared and confused
of the world outside,
everything is so messed up
I just wanna run and hide.
Friends I'm not sure of,
don't know if they'll always be there.
Maybe they're just there for sympathy
not because they really care.
Some people don't like me
because of how I act.
There's no reason to hate me,
if you don't know all the facts.
I look outside to the world,
scared of what I may become.
Why can't it just happen?
Why can't it just all be done?

Shaunte Yowell

Forever Friends

Come the Days
Gone the Years
the shine of Smiles
the Shed of Tears
Secrets spilled
Memories made
Precious Moments
that will Never fade
throughout my Life
you were there
whenever I needed
a Friend to care
Fights were fought
yet We made amends
Together then
Forever Friends

Marissa Mae Gurtler

Simply Speaking

I'm myself, myself is me.
Nobody knows this, but I'm free.
I talk out loud, I run out wide.
Sometimes I'm small and I hide.
I've waited so long for this day,
And now I'm going to fly away,
Fly past your boundaries and your laws,
Fly to my world that I adore.
When it's all over, I will lie,
Rest my head as I die,
Thinking about you and me,
And thinking about how I was free.

Melissa Louise Hardman

More Alone

More alone, than each
time before.
Coming home, while going
out the door.
Every time, while
trying to touch.
Rolling away, with
distance and such.
Crying inside, the
feelings I hide.
Rotting away, like a
road kill's's hide.
Separate each like
good friends flown.
Diminish us less than
being more alone.

Timothy J. Purdy

Dying Dandelions

Dying dandelions and
Twitter-painted signs and
You're so cold to me and now
There is no breath left in me
Lost in thought and lost in
Mind and lost in heart I
Can't see you, you're too far away
I can't voice what I need to say

'Cause I can barely speak and
You're so cold to me and
I can hardly breathe but I am
Strangely still alive
Haunting dreams still make me
Wish you were here now with me
Till then I'll lie here with these
Dying dandelions

Amber MacKenzie Hamilton

A Healing New Home

The beauty of this atmosphere
Makes me feel extremely dear.
Breathtaking the mountains are
And night time sky full of stars.
Here has brought a lesson taught,
Something that I never thought.
A land that holds so much inside,
The people here have lies to hide.
Healing is the sight I see.
Colorado's affecting me.
Without friends and all alone,
At least I have this place as home.
I could be in no better place.
God has blessed me with His grace.
This feels like a dream to me.
It could last for an eternity.

Katey E. Saari

The Lord Will Be with Me

The Lord will be with me,
I'll remember that always.
And Satan won't be there,
No dark and black hallways.
The Lord will be with me
To hold me real tight,
To watch and protect me
All day and night.
The Lord will be with me,
No Satan like a knife.
The Lord will be with me
The rest of my life.

Ashley A. Bodette

Spirit

Spirit soars like never before—
Unbelievable like rivers roar.
Wind rushes like angels in the sky,
Watching down like hawks flying by.
Spirit glides like fish in the sea.
It never hides or lives in trees.
Animals frolic, skip, and play.
It's true to say they have fun days.
Spirit is life all on its own.
It's mischievous, sly,
And never alone.
It's always a friend until the end.
Spirit sails like kites in the sky,
So free and happy as they wail.
Birds fly high with songs of joy,
Spreading the word of never-ending time.

Brandi Michelle Kempfer

Insight

In the moonlight
The caress of light
Oh, beautiful sight
In my arms tonight
I shall write and write
Tonight be right
Love shine bright, tonight

I know, I go
Forward to the love I sow
I sweep her off her feet
I leap towards fate to meet
I know to go
Love low and show
Love right, be right
Tonight and forever
Insight, I endeavor

Calvin Perry Johnston

The Gentleman

A gentleman of our country
Protects the weak and small
Kind words he gave us
To boost our spirits tall
Amazed by the ability
We mothers carry on
To teach our little treasures
Difference of right and wrong
Soon he'll be going
Back to his home
Leaving us his laughter
His smile to linger on
Warmth from below
We send out to him
Our gentleman of this country
Blessed is this man

Carrie Ann Anglin

Stony Bridge

I sit upon a stony bridge,
an azure sky floats above.
The crystal waters down below
usher in sweet thoughts of love.
A flower tossed into this brook,
carried down this gentle stream,
a symbol of my love for you,
angel of my ev'ry dream.
A gentle mist rolls down the hills,
just outside the shady knoll
where you first touched my tender heart
and forever won my soul.

Joseph A. Huddleston

Reflection

As I watch a girl,
just as pale as a pearl,
just standing there
with no worries and no cares,
but when you look closely,
oh, what fools we be,
if you can't see
that she is me.

When you look in a mirror,
does your figure seem to differ
than what is normally there,
since we never really care?
But when you really notice
and you just sit down and focus,
you see that that's the real you
and nobody else but you.

Nadia Arielle Guennouni

Your Smile

When I woke up today
I tripped out of bed
Fell down the stairs
Landed on my head
I poured my cereal in the dog's bowl
Ate it with a fork
Figured out the mix of frosted flakes
And orange juice really doesn't work
I brushed my teeth with triple ointment
Gargled with peroxide
It tasted kind of funny
And I thought that I might cry
This morning was a death wish
I'll be laughed at for a while
But it was a great day
Because I got to see your smile

Chelsy Jo Phillips

Realization

She thought she had a good life.
Now she's not so sure.
The truth is starting to surface.
She can't pretend anymore.
Her past was such a mystery,
With the things she didn't know.
The secrets that were kept;
The pain they didn't show.
Scared of the future,
Hurt by the past;
She's lost in a confusing world—
A world that's moving fast.
But a lesson she must learn
Is time waits for no one.
This battle she is fighting
Has only just begun.

Renee Molony

Only a Minute

It takes only a minute
To say a word of cheer.
It takes only a minute
To dry a falling tear.
It takes only a minute
To lend a helping hand.
It takes only a minute
to try and understand.
It takes only a minute
To brighten someone's day.
So use this very minute
Before it slips away.

Archana Sameer Mahimkar

Pain

You wanted to be together forever,
but forever turned into never;
never had,
never was,
never will be again.
It's a shame to lose then gain,
but all the pain still remains.
Remains here in my heart,
so we're really not torn apart;
apart from each other,
apart from me,
apart from what was never meant to be.
Be heard.
Be seen.
Be met.
Man, I wish we never met. . . .

Ashley Noel Davis

Escaping the Dread That Festers

To Josiah, my heart in Heaven:
May God hold you close.

Throughout these quiet moments,
The silence that I fear,
My life lay still before me;
These times I know you're here.
The sin I clutch with fervence,
In stillness you provide
His rescue to your solace;
In you, my mind abides.
Escaping this dread that festers—
From feeling he's lost and alone,
I call to you for comfort;
Only your spirit can atone.

Erin Formby

Masquerade Ball

I live in a masquerade world
With a masquerade mask
I dance to the tune
Of the song masquerade sound
How I long to loose my mask
And waltz to my very own beat
How I long to make my own tune
And loose the ongoing drone
but the masquerade sound keeps going
and my feet can't break the beat
My mind may wonder
But my feet can't break the beat
I live in a masquerade world
With a masquerade mask
I dance to the tune
Of the song masquerade sound

Chelsea Elizabeth Blackstone

Children

The sweet innocent mind of a child,
their imagination which runs wild.
The sound of their laughter
makes them run faster.
Their delicate being
has so much meaning.
Children's intricate minds,
there are so many kinds.
The purity of their souls,
their fun never dulls.
The magic a child may behold
is more than what could be told.

Diana Michelle Frank

The Day We Said Goodbye

I held your hand till it went cold
Your soul had slipped away
You couldn't hold on anymore
I begged you so to stay
Your time on Earth came to an end
God had now called you home
Part of my heart went with you
So you didn't go alone
Please be there with open arms
When my journey here is through
And welcome me with your embrace
As warm as I once knew
Goodbye, my precious mother dear
And save a place for me
Right in your loving tender arms
Where I was meant to be

Gail L. Hyziak

Foolish

The softest touch doesn't mean much
At least not in your mind
And while you hold me tenderly
I wonder how I became so blind
Staring deep into your eyes
I realize my heart's deception
Stubbornly it clings on
Where there is no connection
I can fool myself no longer
I know exactly where I stand
I'm just a willing slave
Obeying your command
And maybe I really do deserve
The anguish I'm forced to feel
Because you never promised me
That what we had was real

Lisa Marie Majewski

Untitled

My world had begun to crumble.
Piece by piece, my dreams were gone.
I'd lost too many times,
and was tired of pressing on.
The hope I had of love
was quickly disappearing,
but since the day you kissed me,
the clouds have started clearing.
You taught me how to love,
and made me your obsession.
Now you've won me over,
and my heart is your possession.
I used to always fear
of being old and lonely,
but now I'm not afraid
because you'll be there to hold me.

Danli Brooke McClanahan

Family Buttercup

Petals falling softly up
Arrange a giant buttercup
One by one they are picked in place
Side by side and face to face
A lovely flower to behold
Our family members do unfold
Holding hands with gentle care
With love are waiting to greet one there
Oh, so young to float so far
It's okay, love, there is a guide
You swiftly, softly up
To fill your place in our buttercup

Mary Ruth Graham

Bright and Free

The grass sways
In a warm May
Warm sand between your toes
In the sky, birds fly low
The sun brightly shines
Everything is peaceful and fine
The mountains stand tall
With snow tops acting as shawls
The light blue sky
Makes you gasp and sigh
About how beautiful life can be
Beyond the sea
With wisps of clouds
And quiet forest sounds
This is how Earth should be
Bright and free

Colleen Kathrine Dooley

Invisible Man

People look right through me
No one really sees me
When I walk through the hallways
I'm not even there

No one understands me
All that I could be
How can you find me
When I'm not anywhere

Because no one can see me
I don't even exist
I'm just a shadow that fades in the sky
I want to be noticed
But no one is able
To see an invisible man
I am the invisible man

Steve Wilburn

My Smile

I look but cannot see
Feeling joy come upon me
I seek what has been doing this
But can only sense it
For it's like the wind
I know it's there
Because I can feel it
And breathe it
So, a dark cloud rises above my head
The wind will drive it away
And put sunshine on my face once again
For as you said
My smile is what makes the sun rise
Every morning
And you are what makes my smile rise
Every second

Mindy Janell Fadden

When I See You

When I see you my heart beats
It beats faster than ever before
My mind goes around and around
For it is confused because of you
You make my mind go crazy
My emotions are ever flowing
They are flowing through my body
Trying to find a place to rest
My energy is static for you
It seems to have no place to go
But into your heart it must flow
But the love for you will stay with me

Anthony Davis Ziebarth

she was my world

she was my world
and my world came crashing down
the thunder split the skies
and the ground shattered to pieces
all the buildings exploded
and all the people died
the jungles burned to the ground
and all the animals with it
my heart cracked in half
and my soul cried itself to death
just like me
just like me
she was my world
and now my world is in ashes
empty of all existence
and ready for the next destruction

Tyler Matthew Hambrook

Gateways

Eyes, gateways to your soul;
deep blue like the ocean,
gently whispering stories untold.

They tell all or nothing
in the blink of an eye,
whispering truths unknown or
lie protecting your soul
from grief and pain untold.

Revealing all is to hurt like
nothing felt before, to give
complete control of yourself
to the one who knows.

To surrender and reveal all,
love and trust, the gateways
to your inner soul.

Sarah Young

My Name Is Russell

What day is it?
I don't know anymore.
They fuss at me to eat.
I thought that I did.
My name is Russell.

Virile and handsome once upon a time,
Now I'm skin and bones.
So stiff, its hard to walk.
Did you know I once walked on the moon?
My name is Russell.

My Peaches takes care of me.
We once were lovers, you know.
Now I can't remember her birthday.
Oh, to be young again.
My name is Russell.

Beverly W. Johnson

sisters

close to my heart
and even closer to my soul
apart from each other
we collapse in pain
but together
we stand tall with strength
our blood is what binds us
but our love is the true glue
tears fall down my face
as i hold you close
and tell you
i'm here to stay

Andrea Ashleigh Rabbe-Martino

Thankful

The sun so bright and warm,
The rain so refreshing.
The mountains so full of beauty,
The wind so strong and moving.
The birds that sing so sweetly,
A stream of clear water.

A loving wife and best friend,
My children so strong and healthy,
The touch and smile of grandchildren.

A loving and forgiving God,
The brush of angels' wings.
A rugged cross,
An empty tomb,
The promise of a coming redeemer.

So much . . . and yes, I am thankful.

Robert Lee Bankston

Be a Light

You never know
What the day may bring
Whether you'll cry
Or whether you'll sing
You never can tell
What will happen next
Or whether your choice
Was really the best
All you can do
Is pray you've done right
Helping others
And be their light
For tomorrow
Is a brand-new day
And only you
Can find your way

Rachel Denise Saunders

Desert Rose

Legend has it or as the story goes
Deep in the desert
A beautiful flower grows
In a garden of sand
It was placed there by the master's hand
And out of all the beautiful flowers
He chose
This one he calls his desert rose
So, I went to the garden to see
If I could just have one for me
He went into the garden of sand
And you were picked
By the master's hand
Out of all the beautiful flowers
He could have chosen
You were picked my desert rose

Randall Clinton Richmond

A Wish for You

I think of you
and start to cry.
You decided to leave
and I wonder why.
You need not go.
So how can this be
that I sit here and wish
you were alone with me?
It hurts to feel.
Why can't you see?
I didn't want you to go.
Please come back to me.

Jessica Irene Merkes

Do I Love Him

Do I love him
How will I know
Will I skip when I walk
Or will I look all aglow

When will I know that he loves me too
Do I believe when he tells me his love
Is true

Will the feelings we feel diminish
With time

Will I break his heart
Or will he break mine

I wish that I knew without any
Doubt how love really feels
And what it's about

Mary J. Fitzgerald

Beautiful Death

Death can be hard
Taking people we'll miss
But it sends them off
To beautiful bliss
Death is not dark
Just a loss of breath
Harsh words are not true
When they're used against death
So you see
Death can be a beautiful thing
It is God taking people
Further under His wing
Oneness with God
And enlightenment
Passed ones get
First class treatment

Garrett Thomas Sanford

Ryan

Your eyes are so deep
They reflect your soul
Gentle, passionate
Your lips are so soft
Pressed up against mine
Your arms are so warm
I adore your touch
Don't ever let me go
Your hand enfolds mine
The touch is sincere
Your voice is so smooth
Calling out my name
My feelings for you
I want to explain
But words cannot capture
How I feel for you

Amanda A. Basterash

Your Love

From the time it began
Until the end of time,
I know it will be there,
Never changing nor lost.
It will remain constant
And even grow larger.
Though time is brutal
And miles apart,
It never leaves my side.
Inside of me it will remain
And the treasure it is;
Your love I will always keep.

Belen Nevarez

The Roaring Silence

Alone with my thoughts
On a warm summer's eve,
Down a deserted beach
I walk, to relieve
All the tension and stress
Of the daily workplace;
Trying to ease my mind
And smooth my face.
The sound of the surf
Drowns all city chatter.
Hearing nature's noise
Is truly all that matters.
After a soothing stroll,
I feel, once again, sound.
All it takes is the silence
Of the roaring waves pound.

Daniel J. Killian

I Swear

Manipulative ways, narcissistic rage.
Watch the pawns, how they play.
Prey on them till they're feeble,
Move in on them when they're unable.
Twist their fate into need.
Succumb them to your greed.
Fraudulent tears, attention fears.
Tolerated your games for years.
Now you play alone,
Prey on no one.
You can't hide it, when you speak.
I can see through you.
You're weak
And you won't break me.
As time goes by, you'll see,
You were nothing but a toy to me.

Angela Jade Carrier

My Memories

Twinkling eyes
smiling face
gentle touch
whispers of love
I will remember thee

Dancing until dawn
laughter in the air
wealth of advice
fountain of knowledge
I will remember thee

Darkness of the nights
sunshine in the days
moments of joys
forever in my heart
I will remember thee

Shanta Devi Persaud

Fate May Be Wrong

After all these years
I still think about you
I wish you'd come back
And we'd begin anew
But would it all end
Just as it did before?
Or would you treat me right
And make my heart soar?
Maybe fate pulled us apart
Perhaps it was destiny
But sometimes fate is wrong
Were we meant to be?

Bryan Sebrell

Heartaches

We've had our share of heartaches,
but choose to concentrate
on the good things about us
that fuel our family state.
Suffering humiliation
by the actions of our kin
keeps one humble,
compassionate through thick and thin.
Who among us has not
erred once or twice,
been caught up short,
made to set things right?
It is all part of growing;
developing insights,
setting higher goals
to climb to new heights.

Donna E. Gasteneau

Alan to Laura

How could someone enter
My life so soon
And bring me such real
Cheer with just a tune?
Doing things together
To make real love;
I certainly did not need
A big shove.
I thought that you came
Just in time to me
To dance, visit London
And, oh, gee,
So happy to be with
Only just you.
Vita celebrateo est
Amo tu.

Frank C. Hamlin, Jr.

Beacon of Hope

Where there are shadows,
there is fear.
Where there are shadows,
evil is surely near.
Like smoke,
they do consume
as a deathtrap
waiting in the gloom.
To have shadows,
there must be light—
like a beacon of hope
in the night.
Yes, this light is my hope;
it helps me move on.
With each step of faith,
I reach toward its glow.

Tamara Joyce Becraft

A New Love

My world has come crashing down
and my heart feels torn in two.
A new love has entered my life.
What I thought I wanted is not true.
It took me by surprise,
yet he was there waiting for me;
To show me real love,
if I was willing to see.
Should I act on my desire?
Should I take a chance on my heart?
I could gain a new love
or would it tear my world apart?

Arlene Mae Young

Plea for an Angel

Our angel came so quickly
Filled our lives with joy
Only six months longer
To hold our girl or boy
Tears of joy we shed
With overflowing love
After years of trying
Finally, a gift from up above
Suddenly we lose you
Tearing our world apart
How shall I go on
With an empty broken heart
I cradle empty arms
As tears stream down my face
Silently I whisper,
"Where's our angel to embrace"

Tana M. Watson

First Date

Think a moment
Of the butterflies
Beginning as only a flutter,
The start of what

Anticipation itches the wings,
Yet caught in the syrup of the day
Time grows near,
A twinge, a tickle
The butterflies awake,

Feel a smile break
Soft as a kiss,
Sweet as rain
Between moments

A smile that lights
The butterflies

Sandy G. Wheeler

Apart Together

Why do I feel lonely with you?
Unable to touch you while you are here,
I feel apart when we're together.
My heart cries out tears for you.
How can your eyes show no love
and yet your mouth speaks of it?

What happens to the lingering heart?
Will it break too?
Feeling my heart beating,
so rhythmic, so unchanging,
unable to display the way it feels.

I have lost my only love,
but unable am I to give away
something that I don't have,
something that still has me.

Briana Catherine Roeder

I'm Me

You see green, I see blue.
You see a screen, I see a two.
We are different, you and me,
So why don't we all just go live free?
Stop living lives of a copy cat,
Seeing others, and then react.
People need to see me for me,
Not someone they want to be.
Living free is a choice by you,
Not by someone who made you, you.
So get off your butt, make a decision,
And I better not find you up in prison.

Kenny Michael Good

You're the One

You're the one that keeps me smiling
When I go through times like these
You're the one that stops my crying
When I've soaked a box of trees
You're the one that keeps me going
When I want to throw in the towel
You're the one that keeps me running
When I don't want to go the extra mile
You're the one that stays beside me
When my patience runs so thin
You're the one that understands me
When I fail instead of win
You're the one that keeps me strong
When I feel so hurt and weak
You're the one that can do no wrong
When it comes to loving me

Kristin Yvonne Maas

Derek

A man of many hearts of grace
He left without a single trace
His thoughts were of without a haste
But he had such a beautiful face
He had the courage of a bear
But still he had a little fear
I know he's always with me here
'Cause I always feel his presence near
His time went out before his way
An hour of the blackest grey
For Derek I will always pray
That I will see him again someday
He never gave a single shove
He's in Heaven with all the doves
When I look up, he's from above
But no matter what, it was always love

Lisa Marie Gartin

angels, do you hear me

angels, do you hear me
calling in the night
wishing you were near me
to shed a vision bright
give me love and guidance
show me you are real
for your love inside me
must never yield
so, angels, do you hear me
in the secret night
don't forget to touch me
in your peaceful flight
and i will know you're with me
with your light so bright
giving me peace
in the aspects of my life

Alison M. Campbell

Child of the King

I often sit and wonder
just what God claims to be:
a loyal master, a faithful friend,
our Lord, our God, our King?

He's the Alpha and Omega,
the Beginning and the End,
the Father of all creation.
He says, "I am, I am."

And then I stop and ask myself,
"Just what does that make me?"
An awfully special person,
for I'm a child of the King.

Karen Ann Mazie

What I Miss

Dedicated to my son

Playing all day long
singing him a song

Rocking him to sleep
hushing every peep

Reading Dr. Suess
like a silly goose

Giving him a bath
before his daytime nap

Sharing our dreams
because we are a team

Giving him a hug and kiss
those are the things I miss.

LaDonna S. Hatcliff

Only Me

Today I received a birthday box
wrapped in sky blue tissue
amid angels in assorted
wings of flight
The tie that garlanded the sachet
was white lace
I carefully loosened the knot
lightly removed the wrapping
to save it for another time
I opened the box
Alas, there is nothing I grasp
that I too could be a bejeweled box
on the outside
It is up to me to fill the
spirit from within
only me

Mary S. King

Broken Promises

I gave my heart to you.
You gave your heart to me.
We made a lot of promises
and said it will always be.

At first it was happy and carefree,
this love so grand, so new;
but along the way
some promises got broken
and made the trues untrue.

There must be a little
give and take
in all we say and do.
And . . . you cannot fix
broken promises,
but only to start anew.

Diane Leenknegt

My Friend

You were my friend
that laughed with
me and shared my tears.
You shared the
good times and bad
and kept those secrets within.
As a good song
ends and the sun fades away,
our friendship ends
And I don't understand why
it had to be this way.
I will cry a million
tears for you my friend and
you will not be forgotten.

Jill Ann Marquart

on a summer's day

gentle breezes blowing
clear brooks flowing
on a summer's day

butterflies fluttering
pretty flowers blooming
on a summer's day

lovers walking hand in hand
strolling over grassy land
on a summer's day

frogs leaping in the pond
tadpoles swimming
having lots of fun
on a summer's day

Luvennia K. Ross

Before the Teardrops Fall

I feel like my life is falling apart,
I feel the sadness in my heart.
I don't know what's wrong with me,
But nothing seems to make me happy.
The man I love doesn't even care.
My life just isn't fair!
I love him with all my heart,
But we're destined to be apart.
This kills me deep inside,
I just want to run and hide,
To never see the light of day.
Nothing will ever go my way.
As another teardrop falls,
I have to put back up my walls
And hide my feelings for this man,
Before another teardrop falls.

Linda Abukhzam

Amnesia

Who am I,
Do you know?
Will you let me in
Before I go?
Am I familiar,
Have we ever met?
Do you recall
Or would you rather forget?
It's very strange,
Missing my identity.
Can you give a hint,
Eminence or nonentity?
Who am I,
Confused and so bereft.
I remember I let you in,
Just before you left.

Cheryl Anne Mednick

Siren Song

So calls the siren in the night
A vision on the cliffs of death
Soft, angelic in pale moonlight
You love her more with every breath
And on you sail to your doom
Sweet prince with romance in your heart
To your dark and watery tomb
Lost in her eyes, lost in her art

Nancy Jamieson

Petals of a Rose

The little girl
Plucks the petals of a rose
Dropping them one by one behind her
With glowing eyes and a beautiful smile
She leads the bride up the aisle
And slowly she turns
Just in time to see her petals disappear
Beneath the bride's small feet
And as if in slow motion
The girl begins to cry

Ashlee Lane

One Night

When I met you that night
I knew it was right
I never knew
I could fall in love
At first sight
But now I know it is true
Because I fell in love with you
You made me feel special
Yes, it's true
I have never met a guy like you

Jessica Meyerhoff

Broken

As I lie
My head to the clouds
I watch the world float
But it is not whole
not complete
but broken
shattered
into thousands of small pieces
and in this moment
I am happy

Imogen Cathryn Murtagh

Dark Angel

You are my night.
I am your day.
When I look into your eyes,
I see yesterday.
You are my angel.
Day fades to night.
I see you in sight.
We're only together in the night.
You are my angel.
Night fades to day.
I feel you in my soul.
I lose all control.
You are my angel.
Day and night can't be one,
But when we come to each other
The time passes though our lives
We loved as one.

Sherri Jo Thompson

Stress

Life goes by so fast;
before you know it,
the day has passed.
Like raindrops before our eyes,
one can see the drops;
and before one knows,
the ground has soaked them up.

Alonzo Trejo Gonzalez

Fairies

Once upon a starlit night,
With moon rays all around so bright,
Two fairies danced among the springs
With glitter falling from their wings.
Playing and singing right out loud
As carefree as the endless cloud.
Zipping in among the trees,
Laughter bubbling on the breeze.
Squeals of delight ring across the glen,
With bullfrogs and crickets joining in.
A serenade so pure and sweet
Just to start when again they meet.

Kristina Pulliam

Love Combined

To Mom

A mother's love,
strong as the hardest steel,
never to be broken.

A son's love,
changing through the years;
its strength is always unspoken.

Both,
when combined,
this love can stop the aging time.

Leaving both, with endless love.

Shaun D. Muehlheausler

The Perpetual Fallacy

A despairing darkness, cold and deep
A sentient slumber, dreamless sleep
The past and future doth converge
Into the mind of babe, submerged
The dwelling thoughts, tempered soothe
Form the answers, immortal truths
Divulged with first, resounding cry
Mistaken, forgotten, lost in atrophy
And thus, forever, knowledge misplaced
Undetectable memories, lacking a trace
Elders entrusted, children uncouth
Forever we've lost the knowledge of youth

Benjamin Garrett Keipper

Is

Does the blue moon cry,
imagining a horrible dream?
Is the dark silent and cool,
thinking of winter?
Is there a happy rainbow
remembering a friend?
Is the rose garden showing
red love for a bug?
Or is the mountain pretending
to sing for rain?
And yes, this is how
the world really is.

Kaylyn Christina Cooper

Why?

Why can't everyone always be happy?
Because there would be no tears to cry?
Why can't everyone be perfect?
Who knows why?
Why can't we all just get along?
Because there would be no one to hate?
Why?

Meagan Messina

My Sis

I once had a sister
Who was older than I.
Mom had a miscarriage
And so she died.
I wish I'd seen her once
Before she went away.
I guess God was unwilling
To let her stay.
I never got to know her,
Yet I love her very much.
I feel she's close,
Close enough to touch.

Owen Chi Huynh

The Loner

He didn't care,
didn't care at all.
His presence is unknown,
unknown with nothing but his fear.
He wasn't ever there,
never there for the memories to share.
His touch was cold,
so cold you felt it in your soul.
He never understood,
never understood how to love.
His words are never spoken,
words that must burden his being.

Rebecca Ann Reid

The Song inside of Me

Music is flowing inside of me
Encircling the flowing blood in my veins
A drum beat is the beat of my heart
Sharp notes upon the violin are my tears
Clashing of the cymbals my anger
The melody of the flute my happiness
Guitar chords are my daydreaming
The sounds of the chimes my wishing
Quick notes upon the piano my confusion
The noises blend together
Forming an orchestra to play my music
Playing the song inside of me

Amy B. Blizzard

Never an Angel

Afraid to love
Enveloped by fear
Fighting an endless battle
Screaming on the inside
Smiling on the outside
Lost in a pool of choices
Stranded in a sea of debt
Muddled by confusion
Suffocating in hopelessness
Crushed by failure
Always a shadow
Never an angel

Melissa Malo

pandora's prison

she opens her mouth
to create a crisis
every movement, tense
every breath, a plea for sympathy
advice pummels her
Eighteen stories above
as her sighs overpower my thoughts

Jessica L. Hogg

Helpless Hoping

In the forest of forgotten longings,
shaded by mistaken fears . . .
I sent a message through a vision
shrouded in frustrated tears.
If what I wanted, all desires,
was not what was meant to be . . .
Then may the flame of passion flicker,
dying in an amber sea.
Yet in the instant recognition
of the light within your eyes . . .
Helpless hoping, one more chapter left,
before all love belies.

Kathy J. Fuller

Us and Them

It's an us and them world.
We could never unite!
Due to our differences,
We seem doomed to fight.
We're so glad we're not them!
They could never be us!
But, we spring from the same source,
So why all the fuss?
We all work our own way
And variety is good.
We could all get along—
If only we would.

Jackie Athon-Hodsdon

Nothing

I am nothing—
nonexistent, transparent.
The world around me is a dream,
a bad one.
I'd cherish an hour in dark
solitude,
waiting for life to pass me by
without a word.
Silence is the language of the soul,
but I am nothing,
gone without a trace
or never here at all.

Morgan Elise Ashton

Me, Myself, and I

Me, myself, and I,
Stand as the time passes by;
And I'm finally able to see
That my thoughts are catching up to me.
But as each day goes by,
I take one more little sigh;
And hope to take but one single step
Towards my secret goals I have kept.
I know that someday my time will come,
And it will be more difficult for some;
But still I know I must do my best,
For I am the one responsible for the rest.

Marsha Leslie Fiesinger

Preempt to Love

So many thoughts roam uncaptured
by human ears.
Streams of illusive babble wander
the naked space between us.
Crying out, I hear the whimper of
someone lost and hurting.
Thoughts left unexpressed—
Are you afraid I won't love you?

Courtney Bronwen Hilary Pellow

This Day Is for You

This day is for you
To reflect and enjoy
All the prizes in life
God has blessed upon you
On this wonderful day
I want you to know
You have won the grand prize
My love for you

Gary Dean Coe

Death Does Mourn

The very core of a heart does ache.
Sorrow soars, insisting to break;
One lost spirit must it tend.
Perception drives emotion to bend.

Peace must pain drive to make;
Breath does pain strive to take.
Chaos does emotion send;
Forever long it takes to mend.

Shaun Edward Ward

The Unseen

A storm rages as life goes on,
nothing is as it seems.
A silent deadly killer of souls,
our secrets lie unseen.
For, if one should know the horrors
underneath our false facade,
would they still wish to know us
or would they flee from that unseen?

Pamela Dawn Nugent

Nameless Strangers

The world is full of nameless strangers
Another someone in the crowd,
Uncertain of the future dangers
Reckless, young, innocent, and proud
Living every day
In a sea of others just the same,
Trying every way
Not to be just a stranger with no name

Anneke Maia Rachinski

Water Nymph

Snow is falling to the ground.
A water nymph has fallen down.
In a field solitaire,
she laid her bloody golden hair.
Delicate is her skin,
strong the magic she has within.
She is passing slowly away,
deciding she can't end this way.
She takes her dagger made of stone,
and cuts her throat to end my poem.

Dennis S. Lanning

Serendipity

The warmth of a first kiss
The gentle breath against your ear
The arms of comfort
As the sun leaves the Earth
The breeze upon the skin
And the love of all time
All which are the gifts
Of serendipity

Krista May Warren

Living

I come home and there's nobody home.
There's always nobody home.
No more ice cream in the cone.
I'd probably miss being alone.
Like a surf longing for a throne,
I long for messages on my phone.
How does a singer sing at this tone?
How does a singer sing at this tone?

Jonah Jerry Jackson

Night Sky

The sun is covered with the night
The stars will form to make our light
The wind will whisper and will blow
The leaves will join into the show
The little streams will trickle along
The rivers and seas will join their song
The stars go black in the dark lake
As the rays of the sun awake

Paige Katherine Fleming

I Think I'm Falling in Love

Flames blaze through my heart
Like an owl in the dark,
Burning from the inside out.
Not knowing what this is all about,
I get this funny feeling inside,
A feeling that I can't describe.
I think I'm falling in love, I do.
I think I'm falling in love with you.

Heather Jean O'Guinn

Flying Above

Looking down on those days gone by
Smiling at life passing by
Hoping that this is all a dream
Thinking that it's not what it seems
How is it that I got up here?
Why is my family not near?
Flying above, lonely and free
Flying above, does anyone miss me?

Carly Heinle

This and That

This is this and that is that
said the boy who wanted that.
That is that and this is this
said the girl, the little miss.
If I give you this, can I have that,
asked the boy who wanted that.
Not for that you can't have this,
said the girl, the little miss,
Because with one of these
I can get all of those that I want.

Dennis Scott Simnick

A Poem

There once was a reddish fox
Who lived close to Fort Knox
He scratched at a spot
'Cause he itched a lot
And wondered if he had chicken pox

Kate Miller

Cedric

Calmly watch the sunlight drift
Embrace the love your lover gives
Determine to stay forever as is
Remember this day and it
will continue to live
Entwine the life both have live
Calmly watch the sunlight drift

Melody Cecilia Wibisono

Thief

To anyone who has ever been in love

You came into my life,
Set me at ease,
Stole my reason,
left only constant thoughts of you.
You left my heart for the next theft.
Will I be angry if you took it . . .
No, I long for it.

Bill Ulbrich

Just Know

Just know that time cannot
erase the weight on the
human heart.
Just know that time can
only help the human heart
remember the past altogether
different.
A face once HATED, can be LOVED
with one forgetful glance.
A love can be reborn.

Patricia Cox

your eyes are scarlet-ribboned skies

crash into the flames
ashes as the earth again
unseen, yet unforgotten
rise strange and anew
yet no different than before
as they fade
sorrow lingers as they fade
bound to the reverie
perfect pastel

Michael William Klimovich

Life Is Like a Stream

Life is like a stream:
at one point
it's calm and peaceful,
yet further down the way
it's rough and rocky.
No matter how rough
and rocky life gets,
the beginning and end
of a stream
is always calm and peaceful.

Catherine Margaret Sims

Teresa Helen Becker

You're more brilliant than the sunshine
Gentler than the fastime
Worth more than armed, never be the same
But since young graced, never be the same

John H.

A Smile Lost

Wandering eyes that meet by chance
Stubborn minds that keep their stance
Force it out and push away
Somehow, someway, some things just stay

As I walk by and steal a glance
Wonder why I took the chance
Hide the frowns and force the smile
Wear protection in denial

Louis R. Fourquet

Can It Be?

Can it be August?
Where'd July go?
It furnished the heat and
The drought does show.

Will August, likewise,
(With hints of fall)
Bring us the same?
Let's think "snowball."

Evelyn Copple Widner

Song of the Morning

I hear music in the squirrels at play,
Who run among the trees each day!
With swooshing tails and lively feet,
They gaily tap a happy beat.
Birds sing backup to the furs,
Cardinals shrill and blackbird purrs.
Bright sun announces morning's birth,
As nature's singers brim with mirth.
But interloping man within,
Makes music end in rush of din.

Renee D. Robare

The School Bus

The school bus draws near.
Moms' eyes full of tears,
Young eyes full of fears.

The school bus draws near.
Dads' minds full of pride,
Young minds waiting to ride.

The school bus draws near.
Their first day of school,
Only twelve more years.

Ronald Edward Gale

Love

My love,
Why have you left me?
Is it my eyes who have deceived me?
Can it be?
No, uncertainly.
I cannot see for the reason,
Or is it the changing of seasons?
Tell me, my love.
I must know the truth.
Tell me!

Angela Barnett

To a Sea Gull Far from Shore

To fly, white bird, like you,
Far above man and his mediocrity
To view the world
And yet be blind
To somber shadows of the soul,
To rise above my soul's dark night,
Cast off the pain, the hurt, the fright,
And spread my heart in winged flight,
To soar unfettered into the dawn—
This is my dream that cannot be,
For I chose these chains
Of self-forged fears
That bind me to the dust,
And though I dream of wings and space,
I am afraid to fly.

Cheryl Lee Andersen

Life

And in the end of days
You'll find
Some beautiful photographies
Of mind.

And in the end of days
You'll part
With few photographies
Of heart.

And in the end of life
You'll see
That death is like a
Quickly
Shot
Film to be.

Undine Godsent

Far from the Coldness

I was not except a stranger,
Only familiar with the winter.
I was not except a lonely wayfarer,
Passing through a way unfamiliar.
Your "LOVE" made me familiar
With all the beauties,
With all the warmth a heart can offer
In the coldness of the winter.
Stay sweet here.
Stay forever here.
Let fly to a world
Full of roses.
Let go to where
"THE ROSE" has no thorn.
Let stay far from the coldness.

Melina Nazarian

My Internal Agony

Karol, thanks for being there
when I needed you. Love, your sis

His features chiseled into perfection
An expression of frailty in his face
Too vulnerable for the touch
And kept in a miniature box
In need of protection
In need of attention
Too weak for the vicious, violent world

Tired of fighting a futile battle
Life drains from his body
His bones relax and crumble
A last gasp for air
Followed by an eternal peace for him
And an internal agony for me

Dorine Mildred Coello

Ego's Mouth

Careless whispers of ego's mouth
in search of personal gain
How the spiked tongue devastates
Invisible are the daggers of envy
Whispers proclaim inferiority
Demonstrations of broken halos displayed
through selfish vision of pride's dismay

Careless whispers of ego's mouth
cut like swords unsheathed
Improved self-image remains out of reach
for beyond the whispers
others are so willing to hear
only the vacant engage in the
careless whispers of ego's mouth
Afraid and empty they shall always be

Lori Maurizi

Fear

Ice runs through my veins
After breaking from the source.
With one beat of my heart
My brain and toes go numb.
Dizziness washes over me
As my eyes glaze over with frost.
My lunch is suddenly in my throat
And my knees cannot support me.
Old memories wash over me
And suddenly I am not myself.
The voice I hear is distant.
It urges me to stand
And face what lies ahead of me
As I feel the sudden comfort
Of a warm hand.

Casey McFarland

The Bond of Four

To my beautiful kittens,
Ampris, Loki, and Jude

The love I show is strong I know
A bond of four, there can't be more
Still, I think when they go
Then what love can I show
The world itself will forever shake
For it's a bond and cannot break
What then, I find I ask
Must I wear this painful mask
The bond of four is great, you see
And time I know is running out
But it's not too late, so hear me shout
I love them so, by now you know
Please don't make me watch them go

Kari Lynn Holm

His Grace

To Jesus Christ, my Savior and Lord

When in the hour of my filth and shame
I fall upon my knees and cry
I seek your face and call out your name
And get the answers to my question why
I yell with all my heart and soul
Because I am lost without you
And I have stepped in another hole
I pray and hope you make my life new
But at once your peace comes over me
And I start to think of your love
And now I know deep inside I'm free
Set free from the big man above
And gone are all the hurts and pain
And gone are all the tears that stain

Lorinda Hamon Perez

Father

My father is that one
Who works.
My father is that one
Who taught me to read.
That's my father!

My father
Has inspired me.
I hope I'm like him
When I grow up.
That's my father,
Who loves his two countries.

That is my father,
And I'm proud to say,
"That's my father!"

Nelson Fernando Contreras

i am

i am an athlete
i have a dream
to be the best of me

i am a writer
i have a dream
to write what i feel

i am an artist
i have a dream,
to draw what i see

i am myself
i have a dream
to be different from everybody

i am me

J.J. Mercedes Kfoury

Grandpa

You will always be in my heart
I remember you by the way you walked
The way you weren't always that smart
And most of all the way you talked

It has been almost a year
Since the day you passed away
To all of us you were so dear
Yet we will see you up there some day

I think of you each day and night
Dreaming of you still being around
Wishing you were in my sight
Here on the Earth, the ground

So never fear
Because we are here

Ashley Nicole McIntosh

the way things were

the way things were
are no more
forgotten feelings
leave a void
where a heart once was
the call that never comes
a voice you long to hear
the recognition of a time
when all were happy
a distant memory
asleep in a world of our own clique
fear of change
but everything does
sooner or later
we all do

Cathy Blackburn

Father

You are the dawn
The beginning of new life
A gifted artist
Designing and creating
Shaping and molding
Working to create a unique masterpiece
And when your work is complete
You don't toss me aside
Or throw me on a forgotten shelf
But set me free to sail the waters
In search of the trusted lighthouse
The star in the night
Shimmering over the sea
The beacon
That will carefully guide me home

Barbara Jean Michelsen Zimmerman

To Be Yours

These words are for Sonya,
a wonderful friend of mine.

When you smile the sun rises
Turns my knees to water
I see stars and hear sweet music
When I hear your laughter

When you speak my pulse starts racing
Singing in my veins
Knowing we're so far apart
It causes me such pain

I would give up fame and fortune
Diamonds by the score
Just to hold your hand in mine
And wish that I were yours

Darren Cozens

Too Late

My love,
She's wearing a mask,
But I can see her eyes.
Nothing escapes me.
Her mask is transparent.
My love
Is not mine at all.
Her mask is for another.
I don't see it now, but this I know.
Her face would scare him away.
My love,
Her mask is that of flesh
Of which I've never seen.
Her mask is in my hand.
He can see her face.

Chris Kuric Messer

Swimming for the Shore

The diamond is prized for its rarity
As is gold, money and ivory
A grain of silver for a beach of clay

Yet a rare idea is ridiculed
A rare opinion disregarded
A rare point of view is overlooked
A rare heart is brokenhearted

The voices in harmony
Are swallowed by solos
The song of peace
Enveloped in war
The raindrop of love
Lost in a sea of hatred
Is desperately swimming for the shore

Robert J. West

The Reflection and Me

Why are you looking at me
The same way I look at you?
Why do you copy me?
You and I both know you do.
Why can't you go to some far off place
Where no one can trace you?
Not even your face.
Your face?
No, it's mine,
So give it back.
You better get yourself back on track.
I'm losing it myself,
Just looking at me.
The mirror destroys things.
It has destroyed me.

Martine Read

A Fearless Front

Fear is nothing but a silly emotion
which people make up;
an emotion that makes life harder
yet we all fear.
Some would say that I fear nothing,
but I am no different.
I'm not afraid of heights,
nor am I of water.
Enclosed spaces don't bother me,
and darkness is nothing.
No, my fears lie elsewhere—
fears which are hidden deep
until brought out by another.
She is who I fear—
the one I love is who I fear most of all.

J. Hindman

In the Night

The monsters are at night
They tread the dreams
with horror and fright
The cruelty of today
they send upon you
You wake with a heavy start
Close your eyes
The monsters appear
Got to sleep
with haunted dreams
So live with monsters
in your head no one goes
If they did the horror they would see
it will carry to their dreams
No it will be done alone

Brenda L. Schultz

You're the Best

There's nothing left to say
They've all had their day
They were sent away
You're the best
The rest all know
You're here standing strong
A champion among them
They get a feeling in their hearts
When you come near
It's called fear
You're the best
You stand out from the rest
Everything you've done
Shows you're number one
You're a champion

Francis Darcy

November

Piercing gray stillness
Calls forth frozen-frost sadness
Found in fleeting snows.

Look close, see the ground?
The bare, bitter snow-laced
Brown. Fields that never end.

Like an ancient film,
Empty fields, gray and white,
Brown grasses bending.

The touch of the snow
Reflects the sky it's below
And smothers the world.

Theresa Ruth Grate

Baby Footprints on My Mind

Give me comfort all the time
Walking softly through my thoughts
Baby footprints comfort brought
Baby footprints softly there
Reminding me of days of care
Baby footprints on our hearts
As worry and training fill our part
So much love and time we spend
Hoping in them success to send
Baby footprints show the path
Of life's long road when people ask
Baby footprints on my mind
Bring me comfort all the time

Margaret Caroline Rasmussen-James

walking in the forest

as i walk with my basket in one hand
and vito in the other
we walk through the forest
we love the music of the birds
the sound of bees buzzing
and the bubbling brook
in which we wash our hands
as we sit by the brook
i take out the bread
and vito gathers berries
i watch with such joy
just me and my son vito
walking through the forest

Zea Carmela Zingarelli

One Last Chance

Look into my heart,
A heart so lost and broken,
All I wish is one last chance,
I'll give you my life's token.

One last chance, that's all I ask,
To look into his calm blue eyes,
Now staring down at me,
From heaven and the beautiful skies.

One last chance, please can I have?
To feel his arms around me,
In a place so safe and warm,
Where a love overcomes me,
But now, now my heart is torn.

Please, one last chance,
But, I know I'll never have.
To be by his side one last time,
And to tell him how much I love him,
So maybe I could say goodbye. . . .

Maria Creager

Your

Your eyes, your smile
Radiate
And your beauty, your grace
Escalates
As your warmth, your touch
Sensual
For your class, your style
Gravitates
Though your natural, your sensual
Passions
In your innocence, your devotion
I find strengthens
Me

O. E. Cruiser Small

Gauntlet

I cannot escape my destiny.
I cannot flee the dark.
It is closing in around me.
I no longer hear the lark.

I am burning in the hands of death.
I am running in this icy hell.
I am losing all my precious breath.
I have yet to reach the dell.

The light is far behind me.
The moon has turned blood red.
The cold, black, lifeless sea before me.
I fear this is the end.

Jessica Milem

Guess What I Am?

Guess what I am?
I like to suck your blood.
If you're all dirty,
I'll suck right through the crud.

I'll bite you on the neck,
I'll bite you on the knee,
I'll bite you on the elbow,
It's all the same to me.

Did you guess what I am yet?
A mosquito—you're right.
But remember, if you try to hit me,
I'll fly out of sight.

James Edward Shields

Falling

I'm so scared now,
I shouldn't even admit this to me.
I'm falling hard now,
And I'm afraid that you can't see.
I'm trembling now,
I'm truly scared.
Tell me, is this how it feels,
To truly care?
And is there any chance,
That you feel the same?
Or am I alone again,
With just myself to blame?
I'm sure that nothing can stop this now,
So I suppose I'll stop trying,
And, if it's all the same to you,
I'd like to stop crying.
So, tell me, do you see me reaching?
Do you hear me calling?
Do you feel me weakening?
Do you know I'm falling?

Brandee Nicole Norton

Snake!

I went swimming
In the lake
While getting wet
Saw a snake

Out of water
Ran for land
Didn't let snake
Get upper hand

Was not watching
Ran into tree
I fell down
Snake ate me

Douglas Vaughn Miller

A World Gone Wrong

What happens to a world gone wrong?
Does it burn with hate
like the differences between two races?

Or spread like a crowd—
And then go places?

Does it smell like blood?
Or rain and pour—
like a flood?

Maybe it paces
like a lie.

Or does it say goodbye?

Jade

The Sun

Purple, pink, orange, and gold,
I gaze dreamily as these colors unfold.
As I gaze, I wonder who . . .
The sun last gave its smile to.

Maybe someone years from now
Will sit and gaze at this same sun,
And wonder who . . .
The sun last gave its smile to.
Perhaps two thousand years ago
When this world was still young and new,
Someone sat and gazed at this same sun,
And wondered who . . .
The sun last gave its smile to.

Jenny Lawson

The Pain of Tomorrow

Yesterday, I looked into your eyes
And called you mother.
Today, you gaze back at me
And call me daughter.
Tomorrow, I regret to wonder;
Will I call you gone?
How cruel this twist of life . . .
Yesterday, your eyes were bright.
Today, your eyes are searching.
Tomorrow, I regret to wonder,
Will mine be filled with tears?
I curse the summer skies.
I fury at the brightened sun.
These days should be black and somber,
As black and somber as my heart.
I cannot grasp this reality.
Our yesterday is gone.
Our today is filled with doubt.
And tomorrow . . .
May be mine and mine alone.

Sarah Lynn Clifton

Just Like Me

I used to walk the footsteps
that every girl would dream,
but then I moved and suddenly—
I was simply me.
True friends came
who liked me for me,
and I realized
that is all I had to be.
Other girls looked past me
and I wished they could see
that really,
truly,
inside,
they were just like me.

Joanna I. Hamlin

Gift Package

You answer the doorbell and
have a look of wondrous surprise. . . .
This package all neatly done up
with laces and ribbons—your heart fills
with momentous patter.
How fresh and lovely . . .
especially topped by a rose,
colored vermilion.
You throw your arms around it.
It's so long overdue.
You usher it into the drawing room and
sit right down beside it
and admire it oh so,
especially since it is me.

Genevieve Vacca

My Heart

My heart does not ache.
My heart does not break.

My heart cannot bend.
My heart cannot mend.

My heart will not die.
My heart will not cry.

My heart shall not live.
My heart shall not misgive.

My heart gives not affection.
My heart gives not mention.

My heart is lost.
I am lost.

Jeffry R. Cahill

The Angry Goodbye

I say goodbye now to you, lover;
I say goodbye now to you friend.
I lay my rose down on you, cheater;
I close the casket on you men.
Your snake of a heart changed
Like a sudden switch in the tide,
And I'm violently dying inside
Because you won't tell me why.
One day you might just learn
What it feels like to be deceived.
The pain you've caused others
Only makes your snake weak;
Your sugar has spoiled my cream.
They say, time heals wounds,
And time seems to be on my side,
But my time is very valuable,
And I'm still sorry that you lied.

Marla S. Laurin

The Cell

In my tired, weary mind
I dream of the days I've missed:
Mama's mashed potatoes,
my love's first kiss.
I seep into the darkness
of my forgotten soul.
I creep once again to my
memories in this abandoned hole.
Guilty, they think I am.
If they only knew
the heart, the innocence,
the depth of this man.
I seep into the darkness
of my forgotten soul.

Melissa Amy Soller

i'm alright

please don't cry
never say goodbye
never let go of my hand
so i don't drift away like sand
you look, but never find me
just don't follow me
it will be alright
live another night
keep me inside your mind
and thoughts of me only kind
realize i'm gone
try to move on
live your life
don't do what i did with my life

Matthew Edwin Coffin

A Moment's Flight

The day was magenta
filtered through rose, sunlit moments
I took communion
from your fork
stabbed bits of Ritz and brie

We were baptized in white zinn
and shared chicken
shorn of wings
unable to take flight
and follow you
in your haste
to leave my bed
my arms
our times together

Lynn E. Cohen

The Rock Pool

The sun shines warm
The breeze blows cool
The waves roll in
On my little rock pool

I dip my toes
Into water so clear
You call out to me
But I do not hear

The pool draws me in
Like a fish I am caught
To another world
I have been brought

You call out to me
But I cannot hear
I am finally free
In a world so clear

Merey Colquhoun

Just Wondering

What was he thinking,
When he held me close,
I wonder.

Was he thinking to never
Let me go,
I wonder.

Was he thinking,
I love you so,
I wonder.

And will I ever
Know,
I wonder.

Mary Byrne-Solari

Love Remembered

Oh, put your arms around me,
and hold me close again.
Make-believe you never left,
but stayed with me again.

Of all the women in your life,
you should have stayed right here.
I loved you more than life itself
and would have always held you dear.

I am sorry you missed out
on the life we could have shared,
but am sure as time goes by,
you'll wish that I was there!

Maryann Bowden

Loneliness

The sound of a whale is lonely.
All alone out there,
Going somewhere—going nowhere.
Seeking its mate?
Seeking freedom?
Seeking its place in the grand
Scheme of things?

Singing its song, as if to say,
I'm here, I'm me!
I have a purpose;
To interact with something out there,
To be free,
To be me.

Dorothy L. Skinner

My Life

As beautiful as can be
So precious to me
My love will always
  Be given to thee
As dear as can be
Most important to me
You will always be
  All these things to me
The time we share
I will always be there
Now and forever
  I will always care
For you were sent out of love
Sent to me from Heaven above
As delivered to me on the wings
  Of a beautiful dove
You, my son, I will forever love
For you are my life

Cody Jay Franzen

Rodeo Cowboy's Prayer

*Lord, protect J. L. and let his face
reveal Your love always.*

Jesus, as I ride and rope today,
Help me, dear Lord, I do pray
Always to keep my eyes on you!
Help me, Lord, in all that I do.

As the rope spins around my head,
Help me to glorify you, instead
Of seeking all the fortune and fame.
Help me, my Lord, to praise your name.

And when this bull twirls around
And I come crashing to the ground,
Help me, Lord, in what I will say.
Let me only yell praises of you today.

Lord, if this horse throws me tonight
Let all the cowboys see your light
Upon this dusty, weathered face.
Let your love shine through in its place.

Cheri Lynn Cornett

2:00 a.m.

It's happening again . . .
Rusty tears rolling into dark seas
Filled with lobster prongs, mildew
And pain . . . awful pain
They hurt, you hurt, so do I

Your name trails off my lips
Soaking wet from rain
I once hated the rain
With all its thundering skies
That was before bells rang
Before love vanished into air

Now it refreshes my face
And sets my spirit searching
It protects me from death
Like yesterday afternoon
While dying my blond hair black
Like this morning
While sipping my mother's coffee
And now, while missing you

Tamara Sue Gerkin

Only One

As the unicorn sweeps
Across the land
A rider rides
With rein in hand
The beast with white mane
The beast with white horn
A thousand years ago
This beast was born
It was born
In a vast, remote land
A great place
Far away from mortal hands
No normal man
Can ride this majestic creature
Only one with a special purpose
Only one with a special feature
That man is out there
Riding his great steed
I only wish I was him
Riding with great speed

Benjamin Bock

Tree

A tree to a child,
there's so much to see,
a giant with a thousand arms
swinging high and free.
Looking high to the sky
the sun sparkles bright,
leaves rain down from above
like stars from the night.
All the leaves are like fingers,
the roots are like toes
wriggling into the ground
to get a good hold.
"This tree is strong,"
said the tiny meek voice.
"I like this tree lots
I've made my choice."
So here the child lays
in the arms of this tree,
a magnificent protector,
held safe . . . serene.

Laura T. Snow

Giants' Shoulders

To see the far horizons
On giants' shoulders I've stood
Squinting at distant visions
I missed my neighborhoods
While looking for wider vistas
I so often failed to see
The beauty that lies so proximate
And the love invested in me
We all so very often run
On treadmills of our own
Designed to keep us moving
And to keep us from moving on
If I should happen to smell the roses
Then a wrong turn I did surely make
The best things so often escape us
As reality dissolves in our wake
When next I meet a great giant
And should he offer to lift me high
I will politely refuse his kind offer
To concentrate on what is nigh

Charles E. Andrews

E Pluribus Unum

In memory of 9/11/01: Stay strong. . . .

Moments of silence
Interrupted by slamming doors
And stifled cries
Hold me captive.
As the silver screen flickers low,
I can't help but stare
At the soot
That covers
The amber waves of grain
That used to shine
For our purple majesties.
Hold your torch high,
My fair lady,
We won't forsake thee.
Guide us through the night
And hold our flag high,
For one day,
All will become one again.

Cassandra Lynn Kimberly

last morning

awake, as i hear your breathing—
it lingers on my skin
soft and warm
reminding me of honeyed tea
out your window—
i hear the morning sounds:
snow shovels undoing the white mounds
that appeared last night,
children wildly yelling
with no regard for the sleeping
on a thursday morning
opening my eyes to you—
you do not move
these ubiquitous sounds
are unable to penetrate
your dreams
I lie my head on you chest
and pull the covers over my head
i can still hear
your breathing

Heather Diane Fausett

Broken Dreams

I held the secret
close to my heart
right next to where
the boys grew.
Our dreams for them
lay shattered
scattered as
tossed toys
strewn along the floor
of the rec room.
Tears of aching
poured from my heart.
Our dreams for them
were no longer theirs.
We are a mommy and a daddy
with broken dreams.
God sees, God cares,
God repairs
through prayer
one toy at a time.

Kathryn Hartman

My Own Worst Enemy

I finally noticed the cold
As it numbed my soul
I've accepted the fact
That my heart is withered and black
I've felt the lies corrode my brain
Just to hide my pain
My eyes now see
Life's simplicity
You spared none of me
To get what you wanted
I gave so generously
And now I'm haunted
You just couldn't see what was right
Some tried to help you
But you pushed them from your sight
Now what are you going to do
Why didn't you listen to the wise
And make things right
Instead of covering them with lies
I could have saved my life last night

Bryon Alan Schmidt

My Love

With not a tear left to cry
I sit alone and wonder why
A different place, a different face
Still the same tale, merely by grace.
Learned my lessons long time before
Over and over, more and more
A fast pace, a fast race
Seeking love, to end the chase.
A beautiful rose, yet can splinter
Sprouting in spring, withering in winter
Sweet smelling, thoughts dwelling
As my love persists to grow.
Ah, yes, my love, never ending
My heart pounds, forever depending
On your smile, though all the while
My love continues to flow.
Love me once, as you will
But do it forever and never say never
Then my heart will be yours
'Til the pounding halts still.

Rob Hoffmann

Butterflies

Dedicated to my grandfather who died—
I love you!

You are an angel of mine
From the grace of God
My tears come and go
But always in globs

I miss you, Grandpa
You came and went
You are the angel
Heaven-sent

If anything harms me
You are there
I love you, Grandpa
When you were there

I sit sometimes
And wonder why
But then you come
As a butterfly

Rhonda Hoover

Early . . . Late . . . Hurt

I hear your voice.
It's been so long.
I don't know what to do.
Show me how to act.
That's not what I want
To see from you.
You seem too different.
You seem too new.
I know how you are.
I know what we had.
It could be the same.
It could be better.
You won't give it a chance.
You keep it buried inside.
Does it hurt you too?
Do you not care at all?
I'm giving up.
You seem out of reach.
I'm on the verge of tears.
You don't care.

Sean M. Kelly

The Mirror

While we were going out
I would look in the mirror
And see the man I had always
Wanted to be
A man that was strong
A man that knew what he wanted
And had someone that he wanted
In you
A man that knew what his goals were
And was making his way to those goals
Someone who loved someone
And worked hard to keep that person
I saw a man
Not a boy
But now all that has changed
And all I see
Is the boy that I have worked so hard
To grow away from
But I guess I didn't work hard enough
To keep you

Mike Mammel

if i could be

if only i could be
a little bit more like you
and a little bit less like me
i would gain a small perception
of what it is to be
to be consisted of such perfection
if only i could be
just like you
then i could let the world see
the closest thing to happiness
is to have the love you give to me
if only i could be
how you are
always so faultless unlike me
you manage to walk in
when everyone walks out
you shine light in places that are dim
if only i could be
could be to you
what you are to me

Patricia Souchois Mello Braz

Our Love

To Bryan, my love

Our love,
why must it be
that our love is so hard to see?
It is clear to thee
that you are the right one for me.
Old loves don't mean a thing
because you gave me your ring.
But a ring
is only a thing.
Our love is deeper;
it just gets sweeter.
We will grow stronger
and stay together longer.
For the rest of my life,
I would love to be your wife.
We'll live our life in blithe
when I'm your wife.
So why must it be
that our love is so hard to see?

Anngele Rosa Vose

Under/Over

The world spins on a fulcrum,
My mind is out of place,
I cannot see my fingers,
There's a grimace on my face.
I don't remember anything,
My sight is lost to dark,
I wish I knew the magic cure,
Because my life won't leave a mark.
Paranoia shows its ugly head,
Its intention is to get me,
I know I'll never out run it,
The magic cure is the key.
And now the cure has come,
My sight returns to day,
My mind clears up in seconds,
Paranoia is held at bay.
From this day forth I'll leave my life,
And start again from new,
But only on the overdose,
My mind still needs a few.

Alex James Manning

One Moment, a Lifetime

I am here, I stand in the middle.
All things move around me.
Something brushes my conscious.
I feel it. It is you.
We stand together, all things moving
quickly by,
selecting what we want to make us
feel good,
selecting what we need to get by,
ignoring all that we fear,
changing all we can to match our
perception of what should be.
Years went by?
Had not only a moment passed?
I was unaware. It went unnoticed.
I stand in the middle. All things
move around me. Time passes. I blink.
Something brushes my conscious.
I feel it. It is Death,
my moment complete.

Cheryle Lynn Silanskis

My Brightest Light

Sometimes when I'm by myself
I sit and think awhile
My thoughts always turn to you
And only then I smile
It takes me back to times gone by
Before you came along
Days so long and empty nights
It could never be more wrong
You came to me, we sat alone
Just talking and spending time
We soon became much closer
All I wanted was you to be mine
When we touched my body trembled
Your kisses made me melt
Lips so soft and tender
So good I've never felt
As my love for you is endless
Our future forever bright
Loving you is just so easy
For you are my brightest light!

Delyse McFarlane

Letters to the Dead

Letters to the dead
What are they for
For your sanity
For their forgiveness
For your forgiveness
No one can answer me
What if they are watching
What if they are here
What if they surrender
What if they want to know
Letters to the dead
Is it really
Are they really listening
Will they help you cope
I sure hope
Dear dad
Are you listening
Are you there
If you are here goes
Letters to the dead

Jennifer Gail Phipps

Unwanted

No matter what I do,
Despite how hard I try,
Nothing every works.
I want to know why.
I just want to be me
And not be hurt again.
Pain is what I now expect
Because that's the way it's been.
I feel like the stepchild,
Redheaded and alone.
Why aren't I good enough?
It hurts to be on your own.
I can't be someone else,
I am what I appear.
Just what is wrong with that?
You act like you don't hear.
My overtures and gestures,
Everything I hold . . .
Friendship, acceptance, love
And so again I'm left alone.

Keri Roeder

Shattered Trust

Sit back and watch
As the world flies by
Drink your scotch
While everyone tries
Won't you care
While they all talk
All of the things they share
It's your heart they stalk
Can't you see
The bruises and pain
Break free
Before it rains
Do you feel
The scrapes and cuts
We made a deal
To forever trust
Don't you know
It's now they come
Nowhere to go
It's forever done

Alina Jo Corrion

On Him I Stand

I often stand in wonder
at the awesomeness of God;
from the highest point above
to deep beneath this sod.
To create the force of the ocean
and the waves that hit the sand;
to mold the splendid mountains
with the firmness of His hand.
Yet, amidst all of this splendor
some yet can't understand;
that His most wonderful creation
was when He created man.
It is by some men's reasoning
that this happened all by chance,
but I know the truth about my God;
on Him I'll take my stance.
So, in those dreaded storms of life
that plague us in this land,
all you ever need to do
is reach up and take His hand.

Timothy D. Sickmeyer

Seed

Walk here with me, brother,
and I would talk with you
along this rolling stream;
stroll a mutual patch of ground
and discuss nature's scheme.
Likely is it along the way,
and without a glance aside,
in passing our paths crossed.
Prices paid along some ways
made no tribute to such cost.
Because those ways define
by some parts misplaced
from one side in a mirror.
Show me if you see the loss,
so what I see will be clearer.
Here I would sow in time
a single meager seed,
but to make a forest grow.
Light a path back near you,
so I turn the way to go.

Robert Knapschafer

I'm in Love

I'm in love
as deep as the sea.
I saw the man
this boy can be.
We are in love;
I don't think people understand.
It makes me happy
when he holds my hand.
I talked to him the other day,
and I told him I miss him.
I wonder if he thinks of me
or even remembers me.
He and I together
is what I wish could be.
I wish he was mine
'cause he's so fine.
At night I think of him,
and sometimes it makes me cry.
I remember the last time
we hugged and said goodbye.

Jamie Diana Hjort

Fly

Oh, little child,
Fly, fly away, little child
Close your eyes
Wander your dreams
Find your wings and fly
Fly away from this world of real
Ruled by greed and hate
Find peace in dreams and fly
Oh, little child, I beg you to fly
Fear not the mares of night
Faith be your guide
In the wood of fright
Oh, little child,
With eyes full of light
See through the darkness and fly
Fly beyond the world of real
Beyond the sun and moon
Beyond the very stars
Find your dreams and fly
Rest now and be at peace

Brennan Patrick Roorda

A Mother's Prayer

When I can't be there
Mommy wants you to know
That my love is there
So don't let go
Just put your hand over your heart
And I'm sure you will feel
The feelings my heart sends to you
Are, oh, so real
I pray to the angels
To guide you tonight
And to forgive me the moments
When I can't be by your side
I pray tonight
And every night to come
To give me the strength
I need to carry on
There is no place in the world
That I'd rather be
Than home with my
Loving family of three

Tammie V. Gibson

Hatred

The rain pounds down
On a soul so thin
And this will all begin
The hatred of kin
Crying so sound
In love I'm stuck
And torn apart
She leaves me here
With a broken heart
A bleeding mind
A blistered soul
A torn up world
It all unfolds
Upon this page
My mind flows fast
With a steady pace
Tears of blood
Flow down my face
It's all over now
My soul's settled down

Jordan Ryan Smucker

Ruitian and Shirong

Ruitian and Shirong,
two puppies I know,
two Shar-Pei sisters
so ugly they're cute.
Ruitian is all red,
big quivering jowled
head like a sledgehammer,
chest like a barrel.
Shirong's coat is fawn
with a face like a hatchet.
She's an avid hock biter;
turn away and she's gotcha.
Ruitian, she's goat-like,
all leaping and bouncing,
while Shirong is manic
depressed, slightly scrawny.
Hours would be needed
to describe them in full.
Both are insane,
not one moment dull.

Patrick R. MacIntyre

Ill-Fated Voyage

This is a poem about a disaster on a starship.

As the ship drifted
On its sea of inky blackness
The crew slept softly,
Unknowing of their peril.

The asteroid slipped
Beneath their sensors
And plummeted on towards
Their silvery-gray craft.

The klaxons blared—
Too little, too late—
As the rock crushed their hopes
And dreams.

Now all that is left
Are the memories and legacies
That they all left behind
In their families.

Theo David Williams

Chariot of Doves

Sitting on your chariot of doves
Silver stars shine all around
Looking like diamonds in the sky
As you fly away
Looking back and smiling
Seeing all who love you
The tears fall from your eyes
Little stars they become
Shining bright, looking on
You see all of us cry
You wish us not to
Gently rubbing our backs
With your smooth-skinned hands
Kissing the tears away
Soothing the stinging ache in our hearts
Your love for us will never die
It will stay in our hearts
On your chariot of doves
Blowing us kisses as you head home
Giving us love and stars along the way

Josie Leah Smith

Shattered Dreams

My heart is cold
Love is sold
Bound in an invisible cell
A small piece of Hell
Locked by my own key
He looks at me
With eyes clear
Hot touch that can sear
I wonder what he found
Voices sob without sound
Inside my aching head
Echoes of everything I said
Could he be heaven-sent
Maybe he'll make me innocent
The way I used to be
Perhaps his touch could set free
These demons in the shadows
In the dark and dusty hallows
Filled with scattered sunbeams
Beyond my shattered dreams

Kaitlyn Elisabeth Ireland

Life

Life is like a rocky road,
Uneven and unsure,
With ruts and stones everywhere,
Like the problems we must endure.
But if you look so very close,
You will begin to see
The answers to your questions
On what your life could be.
It shows how you can clear away
The path on which you tread,
Put all your troubles far behind
And see happiness ahead.
So, walk on down life's rocky road,
Believing all the while
You're solving your problems one by one
And conquering each troubled mile.
For, at the end of every day,
When you lay your head to rest,
You're feeling good about yourself,
Knowing you've done your best.

Priscilla Louise Waite

Sweet Morsels

So many tidbits
Here they come, here they go
Like a roller coaster
Flooding my soul
Coasting like a ship
On ocean waves of bliss
They're true to the heart
Sweet morsels, I pray never to miss
Life is precious, so profound
Sweet morsels
Just think
They're all around
In the halls of our mind
Looking back to see
God gave sweet morsels to you
He gave them to me
No, they're not a chocolate
That you eat
They're our memories
Sacred memories, bitter sweet

Deborah Paulette Dotson

A Daughter's Pain

Tears flow down my face
As I walk toward his grave
I kneel down
And wonder if he's okay
I brush off the dirt
And read the inscription
A beloved son and father
What a contradiction
I'm filled with such anger
Yet a lot more pain
I stand there speechless
There is nothing to say
My dad, an abuser
One more selfish act
Did he take time to think
He'll never be back
His son and daughter
Dealing with their loss
He just left
And they are paying the cost

Tabitha DeAnn Creech

Horses

Over the years
their help has been cherished.
Through many generations
their kind has not perished.
It started long ago
when their kind was spotted;
majestic and beautiful,
strong where they trotted.
Out of curiosity
they tamed these wild creatures.
Now the deluxe model
comes with many features.
A horse is a friend,
your partner in crime.
When you need a comforter,
you can count on them all the time.
From the past to now,
Their purpose has taken many courses.
We truly owe a lot
to our dear friends the horses.

Logan William Murphy

Passages

If eyes are the passage to the soul,
then what leads to the heart?
The warm touch of your hand
on the back of my neck?
Or is it the kiss that I taste
when we are alone?
Maybe love is just a feeling
left to be unknown.
A slow song played
reminds me of you,
your warm eyes,
and your handsome smile.
As I gaze into your eyes,
I thought I'd be alone
and as you looked back,
I knew my love was known.
You keep me safe
and keep me protected.
I wonder if this is true
or something that will soon be rejected.

Heather Michelle Abraham

A Mother's Love

A mother's love is precious
It can never be replaced
For only a mother has
Enough love in that special space
There will never be a better mother
Than the one God blessed us with
With her loving heart and soft voice
Disciplining when Mom had no choice
We thank you God for blessing us
With the time we had
Lord knows we're going to miss her
And it makes us so sad
There is no more pain forever
She's in our Savior's hands
Can't you almost see it
That beautiful promised land
So Mom, you rest in peace
Someday we'll all be there
Living in our new home
That our Lord Savior has prepared

Bernadette Renee Boyd

Temptation

The want for drugs
Is always near.
The trickster's voice
I often hear,
Calling my name,
Promising pleasure,
Opening his palm
To show me the treasure.
I see the powder,
White as snow,
Close my eyes
And here we go.
The memories are back;
How they entice,
Making me feel
I'd pay any price.
What I'd do
For one more time.
Please forgive me
For this last line.

Tricia Victoria Gutierrez

Our Covenant

Please know there is a covenant
That is running with our land
It is called the Constitution
And its purposes are grand
It guarantees our freedoms
And it speaks of liberty
It guarantees the rule of law
And is there for all to see
We teach it in our classrooms
And we live it in our lives
It makes us independent
In our mansions and our dives
It forms the basis of our country
Is the reason we are free
In us it causes confidence
In others jealousy
Which is why we must defend it
Against foes and saboteurs
And those who would pervert it
So that America endures

Keith E. Spero

In the End

What's my life again?
What does it mean?
Will it tear at the seam?
Can I live one day at a time,
Knowing you will never be mine?
Can it be this extreme
To ride on this dream?
Will I jump off a bridge
Or will it be a ridge?
Will it end all this pain
Or will it last in my brain?
Will they stay constant fears
To drown in my tears
To look down and frown?
It came to this,
To die by my wrist.
Will I be here tomorrow?
Will I drown in my sorrow?
Will I come here again,
Or will it all end?

Joseph Wayne Schumacher

My Fire

You're my fire.
You're my desire.
You are my waiting, hesitation,
For you are whom I admire.
You set my soul on fire.
You give me my temptations.
Then you fill my sensations.
You brighten my world.
My life is a twirl.
My skies aren't cloudy,
Now that you are by me.
Because of you, I breathe.
It is you I will never deceive.
Love taps aren't enough.
Next step.
Take it slow.
Don't be so rough.
Stay with me always and forever
Because without you, my life is never.
You are my fire and my desire.

Dionna Nicole Bittle

hiding in me

hiding fears and fighting tears
silence becomes her friend
minutes that go on for years
her days just never end
looking out at all those faces
but never looking in
can't you see that painted smile
hides the tears within
she's victim to wounds so deep
engraved in her's a hole
only happy in her dreams
the playgrounds for her soul
ambiguous, no place to turn
but no one else can tell
she whispers when she's told to whisper
although she wants to yell
she hides herself so well
and no one else can see
in artificial heart and mind
she hides herself in me

Meghan Schenkenberger

Never Again

The first time it wasn't bad
because all you did was push me;
but it still hurt like hell.

It hurt so much I screamed at you.
I guess that made you mad
because then you slapped me.

I think I hit you back,
so it must have just been a reflex
for you to punch me.

Darkness surrounded me.
I saw blood.
Hate flashed in my mind.

My face throbbed.
I didn't realize I grabbed a knife
until I saw the tears in your eyes.

Now you think I'm crazy.
Isn't that ironic?
You will never hit me again.

Jasmine Renee Polk

Contradiction

I am hate
And I love you
I love you with all of my hate
But hate cannot love
So I must hate you; I'll destroy you
But my love will not allow it
The love I do not feel
I feel no love; I am numb to love
But hate cannot exist without love
Love cannot exist without hate
I feel no hate
I am numb to love, numb to hate
But I am hate
And I love you
Everything I love, I hate
Everything I hate, I love
All that loves must hate
All that hates must love
I am love
And I hate you

Rozlyn Grace Imrie

Untitled

I come from places where
People would care
Especially the bright ones
Who'd visit us there
I listen for car horns
And knocks on my door
And maybe Christ Jesus
And God who would please us
In leadership games
And alphabet fames
Our monthly professions
Makes "D" number one
The others line up
After getting their grades
While I think of ways
To give and get trades
My prayer is for Heaven
And Earth to prevail
And healthy conditions
For me and my pals

Deborah Breither

Silence

The silence from you
echoes . . .
in my head,
pounding
like the green sea outside
on my fragile being.
Lately, the hard
diamond tears I've shed
have bruised your blurry image,
and still no sound
breaks this hateful silence
from you.
I'm caged in the unforgiving
place of obscure "what ifs"
waiting for your
loud silence to rip,
so I can be free,
free from death,
from you
and from me.

Kayleigh Anne Weber

One

I look over at my mother
I see inside her
I know her faults
I feel her pain
And in return she, too,
Feels my pain,
My joy, my sorrow
She knows my faults
And usually can help
There are times
When I feel alone
But then magically
She appears
To mend my broken heart
I look over at my mother
And realize we are like one
We live together
And apart
But we survive
Because of each other

Courtney True Breun

Feelings Within

Pain and frustration
I'm not alright
If you ask me what's wrong
I'm just going to lie
Can't seem to love myself
What made me this way
Were there childhood memories
Or just feelings thrown away
Some say that I'm happy
But don't know I hurt
I smile just for the crowd
And deny the pain inside
Don't want to be judged
Just want to be loved
Stop, look, and listen
I'm saying it's done
Pain and frustration
Won't feel anymore
Only please the ones I love
And the man up above

Artemias Renard Rivers

Why?

I am but a fool of God,
a God which plays
as puppets seem.

Through misfortune, through love,
which in greater light are but equals.
Through light, through dark.

I am but a fool of God.
To be such a fool
is but misfortune, granted to all
such a I.

I am but a fool of God,
whose puppet strings run
through hands and toes.

Though life seems proved,
my strings seem
disappeared.
But I . . .
I am but a fool of God.

Mario Elias Facusse

Courage to Be

When I live, when I die;
There lies a beauty in both.
The purity of love
Surrounds creation.
How can I explain, how can I express
These tensions, these emotions?
It is all too confusing.
I found myself, then I found you.
Life and death, it is one in the same.
It all equals love.
Whether it is for the love of God,
The love of your country,
The love of Mother Earth,
Or just for the love of Mom.
Music serenades.
So does life, so does love;
So does hate, so does death.
All we can ask for
Is peace of mind
In whatever may come.

Carissa Ann Deese

A Wedding in the Mountains

The Green Mountain State
Can proudly say
A wedding took place
One beautiful day.
For the couple's "First Home"
A gazebo stood proud,
While bridesmaids so pretty
Heard loving words vowed.
Twinkling trees in water,
Holding up a tent,
Had daisies' brown eyes
To observe the event.
Candled tables with fare
Prepared for a king
And music as gentle
As birds when they sing . . .
The pond in the background
Reflected the joy
Of that day when it joined
A girl and a boy.

Evelyn E. Murphy

Our Nation's Mighty Strength

The cruel hatred of man
That's thrust upon our land,
It will not prevail,
For the courage of our country
Will not fail.

Unity lives forever in our land.
Together with the grace of God
We will stand!
Our freedom's foundation
Is not shaken.
Always strong, it cannot be taken.

On the solidness of the rock,
Our nation was started.
By the waters of hate, she's not
Washed away or parted.
For America is bound
By a mightier hand
That even in the worst of times,
We stand! We stand!

Rachel Gregouire Gaines

Cross Your Hands

I've searched over hills
and through the woods,
searching for a sign
to show what is good.
I've climbed up high;
I've reached down low,
searching for a path
on the right road.
Cross your hands; lift them up high.
Cross your hands; lift them to the sky.
I've spent all my days
and all my nights,
searching for a sign
to show what is right.
I've worked real hard
many nights and days,
searching for a sign
to show the right place.
Cross your hands; lift them in the air.
Cross your hands; show him you care.

Ronald E. Armstrong

a piece of life

sweet and sour
a tasteful blend
compliments that come
from a jealous friend

bittersweet
pleasure and pain
of love, of hate
shining sun, pouring rain

life uses all flavors
sometimes only one
sometimes all at once

salt to toil
and bring reality
closer to home

bland for no commitment
just passing by
a small piece of life
waiting to die

Edelwina Antero Diokno

My Lost Day

I see far away, the moon is rising.
What has happened to my day.
Did I lose it somewhere along the way?

The sun did shine; did I awake,
or did I sleep and miss the show?
I do not know, I do not know.

I'm left empty, all is gone.
I must arise for tomorrow
to live my joy, to learn my sorrow.

I must cherish each moment anew,
lest happiness leave me behind
or fate be then unkind.

Alas, I lost it, this day is gone,
not one moment can I recall
but tomorrow I shall know all.

I'll live each hour of each new day
grasping all in sight and sound,
hoping, somewhere, my lost day is found.

Elma F. Wilson

Walking with the Light

Don't worry about me anymore.
Rest assured, I'm not alone,
With many friends and loved ones
Here with me in my Heavenly home.
The things we read in the Bible
Are just as they were told,
For the place where I walk now
Are on streets of solid gold.
And here walking beside me
Is a love I can't explain,
But one thing that I'm sure of now,
His death was not in vain.
For all the things upon this Earth
That we didn't understand
Were suddenly made perfectly clear
As I walked holding the Master's hand.
So think of me from time to time,
But know that I'm alright.
Never again will I walk alone;
I'm walking with the light.

Lisa Darlene Jarboe

The Dysthymic Dance

Come one and all
and watch me dance
purely for your pleasure
i cannot mind
i must appease
for my life no longer matters

Would i notice
if the good and pure
were right in front of me
would i bother to look up
from my misery
would i join the festivities
that bring happiness and joy
or would i sit all alone
angry and annoyed

Is there life beyond my realm
where others like me belong
should i seek them out
or shall i not be found

Tasha A. Korby

Friendship

Dedicated to Jonathan Dennis,
the best friend a guy can have

Friendship is like a flower,
Its scent can overpower.
It will show its might
When tragedies strike.
It may have a bite
When not treated right.

Friendship is like a car,
It can go very far.
Friendship is to be admired,
Not to be fired.

Friendship should not be lost.
That will only happen at great cost.
When it's gone it's hard to retrieve.
For that to happen, you must believe.
It is better not to lose.
That will give you the blues.

David Joseph Patrick

Dream

As I sit here
Watching you sleep
My heart fills
With love again
You look so
Peaceful and serene
I try not to
Disturb your slumber
Half of me
Yearns to hold you
The other half
Can't look away
I wonder what
Your dreams hold
Perhaps I live there
I see a smile
Slowly spread
As you awaken
Reaching for me

Kristin Lynne Dudzic

dented

a million different seconds
moments, interactions
that could organize, arrange, themselves
manipulate
changing what may have happened

so many multiple thoughts
floating in your unconscious mind
impossible to pin each down
to understand your finds

some humans dream in color
some dreams drip with emotional
sticky residue
imprinting on your morning
a feeling of yellow
or unsweetened blue

if only this or the other
if only i had stopped to tie my shoe
the universe is happening
design intricate cannot undo

Alison Jo Matulich

Trying to Forget

My stomach didn't flip this time;
Maybe I'm getting over you.
My heart didn't take a leap;
Maybe it's forgetting, too.
I don't know how or when,
But maybe I will stop longing for you.
Why did you choose her
Instead of me?
I loved you so much;
Couldn't you see?
I guess this has to be the end.
I just had to tell you,
I love you, my friend.

Sarah Jane Diener

Within

I lose control
I'm losing the fight
He took my soul
Shaded the light

The demon lashes out
Prepared to make the kill
Leaves you with no doubt
Trying to break my will

The battle's within
I won't submit
The pride kicks in
I'll never quit

Brett Carlton Sivesind

Common Pressure

Common sense is replaced
By a common sadness
In the world that I see.

We are all migrant workers
In this land
Of word and paper values.

Hesitating to lend a helping hand,
Afraid
Of being pulled down.

None can take the weight,
But we all
Feel the pressure.

Alexander John Prindle

Lone Wolf

Seasons come, seasons go;
Still he's all alone.
Lone wolf runs for freedom,
Chased by the guns of fear;
Reckless men are always near.
A danger to themselves,
A danger to all else.

Legs grow weary, senses leery;
Lone wolf cries at night.
Darkness hides what the moon testifies,
And no one sees the tears.
Nobody knows the lone wolf's fears;
Freedom lost in so few years.

John Edward Budris

Kendra's Song

Passages of sweet refrain
Cooling drops of gentle rain
Washing from my heart and mind
Cruel words left behind.

Dreaming dreams that never end,
Living a life that didn't begin
Tracing castles in the sand
Reaching for an empty hand.

Longing for endless starlit night
Sun-bleached beaches hidden from sight
Never quite knowing where to start
Tell me how to fill an empty heart.

C. A. Griffin

A Life Never to Be Forgotten

I look to the sky each and every night.
Are you looking down on us?
What is it like up there?
Are you happy?
Do you miss everyone?
I look to the sky each and every night.
Can you give me a sign?
Are you okay?
Did you get to meet God?
I look to the sky each and every night.
I miss you.
I love you.
You will never be forgotten.

Stacey Ann Blackman

My Christmas Gift . . .

As we share our first Christmas
What a treasure it will be
For Santa has been most kind
By saving you for me
He knew how much I'd love you
And he knew we'd never want to part
For this year for Christmas
Santa truly filled my heart
He's filled it full of love
And full of inspiration, too
He's even filled it full of hope
That's what happened
When he gave me you

Lisa May Grevell

How Much I Love You

The blazing sun rises with you
at the dawn of each new day,
and signals life to continue
with every passing day.
Like the bright and exuberant sunshine,
you light my darkest night.
Like the swiftness of the ocean,
you are always in my sight.

I think of you and me together,
and it's like a fresh, moist scent
of an early morning dew.
It is only then I realize how much
more I love you.

Barbara M. Caroo

A Mother's Heart

A mother's heart is filled with pride
To watch her children grow
She envisions life and what's ahead
So many things to know

A mother's heart is filled with joy
As they become unique
They find themselves and move ahead
Their lives are what they seek

A mother's heart is filled with pain
Watching as they fall
To let them go is hard to bear
Her hand will guide them tall

A mother's heart is filled with love
And always strength to mend
A heart that has no boundaries
A love that's without end

Joanne Marie Schleihauf

Don't Wait

Don't wait for the perfect season
To give your love away.
Don't wait for the ideal reason;
I need your touch today.
For time has a way of ticking
As it quickly passes by,
Like the softly spoken whisper
Of the elder's last goodbye.
Roses don't last forever;
They lose their vibrant red,
While my heart remains unopened,
And my thoughts remain unsaid.
Our love can last eternity,
Just let me in your heart.
Why wait to give your love to me
Because we are apart?
Please do not decide to wait,
For denial will set in.
Just as memories fade away,
Our love will surely end.

Mary Megann Borchardt

Night Watch

You woke me before I fell
asleep, the roughness of your
hands on my smooth bare shoulders.
"Just get up," you said, and I climbed
onto the dewy steel deck.
Dolphins surrounded us, driving through
iridescent water toward the stinking
city. Laughing, I ran to the pulpit
and flew—the green symphony
convulsing below, while my stomach
churned, smelling civilization.
Time had sculpted you into a man
before I was born.
We met going south: I was looking
for myself; you weren't looking for
anything. Your dark, scarred hand
cupped my white breast the last night
we set anchor. Your mouth covered mine.
I remember saying, "I love you," and
how laughter rang out in the darkness.

Timber L. Holmes

adventures in boredom

saviors need bed rest
and superstar status
or they can't get wasted
and give us some vengeance
like seven-year itches
and hitler would grin
if he only got wind
of the evening news

run with some cigarettes
bought me a sickness
and looked at my insides
for good space to enter
i broke through the surface
and laughed at the fact
that i couldn't look down enough
got to be mad enough
pull for the redness
and pushed myself over
the edge of the earth

Jeremiah Christopher Storey

with you

the sea dark navy, the sky light blue
but somehow i can't stop thinking of you
i know how happy up there you must be
but down on this earth it's just me
you must be lucky
but i'm stuck in this would full of hate
that's no mistake
if the world could be better
and nothing was wrong
america could be happy
and sing this song
stand strong, don't go away
we can do this together
united each day
our weaknesses making us strong
america singing along
even though i'm alone
i know someday I'll be back home
with you

Rachel Irene Jones

Lesson Learned

I shake my head
In disappointment
You force me
Through my resentment
All I asked
You couldn't reply
All I wanted
You couldn't comply

Unconditional love not returned
My heart ripped out and burned

Someone new
Offers promise and resolve
Is it true
My past mistakes absolve
Slow down
Lesson learned
Prevent the heartache
Stop being burned

Nick J. Reed

The Visit

The house was different.
Nature and men had rearranged
the things my memory could not.
The walls were torn and split
as they echoed the past.
For a second I heard laughter
of a moment long sought after.
I closed my eyes,
trying to find a time I left behind.
I reached out my hand.
I tried to touch the past,
but the cold, dry remains of a building,
long neglected, would not allow me
to go back.
At last—I understood.
Let my memory keep this house.
Let my heart hold the laughter.
May my soul never quest after,
for I am bound to the future.

Julia E. Underwood

Thou Never Saw Me

Thoust never noticed me
Thoust never looked at me
Thoust never knew
How much I've put in
Thoust never recognized
The sacrifices I've made
Thoust never knew
How hard I've tried
Thoust never noticed me
Thoust never glances at me
Thoust never know
How much I love thou
In thy eyes
Thy see the rest
In thy ears
Thy hear others
Ask thoust mind
Ask thoust heart
Hast thou ever seen me?

Janice Kuek

It's You

It's you
I think about before I go to bed.
It's you
I can't seem to get out of my head.

It's you
Who can tell when I'm not right.
It's you
Who can make any gloomy day seem bright.

It's you
When I'm looking deep inside.
It's you
I see even when I close my eyes.

It's you
From whom my feelings can't hide.
It's you
That I want by my side.

It's you.

Jack Robert Furlong

Widow's Wail

I am the solitary she-wolf,
untamed and unpredictable.
I roam the frozen night,
searching not for prey
but for the pups grown and gone,
for the mate loved and lost.
No pack wolf am I,
neither follower nor leader.
No companion to warm me,
no partner to assist me,
I wander the winter-enslaved forest
endlessly searching
for that which cannot be found.
The moon is my sister,
sole witness to my sorrow.
I howl to her in my agony.
She joins in my mourning,
frozen tears falling from her face,
covering my coat.

M. W. Hows

Love You Still

My love for you
was not in vain;
a loss for words when I see your face.
My heart beats still, I feel no pain.
Do I love you?
I try not to,
though no matter how I try,
I know I always will.
Do you love me?
My eyes cloud up; my lips quiver,
my knees buckle, my words hither.
Silence is heard, an icy stare.
Now I know there's no love there.
You try to hide it with your style.
My eyes drift away, I sadly smile.
I knew your answer, you wouldn't stay.
So take your thing and close the door.
I've said it once and many times more,
I swear I will never love as I did before.

Susanna Michelle Gonzalez

Believing

Believing in giving
you gave
giving from the sum
of all your heart
Believing you could help
you helped those weak
build strength within themselves
You helped those discarded
create value without dissent
You helped those lost
find inner directions home
Those touched by your heart
truly believed in you
To them you were
a guardian, a champion, a hero
and more
more than a mentor
more than a friend
you were family

Kory L. Smith

Bin Laden, Bin Laden?

To 9-11-2001

Bin Laden, bin Laden,
How may your heart feel?
Oh, what terror spreading attitude,
With your fleeing to a solitude,
And your country ready to deal.
What shame you should feel!
Bin Laden, bin Laden,
What does your heart feel?
Loud thoughts of endless killing,
And so much needed healing.
Your people scared and in pain.
When will you see your shame?
Bin Laden, bin Laden,
When will your heart feel?
So heavy with burdens, hellish ways.
Please, sit down and pray.
I care how your heart feels today!
I wish to live the rest of my given days!

Kathleen May Atkins

Make a Grown Man Cry

My fumbling in the dark
Was a certain clear mark
I'd never done this before
Guided by your patient grasp
I undid the final clasp
As your clothes fell to the floor

I couldn't stop trembling
My words sounded like mumbling
Was I doing this right?
And in that warm place
A few tears ran down my face
Hidden, I hoped, by the night

But you let nothing slip by
And even though I cried
You knew what to do
You lie back on the cover
And gently pulled me over
And accepted me into you

David John Kronenberger

I'm Not Afraid

Afraid? Of what?
To feel the spirit's glad release?
To pass from pain to perfect peace,
The strife and strain of life to cease?
Afraid? Of what?
Afraid to see the Savior's face,
To hear his welcome and to trace;
The glory gleam from wounds of grace?
Afraid of that?
Afraid? Of what?
A flash, a crash, a pierced heart;
Darkness, light of Heaven's art!
A wound of his counterpart!
Afraid of that?
Afraid? Of what?
To do by death what life could not?
Baptize with blood a stony plot
Till souls shall blossom from the spot?
Afraid of that?

Mike Yancey

First-Class Enemy

You are my first-class enemy
A hatred which burns whenever seen
You thrive off being mean
You are the colour red
Which lies upon your head
Yet ginger so it seems
Like a ginger cat you beam
Your face is beyond revolting
Repellent to each living thing
Yet your mates think you're a king
To me you're almost beyond words
A monster who beats up birds
I wish my anger could tear you apart
But I'm not like you, not at heart
Not even in my tomboy ways
Have I been like you in past days
Nor in the future will I turn
But in my head my voice will burn
The words I'll never speak

Janet Catherine Nevison

She Who Is Always with Me

In a vision of existence,
I hear a wheel turning,
Scraping over a piece of ground.
I see it moving through a certain space,
And I am merely its sound.

But, oh, I remember
Her lips were soft,
And a voice to touch
All that's hidden or lost!
A creature of dreams,
She cannot die as I will die
When the wheel moves on.

But there are times I must weep
And seem to have forgotten her form,
And there are days so hopelessly drear.
Yet in dreams of caresses,
I hear her voice
When the sound of the wheel moves near!

John Henderson Ayres

Prayer for Writers

God, let my pages be never fabricated.
Help my works not to be bad.
Give me the inspiration I need
To not make other people mad.

Always let my writing
Touch that special chord,
For a person who is grieving
Or someone who is bored.

Finally, let my writing be
A testament to myself,
And let it restore vitality
In someone of little health.

Let it always be a comfort
To those whose eyes will see,
And those whose fingers feel,
And always let me know
Just what to say
To help their hearts to heal.

Lori L. McLerran

Love

Falling through the air
In every park walk
Seeing a boy
And wanting to talk
Listening to his words
And every heart beat
Feeling his pain
In everyday words
Seeing him smile
Loving that everyday look
Seeing him in school
Seeing him at home
Knowing you're friends
Is more then nothing
Knowing he hates you
Is very strong
Loving that boy
As every page turns
Your love follows the page

Ashley Couturier

In Death

Death sprints
an impulsive flash
his heart
Death creeps
a calculating sloth
his cancer
Easter morn finds
the eagle soaring above mourners
the soul lifting to Heaven
Seasons pass
I watch
eagles rest
on oak branches.
Six keep watch
Two drop to the broken ice edge
to refresh
to nourish
A whisper rises, "We're not alone"
Father and son in death are one

RaNae Connie Drexler

The Clink of Clank

I really think there
should not be anymore
poems about love,
flowers,
or happiness.

Let me, instead,
rant and rage,
spitting out phrases of
insanity
and lust.

I've come from the branches
of Heaven.
I can taste ash, and I don't understand
algebra.

It's easier to hate. I trust it.
I understand the freedom of resentment.
I stare at my knees, unable to pray.

Jim Burns

No I Love You's

I am doing okay
Still and always
Missing you
I am truly sorry
For not being there for you
I was wrong
I don't want you
In my life
I also want
To be in your life
We have put
Our plans on hold
And I am in the dumps
It is hard here
And it is lonely
With no calls
No cards
And no I love you's
It makes my mind run wild

Keri Lynn McCarty

Sorrow

And sorrow sat deep in his heart,
Dark secrets lay within,
Trapped within his heart and soul,
The sad things that he'd seen.
Too young to know the difference
Of just how it should have been.
Had pride not been his foremost friend,
Had he the courage to but ask,
He may have seen the truth of it
And gone a different path.
Instead, he had not understood
Quite how to make it work,
He'd lost the game so long ago—
When he lost his sense of worth.
Now sorrow sat within his soul.
He never would be whole.
Each day that drifted slowly past,
He knew deep in his soul
Regret was his best friend.

Barbara Atkinson

The Young Men of All

My father played the game of men;
He served his country well.
Young and brave he paved the day
With bullets and floor-worn shells.
In a desperate past, he drew
His last downtrodden sacrifice.
With his fallen troops
He wore his shabby boots
Down death's peaceful right.
Weapons blazing, flaming fire
Littered an honest land.
Many a man did cut and crawl and
Die by his blood-spattered hands.
The lives of soldiers everywhere
Splintered and tarred;
The life of a man all but gone . . .

But soldiers never fall,
Only do the young men of all.

Dominic William Florentino

life

a bed of roses
sitting quietly
showing its beauty
for all to see

look closely, look and see
ah, thorns protecting me
are we not
just like that bed of roses?
waiting to be admired
yet protecting against harm

a bed of roses
so innocent
deep red pouring off them
your blood or mine, i think both

the pain in the world
raveled so tight
in that small bed of roses
thorns so sharp

C. A. McNabb

Mom

You used to
throw
things at me
mugs, frozen bagels
anything within arms length
Once you
threw a box of tools at me . . .
I was standing
on a flight of stairs
Remember that time I ran away?
You called the police
They brought me back
fighting and screaming
You were so angry
I couldn't brush my hair
for three days

It's been five years since I moved out
Now I call you for cooking advice
and help with crossword puzzles

Elena L. Wadsworth

Through the Eyes of a Child

Morning brings the buzzing of bees
And the dancing leaves
The smell of toast
And Irish roast
As Mommy rolls my sleeves

After messy fun
The waters run
And the bubbles float about
I'm slippery and clean
But Mommy's so mean
'Cause I don't wanna get out

A quick cartoon
And very soon
I'm waking up once more
My eyes open to see
The maker of me
The mommy that I adore

Susan Bridgette Olsen

The Stand

As night slowly creeps forward, the battle rages on;
rearing its hind legs fiercely in confusion.
The smoke remains as heavy as the loss of life.
Tears invade their eyes as smoke invades their lungs.
A constant storm of screams and cries pierce the darkened sky.
Death, they no longer fear.
They fear life.

Kiera Brianne Peacock

The Miracle

There is only one miracle in life
Which only happens to a husband and his wife
It's a miracle that is one of a kind
This miracle, everywhere you can find
It happens every minute of every day
These miracles come to the world in every way
It takes nine long months of care and wait
This miracle may arrive a little early or a little late
As the nine months soon come to an end
To everyone a message the couple does send,
"The miracle is on its way to join us on Earth"
When in just a few short hours the mother gives birth

Shoushanik Palandzhyan

lock of loss

Written by a ten-year-old

a drought in my soul
a montage of madness
an anchor of sorrow below my way
yet there in this world lies one me
my heart is broken and lost no where to be found
along with my soul hidden from more pain
yet in this world their lies one me
understanding how i feel might be confusing
but that is still how my clustered story will tell its tale
yet in this world there lies one me
an angel who cannot be understood

Rosaline Natalie Paronyan

Kiss of Death

Two souls are housed within my breast,
Either of the souls will never know of rest.
Both souls, once good, crossed into Perdition.
Now they only know of eternal damnation.
Even when I die, these souls will never be free
Because the depths of Hell will not leave them be.
They know of their Darkened Father,
They have seen him without care or bother.
Every man, before he dies, sees the God of Darkness.
He presents the chosen with the eternal black kiss.
Make no mistake, this is no lie;
He will come with your kiss before you die!

Marla Katherine Browning

All Is Lost

So much is missing, too much not there
I feel so empty, there's no reason to care
I'm like an unmade puzzle, a half-empty well
An unmowed lawn, I'm living in hell
Trying to bring reason to this dreary little life
Is like piercing skin with an old, dull knife
Clouds are getting darker, it's beginning to rain
If I can't find hope soon, I may go insane
I feel so deserted, I can't find my way
Back to the life I enjoyed yesterday
To be at peace, I'd pay any cost
Is there an end to my pain or is all lost

Joseph Ardoin

Candlelight

Every night I awake in fright in a candlelight.
When I look in that single flame, I think, what a shame,
my life is gone. All I have is a candlelight.
When I look in my heart, I think, what would happen
if the world was only lit by a single candle?
Then I think, what a fright,
all I have is a candle to light the dark dark way.

Lauren Lea Giudicy

Who Will Hear?

Tears of the lost
Is it just that I sit and wonder
Tears that drained the eyes
Sadness, cries, but who will hear the cry of the lost
Like a sheep who is running through the green pasture
Who will deliver the lost from despair
A cry to stand for just one

Cynthia M. Mitchell

Heart

Oh, my heart breaks in silence.
Oh, my heart, it hurts so violently
Why does my heart break?
It is for my love it aches.
It is distance that separates my heart from his heart.
It is distance that tears us apart.
It is togetherness that will mend my heart and his heart.

Cajun Blaze

Isn't This Something

I grew up listening to people tell me
I wouldn't ever amount to anything.
I have joined the Army
and am now fighting for America's freedom.
Isn't this something?
With this, people congratulate
and thank me for my dedication.
Yet, they are the same people
who would try and put me down.
Isn't that something?
With what happened on September 11,
I am honored to fight for the American people;
even, and especially, the ones who would put me down.
Isn't that something?
Now all I ask you to try and see
what kind of person I am.
Well, isn't that something?

Nathaniel Lee Palmer

In Time, You Will Understand

In time, you will understand
That the world doesn't revolve around you
And your needs
In time, you will understand
That everything is not handed to you
On a silver platter
In time, you will understand
There are the haves and the have-nots
In time, you will understand
That there is one God and you are not
In time, you will understand
That you are not God's gift to women
Because there's always someone better
Than you
In time, you will understand
Life is full of lemons
But you will have to make the lemonade

Yolanda Oliver

That's Why I Love You

When I look into your eyes, I feel like I'm in love
My heart beats faster and faster
I see a sparkle that could brighten anyone's day
One look could last a lifetime
You could make a rose bloom with your smile
You're like a unicorn, as beautiful and rare as ever
Neither the light of a full moon
Nor a sunset over the ocean could compare to your beauty
Your love is more than anyone could ask for
And that's why I love you

Matthew Stephen Belt

If I Should Die

If I Should Die before I wake
Don't cry for Bri, don't mourn my fate
My eyes despise this boring place
Don't ask why I died, we're born to break
The thorn of hate has torn this place
Lord, my demise is Yours to take
This is my goodbye, my Lord awaits
I now lie inside His warm embrace and explore His grace
Don't cry for Bri, don't mourn my fate
If I Should Die before I wake

Brian Lee Kuhl

Remembrance

Their impression is engraved on our hearts
Always playing an important part
Showing our gratitude and appreciation
In this pensive revered memorandum
And venerated recollection
Giving a little time and thought now
Remembering those, whose advice we sought
Their knowledge and experience an example
All that they gave to us and taught
May this memorable reminiscence of them
Rebound like the waves of the sea
Upon the sands of time
Shine as the light from heaven upon the waters
Sending ripples upon the ocean's surface
To the depth of the ocean far and wide
Returning with the tide
And like the echo of a cave's resounding
Have an everlasting influence on all
In our thoughts remembered
Never to be forgotten

Sheela Spence

Dear Departed Dog

She enjoyed every day; food in a big way.
"She's too fat," said the Vet,
"No more than two ounces per meal!"
Our dog, Suzie, started to steal:
stole from the horse, stole from us,
until Suzie grew as big as a bus.
That was her downfall, of course,
so we think, and the horse.
Her heart could not cope with her weight;
her tummy was huge, her legs slight.
One afternoon, she lied down on the lawn,
lied there all night till early dawn.
We found her and took her to the Vet
who said, "Is she on her diet yet?"
Too late, however.
She recovered never.
We buried her proper and said goodbye.
Teary, we muttered, "Why did you die?
You lovely dog, you faithful friend,
we'll love you forever until the end."

Christa Hermann

Sound of Silence

Lying alone on the dust covered floor,
the sound of silence for company,
speechless company for me.
If I listen closely, I hear the sound,
the sound of everything, everything around,
and everything is silent, except for the sound.

Having nothing, I could ask for more.
The sound of silence for company,
the only company for me.
If I look closely, I see I have silence,
and silence is everything, at least in a sense,
and everything makes sense, except for silence.

Isn't silence what some people ask for?

Miles Daniel Travis

Celestial Awakening

I was looking at the sky for a while
A star winked at me and the moon began to smile
This elated my heart, my aura enchanted
All of my dreams came alive
All my wishes were granted
A sparkle of life seem to pierce my soul
Once again, at last, I began to feel whole
Never before affected by a celestial being
Delighted in awe of what I was seeing
Chills caressed my body as I stood aghast
I thought to myself, how long will this last
Then the star gave another wink of its eye
And with the brightest smile the moon waved
Goodbye

Karen Johnson

Misery

It's not that I don't know what to say to you,
it's just when I'm with you the words won't come out
I'm afraid you will reject me and never know how much I like you
The way you smile,
I just can't stop staring at those beautiful pearly whites
or how when you say certain words
your accent seems to find a way to be heard
Whatever it is that attracted me to you
won't let me forget how much I like you
I know we will never be together,
but all I can do is hope and wish my dream will come true
Whenever you see me, you always smile and I smile back,
but from now on when you see me,
you won't see the happiness inside of me that glows
That light has been blown out
and is waiting for you to relight it

Elizabeth Corinne Fritz

California Ghost Story #3

It is time someone painted
over the Mona Lisa, while the night
is car-horn thick and there are rocks
to skip over hazy ponds.

The addresses laugh at their houses
early in the morning as pigeons coo in
the attic. Attack by numbers, by the
cleared throat, by breath. It's time
for March and June to be erased.
I read this at night, when streets
shrink behind mounds of gravel and light bulbs.

There are enough specks of people to
hide the coastlines as seconds swell

and the ink shrieks,
appalled at what it conceals.

Robert A. Paredez

Conviction

One good turn may very well be recognized with
yet another during this time of the year.
Even so, difficult choices or decisions may still persist,
even in glee, even in sorrow.
So lifelike, contented, and common in finding themselves
placement at most anytime
They can take a visitor's journey to suffice
as one minimum known 'til tomorrow

If ever a prophet had ever as sin—
it would probably guarantee for the fact that
anyone is even needed at all
And then so—in gift, as there so—
in life and as life goes on there are those
that need and there are those that needed
So, no more sin, Sow

Billy Holiday

Sparkles

The light of our life
She was a gift only weighing three pounds
A mini Yorkshire terrier
She's bright
She's beautiful
Her colors change
She is so small like the rain
When I look at her I feel no pain
For there is always another day
One so close yet so far away
A little love
A little light
A little one so bright
I wish I may I wish I might have
This little one for my whole life

Cindy Unita Kitchell

Coast Guard, Ahoy!

Good seamen they claimed to be.
They were buddies on the R. B. Taney.
Though I wonder as I ponder what I see.
Out for a ride, just out for a row,
Into the boat water began to flow.
Back to shore, bailing as wind did blow.
Out again with the plug in the transom;
The crab pot, the wind and then some.
How did we get so far? How do we get home?
One pushed, one pulled back to shore.
Camera in hand, they were met for sure.
I heard it said, with camera clicking away,
"I can't believe we made it!
Just to think, we were good sailors,
The Taney Terrors of the South Sea."

Sarah L. Cummingss

God Mends the Smallest Heart

Dedicated to all the little children born with hypoplastic left heart

A child was born into this world—
one of God's greatest creations—
with perfect little hands and feet
to reach for goals and walk with nations.

But underneath this little chest
was a heart they could not mend.
Dear God, we prayed, please help this child,
and a miracle please send.

Then God in all His glory
placed His hands upon the surgeon's knife
and as He promised long ago
gave this little one a life.

Nancy Lee Miller

Don't Worry

Don't worry, dear brother.
Please, you don't have to fear.
We have a place for you in our hearts
so you'll always stay near.
How can we forget that smile,
so pleasant and friendly?
You brightened the lives of others, not one, but many.
The hallways are all but joyful,
for your laughter we won't hear,
but always remember, dear brother,
you'll always stay very near.
Life will be all but pleasant,
for you won't be by my side.
But don't worry about me, Trevor, dear brother,
for in my heart is where you will always abide.

Morgan Marie Pigg

Have You Ever

Have you ever looked at the stars
and saw the boy of your dreams there,
smiling down on you from above;
the brightest star,
which makes your heart beat.
The one and only boy for you.
Whatever you do it's with a new strength.
A strength from him beside you, all the way,
lifting you up and dancing with you on a starry night,
miles and miles into your deep dreams.
You smile in your sleep and turn over.
Having you beside me gives me a newfound strength.
Now I think you have looked at the stars
and found what you want—
the boy of your dreams.

Becca Jane Shears

thank you, lord

heavenly father, thank you for the love you gave
helped me through the darkest days
with the light you shined
to help me find my way
kept my motivation headed in the right direction
steering me out of my own conviction
knowing that i was relegated
that you made it the way you made it
always guided me out of the midst of fire
that no one but you could acquire
when i fell along side the road
there you shifted into your heavenly mode
if it wasn't for you i wouldn't be right here
never will your name fall on deaf ear
that's why i say thank you, lord

Monya L. Williams

Last Goodbye

I still can't believe you called to say goodbye!
I never thought you would say those words,
The words that made me cry.
But all my crying is over now.
You shouldn't worry about me.
I am holding up just fine.
I'm a stronger person than I used to be.
I believe in myself and maybe you should too.
I'm definitely hurting, I will admit, but it will not leave a scar.
I'm keeping you at a distance . . .
A distance, but not too far.
I don't regret anything that happened.
I'm glad we shared a part of our lives together.
I will always keep you in my heart..
Part of you will stay with me forever!

Melissa M. Verge

Computers

computers are revolutionizing our world
even more than our friend, the TV
emails and cards are sent by Internet in seconds
viruses are spread to give our computers colds
we sit in our homes and chat with friends miles and miles away
in a few years, there will be so many new types of computers
mine will seem so old
music and entertainment is sent to someone in a flash
soon everything will end up under control
of these rabid and power hungry beasts
why, you ask
because people need something in which to turn
something they can have
to be better and greater
richer and more popular than everyone else

Pearl Joanne Kinch

New York

The state of New York was sure to burn,
and turn heads with many peoples concern.
People died, people cried;
many lives set aside,
like a widowed bride
whose husband never arrived,
her whole family deprived
of a man they wish woulda survived.
But with this metal mountain of death,
you take a deep breath,
close your eyes,
then there's nothing left
except tears that endear
peoples' hearts with fear,
feeling like the end is almost here.

Luke Patton Rosshirt

Out My Window

When I look out my window
I see crime and hate.
When I look out my window
I see a world of misunderstanding.
When I look out my window I see war.
When I look out my window I see my future,
my past, my present, my friends, my family,
But most of all I see the world—
not just hate and crime and misunderstanding,
but love and peace and respect.
So as you can see, the world is a place of diversity.
Enjoy it while you can.
We're only on the world for a short time.
So live your life and I'll live mine and together.
Let's live in perfect harmony.

Amanda Jennifer Teplen

Anything

Being stupid has to be synonymous with love
Because if you could, you would steal the stars from above
Just to show that person you would do anything for them
Just to show that person you really enjoy them
You're even stupid enough to over look major faults
Like when he blackens your eye
Or when she cheats and gets caught
Or maybe you're stupid enough to let pettiness get in the way
By only thinking of yourself when it's her special day
But the damage is done and it's too late to apologize
Now you're all alone and with that I sympathize
But you will still do anything just to get them back
Just to show that person you can make up for that
Just to show that person that things can get better
Anything for the love you had when you first met her

Nick J. Buie

Hurt

Hurting, hurting
Life is what's hurting.
When will this pain go away?
It is not physical pain
But pain much deeper.
So deep it hurts my soul
So tall I can't climb out of it.
So wide I can't step out of it.
Why is it me it hurts?
Why me? Why not that person or that one?
Why me? Why?
Something must've gone wrong.
My life has gone wrong.
If it isn't life,
Then it must be me.

Claudia Shantal Lopez

Counting Rhyme—on a Summer's Walk with My Child

There is one lone palm tree bending in the breeze
And here's a fresh-raked lawn, but someone left two leaves!
There are three dogs running down the empty street
And now a couple, arm in arm, which makes four feet!
Five rose bushes are growing in a row
And six boats are sailing on the sea below.
Over there are seven girls playing in the park.
Soon our walk must end because it is getting dark.
There are eight tall lampposts lighting up our way
And nine cars' headlights beam at the end of day.
Now the moon has risen high—we are home again.
All we need to finish up our rhyme is number ten.
Listen to the sounds of night—hear the cricket's tune,
And hear the ten wild geese call as they fly across the moon.

Ruth Parsons DuVal

What Manner of Man Is He?

He came from holiness to unrighteousness
to free the world from its sin.
He came from a golden throne to a manger low,
make room in your hearts for Him.
He sailed crystal seas, then He calmed Galilee;
He's the master of the wind.
He walked down streets of gold, then down dusty roads,
and still He walks with Man.
He heard angels on high, then the crowds cried, "Crucify!"
and still He chose to die.
He wore robes of white, then a back of stripes
so we would feel no pain.
He came from His father's hands to rise again,
and just for one life He would do it all again.
What manner of man is He?

Pamela Lynne Stanley

Love

Intense for all people
Unbreakable so no one can touch it
They can only feel it
A sensational feeling, like flying
Exhilarating and yet so calm at the same time
Inspirational for some people
Dysfunctional for others
Sometimes going in a steady beat
Other times going in a varied beat
I guess it really depends on you
Like a rainbow,
Love has so many different colors
Which is your color?
Is it true love,
Or a mere illusion?

Angela Deng

Midnight

Rusty iron, dusty keyhole,
Grating metal on decaying wood.
Young hands turn the ancient key,
Staining fingers, rust on pink.
Imagined moans, ashen faces,
Serious wide-eyed stares.
Squeaking and creaking, the door swings open,
Silenced feet on stone stair stepped.
Muffling, scuffling, jostling, hustling.
A whispered dare, a bet.
Then, cobwebs dusted tender faces,
Screams shatter the silent air,
Hearts beat faster.
Childish laughter,
And tonight an empty crypt.

Marie Brignall

Captivated

For my beautiful wife, Connie

As day turns to night and night into day;
the words in my head, so much I wanna say.
All through my mind, I've searched the past,
seeking and searching, to find this, alas.
No one has ever captivated my heart
the way you have, since our very start.
When at rock bottom, you entered my life;
our love so real, became husband and wife.
Some people search their whole life through,
looking for the love, like I found in you.
Since then the years have come and gone
and my love for you still grows so strong.
I hope when they've grown our children will say,
I have to find someone to love me that way.

Jeffrey Scott Gamble

Our Love

Should I have told you, you were royalty,
So I could treat you with all my best?
Instead, you chose to test my loyalty,
Just to say I'm only like all the rest.

So why inside of me a silhouette
Of precious you where love was our band?
With the day of yesterday, I'll forget
The sensation I got holding your hand.

I'll continue to scout like an eagle,
Searching for that one thing that we have lost,
Or did it change, becoming illegal?
I will continue searching at all cost.

And I will feel no remorse or sorrow,
Thinking 'bout you today or tomorrow.

Matthew Lyndon Brett

Two Little Kittens

Peace, tranquility, nevermore to be,
They have taken command of our chateau.
One is called Dennis, a bull you will see.
The other is Mittens, as gentle as snow.

From here to there and all around they ran,
Never aware, never caring of how
They turned an enemy into a fan.
They lived not for the future but for now.

These two little kittens placed their own marks
As they worked their way into our calm life.
By doing so they filled our hearts
With joy, contentment, without any strive.

We remember the precious times we had.
Their spirits are with us forevermore.

Barbara Anne Hersh

Unaccompanied by You

Unaccompanied by you, I chose to see . . .
A garden of love amid this sea of desolation,
Where I might find a stone, yet unturned,
And a golden autumn leaf to carry my soul
Through a myriad of dreams.

Winds of change and unwillingness . . .
Whatever happened to fulfillment?
Wishes can't give you peace of mind;
Inner search not yielding.
In and out of phases, but always consistent;
The search goes on forever!
Leave the trail untouched and go beyond
What never can be.
Cast the ashes to their location . . .
Flowers blossom; even in the night.

RJ

The One for You

Do you think I could be the one
That you could share your heart with?
The one you could turn to when things make you smile.
The one you could run to when people bring you down.
Do you think I could be the one you can invest your soul in?
You know you can trust me with your life,
A choice you'll never regret,
A decision you won't have to think twice about.
I could be the one to take you on a different level or two,
Show the true meaning of love.
What wouldn't I do for you?
A whole other type of man,
One with a mind, heart and soul.
One who values love instead of money or gold.
I could be the one.

Bruce Lee Cunningham

Love from Afar

On the sandy shores, watching nature's beauty and grace.
I'm drawn to majesty, in each and every face.
In the sea of vision, I think of certain faces
One never seen and one never to be seen again,
both in distant places.
A new friend and a distant love.
Both gifts, angels from above.
Fresh friendship and classic infatuation.
Both serve as supreme soul immaculation.
Swimming in the ocean of joy and peace.
I pray that this feeling will never cease.
I want to thank one piece of the elation.
You touch me from partway across the nation.
Thank you and always stay true.
I owe my current cheer to you.

Patrick Kelley Powers

Parents

There is nothing in the world like your mom and dad
They love you whether you are good or bad
They are always there for you when you need a hand
There to put a pillow under you when you land

They lift you up when you are down
Even when you have a frown
Parents should be respected
Not people who are rejected

You may not call your parents honey
But you should love them rich or with no money
They make you laugh and they make you cry
I bet they always teach you not to lie
So love your parents as long as it may last
I promise you, it will be a blast

Brent Curtis Ausborn

Heart and Mind

The mind is an amazing thing
Controlling every emotion
It reaches for things not seen by the eye
Chemical reactions in our brain
Things not possible are made reality
Love pushing me closer to insanity
Stay strong for Love
The mind is willing but the body is weak
My Heart is Humble and my Soul is Meek
Love is Paramount
This onerous look on my face
Love has stripped me of all cognizance
Love has taken me prisoner
And in you I find refuge from the storm in my heart
You mend these broken wings and I fly again

Ryan Mark Spannagle

School

The ringing phone hides you,
But you answer and I listen to sorrow.
Kitchen ants have broken the camel's back.
I hear your voice quiver and I know there is more to it.
Unspoken feelings leak from your understanding
In the timbre of your tongue.
Crystal heart unfolds a deeper infection.
Daylight separates us.
Night segregates us;
Only united by dreams, names, destiny,
And a fear of aquatic severance on the horizon.
This is just a test of strength, phoenix—
An examination of our love.
There is no need to worry.
I have done my homework.

Shawna L. Kiser

Hurt

Now I know nobody knows the pain you're in.
Why couldn't you go slow, man, before the way things have been.
But it's over now; just concentrate on recuperating.
Messed up how you made your family stay up
And hurt emotionally but just glad that you're alive.
But forget about it, all of that bit.
No more bikes, man, or once again you'll really eat it.
You probably not beseechin',
Just stick to the turbo Escort though.
Or I'm an advocate or cajole,
And I'm a be ebullient no more.
But whatever, man, I don't own you, fool.
It's just a word of advice from a close friend trying to be true.
Just please do.
Mank, I love you lots—know you love me too.

Bryan Yoonha Jeon

Wildfires

Yearning, straining to meet
Two wildfires, burning, scalding
In joining they flare bright and all is consumed

Sometimes traveling in different directions
Always seeking a path to coalesce
In that ultimate rush they are fulfilled

Plasma burning bright in many colors
Startling to behold
Awe-inspiring in its beauty

In its wake the embers glow
And keep the warmth
Renewal is bought with a new breeze

Flaring yet again

Colette Woodford

Darkened

When first I saw you I knew it was true
It was a feeling that seemed to last
Then the clouds moved in and darkened
Bit by bit, things fell apart until barely there

Trying to pretend nothing was misplaced
Blindly walking the edge of disaster
Dying finally set in as the storm took shape
Kindly the outside shown hiding the monster

Time passes but it does not magically improve
Still we hang on by a thread only hoping
Slime has set in making this bitter to the end
Will has faded from us both and reason dwindled

Facing truth the storm is cut at the heart
Bracing for the unwilling heart that is cut

Geoffrey Freeland Lewis

A Place to Call My Home

I try so hard to climb the rope of my simple coded life
I yearn to reach the very top and head straight for the sky
There's a road straight up ahead—wonder where it'll take me
Maybe to a place where I can call my home
A place of peace and happiness that is so unknown
A place where the pain won't come, a place where I am free
A place where I can be happy
A place where there's no more fears
A place of no more tears
A place where I can just be me
And my spirits able to fly free
A place where I can sour
And the rain will never pour
A place where everything is fine
A place where the sun will always shine

Amy Marie Miller

My Soul

My soul is experiencing excruciating changes
The loss of everything, the gain of nothing
It has become a starless void of useless hopes and dreams
Intangible objects
Unexpected devotion
I am lost and afraid in this darkness, this eclipse of the soul
Memories flash before my weary eyes
Each one a forgotten dream
Each a knife that pierces the soul
It burns, aches, tears apart sanity
The pain they cause me
The torment that plagues me
I can't escape it
It chases me eternally
It drives me toward oblivion

Davina Williams Benge

An Act of Love

We kissed
And gently touched
And for all the moments
That passed in those innumerable eons of time
The beginning and end of forever
The eternity of existence
We were one
Self vanished with the beginning of oneness
And passed into the being of the cosmos . . . of God
Life was death
Now was forever
We loved
And as eternity vanished away in the conception of time
And existence began
We lived

Russ Perry

The Winding Stairs

Life, like a set of winding stairs,
Many days, a monotonous pattern
The past, present and future somehow connect
Nothing more, nothing less
What could I expect
How many ways can I initiate each step
Should I walk and take my time
Or run out of fear of being left behind
To stumble and fall
It is a part of the journey
To be humble when I am tall
It keeps my determination burning
Life, like a set of winding stairs
My mission, to reach the top
Someday I will be there

Sheva Moore

Space and Time

We all see, from the beginning of space and time,
the need for a good rhyme.
I look to the stars and drive in fast cars.
My time will be
that when I can see.
Through space and time,
I will be free

Set apart,
all for a new start
in my go-kart.
So they say
in order to be free,
all we need is to look
through space and time,
and then think of a good rhyme.

Leigh Michaelieu

The Wall of Tears

The wall that heals
The wall of tears
The wall of pain
The wall of suffering
The wall of courage

The wall that let's them know we care
The wall that's full, but should be bare
The wall of remembrance
For the fallen soldiers
And all the brave nurses

The wall that represents the torn hearts of families
The wall that shouldn't have been created
Because the war shouldn't have been
But the wall for all the slain soldiers

Shane Nangle

Orange

Orange is the splash of the perches' fins.
Orange is the sound of Jack, the jack-o-lantern, being carved.
Orange is the old star burning bright, then fading.
Orange is the bittersweet sound of the macaw
fluttering in the sunshine.
Orange is the color of topaz shining.
Orange is the loud sound of mandarin oranges
falling from the tree.
Orange is the bang of hunting clothes.
Orange is slippery, sloppy messy paint.
Orange is the sand between your toes.
Orange is the spicy scent of peppers
stinging your nose.
Orange is a crisp breeze blowing.
I guess orange is just orange.

Seth Allen Robison

Autumn Love

A precious flower, a thorn so sharp;
a beautiful sweetness
that still pricks my heart.
Vibrant leaves drift, time passes through
an hour of sand;
worry floats away as I am guided
by a trusted hand.
How I forget about my fears, for I know
who brushes away my tears;
on a crisp autumn day I am reminded
of this peace.
It is as sweet as the air
the warm sun sets release.
A breeze whispers a promise from afar,
"I will love you always, no matter where you are."

Sheeanah Cecile Lowe

Heroes

All of us have heroes, special heroes in our lives.
Maybe a man, a woman, a child, or maybe a husband or a wife.
We look up to those heroes often through our days
and follow their paths in all sorts of ways.
Our heroes are a gift, a gift of life and love.
Our heroes watch over us from near and from above.
For heroes are the best of things
and tonight our heroes will know the joys that they bring.
Mom and Dad, our heroes are you.
You are strong and bold and you are always true.
You have our love, our hopes, and our gratitude.
Thank you for being the heroes in our life.
You are the parents,
you are the man and woman,
you are the husband and wife.

Shellie Ann Smith

See the World

See the world through my eyes.
See what I see.
Feel my pain, my love, my emotions.
See the world through my eyes
and experience the misery of a human in agony.
Open your eyes and let the world come
into your heart and mind.
Open your heart and be vulnerable.
Open your heart to the world
and let life come in.
The world as I see it . . . you can see before you.
Open your eyes, your heart, your mind,
and you will experience everything life has to offer.
Then you will see my world.
Come in and share my world with me.

Michèle Stigter

Strangers No More

A stranger sees your face and usually nothing more.
He may think, "how beautiful," or maybe, "what a bore."
His life does not include you and he wants it that way.
He's much too busy to make friends with strangers today.

What a pity—this truth—when you think of it,
that a measure of genius, experience,
and wit is concealed
by the faces of strangers everywhere;
and rarely does anyone take the time to care.

A world without strangers—would it be a happy place?
Would it be difficult to be a friend in every case?
Well, if life could last forever, and if hate could be erased,
there would only be friends to see—
you couldn't find a stranger's face.

Lawanda E. Isbell

A Poem Written by an Eleven-Year-Old

The sunset is so beautiful
with all the colors I could think of.

The rainbow is so magnificent
with so many colors:
red, orange, yellow, green, purple, and blue.

The flowers are so lovely
with their most greatest smell
I've ever smelled.

And the sky is so great
it makes me feel at home.

Everything is so wonderful,
so I don't care if I win this contest or not.
It's all about entering and doing something you love.

Victoria Elizabeth Johnson

Crazy Love

Oh, how I long for you.
Oh, how I ache for you—
your control, your rejection,
your perpetual obsession with my perfection.
Am I a fool?
Or the woman you love?
Or simply a fool who believes in love
and that it controls?
No love is rejection.
No love is your perpetual obsession with my perfection.
My perfect hips, or was it my perfect lips?
No, my perfect smile; or was it my perfect style?
No, maybe my perfect ways or was it my perfect gaze—
that captured you, raptured you, wooed you, subdued you?
I am a fool.

Latonia Valincia Pulley

Apology

Ich liebe dich, Mama.

Impatiently, almost frantically, I unpacked my life,
Eagerly waiting to be left alone and free,
Neither knowing nor caring how lonely free can be.
My sharp and restless words cut like a knife
The hearts of the people who gave me life.
I was surrounded by intruders and all I could see
Were four unwelcome strangers driving hell into me,
And filling my room with unnecessary strife.

I didn't realize I needed them in my life
Till time ran out and I had to say goodbye.
Bitterness had remembered years of strife,
But in the arms of my father's wife,
Love showed my heart that hate always lies,
Then gave me regret and made me cry.

Heather Block

windows to the soul

one is green
the other is blue
long, dark defenders above and below
large and lucent
they make a perfect match

they have the gift of scrutiny
seldom let down their guard
they're mischievous, playful and mysterious
caring, passionate and true

sometimes they show emotions
speaking without words
opening the door cautiously
only then becoming enigmatic
closing it once more

Patricia A. Blessing

Matter of Mind

My energy is fueled heavily by what I seek to destined be
Construct my fated destiny, combining clues to see my apogee
That divine form of me
Hunting through life this thick forestry with plants thorning me
Rain pouring through trees, I write about it cordially
Engulfing the world, the mind's eye extends enormously
In this orderly life, I still see inequity
In this economy of wealth class, the struggle is heavily on
That's word is bond
To sum up all the rest of it, aside from death and living in pain
Not much is threatening
Mental or physical pain, I extract the medicine
People are birds, and most of these birds are running featherless
Trying to get a grip onto wind escaping the treacherous
Nature of pain with hopes to be in glide effortless

Dion E. Baker

First Love

Someday you will lose your love.
Someday you will feel the pain
of being left alone in the rain.
You haven't lost yet, but it's coming soon,
and you, my love, will be left alone.
No one in whom to turn, nowhere to go,
lost in a world with no one to know.
You, my love, have taught me this fear
of pain and rejection, no one to be near.
I've learned not to trust, to let no one in.
I've learned to shut the door, to begin again.
I'm on my way to start anew,
scared and alone with new things to do.
I'll never forget you, for you were my first.
For the love and affection, that lost its thirst.

Christine Lee Walker

Indifferent Eyes

life burns through me,
alighting every fiber of my body on fire
your eyes which once tormented me now bring a new type of pain
the pain of love

your breath is my breath, the breath of nature, of the universe
I have soared on your words,
they alone have flown me to the moon
but your eyes bring me back
eyes full of indifference

do not look upon me
for your eyes sear my soul
with knowledge that my heart cannot comprehend
but I will look upon you
while I dance to the music of love

Valentina Coccaro

It May Be

It may be that you'll never find your way,
But you finally will someday.
It may be that your heart's burned up,
But the flames will vanish,
And it will turn up.
It maybe that you're looking down,
But you can look up and remove your frown.
Every step you take
Leads you farther on.
You will find your way,
Every dusk and dawn.
Every smile you smile
Is another day.
Every tear you cry
Is a dream that's washed away.

Emily Noel McQuarrie

For Members Only

As we bake in the streets of hatred and destruction,
Cars exhaust by, carrying people to a luncheon.
We are brothers and sisters with personalities diverse as twisters.
Ignited emotions search for trust in this scorching blaze.
We are the victims of the blue collar phase.
Our cauterized lives cause amnesia once in a while,
But sometimes seriousness ignites laughter, illuminating a smile.
We are millions located in every town.
As coals in a furnace, our heart's abound.
Don't see us as evil or charred to the core.
We only seek to better our lives once more.
We are part of one fire, as each flame,
Searching for a spark to ease the pain.
We are the plagued, the homeless, the lonely,
A spreading wildfire for members only.

Kathie Anne Glore

Remembering the Day

Our nation grew bold and strong as ever
On the tragic day we will forget never.
As friends and families lost so many,
The pride we gained is forever plenty.
Towers were hit by two birds in the sky,
The planes that contained people with fear in their eyes.
Calls were made to families at home,
Goodbye messages and tears alone.
People scared like never before
As towers crumbled to pieces.
On thousands or more
Songs were made and
Memories shared to help us.
Remember the tragedy that won't last forever,
But will be forgotten never!

Samantha Lynn Woodward

Never Fade

Everywhere, all around,
The flag waves and I hear the sound;
Cries for freedom, cries for life,
Cries piercing the dead silence of the never-ending strife.
Our flag, our symbol,
The glory of our land;
A picture of the hopes and dreams of every man.
Over our nation proudly it flies,
Radiating its beauty across the bright skies.
To our great anthem we slowly rise,
Saluting our banner with tears in our eyes.
I will be true to the red, white and blue.
May the stars and the stripes forever wave.
For the land of the free and the home of the brave,
These proud colors never fade.

Bethany Rachel Hartman

A Sense of Confusion

The hot August days are as such
Mosquitoes continue to bite
Days shorten to night
Summer fades
And while my eyes behold, my body feels
The lingering of Summer's bliss
My senses are amiss
The air is scented of rustic charm
A symphony of leaves falling down
Grass turning brown
Autumn arrives
Too soon the signs, the scents, the sounds
The coming of Autumns' gifts
No taste of rain
The cause, strange shifts

April Elizabeth Hanlon

The Elements

Inspiration; it's just falling into me, turning into words,
floating without wings, a recorded human energy.
It's drifting in and out and in again, feeling paper thin.
Sometimes so full of life and then it's dead again.
The poet in me; he's just an actor,
reaching out for words looking for a stage to be seen
and to be heard, reciting his latest verse.
He's playing God and his own Adam, shaping and reshaping,
being formed and deformed while looking to his audience
waiting for applause.
He floats out and in and then into the other role again,
always feeling paper thin.
Beneath the stage lights he's so full of life,
but when they're out, and no ones listening,
he's just a shadow, shapeless and lifeless.

Leon Baldwin Taylor

Sweet Dream

Watching the distant stars
Beginning of a bright beautiful fairy tale
The pace of the heart increases like a horse race
Your smile like a flower
Lips soft as clouds
Walking through the field of fantasies
My stomach quivers, my body shivers
Tears fall in a blue stream
Sounds like drip, drop, drip
Eyes sparkle, diamonds shine
Bright baby blue
As the wind goes swish swoosh swish
Awaking by the day breaking
Tears coming down like a stream
Realizing it was just a dream

Shawna Marie Ruffner

Remembrance

Ah, yes, the dagger you flung went deep,
its tip so close to tender heart,
and I did leap from tranquil sleep
and blew the horn: a call to arms.
As blood flowed hot from gaping wound,
my allies flanked my swift attack.
Into shadow you slipped,
a smile on your lips,
as those near you paid for your self-righteous act.

Time, however, softens the most firm resolve.
Flesh heals, scar forms, and pain fades.

But mark this my friend,
when we shake hands for them,
my left hand will conceal my blade.

Jessica Lenore Mouser

Flow to Me

Straight down Gutter Way
Through that Sing-Song Mile
Into the intersection of the Crimson Kiss
Just flow to me
Let's reminisce
Crimes against the tongue were spent
Pressure points were near explosion
Dancing visions, angry mobs
Let them lie
Slowly now, just let them die
Come on through those Teardrop Ravines
Right past the Glitter-Chime Court
Into the intersection of the Crimson Kiss
Just flow to me
Let's reminisce

Johanna Rose DeBauche

Plastics

Someone once told me my voice
sounded like a car shifting gears—
rising only to fall and rise again.
But sometimes,
in my mind
it sounds more like air
trapped in a thick plastic bag—
rushing towards one dead end only to turn
and reach another
in a self-imposed jail.
It could be released if the bag is broken,
easy enough,
but I think I'd rather leave it contained—
where there's no risk of it suffocating
me.

Mindy Anne Schuler

On Friendship

Sometimes you need someone
Without realizing you do.
Just someone you know you can count on
To listen to whatever is bothering you.
Not necessarily someone with answers
Or advice on the tip of their tongue.
Just someone you trust to share with,
To not judge you when it's all said and done.
A friend is that someone
God put there for you,
A shoulder, a smile,
No doubt, an ear, maybe two.
The tears, the hugs, shared along the way,
Form the unconditional bond called friendship
Made possible through Jesus today.

B. "Babs" Yvonne "Vonnie" Cowell

The Flower and His Friend

"I am so glad you are here"
Said the flower to his new found friend
It did not answer, so the flower went on
"I was the loneliest little flower till you came along
I cannot wait until you are grown
Think of all the fun we will have
Singing in the rain, helping bees make honey, freshening the air
Oh, what joy it will be to have a friend
To talk late into the night"
Days passed and the flower's friend grew
And the flower talked and talked
And the day came when flower's friend could talk
"What shall I call you," flower asked
"Well, Mister Flower," it said with a smile,
"You can call me Mister Weed"

Eric Anthony Western

impurity embraced

these are lessons in life . . .
as we tiptoe softly and trudge hurriedly
through this garden of earthly delights,
we take not enough time for the sweet
rewards, those sweet scents and sensations
that embody this act of existence.
o, but i do love only you,
though my flesh fools with another,
and i seek to fulfill something akin to desire . . .
just short of passion.
mock my malicious manner and
i might imitate despair,
for thou art mine alone . . .
in my soulful solitude,
in my sacred heart.

Heather Marie Bruce-Malm

The Clumsy Boy

There once was a boy who was really tall.
He sprained his ankle playing basketball.
He fell on the floor
and was really sore.
Then he got up and crashed into a wall.

Erica Y. Chan

Desire

I must be bound by spell
You are my every thought
Now held
I can almost taste your smell
Your presence makes my insides quiver
Natural juices flow like the river
Just on sight, this feeling
Just so right
Too good not be true
I'm hot like hell, with visions of you and I
Love your ambiance and vibe
You have got to be candy
And I must be five
My body speaks as I thrive
Consumed by thoughts of a kiss
My tongue pressing, tracing
The outline of your moist lips
I lie alone, lights off, candles lit

Kima T. Moore

Turning Point

On Tuesday the eleventh, two thousand and one
Our strength was tested, our emotions come undone
Terrorism reared its ugly head
Leaving family, friends and loved ones dead
Tears were shed, the screams of sirens heard
Some just stared, without speaking a word
Debris and papers rained down to the ground
Scattering the pavement without a sound
The great buildings collapsed, buckling under weight
Hours ago, they couldn't have imagined their fate
All through the day, billowing smoke filled the sky
And thousands of Americans wondered why
This terrible tragedy had happened to us
Destroying our city in clouds of dust
One and then growing, candles burned bright
Showing support with their twinkling light
Flags appeared in every home
Letting us know, we were not alone

Alecia M. Gruenemeier

I Am Not I

As I look back on my life
I realize how everything has made me who I am today
I am not possible without
The events or people that have been in my life
I was given a foundation
I built upon it
I was given events to learn from
I took what I needed
I came across people
I gave what I had
I stumbled many times
Yet succeeded many more
In the end I realize that there is no end
I am not I alone
I am a result of what life has given me
I am not I without the world
I am a part of everything
Everything is not a part of me

Maria T. Santi-Rivero

Key West Vacation

Server snaps his tray holder open
and sits his heavy load down.
We're happy and starving—who got the flounder?
I gaze at marina sundown.

Hundreds of boat lights shine tiny sunsets
and line the floated tie;
I glance in awe at son's lit face
and plan how not to die.

Janet Carr Hull

confused

i'm confused and afraid, yet everything but lost
and i want it so badly to drop all my fears
though you must know it will take some time
i'm only hoping that you'll stick around long enough
to help me prove to myself that i can trust you
just the same and as well as everyone else
for i've never fallen so fast, so far, so deep
i promised myself i wouldn't let you sweep me off my feet
and as i pray that you wouldn't drop me and that i'll be fine
i wonder if i'll ever think straight; my heart controls my mind

Tiffany Lynn Meulemans

An Aging Warrior

An aging warrior stands to fight,
But the younger man will win tonight.

The pain and shame touch his very soul.
Was this his future that was foretold?

They said his strength and speed would fade,
But they knew not
Of what his heart was made.

So stand again, again each day,
Until cold and dead he lay.

Michael John Lucio

My World

The world rotates around me
Simply floating upon celestial rings that
Touch my hair
A whimsical tour of resounding light
I fly through my mind and all of care is
Around me
Silence is constant, but makes no noise
Why is that
Perhaps all the flowers have heard the song
Before
For they don't dance, as the trees do when
The wind touches their leaves
The world rotates around me

Steven Edward Eirish

Darkness

Disconcerting darkness behind my eyelids.
Truer sight was never seen.
When my eyes are closed, I'm thinking,
And my thoughts are very keen.

Within this darkness I know my limitations
With their nagging wave of doubt.
It is this self-imposed wall of blindness
That I have to struggle out.

Yes, I have seen my many demons
Hidden for no one to see.
The worst of the demons that I fight
Is the one who's known as me.

Raenelle T. Tyson

We Will Never Forget

Mother, daughter, father, and son
Titles we are given in families
On September 11th we were all united as one.

Our one big family has all the respect,
The Pentagon, Twin Towers, and Somerset,
We will never forget.

God bless the USA!

Kathleen Vennae Seaman

All Hail the Conquering Hero

Life flows from his fingertips.
His hands dance across the keys.
With each touch, he loses lives
and corporate structure thrives.

Although still young, he is old.
His eyes grow dim with each day.
A once quick mind, through red tape
trudges the corporate mile.

With great passion, he began
his life profession and dream.
Now, for him, the passion dies
and corporate nightmare lives.

What once brought life now brings death—
the life force removed forever;
the conquering hero praised
through corporate yearly gains.

Christopher Alan Krajec

Eternity

Sometimes I lay in bed and cry,
Cry because of what we had and still have;
Cry because of loss, love, happiness, forgiveness
And above all, trust.
That trust we once had I feel is gone,
Gone beneath the depths of the ocean.
Why is it gone? I do not know,
But I wait for it to return
Like the geese return to the north
In the spring every year.
Please return, for you are hurting
Yourself more than me;
That trust is what keeps us alive,
Free, happy and to feel love.
Oh, please open up and trust again,
For I feel like I am waiting an
Eternity for it.

Lauren G. G.

Changing of the Guard

Flowing quickly, moving fast
Soon today will be the past
Yesterday's sunset, tomorrow's dawn
Before you know, the years are gone

Tighten your grip, squeeze, contract
Time moves swifter as you act
Struggle on with will and might
Knowing not just how to fight

Now in autumn you've lost the day
Wrinkles, spots, hair turns grey
You've fought the battle that can't be won
But soon to rest, your struggles done

Smiling now, you release your care
But wait, who's that fellow there
Young and strong he fights so hard
Your son, the changing of the guard

Jason James Daniel Eldred

Untitled

Curled up,
like a child in its mother's womb;
wrapped up,
in layers of hand-stitched quilts,
like the patience of their seams,
I wait for her to awaken for those dreams
where when clouds move
they make the wind blow.

Kimball Handle

A Family Is Like a Tree

A family is like a tree.
The mother is the warm, comforting earth,
rich with life-giving soil and nutrients to nurture the tender seed.
The father is that seed . . .
a piece of his wisdom, his knowledge,
and his love rolled into a life-giving shell.
Nursed by the clouds and the rains from heaven,
the roots begin to form and the tree begins to grow.
Then, from the trunk, the branches begin to take shape.
Aided by the support of the stem,
these branches, bounded by birth,
develop to pass on their wisdom to their children,
the young leaves.
And, though there are strong winds and heavy rains
to break the spirit of the tree,
the foundation is strong and holds it together.
Mom and Dad, you are that foundation.

Christopher L. Gorman

Origami

I am dancing on the graves
Of the thoughts that have died in your throat.
Your silence,
Like the hollow you leave on your pillow in the mornings
When you get up before me to brush your teeth,
Your bare feet on the cold bathroom floor,
Pierces my ears.

And I am wearing these absences like earrings.

In this noiseless house we have created,
With walls of melting caramel,
We become paper to one another.
Back and forth,
I fold you into a fan I put in front of my face.
You make me into a plane.

When we look into each other's eyes, we see.
Our pupils are magazines.

Rebecca Pekron

Twilight

Day ends begin twilight,
Your eyes twinkle like a star so bright.
Beauty,
Oh, goddess, what a sight.
Your heart more wondrous than a starry night,
Captivated,
My soul finally screams free of blight.
Eliose's beauty you may be not quite,
Alluring,
Where all kings must bow to you at night.
Finally, awash in your golden light,
Sadness,
My heart cries as you fade like a wight.
There is only darkness, nothing more in sight,
Completion,
I dream sweet dreams of you tonight,
For love starts in the twilight.

Darren Ryan McMahon

Maybe Later

She comes back and lies next to him in bed.
He reaches out for her and draws her near.
He knows her smell, her taste, her form.
She knows he could mold clay into the shape
of her body with his eyes closed, but does
he know what is going on inside her?
She cuddles closer, not wanting to think about the answer.
Maybe later she thinks, maybe later. . . .

Brittany Ward

Abby

Somber days, happy moments, sad tears, joy.
My moods change a lot, it's true.
If only more people understood
What I'm going through.

Retarded, disabled, impaired—ugly words.
Smooth skin, soft hair, innocent, pure heart.
Her eyes penetrate mine and I melt.
For a moment she's perfect; she's smart.

No speech, no walking, no crawling around.
Squeals of delight, happy fingers, smiles.
Unknown life expectancy, medical bills.
This bumpy road has how many miles?

She's only five years old; I've aged ten.
Wisdom comes from adversity and strife.
I like who I have become.
She's made a difference in my life.

Bonnie Jean Tolles

Love Discovered

You asked me how I felt that night when we first embraced.
Forgive me when I say, I feared you,
For at the slight of your touch
My heart leapt with joy as if it was expecting you to come along.
We kissed in the cool night breeze.
The warmth of your kiss ran right through me.
I wished to push you away,
Yet desire led me to hold you even closer.
A sudden rush of fire enveloped us.
The world around us disappeared.
In that moment, we were all that existed,
Two lovers united by destiny.
All became silent except the beating of our hearts.
That night, I became eternally yours,
And since then, our love has stood the test.
In my heart, there are no fears, no doubts, no regrets.
The void has been filled by love discovered.

Debbie DelValle

Nightly Battle

Until tomorrow, today's at an end;
the time between is mine to spend.
A mystical hour, devoid of light,
where in cold timeless terror
the hopeless unite.
Shadows of today stand and fight
to claim a place to lurk tonight.
Ages ago and who knows why
the moon fell softly from the night sky?
The rapier of time, stony and stark,
locked in combat for an end to all dark.
After one hour, the deep shadows fall,
and tomorrow's sun rises at old time's call.
The hour of battle to lift the sun
has gone for a time; today has begun.
Throughout today, the dark hour is gone
till between today's end and tomorrow's new dawn.

Margaret Sarah Ziph

Am I Forgotten?

I know I am lost, yet I know my way.
All I see is darkness, but I have seen the day.
Am I forgotten?
I am not heard, yet I scream.
I have no thoughts, but I dream.
Am I forgotten?
I have tasted success, yet I am at the bottom.
I have felt love, but I am forgotten.

Jeremy Lee Marlin

Your Hands

Dedicated to Ryan Esparza

Your hands so masculine
So strong
Yet so gentle
They always seem to know how to hold me just right
I love the way they look when you are holding me so tight
They always know what to do
Your hands are beautiful
I love them as I love you as a whole
They are there in all times of need
Whether it be you tickling me with them
Or you wiping the tears from my eyes
Or even just holding me out of the love you hold for me
They hold the power to drive me to ecstasy
They know how to move just right
Giving me the tingling sensation all over my body
I love you

Sarah Lynn Kohn

Bittersweet Temptation

No gleam in his eye,
he has no soul.
A whisper . . . his breath
uncomfortably close.
A smile on his lips,
deceitful grin.
Soft murmurs seducing . . .
my last mortal sin.
Forbidden love, burning heart's desire,
sickening sweet in a river of fire.
I crave dawn's light, but forever, it seems,
in the midnight hour,
barely surviving my dreams,
he devours my love, my tears fall like rain;
each moment in time is a century of pain.
My body—so weary—his touch, now cold;
this nightmare is real, he possesses my soul.

Brenda B. Bailey

A Cowgirl's Reward

There is not a lovelier or more peaceful sight
Than when mamma cows lay by their calves at night.
Not only is it for warmth and comfort,
But to protect them from what would hurt.

These little calves live their lives day by day,
Making it important, to eat, sleep and play.
The game they consider the most fun
Is to buck and kick while on the run.

All it takes is one little bawl
And mother is there at a beckoned call.
These adorable miracles seem angelic and shy,
But sometimes they get into mischief and need mamma close by.

It is very easy to lose track of time
When in the company of calves in their prime.
These small creatures grow dear to your heart.
You cannot help but love them right from the start.

Krissa G. Thom

Teddy Bear

Dedicated to Matthew Eslick, my true love

Once I cried a tear into the ocean;
when you find it, you'll see what my love amounts to.
A star fell from the heavens, and you were delivered.
A present from above, saving me from myself.
For that, my honey, I shall love you
to an extent never amounted to.
My little teddy bear, this much I promise you.

Tiffany Lee Rattenbury

The Knot

You can see it,
that deceitful knot rising in her throat.
Control,
it rises up into her mouth and nose.
Choking,
finally it reaches its destination—the eyes.
Resist.
But that salty river will not be restrained,
a reprieve from that hell of strangulation
only to meet another terror . . .
their pity.
It surrounds her immediately,
damming the stream running down her face,
and the laugh—
that "'tis of nothing" laugh.
Visibly, her mind regains control,
but that cursed knot remains.

Jennifer Renee Riggs

Consumed

I look at the sky
in the soft strong summer air.
My being is immediately wholly engulfed
like a sponge absorbs.
I actually feel my pores
expand elastically and open to it.
And I know with one look up
Into that starry, silver slate
I'll be taken far, far away . . .
No longer looking.
I am a part of it, eagerly enveloped.
The stars, so surreal all around,
fall on me like a warm blankie on a babe.
Instantly at peace; indefinitely content.
So natural.
So inspirational.
So real.

Opal Ann Smith

Declaration of Life

Can you see me, feel me
Are you wishing you could touch me now
I have feared you, loathed you and even wished for you
But do not tempt me
I have felt your breath before
Too close for me to willingly describe
Look at me, for you will not embody me yet
I know I am the life you will eventually deny
But for now I am the heart you want
To silence the warm blood you struggle to cool
The curious mind you desperately want to drain
I still warm from the sun and walk against the wind
I breathe in your nemesis with more happiness
With more speed than you can take away
You are denied my life
Until my name too
Drowns in your sea

Abby Mae Berner

Special Key

God has special people, just like you and me.
He loves us all so much so He gave us a key.
Now this key does not work on just any door,
But there is a special door this key was made for.
This is the key to your heart, and if you use it daily,
This door will never be locked.
So, be careful, keep it open and let it swing wide,
And then the Master of this key will step inside.

Wanda Sullivan

Why Must I Die?

I have been living, wishing for death;
Something soft like a cold or a wound.
I wanted to die and be forgotten.
I wish no one thought of me again.

I have lived halfhearted and shallow.
I have waited for my time to come.
I have wasted my years, living in shadows . . .
Wasted my life, living in fear.

But now I realize what I have been missing . . .
The fun and the joy life really is.
I want no more than food and shelter,
But I have more, like friends and love.

I hope I never think of death;
I want to be remembered and spoken of daily.
I wish everyone loved me,
So I could love them, too.

Cary Robert Dean

The Fourth of July

Bright colors in the sky
Bursting with delight
Many down below
In awe of such a sight
Young children and lovers
All gather 'round
To see the sensational show from the ground
I am in awe that such a thing exists
For each bursting color is sealed with a kiss
Why can't all unite?
Like the colors in the sky
Joining all people
Yellow, black, and white
I wish I could reach up
And touch this beauty up high
But for now I am satisfied
In watching the sky

Linda Marie Bommarito

I Am

I wonder sometimes what the world is going to.
I hear cries for help.
I see the world falling apart.
I want things to be better; no more suffering.
I am a patriot and a hero.
I pretend that things are better than what they actually are.
I feel my fate in my hands.
I touch angels every day.
I worry that it may already be too late.
I cry sometimes at the thought of nonexistence.
I am a patriot and a hero.
I understand that only one person can't change things.
I say if we all pull together then anything is possible.
I dream of a better world.
I try to make a stand and represent our country to the fullest.
I hope it can only make a difference.
I am a patriot and a hero.

Joshua Lynn Hart

some days

some days i want to stay home
some days i want to leave
some days all i want is to be alone
some days i just want to believe
some days i can't stop thinking about you
some days you're the farthest from my mind
some days i wish for just me and you
some days i just want you to be mine

Christina Ann Torres

Longing

My pen is my messenger,
The apotheosis of my thoughts far carried
Across the miles to thee.
These words are my dear expressions,
Oh, how they arouse the life in me.
Often, as I am in the midst of furtive
Conversations with those unbeknownst to thee,
I have engaged in meaningful thoughts of what
Life might be like if you shared it with me.
Sometimes in ordinary moments
Of simply jogging, dish washing, or calculating an expense,
I am overcome with a longing mere
Words can only describe as intense.
It would seem that the more of time passes,
This love shall no doubt ensue.
Thus leaving me drenched evermore,
In the essence of we two.

Kelly Marie Marshall

Dreams

Dreams are what everyone has
Dreams make us happy
They make us think about who we are and what we want
Do you dream of living in the country or the city
With or without children
Do you dream about what you want to be
Without dreams, sleeping would be nothingness
A state of boredom would be felt instead of peace.
Life without dreams would be depressing
You never lose dreams
You just don't see them for awhile
Dreams are magical because anything can happen in them
Even bad dreams have a purpose
You dream about what you are thinking or worried about
Don't ignore your dreams, they won't go away
And you will lose the fun
Of floating on a cloud of dreams while you sleep

Caroline Florence Shchegol

A Dream

Stars shimmer and shine above,
While the velvety darkness takes shape.
A silvery moon casts its glow upon me,
While I scan the woods.

The woods,
So silent they sit,
While reaching up to touch the sky.
Tall dark figures against even darker sky.

Yet wait! Motion stirs among their
Heavily laden branches.
A light, its hazy red glow shows
through the darkness.

As the ember snakes its way along
The forest paths, its bearer becomes clearer
And he seems to look toward me.
I know his face, its the one I see only in my dreams.

Athena Jean Simpson

Until Our Time Is Done

Silently, I watch you sleep; this vigilance is mine to keep.
Wanting to touch you is so clear, knowing that you're so very near.
Memories, in dreams, they taunted, keeping your spirit so haunted.
In this I feel so helpless; I know that I can help this.

A loving touch can show the way, but behind your walls you do stay.
You are blind and cannot see the healing touch God gave to me.
So much tension, so much pain, close at hand you've much to gain.
In this, I will try to sway, hurt and pain will drift away.

Let me in to show you how, a loving touch can heal you now.
What was missing in the past, shall you regain enough to last.
In your soul, you feel my touch, trusting in our love this much.
Sleep now my beloved one, sleep now, until our time is done.

Denise Prier

Straight from the Heart

I love you so much, yes, I do.
I don't know how to explain because
These feelings are so new.
I'm not sure if you feel the same about me.
As far as I know, love is blind as far as one eye can see.
You say you love me, always will, and promise;
I do hope it's true, I want to believe this.
My heart is so fragile and I don't want to cry.
I want this to work and last forever; I promise I'll try.
I really want to know, are you sure you feel the same?
Is this for real, or is this a game?
Please let me know, is the magic word never?
Because if it's not, baby, I'll love you forever.

Arlana Dawn Jewer

The American Flag

An expression of patriotism
Toward all that I represent
One nation's history, a sanctuary for liberty
Spread across a continent

A confirmation for the sacrifice
The great experiment to better man
Since my first unfurling
Upon this blessed land

With vigor I wave my stars and stripes
A homage for all that you hold dear
Old Glory, I am your flag unfurled
O'er a land that answers freedom's fears

John C. Osborne

I Believe

I believe in America for which it stands.
I believe in the waters that flow with our lands.
I believe in the mountains and their tremendous height.
I believe in the stars on a beautiful night.
I believe in the sun and how it throws off its ray.
I believe in the snow on a cold winters day.
I believe in the skies, the clouds, and the trees.
I believe in the winds and the soft gentle breezes.
I believe in the importance of what we should conserve.
I believe in our wildlife; we should protect and preserve.
And I believe in our future and what it holds in store.
And I believe in progress through the opening of a door.
I believe we could make a better world if we worked as a team.
And I believe in those who work for their dreams.
I believe in this land, so free and true.
And I truly believe in our red, white, and blue.
I believe in this day and what it stands for.
And I believe in the soldiers that have died in our wars.
I believe in the flag which so honorably waves.
I believe in our land of the free and the home of the brave.

Robin E. Wright

Love

Dark winds blow over life's field
Where small children used to run joyfully
An icy moon freezes old joys
As all remember a time of such innocence
It's not from a loss of life
But a loss from which brings life

Love breathed life into all things new and old
Love created the field of joy and happiness
Love brought forth the many swaying flowers
But like all flowers, these withered away
Then the clouds of depression rolled in
Blocking out love's sun and drying the ground
But then the rains of sorrow came, drowning Earth

In the end, an abandoned waste field lies there
There, where the children frolicked and played,
No strand of true life remains
It's the consequence of thoughts and words
It's the end of a relationship in the blink of an eye
We all have it in our hearts
But once it's gone, so are we

Christopher Lee Warner

You Say

You say you love me
When I despair
You are there to give me hope
Then you crush my hope to pieces
You say you love me

You say you care for me
When I get hurt
You are there to say, "It'll be okay"
What of the pain your hand freely gave me
You say you care for me

You say I can trust you
When I tell you my darkest secrets,
You are there to reassure me
That is until
I find you have betrayed my trust again
You say I can trust you

You say these things until
I do not love you
I do not care for you
I do not believe your lies anymore

Rosa Elena Medina

Poetry Is Not Made Up of Words

poetry is not made up of words
these are not words you are reading here
these are strands of hair from the woman
I lost this year
these are wisps of regret
pieces of bad faith
the last section of last night's nightmare

poems are not made up of words
these strange shapes are not even characters
not letters not spaces between black ink

these are eyeballs baseballs and screwballs
these are Washington's 300 slaves
these are Mickey Mantle's 500th home run
Ruth's strange face and magnificent heart
my brother's black wool sweater
my father's coffin
my mother's small lovely breasts

if there were words
I would use them
you know this more than anyone

Richard Phillip Quatrone

By My Side

When I fell, she was at my side,
Always willing to give me a ride.
She always cheers for the great things I accomplish.
Like a fairy godmother, she gives me a wish.

Through my journey of life, she helps me along.
She is always with me, like a catchy song.
She is the fantastic flowers I love to smell.
My mother always cares for me well.

Rani Lynn Streff

Faith in Our Nation

People might think our faith is gone,
But it just made it strong.
Our nation will not go wrong.
We will fight to keep the red, white and blue
Because America knows what to do.
We reach out just to name a few
Or we may come after you.
America, we love you.

Theresa Beckham

The Secret

As the cold wind blows
My face still glows
For I know a secret
And I cannot keep it.
Jesus came to Earth and died.
He took away my sin and pride.
You can now have this free gift from him,
And he will gladly free you from your sin.

Sarah Danielle Burpo

Born Again

Dark clouds cover my sky
And the rain falls in steady streams
My body drenched, my soul soaked, and my sins washed away
Then a bright light shines
A light more brilliant than the shimmer of the moon
The sky clears and the clouds roll away
I have a cleansed soul
I am reborn in my savior

Britt Michelle Walker

Universe

In this world we're living in,
Is everything we do a sin?
How will we die?
When will it happen?
Is everything a question?
Is everything an answer?
God knows the way, let's take His hand.
Let's live in Heaven on better land.

Leah Paige Hunt

Heaven

Heaven will be a beautiful place
because we are going to see Jesus' face.
We will walk along streets of gold
and there we will never grow old.
We will enter in through pearly gates,
and our minds cannot comprehend what awaits.
The walls are of jasper, they say.
O, I can't wait for that glorious day!

Lana Christina Bush

Sonnet Written in Optimist Park

I met a pessimist walker in Optimist Park
She walked with a walker and a co-walker
Swaying on either side, not in her mark
Crippled, stressed, depressed—a fatuous talker
Troubled by bloodsucking winged insects
"Mosi-ki-toss," many, many "mosi-ki-toss"
Shouted she in her Yugoslavian accents
Waving her palm to drive away foes and woes

Immigrants of different nations and cultures
Come in search of shades of Optimism
Culminating in the Old Testament adage
"He hath made all things good in their times"
Indulging in the mirage of meliorism
Things are bad but can be of better advantage

Ram M. Mehta

Sunbeams

Written for my eleven-year-old granddaughter, Casey

As morning slowly wakens me
And shadows touch my windowpane,
I see a glowing light come through.

A sunbeam dances in the air.
She dashes high. She peeps through rays.
She taps my face to my amaze!

She sits upon my pillowcase.
Bright spears of arrows fill my room
As radiant beams lift my heart.

They greet me on this early morn,
Adorning such magnificence
As morning slowly wakens me.

Arline June Pearce

Dad

To my dad whom I love very much,
I wish I could just reach and touch,
It hurt our relationship when you got sent to jail,
but as my father you never did fail.
It scared me a lot when you were hurtful and loud,
but everything you do makes me proud,
Every night, all I do is cry
because it scares me that you might die.
And if you have to go to the hospital, I'll be there,
holding your hand and in an uncomfortable chair.
If you leave me, I will think of you only,
and no matter what, I will always be lonely.
I just want you to know that whatever you do,
Dad, I will always love you!

Melanie Keeoma Vergara

Salvation

As the wind bloweth over the deep dark sea,
the serpent is out in search for me.

I run and I hide, and I pray to thee,
don't let those demons take ahold of me.

This world in which we live is full of sin,
for the Devil himself dwells within.

He was cast out of Heaven, for he did defy;
the works of the Lord you can't deny.

If not for the word, which he hath gave,
this life of mine could not be saved.

You're burning in Hell from condemnation;
don't you wish you chose salvation?

Patti Jo Keller

The Eyes about My Sidney

Looking at the eyes about my Sidney,
Wondering if others admire him like I do,
Expecting to see all of them a glowing,
Affording him the love that is his due.

But the latest time I looked upon his handsome face,
He must have seen such adoration there.
It caused him just to turn aside with little grace
And treat me with a cold and haughty air.

This Sidney is a handsome man.
When such a prince
Has been for so long absent from my sight,
I cast about me aimlessly and am convinced
An empty soul is like a winter night.

Lilli Lee Buck

My Mom, Ruby

A birthday just past makes you eighty-five,
and you are still vibrant, active, and very much alive.
You've lost a husband, daughter, and son
and maintain an active lifestyle, keeping you on the run.
I guess this must be God's way of saying to you
He's still got things He wants you to do.
If rearing five children of your own was not enough,
adopting two more should have been much too tough.
But you would have it no other way,
not caring what others thought or had to say.
God has a mansion awaiting you in glory
when this chapter comes to an end in your life's story.
I pray you'll keep seeking God's will in all that you do,
as His grace is daily imparted to you!

Joyce W. Warren

The Deceiving Voice

The voice crept into my mind and it deceived me
It told me that my life would be trouble-free
Don't worry about the consequences of your actions
Who cares in society has a negative reaction
It was the source of all my affection
It turned out to be the voice of deception
It deceived me into doing what was wrong
Now it has left me and I am all along
As I lay here my body filled with pain
I know that I only have myself to blame
I let myself be deceived by that voice
Knowing that I had a choice
So as I watch the solemn face doctor come into the room
I knew that my life was over all to soon

Patricia Burden Evans

Ode to His Holiness, the Dalai Lama of Tibet

Your Holiness, most venerable Dalai Lama
Embodiment of Avalokiteshvara
Precious Jewel on Lord Buddha's crown
Turning the Wheel indefatigably around

Your smile and laughter warm the heart
like the rays of the sun in a clear blue sky
Your presence and posture soften the mind
like the milky full moon in a cloudless night

Wherever You go, You spread peace around
like golden flowers from all the skies
Inspiring sentient beings' ignorant minds
with love and compassion so profound

Johan Ysewijn

Waltzing Matilda

Waltzing Matilda, Graham and Fonteyn—
Dancing on toes should NOT cause such pain!

Tippity tap in my clickers with big black bows.
I slip on the hardwood and bloody my nose.

The grace of a swan, how absurd, how bazaar.
As I watch in the mirror, my leg traps in the bar.

Each choreographed move brings shame and despair,
En pointe, pirouette—my poor derriere!

Mother brings me each week in hopes she will gain
An Anna Pavlova or a Margot Fonteyn.

But, alas, my aerobics, to Mother's dismay,
Will earn me no place in the Corps de Ballet.

Anne C. Carmichael

For Daisha

The slow tinkle of her rattle
stops in sleep—
a dream of soft breasts and father's pride
truncated in mirth.

She wears a soft garland of aged violets
and rose smudges blush on cheeks,
tempted by childhood.

Her mother's wishes are lost to mystery,
as delicate fingers peck a piano tune,
perhaps stroking her own baby's head.

These blues rage with the sad silence
of the saxophone,
surrendering its tangent.

Anne Trimpi

Without You

From the moment I saw you
I knew I couldn't be without you
You are perfect from my point of view
No matter what anyone else says about you
Without you I feel blue
Without you I feel like I've been torn in two
I need you to carry me through
Any pain that I might run into
Without you I don't know what I would do
You are the one that I talk to
When I need you
You always carry me through
I'll always need you
I can't be without you

Tammy Marie Smith

To Our Daughter at Graduation

Our Christmas gift in eighty-one,
First girl in generations born.

The Lord had made our dreams come true,
First there was Jason and then there was you.

Blonde hair and eyes as blue as the sky,
So full of life but oh, so shy.

Time has complimented you so well,
The standards you've set, you cannot fail.

Our pride explodes, as we watch you grow,
For it won't be long, we'll soon see you go.

Life's journeys are rough, face them with no fear,
Remember we love you and will always be here.

Teresa R. Monk

Heaven

The Bible says that Heaven is paved in gold.
Is this the place where all souls will be told?
Told of the O Mighty and what you have done in his book,
praying and hoping that he gives you that one last look.

A look to make things right,
something that wasn't done in the living to begin a holy fight.
They say Heaven is a place where things change.
I wonder, do you keep your same name?
Heaven is where youth is never an issue.
O, stop, stop that crying and use God's clouds as a tissue.
The love from God's angels sings
as each soul comes up doing its own thing.
Who says who is saved?
Leave it up to God to tell who will walk his golden pave.

Ketina Joel Rogers

Ode to Stardust

The winter wind blows icy cold my breast.
Our life is held by threads of love and trust.
My aspirations fly, and may God bless
The children as they contemplate stardust.
I see the world and all its great mistrust,
And life is sometimes very troublesome.
It makes me think there's no one you can trust,
And when I wonder what I will become,
I look and see just pandemonium.
I know that I am just misunderstood,
That my life has really just begun,
And soon I know I'll grow to womanhood.
At seventeen, my life is bittersweet;
At twenty-one, I'll live on Easy Street.

Gwen W. Winter-Neighbors

The Crocheter

Like ivy that climbs the garden wall,
she crochets the yarn into a lacy shawl.
In rhythmic cadence each stitch she counts,
as the hook weaves gracefully in and out.
With intricate precision each patterned
thread begins to resemble a spider's silky web.
The rainbow colors spill across her chair,
cascading down in triumphant flare.
At last the final stitch is complete, she
gives a sigh and hugs it to her chest.
Then slowly she turns with outstretched arms,
and to her friend presents the shawl.
And ever so quietly she affirms,
"My friend, you are the very best."

Connie Edmonds

Salt

You are my salt
The salt of my earth
Perfection in white
And yet you sting when you get into my veins
Into the cuts you've created
You make me dehydrated
I feel weak in your presence
I have cottonmouth because of you
Making me sick not because I hate you
But because I wanted to love you
But even now I don't think I could have.
You were my salt
My perfection and pain
But you make everything taste better.

Lindsay Bray Pope

Pain

Is it a cougar about to pounce
on a fawn faithful to silence?
Or the sound of an ambulance
howling, unable to move
in a rush hour traffic jam?
Or is it a force that rants and raves
and won't be tamed
at the bottom of a volcano
about to claim the lives of countless innocent?
Or is it the moment Beethoven went deaf
and was inspired to compose
his greatest symphony yet?
Or is it whenever we forget
God?

Patricia Barthe

You Know Me

You know me.
You know my heart.
You know my thoughts even better than I know myself.
You love me because you know me.

Where can I hide? Where can I run?
This sin-filled body is not worthy or Your presence.
But You covered me with Your blood
And took away my guilt and shame.
I'm no longer shackled, but now free because You know me.

Pure and holy, a life filled with praise.
You cleansed me and now with the eagle's wings I soar,
Running, but not growing weak,
Straight into Your arms of love because You know me.

Cathe C. Morton

The Ocean

The ocean is wide and blue.
Whales and dolphins swim free.
Always the sun shines true.
In the wild is where they should be.
The shore is warm and bright.
Fish are always on the move in schools.
Jellyfish attack with great might.
The ocean world with all its rules—
Crystal clear and abundant is life.
As you look up, you see birds fly high.
Sword fish with their sharp knife.
Birds on the beach eat bread of rye.
So enjoy your walk along the beach,
Because beauty is something it managed to reach.

Kyle Christopher Jones

Forever We Love

A tribute to the victims of 9/11/2001

The sky was blue
the sun was bright
the wind was fresh
and life stood still
But the moment was brief
so was the blue sky
so was the bright sun
so was life that had come to an end
There was grief
there was pain
there was sorrow
but hope, unity and love will always live forever
May those souls find their complete rest and peace

Maria Olivera Tanada

King

I AM THE UNDISPUTED KING OF ALL THAT IS HATE!
Follow me and I will get you everything on a silver plate
There are no questions, just say the word
I will grant you anything from the petty to the absurd
Every luxury is provided, no longer shall you want
Satisfaction is achieved, your life—complete.
Place your trust in me, I would never lie
Run with me forever and you will never die
Look at all that I own, I worked for every part
I am willing to share with you from the goodness of my heart
So will you join me, become part of the family
One with no fighting, soon you shall see
Inject me into your veins, feel me grasp your soul
But pleasure has a price and now you shall pay the toll.

Scott Matthew Kupka

Happy Anniversary

To my parents: Happy anniversary!

You loved each other with all your heart
I'm sure you will never be apart
Remembering us in our carriage
Going back in time of your lovely marriage
Dad loving you because you're so cute
Mom loving you in your handsome suit
Mom being the beautiful bride
If I were there I would have cried
Dad as the handsome groom
I would agree and assume
For being such great parents
And having raised us right
I would right now hug you two tight

Tiffany Marie Colston

A Child's Pain

To my precious children

A child's pain is the worst thing to see
The look in their eyes as they keep it inside
A child's pain is the worst thing to have
The damage that's done by a touch of a hand
Nowhere to run and no place to hide
A child's pain that is kept deep inside
Alone there was nothing I could do
But to stand and watch my babies being
Punished for a crime that they haven't done
They end up as everyone's punching bag
For them to take their anger out on
An innocent child with no strength at all
A child's pain, they know their names

Tammy Jo Wright

Misty Eyes

As I wake to turn to you I realize the emptiness is still true.
Then suddenly my eyes fill with the morning dew.
My mind stands still.
I ponder, is this really real?
How could I've been so crazy?
I didn't mean to be so lazy.
But the fact is still there,
and now more than ever I want to show you how much I care.
I look outside my window at the trees
and imagine holding you close
as we watch the sunset and take in the coastal breeze.
Our bodies warmed by the amber light
and our hearts pounding in anticipation of the night.
Now that I'm with you I know everything will be alright. . . .

Joseph Lawrence Bohrer

Death Is a Shadow

Death is a shadow over your shoulder
Death is a silent whisper in the dark
Death is a chill growing ever colder
Death is a brush that shall leave its mark
Death is a resin that hardens the heart
Death is a place with but a single hall
Death is a game that shall play its part
Death is a fate that shall come to all
But enjoy the time before you leave
For death may be our final resting place
But life is an intricate lace to weave
And fearing death makes that life a waste
Death is a shadow over your shoulder
But life a strive making you ever bolder

Michael Joseph Martinez

More Than Love

To Amber Johnson

Baby, I'm at silence with the emotions
that choke my every breath off when I see you.
My stomach grabs my insides,
numbing my body from movement.
When I hear your voice, close my eyes, hold you near,
my heart races to the highest point in my body,
only to stand tall and proud that I have you.
If my love could be stretched in a straight line,
I would spend every day of forever to find the end,
for you I love.
So you see you, I can't leave because
if there is no more us than there is no more me.
I love you with all of my heart, Amber Marie.

Clifford Charles Weigelt

The Trip

He left his shirt for me to hold,
leaving on the sleeve his heart of gold.
He left with a beautiful kiss upon my cheek.
His voice saying, "I love you," made me weak.
He said that we were meant to be
There could be no other boy more perfect for me.

He would be gone for a whole week,
Even that short time made me weep.
I tried to pass the time as quick as I could,
And watched the news, as a concerned girlfriend would.
At 6 p.m. on that idle Tuesday I saw the tragic story;
A plane had crashed, the one carrying my Corey.
The phone ran and I ran for it, tripping over my shoes.
Was it Corey or his parents with the terrifying news?

Corey Michael Pollom

I Didn't Know

I didn't know it would be my last time seeing everyone I loved
Of course I had to think of this while looking down from above
I would have lived each day to the fullest
Making the best of things
But without even knowing my car spun in a crash
Because I was drinking at this really cool bash
My life just all changed in a flash

I thought it was cool for a few hours of my night
Having people think I'm cool, or a fun little sight
It wasn't worth making everyone sad
It wasn't worth losing my life I once had

It was just a few fun hours and a couple of laughs
Too bad I didn't know those would be my last

Jennifer Lynn Verge

Ouch

A girl as perfect as can be
like the one I met today.
I noticed her smiling at me,
but didn't know what to say.

Not only thinking, but asking too
if I asked you out, what would you do?
Then she came with the terrible reply
I'd like to, but can't. You wanna' know why?

'Cause I have a boyfriend . . .

Should I be sad
or should I be mad?
Should I not care about what they say,
not let them ruin this beautiful day?

Richard Eduard Vittali

Too Much to Handle

It is times like this I wish I was dead,
Wishing everybody will stay out of my head.
Screaming, bitching, and fighting is all I hear,
Wishing I could disappear and forget my fear.
But what would I do? How would I react
To this most dreadful and senseless act?
I'm so confused, with homicidal thoughts crossing my mind,
Trying to figure out a way out of this bind.
The answer is there in front of my eyes,
For me to grasp it and use it, leaving those that hurt me behind.
With this short note, I shall leave you now,
Hoping one day to return with a bow.
So this is goodbye, this is good night,
Leaving you with your desperate fight.

Jonathan Arellano

Inner War

Kneeling, caged, confined;
Watching the road of life unwind.
A single tear and nothing more
Remains of what was before.
The road ahead, uncertain at least;
Fighting the great inner beast.
A war within thyself rages on;
Respect once had, now long gone.
A feeling of sorrow, a thought of despair,
Going someplace but not knowing where.
Stepping outside thy protective home,
The world before you forever to roam.
Break thy chains, exit thy cage.
Step outside, let the war no longer rage.

Jaclyn Renee Tipton

Life

Life is cold, harsh, and bitter
Then you find someone to love
But the light gets dimmer and dimmer
It doesn't matter if you're young nor old
'Cause by the time you die
You're all alone
Whether you're rich or poor
When it's said and done
Someone has slammed the door
Will I make it in this horrid life
No one knows
But here I sit
Secluded
Alone

Scott Newton Arnall

don't feel sorry for me

my name is dewayne and i got the blues
i'm the guy who delivers your shopping news
i'm the guy who asks, can you spare a dime
and you just walk on, not giving me your time
i'm the one who lives under the bridge
because my wife divorced me and took the kids
the shadow walking in the night light
is me asking god for a better life
if that isn't possible, just kill me
because my clothes are torn and filthy
no one will talk to me, my day is full of dirty looks
i can't even walk in the street without being called a crook
this bottle of liquor is my only friend
so god, i ask you, if you won't change my life, just end it

Max Debuque

They Always Seem to Hurt You

Coldhearted people everywhere you turn.
They always seem to hurt you, yet you never learn.
Will you ever find someone who is true,
Or will the one getting hurt always be you?
You put your heart at risk all the time,
And they always seem to hurt you for no reason or rhyme.
After every encounter, you end up crying.
You smile on the outside, but inside you're dying.
Whatever your feelings, they are never shown.
You feel so much hurt, but never let it be known.
You are a brilliant actor and this a great play.
They say they'll be there forever, and yet they never stay.
Everyone always tells you that you are the best,
Yet they always seem to hurt you, just like all the rest.

Rebecca Lynn Dillon

Friends

True friends don't lie, but mine did. She hurt me
so much that I forbid, forbid to forever forgive her
for all she's done. This is a lesson learned.
A lesson to trust someone ever so much, but
little did I know she couldn't get enough. She
kept on going with her lies and name calling,
but she didn't know the end was soon coming.
I made my decision not to forgive, and stop
giving all that I give. I was too nice, gave
too many chances; and how it ended with
only glances, glances that hurt, that tear me
up inside; because she said she would always
stand by my side. Now she was true to her
thoughts, and now she has what she wants.

Stephanie Gloria Silva

If I Were in Charge of the World

Everyone would have the perfect soul mate.
They would live with one another until the end of fate.
They would say, "I love you," all the time,
even if they had to give up a dime.
They would hold each other's hand
and walk through the silky smooth sand.
They would watch one another grow old
as the years would unfold.
They would never have to think of being alone
because they would die peacefully
at the same time and zone.
Then they would lie next to each other in the ground,
but their souls would still be together
as they were sworn to be bound.

Natalie Rochelle Crosby

Eight the Years, Eight the Sign

Eight is the number, eight is the sign
Eight are the years we've been married sublime
Look at the number and notice the line
Goes 'round and 'round like unending time
It's the sign of infinity which means there's no end
Like the love I give you with this poem I send
So happy am I to love you this long
With each passing year it keeps growing so strong
We've passed by seven and now reached eight
Guess it's an omen that our love is still great
Now as we go forward to start on year nine
I give me to you and again claim you as mine
Happy anniversary dear, from your husband and friend
Knowing that my love for you will have no end

Paul T. Miller

The Other Side of Me

The other side of me nobody knows,
It's filled with hurtful truths and down lows
So many secrets hidden and closed up,
If I have to hide anything else, I might just blow up
Now I see how people become mentally unstable,
But if I tell my secrets, I might be labeled
They might interpret my hidden secrets in the wrong way
If my secrets get out, insanity might come upon me on any day
The other side of me might just come out
People will misjudge me, no doubt
I have many secrets that I keep deeply hidden
My secrets get out Oh, no! That's forbidden
So each day I smile and hold my head up high
I hope no one would notice that I'm living a lie!

Sabrina Darlene Polk

Small Country Town

Small country town
Seeing no fast changes
Changelessness in the people; changelessness in the town
The families grow up together for a hundred years
And then the next generation after that
If you take a visit, you'd exclaim, "What a nice town"
Though its inhabitants want to escape
That's what I keep saying to myself
I will leave as soon as I am able
But towns like mine have their ploys
I know some moment in my lifetime I'll wander
Back just as everyone else who's left will
At some point return to that small country town
Of Medway

Michelle E. Droeske

The Journey

The pace is set the journey long and far
The slender body pushes up the stream
Through rocks and boulders to the place afar
Traveling side by side with your straight beam
Yet knowing where to go and never there
The thing you eat may put you on a hook
How far do you go, How much do you dare
Or you'll be gone without another look
I know you're tired, thinking you might quit
But keep the rhythm, keep the obsession
You can contend you know how to outwit
For you will win, for true possession
So look ahead to rapids that you face
Or you will fall behind and lose the race

Ethan Edward Prevost

Pure and White

You helped me see in the dark.
You gave me hope when its loss left a mark.

You gave me faith when all was lost.
You showed to me courage when it was tossed.

You gave me happiness, dreams, and strife,
And also inner beauty, love, and life.

What would I do without you by my side?
You're a guardian angel, so soar and glide.

I need you here to hold me tight
So instead of darkness I see light.

Be sure that my dreams are in sight.
My love, spread your wings, so pure and white.

Callie Elizabeth Fitzgerald

You Are

Someone to share the coldest days
Someone to share the snow fall's beautiful flakes
Someone to greet when I wake
Someone to hold and love when day breaks
Someone to bring smiles and take my breath away
Someone to bring joy and laughter into the day
Someone to light up the darkest nights
Someone to turn the wrongs to rights
Someone to share life's good and bad
Someone to hold when times are sad
Someone to love and treasure
Someone to be yesterday, today,
Always and forever
You are someone

Cheryl Rae Sherman

Lost within Myself

Question: Where are you?
Response:

I'm lost.

I'm trapped in my own self consciousness,
Confused in my own mind.
I can't leave, can't get out—
The force is too strong.

I'm suffocating by every breath I take,
  Falling with every step I walk,
    Drowning in every tear I shed. . . .

I'm my own cage,
Trapped in my own self being.

Lauren Elisabeth Binns

It's Just My Adam and Eve Poem

Adam and Eve were made to be
Perfect portions of you and me
But Eve took temptation and now we suffer eternally
A little girl dies, not physically
She hurts inside, her pride is lost
Forever she's left wondering
About a father who would be better wandering
Instead of staying home
Children suffer instead of play
Parents leave instead of stay
Is it our fault for one mistake
Is our payment rather great
Or are all the things in the world today
Just a punishment that we must pay

Janet Ann Ferguson

Goodbye

Old jokes, old emotions
Remembering the fun times—all the commotion
Old parties, old games
Some still funny—others now lame
Old memories, old dreams
Do you remember any of our old schemes?
Old comforts, old talks
We'd promised each other that we'd never depart
Yet here we are—drifting away
deep inside, I wish we could stay . . .
Stay the same—friends forever
I guess we'll just have to cherish the moments we had together
So goodbye, adios, au revoir dear friend
I'll keep the memories we made together until the very end

Marcia L. Newbert

our nation

our nation was hit like snow in summer
trade center knocked down just like lumber
mommies and daddies never to come home
millions of children left all alone
those still alive trying to regain
our grieving nation filled with hatred and pain
nations need to unite as one
to get through the storm and into the sun
most people in our nation thinking revenge
they think it will help them, they think it will mend
mend wounds that were cut so deep
this event in our hearts we will always keep
so now our nation will try to regrow
get back to what we consider normal, very slow

Amy Lauren Bissonnette

Hurt So Good

Why is it you hurt so good?
Why does the pain you cause make me feel like I should?

Sorrow trickles down past my smile,
As I gaze at you for a while.

All I want to do is embrace you,
So you can suffocate me blue.

I only want to feel your lips,
So your poison I can sip.

You don't tear out my heart; I rip it out for you,
To make it easier to do the evil you do.

I let you ravage my soul, like only you could.
I don't know why, but you hurt so good.

Vincent Edwin Casiano

Manumit Me

You bond me with your stereotypes;

Silicone breasts, red lips,
Soft hair, long nails, round hips.

Strip me of my rituals, my exemptions, my seeds,
To enslave me in twists with your sexist needs.

Nonchalant sarcasm, crude laughter, sophomoric fights;
All to expose, embarrass and rape me of my likes.

Ah, but my heart, my passions, my love, you cannot capture,

As my independence transcendent, your envious servitude.
Do you fear my strength, my passion, my attitude;

Manumit me, for I am all that I am, a woman or fear my rapture!

Nicole Durham

Love Hurts

Love hurts, as you may know,
But the pain you endure makes your love grow

Love is fragile like that of a dove,
So when you spread your wings to fly,
Fly with the one you love

Hold the one you love near,
For they are the ones that you love so dear

If your love falters, I hope you see
Apparently that love was not meant to be

As you all know, love really does hurt,
But my question to you is,
Is it worth the work?

Jennifer N. Harris

Sound of Silence

the sounds of silence I know too well
a lonely feeling, a story to tell
a broken heart, a shattered life
chilling silence, a departing wife
feeling like I might end
waiting for my heart to mend
holding back my tears of pain
hanging to life, trying to sustain
my tears flow a little at first
trying to hold them back not to burst
the morning is here, I tried to escape
my heart feels better, it's mended with tape
the sun rose, the birds sing
hope and healing the warmth bring

Jerry Weston Trimble

Forever This Is Love

I know you love me when you hug me
I know you love me when you kiss me
When I wake up to you watching me sleep
and when you say you miss me
I know you love me when you grab me
when we're sleeping in the middle of the night and hold me tight
I know you love me every time you look at me with your gentle eyes
I know you love me when you say you want to be with me forever
and we haven't even been together a year
I know you love me every time you whisper sweet nothings in my ear
I know you love me when you finish my sentences
and when you come up from behind me and kiss my neck hello
I know you love me when you do all the above over and over until
we see our precious dove . . . forever this is love

Jeannie Marie Rounds

Requiem for Angels

Fallen angels and tattered wings
The Heaven above no longer sings
Forced-shut eyes and outstretched hands
Chaos and madness spread through the land
Satin skin and perfect lips
Crying for something other than this
They know there is something greater above
More powerful than beauty, peace and love
But their fear of death so loudly rings
And to each other they loyally cling
As the angels fall and crash and yell
The world becomes its own living Hell
Because without angels and their wings
The Heaven above no longer sings

Brandy Lyn Hocking

Mommy's Baby

Your tiny fingers and teeny little toes
Those pouty pink lips and button nose
Chubby wee arms and thighs
Gleaming bright eyes that keep me mesmerized
Great big hugs and tender sweet kisses
Isn't this what every mom wishes?
Holding your, oh, so little hand to take a walk
Taking out time to just sit and talk
How these days go by so fast
These early years are gone in a flash
Savor every moment and time
Record them all deep in your mind
So when each memory you replay
Will bring you back to these precious days

Shelley Reneé DeWitt

Philip Edward

Philip Edward . . .
The day I met you I knew there could be no other.
You came into my life and I felt so alive again.
You treat me so good, like no one has before.
You love me for me and not for anything else.
You see the good and bad in me and still love me
Our love has grown so strong,
Strong to where it's more than just love.
I could never see us apart, to see us apart would just destroy me.
I have given to you everything that I have.
No one has ever seen that in me.
I have given to you my life the best that I can
And I have given to you the rest of my life together, forever.
Philip Edward . . . I love you.

Cheryl Lee Brown

Mother's Heart

Mother's love cannot be measured
with teaspoons or rulers.

Mother's strength cannot be shown
by lifting of weights or bars.

Mother's endurance is not tested
on the track or in a game.

But each is tested in her heart as her
children grow, change, and deal with this
life that is placed before us all.

As we each learn to love and grow strong
through enduring life's journey,

may we place our heart in God's hands.

Jessica Erin Lovett

Friends

Friends are here for you, or supposed to be anyway
When you need someone to talk to on those messed up days
Whenever I felt blue
You said that I should call on you and you'd be there
It was just yesterday, I swear, that you told me so
But I found out that when I was low
Nobody would show
I'd take my shower
And wait for hours
I would sit and cry
Then wonder why
I started to realize what was going on
I would ask myself why
Then you came and said, "Goodbye."

Jenna Leigh Centers

The Lost Love

You once were mine, now you're gone.
I miss just hearing your voice on the phone.
I used to sit and wait for the phone to ring,
Now it is only a sad song I sing.
Everything I see or do reminds me of you.
Without you I am lost and I don't know what to do.
I wished we would be together forever,
now that the sunshine is gone it feels like all I have to face is bad weather.
To give up or hold on is such a hard decision to make,
but I want you to know my feelings never were fake.
I love you now and I always will,
though you may not have the same feelings
this is how I feel.

Jennifer D. Davis

How Could He?

I couldn't believe it when they told me what he did.
How can he do that to two innocent kids?

He is now a part of the scum of the Earth—
He took away their innocence that they had since birth.

Does he really think God will forgive him for this terrible act?
A conscience and morals is what he lacked.

His day is coming, it's coming near.
I hope it approaches him with terror and fear.

I hope he feels the pain that he gave to the twins,
But in the end, no one really wins.

Hopefully he'll be locked up and put away,
But the pain and memories for the girls will always stay!

Amy Beth Whitlock

Waiting for a Beer

Standing here so patiently
Waiting for a beer
Got a sawbuck in my hand
Bartenders looking busy now
May have to wait a year
Hopin' it don't cost too much 'cause I'm drinkin' on limited funds
Shouldn't cost too much though
'Cause it hasn't in the past
Gonna' drink it real slow
'Cause I gotta' make it last
Drinkin' ain't the only thing 'round here to do
Like readin' poetry, you know
I made the words all by myself
But now I gotta' go

John Rosenquist

Each and Every Day, By and By

I want to spend the whole night in your eyes,
Each and every day by and by!
I want to feel your sweet lips touch mine!
Each day I want us to bind
With our hearts beating forward
And everything else left behind!
I don't want us to ever part
'Cause I know it will break my heart!
I want to be in your life every day,
And I don't want you to ever go away!
Each and very day I think about you
And you know I love you!
I want to spend my life looking in your eyes!

Tristan Diane Couch

First Sight

The day I saw you, I knew you'd be mine.
The steps you took were in a perfect, straight line.
Everything was in slow motion and I couldn't breathe.
The sound of your voice was more beautiful
Than the birds and the bees.
You looked at me and I looked at you.
I knew you were feeling the same way, too.
Love at first sight is what I called it.
The puzzle pieces of you were a perfect fit.
You stole my heart and I had yours, as well.
We loved each other and everyone could tell.
To this day, I still feel the same. . . .
My whole life grew the day you came.
I love you. . . .

Ebony Anne Dickerson

Peaceful Angel

Sitting here in a silent room,
Staring at the picture of the heavenly angel God sent my way:
The way he looks,
So calm and peaceful,
Brings a tear to my eye,
Knowing I have to wait to be in his arms.
He is my Prince Charming, for now until eternity.
A warmth like never before fills my heart,
Knowing we truly love each other.
I long for his words to say, "I love you."
Every time I hear that,
My heart skips a beat.
I just know God has been watching me suffer and ache.
I also know that I'm the lucky one because he brought me my soul mate.

Tedder Rae Vickie

Frankenstein's Modern Monster

Pieced together from parts unknown,
Quasimodo redefined,
Was given a conscience but no backbone.
His tongue in silver scale is lined.
The monster's limbs, filled with strength and grace,
Are fueled by a pump that feels love but does not know it.
An unblemished hide masks his face.
To fortify the facade, he must show wit.
Throughout his brain is marbled insecurity.
His soul hungers for something to shove.
So he seeks a heart of untouched purity
And cages it like a morning dove.
Now I know why the caged bird sings
And the meaning of unrequited love.

William Chin

Thanks

I never thought I would find
A wife so loving and all so kind.

Without you I don't know where I'll be,
But I sure am glad you're with me.

You've given me more than money can buy.
I'll give you my heart till the day I die.

These feelings I have get stronger every day.
Hoping we stay in love, that's why I pray.

It really doesn't matter what you do or say
Because you're more than my wife in so many ways.

So just wanted to say thanks for being the wife that you are.
You're my best friend, lover, and angel by far.

Kerry Rene Yarbrough

From Within

To shiver, tremble, due to violent wind,
it's those who think of life as dark and cold,
the icy air is from within the soul;
it's only what the heart to brain has told.
The soul has eyes, and yet the heart is blind;
our dreams of hope are what the soul can see;
it searches through an endless maze of blurs
within a locked up heart without a key.
So keep the light so bright within your heart,
yet just remember what is learned by pain;
to know, it's clouds to stars the depth recedes;
it's from inside one makes the flame remain.
It's just the fear of loss we have to end;
without the doubt, our hearts we all can mend.

J. A. Weber

Please Give Me

Please give me bravery to smile each day.
Please give me honor to not look away.

Please give me hope by which to live.
Please give me strength to not take, but give.

Please give me pride so I can be proud of me.
Please give me friends who don't judge what they see.

Please give me openness to smile at all.
Please give me courage to rise after a fall.

Please give me peace to be friends with myself.
Please give me determination to not put the real me on a shelf.

Only when I have all these virtues, you see,
Then I can make peace with those around me.

Shir Lerman

What If . . .

What if the world had never made a gun?
What if the shooters at Columbine had never picked up one?
What if the world had never made a beer?
Would those who were killed by drunk drivers still be here?
What if the world had never made a bomb?
Would people torn to pieces have survived Vietnam?
What if the world had never made up killing?
Would terrorists still find it so thrilling?
Would the world be a better place?
Would millions of loved ones still be here to embrace?
Would humans still destroy themselves and others?
Or would we care for one another like brothers?
We can't change the past, it will be there forever,
But the future, that is ours to endeavor.

Kaitlyn Marie Hurst

love is like . . .

love is like a rose:
there's so many faces,
so many changes.
it can be beautiful
and in so many colors;
some are even mixed.
but as the petals fall off, the love gets weaker.
some love is fake;
some is real,
but love never lasts forever in this world.
eventually, the love dies between two people.
so,
as i said, love is like a rose.
it never lasts forever.

Stephanie Lee Elgin

given the day

Dedicated to September 11, 2001 and staying strong amid chaos

given the day, a grace
a monument in common place
unmoved but for a time, then . . .
weathered down in prime
apart the pieces, floor to shower
unforgiving, broken tower!

given the day, afresh
a stronger outer flesh
erected new with center square, yet . . .
similar burdens to bear
elements pound, remain steadfast
forgive the day, resolve to last!

Anita Lozeau

Questioning Soul

On full moonlight, creativity flows and mysteries reveal,
but what revelations remain untold?
Do the galaxies and stars, these human eyes have yet to see,
hold more answers or yet another key?
Perhaps the latter is best—experience is the greater guide
for my curious, ever-questioning soul.
When my soul dreams, it is not of earthly things;
dreams are my doors to the unseen.
The dreams come during wake and sleep to my third eye,
which wishes never to sleep.
The window to my soul has much to see,
for with knowledge comes one unquestioned truth—
The more I know, the more I realize the vastness
I've yet to have revealed to me.

Jeniffer Ann Harrison

The Auction

The men all came on a cold December day
Most from far away
They looked around to see what could be found
The day the auction came to town

They were bundled from head to toe
And wander to and fro
Until the auctioneer yelled, "And here we go"

All gathered around
As the hammer went down
And one piece at a time was carried away
On that cold December day
When the auction came
And took Grandpa's things away

Marsha Elaine Wright

tears

tears in your eyes, you look so sad
wish you'd tell me why you feel so bad
your heart is full of pain
wish you could explain
a wonderful friendship we shared
i thought you really cared
i promised you the love of lifetime
you promised to be my friend all the time
miss your smile, miss your love
in fact miss you all the time
i love you every day of the year
just the way i promised, my dear
wish you could tell me why you are so sad
tears in your eyes

Saeed Akhtar

Dreamscape

I am escaping life through my dreams
A pirate embarked on a perilous stream
My ship is my mind, the oars are its thoughts
They fuel my emotions; all expectations forgot
Oh, the details my mind can create for my soul
The happiness encouraging my thoughts to be whole
The people who love me are never the same
It's never confusing, deceitful or lame
I move through the shadows, my path never clear
Through mirages of transgressions, not a trail ever near
Each destination, a muse of delight
Never breaking my journey till morning brings light
As I return, my heart will be true
Covered with layers of lingering dew

Laura Lee Probert

The Rose

Butterfly-free, yet planted in soil, roots refuse to grow
I allowed my wings to be clipped; where I stand, I do not know
The morning dew upon my petals, sun begins to rise
A flower here, a pricker there—a bud to my surprise
A part of me begins to grow, despite my heavy heart
Friends come to visit, stay a while, but soon they too depart
My solitude comes creeping back as the moon begins to shine
Dancing lightly in the wind, remembering dreams of mine
To be a rose so plush and red to stand out from the patch
To know a thorn so hard and strong and know I've met my match
Darkness falls, death's upon me, my petals wilting to the ground
I feel lighter, start to rise, flying I turn around
And see a bed of red with a bouquet as sweet as wine
Remnants of a beautiful rose and I realized it was mine

Caryl Lynne Kourgelis

The Stormy Cloud

I run and play outside
And watch the clouds go by.
But when the white clouds go away,
Then the stormy clouds come into sight.
I watch them move in the sky.
Then I see the lightning strike as I run inside.
I look outside the window
As the lightning lights up the sky.
Then I hear the thunder
As it rumbles by.
I like the way it looks
And the way the raindrops patter.
Then, inside of me, I think,
I wish I could be a stormy cloud.

Scott Hammond

Without You

The rain has got even colder.
The sun doesn't shine ever so brightly.
The nights have got even longer.
Days go by even shorter.
The bees don't come around any more.
The flowers don't bloom very brightly.
I want you back in my arms,
So I can hold you more tightly.
Therefore, the rain will be just a mist.
The sun will shine through the whole wide world.
The night will fly through again.
The days will pass just like a fast train.
And bees will sing their pretty songs.
Flowers will bloom as they should.

Alicia Ashley Nutter

My Mother, My Star

I have a star that I call only mine.
I love to sit at the window and watch it shine.

It leaves me calm with peace at mind,
Its rays of light caress my face.
The warmth in my heart, impossible to replace.

I know you're not here, yet through my star,
I'll bring you near.
For a moment I am safe, for I am with you.
I shed a single tear, but when you leave me,
I'm left with nothing to fear.

At the end of the night I apologize to you,
Sending my love to the one . . .
The one in my life most dear.

Nicole Lee Boehle-Kirrane

I Don't Know . . .

I just don't know what I'm going to do.
I've been dreaming of holding and kissing you.
When my nights start getting long,
that feeling of desire is never gone,
as time slowly passes me by.
I wish for the day that you would be mine,
but sadly and painfully,
the truth is plain to see,
because someone else has your hand,
and these days it's so hard to understand.
Now I just sit and pray for a new day to begin,
and that you're safe when the day comes to an end.
These words I've written to you are real,
for in my heart this is how I truly feel. . . .

Randi Lamonte Johnson

Remember Always

You are a very special person
You have a big heart
Always treat people with respect
Smile like there is no tomorrow
As time passes time heals
Do not worry so much
Great things will come
Be patient
Have a strong faith in God
Take time to stop and watch the birds fly
Keep strength in your soul
Most important, remember
Have peace within in you always
The rest of life will fall in place

Monica Jeanne Drolet

Confusion

Your love is so painful
that I turn it away.
I can't stand to be without you,
but I want you to go away.
A love like this is tainted,
but I want it so much.
When you are angry, the colors of black
and blue is what I get from your touch.
I want you to leave, I want you to stay;
Confusion has taken me over today.
So I pray and I pray for the answer to come.
Now, when I open my eyes, all I see is the sun.
No longer confused, now I know;
Love is a beautiful thing, God told me so.

Makanya Patrice Rouse

In the Line of Duty—the Bravest

To New York City's bravest

A servant to all, the protector of sum
In the line of a duty you serve
With resounding alarm, the concern ascertained
To each blaze you bring fortified nerve

Making safety for others a basic detail
Fighting embers, intensive and dire
Each day you go forth chancing life on the edge
With adversities daunting each fire

You are one of the group of the bravest we know
We respect, bid esteem and revere
May you always have strength, be compelled to go on
And conviction to conquer be clear

Diane C. Powers

Untitled

You pass me by, but I don't say a word,
I stay passive and quiet.
Inside, my soul is chasing you, brushing your cheek
with its hand.
My soul is fleeting, like your steps on the floor,
ever changing in rhythm and pattern.
The fear of rejection chokes it and holds it down.
The soul is reckless and carefree.
It should never be left to control you.
It will break your heart and leave you wounded.
I tell you this so you will save yourself from the remorse
that will inevitably follow.
My soul watches you pass and cries from its deep confines,
never to be let go from its prison within me.

Stacey Leigh Bridewell

'Cause I Can

The Original Mister

Why can't I have my way?
That's what selfish people say.
I want this and I want that.
No! I'm the very first to bat.
I get whatever I want.
Just put it right here in my hand.
Know why I do?
'Cause I can.
I don't have any friends!
No! I won't fix those fences that need a mend.
I am always first at what I do.
Know why?
'Cause I don't have a me and you!

Debra J. Cowan Stiles

The Roadside Memorial

Who are you? Why did you die?
Why do I grieve every time I pass by?
I didn't know you or that of your life.
Were you somebody's mother? A lonely man's wife?
A simple white cross burnished with gold
Speaks volumes and tells me you'll never grow old.
My heart skips a beat; my eyes see your name.
The question is haunting: Who was to blame?
The danger that lurked at the crossroad was clear;
Accidents happened year after year.
Now a caution light blinks at four corners, beware.
Where was that light when you passed by there?
Why is it hindsight hides behind eyes
That only see sharply when somebody dies?

Evelyn P. Kemmlein

Thinking of You

When I look at the beach
I think of you
I think of how you touch me
How soft and warm
Like the water on the sand
How I love to be held by you
And hold you
How I can be caught up in that moment
How I can feel so much a part of you
Like the water and the sand
Being pulled together by the current
How two different things come together with a gentle kiss
How it can be so full of energy
Yet completely at peace

Sandy Kay Welch

Let's Talk

Hold my hand and I'll tell you a secret
Listen attentively and promise to keep it
I want to tell you about things of the past
Times we've shared and times we've laughed
Sorrowful moments that haunt our minds
Dreadful memories that we've left behind
Some think we're too young to worry
Little do they know our lives are in a hurry
The world is changing at a very fast pace
It won't be long before we see His face
My life won't be in vain is what I am told
But ruthless people are becoming very bold
I'm holding onto what trust I have left
I just hope I'm not the next theft

Michaelle Helene Page-Gray

Contra Dancing

A night out contra dancing, do-si-do
Go grab with care your partner, circle 'round, swing
The music resounds in next day mindful sing
I don't recall ever asked before to go
From France, the British Isles to U.S. shores
The perspiration expected, go hug
In proper dance position, no tight tug
One hundred couples line up door to door
A waltz tune theme at half-time delights my date
In graceful slides across the hardwood floors
Our hearts find ways to talk through all the noise
The box step dance of past seems just so great
A quiet sit by moonlight; spirit soars
We danced flirtatious cuddles sharing joys

Timothy Scott Margulies

Perfect for Me

Some say that patience won't get a man far;
but a woman perhaps, for here you and I are.
I've heard you felt for me ever since we met
and at first I ignored you, which I now regret.
Now when I hear your voice I look and see
you're anything and everything perfect for me.
So, now as I sit and pour out my heart here,
things are becoming more and more clear.
I don't know if you know this, but I can see
I'm perfect for you and you're perfect for me.
So, now when you see me, do you feel anything at all?
If the answer is no, then my heart and hope will fall.
But if it's yes, and you still feel for me,
then you couldn't understand how happy I'd be.

Levi Deming

Speaking of Clouds

Speaking of clouds
Trying to push above
Pollution
Mangling malnourished limbs
Tossing around like stranded gasping fish
Flapping gills
Deoxygenated
Jumped over the waterfall willingly
To the pinks, purples and grey streaks
Of the soundless soulless screams
Pushed. Shoved. Crammed.
Crux of the Earth remonstrating.
Eruption of saltine geysers
From the bottomless pit of my innards.

Ezaree Modesta Doroliat

The Ravioli

I had a ravioli, it had sauce
But it was for my really mean boss
It cost a dollar for one can
I cooked them up in a frying pan
Without the sauce, it had the color of sand
I held one up with pride in my hand
That was when my boss I found
Standing there all chubby and round
"Where's my ravioli?" he bellowed at me
"Right here," I replied without a hint of glee
He gobbled it down without a thank you at all
I wish I could slam him up against the wall
So I sat there ravioli-free
I had to eat Spaghetti-o's; that's what happened to me

Meghan Elizabeth Landry

Platonic

You madman over the overeasies
and I'm glad to watch you again,
even through this pane of glass
like a greased divider between past
and now. Can you really exist independent of me,
post the reseparation of man from woman, the resieving
of yolk from white over albumened fingers?
You do not know how under the diner
flourescents you are drained of color,
bloodlet like a fork-pricked yolk.
You look to the street now, look through,
and your eyes register nothing, your mouth
as if I were not there, as if I were
no more tangible in air than the smell of frying.

C. Morgan Babst

Sonnet #14

I dwelt unhappy on ancient steppes blue skyed,
Inhaled aromas lost when cities grew.
I coursed the gray Atlantic gloam and died
In search of far off lands where ravens flew.
The pines grew tall beyond the prison gates
As thoughts of home drove hot blood through my veins.
Olive groves shaded my songs of the fates.
Of words intoned today no trace remains.
Recall the ventures to Himalayan heights
Before hobnailed flat feet there intruded.
Campfires in old Virginia's bygone nights
Brightened black fear and reason occluded.
Why sing of scenes and dreams of time remote?
Ask to whose future I these lives devote.

Jeffrey Paul Lee

Friendship

You're a friend to me.
I'm a friend to you.
When we are together there's nothing we can't do.

I'm a friend to you.
You're a friend to me.
When we have each other there's nothing we can't be.

I love you.
You love me.
Together we can both live in perfect harmony.

Tia Marie Lambert

Stranger

All I hear is a voice,
Hard to believe where he lives was his choice.
I hear his voice—but where's the rest?
It's like God is putting me through a heartbreaking test.
Nobody knows what I'd do for his kiss or a hand to hold.
It feels like my heart has been beaten and many times sold.
Why do I still love this man of mystery,
Even though his face I hardly see?
"What?" friends say as they feel so bad,
"That man of mystery is your very own dad?"

Emily E. Cosentino

On Memorial Day

On Memorial day, a time to remember
Days gone by from January to December
Of faces and times we all hold dear
With God on our side, we have no fears
Mother and father, sisters and brothers
Friends so dear, we have no others
We'll travel long distances in our cars
It makes no difference, if they are near or far
We will always remember our lives that are past
The good times and bad, they will last and last and last

James Allen Towle

True Poetry

I'll start with some mushy words
That make no sense
I'll add on a few dark phrases
That no one really listens to
Gotta have some big words
I'll lose the dumb people like that
Now I'll add some spicy phrases
That'll lose the rest of the audience
Then all I'll have left is the people that don't care about life
And I'll call it true poetry

James K. Kosiorek

The Smile of Love

Sitting next to you, I tremble with thoughts.
What are you thinking? Are you caught up in knots?
Slowly, as though it seems forever, you turn to me and smile.
A smile that makes all the waiting worthwhile.
Then it slips from your face as she comes so loud.
The moment has passed, your face is a cloud.
Yet you linger looking at me, while she slips you away.
But you are her puppy, she commands you obey.
We shall never forget those smiles we share.
For the smile of love is always quite rare.

Blair E. Lambert

Hello, Stranger

Hello, stranger, it's been a while.
I've missed you.
Hello, stranger, I'm all grown up.
Life has gone by so fast.
Hello, stranger, the baby teeth are gone.
I am ten now.
I've had some problems, but they're all gone
because now I've seen your face.
Hello, stranger, I know your name.
It's Dad!

Amanda J. Hamlin

A Place That Feels Like a Child

There is a place inside
that wants to dance, sing, skip, and blow out candles.
Children are remarkable
because they love unconditionally, speak little truisms,
jump up and down when excited,
run because they feel like it, laugh, play, give wet kisses,
and look at you with a twinkle in the eye.
Act on those urges, regardless of who's watching . . . I did!
I was elated!
There is a place that feels like a child!

Judith Ann Dunn

Faith

Dear God, oh Lord, the mighty one;
I am here today because of Your Son.
He came to wash our sins away and for that
we are in a debt we can never repay.
He died upon a cross one day
and rose again to pave the way.
You gave Your only begotten Son, so that we
might one day understand Your love.
I thank you for Your sacrifice
And rejoice knowing I can have eternal life.

Helina Cecilia Velazquez

Swan

The crystal rushing water passed beneath her naked feet,
as she flapped her wings, to leave her watery seat.
Standing on land with beauty and grace,
looking at her was no disgrace.
With a long white dress and eyes of gold,
I'm saying now you could never be told
exactly how brilliant she would be.
If she was still here then you could see
her lunge through the air with not a care in the world
and the beauty of the swan would be unfurled.

Matthew Wayne Cottle

Point of View

To my mom

What is life, it depends on what you make it
Where is your soul, it depends on where you take it

Where is the best spot on Earth, it depends on where you go
Who is the most admirable, it depends on who you know

What is the best use of time, it depends on what you've done
What is a favorite pastime, it depends on what you call fun

What is your point of view, it depends on what you see
What lies in your future, it depends on what is meant to be

Jennifer Lynn Lemon

Memory

A single snowflake meets
the lone leaf on a winter tree.

The snowflake was positioned for
the eyelash of one not yet found,
but penetrated to a new destiny.

When that snowflake rested securely
on the lone, yet attached leaf, it radiated
the light of many ages, before slowly
melting into one with the leaf.

Darien Noelle Engelhardt

My Friend

There is an eagle in my tree
who is forever watching me.
Should I consider him a friend or foe?
As of now, I just don't know!
He is as cute as he can be,
methinks a babe, just like me.
Dad and Mom guard me from him,
as he sits there watching from his limb.
I'd love to play with him a bunch,
but really, I think he just wants me for lunch!

Mollie Corene Alexander

Destination Unknown

Down the highway
With only the moonlight leading the way
The wind whips through the golden locks
Entangled with emotions
The gust threading every thread on my head
It summons me to follow
The light is so bright
Increasing my speed so the darkness won't catch up
Waiting for the touch of the hand
Waiting for life to happen

Christy Lynn Bowman

To Reach

The clouds of which I dream
float high above my head.
I will reach for them
as a child reaches for candy
only to fail, for my arms are yet too short.
The stars of which I try to reach
twinkle high above my clouds,.
but I will grow and grow
Then, to pluck them from the sky
will be only to reach once more.

Cindy Angle Newton

A Place Called Heaven

A place with light and love, a place I long to see.
A place I know one day, God will be waiting for me.
Golden roads and pearly gates, a place with all love.
No sin. No hate.
A place where you will go only if you believe.
A place that is so wonderful when you close your eyes,
You can almost imagine and see
A place I will cry with joy when Jesus walks with me.
A place more beautiful than the wonders of the world seven,
Nothing is better than a place called Heaven.

Teigha Lynn Dye

Eyes of the Beholder

Flames so fierce brew fire and might,
walls cold and strong through storm and fight.
Unleashed power greatly unmatched,
monstrous strength and wicked wrath.
A mix of forces unreckoned with,
a formidable defense both harsh and swift.
'Tis the beholder whose magic and knowledge so wise
holds the present and future deep in its eyes.
This fortress is guarded by many, few bolder,
but none so untamed as the eyes of the beholder!

Sara Ann Konvalinka

Death of a Marriage

A few years ago, we said I do.
I was there and so were you.
What happened to us from then until now?
It's like we've forgotten every vow.
All that we've been through, all that we've shared,
I know there was a time when both of us cared.
I don't know how things got so bad,
or how I can possibly feel this sad.
Is this the end . . . 'til death do us part?
The end of our love . . . the death of my heart.

Christina A. Henry

Colors

With my colors over my head I stand tall and strong,
Nothing—and I mean nothing—will ever bring me down.
I am the greatest city on Earth and will remain that way.
I have the blue sky, the red sun, and the white stars
Over my head; what more could I ask for?
The almighty has already spoken; I still stand tall
And strong after September 11
Who I am I?
I am, like I said, the greatest city on Earth.
I am New York City.

Nancy Deboraha Johnson

A Moment in the Window

As winter snows fly, a pioneer am I,
braving the mountains bordered by the sea.
Darker skies bare a small hint of blue,
a hint of spring among the hidden stars.
A veiled moon through this window floats
with a ring of clouds around her
as she plays hide and seek with the trees.
The north wind with its gentle nip
through the tall dark crags it slips
as if it could find forever in the gloom.

Eric S. Julson

Unto My Own

I am an instrument unto myself—
I initiate and bring forth my own melodies;
Others would play upon me,
Call themselves composers and musicians;
Would beat their own time upon me.
Mark!
I am an instrument unto my own self . . .
Composing, directing, conducting and playing.
Others can only interpret me.
I play on.

Jeanne Merritt Bosworth

We're All the Same

I don't want to cry anymore.
I don't want to fight anymore.
I don't want to need you anymore,
And I don't want to love you anymore.
But I do.
These tears that fall from my eyes are for you.
With all the strength I have, I fight for you.
I fight for us.
Every minute, every day, I need you.
And as long as I live, I'll love you.

Kadie Rayann Hutchinson

your birthday

a scotch for a toast
a sprinkle of rain
the bright moon above
and feeling no pain
barefoot in the grass
a little dance with some class
walking and talking in darkness at last
what more can one wish for with a night so complete
but thoughts of tomorrow
for a friendship to keep

Rose A. Offerman

Contentment

Once restless to run, her feet are now planted,
Not needing to fly since her prayers have been granted.
She was reaching for stars, yet fulfillment was here,
Always climbing mountains when doubt drew her near.
Every mile she ran just brought her closer to home,
With no longer a need to search or to roam.
The chase was soon over and she was ready to land.
Life was her teacher and her truth was at hand.
All that she wanted was hers all the while;
Her three beautiful children draw her most radiant smile.

Pamela M. Schnoor

Finally in Love

To find love is a great thing to have.
There is a special someone that you kiss and make laugh.
I smile, you smile; we are happy together.
It can be raining outside, but, to us, it's sunny weather.
I wished for you every night and day.
I wished so much now it's reality.
You are the best friend that I've always searched for,
My love, my heart, and the one I adore.
You bring me happiness and give great hugs.
These are the reasons I am finally in love.

Rochell Marie Provost

Life

Life is like the wind:
it's always pushing things your way,
whether you're at work or outside at play.
Life is cruel, harsh,
and mean, scaring you
with things unseen.
Playing tricks on your mind and soul,
messing up your lifetime goal.
So think of it a lot today,
And listen to what God has to say.

Jasmine Pimentel

Lily Violet

Lily Violet is a dragonfly fluttering and a glistening sunset
And is warm and silky smooth
Lily Violet is the taste of a sparkling fairy's wing
Blooming spring and the fresh breeze
After a rain smell like Lily Violet
Magical freshness makes me feel Lily Violet
Lily Violet is an open prairie,
Jungle wildlife and a flower filled valley
Flying is Lily Violet
Lily Violet is the taste of earth

Kristine Riniker

My Torn Heart

I come home knowing there's a decision to be made,
The wrong choice and a price to be paid.
To love not only one but two
And love them both with a love that's true.
To have to choose only one
Seems too great a task to ever be done.
The sun has set, time to decide.
My choice is now; my feelings I must hide.
I can't tell them the truth; they couldn't bear.
So the truth I promise to never share.

Blair Henry

Things Are Changing

Things are changing, can you hold on?
Here come the clouds, there goes the sun.
Here comes sadness, there goes happiness.
Things are changing, can you hold on?
There goes the rainbow, here come the storms.
There goes the old, in comes the new.
The wheels are set in motion. Surprise! We are moving.
Things are changing. What once was war is now peace,
but can you hold on?
A change is fast approaching, are you ready?

Elizabeth Ann Harrison

It's Amazing

It's amazing how some people can be so cruel.
I really do pity the fool.
It's amazing how many people can die,
Many people wondering why.
It's amazing how such chaos can happen in a day,
In such a manner, procedure, in that way
New York will never be the same,
But who do we really blame.
September 11 was the day
That America slowly drifted away.

Emily Robertson

A Night with Myself

I sit, quietly watching the stars above me.
I lie, half asleep on the sand.
I wait for the moon to glow.
I wade into the darkened sea.
I dive under the water of murky cold.
I surface, looking into the sky.
I laugh, fish waving around my toes.
I walk away from this night.
Waiting.
Waiting for the sun to rise.

Sara Jane Troxell

Life Is Worth Living

September the eleventh got our attention
Made us aware of too much to mention
Like what are our dreams and goals ahead
Unlike the victims we're living, not dead
Will we change our paths, live life to the fullest
Or let the terror remain within us
It made us remember to say I love you,
To strive for happiness in all that we do
Don't ever let anyone take it away
Our future depends on how we live today

Jill M. Langley

My Sons

I watch each day as my little boys
grow into fine young men.
Loving God, loving life
and loving their fellow man.
I watch as they choose
which way they want to travel.
Where will their feet take them?
And all I can do is say a prayer
that our God will guide and protect them.
I love you Aaron, Mike, Andrew, and Daniel.

Anita Quincela Beason

a light in the black

match sticks burn quicker in the dark,
dimming light in the softness of her flame.
burned to a crisp, the wrinkled length curls,
and the dying light makes shadows dance
on the walls.

waving finally, she turns to blue and shrinks,
burns sharply on its way to my fingertips.
she is painful and must be stopped;
blow her out and the black envelopes,
leaving her scent.

Martin Isidro

Crayons

Days of gloom I thought would never end, did
And days of happiness I saw no reason to end
Were brought to a close
We drink and some bubbles bounce inside us
We fart and laughter is hidden
Did you bring your pens? Your paper? Your starship?
Light a course for others to wonder
Color is sumptuous and thoughts are without bound
Until someone sneaks up on them
Have your crayons embellished with glitter and surprises await

Lisa Ingrid Solheim

As the Students Pass

Seeing students race by
Determined to reach their destinations
One thought can't help but come to mind
Of the sea and waves that crash
Together to form one being
With cries of laughter from small children
Chased by a wet blue monster
They are all too soon replaced
With the chatter of older students
As they continue to race by

Stephanie Lynn Haynes

Grandparents' Day

Grandparents are very special people.
They are there when we need someone to talk to.
They are there when you need a hug.
They are there when you need something sweet like a cookie!
They are there to teach you.
They keep you busy,
But most of all, they give you love!

Debra Lynn Bender

September 12

September 11, a day of tragedy!
A day when all of America froze in horror.
A day when evil was at its worst.
A day when we all prayed, "God bless America."
A day which will never be forgotten.
September 12, for those of us still here, a
Day to make a difference for those who
Tragically died the day before.

John Derek Rogers

The Last to Know

Fifteen years have passed me by
and all I wanted was for me to die.
If you were me, you'd understand
that the life I live was not well planned.
To be teased at school and even at home,
you feel like you're in this world alone.
I felt like that for fifteen years
and at night I'd cry those empty tears—
The tears of a girl who feels no love;
who needs an angel from up above.
But all this time I never knew
the angel from Heaven was always you.
Mom, you were my angel in disguise.
All I needed was to open my eyes.
You were there through good and bad
and made me feel special when I was sad.
Our life on Earth is very short,
so complete the mission and don't abort.
Let your love towards your family show.
Don't let them be the last to know.

Katherine Angela King

Without Excuse

Without excuse I humbly press on,
never turning back.
I turn to God, and pray with hope
that I never stray off track.
Without excuse I keep in mind,
the goal I've set out with.
Loving the Lord and reaching the lost
are at the very top of my list.
Without excuse I hope and pray
God's light would shine through me.
For work and play and everyday life
are all that they may see.
Without excuse I praise the Lord
each and every day.
For, I want the lost and the whole world
to know that He is the only way.
Without excuse I know my mission;
I'll follow it through and through.
It's saving the lost one person at a time
and doing it all for You.

Candice Marie White

Mower for Sale

Fire engine red riding lawnmower for sale
must go to a good and loving home.
Very dependable and trustworthy, "as if an
inanimate object has any feelings at all."
Starts every time, in the coldest winter or
the hottest summer. I have tackled many a
large job as well as smaller ones with no
problems. The only reason to sell me is a
larger tractor is needed for the new place
and I have not been used for the last two
cuttings. I will work hard for my new owner
just as I have for my old one. All I ask is
that you do good maintenance on me and keep
my blade nice and sharp. Here comes my old
owner heading towards me now, with tools,
oil, and a new blade. I even see two new
headlights and four tires in the back of the
truck. I humbly withdraw my ad and hope that
other mowers have a owner as good as mine.
The mower.

John Brett McCuan

Nana

You remind me of the wind whistling in the trees.
You remind me of the sunshine coming after the storm.
When I think of you,
I know that I want to be just like you when I grow old.

You make me think of funny things,
like rabbits playing with foxes.
You make me want to laugh at the silliest little things,
like clouds of cotton candy and raspberry streams.

You make me laugh when I feel like crying.
You make me smile when I feel like frowning.

You are the treasure at the end of the rainbow,
the smile on everyone's face.
You are like the little bird that sings in the morning
when everything is still.

You are you,
you are Nana,
my Nana,
and I will always love you.

Tara Marie Clark

Our Children

Our future remains in the little eyes
We see all around us every day
The blue, green, and brown alike

Take care of our children, love them
And need them, the precious little ones
As they grow more innocent and sweet

The homeless and the abandoned
Along with the abused and unwanted
All needing the same love and affection

Teach our children about success
Reading, writing, and numbers equally
As well as good morals and values

Need our children of the future
And keep them safe from harm, wanting
The world to grow and prosper before them

Our children are the future
Challenge them in everything that they do
Remembering that we teach them the meaning of forever

Theresa Jean Kent

Someone Special

There are so many choices I have to make.
That's why I have to give and take.
I could give all my love to you,
but I might be wrong if I do.
You are so sweet to me in so many ways.
Maybe we could mend our ways.
I think of all the times we were together,
and maybe someday we can make them better.
In my heart, I have a special place for you;
all my life, it will be so true.
You really do mean a lot,
that's why I given this so much thought.
I think of your sweet, little face
and how I once had your warm embrace.
I wish I could make you see
just how really special you are to me.
Then, maybe you could forgive me
for the day I had to set you free,
and it could be just you and me.
I guess we'll have to wait and see.

Sharon Denell Mead

Now You're Gone

To my puppy, Daisy, who died in January of 2001

I got you when I was only three.
Your had a bow on your collar and a little pink nose.
You had a short tail and pointy ears.
You also had little short toes.
You ran in the backyard and had your fun,
and went to bed when the day was done.
Eight years later you got very sick.
No one knew why,
but I knew there was a chance you might die.
When I heard the news I began to cry.
You were my puppy, how can I let you die?
I was lying in bed
and Dad came into the room.
He said you have passed away,
and your life was now through.
I started to cry,
but I wasn't sure why,
because now you're in Heaven,
somewhere in the sky . . .

Keli Renee Perault

Real, but Invisible

Starked as a statue, wounded in my heart
I think of the past: my life, my love, my hate.
All wrath I wreak my feelings,
But there's no one to listen.
I wrestle with a pen in my hand
Trying to release myself from pain.
I toddle on my trip to nowhere.
I'm so far away from the truth,
So far away from what I dreamt of,
Because God played another tune.
Just wanted to be visible
In front of your eyes.
I tipple from your look as before,
Even though you never really saw me.
Captured innocent as victim of love,
Remember, on my tomb, your name will be,
With invisible letters that I only can see.
I had a heart once, now I've lost it.
If you try to bring it back to me, as it seems
I won't be lonely when I die at least.

Veneranda Dulaj

Eye of the Beholder

A spell has been cast upon me
A kind of magic that engulfs me
It floods into my lungs, torments my dreams
Soft sounds speak to me
They speak to me and whisper words of desire
My utopia is found
Anything less is merely an illusion
Take me where I have never been
Now it's too late to go back to before
This world I have found
Becomes an escape from reality
I succumb to the magic which sets me free
The mysterious poet that has given me peace
The eternal calm within me
Breaks the long hated darkness
The great white light becomes a clearing
To an understanding
In a moment of weakness, I look into the eyes
Of the beholder
It is you

Robyn Ashley Rose

A Nation without Love

A nation that has no peace
Is a nation broken up to pieces
A center without growth for the people
Without a place to rest in peace
Their children are living in the past
With a gun in their hand
Then an enlightened path to grow on
In a rock that has no place to grow
A few are rooted to death than to an enriched soil
If only they found the switch of our Creator's love
That we are connected as families from afar
Generation from generation of many changes to build on
The sun rises and sets ever day without asking
Knowing we have another day to build our love together
So does our Creator's love with every breathe He gives us
We hope that not in history books they will know peace
But within the hearts of their children
This land was created by a Living God
The just will overcome the few in peace and in love
Returning the nation to a center of growth for the people

Mary Fatima Hoffman

Black and White

She dreams at night in color, the spectrum of her mind
The feelings swirling through the mists of sleep
Each color holding a truth in dreams
The brilliance explodes in hues of meaning she can almost
But not quite touch
Her soul she sees before her, a myriad of shades
With wakefulness she sighs and knows that she must wait again
And seek the day, always looking within
Searching for her heart
Confusion reigns in daylight, wisdom glows at dusk
The greyness creeps in slowly
What lies ahead she must paint, a picture of her life
The pallet trust and truth with love
She longs for the night to dream again
To continue on the journey for that one elusive color
That only she will know
In time to complete her canvas
And the peace will finally come
She dreams at night in color
And wakes to black and white

Cathy S. Staton

if my father were a cowboy it would have made divorce easier

i saw you beyond the rocks
walking eastward slowly
early in the morning
you were watching the finches
in the wet grass
with your back to the sun
there was a glint off of your belt buckle
that strained my eyes
your boots kicked up dusty top soil
i swore i could hear hoof beats
prancing in circles around you
while you hummed low under your breath
clouds passed above you
giving you this ethereal halo
you were out of focus
you moved your body
like a bulk of wheat or a shock of oats
and i silently begged you
to come back home

Lauren Scotto

I Can . . .

I can fly with the birds
And swim through the seas
I can pick wildflowers
And talk to the bees
I can play music all day
And into the night
I can try anything
And I am always right
I can sing songs like no one else can
I can be soft or act like a man
I can cry over nothing at all
I can smile and laugh at myself when I fall
I can climb mountains
And jump out of planes
I can race cars
Or drive a train
I can do anything I like
Any time that I please
I am whatever I want to be
But only in dreams . . .

Meggan Panico

The Perfect Match

Dedicated to my love, Nada (November 14, 2001)

Precious yet bold in its own ways
as the generous sun shares its rays
is my Love for our commitment showing praise
and feeling its warmth,
never feeling its piercing combustion
from being too shallow,
never its frozen immobility
from being too distant.

Perfect as the distance Earth is from the sun
is the Love we extend when we become one,
thorough as the never-ending days to come,
and known as all the days already begun.
Foreseen motions guaranteed from unity
as a morning flower blooms its purity,
watch our Love open up a trinity
and stay with us throughout eternity.

As Earth lets the sun nourish life,
you allow me to represent my Love.

Joseph Daniel Chamoun

Dear Mr. President

My name is Dyanna. I am a U.S. resident.
I love my country and what we share,
but I want to tell you my life is now a bear.
Since the tragedy
our lives have been disrupted,
not only that, our land corrupted.
We are sending our men to battle
in a much needed war,
so many lives were lost, we must get to the core.
I have a lot of family who may be going there,
we'll lose a lot of soldiers,
surely you must care.
I love a man named Ryan
who is ready to fight for us.
I just want him to come back
and not float into dust.
I know there's nothing you can do
to help ease my mind.
I just wanted you to listen,
thank you for your time.

Dyanna Zane Dunlevy

Frustration

Frustration
prodding from the innermost bowels of self
screaming, howling, thrashing
for justice,
for justification.
Confusion
thrusts and juts out
clogging thought,
making you choke
how, when, why, especially why,
questions without answers
choking on doubt
barricaded in the fog.
Lost,
no directions all around you,
glued to one spot,
frozen in disbelief,
forced to withstand, to understand a
thing you're not yet ready to handle
and then accepting it.

Jacqueline F. M. Ward

To My Jasmin

As morning hues of sun-swept fire
Caress your passionate face
Along with you, pure desire
To worship untold grace
Oceans of blue and purple nights
Whisper in envy to the northern skies
Of all that is best of dark and bright
That meet in the loving brown of your eyes
And tenderness of dew drops, on your blushing cheeks,
Written in poems, and written in rhyme,
Speak to angles of mountain peaks
Tales of lovers of another time
Your lips carry the essence of a time long ago
Of fields of wine under the soft moonlight
If you look deep in my eyes, you'll finally know
How I long to drink, and be drunk tonight
Alone in solitude, for so long I fell
My heart longing for that ray of light
But how long had passed; I could never tell
Till I was saved by a Jasmin that blooms in the night

Anas Fouad Hamam

Ode to Leah

Every time I get into my car, I think
Of my niece Leah, adopted at three,
And of how life can change in just a blink.
Oh, what an eager child was she!
At cousin Joe's wedding, we went to a park.
She skipping beside me, holding my hand,
Eight years old and happy as a lark.
That life is quirky, yet to understand!
At sister Lori's wedding, dressed so fine,
Seventeen, a glowing beauty with a fresh GED,
A job and a future, this niece of mine.
Eager to travel and for her future to be!
About a week later, as she drove to work,
A jalopy of a car with a bad steering wheel
That came off when she veered to miss debris
Did for once and forever the life of her steal!
What can we learn for miscues such as these?
Precious children do not belong in jalopies
Any more than do elders of other dignitaries.
Put irreplaceable people in safe cars, please!

Meg C. Steensland

The Playful Pooch

I had a dog I liked to stroke
He only smiled and never spoke
The name I gave him was Slowpoke
To the park I took that bloke
Then, Holy Smoke!
His leash just broke

I cried all that day when he ran away
Why couldn't Poke just stay, stay, stay?
The search went on till the sky turned gray
But still no sign till late in May
We found him on that glorious day
Down the street from Mary's Way

When we found my little Rover
His head was sprinkled with some clover
Oh, no, my pooch was run over

There he laid all surreal
But the car just hit with one wheel
As I watched, I could not feel
I just peered on as they peeled

Samuel Arthur Lima

Immt

In time nothing destroys meaning
In time death forces weaning
I see a hole in my head
Life is being remembered when you're dead
I shake and hunger for feeding
I vomit everything I'm eating
Alone in a world of my own
Intimacy comes in sporadically via phone
When the singing is done
The only music is a moan
Bound up in a hell trap
I carved out of stone
Living in a mind
That is broken
I have a thought
That's a token
The ability for greatness
Violated through to the bone
I slipped in the ferment
That is home

David Curtiss Stout

Drifting

Drifting
I awake again to the loneliness
The half darkness
The shadows

Drifting
I belong to this place, filled with dust and dirt
They are me I am them
The shapes

Drifting
The memories haunt me
They taunt me
The faces

The darkness
It comes advancing towards me
Fear fills my already cramped mind
A question floats to the surface of my already cramped mind
The nightmares terrify me, then the question again

Why

Kathleen Elizabeth Johnson

don't hurt me

don't hurt me now
i love you too much
don't make me cry
i can't handle the pain
please don't leave me this way
i can't hold back the tears
why couldn't i just listen
they were all right
you played me just like the rest
and now i'm stuck here
all by myself
no place to run
no place to hide
please just come back
i need you by my side
i guess i'm too late
you already left
all i have is the memories to hold
i won't forget you but forever remember you
i still love you

TIffany J. Vorlob

Show Me

My Jesus, only you can show me,
when I look in the mirror, what is truly there.
My Savior, you know that I am far from perfect,
but you look back at me and stare.
You seek the things I'm trying to hide;
You seek the things I'm hiding inside.
With each step, I walk my path,
but I know that when I stumble, you look at me the same.
Through this mirror, I stare at your creation.
I see no big gift, no big revelation,
but step by step I'm walking forward, inch by inch.
I'm getting closer to that beautiful person I was meant to be.
Flaws and imperfections are not as easy to
hide as they are to attain.
Striving to be different and noticed are not
as hard as striving to be perfect.
Shine your light upon my face and open up my
eyes to your eternal grace.
Grab my hand, lead me forward, break me away.
My Jesus, my savior, show me your eternal grace.

Karen Weathers

Eternal Infinity

What word can I use to reveal my heart feelings
Which are very pure, deep, sincere and everlasting;
And hardly expressed, though I have tried my best?
You can see it in my eyes.
You can feel it in my smiles;
In our kisses as eternal paradise.
Every minute of every day,
I cannot help thinking of you.
As often as I think of you,
I dream of you as my beloved angel.
I wish you could wipe my tears and sorrows.
I will love you until eternity;
Until God allows us to be.
My glowed love for you is my destiny,
Which is called eternal infinity.
What more can I say and what can I give?
No more, as I have devoted all to you.
What do I have left?
Nothing, but my love and my breath.
I will also offer them to you.

Phi Thisong Nguyen

I Am Free

I found my voice and it is strong.
I found the place where I belong.
I need not hide from the world anymore.
I have decided that I want more.
I have a voice that I will proudly use.
I give rebuttal of your mental abuse.
I have stable gait and will stand tall.
I have a purpose: I now claim life over all.
I have a need that only I can fulfill.
I will not ask permission for my will.
I have declared this time as mine!
I take it with vigor and great pride.
I accept this life that only God can give.
I now allow my soul the ability to live.
I stand firm for myself, even up against you.
I believe in me, regardless of your view.
I hold tight to what I claim, for it is mine!
I no longer give you authority of my time.
I accept God's blessing, all He bestows to me.
I found my way, I proclaim, I am free!

Stephanie Tanner-McDonald

Life's Journey

I imagine golden cliffs
and almond-colored bluffs
that stand before an expanse,
a depth of penetrating darkness.
Continuing up, I scale a mountain like a
climber more experienced than I am
and wonder how I must look
floating, rising simultaneously.
Each angled step
set out in patterns of rhythm,
exhaust more units of energy,
but I strive through the burning in my thighs
making it past goal-points,
struggling and cursing all the same,
but yet happy to have had the chance.
I only hope the ascent will be refreshing
as only a life journey can promote
more visions of lush green rolling hills
and yes, snapshots of golden cliffs
and almond-colored bluffs.

Micah Lee Digre

Whole Association

Everywhere around the world,
You'll find them knocking at your door.
Everywhere around the world,
You'll find them smiling more and more.
Everywhere around the world,
you'll find much inspiration
as you hear the truth around the world
in the Christian congregation.
Everywhere around the world,
You'll find them zealous in the field.
Everywhere around the world,
yes, the Bible is what they wield.
Everywhere around the world,
You'll find an honest person you can trust.
Everywhere around the world,
Love for your neighbor is a must.
Everywhere around the world,
For their God Jehovah they show appreciation.
Yes, anywhere around the world, you'll find
Jehovah's Witnesses as a whole association.

Vanessa Ann Leroux

Stand by Me

When worldly problems weigh me down
And light seems too far and, oh, so dim
When moonlight casts its ghastly spell
And I can hear the storm rushing in
Will you be so near and hold my hand
And will you be my friend and stand by me
When I seem lost and lonely too
When the dreams have deceived that were so true
Will you so care, will you always be there
Will you come my way and stand by me
When I'll go weak and I'll turn pale
And I'll call out, but to no avail
Will you let me draw my strength from your's
Will you urge me to go another mile and more
Will you let me lean on you for a while
And share a smile and stand by me
And when I'm buried under the silent mould
Will you lay a flower and stop for a while
And reminisce of the melodies that ceased to be
Fondly looking at my grave, will you stand by me

Renu Singh

Questions

"Why tomorrow?" I asked yesterday.
But once again I've lived 'til today.
This question I ponder, among many others,
"What would it be like to have sisters or brothers?"
as time marches on to the beat of a band
who play their instruments with arthritic hands.
"Why is love so fleeting?" this one dwelt on quite much,
hearts once tropic warm, now ice cold to the touch.
"What is my part to play and do I know my lines?"
That one is left open, waiting for signs.
"Will there ever be 'the one'?" myself oft asked
or is monogamy for me too demeaning a task?
Too many questions I impose on my soul,
like so many cherries in a crystal bowl.
Will time bring them answers or will they be left open-ended?
Whoops! There's another cherry; my soul's getting winded.
In time, I suppose, they all will have answers
or just be left bruised and bleeding like cancers.
So! Tomorrow has come, good morning today!
At least I know one stem can be cast away.

Bryon Heath Harris

Unknown Prayers

I'm looking up at the stars in the sky
As I sit here in this breezy park
Wondering if what I know in my mind
Is what I'm really feeling in my heart
Convincing myself he's not good for me
I can live without his love and without his touch
Oh, God, please be so kind and friendly
As to believe me when I tell you such
Watching these clouds linger over the moon
While knelt upon these knees of mine
Wanting to take back that dark night in June
As this darkness sends chills down my spine
I'm searching for the goodness of God
To help me through this miracle trial
But this park is settled in the fog
Which tries to cover my hopeless denial
As the wind begins to blow restlessly
I feel myself no longer scared
God was there to rescue me
And to answer my unknown prayer

Melissa Mae Wirth

Your Voice

Gather round, my children,
And listen to my voice.
Hear it in the howling wind
Rushing on swift feet across the plain.
Hear it in the raging rivers,
Cutting knowingly through the land.
Hear my message in the mysterious voices
Calling through the dark green wood,
Hear my message in whisper of the sun.
See it in the glimmering and watchful eye
Of your brother, your sister, yourself.
Hear it in the cries of your loved ones,
Their voices raised in agony and joy.
Listen to my message and understand.
I am your protection from scorching doubt,
Your welcoming embrace from blistering cold.
Hear me ask you to be true to yourself.
For the voice inside your heart is my voice,
Hoping that in the end you'll come in love.
You will come to me and know yourself.

Deidra J. Oxendine

The Truth

Why do we even try
when we hold back the truth?
We disguise the hurt
as if we can truly hide it.
Funny though, isn't it,
how our eyes never lie?
Tell me, what do I do
to show you that I'm not fooling you?
Shall I give you my tears,
which fall from my eyes when I think of you?
Your heart will move for only a second
before memories flood back in, haunting you.
They prevent you from letting go of the day
on which I left you,
the day I let you down
by shattering all your dreams.
Tell me, what do I do
to show you that I am true?
Don't you know the truth?
I really do love you.

C. E. Smith

The Art of Living

Look there. See the sparrows?
Breathe deep the morning air and you will feel alive.
Use your senses. Feel, then allow yourself to feel again.
Touch the sky, then paint its cobalt field
with the accumulated cumulus of your mind.
Observe how sunflowers steal the energy of the earth,
only to replenish our souls with their exuberance.
Smell the sage after a rain and know why the experience
cannot be described. Hickory smoke and perfumed pines.
Listen. Crickets. Aspens in the fall. Do you hear them?
Raining gold. Backlit leaves. Nature's stained glass.
See the rocks on the side of the road,
all covered with the wrinkles of age, and the other smoother ones
that allow the streams to playfully jump over and around them.
Silver streaks of mischievous trout.
Spring. Wildflowers and morning glories. Poppies.
Watch the shadows move and the colors change.
Watch too the sun rise, then set (yes, different,)
But now the moon speaks softly and I must listen.
I lived a life this day. I lived that life in Santa Fe.

Frederick R. Mollner

The Sky

In the woods and their branches
are many birds that sing and fly
not only high above the tide
In between the light
is a bird that can reach the sky, the breeze with plenty ease
They oversee the
plains to which they reign supreme
thus follow their own fleet
That is what I know
Through clouds of deep obstruction
are many birds that sing and fly
in the sky and in the night
I face the clouds and winds
I call these obstacles my own
I know I'm not alone
yet I know how birds can sing and fly
I see my letters need some feathers
to let them sing and fly
Above the ocean's tide
is where a bird decides

Roumen Detchev

Wonder

I can't help but wonder
if tomorrow I die
would anybody laugh?
Would anybody cry?
Or, if I disappeared,
would anybody notice?
If they read this poem
would they wonder who wrote it?
I can't help but wonder
if, to you, I'm just another guy,
another person to pretend you don't see
every time I walk by?
I sit here and wonder
Have I affected anyone's life?
Or if because of me they look at their wrists
and then pick up a knife?
Or if I didn't wake up
how long would it take
to notice I'm not there?
Is there a difference I make?

Cameron Mecham Adams

He Stands Alone

He stands alone, both tall and true
The perfect picture of solitude
The soul of a man encased in bark
With limbs that move in a manly arc
Alone he's faced the storms of life
The wind and rain, disease and strife
Others gave up, but no, not he
And there he stands for all to see
He's had his share of troubles and woes
But he made it through, and still he grows
Like him, I too, know grief and pain
I've faced the wind, I've felt the rain
And like him, too, I still stand tall
Though life may beat me, I will not fall
It may throw punches, I may take a blow
But in the end, I too, shall grow
Each storm I weather increases my strength
And beneath this skin, my soul's to thank
The elm and I, we know what to do
We count on ourselves, and make it through

Ann Marie Rincones

Life

Why can't life be like it is in the magazines?
Life would be perfect and I would always be in the scene.
Then I realized that life isn't so perfect.
It's great one minute and then it gets squashed like an insect.
It's like all your friends turn on you and life goes downhill.
It all gets so bad till you feel like you could kill.
There is this hole and it's dark and cramped,
And it feels like you just can't.
And you wait and wait down here in this lull.
Then out from nowhere you hear this call.
The call had light and a ladder to help you out.
When you get up you learn that there was this whole other route.
This route had flowers and birds singing.
It was this whole other thing.
Then you look down it and see all these other holes,
So when you sit happy you have to pay the toll.
Life has its ups and downs.
It feels like everything is tightly bound.
So I guess everyone knows how it feels,
Because life doesn't throw you a sword and shield.

Melissa Ann Merlotti

As the Tears Fall

As the tears fall down my soft cheek,
I look up and wonder why life can give so much
Only to take it away
As the tears roll down, I fall deeper into despair
I never stopped to think, is this right to love you?
As the tears fall, so do I
As the tears fall, is there a time I don't think of you
As the tears fall, I look up and cry
It hurts to think of what we could have been
I cry at the thought of you
As the tears fall deeper down, I think let it come
I don't want to live without you
As the last tear falls, my heart takes its last blow
And the world is gone
I'm in that world in that last tear
As the tears stop . . .
As the tears fall down my soft cheek,
I look up into the clouded sky
My tears mix with the rain and hide my true feelings
As the tears fall down . . .

JoAnne Rae Tavano

I Remember When . . . If Only

I remember when I woke up to the
sounds of cars honking, and the tap, tap,
tap of the leaky faucet.
I remember when walking to school was
just two blocks this way, two blocks that.
I remember when one day everything
changed.
No longer did I visit my parents in
that big building which they called work.
Because there was no work and there
were no parents.
The leaky faucet was no longer my
biggest problem.
I shared my biggest problem with
millions of people.
If only the many countries of the
world were at peace.
If only the thousands of people had
thought twice about going to work that
morning. IF ONLY . . .

Kimberly Anne Johnson

Long Ago Love

The golden suns of summers past
Seemed somehow destined not to last.
Moreover, shadows now they cast.
A lonely place to be . . .
Walking on a country way,
Laughing at our pauper's pay,
Dreaming of a better day, a tragic irony . . .
Young love in her tender bloom
Blinds us with her sweet perfume;
Too subtle, but approaching doom.
Too late, now we see . . .
Hindsight, which no words may teach;
The student who will dare to breach
The barrier of pride to reach for what had once been lost.
A light at journey's end may be,
For those who dare to willingly,
Brave wind and rain and stormy sea and winter's barren frost;
To onward go and upward grow,
To challenge what we think we know,
To win the love of long ago, no matter what the cost.

R. Mark Laperle

Walk Lightly

Walk lightly on this Earth
Tend with love, consideration and joy
Where you are presently planted
Bask in the warmth and glow of the sun
Absorb the fragrance of heaven surrounding you
Saturate your senses with the music of the ages
Connecting with the energy of creation
Mindfully be still and listen . . . listen
There is a voice waiting to be heard
The wisdom of the ages is waiting for you
Knowledge and wonder to impart
Oh, mystery of life that surrounds us
Every speck and jot has a story to tell
Open your heart and mind to them
Receive the great richness of the ages
History and mysteries in the streams
Grand majesty in the mountains and eagles
Peace, joy, and abundance ours for the asking
Walk lightly and listen quietly
The treasures are yours to be had

Dianna Rae Harrison

Sweet and Sour

Taunting, teasing, pretending I'm not there
Mocking me as if I've disappeared into the air
Only hanging with those everyone likes best
Never caring to see where the others lie
On the dusty road of life
Versatile and complex, just like the rest of us
But for some reason, you think you're better
Set apart
Which you are not
You never pick on those
You consider to be the best
Just those below you
Are the only ones to whom you stand up
Sometimes I wish you would disappear
Just as you made me
Sometimes I want you to be my good friend
For eternity
But I know underneath
What's lurking in your brain
And know that our "friendship" will never be the same

Joy Liu

I Love You So Much

I love you so much, it's hard to explain,
but I hate it when you bring me so much pain.
When I cry it's always for you;
I wish that all my dreams would just come true.
I dream every night that you are there,
but when I open my eyes I give myself a scare.
I'm frightened you will never like me,
and because of that, I don't think we'll ever be.
I try to tell you how I feel,
and I know what I believe is real.
I believe I need you to survive;
if I can't have you, I will just have to hide.
I could speak of a thousand promises, or even bet my soul,
because I'm touched with a feeling that no one can control.
My feelings for you are, oh, so very strong;
I think it would be possible for there to be a wrong.
You are what I'm living for,
I will treat you like no other girl has before.
I cry every night, hoping you would like me,
but then again I realize that wouldn't be reality.

Vanessa Saldana

The One That Changed My Life

I saw you just the other day,
And I hid behind someone,
Hoping I wouldn't catch your eye,
Looking for a place to run.
Although our parting was bittersweet,
I still learned a lot from you:
Not only how far down I could go,
But how far up too.
I owe you for the knowledge of myself,
For all the laughter through the tears,
For all the things you taught to me,
To look at myself honestly in the mirror.
Even though you meant the world to me,
I was never sure where I stood,
So my feet stood there just frozen,
Knowing I shouldn't talk, even if I could.
We have both moved on now
And started our new lives.
I just wanted to say thank you
To the one who changed my life.

Bethany Rae Allan

Nag Champa

the world waits for me
right outside that door
leaves petrified in spite of winds
birds frozen in flight
sound suspended in air . . .
Miles' notes can't reach beyond my door
lying in wait for just one
word from me, grey skies
just dying to turn blue . . . dogs
choking on barks and
conversation spilling with no
rhythm . . .
Grandma's greens, candied yams, and
corn bread cook with no
aroma; love being made with no
cries of passion . . . tears fall dry
shades of red appear dull as
rust, black is pale! and a lover's
breath has no warmth . . .
yet here I sit, nag champa in my oil burner

Jamila N. Gary

A Rose

The deafening aroma of your scent
Solely reminds me of life's repent,
Making every bit of me hurt,
Slowly turning my heart into dirt.

You were there when my loved ones died.
You watched us all lose our pride.
I know you didn't have to choose
The day you heard our sad, sad news.

Running away from all my fears,
While my father got drunk on a couple of beers,
You saw us through lovers lost,
Fights, toils, and angry thoughts.

My baby cousin didn't understand
The day my grandma grabbed your hand,
But soon that hand was tucked inside
A lonely coffin, a place to hide.

Your face on top for all to see,
A beauty wasted so hastily.

Bailey Deane Mills

The Hole

All this hurt you left inside
and the many times I hysterically cried.
These wounds that were left unhealed
left my lips permanently sealed.
You caused me so much pain,
leaving my heart a fatal stain.
You were a deep hole in which I fell in.
I couldn't get out; I couldn't win.
But despite all my effort and tries,
you managed to see a weakness in my eyes.
Keeping my soul in a cage,
it was hard to escape your rampage.
Then slowly you let me fade
and sought for another's life to raid.
It's been some time since you disappeared,
and your return is what I mostly feared.
You make part of what I am today
and all because with me, you had your way.
As I look in the mirror now I see
a half of what you were, not just me.

Isabella Eloise De Yurre

Tears

Sometimes I could cry
Because he's not here by my side
I look around for him
Wondering if we could become us again
As I lay in my bed at night
I remembered all those times when I felt right
With his arms around my waist
And my eyes gazing up into his face
I had then realized that soon this would end
I just didn't want to lose a best friend
Until the day he looked at me
And said, "We were never meant to be"
I felt like my heart was ripped apart
Could we begin with a new start?
I had thought he was the one
When I looked up at the sun
I saw those eyes that I had once trusted before
I have to walk through the door
And begin a life that does not include him
Because we can never become us again

Loreal Marie Arduino

Full Circle

A year has passed since that lovely June day
When you closed your eyes and went away.
Not a day goes by without thinking of you,
And wherever you are I know you think of me too.
Although not together we can never be apart
Because forever you have a place in my heart.
Through my life's journey you're unseen by my side.
I can still feel your love, your affection, your pride.
This last year's been hard without you being there.
I've gone through so much that I've needed to share.
I've cried oceans of tears, I've felt lost, I've felt sad.
I've been so angry with you for leaving me, Dad.
But your spark hasn't diminished, I know that is true.
Because when I look at my son I see him in you.
It's comforting to know that part of you carries on.
For as long as we breathe you will never be gone.
Now this year's finally ended, it's gone, it has passed,
And we're left with our memories that forever will last.
I'm saying, "Goodbye, Dad," because that time is at hand,
And I know that you're watching and you'll understand.

Susan P. Hannigan

Accepting

Tears welling up inside me, demand release.
Yet evasive of the nature.
Frustration? Anger? Despair?
Elusiveness breeds discontent.
Yearning. But for what purpose?
Torrential need overwhelming my senses.
Dictating my logical nuances
To emotional override.
Seeking completion.
Perhaps the staggering need stems from more
Than cleansing the fragmented soul.
Resistance is not recommended,
Can in fact be detrimental to overall health.
Will gives way to flow.
Peace at last.
With walls down, humanity embraced.
Weakness saluted,
Strength recognized.
Unrelenting ocean overrides unchecked.
New beginnings await.

Shelly Lynn Johnston-Ouellette

The Cornerstone

Threads make up the pattern of my life, like
finely spun silver webs of intermingled
thoughts, belonging to me

and others contrived in conspiracy against me . . .
despite desperate futile attempts to pacify the mind.

Comforting fixtures of support,
the cornerstone of my life,
comes from family and loved ones,
which form the intricate framework in challenging times. . . .

To me, as important as faith, hope, and most of all love,
strongest in their foundation truly unshaken,
when the storms of life appear tossing us in its tempest,

then comes to me their love of many forms,
and all those happy aromatic memories
keep me safe and warm. . . .

They have tamed my fears and sorrow-filled sighs,
which now no longer echo in my ears,
leaving me free to live and dream and fly.

Kym M. Bamford

Love's Song

Waves of blue rise and fall, passing me by
As soft white clouds float in the sky
A cool soothing breeze blows over the land
While the suns rays warm the sand
Walking slowly along sandy land
I feel someone take my hand
With a gentle gasp, I stop abrupt
As big strong arms lift me up
He holds me close in a warm embrace
As I smile and look up to see his face
He smiles softly, caressing my back
As the sky turns from blues to black
A beautiful union, like day and night
We let our hearts and souls take flight
Echoed in our voices so strong
Loves beautiful, tranquil song
As the sun begins to set
We both treasure how we met
Walking softly in the sand
Walking happily hand in hand

Jamie Elizabeth Wallace

How Much We Are Worth

She brought so many people on this Earth.
No words could describe how much she is worth!
She always knew how to brighten one's day.
You asked her a question and she knew the right way.

She treated everyone as she felt she should.
If you ever had a doubt, she knew you could!
She was always as positive as can be,
Never underestimating the power of thee.

She was by far the best person ever to live,
If ever the option, she would give, give, give!
She was always there for anyone in need,
Always looking to do a good deed.

She affected so many people as she left us here.
Not one single person shed a tear.
We are all going to miss her so very much,
For she gave us all that special touch.

As one last wish from her, before the end,
Is if we all continued her special trend.

Rebecca Ann McIlquham

Realization

Beautiful, that she is, and you say this to me
as if I don't matter
to you at all.
I cry silently and wish to be
your beauty.
And silently my thoughts belittle me.
I stopped for a moment
within your years of craze
and my stupidity.
I believed in your words.
You humored me with your lack of respect,
though time repeats itself and I doubt myself.
Here my reflection reveals
crystal blue water eyes without tears,
a mind of intelligence,
self-esteem full of endurance,
a body of sacredness,
and a soul of beautifulness.
I said goodbye to you
and hello to my life.

Margo Marie Morlock

The Kite

The kite lays on the ground
With no will to fly,
No will to soar
Or conquer the sky.
This kite is very special.
It means a lot to someone,
But it will never fly again,
The damage has been done.
It sees the skies of freedom,
But closes the door.
Into the depths of darkness
It will eternally soar.
The kite is the loveliest of them all,
Its colors true and bright,
But here it lies covered in dust,
Victimized by the harsh night.
Now you see, the kite can only dream,
It will fly never more.
Its dreams will never take flight
Because its wings, someone took and tore.

Elizabeth Jane Peace

Dark or Light

As night folds into day
The truths lie hidden in the bush
Darkness is only the tip
Of what can be
Sunshine may last a while
But a shadow can live forever
Insanity is only the beginning
Of what can be
A friendship in Light
Is one of common phrases
But a deception in Darkness
Is one that has many faces
So what of inspiration
Rather the choice of a choice
In Light you see all possibilities clearly
But Darkness gives no answers
Only questions for an endless song
The Light may bring laughter
The Dark may bring tears
But in the middle lies true inspiration

Timothy Adam Swafford

The Reasons I Love You

I love you because of your smile,
The way it brightens up the room
Like the sun on a warm day.
I love you because of your deep blue eyes,
The way they look deep into mine.
I love you because of your blonde hair,
The way it shines with every ray of sun.
I love you because of your arms,
The way they hold me tight.
I love you because of your voice,
The way every word soothes my soul.
I love you because of your lips,
The way they softly touch mine.
I love you because of your hands,
The way they touch my face so gently.
I love you because of your sweetness,
The way it lingers in my mind all day.
I love you because you're you,
The way you always know what to say.
And that's why I love you!

Shannon Marie Morse

The Sad Little Girl That Cries All Alone

Her innocence should shine like dew on a rose,
But instead the aloneness inside her grows.
She's far too young to be so aware
And what of her parents; do they even care?
She fears the touch she doesn't like,
The unwanted touches she didn't invite.
The feel of them may fade after a while,
But not the terrible hurt she feels right now.
She feels the anger down deep inside,
Anger that is now too difficult to hide.
She cannot forget the evil she knows
Or the aloneness that inside her grows.
Kisses and hugs are no longer sought.
The price is too high with which they are bought.
The little girl feels so small and alone.
The hate is turning her heart into stone.
No matter if it's right or it's wrong,
Her hopes and dreams are now all gone.
Her future died with her innocence gone,
The sad little girl that cries all alone.

Catherine Lynn Woychesin

Where This Path Is Headed, I Don't Know

Such a foreign and strange place to me,
Nothing here that I can relate to.
Oh, just a small fish in the deep sea.
"I'm Amy Maurer," and they say, "Who?"

But I must stay to achieve my goal.
Still in question, is this what I want?
Where this path is headed, I don't know.

Wandering aimlessly in a daze,
so deep in thought about life itself.
I would like to call this just a phase.
Oh, please, just let me find my old self!

I have to keep moving forward though,
adapting to this new way of life.
Where this path is headed, I don't know.

Just wake up and carry on each day.
Through that thick, white fog just poke a hole.
God will guide and direct the right way.
Where this path is headed, then I'll know.

Amy Jo Maurer

Regret

Why won't you come back to me?
How I need you desperately.
How I long for you embrace,
How I wish to see your face.
I sit up every night and pray,
Then wait for you all day.
Then, when I start to know you are gone,
I sit there as quiet as a fawn.
Once a person is gone, I realize
How much I wish they could hear my cries.
Why can't I just pick up the phone
And get a voice, not just a tone?
I never sent you a letter
To tell you, hope you feel better.
I never took a picture of you.
I don't even have a few.
I need you back with me.
We can finally sit down for that cup of tea.
There is one thing I will always regret,
All those excuses that made it to where we rarely met.

Stephany Lauren Hash

The Only Way to Truly Live

Oftentimes, as I walk through this life
and I ponder why many things must be—
so much tension, confusion, and strife—
where is the good in all this to see?
So much pain, sadness, and grief,
endless death, destruction, and gore;
where can one find sweet peace and relief?
Is there a place where we'll weep no more?
And then I have to laugh and say:
There must be hope or else who could
go about existing from day to day.
Not only who could, but who would?
Who would wish to experience life—
knowing nothing more than what meets the eye.
Bearing that thought—that piercing knife—
the belief that the hereafter is a mere lie.
Oh, what could humankind think to do
to save itself from its own way of sin.
Without the hope of God, Christ living in you,
His Love in our hearts—salvation within.

Michaela Leigh Sheppeard

Me

Everyone remember all the me moments from
When I was little
They never thought I would grow up as quick
As I did
I am sixteen years old and I have come a long way
And it was a fight
I am not a perfect person and never want to be
I want to be me
I don't want to be controlled and don't want
To be held down.
Blood is not always thicker then water and
People have proved that to me.
My parents taught me right and wrong and
They did the best job
My parents mean the world to me and I will
Always love them
I learned to put myself first
I am almost an adult
I will always hold a special place in my
Heart for everyone

Ashley Marie Landis

The Moment

Everything pulled to the top.
See, this is the true me.
I show myself and pray for a miracle.
To have it be true feelings,
the same, from you.
Oh, the fear; eyes show all,
especially under such stress.
I tell you every part of me
and why must you just sit looking?
Just accept and embrace,
take me for who I am.
Hold me tight!
Please allow my dreams, so many, to come to life.
To live in Heaven while on such a painful Earth.
Show me you feel the same . . .
at least on the inside.
All my emotions thrown into a pot,
stirred and at random chosen.
Holding my breath as you move your lips
still . . . Nothing comes out . . .

Nicholas Ryan Partlow

Remembering My Childhood

Childhood is leaving the house without telling anyone.
Childhood is having a brother or sister break your finger
On accident when you are five years old.
Childhood is yelling at your sister and
Getting in trouble when "she's the one that started it!"
Childhood is being scared of the dark, vapid closet
In the damp, creaky basement.
Childhood is cherishing unforgettable letters from people you love.
Childhood is when your dog dies and
You don't quite understand the concept of death.
Childhood is hanging out with friends and
Making memories that will last forever.
Childhood is listening to adults and
Not having the slightest clue as to what they are talking about
To each other.
Childhood is doing things you know you aren't supposed to and
Feeling guilty.
Childhood is growing up gradually, feeling new things, and
Changing emotionally and physically,
While remembering it all for years to come.

Brianne Maree Shropshire

Best Friends

My feelings are hurt
I've been betrayed
You've lost my trust again
I thought you were my friend
But now I know
Your the one that I must let go
All friends fight
This time it just isn't right
You were like the sister I never had
Now you've gone and done it
You made me sad
It's going to hurt for a little while
But we both know it's best if we let go now
You were there for be when i had to cry
But I soon found out
You are one big lie
What's kind of funny is
You were my best friend
Now I hate you
And that's the end

Kayla Nowak

The Haven

Have you ever been to a haven where peace and joy exist?
This is my safe place and I have so much to risk.
Mom and I are in the back yard, watching meteors fly.
Kids are sleeping on the mountain up high.
Everyone is happy, only love and laughter exist.
It is my safe place, my haven in the hills.
Nestled in the mountains, its name is Smoky Cove.
We work and we treasure the history and family woes.
If you don't have a safe place, a haven all your own,
Go on a journey, God will tell you where to go.
Over the covered bridge, you know you're almost there.
It's a haven. It's a retreat: a home away from home.
No phones, no traffic, you'll know when you get there,
When your shoes are off your feet.
On the mountain you can see for miles and miles.
Washington and Maryland are far off in your site,
But not close enough to carry the hustle into this life.
Go find your safe place, a haven all your own.
There is nothing like it, it's a gift from God above.
Enjoy your haven, your own Smokey Cove.

C. J. Brickner

Hello, Stranger

Hello, stranger,
haven't seen you in a while.
Haven't seen your smile and your big blue eyes
that I can see a mile away.
Hello, stranger,
seeing you sitting there in the crowd, smiling at me.
Smiling at me like you were proud of me.
Hello, stranger,
are you here to stay?
I hope we can get to talk.
Hello, stranger
the one who will be there for me!
Hello, stranger,
I hope you stay a while!
Don't leave my side!
Hello, stranger,
I can't wait to see you again.
Hello, stranger,
I hope it'll be real soon.
Until then, hello, stranger!

Jordyn Nicole Bazin

Where Am I?

I remembered her,
I remembered she,
But somehow I had forgotten,
I had forgotten me.
Where had I gone?
Where had I been?
I had forgotten me,
The worst possible sin.
I remembered him,
I remembered he,
But what was wrong?
I had forgotten me.
I remembered my hobbies and the music I love—
But I couldn't remember that one detail
That made me, me when I looked up above.
So I thought, maybe one day I'll remember
What made me, me.
And now I do remember.
I had forgotten everything
When you left me.

Leah Schindler

Eternity

Tingling with every touch,
Drowning in the whirlpool depths of your eyes.
An ache in your heart, so deep, so sweet,
A loss of words at a single glance
Rising emotions you've never imagined.
A swirl of feeling that frightens you and satisfies you,
Sends you reeling for explanation.
Losing your mind slowly, as well as your heart,
And never thinking to care.
Forgetting what you've forgotten,
Learning to forgive.
Listening through your heart,
Sending through your mind a feeling in every bone,
Every corner of your body.
Throwing caution to the wind, never looking ahead.
Spending this one moment,
Living it to its fullest and memorizing it,
It's every detail to store eternally in your heart,
For eternity is the meaning of these feelings,
Eternity is the sordidness of love.

Lauren Taylor Gordon

The Day When Angels Got Together

To my three children, the angel God took home, and my soul mate

The day when angels got together was the day
when we found each other. The day when angels
got together I knew that then fairy tales do
come true. The day when angels got together
was the day that our souls finally gazed
upon each other. The day when angels got
together, that was the day when Heaven was made
on Earth. . . . The day when angels got together was the day
when I let you take my hand in yours
and guide me through your dreams. The day
when angels got together was the day when we
shared our embrace upon one another. The day
when angels got together was the day when we
stood together in front of our family and
friends, and the wings of the angels touched
each other and surrounded us, joining our
souls as one. The day when angels got together
was the day when two worlds became one. . . .

Julie Mae Buie

My Autistic Student

You entered my world seven years ago,
a world that you were not accustomed to.
I taught you to sit in my world, but I
learned that you don't have to be still.
I taught you to be quiet in my world, but I
learned that it's okay to be loud.
I taught you to maintain eye contact, but I
learned that sometimes it's better to look
the other way.
I taught you to keep your hands to yourself,
but I learned that hugs come in different
ways.
I tried to teach you to talk, but I learned
that actions speak louder than words.
In my world, I tried to correct your
imperfections, but I learned that in your
world, you have no imperfections.
As you leave my world, I have but one
question:
Who taught who?

Dwayne E. Rice

Too Late

I always think about you, every single day.
When I talk to you, I don't know what to say.
In my dreams, in my mind, everywhere I look,
You're always there, by my side, even in a book.

Every time I'm down, or when I'm feeling sad,
You've always been there for me, even when I'm mad.
I thanked you once, I thanked you twice, everywhere I go;
It doesn't even matter if you're my friend or my foe.

You always kept your promises, you would never lie.
You always made me happy, and you were always mine.
It made me feel so special when you were around.
It's like the ring you gave me from the lost and found.

You were one in a million, someone really unique,
Like one special flower in a beautiful boutique.

But now it's too late for that, and none of it is true.
It's too late for you to cheer me up when I am blue.
You're gone now and I can never see you again.
You're dead in the ground. You were my best friend.

Tanya S. Chan

Fall in Carolina

Driving down the Blue-Ridge, counting the clouds,
going around curves, you're above them now.
It's colder than it was down below.
The leaves have turned to colorful stones,
singing in the wind with a husky voice,
making my ears freeze with their sound.
The cottages of Linville among the pools of water
warmly welcome me to this quaint town,
making me want to stay forever.
Boone offers home-cooked meals and a place to sleep
before I go traveling with the clouds again.
I want to reach Asheville by dusk.
The detours have taken me to Lake Lure.
its beauty has been aptly named;
I feel the magic lapping on its shore.
The Biltmore is guarding Asheville;
it shines in the afternoon gleam,
answering my call of a peaceful dream.
Fall in Carolina, it never blooms late.
Please come, it's Heaven's only gate!

Karon Denise Brisson

In One Breath

So scared about what's going to happen to me.
Everyone, everything,
Taken away in one breath.
One disaster, totally unexpected
Took away everybody important;
Couldn't prepare for and couldn't expect.
I want to cry, but they won't come out
Because in my heart I know.
My whole life couldn't have just vanished in one breath.
I want to hold onto somebody.
I'm so worried.
Everyone just keeps pushing me away.
I'm determined to stay;
They say there's no way.
What they don't say is there is nobody left to care.
Then the sky opened
And a man in uniform lifted me from the rubble.
He said everything's going to be fine, I'll take care of you.
In one breath my whole life changed
And in one breath I was saved.

Stephanie Jeanine Brabham

Dads

Dads say that they're going to do a lot, but it never happens.
They miss out on a lot of their daughters' lives,
and they don't even know it.
One of these days, their daughters are going to walk out
and never come back and they won't even care.
Now I'm all grown up
and I didn't have that guy by my side telling me what to do
because he didn't know what to do himself.
The person I consider my dad is that person
who was there for me;
who held my hand on the first day of school;
who wipes my tears when some guy breaks my heart;
that's who I consider my dad.
Since today is my wedding day
and I'm supposed to have my dad walk me down the aisle,
well . . .
he's going to, because he's right here by my side,
and he's never going to leave me.
But most people would call him my grandpa,
but, to me, he's been the best dad a girl could ever have.

Megan Kristine Wilhelm

Grief

A blow hard enough to knock you out of life itself,
only to produce a new being of inner respect.
Wonderment hangs blasphemously in air.
A smooth howl shows gratitude to all around
and thrusts forth a burning flame for one's great shame,
giving way to new grief.
A feeling of a lifted burden is hesitant to the wind
of whose self is needed to defend on the way
of facing the old way to send a good news message
to God's followers set afoot to find new ground.
When will labor begin to hurt,
begin to slip through your little fingers?
Let alone to grasp one thing at a time
to challenge a knight of continuous might,
astride his living, breathing, running steed
to follow the sunset past the water reeds
into his father's arms of love, trust and abuse.
A narrow escape won't change the fact
the desire you lack of rescuing me
from love's tormented talent of heartache and pain.

Annie Rosemarie Mitchell

Stop

Why is everything all messed up?
My life, the world, my hair.
I was supposed to be a perfect girl,
And live in a perfect world.
But they hurt me,
My soul, my life.
All safety is lost.
I feel surrounded by hatred.
No peace is in sight.
We are supposed to stop the hatred,
But how can we stop what is not seen?
We are blind.
We want peace,
and we are fighting for peace.
We see it all the time,
But we don't notice it.
Nothing but more fighting is trying to stop the war.
But I've had enough.
I want my life, security and safety back.
I want it all to stop.

Roseann Neusch

A Mother Is . . .

A mother is . . .
A warm blanket wrapped tightly around you,
Keeping you safe and warm from the world.

A mother is . . .
An attentive audience,
Hanging onto your every word and
Remembering it always.

A mother is . . .
A shadow in the night.
No matter where you are or what you are doing,
You know somewhere, someone loves you unconditionally.

As time passes so must a mother and with her goes:
A warmth for the body,
A peace for the mind,
A comfort for the spirit,
And is replaced by a longing of the soul.

A mother is . . .
Waiting.

Cindy Carnes-Rich

Sheri

The stars twinkle through your naked eyes
and I can see your soul shine
upon your sweet smile.
My heart is blinded by fierce attraction.
In my mind we embrace
and a simple breeze is all that passes
between you and I.
Cupid hovers, as bare as we,
showering flower petals
as soft as the skin I stroke.
Our spirits rise and dance in the sky
inviting new twirls into
a whole new realm of excitement.
You fill my time with fresh existence
and we stand still
as I stare at utter beauty.
Your personality breaks my every motion,
my every word and my spirit grows
with every thrust of inner beauty
you share with me.

Lindsey Sue Ellis

Love Hurts

Love hurts when the one you love doesn't love you back.
Sometimes that's all it takes to throw you off track.

Love hurts when they want someone else,
Leaving you to cry alone all by yourself.

Doing what you can to make that person's day,
But they're steadily and always pushing you away.

No one told me love hurt so bad.
Now that I know, I wish someone had.

I wish I could just do it all over again.
Find that true man and also my friend.

I want someone who holds me, caresses me,
and tells me he loves me.
I want us to share our feelings and also be happy.

I want us to do things together and be the best of friends,
Best friends until the end.

No one ever told me that love hurt so bad.
Now that I know, I wish someone had.

Kim Levette Williams

New Beginning

Your smile is what caught my eye;
I had to have you or I'd just die.
Then came your tender loving touch;
I knew I'd love you, oh, so much.
You have such passion and great desire;
When you're near me, baby, I'm on fire.
You make me laugh and have a good time;
I can't believe this is a nice rhyme.
Usually I think only negative things;
It's most unbearable, the pain it brings.
Where do you begin again or get a new start
When all you've ever known is a broken heart?
You have shown me it's good to care;
To take a chance, do I dare?
Thank you for loving me like you do;
It's a totally different world when I'm with you.
I'm holding on, never to let go.
My love for you, I want you to always know,
Is special and kind and wonderful to me.
Isn't that the way true love should be?

Melinda Ann Miller

Daddy Came

I remember that day
A time green vines crawled
Up to the rooftop
Air smelled of caramel rain
It was the night my daddy came
I was in my pajamas
In cold bare feet I jumped from the top step
Into my daddy's arms

He held me warm to his chest
Against his sunny heart
His arms squeezed me
So my cheek matched his

He left two cheeks
Unmatched
On that morning cold
When vines were
Dried
Shattered
My daddy left

Priera Hortenzia Panescu

Rivalry

The war will begin when two destinies collide,
When two dreams become reality,
When only one can endure.

As two fight for existence,
For one must come out on top,
This rivalry will destroy anything in its path.

As obstacles are smashed between life and death,
It's only a matter of time before one is triumphant.

What is all this rivalry about?
This rivalry is about hatred, about who is more powerful.

Will several new heroes be born?
Will old heroes become shattered and ancient history?
Will this rivalry ever stop?
No, this rivalry will never stop.

The war will begin when two destinies collide,
When two dreams become reality,
When only one can endure,
This rivalry will never stop.

Ashley Silvester

Mixed Emotions

He came home one day from vacation,
My friend called him for me, I began pacing.
I "borrowed" my parents car that night
And drove to his house in such fright.
I picked him up, we went back to my place.
I couldn't help but smile every time I saw his face.
Things were going by real smooth,
When things between us began to move.
There was only one problem, he had a girl,
And all my emotions began to whirl.
He called me up a few days later,
Telling me, "We're done, I hate her."
I smiled thinking he was finally mine,
But that would be for the last time.
I found out at work they were talking things out
And I began to do more than just pout.
It seems as though I cried for a straight three days.
No one was there to wipe my tears away.
I see him now and my emotions swirl,
And yet, I still wish I were his girl.

Alysha Vogel

Mandolin Angel

The baby-faced girl rests her head lightly
upon the gold, antique mandolin.
She, herself, shines an angelic light.
Eyes shut contently, rose petal cheeks that color her fair face.
Pink, puckered lips
lightly touching the stem of her beloved instrument.
Blonde, curly tendrils cover her small head.
One strand slightly wisping her cheeks.
Her light arms reach over the top of her instrument.
Her slender fingers gently strum at the strings
while her other hand reaches under,
faintly pressing down on the neck.
As the music plays, wings emerge from her back;
almost as a peacock's would.
Beautiful, bright, brilliant colors changing
with every note of her music.
Her wings flutter once,
then again until she slowly ascends
through the crystal clear sky
and pure cream clouds into Heaven.

Margaux Star Weinberger

Summoning the Ancients

Promise of pregnant clouds
steady trickle into stagnant pools. . . .
Nature's curving finger
signals the Wheel of Return. . . .
I watch for an omen.
Who among us might recognize
a fresh breeze when it comes . . .
blowing minds empty, tossing them full?
Sages whisper in the wind;
few ears stretch to catch their breath.
Bright exposures fade into dark heads—
who remembers the last time
the world felt a star explode?
"Who," I wonder, "is here to guide us now?"
Perhaps, (I hope) there is no cry
that goes unheard.
In winter, it is easy to forget
the sun still warms our humble sphere.
Hanging on a glimmer of spring,
my heart opens to the world.

Erica Velis Brodman

untitled

show me what you've got in your brown paper bag
what will it be, a frog, a shoelace, a frown
a finger, a blossom, a rock, an atom
a galaxy
show me what you've got in your brown paper bag
clutch it
fold the top over neatly
carry it with you
put it on the top shelf in the fridge
open it up and pour it on your head
fill it up with air and pop it
watch its contents spread over the world
disperse, rain down, and settle like dust
over everything, filling the world up with
love and joy and peace and brotherhood and
camaraderie and elation and knowing
show me what you've got in your brown paper bag

Chris S. Popp

Weary at Day's End

The woman sat in the courtyard alone
Her fingers idle at last
A smile on her face, her eyes half-closed
As the gentle wind blew past
She wore a shirt and faded blue jeans
The ties in her shoes undone
A straw hat lay in the grass at her feet
Her silver hair gleamed in the sun
With few wrinkles on her suntanned face
It was hard to tell her age
But a glance at the hands that lay in her lap
Made her years more easy to gauge
The sun on the horizon reflected off clouds
With an artist's pallet of hues
And washed the Earth with a painter's brush
While the woman inhaled the views
Her chores all done for another day
She could calmly sit at ease
Resting her weary body and mind
To enjoy the twilight's breeze

Rita M. Smith

Searching

Standing at the edge of sanity
No one here to help me except me
Can't seem to find myself again
Feeling of hopelessness from deep within
Don't remember how I got here or when
Just remember your face and then
Falling, falling, falling down a dark abyss
You can save me, but you will not
I hear your silence and feel forgotten
Looking over the edge I see
Damnation and Hell staring back at me
The slightest breath and all is lost
Lost, lost, lost my way some time ago
Can't seem to regain control
Finding out all to quickly, that
To live again I must let go
Searching, searching the world is dark
Emptiness has finally left my scarred heart
My soul is free, yet still it aches
Trapped between, searching the eternal gates

Elizabeth A. Despeaux

One More Christmas

To my children, with love

Oh, my loved ones, it's another Christmas Day.
Where in the world have the years gone, I say.
Lord, I feel so bad and always in pain.
I try so hard to be happy and put on a smile,
But just to walk a few steps seems like a mile.
Dear loved ones have passed on,
And lately, my time seems so close at hand—
But believe me, it certainly is not in my plan.
When my time comes, I know I will be ready
For Him to welcome me with an open arm—
Because there will be no more pain or harm.
But until that day comes, I will continue to share
My heart with you all with words of loving care.
I just want to hug and kiss you as much as I can,
To share my knowledge and give you a helping hand.
I doubt you will ever realize what you really mean to me,
But I will know I have taught you to be all you can be.
We need some sharing time in case God has other plans.
I just want to hold you close in my wrinkled hands.

Patricia Ann Mathas

A Dedication to My Friends

As we go down this road together,
you may forget the scenery that passed,
but in my heart those memories will last.
They stay buried in my soul
as a testament of what is true;
that true deep friendship
I have rooted in you.
As our destinations become more clear
and we start to go our ways,
I hope we will stay friends
until our later days.
But after each day we seem to drift further
and all of those memories seem little more
than a murmur.
I will forever be loyal to those who have
touched my life and I keep these memories
because it's hard to say goodbye.
I know sometimes I must and it's the
hardest thing to do, but for all who have
shared with me; I'll always be there for you.

James Louis DeMasi

Poppa's Shadow

You never get any peace and quiet
Toys on the floor are the new diet
Movies to watch are Disney and fables
Haunted by animals embedded in your pillows
No one understands why you get so grumpy
Perhaps they should sleep in a bed so lumpy
Food crumbs in your chair are a definite must
To feed your little shadow, one mustn't dust
Someday when your shadow is out late
Think next time, I'll drive her on her date
Remember each day as you close a door
Always look back and check the floor
For your shadow is a fragile thing
It can disappear like a feather from a wing
But just for the moment, just for now
Cherish your blessings of a shadow and bow
Not many men can boldly claim
They have a shadow of such beauty and fame
To be blessed by Poppa's shadow adorn
Your little wonder, complete with a crown

Melany L. Miller

What Will Happen?

We've been friends for awhile,
and I'm really glad.
But what will happen
when one of us gets mad?
Will we stay friends for eternity?
Will we stay friends for a day?
What will happen to our friendship
when a guy gets in the way?
What about later on in life?
Like, when we get out of school.
What will happen if we don't keep in touch?
Then we'll end up being fools.
I'm glad we are friends,
and I hope you are too.
But what will happen if I
need help from you?
Will you come to my rescue,
or will you ignore me?
But I need to know now
so you won't hurt me.

Emily Jean Berner

Fulfillment

Does total fulfillment exist?
Is it a state of mind
or a distant illusion either in the past
or lingering in the future
just waiting to shower us with
euphoria and the trappings of heaven?

There isn't one road to glory,
for what I have, you don't.
I take your journey, and it makes me lonely;
roll in pain, then feel your pity laden with
deceit.

I reach for happiness, but no one helps me.
It's when I am down,
I realize that my deeds of satisfying many have come to naught.
However, who is true
will always evoke a glimmer of happiness in you.
Yet fulfillment evades the mind,
for if it did not, then desire would cease.
And ultimately emptiness would reign.

Steve Alexander Baker

The Pain Inside

Don't listen to my laughter, don't look at my smile.
Enter my eyes and stay for a while.
There is no warmth or a heart,
For those have been lost or ripped apart.
Do you like the darkness? Can you feel the cold?
I hope you are strong enough,
'Cause there is nothing here for you to hold.
I can sense your fear as you start to cry.
Watch out for the demons as they fly by.
Don't try to stay and defeat the pain
'Cause there is nothing here for you to gain.
I know you are scared, so it is time for you to leave.
You think this is fake—something you can't believe.
You just don't understand why this is here,
Why there is so much pain and fear.
It wasn't here at birth or when I was a little boy.
Back then, I was filled with so much joy.
Just remember one thing!
It was you who entered my eyes,
The person who grabbed my heart and filled it with lies.

Stan C. Ohnmeiss, Jr.

Marriage

The bride is lovely in her gown of white
on that beautiful day so clear and bright.
The groom is there by her side,
vowing their love shall never die.
What happens to them in between?
Was it really love or just a scheme?
As the years pass by, it really seems
we often lose sight of our basic dreams.
Why does it have to go so wrong?
It all began as a lovely song.
The years of fights do take their toll;
the many tears drain the soul.
What is the answer to this plight;
to pass unscathed from morn to night?
There is no answer to my quest,
with each person the answers rest.
How will you fare in this game of life
when you take the vows to be man and wife?
Will there be tarnish on the gold
or will love endure until you're old?

Eleanore Dunn

Longest Year!

Today is the day that marks
The longest year of my life.
One whole year has gone
Since I heard your sweet voice.
Did you think that one year
Would make me forget you?
Not likely, with all that you know
Of me, of my heart, and my soul.
My sweet Bard, my sweet Priapus,
I still cry out in the darkness
To see your hypnotic, blue eyes;
As I, willingly, become your wood nymph.
One year could never make me forget!
My sweet mover, you were the only one . . .
Capable of crumbling my ancient walls,
Built to protect my heart and my soul.
After so many years of construction
And living as the happy pretender,
You burrowed into my heart,
My sweet wind, and I was alive!

Hilda P. Smith

Never Say Never

A new breath of air, a sea of emotions,
That's me . . . just a kid,
Sometimes, I don't want to be a kid,
Why does everyone want me to be one?
They say growing up is like entering a new world,
A world you've never been to . . . and you're unprepared
Beyond your wildest dreams.
Life can take you by surprise, full of disappointments.
It can even scare you at times,
Yet what may start out as the worst day imaginable
May end with the happiest moment of your life.
Life is complicated, and you probably think every day,
"No one understands me, no one cares."
Yeah, that's how it seems,
But there's an easier way—
A friend who will never leave,
Who will never say no.
Put all your trust, all your soul,
Believe in Him, believe in God,
He'll never say never.

Roxanne S. Rahimi

I Remember That Day

I remember that day; I remember it well.
It started out fine, but ended like Hell.
The Towers were burning just five miles away.
How could this happen on such a bright, sunny day?
We stopped in our tracks and watched on TV
Two planes crash into the Twin Towers, oh, how could this be?
The Pentagon was hit and another plane down.
What is going on? This was no time to clown.
We panicked and cried, as it was so surreal.
This was terrorism indeed and such a big deal!
The mayor, the governor, the president, too,
Tried to reassure the people they'll do all they can do.
The search and recovery, with little success,
Showed how we as a nation pulled together in such a big mess.
God bless all the people of this great nation
Who stand up for freedom, our rights and preservation.
To all of the heroes, both dead and alive,
You will never be forgotten and may our nation always thrive.
September 11 has come and has gone
And we know in our hearts we must carry on.

Annmarie Cefoli

A Million Miles Away

When I look at you, I get this feeling
This feeling that says you're leaving
It's not in the way you walk or talk
It's in your eyes instead
Your eyes are saying to me
You would rather be
A million miles away
I've waited for you for such a long time
To be my very own
Now I see you with that other guy
And it makes me feel
So alone
I wanted to tell you
Now it's too late
They've told me you're a million miles away
Well, years have passed and I'm still talking
About the one who got away
I haven't heard from her in such a long time
I guess I feel lucky to say she's gone away
A million miles away

Michael Eric Swanson

The Storm

A clear blue night
Lightning in the distance
Thunder coming closer
I shut myself away to hide
But the lightning strikes
Once again I go numb
Free from pain
Thunder echoing in my head
The sting of lightning on my face
The mist of rain runs down my cheeks
The thoughts fly around in my head
Like a bird with no wings
Lost with nowhere to go
Yet I always seem to be going the wrong way
I turn to find myself alone
Alone but not lonely
I yearn for someone . . . anyone
To come save me from this black hole
That keeps getting darker
Alone, by myself

Peggy Elizabeth Vargo

Standing Still

And here I stand still.
Time haunts me as the years pass.
My thoughts filled with a thousand memories,
and yet I struggle to find just one:
that single one that finds its way to heart,
but also eludes me like a passing dream.
Though I have lost my wings, I presume to fly,
ever attempting to touch those distant
candles etched onto midnight sky.
They torment me,
beckoning my name and holding my dreams.
The winter nights grasps me like death
holding a wilting flower,
and the cold burns within the depths of my soul.
Time turns the winter to spring.
The warmth brings life and the moon guides
my footsteps in the night.
Hope guides me, though I may have lost my way.
I am bound by what was and what will be.
Though time changes the world, I find myself here standing still.

Elm C. Valle

Two Special Angels

All the angels up above
Singing their great song of love
Two special ones watch over me
And help me to know who I am to be
Grandpa and grandpa together up there
I can't imagine the stories they share
They'll tell of times when they were mad
But to think of them now will make them sad
And the stories they'll share about us kids growing up
Will bring the tears that fall into their coffee cup
The stories on Earth we tell about them
Will be ones of happiness and sorrow of two very great men
But one question will always plague my mind
Is why it was you God had to find
There are so many people in this world today
Who do nothing good and have nothing to say
Why he didn't take them is what puzzles me
Because the good that was in you was easy to see
Up in Heaven they must love you a bunch
Because down on Earth we miss you, oh, so much

Tara J. Davis

I Know You Are There

I see your people standing,
praising you each day,
hoping to be near you,
to see you face to face.
Wrapped safe and secure in your
blanket of love,
resting soundly in
your compassionate arms.
I hide myself underneath your wings,
knowing that you are there for me,
for I feel your touch, I hear your voice,
and in your presence I will rejoice.
Your tender mercies
show grace from above,
giving me freedom
and peace like a dove.
Even though a storm may come
and my life is upside-down,
I know I will make it, because Lord,
I know you are there.

Kathryne Ann Yarbrough

Through the Eyes of Miracle

Look closer and don't ignore,
It's through these eyes I will haunt you.
Outer strength and confidence,
The image I portray before you.
"Never judge a book by its cover,"
Look beyond what can be seen.
I've adjusted, therefore no regrets,
This is how my life has been.
"A lotus flower that blossomed in mud,"
My experiences have made me wiser and stronger.
Time will heal this wounded soul,
I have learnt to cry no longer.
Self discovery awakened my mind,
My fears have strengthened my decision.
Uncertain of where this life is headed,
I am only convinced of one solution.
This betrayal, I shall take to the grave,
It is to my life, I have solemnly sworn.
Look closer and don't ignore,
It's through my eyes, a miracle is born.

Maria Cecilia Gallardo

The Wake

I took a seat, my head hanging low
The sadness I felt was easy to show
But it wasn't for me that I felt this way;
my departed friend, in a casket he lay
It surprised me when I found out that day
that he had without warning just passed away
I overheard a lady to another tell
that "part of his heart didn't work too well"
How untrue it was, what she had said
That wasn't the reason why my friend was dead
A woman he loved much more than his life,
a woman he would have took for his wife
left him for another who had more to give,
and my friend, I guess, lost all will to live
And now we all stand on the burial ground
That lady is also here looking down
And then I think, as they plant him in clay,
it wasn't so wrong what she had to say
I guess that we both agreed from the start
we both say he died from a broken heart

Travis Michael Pahlke

I Heard

Coasting on the wings of wind,
The moonbeams dance across the sea.
Opal studded skies above,
The stars sparkle for me.
A cool breeze wisps through the salt air,
And carries the unearthly sound,
As an endless song flies so smooth,
And the notes seem all around.
The mournful crying of the gulls,
And the sound the ocean waves bring,
I look out across the water,
And hear the ones who sing.
I hear the past of human kind,
And hear the present that's here,
I even hear what's yet to come,
And feel the frost of fear.
What will come is what will be,
And what has happened is done,
And what is here is already here,
And I no longer need to run.

Tara Louise Call

Pain of My Love

Ode to the definition of life, what of it?
A spiral of burning incense
Leads my mind scrolling,
Seeing nothing but burning ashes.
In this comes the ultimate appreciation
For a being, a mind, a soul.
Dear Lord, give me the strength to understand;
To be, if not to want, to learn.
Is understanding the passage to human bliss?
I will not be an impressionable thought,
Nor a photograph stamped in memory.
I ache to want this something, this feeling,
Only spoken of in love stories.
May he never cease to engulf my spirit;
As blood churns through my throbbing veins,
Such as a volcano, exploding, hot, and again.
Resistance inhibits my intentions.
What may ease thy pain? Give to thy heart.
What gives you this may comfort the soul.
Demand it, embrace it and so my life be true.

Hollie F. Clere

A Mother's Day Theme

If patience had a name . . .
Once a year is nary enough to attribute
To one who dedicates 365 and one quarter,
One who has done so much for a wretch,
One who has seen a boy into a man
Mimicking her very likeness,
One who has dealt with the turmoil of a tantrum-ridden child,
One who aided a sickly asthma victim, nurturing all the while,
And lived through the collegiate quartet of noninvolvement,
Patiently sat through many a banter of drunken embellishment,
Seen all too often the red and blue lights of misdemeanor.
She still listens to the ravings of an oft crazed,
Overworked contributor to the job market.
And yet, when the world has got me on the edge,
I hear one voice, and it need not utter but one word,
A voice so surreal, it soothes the very depths of my soul,
And suddenly, everything has stopped, a world motionless.
Thank you for raising me to be a good person.
Thank you for always being there whenever I feel beaten.
All in all, THANK YOU FOR YOU.

Wade Barrett Schultz

Rebirth of a Nation

September 11 is when it all started.
That is when our nation first parted.
We sat there in hope for the fire fighting crew,
Hoping they could save most of the lives or at least a few.
When the second Tower finally fell to the ground,
The firefighters raised an American flag on top of the mound.
What is known now as Ground Zero
Brought out some of our nations biggest heroes.
Then we decided to rise and stand together,
To fight terrorism in a new terrain and weather.
The attack on the Towers was a giant slap in the face,
So we sent armed forces to bomb bin Laden's place.
To everyone who has gone overseas,
From the Army Rangers to the Marines,
I would like to thank you for the sacrifice you make.
No one knows the costs or the risks that you take.
So, united we stand, a nation as one,
Who together has never known defeat, but have always won.
We proudly show are colors: red, white, and blue.
These colors don't run, and that is true.

Ron Gene Hageman III

To Find an Angel

Silently I pray to see them
But they are not there
We are supposed to believe that they exist
But where
Can you imagine what it would be like to
See them
Apparently they're supposed to glow
And radiate beauty from Heaven above
God's masterpiece with all His glory
Singing like fine-tuned violins
Reaching their highest notes
Deep in our hearts we do believe
We may not be able to see the angels
But they are here
Watching and praying to God
To help us through our days of despair
Protecting us if it is to be
Maybe giving us a miracle
So we can say
I believe

Bernadette Margaret Bielaski

Our Mother's Love

It was like a mighty river
Knowing only power and might
It never once trickled like a stream
But would always hold you tight
It would go around any obstacle
That tried to get in its way
And would search until it found your heart
Where it would always stay
It never showed signs of any drought
If it did you would never know
Like in winter floods it would burst all banks
And to you it would flow
And the mighty roars of a waterfall
Was her heart making that sound
Because if she thought that she had hurt you
She'd turn that river around
Even now as she rests in Heaven
She keeps that love still going
Watching and protecting all our lives
Her river keeps on flowing

Noel Roche

Sweet Daughter of Mine

The day you were born I thanked God above
For giving me this beautiful angel to love.
I love you more than I could ever say.
You are so special in every way.
As I watch you grow through the years,
My heart fills with love and my eyes fill with tears.
The tears I cry are tears of love
As I pray to God to watch you from above.
I am so proud of you in every thing you do.
You have so much love inside and kindness, too.
If I could wish one wish for you,
I wish for your happiness in whatever you do.
There has never been a mother more proud then me
Because you are the very best daughter there ever could be.
Never forget to thank God above
Because He brought us together out of love.
I will always be here for you with arms opened wide.
All my love for you will always be inside.
I love you, Amanda, with all my heart.
I always have, right from the start.

Melinda Faye Gerschutz

The Hartsuff Six

Six kids
Three girls
Three boys
Individuals are we
Rocking silently with Mom or Dad
Constant energy
Always moving
Love of sports
Hockey and soccer are the key
A poochie black cat
A sophie white dog
Nature surrounds us
Times together
Ride bikes
A swimming pool of life
Reading to one another
Videos everywhere
Ice cream shopping
Trips to Puerto Vallarta and Myrtle Beach
Memories grow

Samantha Hartsuff

An Interior

Majestically gliding through the air,
Her feet adhered to the checkered floor.
You see the maid clearly
Before your mysteriously questioning eyes.
As she walks towards your body,
You are sensationally overwhelmed
With an immense force,
Like an old oak tree crashing to the ground.
She decrescendos through life
While entering your soul.
Engulfed by her magically flowing dress,
Inhibited by her tender-taken breath,
She grabs you with hope of life.
She may serve you dinner,
But when the food touches your lips
A spirit beholds you,
Like the wind wrapping around a lonely rose.
As she leaves the room,
Her spirit is still within you,
Replacing your essence with hers.

Deborah Marie Alfieri

For the Way I Am

Invisible teardrops will never glisten
My unspoken words, who will ever listen
Free me from my locked cage
My book is opening, read my next page
Projecting my soul for the way I am
For being my own fool, for seducing life
For the ways I am cruel, for the hate in my eyes
From the pain I withstand, for the heartache
For the way that I am, for the giving heart
That I cannot give, for the meaning of the life
That I live, for building my walls
So very high, for anticipation
Of love of a lie, for scolding myself
And now knowing why, for silent crying inside
For secret resentments that secretly hide
For not always standing by my own side
For the beauty I hold that nobody gets to see
For doing and saying when I do not agree
For viewing a reflection that I just cannot show
For the people I love that just do not know

Angie Miller

My Dog Bowser

Riding down the boulevard
With my Bowser on my right
Riding down the boulevard
He's howling with delight
Squinting at the head light
Viewing all the sights
As we take the curves and angles
He's squeezing me so tight
Fur flying in the breeze
My hair standing straight on end
We're travelling very fast
Round the route 46 bend
Yelling waving pedestrian beware
We cruise safely in our driveway
With so much extra care
Sitting straight up dead center
So proper and erect
Who could ask for a dog more perfect
Than my dog Bowser so black and so white
Riding down the boulevard on a Sunday night

Natalie Petrukowich

Walking in the Shadow of Your Love

The wind blows gently
Yet the field remains calm
There is darkness around me
Yet the sun is shining bright
I realize I am in the shadow of your love
You make me feel like no other
Something I cannot put into words
I can only express my love for you
But I can't
I want to feel your eyes looking at mine
A warmth that could heat a thousand homes
I want to know that you love me back
When I am with you, nothing is wrong
I want to hold your hand and feel the comfort
Of knowing I am connected with someone
Who means the world to me
But I can't
And that is the hardest thing
If you would only let me move next to you
And our shadows become one

Adam Nickerson

My Old Dress

There's an old wedding dress in my closet
Which I wore over 50 years ago
It's yellowed and aged and unwearable
But I can't bear to throw it away
It holds memories of happiness and secrets
Which I share with the man of my dreams
I married him, still have him, and love him
And I will 'til the end of my days
There's also two rings on my finger
That mean the world to me
My diamond still sparkles and glistens
With the love it represents to me
For it was given to me by a blue-eyed young man
With stars in his eyes and plans in his head
For our unseen future to be
He's given me the moon
As he promised he would
Happiness beyond my dreams
He's my life and my love, the world to me
Outlasting that dress made for me

Evelyn L. Mullins

My Angel of Light

To me my angel of light came,
With comfort and wings of protection aflame.
She came to me when I needed her most.
Very unexpected, her light seen was foremost.
With pleasant smile and assuring gaze,
She engulfed me with the light of her rays.
She came to me when I thought all was lost.
Her blazing wings of positive energy were embossed.
And with them I was totally surrounded,
Shielding me from the mundane of which was clouded.
I could ne'er comprehend how this I deserved,
My angel of light, my soul preserved.
Barriers taking years to construct were torn down for her,
For to me, she was of my heart the trusted protector.
The tumultuous seas of my life continued,
But light, life, and liberty within me she imbued.
And thus, because of her, I was able to continue,
And confidence in life I was able to seek anew,
For you see, I had my angel of light by my side,
And her there I expected to always abide.

D. Alan Frederick

Our Exposures

The photo is taken in order to say:
"Look, all you children, we lived on that day.
Distinguished or foolish, in mourning or gay,
We were what we were; we're not sorry to say.
We laughed, we cried, we lived, and we died.
We paused on the way to picture the ride.
Egotistically acting, we focused in vain.
Exposures expired, yet the memories remain.
We bequeath you our courage, with hopes you shall win,
Forging onward in confidence, through goodness or sin."
The photo exists as the optical claim
To show all you friends how we lived without shame,
Succeeding and failing while preserving good name,
Briefly pausing to smile at the shutterbug's aim.
Ancient treasure remains of our once youthful faces,
Laughter and agony disappear without traces,
Scant evidence in images, froze in stark, silent places,
Exposed in a flash—all our flaws and our graces.
Life stays its course our first day to the last,
We are what we are—future ghosts of the past.

Raymond Saenz

Love of Life

Extremely settled in the mundane
We open the door to the world
Experiencing beauty in its fullest
Memories are forgiven, death is commiserated
Life is loved in actuality
Abundance is explored
The trees etched green, the sky painted blue
Dreams are tested against this backdrop
Our love of life is manifested
Exploring the new, the wonderful
Creatures talk to us with buzzing energy
The energy of one
Externally, we are internal
In a world that can be seen as dark
By those who have not opened their eyes
But we alone stand in union to all things
No matter their make up
Our essence burns bright, intermingled with
Connected to, the world at peace
We opened the door to our love of life

Paul Robert MacDonald

Only When I Dream

I think about you night and day,
In my mind you seem to stay.
What is it about you I like so much?
Maybe it's your lips, someday I dream to touch!
Or maybe it's your personality,
You always seem to be so happy.
Oh, I only wish you were with me
Instead of she.
But until that day
You will stay
Only in my dreams.
This it seems,
But if there ever comes a time
When you wish to be mine,
Let me know,
And you can be my Romeo.
So now that it is time for me to go to bed
I will be dreaming of you in my head.
All night long you will be with me
Until i wake and you are with she . . .

Julie Jean Slattery

Drowning

Tears keep falling like rain.
The waters are rising.
I'm drowning . . . drowning.
Where's my safe shore?
Washed away, gone in the flood.
I grasp at straws and floating jetsam
out of my reach.
Drowning, drowning.
So much hurt and pain like shards of glass
cutting me to pieces.
No longer whole.
Shattered and scattered.
Who am I?
Confused and wandering.
Bereft and abandoned.
My fault, my fault.
No solid ground, no refuge.
Only the lumpy bed I made
and I must lie in it.
A lost little girl in an aging woman's body.

Jenny Ruth Bond

Lost Soul

Lost and confused, so down is this soul
Claustrophobic in these lonely eyes
These vultures stalk my insecurities
Why can't I find myself?
Need to breathe new air, new air for my pain
Why is there so much silence and hurt inside?
Plagued dreams run through my head
Should I disrupt these freeloaders corrupting them?
I need a cleanse, a soulful cleanse
Where have the beautiful perspectives gone?
These tears don't rush for nothing
Everything is blurred
My road to peace has faded
Don't come near me
I'm a one-way street closed for construction
Too many thoughts are scrambled
Am I a fool?
I don't want to become a silhouette in this world
Where is my utopia?
Where is my soul?

Jon William Prettyman

The Trouble Within

I lift my troublesome prayers to You
I look to You for guidance and what I should do
I am going through tough times right now
But I know You will show me the way somehow
I have asked You for patience and strength
I have prayed to You at great lengths
As I watch my world crumble around me
It is in You I find my peace and serenity
Through my worries You are here with me
To carry the burden that, for me, is too heavy
I ask You to help me to control my anger
Before it becomes too much and I put my family in danger
I feel myself losing control every day
Not knowing what action might be next or what I will say
I sometimes think it would be better if I left
But just the thought gets me so upset
So, finally I pray again
Give me the strength to find peace within
And if You can find it in Your heart
Give me and my husband a bright, new start

Shawna Lee Schmidt

Marine's Christmas

Christmas is coming, time to go for leave.
The apprehension is getting hard to conceive.
Submitting leave papers is always fun,
Getting them signed and getting them done.
The day is approaching with increasing speed.
The desire is quickly becoming a need.
Two more days is all I lack.
Believe it or not, I am already packed.
"Enter my Office, Corporal of Marines,"
I enter the office to see what he means.
"I'm leaving to go to destination unknown
And I need you to come. Pick up the phone.
Call your folks to tell them the news
That you are leaving, if you choose."
Trying not to let my jaw hit the floor,
How could he ask for so much more
Then I was willing to give?
I hope my mother could forgive
My absence
At Christmas Dinner.

Joseph Michael Herbeck

United As One

Does war ever make you quiver?
Guns and bombs, flowing like a river.
The Earth could meet its final doom
With just one bang, with just one boom.
It may be one country against another.
It may be brother killing brother.
Where can we find a little peace,
Where fear of war can finally cease?
The only way we can ever fight it
Is to stand together, united.
United as one against this war—
This is something we can all stand for.
Maybe to squash this war like a bug
We give each other a great big hug.
Hug your friend, your neighbor or your child.
Hug the one you thought too wild.
Okay, maybe a hug cannot bring peace
Or cause the wars to eternally cease,
But wouldn't it be great, if for just one day.
Love could take all fears away.

Kimberly C. Tittle

In a Second

To our world today, as seconds pass by
We take them for granted not knowing why.
What began as a plot many years ago
Would bring about America's greatest foe.
Uncertain passengers who didn't seem right
Turned out as the country's greatest fright.
Passengers on board had changed destinations
The landing dismembering our beautiful nation.
In a second, a father would lose his life,
Leaving behind children and a mourning wife.
In a second, a mother whom you loved so dear
Would pass away, causing many a tear.
In a second, an innocent child's face
Would remain in minds to never replace.
In a second, our nation as a whole stood still
With sad empty hearts which no one could fill.
Our country that day would take a turn
To show the world there is a lesson to learn:
We will overcome any countries abroad;
We stand tall and proud, a nation under God.

Coleman Micheal Pierce

You

The first time I saw you
I had a little clue
I didn't know it could get this bad
It's driving me mad!
Wherever I go
Your face seems to show
I look at someone and it's you
No matter what I do
I can't stop thinking about your smile
No matter your style
Your in my dreams
And in my dreams I always tell you how I feel
But when I try in reality
I can't seem to get it out lately
I'm scared that you'll reject
Reject my feeling towards you
When I say I'm going to tell you
I wimp out and begin to be blue
Well, here it goes . . .
I really truly honestly love you . . .

Cherie Desireé Hinkle

Wishing Well

An old 1980 penny dropped through the cracks
of rain-warped boards down in an old shallow well,
dropped by unhappiness wishing for a change.
That penny falls into mud getting dirty,
and over the years, rust starts to build.

But then escape comes, the old well is destroyed,
the penny found and cleaned.
Passed from one friend to another,
passed again to unhappiness to be thrown
down another wishing well for the same change.
This well is deeper and there are more
pennies that have been thrown down.

Worthless by themselves, but together
they are a fortune for the future.
One day they will be uncovered and praised,
maybe to be thrown down another well one day
when unhappiness returns.
That well will be bottomless,
and the penny lost forever.

Denise Margaret del Pozo

impressionistic

immortalized in frozen moments of time spent
with a girl in love mere presence would be
enough to stall time long enough to capture
the poem of him artist's sketch of a man
impressionistic but he stays long enough to
offer shadows light-play edges and colors
realistic in the darkness no shadows are
needed to illuminate the artist asleep
beside a girl in love and night portrays
blurred beauty edges musical silhouette of
strength soft-burning love a fragile heart
encased carefully in strong shoulders and
broad-breathing silent body darkness against
the night I've been known to habitually
watch him sleep to memorize the soft play of
eyelashes on cheeks and relaxed mouth to
close my eyes and imagine an impressionistic
kiss of the artist asleep and as a portrait
unfolds the blurred lines of a girl in love
barely exist in shadows and light-play edges

Jennifer L. McGinnis

Freshman

A senior walked into me.
He dropped his books on the floor.
He commanded me to pick up his books,
So not to waste his time anymore.
I simply replied, "No."
He turned to me in such a furious way.
He said,
"You are a freshman.
You cannot see, you cannot hear,
You cannot speak;
Your opinion does not matter!"
As I pondered those words, I retorted,
"I am a freshman;
I can see, I can hear,
And I can speak.
My opinion does not matter to you.
I am a freshman; my opinion matters to me!"
As I walked down the halls that day,
I stood a little bit taller,
For I knew I was a freshman.

Kayla Nicole Troast

Loneliness

I'm crying for you, can't you see my tears
Or are you too ignorant to see
That you're the cause of all my pain?
I love you without a doubt
I love you unconditionally
You laugh with scorn and contempt
To you I'm just one of your games
Oh, I'll love you anyway
My heart just won't let go
How could someone use another?
I don't want to be part of your games
I'm the one you had though no one else would
I'm the one who's there when you're lonely
I'm your secret that nobody would understand
'Cause you want to forget it
And pretend it never happened
To you I'm an embarrassment
The one that nobody wants
Why do you come back if I'm so repelling?
I guess loneliness gets the best of us all

Audrey Leigh Patterson

Unmistakable Love

Sometimes you think you're never loved,
But it seems to me you're sent from above.
So why do you think you're so alone,
Because within my heart I've only grown
To love you more with each passing day,
And to make you see that in every way.
When your eyes get watery with heartbroken tears,
I try my best to wipe away your fears.
But it's hard sometimes, 'cause you're so confused.
I know you feel like you're just being used.
I'm your friend and I want you to see
That you can share anything in the world with me.
I hate to see that you're living your life
Just to have an old guy call you his wife
'Cause you are much more special than that.
I hope you see where I'm coming at.
So, I'm trying to make you realize you should
Find a man to treat you like I would.
If you do, I know you will feel
A love in your heart that is unmistakably real.

Richard Way

Contemplating Troubled Love

Out of millions and millions of girls to be,
is this young woman the one for me?
I guess I'll just have to wait and see,
but, honestly, I don't believe.
She diddled and daddled and fiddled
and faddled and made a mistake that made my heart ache.
Is she honest and true and completely awake
Or is she still sleeping and utterly fake?
This I don't know because she was young
and dumb and so high-strung.
She never knew what was about to come.
What my heart deserves is truly the test.
I know for sure it deserves the best.
Yet, that's why I'm beginning this quest,
to help my heart discover just one
and relieve its stress from life's long run.
Can I trust this sweet young lust
or will my heart keep pounding until I bust?
I guess I'll just have to wait and see.
Is this the girl meant for me?

Christopher P. Fedorko

Build and Destroy

The sun, moon, and the stars
As clear as they may seem
Cannot touch the beauty from within my dreams
I dream of love . . . mind, body, and soul
Love everlasting that will never grow cold
Here it comes, unconditionally there
Sunrays all around, yet I can't help but stare
No fear of light, whispers words just right
Not committing to stand, I wait at hand
It seems to wait in mine
For what, I'll wait for time
Only he can tell all and bring into light
Man, woman, and child all in the fight
Will weather the storm, only if by tonight
We must remove these blinds and open our eyes
Or we'll walk Earth . . . deaf, dumb, and blind
Body and mind trained for the trenches
How about the heart, let me not mention
Skin of steel, heart emotionally weak
Dare you condemn me without hearing me speak

Jose Anibal Otero

My Enemy

I gaze into the eyes that stare back at me;
I don't like the sadness that I inevitably see.
These eyes show me my faults in vivid detail:
lips that are too small, skin that is pale,
not nearly thin enough, not enough glamour. . . .
I try not to listen, ignore all the clamor.
I vow to myself I won't be ruled by these ideas,
but always I find I'm too eager to please.
Too concerned with the way that others see me,
not caring enough for what I want to be.
It shouldn't matter what people think,
yet, in the end, it causes me to sink
into the depths of dread and despair,
wanting better features or prettier hair.
When will I be happy with how I was made?
I wait anxiously for this brighter day,
a day when I can look into the eyes of my foe
and not be filled with heartache and woe.
A day when the mirror will not control what I see . . .
a day when I can be happy with just being me.

Liz Daulton

Precious Moments in Time

A day's gift of time
Donates a dreamy sunset,
Consuming my sensibilities.

A myriad of thoughts
Begins to pledge themselves,
Creating bonds with my extremities.

A musical massage
Provokes my consciousness,
Pondering the past and future possibilities.

A constellation of visions
Creates a beauteous collage,
Giving tribute to life's tranquillity.

A ray of light
Leads a butterfly,
Reminding of Earth's realities.

A promise of love
Invites a kaleidoscope of joy,
Depending on the taken opportunities.

Jennifer L. Paradise

A Vision of Beauty

As I glance across the room,
I see a beauty I have never seen before.
Patiently she sits in a cloud of
exquisiteness that blinds me in astonishment.
Willingly I amble across the extent
and into the mist of beauty.
Rationally I wait for her eyes to
convey with mine.
Then she glares at me
with an expression of curiosity.
Therefore, I implore my
question to her.
Hasty her face illuminates,
illumination so bright that it
distracts me from her answer of
agreement.
Laughter never sounded so pleasant,
and now her name shall remain in
my deepest thoughts from out my dream
forever.

Jimmy Garcia

Oh, to Be Sixteen

Somewhere between right and wrong
You don't know just where you belong
You want to do what is right
But you seem to fight it with all your might

It is my right for me to drive
Please Lord just let me stay alive
Along with friends who want to be
Free at last I am sixteen

I have my school, which I really hate
But why can't I always be late
I am grown, I hear myself say
Why do I have to get up early to face the day

I run the roads just like a fool
Please don't make me go to school
I need to be independent
Give me money so I can spend it
Get a job the elders say
Laziness will never pay
Oh, to be sixteen

Pat F. Newell

Truce

I crept and silent kept my quest
And in the silence heard a cry.
My heart did leap then from my chest;
Sleeping thoughts yanked forth from rest.
I wished to run, I longed to flee,
Yet deeper magic bid me see.
I could not move, could hardly breathe
Till reason laid her hand on me.
A war of sorts did in me rage
While all the world was sweet with dreams
'Gainst unseen faces did I wage,
Lest my peace be caught in cage.
A truce! Oh, worn and weary warrior,
Come walk the brittle corridor.
Truth shall find you if you're worthy
And bid your anchor here to moor.
I danced and laughter met my quest
And with the moon did my lips smile.
My heart did calm then in my chest.
My thoughts laid down to sleep in rest.

Barbara Jean Kidd

By the Roadside

The loneliness falls down on me.
At times I thought it wouldn't rain.
In the middle of a smile, a song, a memory;
My car breaks down.
I never saw it coming.
Sometimes I just sit by the side of the road,
Not even waiting for someone to break the silence.
As I stare into the waterless ocean of frozen weeds,
I find it funny
How snow can be used as a blanket or as isolation.
Truth weaves such a paradox.
I have visions of a little girl
Spinning with outstretched arms,
And breathing in the warmth
From the sunlight's fingertips.
Exhaling . . .
The leaves have started to color the ground
And the sting of the wind's breath
Burns across my cheeks
As I wait by the side of the road.

Elizabeth Suzanne Winge

When She Was Young

Ancient gravity of sticks I've broken
slippery silence of lurking violence
shaping the ground of jelly I walk
Accidents replayed from time to matter
Particles of lips nourish the flowers
growth of circumstance knock at my temple
Dragging this out and hiding from my parents
shapely I disgrace my inner thoughts
shut the door and lock my words
None too much like creepy crawly
run through my bed
and scream "I'm sorry"
Emotional wreckage has taken mind trips
for fear not, if you laugh this instance
This kidnap you've taken her hostage
she is feathery and silent
my force is with love, no matter how scary
Sweet supply of safety runs
beg for her secrets to be no secret
She seems to cover by living for fun

Christy Lea Simmons

Walk Away

Just walk away from the world is shrinking
minds are controlling your thoughts
of who you are you blind leading the blind
with your eyes wide, you spread 'em.
Sell me your soul is already mine
are the eyes of God won't help you
now you run away from yourself
because that's all you know
the lie to save from the truth is
out there you stand up for yourself
because I've told you to.
Think about it isn't going to save you
from the oppression so heavy is your head
for the door is shut your little mouth
the words but don't really hear the silence
coming out you go to hell if I know the lie?
Open your eyes to the swirling darkness
is oozing from the walls are closing
inside is crumbling to pieces of you and
I can't take this

Justin David Howard

For Jack

Written for Jack, who has been a great inspiration

Shadow people glisten
In the glow of flickering candlelight
Curved and chiseled lines blend
Together and into the black
Moving together and apart
Circling one another
Cinnamon and lavender
Fresh cut grass and pine
Blown by a fan across damp linens
Where dreams are created and fulfilled
Silhouettes of rounded breasts rise and fall
As narrow hips slide forward and back
Into rhythmic breaths
And the fan humming
Light on dark lines
Liquid flowing through veins and hearts
And on skin, one to another
Creating a smooth slide
Toward ecstasy

Laurie Jo Noxon DeGrave

Angel of Earth

There are
Angels of Earth
who still the erratic flight
of the wounded heart.
Just so . . . your love stilled mine.
Thus solace found respite
within my fervent breast,
and spilled over into my mind.
Silent . . . on wings of mercy,
your tread unheard by callous man,
Angel of Earth
you came, unadorned, with Heaven's
scepter in your hand. Your message swept
across my heart, speaking
truths only I need know;
and touched with tenderness
the frantic rhythm within my breast.
Quiet heart . . . made perfect by love,
Angel of Earth,
by your hand.

Geneva Bretches

The Mural

My salsa partner is unmoved despite
the nine-piece band, the fact it's Friday night,
and she's no longer pulling guts from mackerel,
salmon, bream, hake, cod behind the counter
at Jim's Ocean Fresh; her fingers raw
from cubes of ice, synthetic parsley, fairy,
chopping blocks and knives behind the pistes
of squid, shellfish, and eels; her white wellies
hard to control on tiling slick with roe
and entrails, hosed down every half an hour;
weighing, packing, gutting, hacking through
those plastic strips towards the walk-in cold store
out the back to tackle crates of wedged
sea-life, whose staring eyes won't ever get
to quite believe what's happened. The tune subsides
and dancers thank each other, separate,
reform, or head towards the bar. I ask
my partner if she'd like a lift to Camden.
Couples wait. She's staring dead ahead
at turquoise bulls being dragged through sand.

Jonathan Duncan Asser

The Music of His Mouth

Listening only to the music of his mouth
imbued in the aloe-kiwi scent of his neck,
my father stands tall, limbs sinewy,
hands calloused
skin the color of burnt sienna.
He hums Naima
while playing an imaginary bass.

Each time I leave,
my eyes downcast with unvoiced promises beating,
we embrace,
conveying what we can.
He cautions me to remember,
"It's the getting up and not the going.
It's the knowledge and not the knowing."

Coming home,
my father mentions that he has always liked the piano.
I have trouble closing the screen door.
My father reaches,
pulls it violently shut.

Michelle Maria Tweedy

Through Deadening Eyes

If life were all that we hope,
Then why are we in a hurry to end it if we cannot cope?

Abused, misused, infused,
Does hurting me make you amused?
You hurt me with your words;
You cut me with your looks.
I'm trying to be what you want, but I'm so confused.

Wanting to be what you want,
Needing to be what I need:
I cannot do both; I must sacrifice something.
Will it be my needs,
Or will you not be pleased?

Malaika Collette Raymond

My Husband's Love

Shines through the night
Giving support whenever needed
Through thick and thin, good and bad

His love sees me as I am, not as others see me
It sees the inner self and makes no judgment
His love sees the outer and makes no judgment

His love is unconditional
It flows out of him and into me, giving strength
The love he gives makes me shine when he's near or far

His love shows me what I have been, am now, and will be
It helps me see life in a better way, making me better
Making my soul whole for this life and eternity

Serena Doore

Over

All good things fade away,
even if it's at your dismay.
Times change, people do too.
You just got to remember who are you.
This chapter of mine comes to a close
like petals falling off a rose.
I will always remember the emotions in my heart,
From the very end, middle, and the start.
Days go by, so its over and through.
Now it's time to bid adieu.
I will close the box, put it behind and below.
But my legacy will live on,
even though I am gone.

Lauren Ashely Hensley

Nothing Compares to Your Love

If given a choice between diamonds, silver, gold
And living my life without you as we both grow old,
The choice would be simple and easy to make.
I would make you my wife; that is what I would take.
Diamonds are shiny, brilliant, and bright.
They cannot compare to our love's light.
Silver is precious,
A rich mans' quest.
You, however, are my heart's one bequest.
Gold as well is a valuable metal,
Only for you would I ever settle.
Riches and wealth will not bring my life meaning.
This will only come when our wedding bells start ringing.

James Gary Thompson

A Dove

My dove flies bye my window;
as I see his wing he believes . . .
I walk to him in free wind;
as I see me on the haven of all my beliefs.
I hear no sound for the weak is me;
the dove ponders on my mind.
He makes me free.
The dove flies by my window,
as I see there is no me.
The dove beats my heart for he is true to come.
The dove is all that is me.
The dove brushes away my tears
and for now I see he is my haven for that haven is me

Carrie Elaine Evans

Your Eyes

Once upon a summer's day,
a pair of eyes glanced my way.
Like a beam of light, they shot right through
a darkness that I once knew.
To name a color would be a shame;
an unearthly power that knows no name.
Why they shine on me, I do not know,
then I felt the warmness grow
to help me through this life, I suppose;
to give me strength in their glow.
In my final hour, when I'm drowning in life's sea,
I'll close my eyes and hope to see
that pair of eyes that glanced at me.

Timothy M. Quigley

My Darling

There is only one you
Who I can call my darling.
I can also call you any other loving name,
But in my heart there's only one my darling.

I can also call you sweetheart or dear one
Or a truly beloved more than a loving friend,
But in my heart, there is only one so dearest,
My ever dearest one, that's you, my darling.

Yes, there is only one you,
That my heart goes out with lovingly,
The love that goes on forever and unending,
Because I love you, my dear one, my darling.

Nito G. Salon

Her Life

She laughs aloud as they cry in pain—
They deserve this she thinks, they deserved pain.
And as the people's houses burned down,
the people watched stunned and scared.
If she could do this, what else could she do?
She did not know mercy, she did not care.
She had lost her love because of them,
she had lost her soul.
As the wind whistled around her,
she pulled out a dagger.
She plunged it into her,
thinking only of her sadness at the loss of her heart,
the loss of her life.

Colleen Elizabteth Lubs

You Failed

Now once again you failed me
My heart's been broken in two
When it all caved in I looked around
But where I looked I found no you

You're the one I turned to for help
The shoulder my head would cry on
But when fear rose up and the tears came down
You were nowhere to be found

Maybe next time I'll be important
And you'll make time for me
Maybe my heart won't be broken
For someone will love me

Cortney DeAnn Hipp

Memories of Beret, Our Poodle

He had silver hair, curly, clipped short
A gruff little bark, a cute little snort
His eyes were big and warm, loving and brown
When he wanted something, he was hard to turn down

He loved to go for a ride in the car
It didn't matter how near or how far
Hot dogs, a kitten, a tough little boy
These small things filled his life with joy

He asked for so little, he gave so much
He is missed deeply by each one of us
Our hearts are heavy, the loneliness so real
For that little character with so much appeal

Eileen Marie Hallen

Color Blind

Color blind.
A blind man would give an eye to see,
Yet, you choose not to look.
You're stuck on a color so many cannot imagine.
I must be blind, I see nothing you do.
You see a color, a tone, minor flesh.
A blind man uses touch to see;
Though with seeing, I've been touched.
You on the other hand, won't look past a meaningless color.
Judging a book by its cover; a man by his color.
I wonder . . . If you were blind, would you feel the same?
The I remembered,
You are blind, blind by color.

Danielle Marie Metallo

Dante's Question

Shadowed evening and dreamy dawns
In the mountains the wolf will mourn
Follow his pawprints
They lead to the desert
Catch a silver speck
Travel from one star to another
Beneath the pyramid is an open mind
The wolf cries with hunger
And in his simple solitude he finds himself
He's lost, astray
He holds his head with dignity
And at last he finds her
Eight pawprints travel through the desert

Raymond Robert Chauvette

The Delaware River

As we enjoy the River Delaware
We are made so much aware
Of the natural sounds here
When you walk on the small pier

My son learned how to canoe in this place
My, what an expression on his face
When he fell into the canal
And managed to stand up, somehow

The canal and the river are like a daughter and mother:
One doesn't survive without the other
The canal fills up with the river's water
Much like love of a mother and daughter

Mary Litschauer

Depression

A disguised smile to suppress depression
Hesitant to face the light of a new day
Hunger for the feeling of belonging
Alas, to suffer in silence

A new day, yet nothing to offer
Quivering with anticipation as the clock ticks
A lost soul in search of dire hope
A weak heart, a frail physique

Flashing thoughts of suicide
Morbid ideas dagger this bleeding heart
Perhaps love and understanding may heal
Sadly, still awaiting the end, too near

Jecinta John

Sky People

The people of the world are alive
With freedom of life and energy
And spirit and glee!
Sky people are people of extreme insight
And wisdom, and only God can challenge them.
I've seen only the beauty of their eyes.
In my eyes, only the shining glory
Of their hearts fleeing captivity
And restraints.
I've seen their brightness and power to
Forgive all they touch,
For they are the chosen ones.
Eons ago their cries were heard by God!

David James Jeffryes

Never Give Up

Sitting on the porch on a day like this,
One can barely see the trees for the low, fine mist.
The air is fresh, like the smell of a fresh baked pie
The clouds are a beauty in the baby blue sky.

My mind wanders to God's great creation
And the war that is destroying our nation.
Our lives will never be the same,
For the Lord will not let it be in His name.

As I sit here I know how God's heart must be broken;
Broken from all the killing and His name never spoken.
God, I keep trying, and we must never give you up this way,
For I want to see my mother again in Heaven someday.

Mary C. McDonald

Sunrise

All is darkness.
A bird cries.
The sun's rays pierce the naked flesh
of the newborn sky.
Bright crimson rolls slowly and evenly
across the fresh wound.
A desperate battle rages as the night holds
for a fleeting lapse in time.
Day, victorious and boastful,
flashes its gloating smile for the virgin Earth.
Life once again thrives in the night's death.
A bird sings.
All is light.

Jodie M. Beyer

Home

Tears are rolling down my face
As I'm in the car and it drives away.
I am saying goodbye to the house I grew up in,
I have no choice at all with this situation I'm in.
This new place is strange, not a thing like the old.
It seems cold and empty, a place not meant to be called home.
My first night in my new room, is gives me the chills—
Strange sounds and shadows, they make me wanna' shrill;
Scream and cry and go back home—
Even though that was where the roaches roamed;
And the bathroom full of mold, and the windows very much broken.
It was where I grew up.
My place I called home.

Shari Eve Garfinkle

She Sat

She sat.
She sat at the window looking out on the world.
She sat at a desk trying to learn.
She sat listening to the birds sing.
She sat.
She sat and watched the children play.
She sat and watched love pass away.
She sat and heard the buildings crash.
She sat.
She sat in the corner trying not to be heard.
She sat invisible to the world.
She sat alone and scared watching the time go by.
She sat and sat and watched her life pass her by.

Sydney Machel Peters

The Dancing Bee

I must have been an easy prey,
Loaded to the hilt with what I thought was a need.
Hair spray!
What happened?
Need I really say?
Trust me; that was enough, but he had friends.
They too were interested in other stuff:
Lipstick, perfume and lotion.
In the hospital, on my back, when I began to awake;
Swollen and barely alive.
The doctor said it was a miracle I didn't die;
A lesson well-learned, my friends.
Now take this advice and on your way I send.

JoNell Renee Barnard

Epiphany of the Societal Sheep

As I lay in tranquility, lost in thought,
The stars tantalize me.
Their mischief, their distant familiarity haunts me.
As streams of brilliance violently flow through my head,
In an ethereal flash of light,
My shepherd appears.
Lacking direction, I follow the faceless one to a shimmering palace.
Suddenly, enlightened I become
These crystals reveal the light that engulfs us all
My streams amass into a thrashing cataract
As the realization occurs:
We are all just stars, each as mischievous as the other.
Now, I rest in Utopia.

Charles David Clarke

Thunder Brings Comfort

As the thunder rumbled
She buried her curly head against me
As we sat cuddled up on the big
Comfy chair in front of the big window

She was afraid of the noise that the thunder made
So I used to tell her it was the angels
Throwing their toys down Heaven's steps
And she would giggle that little baby laugh

Now, when there's an old-fashioned thunderstorm
And I'm sitting all alone listening to the rumbling
I can still feel my baby cuddled up with me
In that big comfy chair all those many years ago.

Lucretia Arlene Fike-Beers

The Unbroken Spirit

They tried her for breaking the rules, not the glass.
They claim she was corrupt and should never pass.
And when she stood behind the bars
The muscles of her heart imagined cars,
Accelerating towards the bitterness of her innocent shame
That has the right to shatter the guilty silence with no frame.
Her salty tears are fighting to appear and defy an arrogant judge,
Who feels coldness towards the terror gripping her heart
With a meaningless grudge.
She would die like a flower without sunlight,
But her unbroken spirit gave her a transparent delight
To overcome the grief dwelling in her sophisticated brain.
Recalling the terrible emptiness assaulted her in vain.

Muneer Tuma

Life Is Not a Bed of Primrose

Life is not a bed of roses when things are so hard,
but if you have courage, you will conquer.
Then you must survive.

Life is a puzzle, you have to find it.
Get out there and fight it, have the faith to uphold
and stand in it. Just handle it, for life is not a bed of primrose.

Life is not the pursuit of pleasure all the time, no, no,
it's pressure and all that's sour.
To go through life, you have to just stand strong,
especially in this yaw land.

We seem to get the harder part,
for our life is not a bed of primrose.

Feliecea Rose

Robin

This full-bellied bird in its orange-brown clothes
Lands in a spot close to you.
This full-bellied bird, full of good fortune, blows
Through strong winds and misty dew.

Off in the distance, it waits its chance
To bring forth an omen that's trusting.
Off in the distance, it whirls through its dance;
Light wings give a gentle dusting.

Tethered to no one, this bird flies free
Like the air it gladly takes to.
From this same air, in which we breathe,
May this good omen you sense come true.

Elizabeth Ann Stoppleworth

if

if i could fly, i would fly to you,
if i could sing, i'll sing just to you,
if i could love any stronger, it would all go to you,
if i could dream, i'll dream of no one but you,
if i could have all i want, it would be only you,
if i could have you in my arms today and forever,
i would never of let you go,
but now all i can do is think of if.
if you was here today, i would of made you take your pill,
if you was here with me, i'll tell you just how much i loved you so,
but now you're gone, the angels have you in their wings,
if only i could turn back time,
if only i really could.

Lesley Carol Cope

Life . . .

Is a beautiful work of art, all in all.
You might at times think it's ugly.
Of course you would.
You go through trials in life.
You have times of happiness and sadness,
But in the end, it's beautiful,
A work of art,
A collage of things past.
Follow your heart through it all; it's God speaking to you.
That way, in the end, you'll have a beautiful work of art
For people to admire and say, I wanna be just like that person.
Life a beautiful work of art; live it well.
Then in your last days, you'll be proud of it.

Jamie Lynn Nettles

Perfection

It's that closeness I miss so much
I miss your kisses
And I miss your touch
What means so much is when we laid there and talked

You always showed me, to the extent, tenderness filled with care
And I knew then that you would always be there

You fed me strawberries and cream
And to me it was like an ecstasy-filled dream
Your lips were so soft and your hair was smooth
Lying there with you, I didn't want to move
When it comes time to say, "I do"
I hope now that it will be with you

Angela Christina Skipper

Ancient Secrets

Ever wonder what ancient secrets lie within yourself;
Old secrets from the past, born of nature's wealth?
Retired from use, but saved for us in a vaulted store,
They number at least a thousand, but could be many more.

Do we really want to know the secrets in history's trunk?
They could be a treasure trove or just a pile of junk.
Should we worry that therein lies a poison pill or two,
That just might find their way into our twilight brew?

So now, in anticipation of that sad event,
What can or should we do in order to prevent
The looming ills and sickness of past genetic sores
That have cursed mankind, now and evermore?

Craig G. Gosling

What You Took

When you take from me,
You have taken everything it took to look at you.
Now I look through you . . .
Past you; you have become a figment of a man
As I would imagine a man to be.
No wonder there is nothing left between us.
You have become a shadow
In the darkest part of my heart,
The part you shattered like
The broken promises you made
Under the wind chimes that
Remind me of the beautiful
Sounds I once heard from you.

Faye Antoinette Williams

The Old Ways

'Twas in a land called Avalon
Where magic and mystery reigned
That wisdom of the Earth and her seasons
Was the knowledge that young woman gained

They followed the path of the old ways
Weaving spells by the light of the moon
But their practices soon were forgotten
And darkness shadowed their moon

Once again we lift up our voices
And follow the old ways of yore
With respect for the Earth and our Mother
Like the daughters of Avalon before

Deirdre Musser

The Pain

Running down the streets in pain
I think about my side again
The gaping hole left in me
Was caused by her, caused by she

She tore me open, left me to die
When she led me to the door and said goodbye
She said our lives we not going right
For all I care, my life ended that night

I stopped there, standing in a daze
My life was clouded in a haze
I asked myself why, oh, why
And at that moment, I started to cry

Sean Murphy

You

Wherever you go, whatever you do,
My love will see you through.
I am here for you in the darkness and light.
I call your name.
I hear your voice, your prayer, your call.
I feel your pain.
I am here for you.
I will be the sunshine in your darkness.
I will be the hope in your despair.
Come to me.
I will hold you, carry you, embrace you.
I am with you always.
My love will never fail.

Carolyn M. Binninger

Remembered

To the little girl whose father is gone
To the mother whose son will never come home

To the husband who has lost his wife
To the wife who is left with just memories

To the boy whose mother will never be seen
To the father whose daughter will never return

Those that are gone will always be
Tucked away in our memories
Safe and sound they will always be

Forever remembered as heroes
Silent and true

Amanda L. Smith

The Letter I Never Wrote

When I think of you, my dear fiend,
I wish it never came to an end.
Remember our talks, the precious talks.
I will cherish it all in my heart's deepest docks,
closeness ending all so soon and abrupt.
Oh, it makes my core and all my emotions erupt.
If I could ask, why did it go this way?
Why did our hearts stray away?
Deeply, strongly the memories I hold of you will never fade,
even if we never cross paths again,
I still remember where they were made.
So, my dear fiend, here are all my feelings showed,
and I shall let this be the letter I never wrote.

Jessica Ann Kondratenko

ponder

a silent cry
no one will ever hear
crys out in the night

has love given up on me
deserted me here
as left contemplating the end

do all distress calls get heard
what will happen to my thoughts
as they slowly fade away

as i drift slowly away from you
i wonder why broken hearts hurt more
than simple paper cuts yet bleed only tears

Jessica Lynn Peters

Undying Flame

There is a flame that burns without light
Without heat, invisible
A flame that is a line on life
Our line on hope, our connection to hate

This flame is in all of us
But goes unseen

The most important fire
That contains an invisible flame, which is also our line
Untouched by others
But always holds us down

The fire of our very fabric
A flame that is our soul

Emily Jean Walden

Desire

To desire is to want something so bad
you can taste it, to crave something, or
to give up anything in order to obtain it.
Desire is based not on what is needed in life,
but what is wanted and what is yearned for
every day of someone's life.
Desire is what keeps a clock ticking.
It is the lust for more when there is no more.
Something desirable is appealing
to the eyes, mind, and heart.
And to obtain these desires is to feel
the most accomplished feeling
one could ever feel.

Brittany D'Lise Stanley

The Placid Dawn

The virgin silence composed and soothing,
a soft breeze quietly cools.
Twilight stars wink.
The first moon smiles.
Cirrus blush and
dew drops on leaf and petal
mirror the perfection of
this placid dawn.

I gaze upon thee in repose—quiescent, tranquil—
inebriated by thy beauty, pristine.
I covet thee, and,
if perfection be a metaphor,
Thou art it!

Anthony P. Ortega

Angels' Wings

Just a little bug crawling around
As it gets older it is told to change
It listens to this voice inside
And builds a cocoon in which to hide
As it hangs there it begins to change
A wiser more graceful being now inside
So out it pops in God's sweet light
To fly and flutter with life anew
Grateful to be so changed because now it knows
Life's full journey is a road of change
'Til one day every soul will develop
Its own cocoon in God's love and grow
Wings to fly with the angels above

Penny M. Lund

The Winter Tree

I am as the Winter Tree
Shivering in the cold breath of autumn's harsh elements.
The sunshine casts only shadows upon the scarce leaves,
Once rich and green, now falling for the lack of warmth once known.
Soon the sap of the barren trunk will slow its life-giving flow
That once enriched its branches and fed its soul.
Birds and butterflies no longer grace the arbor's arms
With song and beauty as it stands alone.
The Winter Tree does doubt that the miracle of spring's reawakening
Will indeed come again to bring back the summer.
The Winter Tree and I wait as winter nears for the
Promise of the season's change,
Waiting for the sunshine to return.

William Charles Booth

Seek Him

My conscience echoing to my soul, I must unfold
Let go of this worldly way that my heart consoles
Living in fornication, fabrication, false precepts
I clutch as if it's saving me from falling in the depths
Mortified of the light, so in the dark, I embellish
Embodying what is tangible so it's Satan's motives that compel us
So fastidious our pattern tedious choosing what we believe is for us
In fascination with man's creations, the flesh intrigues lust
As mercenaries, our excursions drive us into damnation
The cost, our mortal soul for some worldly sensation
So many are mislead believing we live a fair life
But the only way to our father, is through our Lord Jesus Christ
Seek Him

Russell Devon Burton

God's Mixed Palette

The ground is lightly sprinkled with God's heavenly tears.
The trees have all just showered and bathed away the years.
The clouds above had their burst, sagging with the rain.
Mother Nature takes her towel and dries off once again.

A rainbow painted across the sky gives us just a taste
Of the endless beauty that we all will get to face.
A glimpse into the heavens the artist to us shown,
His very brush strokes in our skies that we are not alone.

The night is just a background to give our souls a pause,
So when the light comes back again, the color gives us awes.
A balance and a comparison, an exhale and a breath;
Our planet the perfect scene for this masterpiece God has left.

Sarah Clare Goff

Inner Thoughts

My heart burns like a raging fire,
Burns from pain, burns from desire.
My thoughts race like speeding trains,
Thoughts of the past, thoughts of what remains.

Pain from the past leaves scars visible to no one,
Scars from sadness, scars from love.
Happiness from the past leaves an inner smile,
Times of joy, times of survival.

Will the burns and pains go away,
Will they stay around another day?
Will the happiness fill my heart,
Will the happiness fall apart?

Jennifer Stein

Horses

To Barb Langly

When you are at horse shows,
You experience a great wonderful rush,
And it goes through your body,
Then goes into the horse.

You have to be careful.
You don't want the horse going fast.
Think of the "Row Your Boat" song.
That way you don't go too fast
Or too slow.

As I say,
Canter that pace smoothly,
Not rough or unrhythmic pace,
Not too slow either.
So, ride them safe!
Don't make them sweat too hard
Or let them store too much energy,
Or you might end up hurting the horse in a fall.

Colleen Ellen Marshall

The Double

In the midst of health, hearty as an onion,
you fear your dotage. Sometimes you spot
your aged doppelganger,
wearing an apron over her
gown, furred booties on her feet. She
hums a rock anthem off key and smiles at you.
She is more or less than you can bear.
Her bunions pain you; her thinning hair pulls
from your scalp. Deafened, she forgets
the call of robins.
On your morning porch you listen
carefully, a hoarder. Under your glance,
her skin withers, pocked with the touches
of those you've not possessed or even met—
an oblique line of masked men.
If they saw her squinting
over your shoulder, they'd fall like tiles.
They smell death on your collective breath,
your million exhalations.

Pamela S. Davis

The Blind

Do not look for dreams in my empty eyes,
Neither look for me in my walking stick
And in the dark glasses;
For I live in laughter too.
My morning comes as yours in birds' twitter
And with a new sun,
As I finish my dreams
In lines of nameless colors
In the images of sounds,
Or in the wistful dream of lights,
Or in the lights-come-dream.
I miss in me your blissful childhood days;
But then these days of wild youth
Have not come to stay either.
For sure I know how beautiful is the beauty;
And what is it that makes the flowers and the bees
So happy between them.
You are but a visitor in the world of visuals;
I go beyond the darkness from here forever.

Rakhal Choudhury

Nancy

Silence was never louder.
My nights prolong without her.
I long for her voice,
and I crave for her touch.
I can't live without her.

Tranquil brown eyes and cinnamon skin,
this woman, my queen, this yearning within,
a subtle bewitching, the sweetest of sins.
My actions restrained, my love shall suffice,
hands idle and fretful, my only device.

Though long, I shall strive
for she is my drive.
Whether wearied or down,
we will wear love's crown.

So patience, anxious heart;
time's painstaking and stark.
Her pledges trust and cherish;
without them you will perish.

Michael E. Ortiz

Vanity

To Dean and Reed

Self-induced deception, self-inflicted pain.
I am the master of demeaning. I have played this game.
Sharp edged self-doubt cutting through my life.
Fears unclothed, exposed and pulsing in the light.
As if fright had an existence and could breathe, could stand.
Bungling physician tools in my own maniacal hands,
Carving a loathing self-portrait on my blameless soul.
Thus aiding in my own demise, destruction is my goal.
Ripping, tearing, rending; I must remove the good.
Speak nothing benign of me.
I feel a malignant tickle galling in my throat.
I tell myself, "Your value has not exceeded your uselessness.
Your life has been the cruelest of jokes."
So I comfort myself with criticism, as in the mirror I peer.
Each innocent flaw exaggerated, magnified, inflated
And I see acceptance and sigh. Can anything be so ugly?
Then suddenly hope emerges and excitement gives me cheer.
I blow a kiss and wink at myself. Maybe ugly is in this year.

Diana Ramey Failing

Mothers

They laughed at the clothes we chose to wear
They laughed at the way we did our hair
They asked us where we planned on going
And who we'd be there with they insisted on knowing

They cared about the grades we made
They cared about our pains and ache

They were always pushing us to be our best
And negative attitudes are what they detest

And as we started to mature
We realized what they had to endure

All of our grumbling they had to take
And our bad habits they had to break

Today we stand better girls
Because of our mothers transversals

I want to thank you mom for all that you've done
Just look at what I've become

Rachel Brooke Schallom

Loved by You

I know you can't see me, but here I am.
I know you can't hear me, but here I am.
Even though you can't see me or hear me,
I'm still going to try.
So here goes . . .
What do I have to do to get you to notice me—
Lie down in the hallways until you come to me?
Because you know I will!
What do I have to do to get you to hear me—
Stand on top of my desk and yell to you until you answer me?
Because you know I will!
I don't know how I'm suppose to deal with this because . . .
One day I meant the world to you and the next I did not!
So, please answer this.
What did I do so wrong, or was I just confused
With all the things we've said and done?
And listen to me just once more, if you don't mind.
I never wanted to hurt you in anyway.
I just wanted to love you and be loved by you.

Tina M. Laverack

If She Only Knew

She felt the rain shift
Through her fingertips
Breathing through the moon she saw
Dreaming, believing, without a taste of fear
Holding to her body
Things that were never seen
She held inside so deep, in her starry eyes
A living dream, a hidden sleep
She left to find a minds eye
Her inspiration led her there
She faced her walls of righteousness
The end would not be fair
How her smile misled me
To make me wonder away
If she only know she had me
She wouldn't have gone away
Words she said, grabbed to my openness
She spoke of trust and honesty
And left no room for closeness

Alana Dawn Short

Taking Flight

Your wings first clipped
When you were a tiny chick
This taught you all you know
Birds like you mustn't fly too far
The world is too big for you
So clip your wings, stay in your cage
And stop your chirping too

The smallest song inside your heart
Knows that birds are meant to fly
If only cages had no bars
And wings were never clipped
Time and again the scissors are brought out
And you allow your feathers to be stripped

Let your voice sound its song
And step onto your golden perch
The cage is still yours, no need to cry
A bird knows it's true destiny
Is to take to the wind and fly

Monika Sprott

Do You Know?

I get weak in the knees
At the touch of your hand.
Then I don't know anything,
Until you help me understand.
Do you know . . .
That because of your love,
I need nothing more,
That there's no one else,
I could ever adore?
Do you know . . .
That I get lost in time
With one glance in your eyes,
That I would be bound and broken
If you hadn't protected me from the dark skies?
Do you know . . .
That you're the one and you always will be,
That no matter what happens,
Together will be you and me?
Do you know?

Amanda Beth Churchill

Gone

Each night I lay my head down and think of you
I lie there imagining how it would be to
feel your body against mine once more
Your arms were my shelter
your breath my air
Now I feel like I am choking
because without you I am in fear
one with no shelter
I have no air to breathe since you have left
so I lie here without you all alone
As I raise my head and disturb my sleep
I feel I am dead
because without you, I am nothing
just another lonely soul quivering
with no love left in my heart
no emotions left to feel
no warmth around my flesh
and no you beside me
I am dead.

Rebecca Sue Winiecki

Unforgiving Conscience

I was . . . in a hurry
aren't we all?
Driving my work van
as fast as I could,
then I saw her, blind, young—panic,
she tapped, tapped, tapped . . . lost
on busy city sidewalk
tears streaming from dark glasses.
My heart pounded and a voice strong as
God from my head said, stop, help, love,
but . . .
I was . . . in a hurry
I am sure someone helped her . . . surely
she made it home.
Surely . . .
Thirteen years gone by. I am sure she is, out there,
safe, warm, happy, loved,
and I on sleepless nights can only hear
tap, tap, tap . . .

George Claud Eggleston

That's Why I Love America

I love America! Let freedom reign!
Where children laughing, singing, play all day long,
And politicians freely can campaign.

Democracy where treatment is humane.
We're taught from birth to know what's right or wrong,
And immigrants are welcome to remain.

See flow'ring rhododendron's pinkish grain.
And trees, each shade of green, so tall and strong;
From sunlit days and intermittent rain.

While imitating other birds' refrains,
The mockingbird keeps singing all day long.
The squirrels and rabbits run and entertain.

I love America! Let freedom reign!
This land that's free 'cause soldiers, brave and strong,
Have goals and moral values,
So they train to fight for liberty for us year long.
That's why I love America!

Catherine A. Dower-Gold

Expiration in Slow Motion

Life's passing brings humor in darkness
No light bright neon glow sharpness
Cancer sticks and drinks with little umbrellas
Marlboro, Winston, Camel, Newport,
the chosen brand of storytellers
Along empty streets I ran and watched the broken lines
And tripped and fell and hurt my leg and made cries and whines
I should have been walking or just slowed down
or sat and watched the cars pass
Did anyone see it a spectacular sight
of yellow and black and crimson too fast
Expiration date today
I want to be somebody when I grow up
I don't want to grow up
I want to stay a kid
I don't want to grow up
It's over, it's gone, it's done, it's finished
I wasn't done, I still haven't finished
It's too late, time is up, I didn't even get to say goodbye

Jay Matthew Arnold

Addiction

Crave, crave, crave, concave
Bending my mind and I don't know why
Help me with this feeling
From which my soul cannot shy
This pain, just take it away, take it away
Its no joke

Why, why, why, wisdom
Guiding me in the wrong direction
Give me a reason to live
All I ask is for compassion and affection
Don't abandon me; help me, love me
I need love

Life, life, life, whatever
No one can help me but me, you say
I don't know if I'm strong enough
Will you help me to find the right way
I want to live, want to live, want to live
I choose life

Kelly Watson

Gratitude Eternal to Chester

Barely audible, "Time out," murmured the exhausted mind, body.
A solo ticket for a lone journey destined to be traveled was issued.
Entombed an inescapable web of abject despondency
Spun the entrance, to the endless dark tunnel, no exit offering.
Merely the shell of the man, minus his spirit,
Traversed mechanically, the yawning abyss, submissively.
Fragile threads of reality, floating in mists of obscurity
Tenaciously clung to umbilical love-chords of those dearest.
Considered abandoned, inaudible anguished cries were detected,
Understood by his companion of tender months.
The birth of empathy, hitherto unknown evolved.
Woven, intangible threads of communication acknowledged shared
Were nurtured by an inseparable daily vigil spanning seasons.
Displaying explicit trust, the vigilant brown eyes of the collie
Consistently, ever patiently, always encouragingly
Willed his master, the underdog, to follow
The route, leading to gradual recuperation.
Time out, time to ponder, time to evaluate. Conclusion.
Bonded love. Testimony to the healing power of a beloved friend.

Peter Wells

Mañana

Sometimes she would tell him how she felt
She gave herself props on her bravery
She waited for the perfect day
Every time she woke up she wasn't up to it
Up to the possibility of rejection
She decided next Tuesday was the day
Too bad the world ended on Monday

Sometimes he would travel the seven seas
He gave himself props on his outlandish decision
Every paycheck went to the watch he wanted
Or the pants that looked great on him
So the next paycheck was always it
Too bad the world ended in the middle of the week

Sometimes she would do what was expected of her
She gave herself props on her responsibility
Every expectation could be fulfilled later
Everyone could wait, she was going to get to it
Eventually everything can wait, except the end of the world

Claire Lebeau Fromme

untitled journey

indiscernible feelings of worth and worthlessness
i walk amongst the trees the shadows striking my face and body
bruises of nonexistent love make my soul bleed
past, present, and future
expanding shadows
the wind moans, laughs, and screams inside my head . . . stop

cause and purpose reflect in a small pool of glistening water
to create images of guidance to stimulate growth
i bathe my feet for the long journey
the shadows of my past haunt me still
i gather twigs of endurance to free myself from the darkness
the dew of twilight settles on the foundation under my feet
i keep walking, searching
rain falls, cleansing my feet

thunder rolls to unleash the last shadows
for the arrival of the moon
lighting burns, guiding me through the thickening darkness
beckoning the sun to illuminate my transformation

Geoffrey Sean Mazon

We Met Julia and Marie

We patched together a conversation
in Romanian and English.

The girls held hands and giggled loud
totally oblivious.

The evening sky sun burned out slow
that corner of the park.

The music playing without words
had danced up to the stars.

We parted ways with whom we'd met
earlier in that day,

A sort of sadness and gladness too, that
things worked out that way

In an unquiet time where difference
tears the world apart.

Our differences made simplified, the
pleasures of the heart.

Lindsey K. Langmaid

My Thirst-Quencher

Lord, I thirst for You
There's nothing else I want more than You
I don't want anyone to come in
To take Your place
Because there's none like You
You're the only one
Who can provide for me like You do
My needs even my wants
You satisfy my soul so much more
Than I could ever dream
You're the only one
Who can heal me like You do
So that I'm completely whole
As though there was nothing ever wrong to start
I've gotta give You the best I've got
That's what You did and You keep on giving
Lord, I thirst for You
Keep filling me up
Keep quenching my thirst

Lisa M. Watkins

Infection

Nothingness all around
All my life, gagged and bound
Nothingness all around
Something lost now is found

Spread through me with a narcissistic vanity
Push me to the edge of my withering sanity
Its voracious hunger spreads within my soul
Clawing its way through a widening hole
A darkness engulfs all thoughts in my head
My wisdom and ignorance, ungodly wed
Hollowing out all of my hopes and dreams
This lecherous creature rips deep at my seams
Bear witness, for my blood has been spilled
Inside, a part of me has been killed
Repent, for I have none left of my kin
Run now, because my death is my sin

But if everything was good,
Then how would you know it?

Allen Eric Harrold

But Then, Grandpa, I . . .

I cry
Because you are no longer with me.
I sob
Because you never will hear me say I love you.
I weep
Because I could not give you one last hug.
But then, Grandpa,
I smile
Because I know somewhere you are smiling back.
I laugh
Because somewhere you are happy.
I am happy
Because I knew and loved you.
I am strong
Because somewhere you are helping me.
I hope
Because I know we will be together again.
I have faith
Because I know you are still with me and your love transcends death.

Megan K. Church

My Home

A place of peace where love might grow.
A place of terror I've come to know.

Shaken with fear, overcome by stress,
Each day I become more, less and less.

Sworn to secrecy by my own shame,
Locked up, sealed shut in life's own game.

As if it's fire, it ignites so quickly;
Constant torment will echo sickly.

Deceptions and lies will break family ties.
No one will notice, yet love slowly dies.

Tortured and teased while still in fear
Of what is yet to come, very near.

Nowhere to run, nowhere to hide,
Searching for somewhere I can confide.

A place of peace where love might grow,
My place of terror I've come to know.

Jihath Ghaznavi

Why Must We Live?

Why must we fall into this hole of darkness
And be overwhelmed with such madness?

In all of life's expectations
The worst are those in relations.

Why must we roam around like dead souls,
Which are damaged with penetrating holes?

We expect too much
And accept realization of such.

Why must we listen to the unknown
When truth is always there but never shown?

We think we know it all
Until we trip and never stop to fall.

Why must we live forever
If we can't even live together?

People are so tolerant,
But it's due to being ignorant.

Mayra Griselda Gonzalez

Depression

Depression is standing in a room full
of people and realizing, ultimately,
you are all alone.
Words of nothing, hopeless dreams, heartache;
Gasping for air in an ocean of sadness.
Writing your feelings on paper
with many intentions and not
meeting one of them.
Wishing, wanting, waiting;
Looking for something that was never there,
desiring more than you can ever
hope to receive.
Watching the people you love slip
through your fingers forever and
there is nothing you can do to stop them.
Reaching into an empty gap for
something to hold onto,
something to keep you standing.
Love.

Kandis Lorena Kirk

No Clue

I have no clue as to what I can do.
The sky is cloudy and no longer blue.
I look at the clouds as raindrops slip through.
I have no clue as to what I can do.
Maybe look at a book
Or go to the mall and take a look.
I can stay out of the rain
And play a computer game,
Or I can stay at home
And talk on the phone.
I can do my chores and clean my room;
That would surprise my mom, I assume.
A knock on the door sends me to peek outside,
Only to see the sunshine smiling at me.
I now have a clue as to what I will do.
I will swim with my friend in the pool,
Ride bikes and play football as the sun sets
And the weather becomes cool.
I now have a clue as what I will do.

Matt Allen Alford

Autumn Leaf

Look at me! Look at me!
Down here, under your feet!
Can you see the mud on my veins?
Can you see that my veins are broken?
In so many places they broke.
But it's a dance! Dance of continuity.
Look at me! Look at me!
Did I say my veins are not complete?
And the bird is tearing the rest off!
Clawing through for the unsuspecting worm!
But it's a dance! A dance for a leafy spring!
Yes, it's a dance! A dance for sounds of life!
Look at me! Look at me!
Did you see the ladybird walk?
Through the hole in my heart, it walked!
But wait! Tomorrow, when ice is gone.
I will be giving cover to the nests.
Keep the sun from burning those claws.
We need these claws to continue the dance!

Fred O. Aboge

The Woman in the Night

Heavy eyelids slowly meeting,
constant heartbeat slowly beating.
Arms, legs, and body light,
getting ready to rest the night.
Falling asleep in a trance-like stage,
mind wandering in a foggy haze.
Straps and shackles tie me down,
when a woman approaches wearing the night as a gown.
When I look around, nothing holds me,
yet I'm as immobile as a great oak tree.
Is it normal to fear a face with the beauty I see before me?
How can such elegance, grace, and beauty
make me cower this easily?
Something is wrong, this isn't right.
I will not give in to the torture tonight.
When I look around another time,
would make any man start to whine.
Before the edge of the darkness is gone,
I have often wondered what had begun.

Andrew James McCaslin

Love Is What Love Does

Love is what love does
Love is saying, I love you
Love is saying, I'm sorry
Love is saying, I'll watch the kids for a while; you need a break
Love is having patience
Love is being thoughtful
Love is full of surprises
Love is saying, let me help you with that
Love is kind
Love is precious
Love is never forgetting important dates
Love is intense
Love is wild
Love is untamed
Love is unprecedented
Love is giving love
Love is world-wide
Love is understanding
Love is what love does and so much more

Sonya Lorraine Martin

Where Are the Horses?

The horses are gone
They took them away
Why didn't they just give them some hay?

The cost would be less
There is another motive I guess
Bicycle riders are more important
I don't think so
Does land get more money for them
Are houses more important to them?
The horses have been there a very long time
We signed a petition
But I guess they don't care
Because the horses are not there
Water is short, but it always has been
They survived even when the water was thin

The horses are gone
They took them away
Why didn't they just give them some hay?

Carrie Sneed Vowell

It Could Never Happen to Me

It could never happen to me . . .
Consequence pushed to the back of my mind;
Didn't stop to think about it,
I was just along for the ride.
It could never happen to me . . .
Now my actions take effect, I begin to detect
Something different, something wrong;
Something inside of me that doesn't belong.
It could never happen to me . . .
My previous thoughts were sheer ignorance;
All my wild nights seem to lose all bliss.
I am now stuck, at fourteen;
Looking down an unfamiliar road,
Passing up my hopes and dreams.
It could never happen to me . . .
Until I hold you for the first time;
Mixed emotions rising, I find myself smiling.
I start to think, as I breathe you in,
I'm glad it happened to me.

Tabatha Nasha Culver

Caught by Rain

I feel a droplet sliding on my cheek,
so fresh and gentle, like love.
A soft touch, making everything alive again, shivering,
and you can't resist the emotion of love.
I was caught in love by rain, and I'm not trying to hide it.

He's guilty of the rain discovering my deepest secret;
he's guilty I'm walking bare-foot in puddles,
seeking a way to an unknown world, full of joy and passion;
he's guilty for these new feelings overflowing my body.
And yet . . . I'm not angry,
because I discovered love.

My favorite movie,
a beautiful love story everyone wants to experience.
But as you look at them, you think
that that one couple, sitting in front of you,
is in that story just now.
And I hope I'm in it soon too,
because now love is all that counts.

Lara Vidmar

Last Night

He knocked on the door, wanting to get inside
Should I shudder to the thought,
So I let him in
He talked so fast, so rapidly
He winked his eye, he held my hand
Pleasure has hit, pleasure shall stand
As I relax with this man.
He came to me, and held me close
I melted for love; is what I needed the most
He took me past the hallway,
And through a corridor
Where water lay so motionless,
I fell against the floor; hoping.
I got up in a hurry, tried to fix my clothes
He looked at me and smiled,
As he kissed my nose
How odd I thought the notion,
The idea seemed so strange,
Then without a warning, I yelled and screamed his name.

Sabrina Naomi Caldwell

Love

Love is like the song of the birds,
When it is around you are happy
And when it is gone, you want it to come back.
Love is like money,
You work really hard to get it
And even harder to keep it.
Love is like a child's favorite toy,
They never want to leave it be
And if it is lost they are devastated.
Love is like a life raft,
It keeps us afloat if we need someone
And if it wasn't there, we wouldn't be able to survive.
Love is like the ocean,
Everyone wants to be near it,
Even if they are scared of everything that goes with it.
Love is everything to some people.
They search to the ends of the Earth for it
And will do almost anything if they find it.
They are content with that one and only word in their lives, love.

Eryn Jacquelyn Wilson

My Efforts Fail

Appearing in a moment of time
The gift to exist is given to me
All things new, fresh, and alive
Unaware of the darkness I learn what I see

Protected by love I develop and age
Receiving what my teachers believe
All the while it waits for me
A different world than what I perceive

Touching life results in pain
Unprotected I start to fear
Maturity means innocence lost
The darkness starts to appear

Seeking to escape that which I've become
My efforts fail, my efforts fail
I try to run but where I go I find
My efforts fail, my efforts fail

I fall, I cry, I reach and touch the sky

Timothy Gene Ware

Why

Why does everything have to suck so bad
Nothing but bull, all the things I had
No one helps, no one cares
All these fears I could probably break down in tears
I have no money, no luxury
Constantly losing faith
Where the hell is God's good grace
I have no power, respect, or future
The best thing I own is a crappy computer
I look around and what do I see
Another punk trying to start a fight with me
And why, to make my life worse
I swear my life is nothing but a curse
Can't ever do anything with ease, constantly
Have to please, it's like a disease
Doomed to a life of eternal misery
It has to be a conspiracy, everyone's
Against me, seriously, truthfully, hopefully
Soon it will be the end of me

Alex Chatham

I Love You for You

I love you not for the color of your skin
The religion you choose to follow
The country from which you come
The political party you believe in
The nature of your sexual preference
Or your outer appearance
I instead love you for you
For what you represent to me
I love you for you
The color of your skin
Whatever color it may be
The religion you choose to follow
And the name of your God to whom you pray
The country from which you come
Your political beliefs
Your sexual preference
And your outer appearance
Yes, I love you for all of these things
Because it is these things that make you, you

Mari Beth Mashburn

Waking

Pale, void, unrecognizable.
Empty of life, but have been for long.
Just recently lain, entered new world.
Long ago deceased,
Worthless, crumbled, broken.
Simplistic ceremony renders end of it all.
Tear-streaked faces look upon once so struck face.
Tears are absent from all. Illusory.
Pain begone instantly . . . or seconds past,
Whatever.
None care. None should. Why?
Expected it should be,
Every end as this.
Nothing to shed liquid sorrow over.
For when one knows only sorrow then sorrow
is nothing.
Joy long lost. Reaching to recover results pain.
Ends in current situation.
Warm, soft velvet touches life-withdrawn fingertip.

Timothy Scott Campbell

The Unknown

The unknown stares me in the face.
It calls forth to me.
Some may fear it.
It's a promise of something new and different,
Or maybe the same and boring.
That doesn't bother me,
I love the unknown.
The very fact that I don't know,
That I don't know what tomorrow holds,
What it may bring,
Enthralls me.
It stimulates my senses.
It means that I will always be surprised,
That I will always be challenged.
It makes me happy to be alive,
Happy to be on this Earth,
Happy to be in a place where I do not know,
Where every tomorrow is
The unknown.

Alan Jeffrey Eversole

Waiting for You

Across the lands of my mind and deep within the oceans of time,
I wait for you and each day flew beyond the horizon
Covered in morning's dew and evening's blue.
The sun drew its path, and the moon just laughed,
For how could one sole grain, I, the Earth's rain,
Await another, in this shore of grain brothers?
Silver dragon fate, she awaited till late,
But even she could not last in this desert of days past.
The wind lifted the voices of those trees whose choices
Were to sing the song of light
And make my patience bright in this incessant night.
The song did not die and my heart did not lie
As I saw your face, empty of a trace
Of lost love or exposure
To the silver dragon's exiting closure,
Bringing you closer to me.
So join me, for if you do,
The song of love will be sung
To you.

Marina Cristin O'Neill

Government Assistance

Take me to your leader.
He's standing right behind you,
watching you,
observing every move you make,
every breath of air you take.
Don't try to destroy me.
You can't overrule me.
I am invincible,
and you are merely my slave.
So, get to work and I'll watch you once again,
with the eye of destruction
and the desire of non-intentional fun.

I have fooled you once again.
Go to your wheel in your cage that you call home,
that you call freedom.
I've taken that away from you.
Of course, you can't see that.
You're blinded too tight.
You're damaged to my delight.

Michelle Joy Gingrich

Let Her Bloom

What are friends?
You are her friend. I am her friend.
What's the difference?
When she's happy, she runs to you.
When you hurt her, she crawls to me.
Now, what's the difference?
True friends are a shoulder to cry on.
She is a flower.
Without your water, she could slowly wither and die.
I can only help to fertilize your garden.
If you fail to provide her water,
your beautiful rose may die.
Just as a rose needs water, friends need love.
A love that is not cared for will wither and die,
and just like a garden, you don't just plant one kind of love.
If you kill your crop, you will leave me to replant the rose.
She needs you. Help her to grow, I'll be there,
but when she starts to wither,
show your love, give her water, and let her bloom.

Shawna Marie Seurer

Blood and Ashes

I now lie in a bed of crimson red
As black souls give me back to the original mother
Black like the night I found my rose
In another's hand
Two sounds rang out louder that complete silence
Two hearts were breaking

Blood and ashes, ashes and blood
The blood of a secret and true
Mixed that cold September night
Soon only ashes will be left of me
To cover graves and help roses grow
To be tossed in the wind and never seen again

That night the rose's heart was split in two
Her thorns of deceit dropped one by one
Leaving her bare
Her soul was wrecked
That night she wilted alone
That night three beds of crimson red were made for three dead

Denali Rose Halsey

It All Started in the Forum

Dedicated to Rich

Richie Rich, his heart is sewn with the finest golden stitch,
A friend you can count on easily in a pinch.
"Richie Rich, what makes you this way?"
"Not the money," he'll say.
"It is the thoughts that are deep, that come into play."
Women often wonder the spell they fall under,
Wondering, how could one make their soul's roll with thunder.
A spirit so strong only God wouldn't fear it.
Men, they could only learn by being near it.
A priceless friendship to be treasured.
A friendship that can always be weathered.
Handsome Richie Rich, gorgeous deep eyes,
Which hold the aura of the wise.
A smile, to which can melt the sadness of the unkind.
Those who take him for granted are weak.
He is a friend we all should seek.
Richy Rich, I'm a better person for knowing.
May my friendship with you, keep forever growing!

Jean J. Conrad

Life's Stream

Life isn't an ocean of problems needing to be solved.
It's a stream of adventures waiting to be lived.
Its cool waters quench the thirst for wholeness.
Its current carries us to new heights, new realms.
True, it can be hazardous; whirlpools and rapids lurk in its depths,
waiting to drown us in its grasp,
the fear of which may force us to cower and hide.
But without the risk of treading its terror,
we forfeit its hidden treasures: challenge, wealth, and love.
For with God's helping hand,
all our life's troubles will become as calm as a mountain lake,
and we will see as clear as it is blue:
crisp and clean.
Therefore, my friend,
we must continue to search and wonder,
and let the sun set on our sea of problems,
for it is God who will deal with them,
while we find our dreams come true
in life's never ending stream.

Craig G. Korth

On the Soap Box

I may not love him,
But I know God.
He is the angel without wings
And the atheist without a master.
I speak, not because He told me to do so.
I speak because He wanted me to do so.
Prayers. I do not pray.
Gratitude. I give thanks.
If my quest ends in Heaven I will be loved.
If my quest ends in Hell, I will be loved.
For I know the evil
And the good.
The only neutral entity is love,
For one can love God.
He brings both joy and sadness,
Destruction and prosperity,
Which is balance.
Hate me. I know someone who loves me.
God? Yes, He loves everyone, doesn't He?

Bryson Ashton Bost

High Dreams

To fly into space has been always my dream;
into the onyx blackness of the heavens that never ends.
To share in this tranquil experience that few have traveled,
through the paper-thin layer of clouds to the bounds of my home,
and then beyond.
Now I am out there:
behind, a voluptuous blue outpost in the vastness;
front, a spot of blood in the night sky, I travel.
Now I stand in the future
on the rusted surface of our new home, Mars.
Yes I stand here,
on this place that will be mutated in the next century
to a thriving red outpost.
For thousands of years both blue and red places will survive
in harmony until it is time to find a new outpost,
for we have now ruined our red home like we did our blue.
So I stand in our future,
and wonder—
this dream that I had, is it really a nightmare?

Chase Jared Kramer

Him

He pushes me to the edge
Until I have no room to walk away
Or I'll fall farther than I ever have before
Then he always leaves me crying
Not even caring
All I see is black
Flashing into nothing
Coming back to haunt me
Sometimes I wish I could just drop
And disappear at the bottom
But he would follow me
Use me again
Pushing me farther every time
He has power over me, even in my sleep
He never stops
All hope is lost
My strength is gone
There's no point in trying anymore
Nothing's left because of him

Megan Christine Thorson

Bedroom Window

I look outside my bedroom window, the eye of the world.
I could watch the world go by from my window,
Maybe even for eternity.
I see the people walking by,
Noisy teenagers and neighborhood kids.
Am I the only one who watches?
Is there anyone else observing the things I take in?
You could freeze time from my window,
Paint a picture or take a portrait of the world behind,
The stars and moon shining above.
The winter snow, covering the rooftop like a blanket.
The fall trees and spring flowers,
The summer's nature.
You could almost think of my bedroom window as a portal
To the world that lies within or even ahead.
To anyone else it may just be a bedroom window,
But somehow to me, it's much, much more, something special even.
I may seem crazy, but I don't even think I can explain it.
I mean after all, it is just a bedroom window.

Nikki Christina Podnar

Angels—September 11, 2001

We felt the angels rising, like the smoke to up above.
We felt the angels rising through our sorrow and our love.
The angels go on rising, though we wish it were not so.
We want them here, we need them here, but still they have to go.
The first will wait and greet the rest,
with arms outstretched in peace.
Their heavy burdens slow them not;
their work, it will not cease.
For those of them that linger near,
we know they cannot stay.
With candles lit each night,
with love, we guide them on their way.
They'll guard us during our daily toils
and help us through each day.
They'll keep us safe, watch over us, and hold all harm at bay.
Forever in our memory, through all our pain and tears,
we will prevail, we will go on, despite our many fears.
And so, dear guardian angels, please listen to what we say;
forever in our hearts, please hear us as we pray.

Donna Lee Hardesty

sometimes

sometimes when the world falls silent
and the ocean floor runs dry
all that is left is my writing
that you never got, 'cause i never tried
sift through my empty thoughts
i arrive at you
alone i sit here left to rot
still i hang on
to the one memory of you
sometimes when i can't think straight
i tell a little lie, 'cause i tried to speak
but it couldn't come out right
sometimes i can picture you and me
and it makes me want to try
sometimes i picture myself alone
livin' my everyday life
sometimes i hear the ocean whisper
it tells me not to give up
that's when the memories start

Brian Christopher Spurgeon

He Is Coming

Yes, the Lord shall come in glory
With a shout of joy and victory.
This victory is ours by faith
In His atoning death.
For without the shedding of blood,
There is no forgiveness of sin.
Praise God for the blood of the Lamb
That washes whiter than snow.
The redeemed of the Lord have victory,
Yes, justified by grace through faith.
In Christ we have peace with God
Through our Lord Jesus Christ.
Yes, Jesus is coming, we know not when.
Only help us, Lord, to be ready that we
May see Him then, when in victory He descends.
So trusting and obeying each day,
Truly walking in the way
And looking for His return,
Lord, make us faithful thy will to learn.

Kimberly Denise Orr

Failed Expectations

A portrait of perfection painted with lies
With each brush of stroke, a color unwinds
With red they gave her passion that she truly needs
Crimson blue to remind her of the love she left behind
Pitch of black, which made her strong
Serenity of green that declared her bold
With all this and more
She was clearly a star
Forever beautiful and eternally scarred
When people saw her from afar
They saw this all
But with each forward step
They became appalled
Her colors were fading
Because it never really existed
Her spirit was fleeting
Because it wasn't hers
So as people screamed "This is not what I thought it was"
She silently cried, "I never said I was"

Raseefa Anwar

The Lonely One

The everlasting pain of this heart,
How long shall it go on?
The knots in the stomach
Grow tighter and tighter;
The knife goes in,
Twisting and turning,
Dripping the life out slowly,
Slowly killing the one that has tried
Over and over again to love.
But with each new day,
It goes deeper within the darkness.
The darkness gets stronger
With each new twist of the knife.
The eyes have saddened
From the pain the heart has endured.
It only wants what it deserves,
But the journey is painful and hard.
Will the pain ever end?
Where is the happiness this heart deserves?

Diane M. Cerasi

What Do You Say?

What do you say when love is astray
and your meaning in life has gone wrong?
"I will change," leaves you to question.
"I won't do it again," makes you a liar and,
"I'm sorry," is an old, worn out song.
You rationalize, try to compromise.
You make promises you know you won't keep.
Deep inside, you try hard to hide,
as the pain rolls down your cheeks.
So, you pass the blame, swear to quit playing the game,
yet you are blind to who's pulling the strings.
As you lay in a daze, you search through the maze,
only to find that days add to weeks.
What do you say? Time keeps ticking away.
It is all too easy to speak when all you've said
has become wasted breath and your words
are like slaps in the face.
You will find it's hard to say, as your life is choked away
by the ones whom your words have disgraced!

Danny Lee Hall

Time

If time could stop
what would this world be?
What is a fragment of our imagination,
the sky or the sea?
Love would come and hate would go;
if we knew we could stop this sorrowful flow.
Things are dying,
people are crying.
Murders are committed,
without even trying.
We could stop what we see,
rewind what we don't want to be.
See our future and live it too,
knowing what we're going to do.
Thinking again about those stupid mistakes,
making them better.
But no, time won't stop or rewind.
Live with what you have
and learn from what you did wrong.

Lauren Elizabeth Ebersbach

Here in Alaska

Here in Alaska on this warm summer day
With the sun in my eyes here where I lay
The grass fresh cut with a wonderful smell
Surrounded by trees growing so well
My lemonade fading into my mouth
It's fine right here no need to go south

Here in Alaska on this beautiful morning
Looking at eagles flying and soaring
Rising high over my yard
A gigantic hemlock growing so far
I still wonder why anyone would leave
A place so perfect and beautiful to me

Here in Alaska is a treasure so deep
Mother nature with miles never seen
Growing up here is an exciting journey
With so many things to do and see
You'd have to be crazy not to enjoy this
Because here in Alaska there is a story

Jessica Marie Lewis

The Light

Written at age eleven

I see it
I see it coming
I see it coming faster
I run
I run faster
I fall
I regret
I close my eyes
Seeing my whole life flashing before me
Then I realize
The Light
The Light that I was scared to death about
Was a friend
A friend who is coming to help me
From the woods, in the dark
With a flashlight
And a smile
I smile back

Kelly Anne Dellisanti

Dreaming

To anyone who has had a dream and the courage to make it happen

Have you ever had a dream you wished would come true?
Do you sit up at night, thinking what will make it come true?
Have you ever longed for something to fall right into place?
When you close your eyes, can you see it come alive?
Your dreams can be real, so don't give up.
No matter what people say, you can make it if you really believe.
God will stand by you and your dreams.
He'll help you turn them into magical things.
If you work hard, it will pay off.
If people don't like it, then that's their loss.
They will try to put you down or make you frown.
You must stand your ground and just believe.
Believe in you, believe in me.
Believe your dreams can be reality.
Believe you can make it and you can take it.
Believe you will win and remain positive in the world we're in.
Never stop dreaming.

Nicholas Bernard Mondi

The Distance . . .

To my bothers and sisters . . .

We would go the distance to be together . . .

A family so far apart,
But yet the love our family shares
Is far from what distance means.
Separated during life,
It's become a mission
To hold one another together.
We all hold a career of greatness,
Which we express, accomplishments to one another
Never to judge the good or bad;
We are proud of who we are.
Through good times and bad
We are there for each other.
We keep a piece of each other in our hearts.
No matter how far or near
Our love for one another
Is far from fallen apart
Because we are all strong, in our own ways. . . .

Melissa Lynn Manitowabi

Unconditional

As I lay in bed and stare at you,
I am left in awe by your beauty.
In the words of my friend Mona,
"a strong, physical creature."
I watch you sleep and marvel.
Your brow at peace,
your breathing—slow and quiet;
Delightful dreams fill your REM.
You move to turn and open your eyes.
Am I here? Yes, I am.
You don't believe in yesterdays
nor tomorrows, only today.
You offer love without strings,
unconditional.
I am now left vulnerable at the thought
of losing you and silently suffer.
As if sensing my sudden distress,
you wake and look at me . . .
and then bark and approach to lick my face.

Tanya R. Corona

to leave without saying goodbye

is like saying hello without saying hi
i know it doesn't mean the same thing
but that's the way my mind thinks

to leave without saying goodbye
is something i can't get over, no matter how hard i try

distance only makes my heart grow stronger
this feeling i can't hold in any longer
the feeling that i get whenever i am with you
the feeling that i get whenever i think about you

time is something not controlled by you or me
time is something that i can't see
time goes on, no matter the situation
time is something i need, to help with this separation

that one moment that we had
is a memory, i will always have
no matter what you say or do
i will always love you

Patrick Joseph Ryan

Who's to Blame

There you are and here I am,
Two different people in this promised land.
The freedom of speech,
The freedom to die,
What's happened to this world, I ask, and why?
Racism, drugs, gangs, and more,
That's not what God made this world for.
From the darkest skinned sister
To the lightest skinned brother
And think of all the expectant mothers
Whose children will carry on
What we've left behind
And you ask who's the cause of this?
Pointing fingers, yet so blind,
Ask yourself one question,
What part of this is mine?
You see, the one to blame would be ourselves
From the past to the present
And for all eternity and time.

Juli Anna Daulton

Missing You

A tear in my eye is the ocean,
And by this we are separated.
So close we were,
So far we drifted.
The best times of my life,
Now just memories.
But, as friends,
Together we fought our enemies.
Our friendship is limitless,
And there are parts of you I really miss.
Your joy and pain,
In my longing heart is where they'll remain.
Fear of living but never seeing you,
I'd rather be gone,
I'd rather be through.
Twelve wonderful years you bestowed upon me.
Instead of returning the favor, I left thee.
Indulged in what you had to offer,
This prepared me for the future.

Maxine Gaenor Christians

Wanting

I long to see your face
To taste, if nothing else
The pleasure of your insult
I yearn to touch your skin
To walk with you and once again
Speak of nothing and everything between us
I dare to flow
You know
The words I need to show
To you to me
To set again my soul so free
Walk with me into yesterday or tomorrow
But never today because it's cold here
And I much prefer the beach
I am cheap, you say—or want to say
But not so much as the movie
Or the play
So you stay
Away

Jeremy Brian Manning

Apologize

Walk with me my little child and we shall
explore the depths of the wild. Take my hand
and explore the land. Dunnea worry, I am your
friend, we shall be together to the end. You
trust me, I trust you. Together we can face
the through and through. The beginning and
the end, you shall be my friend. Betrayal and
hope, you think you could possibly be the
Pope. You try to run my life, you betrayed me
because of a small strife. The quarrel grows
as do we, even though we think we are free.
The guns, the war, the killing is our chore.
We finally meet despite our years, and we
both express we have no fears. You shot me
and I shot thee, yet I still bury you under
your favorite tree. I see that despite our
untimely end, you truly were my best friend.
Should you still be alive, I know I would
strive, I would strive to apologize.

Matt Henry Arrell

Cry

To everybody in need of it
You're flying high—
Then your dreams die
Don't try to hide behind the mask you always wear
Because life just isn't fair
And, besides, it's better to just cry
Until the hurt gets washed away
And you look out the window
And see a new day has arrived
And your dam of tears has run dry
Put your head up and throw away your fears
For I am here to take your hand
And take you to God's promised land
You and me, we're friends
Until the river ends
And the strong ones cry
Without an ounce of shame until they've run dry
So cry
Until you can smile again and your eyes are dry

Diana Carmen Carcamo

Confusion

I took a breath
Only silence remained
Along with the prevalent beats of my heart
I was alone
A body intrepid
A body so unusually calm, tranquil
With eyes so placid
Smothering all awareness of previous fear
Location unknown
Present and future destinations undesirable
I have no emotions, unemotional
I feel cold, damp, and completely surrounded by the indescribable
I can see nothing,
Only vast darkness, black
As if my eyes were tightly shut
My mind, frivolous
No sense of curiosity
I am confused
Severely confused

Chrissy Lee Petty

Taken

I stare at a crescent moon with my hand on my pulse;
I think of what I've gained, I think of what I've lost.
I feel my heart still beating, cold chambers of emptiness,
And I ask myself how much longer I can house this pain.
When I dream a dream of you, of ambrose perfection,
When I feel the hurt inside, the lingering rejection,
When I know I've lost my pride, loving you more than ever,
I wake in a cold sweat, and the dawn tells that I'm alone.
Know a hollow in my heart and the everlasting emptiness.
Were you an angel or a demon? A siren all the same.
And my trying infidelities were overlooked.
Yet it was taken; you were taken; all was taken.
I guess God needed you more than you needed me.
I place a rose near the cross on the side of the road
Where a fallen angel lies, shedding her wings.
Here lies my harsh reality. Here lies my time of need.
Here lies a memory I can't grasp, I can't touch.
Here lies my hopes and dreams.
I'll miss you.

Will Herring

family

life has many twists and turns
up and downs
ins and outs, but no matter what
your family is always there
even when
mom and dad get in a fight
or grandma yells at dad
even when uncle tim hates mom
your family always loves you
remember that when your stuck in the middle
and when you don't know where to turn
remember they all love you and won't care
who you turn to
all they care about is you
and your happiness
so never feel sad and lonely, there's always someone who loves you
never feel neglected or stuck in the middle
remember they just want the best for you
because your their family

Meghan Alison Souza Glidden

The Forty Side of Thirty

Here I lie in the dark,
On my bed, in my room, in my apartment, alone
On the forty side of thirty.
Looking back, I wonder where the years went;
The time, the money—spent.
How could they have all slipped away
To the forty side of thirty?
Being asked by mother, aunts, and friends,
Have you met "him" yet?
Or being introduced to men
Who seem to want no part of me,
Or finding I want no part of them,
Seems to be the fate to which I am doomed
On the forty side of thirty.
So here I lie in the dark,
On my bed, in my room, in my apartment,
Alone and crying to myself.
This isn't where I wanted to be
By the forty side of thirty!

Nancy I. Worster

Untitled

Could I have this dance?
You're like a sparkle that caught my eye.
So I causally walk across the dance floor.
Since I saw the chance, I gazed a little more.
As the music played we seemed dazed!
We were both at a loss for words.
Deep inside, my heart was on the curve.
Each time that you spoke my body swerved.
I really thought this was a dream come true.
I never thought that I'd find you.
In reality I seem to be laughing.
My reactions was, this can't be happening.
So I slowly ask, "Hi, what's your name?"
Within a few seconds you do the same.
Now we're looking at each other strangely.
It seems to be a scene of a movie.
Now I have you standing next to me.
So, would you like something to drink
Or examine different colors of ink?

Kevin Lee Ingram

Wisps of God

Wisps of God
Weave their winding way
Through the darkness of my soul,
Offering glimpses of light
When I feel there is no hope.
Here a glimmering, there a gleaming . . .
A path illuminated by the breath of the one
Who first spoke the Word into being.
Wisps of God.
Breath of Heaven.
As subtle as lightning
Captured from the corner of my eye. . . .
Now I see it, now I don't.
But always it is there . . .
Waiting for me
To turn my face
Fully toward the light,
Drawn by
Wisps of God.

Sonna Marie Berghaier

A Bus Driver's Quandary

"Now go on Mrs. Parks, you ought to know
better than that, to sit in the front when
your place is in back.
You had better get movin' now, I've got a schedule to keep.
If you sit there any longer, you'll be in
trouble deep."
"Like I told you already, and just as I
said befo', I ain't movin from this here spot
no mo'."
"The view is no better from the front, can't you see?
So let's move along now Mrs. Parks, where you're meant to be.
We're all a little tired and it is getting awful hot,
are you going to move to the back or not?"
"Like I told you already, and just as I
said befo', I ain't movin from this here spot
no mo'."
"Of all the stubborn woman on this side of
the Mississippi, you got to be the most
stubborn of 'em all now missy."

Kitchener Lopez Harding

Lost in Thought

I wander in and wander out
It seems like I'm lost when I pout
I am not lost because I've lost my way
I am lost because it's part of my day
I need to be lost so I can think
Thoughts that only my heart could drink

I walk in a cloud and in a daze
All the thoughts in my head could set the world ablaze
I think of many things, important or not
Some thoughts stay cool, while others get hot
All of these thoughts keep me alive
It is for their very existence I strive

Now more than ever I am lost in thought
Lost in thought of what fate has brought
I will be lost for a little while more
While the boat gets rowed ashore
I will be found when the end is near
And I will have nothing more to fear

David Patanella

Speaking the Language of My Heart

For my husband

I love you more than all the pretty flowers and trees,
The warm morning's sun, or the air which I breathe.
More than any wealth the world could provide,
The comfort of home, or my food to survive.
More than my life, which is nothing without you,
More than all memories, or good times I've been through.
I love you more than the ability to see,
To be able to hear, to touch, or be free,
More than all luxuries or the gifts I've received,
More than all rivers big oceans and seas.
I love you more than could ever be known,
More than bright lights to ever be shown.
More than the right to do things my own way,
More than the sun which brightens my day.
More than the rain I love to hear fall,
More than the mountains standing lovely and tall.
I love you more than anyone else,
All of life's pleasures, or concerns of myself.

Audrey R. Jolly

September 11

The two tallest buildings stood so high
Whoever thought so many would die
September 11 was the tragic day
When terrorism had its evil way
They hit us hard when we were weak
Now bin Laden we viciously seek
Many suffer, weep, and cry
Why did their loved ones have to die
Let's hunt them down and make them pay
For what they did on this horrible day
They can't take or bring anyone back
I wish Bush would just say, "attack"
Months have gone by, so many still cry
America is now up and alert
But why did it take this, for so many to get hurt
Why is this going unpunished for so long
When God Himself knows they were wrong
They should die and suffer as we
But I can't do much, I'm only me

Serena Christine Russo

The Dark Days

In the darkened darker days,
The rain falls many ways.
The sun lets out no light
Behind the clouds, which once were bright.
Oh, those are the dark days.
No birds are flying, just many dying.
The children lie in their beds
As the parents try to clear their heads.
Those are the dark days.
No flowers ever bloom; there's only gloom.
The neighbors walk through their homes,
Walking with a weep, weep,
As they silently creep, creep.
Too much for them, too much to see,
Just too much to be, oh, it's too much for me.
Those are the dark days.
No one ever in, no one ever out,
It's just always pout, pout, pout.
Those are the dark days!

Cassie N. Beaudoin

Forever, Angel

She came here
Hopes, dreams
Yet to be pondered
A child full of innocence
Yearning for love, appreciation
Imagination running wild like wind
through her golden locks
No fears yet discovered
Pure curiosity consuming her
Gradually developing into a beautiful being
Full of adventurous dreams
Full of lifelong hopes
She loved, trusted with all her heart those that came near
And touched the souls of those that loved her
As quickly as she appeared she was stolen away
Her time was short, overflowing with love
Memories of her will forever embellish our hearts
Gone from this world she may be
But her soul survives forever

Shelby Lynn Knocker

drifting into silence

the death of a hero has come
and my flame has been extinguished
for the man through which my fantasies lived
has been torn from this world, my dreams with him

my hero has found the ultimate silence
that i have come to fear and loathe
how portentously soothing I fear it is

my hero had a legacy of no other
it seems a mistake that it ended this soon
surely God will realize he has made a grave error
and bring my hero back along with my flame

but i know my prayers go in vain
this mistake will never be corrected
so i lay here in a lifeless gaze

while drifting into the bothersome silence
to dream of my hero
and his legacy never to be fulfilled

Douglas Seth Hewatt

Africa

Ripped from their homes,
Shipped overseas
Whipped so hard that they fall to their knees

Put on the market, sold for money
Thrown to work for years and years
Worked so hard they can't sit up

People disagreed and started to stand
And others said, "We live off these slaves
We will not let them go"

The North and the South went to war
For days and days, blood poured

And then finally the war ended
And slaves were free

The sun had set
The moon was out
And finally for years and years
They had been slaves but today they are free

Joseph Lawson

All in a Dream

Somewhere east of the Moonshine Water
Lies a golden plain that is like no other
And somewhere to the north of that
Stands a mountain range called Berksanbat
Within that chain of silver might
The purest river takes its flight
It flows and streams
Through children's dreams
And comforts them in the night

Flowing so calm through jungles of fear
Making the bad things all steer clear
With their claws and paws
And gnashing maws
Their eyes and scales
And rat-like tails
The purity of this river blue
Keeps them from me and you
And so we're safe, snug in our beds
To sleep and dream till the night ends.

Brenna Dixon

Thinking

Shh! Please! I'm trying to think!
I can't remember, was it about a sink?

Or it could've been about a cow,
but whatever it was, I can't remember now.

Was it short? Was it small?
Was it fat? Was it tall?

I think I thunk
about an elephant's trunk.

Nope, that wasn't it;
it might've been a baseball mitt.

Well, whatever it was,
it must not have been more important than fuzz.

Oh, thank you for agreeing
and giving me a wink!

You made me remember,
I wanted a drink . . . I think!

Rachel Christian

Cumulus Clouds

Dawn breaks as painful as ice,
Stabbing its way through cumulus clouds;
Citrus colors painting the desert floor a bright orange.
I creep with a slow pace out of my lonely bed
To greet the day with an empty belly
And complaints of hot days and cold nights.
So, where am I to go from here?
I honestly don't know.
I'd like to live life with a steady pace,
Taking what it gives to me in steps;
But all life seems to do
is throw one thing after another in my face,
giving me no time to absorb
and contemplate aspects of the situation.
The only constant I can depend on is change,
and change seems to favor me.
I can only hope
That the rising of the citrus sun
Will bring a better tomorrow.

Gwendolyn D. Garrison

Time to Love

The sun comes up and the sun goes down
When you stop and think about it we're
Forever spinning round
In this crazy kind of motion
In this lonely part of space
It's ironic that we're called the human race
And doubts creep in and your faith dries up
But with confidence like children
We will see that there's one thing that's
For certain and I know you will agree
If you're brave enough to be you I'll be me
And the sun comes up and the sun goes down
When you stop and think about it we're
Forever running 'round
And I've this crazy kind of notion in this
Lonely part of space
If we just slow down we'll win this human race
It's time to live and it's time to learn
That it's time to love

Paul Vincent Le Claire

Lovraea

Humble and patient
Yet dry from the thirst
Lonely and unfaithful
Which one is worse?
Putting your all into it
It wouldn't be the first
Or keeping in touch with old flames
Trying to do a little dirt
But I love you
A phrase heard from time to time
But pain is love
And love is blind
Sacrifices are often made
You give one while I give four
And for some reason we don't even talk anymore
Holding on by love
Or just afraid to leave
Trust is all that we have
And you are all that I need

Cainan Bailey Howard

Sanity or Insanity

A cloud gathers round
A soft breeze slips by my cheek
Like a bad dream that touches the soul
One that won't let you wake up
Things seem up then down
Right then left
Back to front wrong and right
Tight yet loose
Crystallized and plasmatic
All at the same time
Is this possible?
Let your imagination go
Drift into emptiness and darkness
Float away on a sea of emotions
Is there an inner sensation deep within
One that makes you think you're in touch with yourself
Does any of this sound familiar
Certain experts believe in the philosophical aspect
But do you

Marilyn Terese Demoss

Love's Sweet Lullaby

Look into my eyes and wipe the tears away
Please don't go, your departure will fade my glow
The pain inside is fear
Of losing my friend never again able to spend
Can you hear what my heart can't say
Listen closely, can you hear my heart beat
As it skips a beat, a sound so clear it's piercing
I want to reach out, and never have to let go
My feelings for you I try to confide
Look into my eyes and see into my soul
Can you see my inner thoughts the real me
How do I explain to you what is felt within
I want you to pull me in close
And hold me tight all though the night
Let your heart beat by mine, a sound so divine
As I close my eyes and drift off to sleep
You stroke my face and kiss my lips
And whisper in my ear
Loves sweet lullaby so clear

Angel Lakeisha Hammond-Edwards

Matt

Don't tell me now that you are free.
You're flying far away from me.
I'm scared you'll never join me here.
I'm waiting for you, holding back a tear.
I'll cry myself to sleep at night,
while you're soaring like a kite.
I miss you, Matt, and I'm scared to say;
I fear you won't come back today,
not today and not tomorrow.
I'm drowning now in my own sorrow.
I miss our talks on my back steps.
I miss our walks and all your peps.
I miss your eyes and the deep sincerity
of your soul that never lies.
You're one of a kind, one whom I love;
try now to regain your mind.
I will always care and wish you well
and when I think of you in my eyes,
another tear does swell.

Heidi Leanne Kroiter

Arrested

Click, click,
This sound makes me sick!
Cold hard steel wrapping around,
I begin to cry, can anyone hear the sound?
The officer says, "You are under arrest."
Getting into the patrol car,
I am feeling depressed.
Again placing myself at the hands of the law,
All I can do is think of my mama.
Someone sees my arrest on the
Eleven o'clock news,
Can only imagine their thoughts
As they viewed
My name flashing across the screen.
Tell me, please, what does all this mean?
What is my crime,
This time?
Prostitution, drugs, a shopping cart?
Give me a break, have a heart.

Linda Sue Wendrick

Adoring and Loving

Dedicated to Sarwer Sultana

As you wake up and go about with routines of the day,
my dear Mom, may you always live and here is what I say—
You have molded me into what I am today?
You taught me growing up, manners and life's way.
You made me sensitive, caring and brought faith into me.
I am beholden to you, for this, in every way,
For all these years near and far away from you.
Your unyielding prayers, communication and link with me
Have kept me going and upheld me in life.
How magnificent and bountiful God has made thee.
You are my source of wisdom, guide for life and end
mirror of time, mentor, and strength that transcends
to help me in my life to act as a man, father, and husband;
in my own way and own time and stay independent.
Your supple and soft love; care and prudence lives in me,
my heartbeat is subject to the motion of beads in your rosary.
I transcribe these few lines, for you, as my tribute.
It is true you have my fondest love and unequivocal gratitude.

Ellahi M. Ishteeaque

helpless jessy

jessy feels helpless
shattered and confused
her world has died
and her mind severely abused
everything backwards and gray
she calls me up, silent and scared
then lets out a scream
all the anger and the silence explodes
destroying me, destroying you
her body aching and twisted in knots
walking on broken glass
avoiding her shadow
wrecked and torn
washed away by her shadows
swimming in her mind
she says, will you catch me if i'm falling
will you hold me together if i'm breaking
will you release me when i'm flying
will you love me when i'm dying

Marc Lewis Gratch

Stay the Course

Once again I find myself searching for the shore
Waves brake hard, the current's strong, I've been here once before

Now what lies ahead is the fear of the unknown
The course that I've been plotting was not His but was my own

Uncertainty lies before me, the direction is unclear
The mist rolls in the sea grows rough, a test of faith is near

Far off in the distance a brilliant light shows through
Stay the course stormed through my soul, it was then I knew

It had to be a lighthouse, what else could it be?
I changed my course, I followed God to where He now led me

The way was not easy but I chose to do His will
My faith grew strong, the wind fell calm, the seas became still

As I looked upon the course that I had planned to drift
The fate I would have met there upon the cliffs

The lighthouse was a guide that God had given me
I turned to gaze upon it but found only the calmed sea

Kristina Luella McGee

Life

Born of innocence,
thrust into the world;
questioning, comprehending,
enthralling and maintaining.

Time flashes by,
granting individuals a window frame;
a window in which to grow,
fortuitously to expand our wings.

Tumultuous dark clouds obscure our vision,
leaving us to flounder and stumble.
Thereupon within us an energy burns,
enabling us with new found strength,
to heal our wounds,
leaving scars of lessons well learnt.

I wish to grow old within my window,
my soul filled with only love.
Content with no regrets,
knowing I gave it my all.

Lisa Jane Brouwers

angels and demons

angels, demons
god's warriors, satan's minions
both warriors in their
own right
they may take human form for means of might
angels—fair
demons—harsh, cold
but both bold
but when two enter one body
that body is often crazed
by right
and wrong
often in a haze
out of sight
many are persecuted
which are you?
angel, demon, both, neither
only one can change the world
the only one is everyone

Benjamin Levi Crabtree

romance language

i remember the day that i met you
your arms a flurry of motion
your legs crossed like an indian
you took the form of a noble race
for they are one with the world
and though you are set apart from it
constantly moving away
you pass through open gaps
with the fluid grace i have never seen any besides them wear
like the effortless deer your brother's hunt
and then cut open
releasing the ghosts within
you move softly with a gentle touch
never spilling water from cupped leaves
or crushing the long grasses
that are whipping in the wind we walk through
i romance you
because i love you
because of who you are

Benjamin J. Bishop

My True Secret

A field of daisies,
A patch of corn,
Let me blow my wonderful horn.
For when I look into your eyes,
I see nothing but true beauty, which lies inside.
Come, come and you will find
You can be free—heart, soul, and mind.
Here is where I will tell you my secret
Of how all your beauty may shine.
Now come and sit, sit with me.
This is how it feels to finally be free,
Free from worries, free from the world.
All you must do is sit here with me,
Rest your head, and go to sleep.
I shall surely see you very soon.
Until then, keep shining
Like the moon, the stars, and all that is nice.
My true secret is,
When you believe, magic will come true.

Karissa Lyn Dold

Battle Scars

A dark line runs from your navel
to your pubic bone.
I call it your equator and rub cocoa butter
on your swollen belly.
You call it your war wound and hide
it with elasticized trousers.
If your line of demarcation is a wound
from battle, then we both
are permanently scarred,
only my mark of injury is internal,
created the day you said,
"Let's make a baby,"
as if I could.
But modern technology makes
lots of impossibles possible,
and so we engaged in the battle
to find a daddy
who was passionate about the cause,
yet practiced neutrality.

Crystal Sherrod

panthers

kimonos are hanging out at the end of the words
their sense commit seppuku
solemnity sleeps on nails
and the festivities crouch under wooden foreheads
little sticks make them resound in the brain
something started to change and you cannot name it
lets impale the moles gnawing inside my heart
seeking the absolute
life is like a sake and appearances are wandering through it
the shadows started to disappear into things as if things
became pouncing panthers devouring everything around
floating panthers devouring everything around
don't need the body of the desert any longer
for the soul of the word is carried to another world
by floating panthers

since the shadows have disappeared
everyone is his own sun his own earth
floating panthers devouring everything left
in an invisible place

Liviu Georgescue

At the Dock

There is quiet peace about fishing you know.
Just watching all these little Filipino boys;
who they are, I do not know.
From three years to teen
there's not one who's mean.
Each Filipino daddy has three or four,
and all his sons cheer him on to catch more.
Oh, how their daddy is such a big man
because he catches fish for the frying pan.
There's even a grandfather or two
and talk Tagalog; yes, all the dads do.
Daddy's got soda pop, chips, even tea.
He takes care of his beautiful boys
fishing by the sea.
These little boys, they're so close to their dad;
a more beautiful sight couldn't be had.

Steve Kent Morton

The House Has Lost Its Children

Brittle paint peels off in great strips
Exposing weathered wood

Ivy engulfs the sides
Neglected for years
The house wears a mourning shroud

Dilapidated stone steps
Worn in the center from many feet
Still beckon invitingly

A porch littered with leaves
Patiently listens for children's voices
Even though it is already deaf

The children drive by
See its shattered windows
Witness the dying house

They turn away, leaving the past to wander
Through empty rooms

Allison Kendrick Posner

sam adams

passing by sam adams on my way to check-out
i was pulled
like the ground pulls a fighter
whose taken one on the chin.
and through my hollow body
a yearning expanded like a flood . . .
i'd never ached to drink a beer
so intensely in my life.

and i never knew one could carry this much
sadness and still will to live.

sorrows really can be drowned,
but when spirits recede, sorrow remains.
and maybe that's how i was able
to keep on walking, walking on by,
with my eggs, and my oranges, and my milk.
i wanna see it clear
when the green grass grows over those
carcasses of my regrets, and not wash
those tender shoots of hope away.

Daniel Kim

Will You Marry Me?

Will I ask it? Will I say? Will I hold it out this day?
The sign of truth, confirmation of love;
not an empty promise, but a gift from above.
Desperate for eternity, I look to you to share it;
needing only your company, I ask for you to bear it.
Holding on ever tighter, never letting go,
seeing my true loving, never untrue show, calling out, "I need you."
Accepting I need you, sharing every moment.
The universe to what we hold on, letting it surround us;
guiding as we move, we piece together future,
our minds accepting new, when we are together.
Man and woman, we find a way;
if you will accepts this, the ring to lead the way.
Will you but take me? Will you let me stay?
Will you open your arms to this man every day?
I ask you now in earnest, meaning forever true.
I ask you to be my wife, will you say I do?
Will you marry me?

Quentin Gammon DeWitt

Ode to Open Space

Sunlight sparkles between glossy green leaves.
Red juicy apples hang voluptuously.
Twisted tree branches tempt climbers.
Imagination swirls thickly,
Transporting young minds to new settings and adventures.
Then, the bulldozer digs a trench and pours concrete,
Replacing our neighborhood orchard
With a steel fence and a growling guard dog.

We explore a pond and field;
Hide between tall green corn husks;
Capture tadpoles and painted turtles;
Delight in a swampy paradise,
But a bulldozer levels the field.

Why must the bulldozer destroy our fragile ecosystem?
Why must we regulate our imagination?
Why must we be forced us to accept structure and concrete
As signs of progress?

Stephanie Eve Arado

People

We different emotions,
And different ideas.
We have different views,
And different feelings.
We are all different,
but uncannily the same.
We never fully trust one another,
Yet we marry each other.
We never fully understand the human race,
Yet we add to it.
We are never fully accepted by each other,
Yet we don't accept everyone else.
We hurt each other
We love each other
We murder each other
We create each other
What is the human race?
What are we?

Lexi Judge

Maegan

The twinkle that greets me as you softly say,
Grammy, I love you, melts my heart away.
Snugglebunny me, Grammy, as you squeeze me close.
What more could a grandmother ever ask for?

Go swimming with me, watch me ride my bike.
Let's play with the puppies, but you have to be gentle.
They are all little sayings that will stick in my mind,
Forever and ever, till the end of my life.

I watch as you grow, in size and in mind.
I want to put you on hold, but I know there's no time.
Life wasn't meant to leave you behind.

As we both grow older, I hope I'll still hear,
Grammy, I love you and snugglebunny me, dear,
Then I'll be the one with the twinkling eyes.
The tears will fall softly and I will know
I've given you something to hold in your heart,
And may Grammy's love be the biggest part.

Hazel L. Martin

Emotional Thanks to God

Thank you for your peace and your love
for living inside of me while still reigning from above
for your joy, all the beauty in life I saw, for the rain
and helping me come out the past year sane
for the sun, moon, Earth
and the reason for Jesus' birth
that I'm found and no longer lost
for sending Jesus to pay my cost
for never answering my prayer too late
for my one and only darling mate
for strength and getting me through 1998
for the good opportunities in the new year that awaits
for protection taking good care of me
for correction, blessing my destiny
helping me forgive, love, care
letting me know you are always there
most of all showing me your way
giving me hope on a brand-new day!

Chelisa R. Rodgers

Your Laugh

Your laugh, innocence and maturity both.
The shyness of your innocence
and the warmth of your maturity,
it draws me to you unlike anything on Earth.

Your laugh, so beautiful is the air of breath
like a child; it comes fast and direct.
It comes untwined from wild reeds, clear
as the flow of mountain water, unrepressed and pure.

The water of your laugh refreshes me,
cleanses me of the day's dirt,
relieves me of the heat,
and quenches my thirst.

Your laugh I would like to conceal in an echoing cave,
the echoes in the cave,
the wetness of your eyes,
and the reality of your gift
come to life in the illusion of your water.

Ophelia Kwong

Salvation

Satan snuck up on me one day
He came into the place I play
He drug me down through that fiery gate
He knows only anger, fear, and hate
He dumped me there before a great demon
Getting past it would make me a free man
I knew I couldn't survive alone
Since now, a sword it began to hone
It turned towards me and raised its blade
A brilliant light made it falter, afraid
The demon reared its ugly head
Then, tail between its legs, it fled
My Savior had come to rescue me
He came along to set me free
He held out His hand, I took it in mine
He embraced me and told me all would be fine
Now I spread the news to all creation
Of Jesus Christ, our Rock, our Salvation!

Nathan Lewis Johnson

Doorway to Heaven

Death is the doorway to my heavenly home.
Thank You, Lord, I need no more to roam.

Because of Your love for me,
Now I fully see
All that You have done for me.

Thank you for Your grace.
It really helped me in my race
To keep me in my place.

What a joy to follow Your leading
So that my life was succeeding,
As I, Your word, was reading.

Now, as I come to the end of the way,
There is just one thing I want to say,
I am happy Your presence is with me this day.

Ah, Heaven is here at last.
Oh, boy, this is a blast!

Melvin A. Sellers

Heart Aches

Why is it that the one man you love
is the one man that leaves your heart to ache, day-by-day?
Why does he make you cry,
and take a piece of your heart that's
hard to give away?
Why does he tell you he loves you?
And if a relationship is not a game, then why does he play you?
If you know he's doing wrong, why do you stay,
knowing all your heart would do is ache,
telling yourself over and over, being with him is not a mistake?
The things he does to hurt you are only blinded by your way:
seeing it, but not wanting it to be true, so
you make your heart believe he's going to be
faithful to you;
knowing deep down inside this is a lie
but you take the pain he brings your way, but why?
And here you go covering all his
lies with an excuse, and you know this is true.

Trina Reneé Byarse

June Third

Life is so different now.
I stay up at night just thinking, wow,
how could this have happened to me?
Now I know my soul will never be free.
A part of me will be missing forever.
I just wish that one day everything would all come together.
I was hopeless and blind,
because I didn't get to see you that one last time.
But I was obviously too late,
for Heaven has closed its gate.
Emptiness is now all that I feel.
I just wish that none of this was real.

I will always remember the times we shared;
nothing else has yet compared.
And the things you have said,
your words always flow through my head.
In the future, I'll try not to fear,
because I know you'll always be right here.

Tegan Nicole Hattle

The 9-11 Tragedy

I know times have been tough
Everybody's been through enough
Has the world come to an end
Jesus Christ is your friend
Why can't we all learn to love
See His light from above
I see His love everywhere
Take His hand—don't be scared
God bless America, God bless America
All the prayers, all the tears
Listen closely, you can hear
I feel awful, I'm in pain
Hopefully peace will come again
The days go by very slow
I feel like there's no place to go
Every night in my bed
I've got a million things racing through my head
It could have been me, it could have been me

Courtney Danielle Kisamore

Excerpt from Shadow Wall

Building castles in the sand with no thought of permanence
For it is not in this castle I dwell
It is not in this castle my fortune is stored or my future secured
Only here where I rest I shall find these things
Only here as I wait for the invitation to watch the wall sink again
Into the sand as the ocean recedes to bring back the soft earth
To allow light to shine where the shadow is cast
To once again feel cool comfort on a hidden hand
Here I rest as the silence overcomes the breeze
And the words of my past are heard without change
Above me etched in calm strokes upon the cornerstone
Words my weary eyes capture as no import
I settle into a gentle sleep, waiting a time
When my eyes may behold the sun without pain
This sleep is the sleep of dreams
The easy fluttering of the leaves and trickle of the stream
It is here I shall wait, it is from here my journey will continue
Upon a different day

Christopher J. Babin

In Chaos

Time surpasses me as I chase behind,
Trying to grasp a hold on a dream that dies slowly in my mind.
Living in fear for the karma of my sins,
Trying to justify the things I said with the things I did.
I want to break free of it all,
Unload the weight on my shoulders as, to my knees, I fall.
I reach for you now, but you're nowhere in sight;
Save me from the chaos, illuminate my nights.
Quiet the whispers of despair;
Show me I was never alone, that you always were there.
Watching in silence, but watching nonetheless;
Waiting for my faith to dissolve with my confusion and distress.
But here I am, arising from the fall;
Wiping my tears away, learning how to crawl.
Wasn't that your greatest lesson?
I never stopped loving you, that's truly my confession.
Worry not, for I'll be fine.
I simply mask my contempt and pain, and leave it all behind.

Ana Maria Osorio

The Journey

As we journey through this life,
We grow, learn and mature.
When we were babes, we were dependent.
As we grew, we became more able.
When we were children, we thought only of day.
As we grew, we thought of weeks and months.
When we were teens, we lived for the here and now.
As we matured, we lived for the future.
When we were young adults, we lived for success and wealth.
As we aged, we lived for retirement and travel.
When we were middle-aged, we were independent.
As we grew elderly, we became dependent.
Life is a cycle, a journey.
We travel through this life growing and maturing.
We learn sooner or later the truths we are meant to know.
We travel through this life to the next.
We either gain wisdom or we become fools.
It is our choice, our journey.

Laurene Birmingham

Forgotten

Left behind are the feelings of love and kindness
Held between us are the feelings of anger and hatred
Long lost is the time spent together as father and son
Found is the distance between two strangers
Memories faint and distant of your kindness scarce
Fresh and new is the pain of my failures brought to light
No longer heard are the words of your praise
Ringing in my ears is, "Son of mine no longer"
Warmth from an embrace of love felt no more
Coldness felt from being disowned
"Father," a word not said from my lips or thought of
"Son," a word with no meaning to your heart
Days of happiness replaced with emptiness
Months apart giving comfort to our inability to forgive
Thoughts, fears, anger, hatred, love, longing; forgotten
Remember what was had
Forget what was done
Continue now with what you have

Amadeo Gonzales

The Game

Fire and ice, you always elude me
Desire for you has always consumed me
A word, a touch, a single kiss
Always in you I find my bliss
Your passion rises, so does mine
Yet ne'er the two do entwine
When I run hot, you run cold
And still this game never grows old
What must I do to win you once and for all?
Name your price, and hear my call
To the ends of the Earth and beyond I would ride
Be undone and made anew, ever at your side
And still we play this age old game
From one day to next, you're never the same
But if playing this game is your price
Then I shall gamble, and roll the dice
For I know the value of the prize once won
Lovers at last as we two become one

Melissa Lee Holmes

Liquid Earth and Magic Skies

Withered man that life has aged sits alone on a bench for two,
Broken smiles but one last dream of his own to see him through.

I touch the sky with broken hands in prayer for what had been,
In hopes that what had blown away would turn against the wind.

Every day is the same; I am only passing by.
I need to heal the pain and mend the broken time.

He sits alone to feed the crows waiting for his Robyn. . . .
Passersby they seem to stare.
But no one knows his name, and no one feels his pain.

So what do you find tomorrow when you live in yesterday?
Where do you breed your sorrow when the past is washed away?

On his grave, left undone, an angel carves a name
To be his own, etched in stone, to wipe away his pain.

She's all I need to fly, pointless my goodbyes.
I will never die with liquid earth and magic skies.

Wil Mendenhall

Fall/Winter

Remember when we played for hours while
The electric fan stood silent in the window
As if it held its breath in sacred wonder
At paper dreams unfolding on the floor.
On summer afternoons with garnered treasure,
A castoff Sears and Roebuck catalog,
We shopped for babies, bassinets, and husbands
That looked like Herman's Hermits or the Beatles.
Our kitchens had the latest model Kenmore
Refrigerators with doors that never close,
While rows of beds with ruffled canopies
Defined the boundaries of our fragile houses.
We dramatized store-bought domestic scenes
And when our lives grew stale, we started over,
Renamed our children, browsed through tattered pages. . . .
Our scissors cut a trail into the future,
Our leavings piled in heaps like burial mounds
Of lives not chosen, dreams we swept away.

Sarah McFarland

Visions

We gaze at our image
painting portraits on cobweb
strands of hair straightened under a hot iron
disowning nature's
curve of mountain rivers

We choose lives
lived like box cars tied to metal rails
blurring past open fields
chasing sand pebbles
falling like elevators in vertical shafts

We think with whirlpool minds
devising codes of zeroes and ones
weaving unseen webs
catching fish
walking with open eyes
blinded
pretending to see

Marilyn Brodhurst

No More

Through the skin it goes
Sliding from wrist to elbow
Life in the form of a liquid flows from the wound
Staining all it touches a dark crimson color
A smile on the face for the sin within is flowing out
Wobbly did the knees become
The body succumbing to the weight
While on the knees the left arm opens the right
More life flowing from the veins
Soon even on the knees is too much
Falling backwards squinting into the darkness
Then the sudden realization that nothing
Wanted would be accomplished
Tears ran from the eyes soaking the now crimson colored clothing
Shortly even the eyelids are too heavy and they close
Finally no life is left to even beat the heart
Laying in the darkness a wasted body of a good person who
Wasn't ever given the chance to be proven

William Bruce Howell III

The End

As I watch the plains fly by
Something always goes through my mind
Something horrible and gray
I can remember the collapse
The screams and cries

Even if I'm not there
It is gray and ugly

I'll think our world has come to an end
As I think how could God let this happen
For all those people that have lost their lives

On that morning of 9/11 and every other morning
I say those pledged words with meaning not just things
Things that come out of my mouth

I hope we catch him; if we do, he will suffer
That horrible man that made us feel
Our world has come to an end

Alison Hinton

Missing Children

Big tears from little hearts are crashing on our land.
Where are they? We cannot say. Delicate shells on shifting sand.

Their tears should flood our hearts;
We're too busy flowing with the go.
Where are we? Wherever we want to be.
Somewhere in a polluted sea, little hearts sink below.

Big tears from little hearts:
Hearts—pounding pain; tears—torrential rain.
Where are they? Do we even want to know?
Possibly tormented, enslaved, or slain.

We engulf ourselves with worldly gain,
Harboring our own ego.
Yet there is no world without children.
Why is this soaking in so slow?

Drowned out by a blatant society, no one hears their salty plea:
"Please rescue me!"

Edie Edwards Lawson

My Best Friend, My Son—on Graduation Day

Once upon a time, when my son looked up to me,
I saw myself in his little eyes.
And now that my son is all grown up,
I look at him as he stands tall among the skies.
We've done so much together.
He is now my very best friend.
I know what he's going to say,
even before his sentences end.
He knows everything about me.
He's heard every story I've told.
And he's lived many of the same experiences,
some of which are rich as gold.
I know that the apple doesn't fall far from the tree,
and my son is like a ripe little apple trying to set itself free.
He is my only son and I am his dad,
and that's always the way it will be.
He's also my best friend, my buddy, my pal,
and I'll miss that apple under the tree.

Bob Ortt

The Quilt of Colors

The many faces of a quilt
Oh, how they shine
In many colors, shapes and sizes
And features formed so fine
The brilliant coppers, blacks and browns
The radiant yellows glitter
These smiling faces of the quilt
Will never be found bitter
Each square is different from the rest
They have their own sole traits
And every personality is always at top rate
The beauty of this special quilt lies beneath the stitches
The single thread of trust helps the faces share their riches
As this special quilt grows in size
The people living within it
Will begin to realize
The wonderful joys of love
And the splendors of their lives

Cameron Steele

A Moment and Then Some

Waking sparkle
And I notice my doubts
Like an ice sculpture melting away
I can feel the warm waters of tranquillity
And the softness of hopes it brushes upon
Thinking of all, I wish I could say
I make myself translucent
To let you reach for the words unspoken
Shimmering candle light
Illuminates our joy
While we sink deep into each other's eyes
Far beneath the surface
Our thoughts are still inseparable
And we wonder if we are real
There may be no explanation
For this connection
But I feel His gentle hands
Embracing the eternity

Tina Boljevac

What Do You Live For?

I want to open my eyes
Let the water drip down my face
Be cool; refreshed, renewed, enjoy it all 'til I die
I want to hide from the fools and play no more games
The city, the hurried rush, hatred, greed, and lies
The people who hide to cover their face
For those do not belong in my place
I want to wrap myself around the world and back
I want to end all the painful attacks
Give me my lake and trees, give me a hand. . . or let me be
I want to wake up to the sounds of birds
Clear my eyes and make myself eat my words
Give me a hand and I'll give two
Give me a child and I'll make him true
Open a wallet . . . to me that is not enough
For it is I who always wants to help out
Wake me up, kick me around, I don't care
For it is the meaning of life that I have found

Chad Gregory Anderson

Prisoner of Myself

Shadows of shapes spinning uncontrollably
Sounds so unfamiliar
Buzzing
A constant aggravation in my ear
Torture
Nothing but pain
Colors everywhere seem to flash before me
My throat is so dry
Pounding in my head, echoes and knocks
They want in, they are all
Trying to control me . . . keep them out!
GO AWAY
Terror
I'm so afraid
Shadows, strangers
Who do these voices belong to?
They are screaming, yelling, demanding me
I'm so afraid

Michelle Lynn Tanner

One Drop in a Pool

Our actions are like
One drop of water
In a vast still pool
Sending out hundreds of ripples
It starts with one person
And soon many others feel the repercussions
Our every action in life
Affects so many others
Most often in ways we never even realize
One tiny misdeed can cascade into a deluge
Of cynicism or hate
One thoughtful act blossoms
Into a huge circle of kindness and caring
And becomes a growing ring of understanding
Be not the drop of failure to mankind
Be instead the drop of compassion
Which spreads throughout
The entire vast pool of humanity

Debra K. Webster

That Horrid Night

To Devin Rae Stage

I think of that horrid night
When everything didn't seem so right.

I remember the sights,
I remember the sounds,
Along with the feelings that pound my soul.

I remember that fright that ran through my mind.
I felt my heart fall out of my chest
When the dear Lord took the best.

You are gone off this Earth,
But you are still with me in my heart and mind.

I will never forget you
And all your kind and loving ways.

When I sit and think about you these days,
I know it will always stay true.
I'll never forget you.

Trevor David Evans

To a Graduate

A path has been laid before you.
It is yours to choose what to do with it.
You look at your past you grin.
Remembering the laughs.
Like when Tommy wrote Cindy a love letter
and Ms. Arch read it to the class.
Or Suzy fell asleep in French.
You shed a tear remembering the sorrows.
Like when your dog died.
Or your friend lost her mother.
You look toward the future you give a grin.
You vision yourself as a pro ball player.
Or a future Nobel Prize winner.
You shed another tear.
Knowing you're leaving home behind.
Knowing home will change.
Now you venture on to the path before you.
Your journey has begun.

Erica Dawn Welsh

Andrew

Always missing you, Andrew—love, Mom

It's your fourteenth birthday and I miss you more than ever.
I can't believe you're not here, not now, not later.
Oh, how I wish it wasn't forever.
This year was hard 'cause you weren't 'round.
Time came to graduate junior high school,
you were nowhere on Earth to be found.
You should have been at your cousin's sweet fifteen,
at church and riding to the reception in a limousine.
You would have been dancin' and stylin'.
Deep down, I knew you wouldn't miss it.
'Cause all the way from Heaven I felt you were smilin'.
When high school began, how I wished you could start too.
I want things to be the way they were 'cause that was our life,
it belonged to me and you.
I remember your last birthday, you were so glad to pass eleven.
I had no idea that three days after,
I could only see you again in Heaven.

April Virginia Jeter-Gamboa

The Silence Is So Loud

Dedicated to 9-11 and the people of the United States of America

Thoughts so overwhelming,
The silence is so loud.
Sky so very quiet as we look up to the clouds.
The answers, we have nothing.
The reasons, we know none.
Peace once in our mind, will it ever come?
Innocent knew nothing as awoke upon this day.
Tending to business, going about their way.
Any thought today of what would be their fate?
Any thought today as kissed goodbye a mate?
Strength of a great nation tested here today.
God bless America and never shall we stray.
Time now passed and still we wonder why?
Hearts still heavy as we look up to the sky.
God protect and keep us, hold us in His hands.
God protect and keep us forever in His plans.

Ramona A. Webster

Life

What is life
Is it something that can be ended with a knife
Should it be lived one day at a time
Could a simple mistake be classified as a crime
Can the metal that's turned into a gun
Cause someone to live in fear and run
Can the blood spilled in a fight
Make a man live in jail for 365 nights
Or flee on the next flight
When a child's life is ruined with a parent's mistake
And they have to spend their birthday without a cake
All because a man decides to abandon his wife
Is this considered life
Ask yourself one night
Is what people do to each other right
The only way to live
Is if people take action and forgive
What is life

Eric Anthony Oberdorf

stardom from the windmills of the gods

like the shadow of a flash
inyenzi emerged from the blues
vineyard belatedly bloomed with fruits
little drop of dew on a calabash
fostered to the ends
and became widespread
resulting in a warrior
though cajoled by mouth
of sword bearer's sword
and wrestled by fiends
but not strangled by babblers
an intercourse with zeus
consolidated a tremulous stay
of inyenzi dwarfed by fate
what a fossilized history

Okey Christopher Anachuna

If Time Were a Window

I'd sit on the sill and watch the snow
As it falls down to the world below
And if time were a window
I'd watch the world pass me by wondering
If any of the lives I see wonder why
But if time were a window
Could I correct the mistakes I've made
Or close the drapes and forget they stayed
Say, if time were a window
Would you sit there with me
As we laugh and cry over all these things
Yet if time were a window
Would I see the lessons so long forgotten
By those biased hands that call themselves historians
If time were a window
I would not sit idly as my life passed me by
But I would open my arms and pray
That these invisible wings would let me fly

Derek Tyler McDaniel

My Son's Hands

For my son, Drew, on September 16, 2000

My son's hands were tiny at birth,
the cutest little hands on all the Earth.

My son's hands, at the age of three,
held onto my finger as he walked with me.

My son grew to the age of ten;
his hands did much to help him then.

When my son went to junior high,
those hands began to really fly.

Football, basketball, even track;
up, down, and around the back.

Now at sixteen, he trains those hands
to do his bidding, to follow his commands.

But there is one thing for sure, I find,
my son's hands look just like mine.

Kimberly Ann Rice-Thueson

Won't Matter

Doesn't matter if you are a boy or girl, if you are kind,
consider yourself a friend already.
You can be short or tall, thin or bald,
and you won't be judged any less for any physical flaws.
You will always be known as simply my friend.
We may argue for whatever reason and yet
your throne of friendship would always be saved especially for you.
You can be overweight or big-eared,
and yet my feelings for you would still remain true
because friendship is based on love and support,
not on material things you can give or outer looks.
What is of greater value comes from within your soul, which is gold.
You don't need to impress me with any riches
or with who you know in Hollywood.
You already earned a special place within my heart.
You can be young or old, Hispanic or Black.
To me friendship is nationwide love, given free of charge.
You can work at a fast food restaurant or for the president
and it would not matter at all.
Our friendship would exist solely on brotherly love.
It doesn't matter what you do or say;
our friendship is sure to last because it's made up of heart.
Doesn't matter what comes tomorrow or happened today,
you can be sure my hand in friendship
will reach across the many miles just to hold your hand
because no matter what, I will be there as a friend.

John Paul Padilla

A New Beginning

The road of sorrow and grief often seems endless,
But the grace of God and the warmth of His love is boundless.
So along the way, find peace and contentment though Him,
For there is joy in the hope we have in Jesus of a new life to begin.
When we trust in Him, we find a new freedom and forgiveness of sin,
And peace through his cleansing from within
Through the great joy He gives for a new beginning.

James Paul Maxwell

Teenage Girl

I wake up every morning my hair is a mess,
I spend twenty minutes in the shower and fifteen to get dressed.
My bathroom is a sty and I have mascara in my eye.
I've already spent thirty minutes on my hair,
and I'm still not sure if what I'm wearing is really what I want to wear.
A quick breakfast if any, I have a few minutes but not too many.
I grab my books and maybe my lunch,
I have a good hunch this day is getting better.
I get to school I look great, my hair, my makeup, everything is straight!
There he is what a hunk, but what's this,
he's walking with a piece of junk!
My day that was great is now a mess,
now I have no date and just a homecoming dress.
Just my luck, this really sucks; another day as a teenage girl!

Dana Brittney Hazell

My Silence

Lost are all my hopes
And shattered are my dreams
Although I hold my silence
My mind echoes with my screams

For naught was all my sacrifice
All promises are broken
Although I hold my silence
My heart rips from words unspoken

I wander blind and numb
As darkness covers all
Although I hold my silence
I hear my soul's lamenting call

As chaos crashes upon my head
And I cannot feel or see
I sit locked within my silence
Alone for now and eternity

Shanaar Arakan diCrystala

This Is Home

Morning crisp, the air so fresh
The sun, it rises to warm the earth
Fields of corn that reach the sky
Seasons come then pass you by

It is so beautiful for one to see
This life it gives to you and me
We are alike and all do need
Everything to please our human greed

Though seasons change so many things
Love and guidance is always there
Nature provides what is needed
Everything, remember our life is seeded

When night falls and darkness prevails
Tomorrows to come but only to go
Your life is yours, for that I know
This is your home, Ontario

Larry Daniela

Ruins of Bellona/Ode to Dhalgren

To wound this autumnal city,
The approaching sun,
Twin moons of night
Sneak out of the sleeping well.
Reflections of perpetual burning,
Crimson red eyes and pupils
In fluorescence,
They illuminate
The otherwise obscure morning.
In the ruins of the city
That resides in currents,
Etched in stages,
We chase time to fathom.
The hallowed city continues
To bloom in our minds
As an orchid.

Stephen Emil Palahach

Devotion

Sonya crayoned starlight
In a dark room.
She swept her hand skyward,
Arcing white light behind her.

Outside the house,
The mailbox stared
With blind intensity in the gleaming window,
Wishing, just for an instant,
She would pause to notice a little red flag.

Suddenly the wax was melting;
Glimmering stars turned to searing drops
Branding her skin.
The rusted flag swung down outside.
Red with forgiveness . . .

Sonya wept to fall fast asleep
In the bleeding room,
A fresh box of 36 Crayolas in the mailbox.

Samantha Leigh Wagner

Eurydice, My Sister

Did they ask the Moirae before they whipped away the carpet
from beneath your feet—
verdant, vibrant, springtime carpet?
People get hurt that way.

Was it Clotho complaining about her fine thread wasted?
What did Lachesis see ahead? Was it she who sent you back?
Why did Atropos hesitate to make that final cut,
or did she wait too long, and you slipped her shears?

And was the tree consulted, the old one,
Yggdrasil, where the river bends and sighs?
He, the sea eagle, and the swifts
would never have agreed to that dirty trick—
to leave the life but take the life.
And who asked me my opinion?
I had no note from Atropos, no option in the matter,
but neither did you, Eurydice,
or do the gods, where even Orpheus failed.

Bronwyn Blake

My Prayer for America

Today our flag was waving, my eyes were dimmed with tears.
Another war beginning brought back so many years.

Once more an evil monster had raised his ugly head
And many innocent people will soon be lying dead.

This lovely country, crowded with folks of every race,
Afraid to go about their life, afraid to show their face.

There will always be evil people who only live to hate,
But love is stronger and we must trust each other while we wait.

To see the sun arising and chasing off the rain
And pray our God will help us live the good life again.

I've seen the face of evil many times before,
And my heart is filled with sadness to behold it all once more.

Dear God, please help the good men who are running our country now

And give them help in every way.

My head to thee, I bow.

Mercia V. Tillman

Appliance, 1978

For a heavy woman
She's not much of a cook, but
Mother always keeps her kitchen
As clean as one might hope
A Pine-Sol forest rises and falls
Between the harvest-yellow fridge
And the harvest-yellow oven—
Evening sun and evergreen towers
Of solutions
Her sister noisily sets down a glass
In the hall, towards the cool kitchen
Aunt will kiss her cheek
And in her travels discover
The elephant graveyard
Of fruit flies beneath the
Four elements on the stove
Father will come home from
His office and find his kitchen
The same

Samuel Means

Playground

Last night, my old headmaster came visiting.
Elderly, smiling, he put his papery hand in mine.
Did he visit, too, the middle-aged dreams of my class mates?
Somewhere, will we all line up on the asphalt?
The one who lost a sister to the drink,
the one who ate himself to freedom,
and all the ones I cannot name—
could never really name.
And will we go there again yesterday?
My young daughter asks hopefully
of the playground we left so recently—
the empty swings still moving, to and fro,
in the mild violet of the long afternoon.

Tui Chi

Midwestern Mythology

Past the unraveling steel ribbons of Baltimore and Ohio,
past the ashen tundra of Indianapolis warehouses,
and the flaccid spires of Cleveland's art-deco skyscrapers,
past the charred-black Monongahela floodplain in Pittsburgh,

boys load themselves
around supple tales
of fathers.

Forged leather, skinned from ancestral slag,
poured into pressed white shirts with collars and ties,
sowing the beautified valleys
of our widened mothers,

daily supplicating for a yield
in the blue reek of paper mills
or pyorrheal office towers

until weary of journey,
they shoulder shotguns to the backyard,
hoping we count their spilt blood
as holy sacrifice.

Erik L. Peterson

Poet Profiles

ABELA, DIANA

[a] Attard, Malta [title] "There Was Peace That Day" [pers.] This poem is about the day my husband passed away at the age of thirty-nine, and is dedicated with love to our four children: Rebecca, Sarah, David, and Susanna, who were only eleven, nine, seven, and six years old at the time.

ABRAHAM, HEATHER

[a.] La Crosse, WI [title] "Passages" [pers.] This poem is written about a true love I once had. A lot of bad things were happening and he gave me strength to get through it. I owe am grateful for his help. I am a sophomore at Central High School in La Crosse Wisconsin. I want to major in education. I have two wonderful parents and a great older brother. They keep me motivated to write more. I have a hard time explaining things face to face to people, but through poetry I can explain anything.

ADAMS, LANIE

[a.] Germantown, TN [title] "In the Whipper Ends Eves" [pers.] I wrote this in honor of the millions of hunters that are being discriminated against in England and here in the United States. As a fox hunter myself, I feel that I can only help through one small contribution, and that is through my writing.

AGNES, BRIAN

[a.] Duluth, GA [title] "I Still See" [pers.] Writing poetry has always brought my passion to paper. As a younger man, I believed that flying was my only love in life. I found later on, that my true love is and forever will be, writing. I wrote and dedicated this particular piece to the men and women who lost their lives on September 11, 2001. As a fellow New Yorker and citizen of the United States of America, my heart goes out to every family in the world who lost a loved one that day.

ALEXANDER, MOLLIE

[a.] Oklahoma City, OK [title] "My Friend" [pers.] I have always been interested in writing poetry, but never really pursued it. I wrote this poem for my sister Dee's Min Pin pup, Prince. In my dream, an eagle had hatched and was raising a chick in a tall tree just outside their front door. Fearing for the pup, I sat down one day with scratch pad and wrote the poem and sent it to Dee. My sister-in-law, Syble, after hearing it, insisted I enter it into your contest and helped me do so.

ALSTON, SHERINE

[a.] Sicklerville, NJ [title] "Yesterday" [pers.] This poem is dedicated to the person who has constantly inspired me to continue to write my thoughts, inspirations and poems; the man in my life. I was thinking about the old days and I decided to write a poem about yesterday, and this is what I wrote. I hope that you and others will enjoy my style of personal writing, and there will be more writings to come. Thank you for reading my words. The words you will read will always come from my life experiences and my heart.

ARNALL, SCOTT

[a.] Alice, TX [title] "Life" [pers.] There are many people that have influenced my poetry. Each one has contributed to unique episodes in my life. I would like to honor them at this time: Rochelle Pratte, who believes in me more than I do at times; her son Josh; my sons, Jessie Brown and Chance Woods David, a.k.a. "Peanut" Adams; Laura, and my niece, Dana Carr Vickie, a.k.a. "Goat" Adams Kelly Leedy; Gary Arnall and of course, my grandparents, Farris Carder and Rosa "Rosebuds" Carder. Thanks, Grandma, for never giving up on me.

ARROW, DEIDRE

[a.] White River, SD [title] "September 11, 2001" [pers.] The poem I wrote, "September 11, 2001," not only reminds us of the heartache and tears shed, but of the love that carries on. Many families lost loved ones to the September 11 tragedies, but instead of dwelling on what could have been, we need to appreciate what is now. September 11 will always be a day we remember with great pain, and the souls that were lost will never be forgotten, but with the strength and the love of others, we will learn to carry on.

ASTON, MARK

[a.] Canandaigua, NY [title] "Self" [pers.] My poetry is based on the abstract and the artistic venue of society. Some of my work is about tragedy, love, loss, and experiences from my own life. I find that the indifferent emotions that people present in their lives are complex and simple at the same time. By writing about these, I believe I am showing creativity and reality as a partnership instead of individualistic ideas. To enhance people's perceptions of my work, I include metaphors and symbolism. Always remember to open your mind to the abstract meaning of words.

ATKINS, KATHLEEN

[a.] Gallatin, TN [title] "Bin Laden, Bin Laden?" [pers.] Inspiration to write this poem came to me after the twin towers of the World Trade Center were attacked in New York City, NY on September 11, 2001. This day was my 47th birthday; a special day for so many others, which turned out to be a great tragedy in our country, the United States of America. As I prayed for so many on that day, many questions kept coming to mind. So I wrote this poem of questions to Bin Laden. Inspiration comes in many forms, and this one came from my heart and soul.

ATSUTA, HIRO

[a.] Tulsa, OK [title] "Appreciation Letter to Friends" [pers.] This poem was created after my hectic experience; I was unfairly about to accused of a serious crime. It took all of the value away from my life. During the tragic period, I was supported by lots of my friends. Thanks to them, I was able to regain my strength. This poem is for my friends, but also for myself to remember the experience that I will have to live with for the rest of my life. I want to especially thank Sheryl, my American mom.

BAMFORD, KYM

[a.] Gold Coast, Australia [title] "The Cornerstone" [pers.] Hello to everyone. My name is Kym. I am thirty-four. I live in Australia, on the beautiful Gold Coast. I am a mother of five children, and writing poetry always been my favorite hobby. This verse has special meaning to me, as it represents the true value of family strength and how I feel about that. I dedicate this to my family and loved ones, and my five children: Michael, Annalise, Cory, Kale, Madison, Helene, Morgan, Mike, Chris, Nan, Troy, Tash, Finlay, Neil, Lyn, John, Ashleigh, Michael, Lizzie, and many others. This is my way of immortalizing my love for them and saying thank you.

BANKSTON, ROBERT

[a.] Adrian, GA [title] "Thankful" [pers.] Each year, late in the fall, we are reminded at Thanksgiving that we are to remember all that we should be thankful for. Yet to me, each day is a day to be thankful; our families, the beauty of our land, and most of all, the promise of a better life after this one is over.

BARRON, FLORA

[a.] Coto De Caza, CA [title] "The Girl in Me" [pers.] I have always found poetry creates itself. It is as natural as the rhythm of your feet, the breath you take, the beating of the heart, and pen on paper. When I wrote this poem I was not only creating this piece of work, but I saw a new side of me. It is a feeling that I hope will be contagious.

BAUMANN, HOLLY

[a.] Topanga, CA [title] "Half a Jar of Peanut Butter and Van God's Soul" [pers.] Art is my life, my soul, my heart. To be an artist, in the truest sense of the word, means great sacrifice; a beautiful sacrifice you give willingly and wantingly. I am a singer, songwriter, and poet. This particular poem was written when I was off the road touring and living on, literally, peanut butter. To live with such conviction there is room for little else. My heart breaks at least a hundred times a day. Thank God for that.

BECRAFT, TAMARA

[a.] Mountlake Terrace, WA [title] "Beacon of Hope" [pers.] I hold dear the poem "Beacon of Hope," for it reminds me of the light that shines through my dark days. Poetry is my "hope in the night." I truly hope this poem might help someone else through a difficult time. It was not long ago I discovered this art, and with it, the solace of the pen.

BELL, HELEN

[a.] Westland, MI [title] "Freedom" [pers.] To me, poetry is a simple, but elegant avenue by which I can express my philosophy, while utilizing my talent to provoke people's thinking. This poem is dedicated to my son: Jimmie Kotrail Bell, United States Navy. Thanks for your support.

BERGHAIER, SONNA

[a.] Linton, IN [title] "Wisps of God" [pers.] Coming from a family of educators, growing up on a farm with few neighbors, and being shy, books were my best friends. Therefore, since childhood, words have been coursing through my mind. I love the sound of words, their cadence, those pauses between good phrases which allow one to intently listen, the look of words strung together on a page. Upon turning fifty, I decided it was past time to be brave, and began sharing my words. So, here I am, a published poet, thanks to two dear friends who convinced me of the worth of my words.

BIGHAM, DIANA

[a.] Vienna, IL [title] "My Son" [pers.] This poem is very dear to me. I was told by doctors I could not have any kids, and God blessed me with my son, Nathan Scott Bigham. He is my only child and I thank God every day for such a precious gift. I do believe he is my miracle from Heaven.

BISHOFF, SUSAN

[a.] Reedsville, WV [title] "My Teacher" [pers.] This poem is about my mother. She raised me, my brother, and my sister all alone. She never complained and showed great strength, no matter what she faced. I wanted to express my love for her in a way that would live on. I lost her last year to cancer and miss her very much.

BISSONNETTE, AMY

[a.] Slidell, LA [title] "Our Nation" [pers.] I am fourteen and live in Slidell, Los Angeles. I live with my brother, Troy, and my Dad and Mom, Mike and Jewel. I have two dogs and I am a freshman at Slidell High. I'll probably write poetry all of my life, but my goal is to open a kennel for dogs. Many died on September 11th and the pain of our nation was so strong. I had to put that into words. My dad is a U.S. Marine and we were stationed in Okinawa, Japan on September 11, 2001.

BLIZZARD, AMY

[a.] Chandler, IN [title] "The Song Inside of Me" [pers.] The poem published in this book is very dear to my heart. It was written as I fought to find the strength I held inside, and understand the emotions I possessed. I would like to thank my family (I love you all) and my friends Liza and Kat. Every day they continue to inspire me, encouraging me to write every day and reach for the stars. I have been performing and writing for local events and hope branch out into writing my own novels, articles and plays. I'm currently taking courses through Gotham's Writer Workshop and will then move on to study freelance writing.

BLOMDAHL, ANDERS
[a.] Skarpnack, Sweden [title] "Life" [pers.] As the name Sufi indicates, I am an explorer. I am a survivor of a car bomb; having the great privilege of being "Bombed to Life." The real life, invisible to the eye, is found within ourselves while searching.

BOMMARITO, LINDA
[a] Berkley, MI [title] "The Fourth of July" [pers.] I am a dental hygienist practicing in Grosse Pointe Woods, Michigan. I really enjoy people and life in general. The smallest things in life make me most happy. Family and friends are very important to me. I am truly blessed to have each of them in my life. My passions include gardening, travel, and expressing myself through poetry. After 20 years of writing, I am thrilled about this publication! My poem, "The Fourth of July" ironically signifies unity rather than independence, joining all nationalities. I hope others enjoy this poem, and pray for peace and unity throughout the world.

BORDA, MARYROSE
[a] Flushing, NY [title] "Love's Overcast" [pers.] Poetry for me is a spur of the moment journey to the far corners and crevices of the mind. Sometimes we go just for the escape, allowing our senses to experience greater depth. On the other hand the power of poetry can even intercept and prevent a trip from happening—like the one to the therapist!

BOUCHER, LORI
[a.] Gardiner, ME [title] "Who Me Be" [pers.] Creating poetry is a therapeutic process for me. It is how I express the thoughts and feelings that are typically hidden deep within. While the themes of my poetry range from indifference to deep emotional turmoil; I recently started writing on a brighter side due in part to my soul mate, Tom, and the undying support of my mother. I have an additional reason for writing in this dark manner; hoping that others who suffer within themselves will benefit from hearing that they are not alone.

BRETT, MATTHEW
[a.] Portland, ME [title] "Our Love" [pers.] I wrote this sonnet after breaking up with a girlfriend, and believe it or not, I still hold true to the last two lines of my sonnet. I sometimes become annoyed when someone thinks that I am like everybody else, even when I forget that they might not know that I am an Eagle Scout.

BRICKNER, C.
[a.] Tiffin, OH [title] "The Haven" [pers.] This poem was written for and dedicated to my mother, Leah L. Bulger, for teaching me the quality of life through hard work, dedication, and faith in yourself. Thank you Mom, for being you.

BRISSON, KARON
[a.] Apex, NC [title] "Fall in Carolina" [pers.] Autumn in North Carolina is magical. It can lift your spirits on the worst of days. I learned this as a teenager when I moved to a small town in the North Carolina mountains. My love of poetry is shared by my mother, who is a wonderful writer in her own right. I began to love and appreciate poetry when I was given a copy of "The Best Loved Poems of the American People." This book was the most magical thing in my life, except for my family and the North Carolina mountains in fall.

BROWN, CHERYL
[a.] Newton, NJ [title] "Philip Edward" [pers.] My poetry reflects my life, without it I would be lost. Expressing my feelings helps me to deal with everyday life and stress.

BROWN, IGNATIUS
[a.] Brooklyn, NY [title] "Portrait of Katherine" [pers.] Ignatius had a special gift for writing, especially poetry. He enjoyed writing poems, always including them with gifts on special occasions to loved ones. Ignatius left this world on April 22, 2002 at the tender age of thirty-two, but his writings have helped those he loved and respected to carry on his legacy.

BROWN, MELISSA
[a.] Sublette, KS [title] "My First True Love" [pers.] "My First True Love" was the first poem I wrote without the prompting of a school teacher. I went through a depressed period when this guy Aaron broke up with me; that's what really started me in writing poems. I'm an avid golfer and basketball player, and I plan to someday play on the LPGA tour as well as being a psychiatrist somewhere I can speak all three languages I know; Spanish, French, and of course English. Poetry is how I vent, and I just hope it means something to someone other than me.

BROWN, THOMAS
[a.] Gilbert, AZ [title] "Love" [pers.] I was reunited with my soul mate after nine years of no contact immediately after finishing this poem. Life is euphoric when love is devoted.

BUCK, HILDA
[a.] Greendale, IN [title] "Eventide" [pers.] After my husband's accident and subsequent months of hospitalization and years of nursing home care, I was totally devastated watching him deteriorate. In order to relieve the pain and get on with my life, I took classes at a nearby college. There I learned about writing poetry at seventy-eight years of age. This was my outlet and it helped me survive those difficult years. My poem is what I experienced one evening in my backyard—a place filled with happy memories.

BUGBEE, JOYCE
[a.] Higganum, CT [title] "Go to Sleep Little One" [pers.] I wrote this poem for my daughter when she was fifteen months old. She kept me going from day to day, especially after September 11, 2001. She is my angel from God. Both of my children are my hope for the future. I now realize how important every day of life is and how quickly that can be taken away.

BURGER, SHERYLE
[a.] Shelburn, IN [title] "Take the Time" [pers.] I write poems for different occasions. I do it for fun. I guess I inherited this talent from my mother. I'd written a poem for a friend, Betty, who was retiring. She took it home and framed it. She inspired me to enter your contest. I never dreamed it would go anywhere! Time is passing by so swiftly, that if we don't take the time today—tomorrow may be too late. It only takes a second to give a smile, a hug, a handshake, whisper a prayer or show someone you care.

C., ASHLEY
[a.] Tivertown, RI [title] "Love" [pers.] Friends mean everything to me. Getting into arguments with friends is the worse thing for me. I had gotten into an argument with my friend, Pete; I felt dreadful. I wrote the poem "Love" because it was truly how I felt. Poetry and writing things down is a way I express myself. I think that writing my thoughts and affection down helps me get through my emotional problems. Composing how I felt about Pete helped me work out my problems. The statement, "Everything is okay in the end, and if it's not, then it's not the end," is precise.

CANNON, ELLEN
[a.] Naperville, IL [title] "Masters" [pers.] A resident of the greater Chicago area, and mother of four young adults, Ellen is a poet and visual artist by affinity; a heath care professional by choice and necessity. Author of more than one hundred poems, she attempts to give an adult voice to the child-spirit residing within the secluded corners of her heart.

CASIANO, VINCENT
[a.] Albrightsville, PA [title] "Hurt So Good" [pers.] I wrote "Hurt So Good" for my sister, Virginia. She, like many others, loves someone who isn't healthy for her. She is one of many people who hurt themselves in hopes of finding reciprocated love. I meant this poem to be a wake-up call for her, and others. Although people often say, "You can't choose who you love," you can choose to love yourself, and loving yourself begins with not allowing people to mistreat your heart. If I can help at least one person love themself, then I've succeeded.

CELIA, SOPHIA
[a.] Wilmington, NC [title] "The Observer" [pers.] The artist and the poet share the gift and the obligation to serve as truth's observers, to open the door to the light. My husband Saant, a fine artist and art instructor, and I work as one toward the plane of a new reality. We are blessed with a son, Sam, and two daughters, Theresa and Bonnie, all of whom are working toward that vision.

CHANNEL, DIANA
[a.] Eustis, FL [title] "Love" [pers.] I am a hopeless romantic, never giving up on love or the power that it holds within itself to bring sunshine to a life that has seen so many dark nights of endless tears. I would like to thank my two dearest friends, Bijosh Mathew and Jen Brown, for sharing my passion through their loving friendship. They've both brought to my life, as my loving husband Don and daughter Carolyn have.

CHAUVETTE, RAYMOND
[a.] Warwick, RI [title] "Dante's Question" [pers.] My poem was inspired by my fiance Melanie, to whom I give my thanks and all my love too. "Dante's Question" has never been changed. It stands the same now as the day it was written. I could make an attempt to explain my poem, but I would rather not. I believe that the beauty of poetry is formed not only by the writer, but the reader who changes it to his own thoughts. Poetry has no limits, nor does the writer or reader. Think what you would like.

CHRISTIANS, MAXINE
[a.] Agoura Hills, CA [title] "Missing You" [pers.] I'm Maxine Christians, and I'm seventeen years old, I love to hang out with my friends. I moved to America from Kimberly, South Africa in 1998. It was a huge change for me. That's what the poem is about, about missing my home country. I started writing poetry at age thirteen. I just liked messing around with words. I've loved it ever since. It's my way of expressing my feelings.

CHURCH, HELEN
[a.] Birmingham, AL [title] "Life's 9/11/01" [pers.] I have always loved poetry, and started writing short poems when I was a young girl, at the encouragement of my precious family. This poem came to me after the aftermath of the crumbling of the Twin Towers. When I saw on television the heroic efforts of all the crews and helpers involved during this tragedy; this poem just flowed in my mind like water in a stream. I was able to finish it in no time.

CLERGET, DAVID
[a.] Muncie, IN [title] "Night of Sapphires" [pers.] "Night of Sapphires" was written for a very special friend of mine. On a crisp, fall night on the B.S.U. campus, she captured my heart in much the same way that I captured her here. Her eyes, so blue, were like sapphires shining into my soul.

COLBY, FREDERICK

[a.] Port Orange, FL [title] "Roots" [pers.] My wife liked to have me read poetry and recite from memory my favorite poets. My pilgrimage to Great Britain inspired me to write for my genealogy hobby. My name, Colby, dates back to 1590 and has traveled from America to the moon.

COMER, MISSY

[a] Kansas City, KS [title] "U.S.A." [pers.] Wherever I am, I am always writing a poem. Writing poems just takes my mind off everything else, it's really relaxing. A lot of people may think a poem is boring, but if you just take your time to read it, you might be able to relate to what the poet might or might not be saying. By writing this poem I was saying that, hey, this is the United States. We are going to be strong and stick together till the end, no matter what. I hope that you enjoyed "U.S.A." and shout what you believe.

COMERFORD, DANIELLE

[a.] Abington, MA [title] "Sammy" [pers.] Poetry is my way of dealing with the problems I face with my friends and family. Each poem of mine has a unique problem. I hope with my poem "Sammy" it shows how others feel.

CONTRERAS, NELSON

[a.] Fort Hood, TX [title] "Father" [pers.] My dad is an American soldier. His deployment overseas made my family and I really sad. One night my Mom told my brothers and I to write something about how we felt when my Dad was gone. That is when I started writing. I wanted to write a poem about my father and everything he has done. In this poem, I thank him for everything he has given me. I am really proud of myself and my writing. I hope my father is too because he was part of Operation Enduring Freedom and I will never forget September 11th.

COONTZ, PETER

[a.] San Clemente, CA [title] "Angel of Light" [pers.] I see so many of us condemning each other, and ourselves, for what we create, what we think, what we say, and what we do. This seems to be such a waste of our own creative potential, to create negativity toward someone who's creating something that works for them. I say create what you want, and if someone sees you as a devil for it, maybe that's merely an acknowledgement for being courageous in your creativity, where they are stopped by their fears.

COPE, LESLEY

[a.] Baldock, United Kingdom [title] "If" [pers.] "If" was written for John shortly after his tragic death in March 1995. John was everything to me; we were to be married in August. A few nights before he died, we argued. That was the last I spoke to him, until the night I found him dead. "If" expresses my guilt over the argument we had, not realizing I would never see him again. It also expresses what I truly hope John knew—that without him I am desolate, and that all I want to do is reach out to him and hold him again.

COSENTINO, EMILY

[a.] Elyria, OH [title] "Stranger" [pers.] My poetry is the way I can express the pain within myself. My poem, "Stranger," represents my feelings to be near my father. Knowing he'll never visit is the worst feeling ever, especially for me, since I'm only twelve years old.

COWELL, B. "BABS"

[a.] Brainerd, MN [title] "On Friendship" [pers.] This is only the third poem I have written. I write when I am inspired, usually when I'm alone. This particular one is about a friendship between two very special people in my life; a friendship I hope will be forever, no matter what our flaws.

CRAWFORD, JAKAE

[a.] Houston, TX [title] "It Is You That I Seek" [pers.] This was the first poetry contest I entered. Therefore, I wanted a grand, yet, pure introduction of Jakae K. Crawford, the poet. This poem comes from the center of my being; it represents the essence of who I am. Many thanks to the family for your encouragement and support.

CSRMAN, GERALD

[a.] Lexington, KY [title] "What of Trouble and Sorrow" [pers.] On April 26, 1992 my Lord allowed me to survive a cerebral aneurysm. My poetry is one way I witness my faith and love for Jesus Christ.

CULVER, TABATHA

[a.] Guyton, GA [title] "It Could Never Happen to Me" [pers.] I was blessed with two wonderful gifts; poetry and my son Tucker. Tucker is the inspiration behind this poem. I learned I was pregnant at age fourteen. I was then faced with many decisions. I composed this poem in hopes that other young mothers could relate to my situation. My family also promotes my creativity. My brother, Brian, sister, Leighann, parents, Tamberly and Dennis, and last, but not least, my numerous family members; The Allers and the Hemphills of Dodson and Winnfield, Louisiana. What was first a mistake, is now a miracle. Thank you God.

CYHOWSKI, MARION

[a.] Ludlow, VT [title] "Mother's Love" [pers.] After many years of drinking and abuse, I finally got sober. My son and I became separated for a period of time, we were homeless. The only thing that inspired me to keep putting one foot in front of the other was remembering his smile, his laugh, his words, "I love you, Mommy." Now, nearly twenty years later, recalling those words still brings tears to my eyes. I've watched him struggle through times of injustice, put one foot in front of the other, and tell me that I'm his inspiration. All the writing which I've done has come from his encouraging words.

DANKO, MELANIE

[a.] Brooklyn, NY [title] "Orphan" [pers.] This poem was inspired by a Picasso painting. Poetry is my release for emotions, happy or sad. Many things inspire me to write, sometimes music, sometimes personal experience. Writing is a very personal thing for me. What I write is a part of me.

DASHIELL, ERIN

[a.] Fayetteville, NC [title] "Mother" [pers.] This poem is special to me because it is a poem for my mother. She means the world to me because she is always there for me when I need her. She is also my best friend. I would have never written this poem if my 10th grade teacher Mrs. Carraquillo had not been having a Mother's Day celebration. She made us write a poem for our mothers. Right now I am in the 11th grade and on my free time I like to write stories. I was surprised when I received the letter in the mail about my poem because I didn't expect something like this to happen. I really can't write poems, and I just entered my poem for fun. I had never thought about winning or anything.

DAUGHERITY, MICHAEL

[a.] The Dalles, OR [title] "My Paradox of Love" [pers.] My writing, my soul and my spirit of life all come from my mom, Marlys.

DAULTON, JULI

[a.] Portland, OR [title] "Who's to Blame" [pers.] This poem is very personal. It is a reflection of the violence, corruption, and injustice I witnessed growing up in Los Angeles. I have always believed that the moment we stop blaming one another and become accountable for our own actions, we become the solution to the many problems of the world.

DAVIS, KATHLEEN

[a.] Great Bend, KS [title] "My Mystery" [pers.] I live in Great Bend, Kansas with my husband, Mark and my children, Jessica, Kaili and Aidan. I wrote this poem when I was fourteen years old, along with many others that I've kept in a folder all these years. I've written other poems, but my earlier attempts hold a special place in my heart because they reminds me of my youth. Years later, my children are healthy, my husband loves me and I no longer wonder about life, but cherish it.

DAVIS, MELANIE

[a.] San Diego, CA [title] "Haiku" [pers.] This poem was written when I was an eigth grade student. I loved it. It came from my soul. As an English assignment, it was well received by my teacher. I am now forty-seven.

DE YURRE, ISABELLA

[a.] Hialeah, FL [title] "The Hole" [pers.] Poetry is very special to me. All my life I've been involved in the arts. However, poetry is more than just a form of art. It lets me express how I feel in more ways than that of a painting. Poetry has developed my personality in amazing ways. I write what I feel, and that to me is what's most valuable.

DEBUQUE, MAX

[a.] Beloit, WI [title] "Don't Feel Sorry for Me" [pers.] This poem is a statement by a guy who is down and out, and is feeling fed up with his life. He doesn't like how it has turned out, but isn't willing to change, so he is asking for the easy way out. The title, "Don't Feel Sorry for Me," is my view on people like him. He has been dealt a raw deal, has the ability to change but won't. So don't feel sorry for him.

DEMPSEY, TAMMY

[a.] Central, SC [title] "American Pride" [pers.] Writing is a way I express my true feelings. This poem is written to support of the president, the victims and their families. To my family: Dad and Mom, Orville and Pearl Colegrove, I love you very much. Dale and Sarah, thanks for brightening my life. Danny and Barbara, I miss you both. My husband, Ewell, thank you for always showing me love and your unconditional support. You are the love of my life. Special thanks to Toby Keith for your song "Courtesy of the Red, White and Blue," it gave me the push I needed to send this poem in.

DESPEAUX, ELIZABETH

[a.] Trinidad, CO [title] "Searching" [pers.] I wrote this poem one night when I was feeling lonely and pensive. I needed a way to vent frustration; writing this poem was the cure. Poetry, to me, is one of the best forms of expression. I can write things that may seem like useless garble, but in another light, it may make perfect sense. Writing poems, is a very enjoyable and stimulating process. I enjoy writing and reading poetry, very, very much.

DETCHEV, ROUMEN

[a.] Pasadena, CA [title] "The Sky" [pers.] I believe poetry is an excellent way to express one's innermost feelings. Poetry with meaning and feeling can move you and make you feel the writer's mood and emotions. In this poem, I am facing the decisions to succeed or fail, to move on, or to stay the same. A person will always have obstacles that will attempt to prevent them from achieving their goals. This poem is about what people do to overcome these obstacles and reach their goals.

DHAWAN, SHANTI

[a.] Gaithersburg, MD [title] "Fear" [pers.] Writing has been a part of me ever since I was a little girl. While I plan to write a short story or a piece of creative non-fiction, when a good idea crosses my mind, poems just happen. Whatever the genre, I love to write. The person who inspired and motivated me the most to write was my father. I wish you were here, Appa, though I'm sure that you know my writings are getting published.

DICKSON, CANDICE
[a.] Bowie, MD [title] "I Found You" [pers.] I am a thirteen year old, eighth grader at St. Mary's Catholic School in Landover Hills, Maryland. My English teacher had been teaching me different writing styles over the last three years, including poetry. I wrote this poem to express how I feel about someone very close to me, my boyfriend. My hobbies include sports, Girl Scouts, chorus and band. I will continue writing because my Mom tells me that I can do anything if I put my mind to it.

DIOKNO, EDELWINA
[a.] Los Angeles, CA [title] "A Piece of Life" [pers.] Half-asleep, tired and longing for rest, I started to write a poem, hoping to play with words associated with cooking and food. I must have dozed off while writing this because I ended up describing what I felt about people who are afraid of making choices and commitments; people who are important to me, people like me.

DITTMER, DANIELLE
[a.] Michigan City, IN [title] "Darkness" [pers.] Writing is what gets me through my adolescent stress. I wrote this poem with built-up anger and sadness, and the burden of family dysfunctions. I was going through one of the many times that I've reached my last straw. Instead of letting it be my last straw, I wrote about it. I hope that when people read my poem, they can relate to how I felt when I wrote it. Perhaps they've felt the same way before.

DOLAN, CHERYL
[a.] Noblesville, IN [title] "What I Am?" [pers.] I have always loved to read and write poetry. I feel you can express a lot through words and writing. With an upcoming marriage, this is the way I see the symbol which is a wedding ring.

DOOLEY, JOSEPH
[a.] Portland, TX [title] "The End" [pers.] I've loved writing since I was a kid, and short stories and poems are my favorite. "The End" satirizes the inherited fear of the end of the world, which all people have. I think the strength of this poem lies in the fact that it blends drama and humor. That's what poetry is all about, combining elements to make the entire work of art appealing to a variety of people. I love to write. I hope in the future I produce art with this kind of quality.

DOTSON, CARISSA
[a.] East Haven, CT [title] "Empty Bottles" [pers.] I'm Carissa Dotson, a fourteen-year old freshman at East Haven High School. My mother is a recovering alcoholic, and I currently live with my grandmother. I love to write, I always have. Even though I want to be a pediatric psychiatrist, I also plan on writing in my spare time.

DOTSON, DEBORAH
[a.] Grundy, VA [title] "Sweet Morsels" [pers.] This poem is very special to me. I enjoy expressing myself through poetry. Inside my soul is a spring of lovely and wonderful thoughts as well as memories. They are like presents as well as memories. I began writing two years ago after being diagnosed with cancer. I had just lost my oldest brother, Gary Taylor. This poem is in memory of him. I am a wife, mother, daughter, sister and Christian. I give God all the glory for my poetry. To all family; Gary, Mom, Chad, April, Wesley and Gary. Thanks for inspiring my life in Christ's service.

DOWD, CRYSTAL
[a.] Orangeburg, SC [title] "Spring Time" [pers.] It was quite ironic that I was selected as a semi-finalist in a poetry contest. Poetry does not play a big part in my life. I like singing. In fact, I am enrolled in William J. Clark's chorus. The poem, "Spring Time," came right off the top of my head. That was the first topic I had in mind when I was entering this contest. I guess the only reason I entered a poetry contest was because of my mom, Christine. She inspired me to partake in a variety of events. I look forward to being in the final competition. I wish every poet the best of luck.

DROLET, MONICA
[a.] Humble, TX [title] "Remember Always" [pers.] I wrote this poem for my son, who was in a nearly fatal car accident. My family has lost a brother, mom, two uncles, a cousin and an aunt these past two years. These words came from my heart to all that suffer such personal tragedies throughout their lifetime.

DUCHARDT, COURTNEY
[a.] Halt, MO [title] "As a Child . . ." [pers.] I really appreciate my parents' support of my writing, and want to thank them. This poem is about growing up, and how sometimes, in their own way, kids are wiser than adults.

DUNN, JUDITH
[a.] Goddard, KS [title] "A Place That Feels Like a Child" [pers.] Rising early, I poured a cup of coffee and sat down to put my thoughts on paper. My parents separated when I was two, and Mom raised Donald, Marcia, and myself. We lost our beloved mother in 1999 and after a long absence, my father moved back to Kansas about a year after Mom's passing. This day, Sunday, March 10, 2002 was my birthday and Dad was cooking me a birthday dinner, including a cake with my name on it and candles to make a wish. This being the first birthday party given me by my father, childhood feelings of loss flooded my mind the evening before. By morning, I had written "A Place That Feels Like a Child." It was my fifty-eigth birthday.

DURAN, JOHN
[a.] Santee, CA [title] "You're the Apple of My Eye" [pers.] My daughter inspired me to write this. This poem is for her, Janice Duran.

DURBIN, LETONYA
[a.] Philadelphia, PA [title] "Woman of Valor" [pers.] Ms. Durbin is a licensed minister, certified Christian counselor, writer, business owner and consultant. In these roles, she understands the transformational power of the written and spoken word. Writing is an integral part of her life. It is her joy and her legacy, and through it she has discovered her voice. Her father, now deceased, was her mentor. Her mother and her sister are her most enthusiastic cheerleaders, and her fiance, Alvin L. Clark, Jr., is her constant encourager, motivator, and biggest fan.

DUVAL, RUTH
[a.] Ashland, OR [title] "Counting Rhyme—on a Summer's Walk with My Child" [pers.] The images are from a coastal California city where our family lived for a time. Christopher, my son, is now an actor in Ashland. At the time he was just learning to count. He can now count higher than ten!

DYE, TEIGHA
[a.] Black Rock, AR [title] "A Place Called Heaven" [pers.] My name is Teigha Dye. I'm thirteen and in the eighth grade in my hometown in Arkansas. I wrote this poem for my very religious grandmother on her birthday. I'm a regular teenage girl. I listen to my radio, talk on the phone, and gossip on and on to my friends. Heaven, family and friends are my biggest motivations. One day I hope to read this poem to Jesus in Heaven.

EITREM, ARIANA
[a.] Birmingham, MI [title] "Drowsy Past" [pers.] My name is Ariana and I write poetry to express my life in words that are very hard to understand what I mean. For instance, each line of "Drowsy Past" has a story behind it. People look at it as art, while I look at it as a journal entry.

ELGIN, STEPHANIE
[a.] Virginia Beach, VA [title] "love is like . . ." [pers.] When my ex-boyfriend Trevor left I wrote this poem. What we had was special, but when he left, it was very sad. But life goes on.

ELISSEN, CHRISTINA
[a.] Tilburg, Netherlands [title] "Trust" [pers.] Hello, dear poem reader. I wrote this poem to tell you that no matter how hard your life may be or how unhappy you are, there is always a way out of it. There is someone that loves you unconditionally, God! He only wants the best for you. You only have to ask Him for help and He will show you how you can be free. He will lift you above all your pain and hurt and fill your heart with love and joy! You are never alone. He loves you and waits for you to ask Him for help. Good luck on your journey, you'll be fine!

ELLIS, LINDSEY
[a.] Honolulu, HI [title] "Sheri" [pers.] This poem was written for a secret crush I had at the time. I wanted to reveal my true feelings to Sheri, and this poem gave me the courage and confidence to do that. Poetry is a great way for me to express my thoughts, ideas, and feelings with others.

ELLWOOD, JEREMY
[a.] Kalamazoo, MI [title] "Disbanded" [pers.] I have an Associates degree in Theatre Performance and Dance and a B.A. in Theatre Lighting Design. There is nothing more important in the world than truth, and the arts are nothing but. This poem solemnly danced in my head the day Mia left for Ireland. No worries. She's back. May the Goddess and God bless you all in their right.

EMERY, NICHOLAS
[a.] Wyoming, MI [title] "Daylight" [pers.] This poem is dedicated to Dionna Karczynski. My name is Nicholas James Emery, I'm twenty-four years old and love music. To me music is the way to Heaven. If you people could only know this girl I speak of, you too would love her to death. This is for you Dionna, only the moon separates us now.

ENGELHARDT, DARIEN
[a.] Christiana, DE [title] "Memory" [pers.] "Memory" is the very idea that where you are in life can change. It is the vision of eyes becoming wide open to possibilities. Someone can be locked into a routine and see no alternative. Then fate steps in and shows him there is more. By way of various geographical trails, someone was traveling the same route in life until we crashed into each other. That person saw a light in me. They gave me the strength, encouragement, and love to realize those dreams. The unity I have with that person gives peace and completeness to my restless soul.

ESTICK, PATRICIA
[a.] Brooklyn, NY [title] "The Battle Cry" [pers.] This poem was written when I was at a very low point in my life. It was a period of such despair that I felt the urge to withdraw from life itself. Then I felt the Lord inspiring me to write "The Battle Cry." I hope this poem will be an inspiration to others to keep holding on through life's struggles.

FACUSSE, MARIO
[a.] Melbourne, FL [title] "Why?" [pers.] This is dedicated to Mom, Dad, Tania, Grace, Monica, Erika, and Jessica, and to all the people in my life

that have helped me survive my many troubles and pains. I would also like to thank God for putting up with me through all these years, and never leaving me in the dark.

FADDEN, MINDY

[a.] Tracy, CA [title] "My Smile" [pers.] One night while my boyfriend and I were talking he said one of the sweetest things to me. This inspired me to write a poem about it. This poem expresses my love to one person and I hope that others can relate to this poem as I do, and share it with the people they care deeply for.

FAW, JARED

[a.] Raleigh, NC [title] "With Love in Our Hearts" [pers.] There are times in life when the heart sings and love casually flows from it. This poem is dedicated, with love, to Martha Smith, for everything she has done for me. It was inspired by Virgo Mortensen. Thank you both for everything.

FLEMING, PAIGE

[a.] Haslett, MI [title] "Night Sky" [pers.] Poetry has its own dimension. It is like travelling to a new world. Writing poems is a way for me to get away from the everyday things I do. I started writing poems about two years ago and "Night Sky" is by far my best one. Finishing a poem is so refreshing and wonderful I don't think I will ever stop writing them.

FLORENTINO, DOMINIC

[a.] San Diego, CA [title] "The Young Men of All" [pers.] Poetry is my spontaneous burst of life; it comes quick and withdraws even quicker than I would like most times. Poetry is a surreal dialect that, translated into any language, transcends the boundaries of the mind. It is writing in its purest form, my confession room, a way of relaying my fears, my regrets, hopes and desires; a way of apologizing or venting frustration with the world. The next best thing I can think of is surfing, but that's a different story.

FORMBY, E. RALPH

[a.] Lafayette, LA [title] "The Rain" [pers.] I wrote this poem in 1961 when I was a junior in high school. Forty one years later, it still gives me the same "feel good feeling" as when I originally composed it. I hope you get that same feeling when you read this short verse.

FOX, VERONICA

[a.] Orillia, Canada [title] "The Flight of the Dove" [pers.] "The Flight of the Dove" is in honor and recognition of a very special person, my grandmother. Always encouraging me to reach for my greatest of dreams and aspirations, she believed in me long before I ever did. She had the rare courage of being able to share her weaknesses as well as her strengths. She did not live a life free from challenge and adversity, she always met each one boldly and head on. She was the foundation upon which our family was built and I will be forever grateful that she chose to share her journey through life with me.

FRANCO, ERLINDA

[a.] Brooklyn, NY [title] "Unforgettable Memories in My Seventh Floor" [pers.] I've had health problems since I was a child. Illnesses were no strangers in my life. Moments I am down or feel blessed, I resort to writing poetry to release my feelings. I love reading and writing poems. I wrote the "Unforgettable Memories in My Seventh Floor" when I was admitted for Chronic Inflamatory Demyelinating Polyneuropathy (CIDP) for twenty-six days to the Long Island College Hospital (LICH) in Brooklyn, New York. I was greatly inspired by the overwhelming attention, care, and untiring services extended to me by the medical staff, especially Dr. Roger Kula, the head of MDA-Neurology. I thank the Lord for the medical staff and personnel, my family, relatives and friends. They are heaven-sent, my angels in disguise. I dedicate this poem to them.

FREELAND, CARRIE

[a.] Gaylord, MI [title] "Seasons of Emotions" [pers.] I am the eighteen-year old daughter of Dr. Theodore and Susan Freeland of Gaylord, Michigan. I currently attend Albian College, where I am majoring in Biology. I play on the Albian basketball team. My hobbies include singing, playing sports, writing songs and poetry. I write about what I am feeling. It helps me express my feelings to other people.

FREITAS, BRANDI

[a.] Chamlin, MN [title] "Dying" [pers.] I wrote this poem after my grandmother died in 2001. Tough as it was, I got through it by writing poetry and with my family's support.

FULLER, KATHY

[a.] South Pasadena, CA [title] "Helpless Hoping" [pers.] Kathy Fuller is a professor of education at a private college in southern California. She lives with her daughter, Samantha, and an assortment of furry friends. She enjoys painting, writing, riding horses, golf, and volunteering with her dogs as pet therapists at a local retirement home.

GAINES, RACHEL

[a.] Salisbury, NC [title] "Our Nation's Mighty Strength" [pers.] I wrote "Our Nation's Mighty Strength" in the month after September 11, 2001 through divine inspiration. It is in honor of Him, and in memory of all the precious ones whose lives were lost on that tragic day. Dear people, as you read this poem, I hope it will remind you of how blessed we really are as a nation, and that our blessings and strengths come from Him, whose guiding hand is always with us.

GALBRAITH, RUTHANN

[a.] Dewitt, MI [title] "Bless Our Home" [pers.] My inspiration for this poem is related to my personal experiences. Whether young or old, there are no promises that life will go on, not only for us, but also for those who share our world. I hope my poem will encourage the individuals who read it to experience life in the moment, to focus on what truly is important. In this way, we may behold the joy of life and in the process make memories that can live until the end of time.

GALLARDO, MARIA

[a] Sydney, Australia [title] "Through the Eyes of Miracle" [pers.] This poem represents my life, a life of challenges, triumphs, and sorrow. Through poetry, people get the opportunity to view life through its windows of feelings and emotions. The word "Miracle" in this poem has two significant meanings: firstly, I believe that my life experiences have been miraculous. Secondly, to many people, I am referred to by my real name, Maricel, which rearranged, actually spells "Miracle." Everyone's life is filled with miracles. It is just a matter of searching for their true meaning.

GALLIMORE, SYDNEY

[a.] Greer, SC [title] "When War Is Calling" [pers.] I wrote this poem, to let out all of my emotions and to let everyone know how I felt. I used the form of a letter because I wanted to let all of those who are fighting for us in the Middle East that I know and understand what they are going through.

GARCIA-LARA, ALMA

[a.] Houston, TX [title] "I Cried" [pers.] The reason behind this poem is to thank my God almighty for delivering me from cancer. I cried, and He listened. To Him be the glory always!

GARFINKLE, SHARI

[a.] Long Beach, NY [title] "Home" [pers.] I always found that poetry was a good way to get my feelings out during tough times. Everyone needs an outlet to express themselves. Poetry is one of mine, as is music and art.

GIBSON, TAMMIE

[a.] Davenport, IA [title] "A Mother's Prayer" [pers.] Leaving my kids, Brianna and Michael, behind with my parents to head to Palmer College of Chiropractic was extremely difficult. My passion and belief for chiropractic and the need to give my kids and disabled parents a better life facilitated my decision. I wrote this poem to ease the pain in my heart that only a mother knows. I give thanks to my family; Robert, Ann, Bobby, and Jason Gibson, my mentor Dr. Celine Williamson, my dear friends Robert Loeu and Dr. Victor Flynn, my boyfriend Chad Meirhaeghe and my support team, Gina Meirhaeghe, Alicia Farrell and Drew Neville.

GLORE, KATHIE

[a.] Hickory, NC [title] "For Members Only" [pers.] This poem was written in hopes to bring awareness that there are people who have found themselves homeless because of situations they had no control over. The homeless population is growing. Sometimes we get so caught up in our own lives, we don't see the simple things. I hope to put my poem with music. I am a guitar player and singer.

GOFF, SARAH

[a.] Redlands, CA [title] "God's Mixed Palette" [pers.] Everyone hears the music of the universe and converts it into their own creative energy. Some might write songs, while others might sing them. Poetry is the music my soul hears. Maybe I am only a conduit, relaying an already sung universal song. The poem "God's Mixed Palette" seemed to find me and use my pen as it's voice. I am like others seeking the truth and looking for God. If He does exist, then this poem is a tribute to Him. If He does not exist then let this poem sit next to all of the other fairy tales in the archives of time.

GOLDSMITH, COREY

[a.] Petoskey, MI [title] "Mother" [pers.] Though I didn't realize it for a long time, my poetry was a release. I'm bi-polar and have used a lot of drugs. My poetry helped me through my drug addiction. I wrote this poem alone in my room. It defines my mom to the t. My mom always lied, always stole, and is a hateful person. Maybe someday she will learn only love can makes you feel good. I'd like to say, "I love you" to Stephanie Neal. Take it day by day. Have fun. Party. Love everyone; it's not that hard. Love is what makes us, love is what keeps us alive.

GONZALEZ, ALONZO

[a.] Fresno, CA [title] "Stress" [pers.] I'm living in Fresno, CA. I've had a desire to write since I was fifteen years old. Poetry has always been a part of my life. It allows me to express myself when I can't verbally. Sometimes I feel mute without a pen. One day I woke up in a rush to get to work. I ran down the stairs and jumped onto the bus. I had so much on my mind. The next thing I remember was walking down the street with two large black garbage bags towards the laundry mat. That's when I realized life goes by so fast.

GONZALEZ, AZALEA

[a.] Modesto, CA [title] "Trees Remind Me" [pers.] I wrote this poem for my Aunt Irene who was ill at the time. It was my way of telling her not to worry, that she would be fine because she is strong. I write poems to express my feelings.

GONZALEZ, LIDIA
[a.] Astoria, NY [title] "Silence" [pers.] The words in my poem helped me express something which I could not bring myself to say aloud. They served also to legitimize what I was going through at the time. I am happy to be able to share them with others, as they spent years tucked away in the back of an old notebook.

GONZALEZ, MAYRA
[a.] Torrance, CA [title] "Why Must We Live" [pers.] Poetry has become my life and my personal therapy. This poem describes my feelings on how humans today act in our society of madness and destruction. We don't realize how much we suffer because of our own ignorance of what's going on in the world. Alas, I want to thank L.D., Susy, and all the people who have inspired and motivated me to write.

GONZALEZ, SUSANNA
[a.] Hialeah Gardens, FL [title] "Love You Still" [pers.] I've never dreamed of sharing my poetry with the world, but now that it is a reality, I'm glad all my tears shed when writing "Love You Still" were worth the happiness brought to me today. I would like to thank my mother, Alina, and my father, Rafael, for supporting my dream.

GOSLING, CRAIG
[a.] Indianapolis, IN [title] "Ancient Secrets" [pers.] All my poems contain lessons from science. "Ancient Secret" deals with the human instincts that determine who we are and why we love, hate, and forgive. Instincts, that assured the survival of our ancient ancestors, do not always serve us as well today. Our passions are too seldom recognized for what they are, and too seldom controlled. They offer worldly bliss or untold agony; the choice is ours. All past and current human conflict, including terrorism and genocide, is fueled by those ancient secrets that lie within us. Superstition may be beyond scientific inquiry, but our DNA is not.

GRAHAM, MARY
[a.] Darien, GA [title] "Family Buttercup" [pers.] My children's father was killed at the young age of thirty-five. My parents and two brothers, several in laws have passed, and a beloved sister has died. But when my fifteen-year old nephew was killed, I wrote this poem. It has brought me comfort many times. I mostly stay at home now and do some sewing and quilting.

GRAY, NOBEL
[a.] Athens, OH [title] "Bat" [pers.] I am an extremely intelligent, schizo-effect in recovery whose hobbies include reading and weight-lifting.

GREEN, BRIANNA
[a.] Gig Harbor, WA [title] "America" [pers.] My name is Brianna Green. I am nine years old. At the age of two, I come to know the Lord as my personal Savior. Since that time, I have enjoyed learning what talents and gifts the Lord has given to me. The Lord has allowed me to become a prayer warrior, and he has helped me to excel in piano, drawing, and poetry. I also enjoy reading, swimming, and karate.

GRIFFITH, CAITLIN
[a.] Cordova, TN [title] "You" [pers.] Hi, I am Caitlin Griffith. I believe that my poetry comes from the stresses I have been through in my life, like my parents' breaking up. I try to channel this into something that is beautiful. Also, I would not be writing poetry if it were not for my mom. She is always looking out for me.

GUTIERREZ, TRICIA
[a.] Miami, FL [title] "Temptation" [pers.] For all those who can relate to my poem, I hope you do not give into temptation, for I, at sixteen years of age, am gratefully, a recovering addict.

H., JOHN
[a.] Winfield, KS [title] "Teresa Helen Becker" [pers.] I am an award winning poet whose intention is to write simple rhyming poems so all may enjoy and understand!

HACKETT, ASHLEY
[a.] Katy, TX [title] "Because of You" [pers.] I want people to know, right now, that all of us are going to face problems. I want people to know, right now, that there is no magical part to life. I also want people to know that we are in charge of our lives, and we can't count on other people to change them for us. This poem helped me realize all those things and so has *Letters from the Soul*.

HAMPTON, LINDA
[a.] Indianapolis, IN [title] "The Breakfast" [pen] Indalay [pers.] I love listening to people because words are so powerful in understanding who they are, and what they feel. In writing "The Breakfast" I had friends over to eat. One asked, "How did you make those eggs so good?" I excused myself and began writing. I have written many poems and turned one into a children's book about a child discovering his shadow. The artwork has been completed, but I don't know how to get published. I love writing poems and short stories. I am blessed with a good husband, Dave, daughter Moritta, son Stephen and five grandchildren.

HANLAN, JONATHAN
[a.] Port Saint Lucie, FL [title] "Death Awaits" [pers.] I thank God for my life, my talent for rhyming, and everything I've experienced. I thank my parents and family for the sacrifices they've made, my friends for their criticism and support and my teachers throughout life, for what they've taught me. Thanks to V. Hernandez for introducing me to the Poetry.com web site. I want to thank Hon. R. Marley, R. Price, S. Henriques, E. Simmons, T. Shakur, C. Wallace, N. Jones, and S. Carter for inspiration. And a special thanks to A.M. Brocon, for being there for me in times of need.

HANNIGAN, SUSAN
[a.] Canton, MI [title] "Full Circle" [pers.] This poem is dedicated to my father, Patrick McGuire. It acknowledges how the years have come full circle since his death. It has been a year of firsts without him and a difficult journey, but we all made it through. We miss him greatly. My father was a scholar and a gentleman who loved to read and would be so pleased to see his name in print in one of his beloved books. So here is your name, Dad, finally in print. I hope you like the poem, love you always.

HARRIS, BRYON
[a.] Lexington, NC [title] "Questions" [pers.] This poem is from a point in my life where it seemed like every breath was a chore. I see myself as being blessed with the ability to express my feelings and emotions through verse, a gift I received from my wonderful mother. I am both proud and humbled that I have shared part of my soul with the world.

HARRIS, CLAUDETTE
[a.] Bronx, NY [title] "Time" [pers.] This is dedicated to my two uncles and three aunts who all died in the span of two years. I though would have had more time together. Valaster Harris, Michael Harris, Hilarie Harris, Priscilla Buntin, and Ohalda Brade; I miss you all so much.

HARRISON, JENNIFER
[a.] Johnson City, TN [title] "Questioning Soul" [pers.] Love is the source, the substance of all that is past, present, and future. Listen to the love inside—then speak, act, and think according to the love within, and you will always be in alliance with your soul. I have had so many special souls surrounding me on this journey. It is not possible to name everyone, however, a special thank you, with love, to Jason, my soul mate and husband, Justin and Lorelei, my joy, my children, and Vicki, a kindred soul. Thank you all for your blessings.

HARTMAN, BETHANY
[a.] Deer Park, TX [title] "Never Fade" [pers.] "Never Fade" was written less than a month after September 11th, 2001, when I was fifteen years old. I didn't even intend to write it. I was sitting in my front yard, and noticed our flag waving in the breeze. It made me think. In September, our nation was attacked. The intent was to tear America down and break us up. But, if anything, it only brought us closer together, and made us stronger as a country; a country I am proud to call home. Jesus Christ, thank you for being my inspiration; may it be for your glory.

HARTSUFF, SAMANTHA
[a.] East Lansing, MI [title] "The Hartsuff Six" [pers.] This poem is about my family and I. We love sports and I especially like to play soccer. My new love is our puppy, Sophie. I am in the 4th grade. The family I have loves to swim and eat ice cream together. I am a lucky girl.

HASH, STEPHANY
[a.] Carson City, NV [title] "Regret" [pers.] I wrote this poem for four different people in my life! These people are my aunt, my uncle, my grandfather, and my grandmother. All were lost within a year. I miss them and this is a poem from my soul. Poetry is my way of saying goodbye. All of them are included in different aspects of the poem. I wrote this poem for anyone who cares or relates. I hope you enjoy it!

HENDRY, JONATHAN
[a.] Golden, CO [title] "Roses and Violets" [pers.] My thanks to my parents for doing their part, and for my three brothers whom I love with all my heart. As for my granddad and grandma whom are still there, I do so miss thine chats. For my aunts and uncles and cousins alike, many happy days have been spent. Well, adieu to all whom I love, bestow upon others this kindness, and don't forget the simple ones out there!

HERBECK, JOSEPH
[a.] Yuma, AZ [title] "Marine's Christmas" [pers.] Sitting in the barracks watching television, I came across a show where poets were performing their poetry. I was immediately inspired to write, and I went online and submitted this piece. I am in the U.S. Marine Corps and have been for several years. This piece is about my first experience away from home for Christmas, and it had a huge impact on my life. Where I went or what I did I still cannot say, but the experience changed me forever. Poetry is something that helps keep me alive, and this is just an expression of life.

HESLIN, PRISCILLA
[a.] Brooksville, ME [title] "Midnight Angels" [pers.] I have been writing poetry for twenty years and there has always been a spiritual base to the writing. I am a psychotherapist and only recently have begun taking my poetry more seriously. This poem was written for a husband who had lost his wife at the age of fifty-two. Since then, I have sent it to family and friends who have lost a loved one.

HICKEY, KATHY
[a.] Arlington Heights, IL [title] "A Definition of a Man" [pers.] This poem is written in memory of my father, Ed, a great man. Poetry is a way to bring beauty to a sometimes hard life. I've had four poems published through the International Library of Poetry. In the future, I hope to get a book of my poems published.

HIGGINBOTHAM, JUNE

[a.] Council Bluffs, IA [title] "Life Is but a Blink" [pers.] In celebration of thirty years of marriage, seven children and a wealth of emotions; I dedicate this poem to my beloved late husband, Frank.

HINDMAN, J.

[a.] Lynnwood, WA [title] "A Fearless Front" [pers.] "A Fearless Face" is a poem spoken from my heart. It is about a time when I felt I was losing the one I love, whether it was her losing interest or falling out of love with me. I never thought I feared much of anything until I met her. I realize now that a broken heart is the one thing I fear the most. I dedicate this to my grandma, for passing down a gift I could never imagine having: the gift of art through words.

HIPP, CORTNEY

[a.] Carnesville, GA [title] "You Failed" [pers.] For me, poetry is a unique way to express my thoughts and feelings. I once said to a friend, "Poetry is your heart's secret prayers." I wrote this poem when I was going through a very difficult time in my life. I needed a friend to be there, but he was too busy. I felt betrayed and thought that I should have been more important. I finally told him how I felt; he had no idea that this was going on. I strongly believe you should tell people what you want or need from them so that they can help, rather than finding out too late, or you simply becoming angry.

HOFFMANN, SHARON

[a.] Ann Arbor, MI [title] "You Are" [pers.] I wrote this while taking African American Literature in the fall of 2001. We learned so many things that moved me, my perspective was challenged in a number of ways. This poem not only applies to people of different nationalities here in the U.S., but to people around the world. I think we need to listen to and really try to understand each other. We came from each different backgrounds and have our own individual, priceless story. That's what this poem is about.

HOLLIDAY-EVANS, BARBARA

[a.] Arden, NC [title] "Song of Silence" [pers.] This poem is dedicated to Harold Nelson of New York, who lost his right arm in a motorcycle accident. He saved my life when I had to leave work because of multiple sclerosis. The time he took and the care he showed made me realize life was worth living. Oddly, he suffered the same fate as Admiral Horatio Nelson.

HOLLIMAN, RITCHIE

[a.] Clarksville, TN [title] "Remembering Lost Love" [pers.] Hi! My name is Ritchie B. Holliman. I have been told I have a way with words. I write hoping to help others feel good about themselves. I have written poetry since childhood. My mother has always been the biggest supporter of my writing. I have written inspirational verses during my family's time of bereavement and for reunions. I am a very spiritual person, and I see poetry in our daily lives. Poetry is my outlet of self-expression. My family has always been the inspiration for me writing poetry.

HOLM, KARI

[a.] Sutherlin, OR [title] "The Bond of Four" [pers.] I am fourteen-years old. This poem is about the first litter of kittens that I was allowed to raise. I was supposed to find homes for them, but as my poem says, I could not stand to be parted from them. Poetry is away to express my feelings.

HOLMES, MELISSA

[a.] Lakewood, WA [title] "The Game" [pers.] This poem is about love, and the games we play to keep from revealing ourselves too quickly. Long live "The Game!"

HOWARD, CAINAN

[a.] Havelock, NC [title] "Lovraea" [pers.] Everybody knows that there is no such thing as the perfect relationship, and this was no where near perfect. The distance between us, the attitude problem; financially and physically it was going downhill. It's sad when you can't even touch the one you love. I thought I could spend the rest of my life with this person. We all make mistakes. It just depends on if we learn from them.

HUBER, ARIEL

[a.] Sanbornton, NH [title] "When Their Faces Change" [pers.] This poem represents how I perceive the people around me. I like to think of this poem as a reminder that people are sometimes far different than they appear. There is always something much greater and intriguing behind every face. Fear, is sometimes the only thing holding us back. I'm a junior at a small boarding school in NH and it was just recently that poetry became important to me. Poetry for me is a getaway, it allows me to focus on the issues that can only be explained in words.

HUBER, KRISTA

[a.] Richester Hills, MI [title] "Untitled" [pers.] Poems are essential to me as a person to express my feelings about life. When I sit and write, my mind is focused on the one and only emotion that particular verse is portraying. This verse has the most meaning to me, as it holds what I believe to be the key to my happiness: dreams.

HUBERT-BLAIR, SHARYN

[a.] Rockdale, TX [title] "Something Inside" [pers.] I wrote this poem for my sweetie, Robin. One evening while we were together it just came to me. I was overwhelmed with his love for me. When he left the room for something, I jotted this down on a scrap piece of paper. I gave it to him on our anniversary. Although we are no longer together, we still mean much to each other, but those feelings are now kept deep inside.

HUELSMAN, ROBIN

[a.] Celina, OH [title] "Just a Moment" [pers.] This poem was actually written as a prelude to a very lengthy poem, that was the result of much soul searching and cleansing after a bad run of years attending too many funerals and viewings. Closure is not always attainable, but often conclusions are inevitable. At least for me, it helps to find some point of perspective conducive to contemplation. At the very least, it's an excuse for star gazing.

HUI, WING PONG PAUL

[a.] San Francisco, CA [title] "If You Want to Marry Me, You Must" [pers.] I hope everyone will find their other half and pass through life with bravery and what they desire.

HULL, JANET

[a.] Seabrook, SC [title] "Key West Vacation" [pers.] This poem celebrates the joy of being with my son while on vacation in Key West, Florida; a place of jaw dropping beauty, with aqua water as far as the eye can see. Jacob was four at the time, and I got to see this beautiful vacation destination through his eyes, with all the wonder and excitement of a sweet, happy child. I dedicate this poem to him, and thank him for all magical moments we have shared.

HUNT, LEAH

[a.] La Marque, TX [title] "Universe" [pers.] I enjoy writing poetry very much; I just say what I believe or know. I'm ten years old, and I am going to write a lot more poetry.

HURD, AMANDA

[a.] Kansas City, MO [title] "She" [pers.] I am currently seventeen years old. I started to read poetry at a young age. I also started to take poetry classes. Then I got really serious about writing. Edgar Allen Poe is a big influence on my writing. The poem "She" is one of my life experiences. But who is she really?

IRELAND, KAITLYN

[a.] Madison, AL [title] "Shattered Dreams" [pers.] This poem has to do with my wish for true love. I've always dreamed of it, but reality has always been bland. After the breakup with my first boyfriend, I felt as though my dreams has been smashed. This poem was written long after that episode, once I'd managed to regain confidence in myself and rebuild my world of glass. People say I'm silly to live like that, but it's what allows me to write vivid characters and settings that bring the reader into my world, if only for a short time.

JACKSON, JONAH

[a.] Albuquerque, NM [title] "Living" [pers.] This poem is about being afraid to trust again. The confusion starts to affect the way you live and do things. I would like my words to relate to any similar situation that the reader is in. Thank you for taking the time to read a piece of my life.

JENNINGS, CALVIN

[a.] Pinehurst, TX [title] "Ode to Diane Allison" [pers.] I am a forty-six year old disabled American. This poem was about how I met my third wife, who was the only woman that loved me "till death do us part." I met her while staying at a friend's house during Hurricane Allison. She took care of me when I became disabled. When she developed cancer, it was my turn to take care of her. Due to my declining health, as a result of nerve damage, I was unable to care for her as I wanted to. I did do the best that I could under the circumstances. But in my mind, it wasn't enough to make up for the ways that she took care of me. Since she had bi-polar disorder and would not take her medication, she would go on all day griping fits. This caused tension which prompted me to attempt suicide. I checked myself into a clinic for psychological help. I learned that the condition was not her fault, but neither of us knew that she had cancer until a year before she died.

JERICEVIC, EVA

[a.] Toronto, Canada [title] "Socks" [pers.] I was born in 1991 on April 23. I love to write and I love art. I especially love for animals. I have fish, a dog, a wild sparrow that we raised, and two guinea pigs. I sometimes like to write funny poems in my spare time. I dedicate "Socks" to everyone I love.

JOHNSON, BRANDON

[a.] Carmichael, CA [title] "In the Field" [pers.] Poetry has not come easy for me. Now at age thirty-two, my writing have just begun to blossom. My high school English instructor said poetry is not for me, and at the time she was correct. However, later in life I found poetry as a way to express my deepest thoughts and emotions about my experiences. I have considered taking classes to improve my writing skills, but for now my poems will remain raw and simple.

JOHNSON, KAREN

[a.] Brooklyn, NY [title] "Celestial Awakening" [pers.] I have been blessed with the extraordinary ability to write poetry without effort. I wrote "Celestial Awakening" on one sleepless night. I peeked out the window and the words began to flow. I graduated from Long Island University with a BA in psychology. I started writing at the age of sixteen. Throughout my school years, I've been encouraged by my professors. My poetic ability is merely a pastime I've decided to take seriously. Give me a subject and I'll write a poem in minutes. I am so grateful to be blessed with this ability.

JOHNSON, KIMBERLY

[a.] New York, NY [title] "I Remember When. . . If Only" [pers.] The day of September 11 affected us all differently. I live in New York and it was quite a shock to me. I remember visiting one of the Twin Towers when I was younger. I was very scared there would be another bombing, even though it was highly unlikely. But never had I thought of something this terrible. I couldn't believe it that day and I don't think I will believe it years to come. September 11 was a day we may never understand.

JOHNSTON, CALVIN

[a.] Honolulu, HI [title] "Insight" [pers.] The purpose of my poetry is to provoke thought or paint vivid imagery to inspire the imagination. If my poetry does both, so much the better.

JOHNSTON-OUELLETTE, SHELLY

[a.] Hillview, Canada [title] "Accepting" [pers.] This poem describes a time of change and personal growth in my life. It is the recognition of my undaunted spirit. I have just moved to Newfoundland, Canada with my husband Marcel and my two amazing children, Cody and Ashley. My children are the twin lights of my soul. I am blessed every day with a wonderful family and friends. Thank you Mom, Dad, Grampy, Sylvie Amanda, Shirley, Don and my good friend Jen, who inspired me to take a chance and believe in my abilities.

JOLLY, AUDREY

[a.] Spokane, WA [title] "Speaking the Language of My Heart" [pers.] Love is a very special gift. I am so lucky to have someone in my life who inspires me so much. This poem was inspired by my husband and the creativity in my mind and heart. I hope the reader receives as much from it as I have. I hope this poem reaches other writers' hearts. I hope they can feel the emotions I had as I was writing it. May love find you the way it found me.

JONES, DAVID

[a.] Brisbane, Australia [title] "Eternity" [pers.] Living in Australia, I believe sometimes we do not appreciate how lucky we are. Sometimes it seems the conflict is not as real, as we see on TV or in photographs in the newspaper. I was once caught in the one of our city's worst floods and some people who watched or read about it said they felt so far removed, even though they were close in proximity. This poem is concerned with the realisation that life as we know it could end any time. I am married to my lovely wife Anne. We have four sons.

JONES, RACHEL

[a.] Tiskilwa, IL [title] "With You" [pers.] I was only eleven years old on September 11, 2001, but I was greatly affected by the lives lost and the sorrow felt by our country that day. Now that I am almost thirteen, I have realized that ever since the attack, Americans have united and become stronger than ever. My poem is mostly about how although something so terrible happened the effect on America was so great, someday we will all be together in Heaven.

JONGBLOED, BILL

[a.] Hurley, NM [title] "Thoughts That Matter" [pers.] My name is Bill Jongbloed (pronounced Youngblood). I was raised surfing, diving and sailing in Newport Beach, California, and soon realized my thoughts often rhymed. This led me to write poems and songs even though I make my living in the racing car industry. My poem, "Thoughts That Matter" urges the reader to stay positive and focused in life. My father, Hans always told me to live my life with love, but to temper it with logic. This is the focus of the poem. All my poems rhyme and most speak of simple truths I feel are timeless.

JUDGE, LEXI

[a.] Victoria, Australia [title] "People" [pers.] Every day stories of heroism and terrorism are reported in newspapers across the world. A child is saved from a burning building here and another is a victim of a car bombing there. I asked myself how these things could happen and "People" answers that question for me. I still don't understand and I doubt anyone ever will. I do hope world peace is not simply a myth passed through generations, but something we can achieve.

JULSON, ERIC

[a.] Brinnon, WA [title] "A Moment in the Window" [pers.] This poem was scribbled on a folder some time ago and I ran across it while looking for a piece to enter in the contest. It reflects where I live with the Olympic Mountains starting in my backyard. Here in Washington, clouds are a beautiful fact of life. I am a writer who spent thirty-five years in the music business here in Brinnon. I am very happy Poetry.com picked my poem!

KASSOFF, ELLIOT

[a.] Los Angeles, CA [title] "Afraid of the World or Yourself?" [pers.] Wherever I go, whatever I do, whomever I meet . . . I am who I am and can always go home again . . . because of my family! Thank you . . . Mom, Elesa; Dad, Edward; Eric; Rerry; Jared; Bergen; Raelle; Ernie; Anya; Masha; Todd; Ellen; Harrison; Sampson; and Hershey.

KELLY, JOSEPH

[a.] Sterling, VA [title] "She Brings the Light" [pers.] This poem carries with it a very special message to someone in my life, someone I continue to cherish each and every single day. Who is she? She's my best friend and her name is Kell. Her beauty, her courage, and her strength are inspirations to me, and I hope this poem in some small way symbolizes just how much she means to me.

KEMMLEIN, EVELYN

[a] Newton, NJ [title] "The Roadside Memorial" [pers.] Poetry has always been my favorite expression of writing, as well as my chosen form of reading. I like reading both the most celebrated poets to the simple greeting cards. To me, words in rhyme are the music of the soul, and I enjoy playing with words. Most of my writing through the years have been for special people in my life and descriptions of special events we shared. This poem touches a different chord—a sadness in my soul for every known and unknown person whose roadside memorial touches my life.

KENNEDY, JOAN

[a.] Woodbury, MN [title] "Addiction" [pers.] This poem is especially dear to me, as the person for whom it is written came late in my life. I have always enjoyed the economy of words that poetry brings to my thoughts and emotions. Poetry releases my inner spirit. It gives me the freedom to soar above the universe. It enables me to express the music of my soul. I began my career as a first-grade teacher and ended it as a college professor. Currently, I am a Native American storyteller and consultant. Growing up a middle child in a family of ten, I needed something to define me. My writing helped to do so.

KENNEDY, NORMA

[a.] Marion, IN [title] "I Had an Old Nannie!" [pers.] My poem was created on the spur of the moment. It was for my beloved grandmother, Jannie Davis. She left a deep and abiding purpose in my life, but until that instant, I never truly felt the full appreciation of her existence. Creating this poem made me think about my early childhood and the importance my grandmother played in the building of my character and that of my sisters and brothers. I hope this poem helps others appreciate the people who are important in their life, as it has helped me appreciate mine.

KFOURY, J. J.

[a.] Great Falls, VA [title] "i am" [pers.] This poem means a lot to me. It tells me who I really am and it shows people what I really am like. I am twelve years old and I am a student at Flint Hill School. I live with my mom, dad and my three older brothers Geoff, Greg, and Robbie. I play ice hockey and I ride horses. I love to write poetry. Poetry means a lot to me because it allows me to express my feelings.

KIM, SUNG

[a.] Elk Grove Village, IL [title] "Moon Night" [pers.] I came to the states in 1985 to study. I have an MA degree from the University of Illinois at Urbana-Champaign. Currently, I work at an international trade company in Chicago. I post my poem with my photography on a couple of Korean websites. I am a poet and essayist in Korean-American society. My poem is especially a short-sentence poem in haiku style. So far, I have composed about 2000 haikus. I wish to publish a book in English for those works. Recently, I am constructing an English haiku website.

KING, MARY

[a.] Bennington, VT [title] "Only Me" [pers.] On January 2000, I decided to enroll in a creative writing class. My goals—to share my story of trauma and to help others understand they are not alone. My husband is a Vietnam veteran suffering from post traumatic stress disorder. Much to my amazement, I completed my book. While writing my manuscript, it was necessary for me to dust the shelves of my inner self and reflex. It didn't take too long to realize I had essentially lost my individuality. My poem is about my awakening and realizing I am responsible for my own spiritual well being.

KING, SUE

[a.] Choudrant, LA [title] "Always Remember Our Day in the Park" [pers.] My grandchildren, Sara Grace and Will Boney are God's gifts to me. They pick me up when I am blue and can change my whole day. My son and daughter-in-law, Travis and April have made my life complete and I thank God for my precious family.

KING, VALARIE

[a.] Covina, CA [title] "Little Girl" [pers.] I was inspired to write this poem by my little sister. I would always watch her and notice how happy she was. For the longest time I wanted to be more like her. I love to write poetry. It allows me to relax and get away from the world. There is a little world to which I go whenever I'm alone. This world I have created is the only world I know to be safe. Yet, little by little, I like to show people this world by writing it down on paper.

KINGCAID, MICHAEL

[a.] Allentown, PA [title] "Elegy for Some Guy Who Died on a Farm" [pers.] This poem is over fifteen years old and was inspired by my college poetry professor, John Haag. Instead of expressing a point of view of "what is," it expresses a point of view of "what is not." This is a perspective not often taken as obvious as it is in this poem. I am a Pennsylvania State University graduate and I currently work as a project manager of digital composition for Creative Graphics, Inc. I write music lyrics as well as poetry. I would like to thank my wife for leaving me and indirectly inspiring me to rediscover my writing.

KIRISH, DUANE

[a.] Canyon Lake, CA [title] "Indiana Summer Dreams" [pers.] I was born in Korea during the Korean War. My Korean mother gave me up for adoption because I had TB and needed medical care she could not provide. I was raised by Otto and Dorothy Kirish in Granger, Indiana. I served with the 82nd Airborne Division, a graduate from Indiana University. I married Bonnie Wenger and have been blessed with three wonderful children, Andrea, Ben and Christopher. I only recently began writing poetry to remember and honor those I love.

KLAUSING, ALANDRA

[a.] Yucca Valley, CA [title] "Love Poem" [pers.] I wrote this poem because of it is loving, kind, and it was the only poem in my mind. I like it because it shows love like America should be loving.

KLIMOVICH, MICHAEL

[a.] Clifton, NJ [title] "your eyes are scarlet-ribboned skies" [pers.] This poem was about stopping to stare at the evening sky and losing myself in it; replaying images and memories of people, old relationships, good times, and old ways of life. It is a message to move on, but never forget. This poem is also a song. I am a young musician who plays an acoustic guitar. I write music and poetry out of passion, and also out of necessity. Music and writing provide an outlet for my emotions; one in which I can illustrate my perspective of the world and in a way others can appreciate.

KNOCKER, SHELBY

[a.] Palmer, AK [title] "Forever, Angel" [pers.] This poem is the memory of my best friend. Though her life was very short, it was full. She had accomplished so much during her short time here and has always been such an inspiration to me. She will forever be my guardian angel. I hope others have been as lucky as me have to have someone as special as her in their lives.

KOERTING, PAT

[a.] Aurora, IL [title] "The Gorilla and Orangutan" [pers.] This poem was written and sent in a card I made to cheer up Mrs. Natalie Vining, who at the time, was suffering from pneumonia in the spring. The last two lines come from quote I learned from Mrs. Marjorie Minor the preceding fall: "Yesterday is history, tomorrow is a mystery. Today is a gift and that's why it's called the present." Without these two ladies, the poem may have never spilled out the end of my pen. . . .

KORREIS, DANIEL

[a.] Clifton, NJ [title] "Tom-Tom Drum" [pers.] This verse is a tribute to all those who have never given up in pursuit of a goal. It is the lyrics to a song I have written. I hope this verse will inspire others to persevere in their ultimate goals. The selection of my poem in this publication was very gratifying. Thank you!

KOURGELIS, CARYL

[a.] Mahwah, NJ [title] "The Rose" [pers.] Poetry is a gift that comes to me in the quiet spaces of a hectic life as a wife, a mother of four, a daughter, a sister, an aunt, a friend, and let's not forget chauffeur! I believe this gift comes from my father's Aunt Claire, along with my higher self. I thank God for all of creation and my favorite four-letter word, love!

KRUCKOW, LISA

[a.] Philadelphia, PA [title] "My Treasured Friend" [pers.] My dad passed from cancer when I was thirteen. I have survived due to my faith in God, choosing to honor my father's influence of strength and hope. I was moved to honor my friend when I recently found out he passed two years ago! I am certainly humbled and grateful by your acknowledgement. Writing has enabled me to cope with my loved ones' passings. I choose to only uphold their goodness and cherish the ways in which my life has been enriched by each soul that has crossed my path.

KUHL, BRAIN

[a.] Hutchinson, MN [title] "If I Should Die" [pers.] I am an unsigned, underground rap artist and this poem is actually the chorus to one of my new songs. Last summer, I completed my first LP entitled, *World-wide Prophesies*. Most of my songs are soul-searching, spiritual songs, similar to my poem "If I Should Die." I feel that self-expression and creativity are God's greatest gifts to humanity. I am currently working on a second album, which I hope to release in the summer of 2003.

KULACZ, CHEYENNE

[a.] Boscawen, NH [title] "Forevermore" [pers.] I am sixteen years old and a junior in high school. I express myself through my poetry, song, lyrics and other creative writing. I feel honored and very excited to have my poem published.

KWONG, OPHELIA

[a.] New Brunswick, NJ [title] "Your Laugh" [pers.] The inspiration for this poem was the laughter of someone I liked. I grew up in England, then went back to Hong Kong where I was born, and am currently in the United States for college. I really love to write poetry. Sometimes, things are so much more easily expressed written down than orally. I would like to dedicate this poem to my parents, who always seem to be there for me no matter what. I want to say thank you to my old friends, Emily, Kathy and Carol; my cousins, Angela and Lillian; my Rutgers friends, Marcia, Alicia and Tammy; and my little dog, Tommy.

LaBARBERA, VINCENT

[a.] Plantation, FL [title] "I Say Bye, Not Goodbye" [pers.] I always knew I had some kind of gift to write. I always felt putting my feelings on paper would pay off one day. I wrote this poem as my way of saying goodbye to all my loved ones and the world. For I have Aplastic Anemia with only a sixty percent chance of life after a transplant of bone marrow. I have also been disabled for three years now from a work-related accident, which lead to this illness. The moral to this story is never take everything your doctor gives you.

LAMBERT, TIA

[a.] Claremont, NH [title] "Friendship" [pers.] I wrote this poem for a friend when I realized we would no longer be going to school together. I didn't want him to think I would ever forget him! Reading and writing have always been fun for me. I really enjoy writing poetry. My dream is to be a great writer.

LANDIS, ASHLEY

[a.] Lapeer, MI [title] "Me" [pers.] This poem is very important to me. It tells me I am growing up. It shows I am thankful for everything my parents have given me. Poetry has been a wonderful way for me to escape and to appreciate everything I have in my life. I just want to thank my mom; my stepdad Chuck; my dad; my stepmom Sheri; my brothers Josh, Chip, Jeremy; my little sister Marian; and to the rest of my family. Thank you for always believing in me.

LANGLEY, EDWARD

[a.] Alpharetta, GA [title] "Surrounded by Darkness" [pers.] I would like to thank the many people who requested more of my writing and those who inspired me to write once again. Through poetry, I find I can escape reality for a bit and go to an exaggerated dream world to let my feelings loose with no limits, good or bad. I live by the philosophy, "live and let live."

LANGLEY, JILL

[a.] Reidsville, NC [title] "Life Is Worth Living" [pers.] September the eleventh changed every American's life. It taught us how precious life is and how quickly it can be taken away. I refer to the saying, "the only thing we have to fear is fear itself." We cannot let terrorism grip us with fear, nor let it rule our lives. So, let us cherish our families, treasure our friends and be forever grateful for the land in which we live. May God bless American again.

LATHAM, PAUL

[a.] Key West, FL [title] "Bodily Woes" [pers.] Originally from England, my wife Maggie and I moved to the U.S.A., and eventually to Key West, Florida. We are surrounded not only by the beauty of the island, but also by the diversity of the people. Many of our neighbors are also artists, writers and poets. Indeed, Key West has been the home of many a famous author. I started writing poetry in 1973 at the age of thirteen. "Bodily Woes" was written to give a light-hearted look at ourselves, as we slowly change and grow older.

LAURIN, MARLA

[a.] Palatine, IL [title] "The Angry Goodbye" [pers.] Often, society underestimates the damage and disruption caused by emotional pain, in addition to the cathartic measures used to dispel this inner-trauma. Not only does this poem seek to capture the essence of emotions typically involved in relations tainted with deceit, but also it tries to validate the universality of those emotions by underscoring self-regard in the wake of its finality. I credit my mother, Barbara Laurin, who is the sole cause for my existence as a poet. Her belief in me provides unparalleled inspiration.

LAWSON, JENNY

[a.] Salmon, ID [title] "The Sun" [pers.] It came as a great shock to me when I first found out not only was I a semi-finalist, but I was to become a published author. I know this is a great honor for any poet, not to mention a twelve-year-old. I hope this will be the first step towards becoming a writer, so I can share my gift with the world.

LAWSON, JOSEPH

[a.] Salmon, ID [title] "Africa" [pers.] About a hundred and fifty years ago, white people didn't think how horrible it would be if their skin was black and not white. I wrote this poem because this issue matters to me. I am ten years old. I have a mom, a dad and a sister.

LEAL, E.

[a.] Dallas, TX [title] "The Day" [pers.] I am something of a renaissance man. Writing has always been a great passion of mine. It has helped search the true feelings within me. Poetry is a gift of this passion. I also write screenplays and manuscripts. I am very active with theatre and have directed in film. Writing has also inspired me to become an inventor. I look forward to sharing my work with others.

LEWIS, ALEX

[a.] Warrington, United Kingdom [title] "Dreaming" [pers.] I started writing poetry in February of 2002. I became completely consumed and within three weeks from inception, I had written sixty two poems. I now feel such a sense of freedom. This is what poetry has done for me. Some of my poems take five minutes to complete and some a little longer, but the sense of achievement is always such a positive thing. What better way to show your love for someone than to write an original poem? Inspiration is everywhere. Just look at our beautiful world and if you don't see it in your world, then just dream.

LEWIS, DEVIN

[a.] Callahan, FL [title] "Sister" [pers.] This poem was written because I wanted to show the world how I feel about my little sister. She has had juvenile diabetes since she was seven, and this is just my way of showing the world and her how much I care. I also think it's really neat that my name means "poet," and I am glad I am living up to it. I thank God for the poem I wrote, and for its inspiration, my sister Ravyne. I live with my mom, dad, sister and three cats.

LEWIS, JAKESHIA

[a] Houston, TX [title] "The Reality: Life on the Other Not-So-Greener-Side of the Grass" [pers.] This poem was written from the heart. It's about reality through the eyes of a struggling, young, black female. It is very sincere and deep. I hope that others who are

going through difficult times can understand, see that others are going through worse, and always know that God is the way, and He will not let you take on more than you can handle. This poem is dedicated to a man and woman and a little girl who loves and inspires me to do my beat in everything that I do. I love you, Timothy Duane Gibson.

LONGEWAY, KATRINA

[a.] Leesburg, FL [title] "Blood-Red Sea" [pers.] To me, my poetry has always a very private thing; something I shared with a few of my close friends. I never thought it as written well enough to share with anyone else. However, my friends urged me to pursue my poetry. So, here I am. My advice to other aspiring writers is this: You are your own worse critic. If your dream is to get published, remember this. It never hurts to try.

LUTZ, JUDY

[a.] Hickory, NC [title] "When I Was Young" [pers.] Life is a collage of tragedy and humor, misfortune and blessing, disgust and beauty. We learn so much on our journey from child to adult. There has been hardship, but there have also been miracles. For some time, I've had a desire to share some of my life lessons with others in order to help them over the rough spots. The things that keeps us going are experiencing the gifts we're given and having faith in tomorrow.

MADDIX, NICK

[a.] Iowa City, IA [title] "Forevermore (Short Version)" [pers.] I've been writing for the past few years, and I must say it is an honor to have my poem "Forevermore" published in this special book. This poem is about a guy who finds out about a girl's relationship that has gone horribly wrong. Upon seeing her crying, he does the only thing he can do. He hugs her with love and whispers the feelings of love he's always had for her. It's an experience I'm sure has happened in everyone's life and it really does make you realize who your true friends are.

MAJEWSKI, LISA

[a.] Brooklyn, NY [title] "Foolish" [pers.] Writing has always been important in my life. For as long as I can remember, it has been the way I express myself. I never dreamed I would be published. It left me a little dazed. There are some who have said my poems are too simple. What I write has never been simple. I write from my heart. Everything I create is a small piece of who I am.

MANITOWABI, MELISSA

[a.] Wikwemikong, Canada [title] "The Distance" [pers.] This poem is very special to me. It's for all my brothers and sisters: Vivian, Archie, Carol, Hank, Timothy, Arlene, Linda, Debbie, Wayne, James and Alvin (who passed away,) Brian and Stephanie. Also, this is for Nunghose, Gina, Joey and Isadore. It's what's in our hearts that keeps us strong. . . . This is for you!

MARGULIES, TIMOTHY

[a.] Flagstaff, AZ [title] "Contra Dancing" [pers.] The poem was inspired by my first contra dance with my fiancée who regularly attends contra dances. I was born in San Francisco, California and reside in Flagstaff, Arizona. I have been writing poetry and have published poems by Timothy Scott in 2002, focusing on spirituality, peace, religion, sports, current events, romance, and perceptions of nature.

MARSH, LADONNA

[a.] Valdosta, GA [title] "Because of You" [pers.] Poetry is a beautiful and short, but impacting, way of expressing emotion. I have written poetry since I was thirteen years old, but never entered a contest until now. This publication is a dream come true, an acknowledgement for something I enjoy. "Because of You" was written to summarize my relationship with my fiancé. His love encourages me to continually reach for new heights. I want to dedicate this publication to him; my son, William; my daughter, Krystal; my grandmother, Betty Hiatt; and my soon-to-be-born niece or nephew.

MARTIN, SONYA

[a.] Collins, MS [title] "Love Is What Love Does" [pers.] I never thought about my poem being published in a book. How excited I was to get the news that it had made it to the semi-finals. I often think of things related to love, but this was the first time I actually put my thoughts into words. So many people say, "I love you," but they never show love. My dream is that others will read my poem and be inspired to show love in any way they can.

MATULICH, ALISON

[a.] South Lake Tahoe, CA [title] "Dented" [pers.] Poetry is a way for me to reflect, like a mirror, that which I see in the hearts of others, as well as expressing the emotions and ideas that dwell within my own soul. Through writing, I choose to provoke thought, inspire hope and send a message of love.

MAURER, AMY

[a.] Waterloo, IA [title] "Where This Path Is Headed, I Don't Know" [pers.] After receiving my undergraduate degree in May 2002, I entered what I call a transitional period; one of significant life changes and individual growth. I knew the decisions I was about to make would forever alter my life's path. So, I began writing a collection of poetry and songs as a means of coping with the problems I faced at the time. This poem reflects my thoughts and feelings as I moved from a comfortable lifestyle to one completely new and different. I hope my poem's message will restore faith in those who've lost their way.

MAXWELL, JAMES

[a.] Shawnee, OK [title] "A New Beginning" [pers.] I have served in Oklahoma as an associational director of missions for Southern Baptist in Oklahoma for thirty-eight years. I have served as a director of the Baptist Student Union at Northwestern State University for nine years. I am now retired and serve as a volunteer chaplain for Shawnee Police Department and Unity Hospital in Shawnee, Oklahoma. My wife and I are graduates of Oklahoma Baptist University, in Shawnee, OK. He is a member of First Baptist Church, in Shawnee, OK. This poem is the basis for hope for many broken lives in the difficult time we live.

McCALL, JAMES

[a.] Centennial, CO [title] "Change" [pers.] I wrote this poem right after I moved from my home city. I wrote it based on my own memories. I hope other people can relate to this poem and know the same feelings I feel. I am currently in tenth grade in high school. I enjoy writing songs and playing guitar. I think people should be able to enjoy life as much as they can without worrying about what other people think of them.

McCRAY, JAMIE

[a.] Kissimmee, FL [title] "What Am I without My Father?" [pers.] My poems are a dedication to my mother Evangeline and my grandmother Viola. Both women have inspired me to be the strong, independent woman I am today. I cannot imagine what my life would have been like if my mother was not there pushing me to do my best and be successful. This is my way of saying thank you to my mother and grandmother. I love you both!

McCUTCHEON, J.

[a.] Sylvan Springs, AL [title] "The Fall" [pers.] The poem is best described by what it is not, rather than what it is. It is not about any person or a special love, but it concerns a feeling from the soul. My mother, Annie McCutcheon, connected the fall season with death and conveyed this to me early in life. As time passed, this connection and early romantic experiences coalesced. There is not one word in this poem that is not from the heart and a true echo of the soul. In the last four lines of the poem, despair arose and a sudden hollowness of the soul transcended.

McDANIEL, DEREK

[a.] Troutdae, OR [title] "If Time Were a Window" [pers.] I am proud to admit I am a follower of Jesus Christ. This poem, "If Time Were a Window," is a reflective piece on my own life. It does, however, show how people sometimes live their lives in regret. The basic message of this whole thing is to let go of the past. Sometimes things just pile up and bog us down, which is why the last three lines of the poem are about letting go and moving on. It was Jesus, who is God Himself, who allowed me to see this. I am eternally in his debt for it is to Jesus to whom this poem is dedicated.

McFARLAND, SARAH

[a.] Atkins, AR [title] "Fall/Winter" [pers.] The poem "Fall/Winter" commemorates countless hours spent playing paper dolls with my sister, Peggy. Currently, I am married with five children. I work as a psychotherapist not far from the town in which I grew up.

McGEE, ROBERT

[a.] Calhoun, LA [title] "For a Better Life" [pers.] For years, I performed as a singer. During those many years, I wrote songs, mostly country and religious. I also wrote poetry of all types—serious, humorous, prose! As a senior citizen, I still write "For A Better Life" because of current experiences, at home and abroad. I try to live by the words expressed in this poem.

McILQUHAM, REBECCA

[a.] Elk Mound, WI [title] "How Much We Are Worth" [pers.] I am very thankful to be entered in a contest! I never imagined my poems getting me anywhere. I would like to share what my poem was about. . . . My poem was written for my grandmother, who had cancer. I wrote this poem for her and about her. I would love to share this poem with whoever else lost their loved one and feels the same for them. I'd like to thank you so much.

McWAINE, LILLYE

[a.] Chicago, IL [title] "Let Go (I Have to Let Go)" [pers.] This poem, like all my poems, is special to me. What I write are private thoughts that come from my heart. After the death of my husband of thirty-two years and my youngest son of twenty-five years, who died less than a year apart, my heart was broken and shattered into many painful pieces. I buried myself in my writing which led me to write "Let Go (I Have to Let Go)". I was holding onto the past. I realized I had to let go in order to save myself.

MEDLOCK, JASON

[a.] FPO, AE [title] "Underway" [pers.] I am in the U.S. Navy and I was inspired to write this on my first deployment. I think this is how a lot of our sailors feel, but don't know how to put it into words.

MEEK, HOPE

[a] La Jolla, CA [title] "Overconfidence" [pers.] I am a retired VP of sales and marketing. I am seventy-four years old and am seeking an MFA degree in Poetry at SDSU. I write for personal amusement. It's better than Scrabble.

MEHTA, RAM

[a.] Charlotte, NC [title] "Sonnet Written in Optimist Park" [pers.] I was nominated in 2001 and 2002 as World Champion Amateur Poet at ISP Conventions. My three poems: "Iris," "Ode to Earthquake" and "Niagara" are published in two volumes, *Nature's*

Echoes and *The Silence Within*. My five poems will be published in *The World Anthology of Contemporary Poets*. My works are also published in *Poetry Magazine*, in New York and Tintota, Australia, and in *The World Congress of Poets' Anthology*. This poem was written while visiting my daughter, Luna Joshi, and son, Miraj Mehta, in Windsor, Ontario. Optimistic Park is located near my daughter's apartment.

MENDENHALL, WIL

[a.] San Marcos, CA [title] "Liquid Earth and Magic Skies" [pers.] Have you ever been face-to-face with an angel? I captured one for a moment. I taught her to say, Daddy, and then I let her go. This poem was written for Robyn, a little girl I raised as my own, only to find she wasn't. I do not consider myself a poet. I'm actually a songwriter. I also play guitar and practice martial arts. Through the repetition of life, we sometimes forget how to be fully conscious. I enjoy writing because it makes people think.

MESSINA, MEAGAN

[a.] South Glastonbury, CT [title] "Why?" [pers.] This is a very special poem to me. When I was writing it, I wanted to say how I was feeling and hoped other people could relate to it. Writing poems about how I feel always make me understand everything in life.

METALLO, DANIELLE

[a.] Rochester, NY [title] "Color Blind" [pers.] I live with my parents and three sisters. When I wrote "Color Blind," I was dating a mixed guy and my father disapproved. It was hard to keep a steady relationship knowing I was a disappointment to my father. Though I couldn't see my father's point of view, I wrote this poem for him because I know he isn't color blind.

MICHELSON, KATHRYN

[a.] Holyoke, MA [title] "My Fight" [pers.] This poem is very personal. I used my life experiences as the material for it. I do not consider myself to be a poet. It's not something about which I'm passionate. I had to write this poem for school and it was the hardest for me to write out of three poems. I also wrote a narrative and a dramatic poem. I think this one's the best.

MILLER, DOUGLAS

[a.] Columbia City, IN [title] "Snake!" [apers.] My poetry is my story: the lives, loves, petty irritations, major annoyances, horrors of war, the quiet moments, fond memories, whimsical, absurd, and frustrating times, as well as the simple joys of being alive. Humor permeates my poetry because when you cease to laugh, you cease to live. I have been a professional storyteller for many years and frequently use my poems in the stories.

MILLER, MELANY

[a.] Lawrence, KS [title] "Poppa's Shadow" [pers.] "Poppa's Shadow" was inspired by the special relationship between my father and my six-year-old daughter. Nothing can come between this bond. Our hearts are a tender, breakable thing. We must cherish the blessings God has given us.

MITCHELL, CYNTHIA

[a.] Kenosha, WI [title] "Who Will Hear?" [pers.] I was born in Louisiana. My parents died when I was six years old. I moved to Wisconsin when I was twelve years old. I have two brothers and two sisters.

MOORE, INEZ

[a.] Granite Falls, NC [title] "Mercy" [pers.] I was living life my own way and in my mind, a great life. I had a good-looking husband and a beautiful baby (God could wait for a more convenient season), then suddenly I became very ill with not too much hope of recovery. I called on the God of Abraham, Isaac, and Jacob . . . and also the God of my praying mom. He rescued me, gave me health, and now I say to one and all His name is Jesus and His mercy never fails.

MOORE, KIMA

[a.] Perth Amboy, NJ [title] "Desire" [pers.] This poem was written to describe a precious moment. I remember so vividly the love I couldn't hold onto because of life's pressures and my own confusion. I dedicate this poem to my other half, with the last name Lavine, what I always wanted to be! I'll always love you, together or apart.

MORAN, JESSICA

[a.] Chippewa Falls, WI [title] "What's Done Is Done" [pers.] A very special person in my life was diagnosed with cancer and I wrote this to give myself a sense of hope.

MORIARTY, HANNAH

[a.] Holyoke, MA [title] "Dyslexia" [pers.] At the age of seven, several close friends and relatives died. I became so depressed and wrote poetry to help me express my feelings. I also was experiencing difficulties due to dyslexia. Many peers didn't understand that I wasn't stupid; I only had difficulties in learning. I wrote this poem to let people know how it feels to have dyslexia. Writing poetry helps me cope with life's challenges.

MORSE, KENETH

[a.] Metairie, LA [title] "Vietnam Veteran's Legacy" [pers.] This poem comes from deep within my heart. I spent twelve months in combat in Vietnam and witnessed several friends die in vain. To all the veterans, both living and dead, and to their families that had to endure the pain and shame of America's tragedy; to all veterans suffering from PTSD, God bless you brothers; to my wife Lupe for your understanding and love and to my sons, Kenny and Richmond, for also loving your dad.

MUNOZ, BRIAN

[a.] Long Beach, NY [title] "Letter from the Field" [pers.] This poem is very special to me, as it represents exactly how I felt while undergoing training in the forests of Quantico, Virginia. I was a marine officer candidate and anticipating the birth of my first son, never knowing if I would be there for his birth, but always hoping I would be.

MURPHY, EVELYN

[a.] Pembroke, MA [title] "A Wedding in the Mountains" [pers.] "A Wedding in the Mountains" was a family affair which took place in a beautiful area in Vermont where ski trails and sun sets connect. I grew up in that area and poetry was in my head since the fifth grade when I wrote such silly verses as "Burning Toast" and "Broken Mirrors." Now, I enjoy writing meaningful, rhymed stories about events in our lives. My children, Shay, Kennie, John, and Kim are all poetic, artistic, and fun-loving, which makes it so great when we all together. Poetry is surely good for the soul.

MYERS, DOUGLAS

[a.] Apple Valley, CA [title] "Centuries Old" [pers.] This poem came to me in a writing class. I was given an assignment to personify an object and chose a rock because it's old and has a lot to reveal. A poem appeared to be the ideal way to disclose the rock's feelings, so I wrote it as you see it. I express my gratitude to my English teachers and my family for their support and inspiration.

NEELY, DARREN

[a.] Florence, KY [title] "What Trust Built" [pers.] "What Trust Built" is just a little over a year old. One key event touched all our lives and another touched me. The key event in common is September 11, 2001, and my personal event is when I lost Audra. I didn't lose her to death, but I lost her to life. The date now is September 16, 2002. The one year anniversary was a time for reflection. Upon reflection, I see that every line of this poem is still true.

NESTICH, PAT

[a.] Travelers Rest, SC [title] "Roses" [pers.] Poetry is an expression that comes from a love for God and the Bible. God says you're forgiven and God made you. He asks of us to love one another. May you know you're special. Special as each rose is, so beautiful, it is so!

NETTLES, JAMIE

[a.] Florence, SC [title] "Life . . ." [pers.] I wrote "Life" while going through a tough time in my own life. It's kind of based on the last two years of my life. I'm so honored to be published since I'm only thirteen years old and in the eight grade. Poetry has really helped me at times when I just feel like breaking down and crying. There are some people I have to thank for it: Victoria Houghtling, Brad Kennedy, Chris Attey, and Mrs. Graves who, through their encouragement and poetry, have inspired me to write my own. Most important of all, I thank God for giving me this opportunity.

NICHOLS, ELIZABETH

[a.] Glenview, IL [title] "The Height of My Heart" [pers.] My family has always shown support for anything I do. They bring out the best in me. This poem would not be written if my family were not by my side. My inspiration comes from their caring and love. Even though we are not always together, our thoughts and feelings are.

NOTWICZ, DANIEL

[a.] Brooklyn, NY [title] "Why" [pers.] I've lived in Brooklyn my whole life. Throughout my life, my views haven't really been changed, but rather added upon; usually after meeting new friends. My poem refers to one of these special friends.

OLIVER, YOLANDA

[a.] Charleston, SC [title] "In Time, You Will Understand" [pers.] Writing poetry has been a blessing from the Lord, to share my thoughts and say something positive to the world. My inspiration stems from life experiences and topics to which everyone can relate. I could only hope to touch a life through the written word. "In Time, You Will Understand" was written when I had to tell a male associate off in a way that would not be offensive. I am very pleased to have this poem published in this book.

OSBORNE, STEPHEN

[a.] South San Francisco, CA [title] "The Voice" [pers.] I have written many poems since "The Voice;" however, the most amazing and beautiful thing is I never knew poetry existed within me until a woman came into my life and touched my soul, forcing it to the surface. Her name is Charlotte Morris and not only is she the most inspirational and wonderful person I ever met but she is also my best friend. "The Voice" and my love are for her always. Thank you, Charlotte.

OSTROVSKY, RACHEL

[a.] Brooklyn, NY [title] "Where Are the Boys and the Girls?" [pers.] I was born in Russia where poetry was taken seriously: you were a professional or you didn't write at all; it was never a hobby. I had my books published and my poetry appearing in a lot of magazines, but in 1980, being in confrontation with the Communist regime, I found refuge in the United States. I am proud and happy to say that for the last twenty-two years the land, the people and the language got so deep into my heart and my blood that I am writing songs and poetry in English as well.

OXENDINE, DEIDRA

[a.] Merom, IN [title] "Your Voice" [pers.] This one is for my Dad, David Oxendine. I love you Dad. I miss your voice, your hand in mine, and your heart.

PAGE-GRAY, MICHAELLE

[a.] San Diego, CA [title] "Let's Talk" [pers.] Poetry has recently become an essential part of my life. At an early age, I began experimenting with words, attempting to write fairy tales and poems. My passion for the art has been rekindled. I am inspired by personal events involving family or current world issues. "Let's Talk," the featured poem, reflects both. This piece captures a conversation between siblings relieving past issues and relating them to the recent abductions and murders of young children. It's a release for me to express my thoughts and innermost feelings through poetry. I am grateful to have been endowed with such a gift.

PALANDZHYAN, SHOUSHANIK

[a.] Los Angeles, CA [title] "The Miracle" [pers.] This poem is a gift from me to all the new mothers in the world who have experienced the joy of bringing one of these miracles into the world. It is my dream that I too one day will bring a miracle into the world—a miracle I can call my own, just like my parents did seventeen years ago.

PALLUZI, LAUREL

[a.] Basking Ridge, NJ [title] "Lafayette Escadrille" [pers.] This poem was actually part of an English project for school in seventh grade. It's about an aircraft from World War One. I hope people will get an understanding of what it's like to be the last one standing. This poem is about a pilot who was the last man left in his aircraft. Many had died, but he stayed with that plane. I would like to dedicate this poem to that pilot. May you rest in peace. I would also like to dedicate this poem to my English teacher, Mr. Steve Sauter.

PALMER, NATHANIEL

[a.] Fort Campbell, KY [title] "Isn't This Something" [pers.] My poem is meant to show people no matter what anyone may say or do to you, know you are and can be the person you want to be. Don't let anyone make you anybody you don't want to be. Your life is yours, so be happy with yourself and the Lord will shine in you!

PANESCU, PRIERA

[a.] San Jose, CA [title] "Daddy Came" [pers.] I wrote this poem to explain my emotions for my dad. When Daddy travels, I miss him so much. I knew the best way to explain my feelings for him was through poetry. I hope people who read this poem will share my feelings because parents play such an important role in a child's life. They are the ones who help you with your homework, problems in your life and most importantly, they love you. This is the reason why I love it so much when Daddy comes!

PARONYAN, ROSALINE

[a.] Studio City, CA [title] "Lock of Loss" [pers.] I am a ten-year-old who enjoys writing poetry, playing the piano and sports. My poems come from the heart and are free style. I have to receive inspirations in order to write them down. I have several other poems and hopefully will publish them in the future.

PEACOCK, KIERA

[a.] Honolulu, HI [title] "The Stand" [pers.] Fear knows no end and sorrow no beginning, and because of this we must live our lives the best we can, hoping and praying for remembrance. Being remembered will provide a whisper of immortality. For those who died, while putting their lives at risk and protecting the lives of those held dear, age will never bind them. Writing this poem, my thoughts never ceased to wander. Perhaps, my writing is a vague eulogy in which people may remember what was lost and what was gained.

PEKRON, REBECCA

[a.] Elmhurst, IL [title] "Origami" [pers.] I'm currently a junior at Stanford University. Writing is my passion, and it is such a gift for me to be able to share it with other people. Thank you so much for taking an interest in my poem.

PIPPIN, SARA

[a.] Franklin, IL [title] "I Guess That's Why I Look Up to Her" [pers.] Poetry is a gift I discovered from a rainbow. Its peace and serenity made me pause to enjoy and compose a permanent reminder of how beautiful life can be. This poem came from deep inside, as well as the other poems which followed. I hope this opens your eyes and your heart.

POLLARA, LEONARD

[a.] Haskell, NJ [title] "United We All Stand Together" [pers.] I feel that writing poetry is a release of stress and loneliness for me. It is a way of portraying my thoughts and feelings. This poem is a vision of hope for our everyday lives. Living among diversified cultures, we strive to fulfill our goals and work together to find peace within and among us all. If you have a strong belief in something, follow your heart and inspire others.

PORTER, M.

[a.] Pinellas Park, FL [title] "Sweet Anise" [pers.] I wrote "Sweet Anise" for my sister. She has been a great source of strength and inspiration for me. I am glad I can share my gift to her with those who love poetry as much as I do.

PORTER, MAGGIE

[a.] Largo, FL [title] "American Pride" [pers.] I wrote "American Pride" in memory of those who lost their lives on September 11, 2001. I dedicate this to their families, their loved ones, and those who protect and serve our country. You are all true heroes.

POUPARD, HELEN

[a.] Williston, FL [title] "You're the Only One for Me" [pers.] I've always had a romantic soul, so it isn't surprising that a lot of my poetic attempts embody that theme. Most of my poems are accompanied with music which I have written, setting the mood as well as delivering a message. I am seventy-two years young. It took the International Library of Poetry to provide the opportunity to publicly express my humble talents.

POWERS, PATRICK

[a.] South Glens Falls, NY [title] "Love from Afar" [pers.] Well, poetry is a natural way for me to express myself. I found I had talent in about the second grade. I didn't realize my prowess in poetry until I fell in love. I was so overtaken by the presence of this beautiful being that I went into what I call rapid-fire poetry. I was up late one night, thinking of my biggest motivation and I just started writing about her. This poem obviously is not it, but just a little thank you to my lost love and my friend. So, thank you girls. I love you both.

PRINDLE, ALEXANDER

[a.] Asheville, NC [title] "Common Pressure" [pers.] To me, poetry is a certain special type of expression simply stating a complex idea or emotion. It is the idea that is poetic to me, and not merely the sound or rhythm of words. My poetry expresses my consciousness, or my conscious paradigm. I attempt to express those things in my poetry that are difficult to approach in other avenues of expression—ideas that may otherwise not be appropriate when a person has a revelation or an epiphany. To me, this is the poetry of the consciousness as it effects the whole of that person.

PROBERT, LAURA

[a.] San Jose, CA [title] "Dreamscape" [pers.] This particular piece proclaims my ability to escape the harsh reality of life. My poetry is the engine to express my emotion and show my appreciation. Words are my therapy and hold the key to my soul. Poetry is my way of sharing that appreciation for the things around me. It teaches my children to enjoy literature and the arts. I dedicate this dream to them: Chelsie, Kristopher and Emily—all my love!

PURDY, TIMOTHY

[a.] Portrage, IN [title] "More Alone" [pers.] The sudden realization that my marriage was approaching an end is what prompted the writing of this poem. I'd like to thank Holly for still being a friend; and, I would especially like to thank Becky for encouraging me to submit my first poem.

RASMUSSEN-JAMES, MARGARET

[a.] Marion, IL [title] "Baby Footprints on My Mind" [pers.] As I traveled to work one morning, thinking about my oldest son Michael, so kind and helpful to me, my thoughts drifted back in time to my sister's mother-in-law, Helen. We were all visiting my sister Del, and Helen asked me if I was "surprised at how gray her son Doug was?" This poem reflects that surprise as our children not only grow up but old. The memories that a lifetime leaves on our minds are like precious imprints of events. This poem celebrates that walk through life and how this one mother feels about the experience.

REAVLEY, COLLEEN

[a.] Des Plaines, IL [title] "My Pain" [pers.] This poem describes how I felt after my mother passed. I dedicate everything I have become to Emily. Always and forever and each day, I thank my mother for bringing the love of my life into my world in 2002.

REID, ROBERT

[a.] Queens Village, NY [title] "The Wonderful Falling Snow" [pers.] I have always loved it when the weather would make the decision for me. It takes all the pressure of you and gives you a legitimate excuse to take a day off.

RENAUD, ERIC

[a.] Stillwater, NY [title] "Silence" [pers.] I spent a lot of time alone this year and writing poetry became an emotional outlet. There were no particular patterns and no particular sense at times, but I was just pouring out my emotions. "Silence" was written about the quiet present while you dream when dreams occur. This poem means a great deal to me. My beautiful wife, Dawn, is the inspiration for this poem because it is the beginning of an epic journey. This is merely the starting point for my artistic expression and I am honored to share my dreams and feeling with all you.

RICHEY, ERIC

[a.] Mason, OH [title] "Dream World" [pers.] Poetry is a way to pose the most important feelings and experiences which shape who I am. When I write, I usually express the images in my head with words, which automatically conjures up feelings I have. It's also a way, as a teenager now, to imprint myself into history so I can look back and remember the person I was and see into who I have evolved.

RINCONES, ANN MARIE

[a.] Harlingen, TX [title] "He Stands Alone" [pers.] This poem is about the life of an elm tree and how it resembles the likes of a man. Like my great-grandfather who knows pain, I too shall grow and stand tall like him. Thank you Great-Grandpa, Mom and Dad, Grandma, and Mr. R., for all your support. I love you all.

RIVERS, ARTEMIAS

[a.] Jacksonville, FL [title] "Feelings Within" [pers.] This poem was written to describe how I was feeling at a certain time in my life. I was not able to openly express my feelings to anyone, so the only way I could let my feelings out was to write them down. I hope this poem helps those who read it who might be experiencing the same problems I have.

ROBINSON, CHRISTOPHE

[a.] Columbus, OH [title] "This Vanquished Emotion" [pers.] This poem is dedicated to my sister, Danielle, whom I love dearly. She was fourteen years old when she passed away. This poem captures youth, the transition into adulthood, and how things change, yet stay the same. We sometimes, as adults, take life for granted and miss out on the little things that are truly important—the things that make us who we are and the light that is our soul. This is what my expression brings to me and I hope someone feels the way I do. I love you, Danielle.

ROBISON, SETH

[a.] Longville, MN [title] "Orange" [pers.] I am writing this to my son. This book will be a Christmas gift to him from me. God has given my son beautiful visions and senses. This poem is so much like him. He is only ten years old. I wanted him to cherish this book forever. I am proud of you, Seth; you are wonderful boy and I am so glad you are my son. I love you always, Mom

ROBLES, BERNAL

[a.] Austin, TX [title] "Life" [pers.] I am really flattered to have my poem published and I hope readers will like it.

ROCHE, NOEL

[a.] Plainville, CT [title] "Our Mother's Love" [pers.] This poem is dedicated to my mother who lost her life in a car crash. The person responsible was never caught. They have been forgiven for what happened that day. They brought my mom and me closer together and showed me how much love she gave to me. Rest in Heaven, Margaret Roche, my angel—a wonderful person who lives in our hearts forever.
Your son, Noel

ROEDER, CYNTHIA

[a.] Carrollton, KY [title] "Unwanted" [pers.] I was really sad when I wrote this. I felt as though no one cared about me, but obviously I was mistaken. No matter what, my family will always love me. There's a phrase I really like: "To the world, you may only be one person, but to one person, you may mean the world."

ROGERS, KETINA

[a.] Saint Louis, MO [title] "Heaven" [pers.] I want to thank God for all He has done for me, because without him I couldn't survive. I want to say, I love you to my family; Vernita Maria Pittman, my best friend; and my God-daughter, Stephanie Frenita Marshay Goodlow. They have stuck with me, while I was dealing with my depression and mental illness. I thank God for keeping them in my life.

ROSENQUIST, JOHN

[a.] New York, NY [title] "Waiting for a Beer" [pers.] The nice quality poetry has is that it can be spontaneous or planned, as desired. Someone can jot down a poem while engaged in any other activity. A few years back, I would frequent coffee houses that had an "open mic" night for poetry. When I went there to read, I would always write the poems I read for the night just before I actually read them. I believe this practice illustrates the essence of fresh thinking and writing. I wrote this poem while sitting at the bar, waiting for a beer.

RUSSO, SERENA

[a.] Fort Lauderdale, FL [title] "September 11" [pers.] The key to poetry is to write what you know and feel. Many people relate to my poems because I always try to express a realistic point of view with anything I write. Whatever happens to be on your mind can turn into some of your greatest poetry. A major person that inspires me to write is my mother. I want to make her proud of me. Since I'm not a genius at academics, I had to search deep down for not only something at which I excel but something I enjoy—poetry. God bless!

RYAN, TANYA

[a.] Dania Beach, FL [title] "Soldier" [pers.] It is no accident that my poem has been selected for this particular series, *Letters from the Soul*, because my work is always inspired by the soul. This particular poem is dedicated to a soldier who accidentally ended a young girl's life and was not able to forgive himself. He is a remarkable soul, full of love and compassion, and I hope one day he will see the truth.

SAAVERDA, ROSEMARIE

[a.] Bronx, NY [title] "Dreams" [pers.] My inspiration comes from my husbend. He is a very hard worker and good provider. I thank him for everything he does for our family. To all who read my poem, all we need is a dream to make us happy.

SCHATZMAN, NICOLE

[a.] Sicklerville, NJ [title] "Friends to Love" [pers.] This poem refers to the relationship my boyfriend and I have. We started out as best friends. Then it turned into love and still remains that way. I feel that poetry is the best way to express one's feelings.

SCHLEIHAUF, JOANNE

[a.] Port Robinson, Canada [title] "A Mother's Heart" [pers.] "A Mother's Heart" was inspired by the unconditional love of my mother and my grandmother. I'm blessed to have them in my life for they prove that true love really does have no boundaries. To my stepfather Sam who always had faith in me and encouraged me to put my heart on paper and publish it. So, Sam here it is.

SHIELDS, JAMES

[a.] Slidell, LA [title] "Guess What I Am" [pers.] I am very pleased with this poem. The only reason I actually entered it was because of my reading teacher, Ms. Mannin, at Lake Castle Private School of Slidell, Louisiana. I wrote this poem because of the mosquito-infested area in which I live. Although I have written many other poems, this one is very special to me. I hope my work will bring joy to your life.

SICKMEYER, TIMOTHY

[a.] Kilbourne, IL [title] "On Him I Stand" [pers.] I started writing poems for my wife, Leslie, in 1983. It started out light-hearted, but quickly turned more purposeful as I saw how they delighted her. It seems as I grow older, I take longer notice of things I used to take for granted. It humbles me to watch a thunder head tower up into the sky; to see the intricacies of a hummingbird as it zooms past my head. When I take my daily drive to work, I look at the wonders of nature and get inspired. The true feeling of my poems captures my senses like a snapshot in time.

SINEX, TAMARAH

[a.] Hummelstown, PA [title] "I Call on You" [pers.] Paper and pen, a whirlwind of thoughts, and that's all you need. My poem plainly describes the senses that come to mind whenever I'm with my boyfriend. He has made such a difference in my life. Here's to always loving you!

SISKIN, SARA

[a.] Grapevine, TX [title] "bulimic" [pers.] The poem I wrote was about having passion for someone or even something. I dedicate it to my inspiration for writing, Kurt Cobain, because he was an unbelievable writer. I have always looked up to him for his writing. I also want to dedicate it to my best friend, Beth, and my friends, Meagan and TJ. Also, to my father and my sister Nicole, brother Eric, and mom Doreen. I thank them for their motivation and love. Anyone who knows what it's like to feel such passion for someone or something can feel free to use my poem. Thank you.

SMALL, O. E. CRUISER

[a.] Salem, NH [title] "Your" [pers.] This poem was written for someone very special in my life, so it has a deep personal meaning. I am from Maine originally, but live in Neco, NH, now. I am a consultant in the business industry and a chef. My friends call me "The Lighthouse Chef" as I collect lighthouses and covered bridges. I enjoy the forests and the beaches and go there to think and write my thoughts. I am also a consultant in the exotic pet and plant fields and an expert on chameleons—the old world type.

SMITH, JOHN

[a.] Manchester, CT [title] "No More Please" [pers.] I was born January 13, 1924, in Hartford, CT, the only boy with six sisters to parents Jack and Anna Smith. I was employed as a quality control manual editor until I retired in 1975, and then as a paralegal until 1992. I have been writing a book, *Tales from My Kinderhook*. I have poems published in local paper *The Hartford Courant* and I published a short story in *Reminisce Magazine*. I thank God for my basic inspirations: my wife, daughter and four sons. I would like to thank you for having the convention in Florida this past year.

SOLOMON, JOE

[a.] Palm Desert, CA [title] "I'm Back" [pers.] I needed good health, positive energy and luck to survive the collapse of a six-year relationship and facing bankruptcy. I managed to start a successful development company while never losing sight that my children are my two greatest successes. One day at a time I need to stay positive and work at staying healthy. I have been involved in many marketing and real estate ventures. I am now the senior general partner of Bella La Quinta, a real estate development firm in La Quinta, California.

SOMMERS, NANCY

[a.] Desert Hot Springs, CA [title] "April in Aries" [pers.] This poem is dedicated to my granddaughter, April, who is an Aries. It reflects my deepest feelings about her and the type of person she is. Publishing it is my gift to honor her life. I also believe it reflects the type of poetry I will continue to write—about the family and friends in my life.

SPENCER, MATT

[a.] Trabuco Canyon, CA [title] "Beth" [pers.] I've always been fascinated with the feelings which occur between waking and falling asleep. This poem was my attempt to express the emotion involved in waking up alone and the distance of dreams from reality.

SPERO, KEITH

[a.] Edwards, CO [title] "Our Covenant" [pers.] I am a semi-retired lawyer. This poem was inspired by the events of Sept. 11th and the conflicted emotions many Americans felt. We were all torn between the desire to protect our country from terrorists and a need to protect our civil rights at the same time, so the essence of our country is not destroyed—not by enemies from abroad and not by ourselves. We must not destroy the things that make our country unique and wonderful. If we allow this to happen, the terrorists will have won.

STANLEY, PAMELA

[a.] Boothwyn, PA [title] "What Manner of Man Is He?" [pers.] This poem has special meaning to me. I wrote this as a song and I've sung it in church. I believe the words express how much my Lord Jesus gave up by giving His life. He chose to die so we might live. When He rose again, He showed His power over death. I come from a strong Christian family. My mother is one of my greatest inspirations. I hope, as a mother myself, I can instill in my children the faith I have been taught.

STAVES, SHARON

[a.] Stettler, Canada [title] "Faery Steed" [pers.] "Faery Steed" is part of a collection written for a childhood friend who had terminal cancer and died in the fall of 2001. The writing and accompanying sketches were sent as cards to keep in touch without intruding too much on her privacy, and also as a journey of acceptance on my part. It's hard, even when you are a "grey-haired granny" to accept the death of someone you have known all your life. My family have been the recipients of my scribbling and doodling, albeit without choice, for a long time. Now it's somebody else's turn.

STEFANIK, AMANDA

[a.] Wheaton, IL [title] "Family" [pers.] I'm often struck by how so many people make poetry sound so aristocratic. I don't see it as an elite "gift." Usually when I write, I'd rather not have the feelings I do. Writing's an outlet for all my negative thoughts. I don't set out to compose the next *Odyssey*. I just write how I feel. You don't have to know about rhyme schemes to be a poet. Poetry's not about that; it's not about being beautiful and rhyming about nature all the time. You just write what you feel, what's real, and that's poetry. That's beautiful.

STREETS, REBECCA

[a.] Ashtabula, OH [title] "A Poem for Daniel" [pers.] This poem was written late one night, while searching for answers from God. I lost my six-year-old son in July of 2001, due to long-term QT Syndrome. I put him to bed, gave him kisses and he faded away in his sleep. This poem is how I feel every day. I wrote it without stopping my pen. My heart won't stop breaking, but having this poem published gives me a chance to let Daniel live forever! Daniel is missed by his daddy Billy, brother Nicholas and sister Delaina, but never forgotten!

SULLIVAN, WANDA

[a.] Poplar Bluff, MO [title] "Special Key" [pers.] I have lived in Poplar Bluff, Missouri, for sixty years. I was married in October of 1945 and have been married to the same man for fifty-seven years. We raised seven children and now have several grand-and great-grandchildren. I write poems because I feel inspired by the Holy Spirit. I also enjoy playing gospel music. I have a hobby of raising different types of house plants and I do outside gardening. We have been fortunate in having good support from a lot of friends and family in our marriage. Thank you for the opportunity of acknowledging my poem.

SWAFFORD, TIMOTHY

[a.] Chattanooga, TN [title] "Dark or Light" [pers.] I am a fourteen-year-old poet. This particular poem is about happiness and unhappiness. My theory is that happiness is the light, which is obvious and blatant in life. You always know what you're getting, but with unhappiness, symbolized as "dark," there are unlimited possibilities to what can inspire you because you don't know where the road will take you.

SWANSON, MICHAEL

[a.] Buffalo Grove, IL [title] "A Million Miles Away" [pers.] I didn't start writing poetry until I took a class at a small liberal arts college in Minnesota. It really slowed my thought process down. That was twelve years ago and I never picked it up again until I found your website. The poem is about my frustration while chasing an old girlfriend. I'm looking in joining a poetry club. I'm impressed and feel very good about your feedback.

SWANSON, REBECCAH

[a.] Redding, CA [title] "Old Glory" [pers.] After September 11, the citizens of America suddenly developed an amazing sense of patriotism. My poem is my way of expressing my true love for my country. These words began as an assignment for school, but as my friends and teachers praised my work, I figured I might share the passion for my country with anyone I can reach. I am pleased God gave me this opportunity. I was thirteen when I wrote "Old Glory." This gift of words is inherited from my mother and father, my role models, best friends, and those who encourage me in life.

TALBERT, LORI

[a.] Virginia Beach, VA [title] "Rhythm Of" [pers.] My dad is a retired biochemest who resides in Trenton, NJ. My mother, Bettye Hodge Culbreth, is a retired school teacher. My eldest brother, Keith Culbreth, resides in Trenton, NJ. My younger brother, Mark Eric Culbreth lives in Charleston, SC, and is very dear to me. My baby sister, Cheryl Lynne Bethea, resides in Franklin Park, NJ, with husband Clyde Bethea. I am in active duty in the US Navy and have served for fourteen years. My husband, Charles Talbert, also in active Navy duty, supports me in my artistic endeavors. My family inspires me in all I do.

TAYLOR, JULI

[a.] Hayden, CO [title] "Beauty" [pers.] This poem was inspired by my mother who adopted me seven years ago when I was twelve years old. "Beauty" is a description of what I see when I look at her. It also describes the type of person I would like to be.

TAYLOR, TERESA

[a.] Beavercreek, OH [title] "God Is There" [pers.] I would like to first and foremost give all glory and honor to Lord Jesus Christ as my Savior. I thank the Lord for giving me the gift of writing. Through this gift, I am obliged to edify his glory. People everywhere are experiencing trials and tribulations. I hope and pray my words will heal the misunderstanding of God's love. God is love and he loves everyone. May everyone experience peace, love and joy in their heart.

TEPLEN, AMANDA

[a.]Fairfield, CT [title] "Out My Window" [pers.] My poetry is a reflection of September 11, 2001. The parts about crime, hate, misunderstanding and war are about the Twin Towers falling down and children like me who didn't understand why the terrorists could do such a thing. All the wonderful things I said were about how America united in a time of pain. That was my poem's inspiration. I have the best family: my mom, dad, brother Will, my Nana, Pop, Grandmama, Grandpapa, aunts, uncles and cousins. I'm in the sixth grade. My hobbies are tennis, soccer, softball, basketball, singing and poetry.

TETER, ERIC

[a.] Hayward, CA [title] "Presence" [pers.] As a child, I was diagnosed with a learning disability. Today, as an adult struggling to get through college, I look back and see my disabilities have enriched my own personal journey. In and upon this journey, I met a number of special people. One such person introduced me to the world of poetry. Through poetry, I have discovered strength, acceptance and the voice to my soul. Thank you, Linda.

THOM, KRISSA

[a.] Marlette, MI [title] "A Cowgirl's Reward" [pers.] When I wrote this poem, I wanted to express the enjoyment I get out of watching our calves. It is always amazing to see the birth of the calves and then watch them grow. My three brothers and I own four-hundred-fifty head of beef cattle and one-hundred-sixty of those have calves. Although I see many calves born each year, each and every one of them is special to me.

THOMAS, CHANDA

[a.] Atlanta, GA [title] "Gift for You" [pers.] I believe when one lives life purposely, they aren't afraid to explore every crevice of their being. Upon these reflections, poetry serves as a means of capturing our explorations through ultimate intimacy. My poetry is my soul's voice yearning to be heard, even by me. My poems teach me about myself. "Gift for You" reflects the pain we experience in our relationships. Though we cry and lash out when we hurt, our deepest pain is never visualized. Poetry is oftentimes a frantic cry just to be heard. It allows others into our world in a special, intimate way.

TILLMAN, MERCIA

[a.] Seminole, FL [title] "My Prayer for America" [pers.] I have written poems since age six. I am also a musical entertainer. I was Ms. Senior Florida America in 1996, and an inductee of The City of St. Petersburg, Florida Senior Hall of Fame 2000. I believe life gets even better after eighty (years, that is). This poem was written September 11, 2001 when the airplanes struck the WTC. I could not believe it was happening. It was horrible. As I watched it on TV and listened to the news, in a few minutes I wrote "My Prayer for America." This little prayer expressed my feelings at that very moment.

TREMBLETT, DENISE

[a.] Toronto, Canada [title] "Impregnability" [pers.] I work with people who have developmental disabilities and I have a graduate degree in education. Poetry has always been a way I could express my innermost thoughts and feelings. Writing poetry and reading bring great pleasure and satisfaction to my life.

TUMMOND, PAMELA

[a.] Vero Beach, FL [title] "A Parent's Prayer" [pers.] My poems are very personal expressions of my deeply felt love. I was inspired to write this poem for my daughter. It was modified years later for my son, the day my daughter graduated from high school. I wanted to express how much her father and I loved her and how proud we were of her accomplishments. Also, I felt it was important to use the occasion to teach my child the way you approach life reflects back on you. I hope other parents will share these sentiments with their own children.

VACCA, GENEVIEVE

[a.] Stamford, CT [title] "Gift Package" [pers.] I enjoy writing poetry, for it allows me to capture sadness and hope into a few lines. I was encouraged by my English teacher, Miss Nelson. Music and art inspire me. My parents were great help. Also, I have two sisters, Evelyn and Rosemarie, one of which is a religious sister. My late father was an architect, so we were surrounded by paper and colorful pencils. When I did interior decorating, I always enjoyed working with unique textures and color. I now work for Sears Roebuck in home fashions. This poem I dedicate to my deceased, wonderful mother.

VAIRO, GINA

[a.] Doylestown, PA [title] "A Fragile Thing" [pers.] A poem comes into everyone's life at one time or another. The words silently stay with us and give us peace at times. I am so glad to have a chance to share this particular poem I wrote about a friend who is now my husband.

VAN DYK, GINNY

[a.] Dublin, VA [title] "Lonely" [pers.] This poem was written over this past summer. I wrote it for all my friends I missed. I have always loved poetry and have thought it to be very important for everybody. I believe poetry is expressing how you feel. So, I decided to try hard at it. My opinion of my poetry is that it is not very good at all, but a friend of mine thought otherwise and posted one of my poems for me.

She then forced me to post the rest because they're "good." I guess she was right.

VanANALSTINE, PATRICIA
[a.] Jessup, MD [title] "Untitled" [pers.] This is not just a poem. This is several fond memories and heartfelt expressions formed into few words; too few for anyone to know how great of a person Maw Maw really was and of how much her presence meant to me. I had not thought so greatly of her until she passed away and I could not spend time with her. Only now can I see my grandmother, Pansy Testerman's, inner beauty—an inner beauty I feel can be expressed through my eyes and transformed into this poem.

VASQUEZ, ANGELA
[a.] Houston, TX [title] "Dear God" [pers.] I was born June 23, 1980. My parents are Janie and Joe Vasquez. My sisters are Sonya Vasquez and Belinda Ratcliffe. My brothers are Joe Vasquez and Joe Vasquez, Jr. I completed college. I love to write poems and I've written for a long time. Poetry is an easy way for me to express my own feelings. I would like to dedicate this poem to my mother and to my grandmother, Ophelia Garcia, whom I love very much.

VAUGHAN, CHRISTINE
[a.] Hyde Park, MA [title] "The Flesh Constantly Bleeds, but I Live" [pers.] I am a local Boston poet and author of *He Raised the World from My Shoulders* and *Epiphany—Third Eye Poetry*. I enjoy the liberty of spoken words. It is medicine for my soul, especially when people and society's constraints try to hold me down. They cannot keep me down. "The Flesh Constantly Bleeds, But I Live" personifies a revelatory manifestation of a divine life not perfect. Read it with a third eye.

VICKIE, TEDDER
[a.] Enumclaw, WA [title] "Peaceful Angel" [pers.] Poetry is a way I show my feeling without saying a word. The poem is very special to me. It is about a guy I love and for whom I care very much. He has made me a stronger person. He will always be in my heart and prayers.

VITTALI, RICHARD
[a.] langezwaag, Netherlands [title] "Ouch" [pers.] I am a nineteen-year-old, second-grade student teacher in college. My parents are Grada van Roon and Han Vittali. I was an exchange student in 2001 in Splendora, Texas and stayed with the Ipes family. When I came back for vacation the following summer, I saw the girl that inspired me to write the poem working in the Mall in Humble, Texas. She was selling ice cream. A day later, I asked her if she wanted to go see a movie, but . . .

VOGEL, ALYSHA
[a.] Warrington, PA [title] "Mixed Emotions" [pers.] Poetry means a lot to me. It's often hard for me to express to others exactly how I am feeling, so I write it down in the form of poetry. For some reason, it seems to help me get through the times when I feel down. This poem in particular is a memory. Those who know me may know exactly who and what it's about. For those who don't, I'm sure some may be able to relate to the feelings expressed through my words. I feel blessed to have the gift of poetry in my life.

vON HANNA, SILVIA
[a.] Stouffville, Canada [title] "I Must Not Scream" [pers.] I am a medical doctor who gets upset when I perceive an injustice. This poem was written when the chaplain to whom I was talking went inside to answer a phone call. She came out less than five minutes later. I showed her the finished poem. We prayed together for my patient. She said my tears showed I cared.

VOWELL, CARRIE
[a.] Las Vegas, NV [title] "Where Are the Horses?" [pers.] I grew up in a small town in the mountains in Red Rock Canyon, Nevada, near Las Vegas. The wild horses came into the village at night and we would see them in our yard. It is sad to know they are gone. So, this poem is how I feel. I'm a sixty-one-year-old mother of four and grandmother of five. I started writing this summer on a trip to the south, where I was born.

WAHLEN, ANN MARIE
[a.] Kingston, NH [title] "When Tomorrow Is Gone" [pers.] This poem exists because of my best friend, Jill, and my English teacher, Ms. Meyers. They both gave me strength and confidence in my writing. I'd also like to thank my family and friends. I hope this poem touches at least one person because then it would be worthwhile.

WAITE, PRISCILLA
[a.] Raleigh, NC [title] "Life" [pers.] My poem entitled "Life" is an expression about how I view life itself. I have gone down many rocky roads before reaching this place in life where, by doing my best, I feel good about myself. In sharing this poem, I can only hope you feel it reaching out to you and showing you that in life you are not alone.

WALDRON, TIFFANY
[a.] League City, TX [title] "Left Alone" [pers.] Since I was a little girl, I have loved to write my feelings down. This was a poem my mom asked me to write. She has been researching our family history. My great-grandfather hung himself in his barn in the early 1900's. His son, my grandfather, was a good man, but he always seemed so distant. It makes me wonder if this story is the reason why. It has been great hearing my mom tell me about my family and their history. I'm sure it will give me many feelings about which to write.

WALLACE, JAMIE
[a.] Rogers City, MI [title] "Love's Song" [pers.] When I wrote this poem, I was thinking about what the first love means to everyone. My poem shows, in the simplest way, just how special first love is. As my grandparents would say, love is the most beautiful thing we have. This poem is written in memory of them and of the love they shared until their deaths. If my poem does nothing else, it will remind people of the love in their lives.

WARD, SHAUN
[a.] Barrington, NH [title] "Death Does Mourn" [pers.] Poetry is not the arrangement of the words, but the deeper understanding of them. To write poetry is to write a symphony of the greater essence of the poet behind it. However, when a poet is able to write poetry that illustrates the greater essence of all mankind, it is but a great gift bestowed upon him by a higher power than him.

WARE, TIMOTHY
[a.] Saint Charles, MO [title] "My Efforts Fail" [pers.] "My Efforts Fail" is a view of the struggle of my soul. It expresses the loss of innocence and the desperate effort to regain it—the reality of becoming self-aware and the realization that I cannot achieve deliverance in my own power. The poem expresses gratitude for life in light of the evolving perception and influences of the world. I believe many will connect with this poem and reflect on the journey of their maturity in this life.

WARREN, JOYCE
[a.] Pinehurst, TX [title] "My Mom, Ruby" [pers.] My mom has lived an exceptional life. As evidence in this poem dedicated to her, God has been faithful through the years to provide for her needs and give her joy and blessings beyond what mere words can express. Mom read the poem and now eagerly awaits her copy of book of poetry in which it is featured.

WARREN, KRISTA
[a.] Osburn, ID [title] "Serendipity" [pers.] Have you ever met someone only for a moment, but felt like you've known them all your life? That's serendipity. I love writing. I have been writing since I was a little girl. I have sixty-three of my own novels and multiple poetry writings. Being a child of a military father, I had a lot of time on my hands. I picked up my diary. I started writing and now I can't be seen without pen and paper.

WATKINS, LISA
[a.] Warner Robins, GA [title] "My Thirst-Quencher" [pers.] The poem, "My Thirst-Quencher," comes out of a fulfilling relationship with God's Son, Jesus Christ. No human relationship can match the relationship I share with Jesus Christ. The way He loves me by meeting my needs and caring for me surpasses all others. I am thankful to be able to share it by writing poetry. I hope my relationship with Him shines through in my writing.

WEBSTER, RAMONA
[a.] Keller, TX [title] "The Silence Is So Loud" [pers.] Driving home after the events of the day of 9/11, I was so overcome with sadness. I pulled over and wrote this poem.

WELLS, PETER
[a.] Nelson, NE [title] "Gratitude Eternal to Chester" [pers.] At fifteen, our eldest son repeatedly requested a dog. Earlier, dogs in a residential area were continual problems. Reluctance on my part dissipated and Chester, a rough-coated Collie pup, won all our hearts. Chester was my constant daily companion, as I painfully struggled the road back to recovery from a total physical/mental "burnout." An immense empathy evolved. At an old age, his life ended. For years, I have wanted to express the deep gratitude I owed Chester. "Gratitude Eternal to Chester" attempts to relate that empathy's depth.

WENDRICK, LINDA
[a.] Bakersfield, CA [title] "Arrested" [pers.] Over forty years of life, I have passed through many doors. Some have closed permanently; some remain open part-way and continue to haunt me; others I choose to leave accessible, to look back and deal with these issues. I have been homeless, a prostitute, a drug addict/alcoholic, kidnapped, beaten, raped, and abandoned. I have been jailed, institutionalized, and imprisoned. I have changed my life for the better. I attend a private junior college with a 3.73 GPA, and am on the honor roll every semester. I am very proud of myself and strongly encourage others to never give up.

WILBURN, STEVE
[a.] Downingtown, PA [title] "Invisible Man" [pers.] "Invisible Man" is the story of my fears of rejection and my desire to be understood by my peers. I believe everyone feels invisible at some time in their lives. I also believe everyone desires for the world to see beyond the superficial, and find the true depth in their lives. Unfortunately, humans can't satisfy that desire, but God can. He is the only one who knows us better than we know ourselves. With Him, it is impossible to be transparent. So, even though the whole world may pass by you as if you're not even there, God still sees you and loves you. That is enough.

WILHELM, MEGAN
[a.] Decatur, IL [title] "Dads" [pers.] I am thirteen years old. My parents have been divorced since I was a little baby. This poem expresses how I feel about my dad.

WILKINSON, ALEXA

[a] Park City, UT [title] "Miss the Dust" [pers.] "Life is not measured by how many breaths we take, but by how many times life takes our breath away." This poem is for a dear friend, who never knew the meaning of this quote.

WILLIAMS, ALLISON

[a.] Brookfield, CT [title] "A Place in My Heart" [pers.] I was going through a tough time and poetry helped me with my feelings. My family and friends helped me a lot as well. Mom, Dad, Shannon and Jake, I love you! This poem is something to which I think a lot of people could relate. I hope it has some effect on their lives. To my friends, Naomi, Krysta, Shawn, Liz, Doug, Becky, Jess: you have inspired me in ways you'll never know. You all mean the world to me. I love you!

WILLIAMS, GWENDOLYNN

[a.] MCBH Kaneohe Bay, HI [title] "Unspoken Words" [pers.] I am a resident of Hawaii. I am a 1999 graduate from South Houston High School. I enlisted in the United States Marine Corps in December 1999. I am currently stationed at the Marine Corps Base in Hawaii, Kaneohe Bay as an administration clerk. I was introduced to Poetry by my childhood friend, Samarys Roman, and have been writing since the age of thirteen. My goal is to publish my own poetry book. I am honored that my poem was selected for this collection and I look forward to its publication.

WINTER, KATHLEEN

[a.] Syracuse, NY [title] "The Cape" [pers.] This poem is for Miss Leigha, my beautiful friend with whom I vacationed at the cape. The inspiration for this poem was drawn from an evening on a beach in Provincetown, Massachusetts. Thank you to Leigha and Poetry.com for allowing me to share this memory.

WISCHOFF, KATRINA

[a.] Canandaigua, NY [title] "Alone" [pers.] I dedicate this to my best friend in the world. Ashley is the best friend anyone can have. I wrote this poem as an idea for a song for my band. I had no idea it would be published. Ashley taught me many things; one thing being, do not allow yourself to be walked all over. I thank her for that advice. I like to write and hang out with my friends. I want to thank everyone at school with whom I had a pleasant conversation. You are very kind. Thanks, everybody.

WOODFORD, COLETTE

[a.] Bungendore, Australia [title] "Wildfires" [pers.] This poem reflects the deep love I have for the person who changed my life for the better. He gave me confidence and encouraged me to laugh once again. Our passion is as strong as ever and is renewed every time we are together. I hope others find the same sense of enduring passion we have.

YADAV, MONIKA

[a.] Jersey City, NJ [title] "Response" [pers.] I feel that poetry is my best friend. I see myself in every poem I write and in its every word. If you think my poem is a fantasy or just a made up story, then it would be a weakness in my writing. I dance my feelings off in my poems. I act with passion to create emotions. I use the art of dance and acting because I hold a passion for both. I am an artist, a dancer and an actor. I live in a world which I create and I remember myself for being a poet. Too many people of which to think, but I have to tell her she was the one who influenced me more . . . I love you, Mom.

YOUNG, MICHAEL

[a.] Society Hill, SC [title] "Beans and Peas" [pers.] First, I want to thank God Almighty for allowing the United States to be a great and free country. I want to thank my wife, Roberta, for her support. I want to thank my mom, Bobby, and thank our Saviour for my daughter Azlyn. Poetry.com is the best. I know I had a talent for writing poetry back in high school. I hardly used it until I was disabled for a few weeks after hernia surgery. My wife bought me a new computer, so I put it to use. A word to the wise: trust in yourself and never, never, never give up.

ZINGARELLI, ZEA

[a.] Irwin, PA [title] "Walking in the Forest" [pers.] I live with my parents and my two sisters. I am in the seventh grade and love it. Ever since I was a little girl I would insist that my mother or father read stories that rhymed. When I got older and began to read, I started reading little bits of poetry and found that I really liked it. Since then, I have been experimenting with a little poetry of my own. When I heard about the poetry contest, I thought this would be my chance to share work. Please enjoy.

Index of Poets

Index

A

B

C

D

E

F

G

H

I

J

K

L

M

N

O

P

Q

R

S

T

U

V

W

Y

Z